Ford Mustang Mercury Capri Automotive Repair Manual

by Larry Warren, Alan Ahlstrand and John H Haynes

Member of the Guild of Motoring Writers

Models covered:

All Ford Mustang and Mercury Capri models
1979 through 1993

(5G20 - 36050)
(654)

ABCDE
FGHIJ
KLMNO
PQRST 3

AUTOMOTIVE
PARTS &
ACCESSORIES
ASSOCIATION MEMBER

Haynes Publishing Group
Sparkford Nr Yeovil
Somerset BA22 7JJ England

Haynes North America, Inc
861 Lawrence Drive
Newbury Park
California 91320 USA

About this manual

Its purpose

The purpose of this manual is to help you get the best value from your vehicle. It can do so in several ways. It can help you decide what work must be done, even if you choose to have it done by a dealer service department or a repair shop; it provides information and procedures for routine maintenance and servicing; and it offers diagnostic and repair procedures to follow when trouble occurs.

We hope you use the manual to tackle the work yourself. For many simpler jobs, doing it yourself may be quicker than arranging an appointment to get the vehicle into a shop and making the trips to leave it and pick it up. More importantly, a lot of money can be saved by avoiding the expense the shop must pass on to you to cover its labor and overhead costs. An added benefit is the sense of satisfaction and accomplishment that you feel after doing the job yourself.

Using the manual

The manual is divided into Chapters. Each Chapter is divided into numbered Sections, which are headed in bold type between horizontal lines. Each Section consists of consecutively numbered paragraphs.

At the beginning of each numbered Section you will be referred to any illustrations which apply to the procedures in that Section. The reference numbers used in illustration captions pinpoint the pertinent Section and the Step within that Section. That is, illustration 3.2 means the illustration refers to Section 3 and Step (or paragraph) 2 within that Section.

Procedures, once described in the text, are not normally repeated. When it's necessary to refer to another Chapter, the reference will be given as Chapter and Section number. Cross references given without use of the word "Chapter" apply to Sections and/or paragraphs in the same Chapter. For example, "see Section 8" means in the same Chapter.

References to the left or right side of the vehicle assume you are sitting in the driver's seat, facing forward.

Even though we have prepared this manual with extreme care, neither the publisher nor the author can accept responsibility for any errors in, or omissions from, the information given.

NOTE

A **Note** provides information necessary to properly complete a procedure or information which will make the procedure easier to understand.

CAUTION

A **Caution** provides a special procedure or special steps which must be taken while completing the procedure where the Caution is found. Not heeding a Caution can result in damage to the assembly being worked on.

WARNING

A **Warning** provides a special procedure or special steps which must be taken while completing the procedure where the Warning is found. Not heeding a Warning can result in personal injury.

© Haynes North America, Inc. 1990, 1992, 1994, 1998, 2004

With permission from J H Haynes Co Ltd

A book in the Haynes Automotive Repair Manual Series

Printed in the U.S.A.

ISBN 1 56392 130 8

Library of Congress Catalog Card Number 94-79926

Contents

Haynes photographer, author and mechanic with Mustang

Introduction

The Mustang and Capri have the conventional front engine/rear wheel drive layout.

Various engines have been used over the long life of these models: A 2.3 liter four-cylinder, a 3.3 liter inline six-cylinder, a 2.8 liter V6, a 3.8 liter V6, a 4.2 liter V8 and a 5.0 liter V8. Some models are carbureted while others are equipped with fuel injection. Some four-cylinder engines are turbocharged.

Power from the engine is transferred through either a four or five-speed manual or three or four-speed automatic transmission to the solid rear axle by a tubular driveshaft incorporating universal joints.

Suspension at the front is a modified MacPherson strut design. The rear suspension features coil springs with trailing arms used to locate the axle.

Rack and pinion steering is used, with power steering optional on early models and standard on later models.

The brakes are disc at the front and drum at the rear (rear disc brakes are used on the Mustang SVO). Vacuum assist is optional on early models and standard on later models.

Vehicle identification numbers

Modifications are a continuing and unpublicized process in vehicle manufacturing. Since spare parts manuals and lists are compiled on a numerical basis, the individual vehicle numbers are essential to correctly identify the component required.

Vehicle Identification Number (VIN)

This very important identification number is located on a plate attached to the left side dashboard just inside the windshield **(see illustration)**. The VIN also appears on the Vehicle Certificate of Title and Registration. I contains information such as where and when the vehicle was manufactured, the model year and the body style.

Vehicle Certification label

The Vehicle Certification label (VC label) is attached to the front of the left (driver's side) door pillar. The upper half of the label contains the name of the manufacturer, the month and year of production, the Gross Vehicle Weight Rating (GVWR), the Gross Axle Weight Rating (GAWR) and the certification statement.

The VC label also contains the VIN number, which is used for warranty identification of the vehicle, and provides such information as manufacturer, type of restraint system,

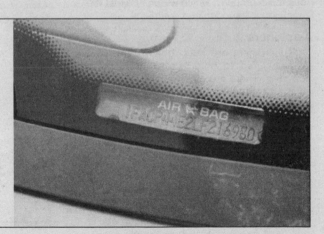

The Vehicle Identification Number (VIN) is visible through the driver's side of the windshield

body type, engine, transmission, model year and vehicle serial number.

Engine numbers

Labels containing the engine code, calibration and serial numbers, as well as plant name, can be found on the valve cover, as well as stamped on the engine itself.

Manual transmission numbers

The manual transmission identification number and serial numbers can be found on a tag on the left side of the transmission extension housing.

Automatic transmission numbers

Tags with the automatic transmission serial number, build date and other information are attached to the transmission housing with a bolt, usually at the extension housing.

Vehicle Emissions Control Information (VECI) label

This label is found under the hood (See Chapter 6).

Buying parts

Replacement parts are available from many sources, which generally fall into one of two categories - authorized dealer parts departments and independent retail auto parts stores. Our advice concerning these parts is as follows:

Retail auto parts stores: Good auto parts stores will stock frequently needed components which wear out relatively fast, such as clutch components, exhaust systems, brake parts, tune-up parts, etc. These stores often supply new or reconditioned parts on an exchange basis, which can save a considerable amount of money. Discount auto parts stores are often very good places to buy materials and parts needed for general vehicle maintenance such as oil, grease, filters, spark plugs, belts, touch-up paint, bulbs, etc. They also usually sell tools and general accessories, have convenient hours, charge lower prices and can often be found not far from home.

Authorized dealer parts department: This is the best source for parts which are unique to the vehicle and not generally available elsewhere (such as major engine parts, transmission parts, trim pieces, etc.).

Warranty information: If the vehicle is still covered under warranty, be sure that any replacement parts purchased - regardless of the source - do not invalidate the warranty!

To be sure of obtaining the correct parts, have engine and chassis numbers available and, if possible, take the old parts along for positive identification.

Maintenance techniques, tools and working facilities

Maintenance techniques

There are a number of techniques involved in maintenance and repair that will be referred to throughout this manual. Application of these techniques will enable the home mechanic to be more efficient, better organized and capable of performing the various tasks properly, which will ensure that the repair job is thorough and complete.

Fasteners

Fasteners are nuts, bolts, studs and screws used to hold two or more parts together. There are a few things to keep in mind when working with fasteners. Almost all of them use a locking device of some type, either a lockwasher, locknut, locking tab or thread adhesive. All threaded fasteners should be clean and straight, with undamaged threads and undamaged corners on the hex head where the wrench fits. Develop the habit of replacing all damaged nuts and bolts with new ones. Special locknuts with nylon or fiber inserts can only be used once. If they are removed, they lose their locking ability and must be replaced with new ones.

Rusted nuts and bolts should be treated with a penetrating fluid to ease removal and prevent breakage. Some mechanics use turpentine in a spout-type oil can, which works quite well. After applying the rust penetrant, let it work for a few minutes before trying to loosen the nut or bolt. Badly rusted fasteners may have to be chiseled or sawed off or removed with a special nut breaker, available at tool stores.

If a bolt or stud breaks off in an assembly, it can be drilled and removed with a special tool commonly available for this purpose. Most automotive machine shops can perform this task, as well as other repair procedures, such as the repair of threaded holes that have been stripped out.

Flat washers and lockwashers, when removed from an assembly, should always be replaced exactly as removed. Replace any damaged washers with new ones. Never use a lockwasher on any soft metal surface (such as aluminum), thin sheet metal or plastic.

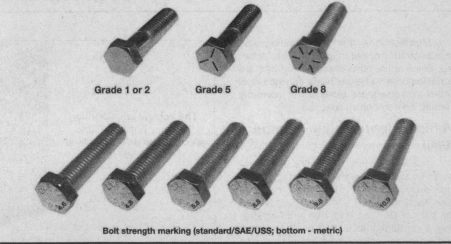

Grade 1 or 2   Grade 5   Grade 8

Bolt strength marking (standard/SAE/USS; bottom - metric)

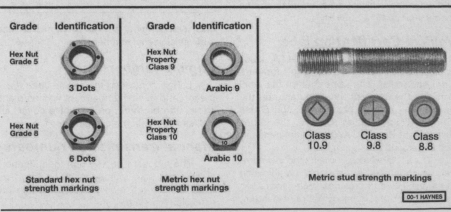

Grade	Identification
Hex Nut Grade 5	3 Dots
Hex Nut Grade 8	6 Dots

Standard hex nut strength markings

Grade	Identification
Hex Nut Property Class 9	Arabic 9
Hex Nut Property Class 10	Arabic 10

Metric hex nut strength markings

Class 10.9   Class 9.8   Class 8.8

Metric stud strength markings

Fastener sizes

For a number of reasons, automobile manufacturers are making wider and wider use of metric fasteners. Therefore, it is important to be able to tell the difference between standard (sometimes called U.S. or SAE) and metric hardware, since they cannot be interchanged.

All bolts, whether standard or metric, are sized according to diameter, thread pitch and length. For example, a standard 1/2 - 13 x 1 bolt is 1/2 inch in diameter, has 13 threads per inch and is 1 inch long. An M12 - 1.75 x 25 metric bolt is 12 mm in diameter, has a thread pitch of 1.75 mm (the distance between threads) and is 25 mm long. The two bolts are nearly identical, and easily confused, but they are not interchangeable.

In addition to the differences in diameter, thread pitch and length, metric and standard bolts can also be distinguished by examining the bolt heads. To begin with, the distance across the flats on a standard bolt head is measured in inches, while the same dimension on a metric bolt is sized in millimeters (the same is true for nuts). As a result, a standard wrench should not be used on a metric bolt and a metric wrench should not be used on a standard bolt. Also, most standard bolts have slashes radiating out from the center of the head to denote the grade or strength of the bolt, which is an indication of the amount of torque that can be applied to it. The greater the number of slashes, the greater the strength of the bolt. Grades 0 through 5 are commonly used on automobiles. Metric bolts have a property class (grade) number, rather than a slash, molded into their heads to indicate bolt strength. In this case, the higher the number, the stronger the bolt. Property class numbers 8.8, 9.8 and 10.9 are commonly used on automobiles.

Strength markings can also be used to distinguish standard hex nuts from metric hex nuts. Many standard nuts have dots stamped into one side, while metric nuts are marked with a number. The greater the number of dots, or the higher the number, the greater the strength of the nut.

Metric studs are also marked on their ends according to property class (grade). Larger studs are numbered (the same as metric bolts), while smaller studs carry a geometric code to denote grade.

It should be noted that many fasteners, especially Grades 0 through 2, have no distinguishing marks on them. When such is the case, the only way to determine whether it is standard or metric is to measure the thread pitch or compare it to a known fastener of the same size.

Standard fasteners are often referred to as SAE, as opposed to metric. However, it should be noted that SAE technically refers to a non-metric fine thread fastener only. Coarse thread non-metric fasteners are referred to as USS sizes.

Since fasteners of the same size (both standard and metric) may have different

Metric thread sizes	Ft-lbs	Nm
M-6	6 to 9	9 to 12
M-8	14 to 21	19 to 28
M-10	28 to 40	38 to 54
M-12	50 to 71	68 to 96
M-14	80 to 140	109 to 154

Pipe thread sizes		
1/8	5 to 8	7 to 10
1/4	12 to 18	17 to 24
3/8	22 to 33	30 to 44
1/2	25 to 35	34 to 47

U.S. thread sizes		
1/4 - 20	6 to 9	9 to 12
5/16 - 18	12 to 18	17 to 24
5/16 - 24	14 to 20	19 to 27
3/8 - 16	22 to 32	30 to 43
3/8 - 24	27 to 38	37 to 51
7/16 - 14	40 to 55	55 to 74
7/16 - 20	40 to 60	55 to 81
1/2 - 13	55 to 80	75 to 108

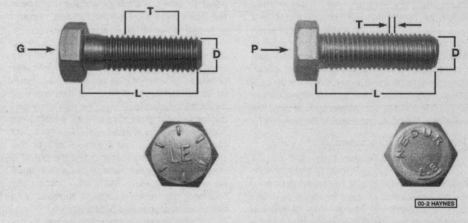

Standard (SAE and USS) bolt dimensions/grade marks

G   Grade marks (bolt strength)
L   Length (in inches)
T   Thread pitch (number of threads per inch)
D   Nominal diameter (in inches)

Metric bolt dimensions/grade marks

P   Property class (bolt strength)
L   Length (in millimeters)
T   Thread pitch (distance between threads in millimeters)
D   Diameter

strength ratings, be sure to reinstall any bolts, studs or nuts removed from your vehicle in their original locations. Also, when replacing a fastener with a new one, make sure that the new one has a strength rating equal to or greater than the original.

Tightening sequences and procedures

Most threaded fasteners should be tightened to a specific torque value (torque is the twisting force applied to a threaded component such as a nut or bolt). Overtightening the fastener can weaken it and cause it to break, while undertightening can cause it to eventually come loose. Bolts, screws and studs, depending on the material they are made of and their thread diameters, have specific torque values, many of which are noted in the Specifications at the beginning of each Chapter. Be sure to follow the torque recommendations closely. For fasteners not assigned a specific torque, a general torque value chart is presented here as a guide. These torque values are for dry (unlubricated) fasteners threaded into steel or cast iron (not aluminum). As was previously mentioned, the size and grade of a fastener determine the amount of torque that can safely be applied to it. The figures listed here are approximate for Grade 2 and Grade 3 fasteners. Higher grades can tolerate higher torque values.

Fasteners laid out in a pattern, such as cylinder head bolts, oil pan bolts, differential

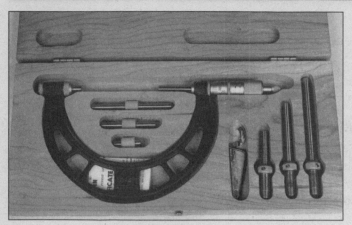

Micrometer set

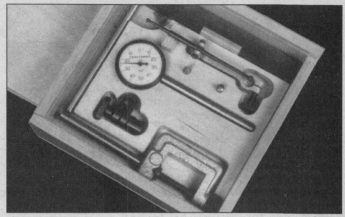

Dial indicator set

cover bolts, etc., must be loosened or tightened in sequence to avoid warping the component. This sequence will normally be shown in the appropriate Chapter. If a specific pattern is not given, the following procedures can be used to prevent warping.

Initially, the bolts or nuts should be assembled finger-tight only. Next, they should be tightened one full turn each, in a criss-cross or diagonal pattern. After each one has been tightened one full turn, return to the first one and tighten them all one-half turn, following the same pattern. Finally, tighten each of them one-quarter turn at a time until each fastener has been tightened to the proper torque. To loosen and remove the fasteners, the procedure would be reversed.

Component disassembly

Component disassembly should be done with care and purpose to help ensure that the parts go back together properly. Always keep track of the sequence in which parts are removed. Make note of special characteristics or marks on parts that can be installed more than one way, such as a grooved thrust washer on a shaft. It is a good idea to lay the disassembled parts out on a clean surface in the order that they were removed. It may also be helpful to make sketches or take instant photos of components before removal.

When removing fasteners from a component, keep track of their locations. Sometimes threading a bolt back in a part, or putting the washers and nut back on a stud, can prevent mix-ups later. If nuts and bolts cannot be returned to their original locations, they should be kept in a compartmented box or a series of small boxes. A cupcake or muffin tin is ideal for this purpose, since each cavity can hold the bolts and nuts from a particular area (i.e. oil pan bolts, valve cover bolts, engine mount bolts, etc.). A pan of this type is especially helpful when working on assemblies with very small parts, such as the carburetor, alternator, valve train or interior dash and trim pieces. The cavities can be marked with paint or tape to identify the contents.

Whenever wiring looms, harnesses or connectors are separated, it is a good idea to identify the two halves with numbered pieces of masking tape so they can be easily reconnected.

Gasket sealing surfaces

Throughout any vehicle, gaskets are used to seal the mating surfaces between two parts and keep lubricants, fluids, vacuum or pressure contained in an assembly.

Many times these gaskets are coated with a liquid or paste-type gasket sealing compound before assembly. Age, heat and pressure can sometimes cause the two parts to stick together so tightly that they are very difficult to separate. Often, the assembly can be loosened by striking it with a soft-face hammer near the mating surfaces. A regular hammer can be used if a block of wood is placed between the hammer and the part. Do not hammer on cast parts or parts that could be easily damaged. With any particularly stubborn part, always recheck to make sure that every fastener has been removed.

Avoid using a screwdriver or bar to pry apart an assembly, as they can easily mar the gasket sealing surfaces of the parts, which must remain smooth. If prying is absolutely necessary, use an old broom handle, but keep in mind that extra clean up will be necessary if the wood splinters.

After the parts are separated, the old gasket must be carefully scraped off and the gasket surfaces cleaned. Stubborn gasket material can be soaked with rust penetrant or treated with a special chemical to soften it so it can be easily scraped off. A scraper can be fashioned from a piece of copper tubing by flattening and sharpening one end. Copper is recommended because it is usually softer than the surfaces to be scraped, which reduces the chance of gouging the part. Some gaskets can be removed with a wire brush, but regardless of the method used, the mating surfaces must be left clean and smooth. If for some reason the gasket surface is gouged, then a gasket sealer thick enough to fill scratches will have to be used during reassembly of the components. For most applications, a non-drying (or semi-drying) gasket sealer should be used.

Hose removal tips

Warning: *If the vehicle is equipped with air conditioning, do not disconnect any of the A/C hoses without first having the system depressurized by a dealer service department or a service station.*

Hose removal precautions closely parallel gasket removal precautions. Avoid scratching or gouging the surface that the hose mates against or the connection may leak. This is especially true for radiator hoses. Because of various chemical reactions, the rubber in hoses can bond itself to the metal spigot that the hose fits over. To remove a hose, first loosen the hose clamps that secure it to the spigot. Then, with slip-joint pliers, grab the hose at the clamp and rotate it around the spigot. Work it back and forth until it is completely free, then pull it off. Silicone or other lubricants will ease removal if they can be applied between the hose and the outside of the spigot. Apply the same lubricant to the inside of the hose and the outside of the spigot to simplify installation.

As a last resort (and if the hose is to be replaced with a new one anyway), the rubber can be slit with a knife and the hose peeled from the spigot. If this must be done, be careful that the metal connection is not damaged.

If a hose clamp is broken or damaged, do not reuse it. Wire-type clamps usually weaken with age, so it is a good idea to replace them with screw-type clamps whenever a hose is removed.

Tools

A selection of good tools is a basic requirement for anyone who plans to maintain and repair his or her own vehicle. For the owner who has few tools, the initial investment might seem high, but when compared to the spiraling costs of professional auto maintenance and repair, it is a wise one.

To help the owner decide which tools are needed to perform the tasks detailed in this manual, the following tool lists are offered: *Maintenance and minor repair, Repair/overhaul* and *Special*.

The newcomer to practical mechanics

Dial caliper

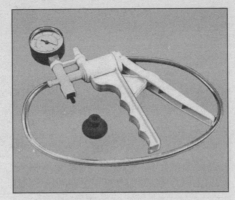

Hand-operated vacuum pump

Timing light

Compression gauge with spark plug
hole adapter

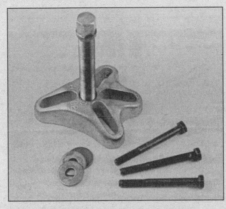

Damper/steering wheel puller

General purpose puller

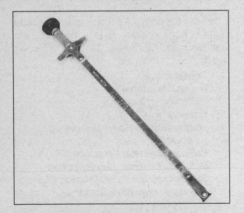

Hydraulic lifter removal tool

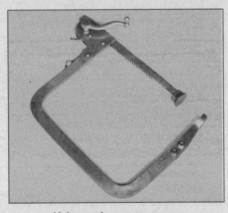

Valve spring compressor

Valve spring compressor

Ridge reamer

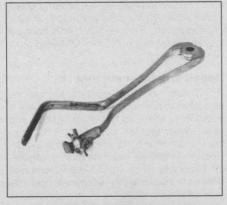

Piston ring groove cleaning tool

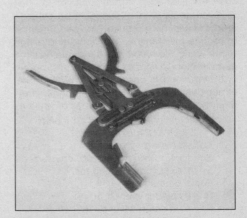

Ring removal/installation tool

Ring compressor

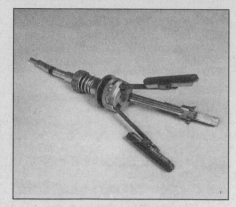
Cylinder hone

Brake hold-down spring tool

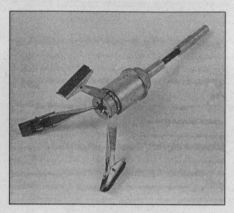
Brake cylinder hone

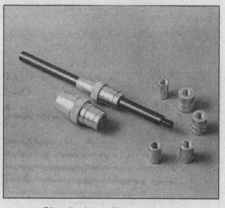
Clutch plate alignment tool

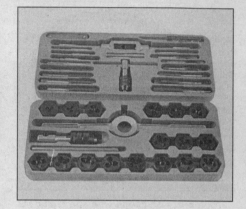
Tap and die set

should start off with the *maintenance and minor repair* tool kit, which is adequate for the simpler jobs performed on a vehicle. Then, as confidence and experience grow, the owner can tackle more difficult tasks, buying additional tools as they are needed. Eventually the basic kit will be expanded into the *repair and overhaul* tool set. Over a period of time, the experienced do-it-yourselfer will assemble a tool set complete enough for most repair and overhaul procedures and will add tools from the special category when it is felt that the expense is justified by the frequency of use.

Maintenance and minor repair tool kit

The tools in this list should be considered the minimum required for performance of routine maintenance, servicing and minor repair work. We recommend the purchase of combination wrenches (box-end and open-end combined in one wrench). While more expensive than open end wrenches, they offer the advantages of both types of wrench.

Combination wrench set (1/4-inch to 1 inch or 6 mm to 19 mm)
Adjustable wrench, 8 inch
Spark plug wrench with rubber insert
Spark plug gap adjusting tool
Feeler gauge set
Brake bleeder wrench
Standard screwdriver (5/16-inch x 6 inch)

Phillips screwdriver (No. 2 x 6 inch)
Combination pliers - 6 inch
Hacksaw and assortment of blades
Tire pressure gauge
Grease gun
Oil can
Fine emery cloth
Wire brush
Battery post and cable cleaning tool
Oil filter wrench
Funnel (medium size)
Safety goggles
Jackstands (2)
Drain pan

Note: *If basic tune-ups are going to be part of routine maintenance, it will be necessary to purchase a good quality stroboscopic timing light and combination tachometer/dwell meter. Although they are included in the list of special tools, it is mentioned here because they are absolutely necessary for tuning most vehicles properly.*

Repair and overhaul tool set

These tools are essential for anyone who plans to perform major repairs and are in addition to those in the maintenance and minor repair tool kit. Included is a comprehensive set of sockets which, though expensive, are invaluable because of their versatility, especially when various extensions and drives are available. We recommend the 1/2-inch drive over the 3/8-inch drive. Although the larger drive is bulky and more expensive,

it has the capacity of accepting a very wide range of large sockets. Ideally, however, the mechanic should have a 3/8-inch drive set and a 1/2-inch drive set.

Socket set(s)
Reversible ratchet
Extension - 10 inch
Universal joint
Torque wrench (same size drive as sockets)
Ball peen hammer - 8 ounce
Soft-face hammer (plastic/rubber)
Standard screwdriver (1/4-inch x 6 inch)
Standard screwdriver (stubby - 5/16-inch)
Phillips screwdriver (No. 3 x 8 inch)
Phillips screwdriver (stubby - No. 2)
Pliers - vise grip
Pliers - lineman's
Pliers - needle nose
Pliers - snap-ring (internal and external)
Cold chisel - 1/2-inch
Scribe
Scraper (made from flattened copper tubing)
Centerpunch
Pin punches (1/16, 1/8, 3/16-inch)
Steel rule/straightedge - 12 inch
Allen wrench set (1/8 to 3/8-inch or 4 mm to 10 mm)
A selection of files
Wire brush (large)
Jackstands (second set)
Jack (scissor or hydraulic type)

Note: *Another tool which is often useful is an electric drill with a chuck capacity of 3/8-inch and a set of good quality drill bits.*

Special tools

The tools in this list include those which are not used regularly, are expensive to buy, or which need to be used in accordance with their manufacturer's instructions. Unless these tools will be used frequently, it is not very economical to purchase many of them. A consideration would be to split the cost and use between yourself and a friend or friends. In addition, most of these tools can be obtained from a tool rental shop on a temporary basis.

This list primarily contains only those tools and instruments widely available to the public, and not those special tools produced by the vehicle manufacturer for distribution to dealer service departments. Occasionally, references to the manufacturer's special tools are included in the text of this manual. Generally, an alternative method of doing the job without the special tool is offered. However, sometimes there is no alternative to their use. Where this is the case, and the tool cannot be purchased or borrowed, the work should be turned over to the dealer service department or an automotive repair shop.

Valve spring compressor
Piston ring groove cleaning tool
Piston ring compressor
Piston ring installation tool
Cylinder compression gauge
Cylinder ridge reamer
Cylinder surfacing hone
Cylinder bore gauge
Micrometers and/or dial calipers
Hydraulic lifter removal tool
Balljoint separator
Universal-type puller
Impact screwdriver
Dial indicator set
Stroboscopic timing light (inductive pick-up)
Hand operated vacuum/pressure pump
Tachometer/dwell meter
Universal electrical multimeter
Cable hoist
Brake spring removal and installation tools
Floor jack

Buying tools

For the do-it-yourselfer who is just starting to get involved in vehicle maintenance and repair, there are a number of options available when purchasing tools. If maintenance and minor repair is the extent of the work to be done, the purchase of individual tools is satisfactory. If, on the other hand, extensive work is planned, it would be a good idea to purchase a modest tool set from one of the large retail chain stores. A set can usually be bought at a substantial savings over the individual tool prices, and they often come with a tool box. As additional tools are

needed, add-on sets, individual tools and a larger tool box can be purchased to expand the tool selection. Building a tool set gradually allows the cost of the tools to be spread over a longer period of time and gives the mechanic the freedom to choose only those tools that will actually be used.

Tool stores will often be the only source of some of the special tools that are needed, but regardless of where tools are bought, try to avoid cheap ones, especially when buying screwdrivers and sockets, because they won't last very long. The expense involved in replacing cheap tools will eventually be greater than the initial cost of quality tools.

Care and maintenance of tools

Good tools are expensive, so it makes sense to treat them with respect. Keep them clean and in usable condition and store them properly when not in use. Always wipe off any dirt, grease or metal chips before putting them away. Never leave tools lying around in the work area. Upon completion of a job, always check closely under the hood for tools that may have been left there so they won't get lost during a test drive.

Some tools, such as screwdrivers, pliers, wrenches and sockets, can be hung on a panel mounted on the garage or workshop wall, while others should be kept in a tool box or tray. Measuring instruments, gauges, meters, etc. must be carefully stored where they cannot be damaged by weather or impact from other tools.

When tools are used with care and stored properly, they will last a very long time. Even with the best of care, though, tools will wear out if used frequently. When a tool is damaged or worn out, replace it. Subsequent jobs will be safer and more enjoyable if you do.

How to repair damaged threads

Sometimes, the internal threads of a nut or bolt hole can become stripped, usually from overtightening. Stripping threads is an all-too-common occurrence, especially when working with aluminum parts, because aluminum is so soft that it easily strips out.

Usually, external or internal threads are only partially stripped. After they've been cleaned up with a tap or die, they'll still work. Sometimes, however, threads are badly damaged. When this happens, you've got three choices:

1) *Drill and tap the hole to the next suitable oversize and install a larger diameter bolt, screw or stud.*
2) *Drill and tap the hole to accept a threaded plug, then drill and tap the plug to the original screw size. You can also buy a plug already threaded to the original size. Then you simply drill a hole to the specified size, then run the threaded plug into the hole with a bolt and jam*

nut. Once the plug is fully seated, remove the jam nut and bolt.
3) *The third method uses a patented thread repair kit like Heli-Coil or Slimsert. These easy-to-use kits are designed to repair damaged threads in straight-through holes and blind holes. Both are available as kits which can handle a variety of sizes and thread patterns. Drill the hole, then tap it with the special included tap. Install the Heli-Coil and the hole is back to its original diameter and thread pitch.*

Regardless of which method you use, be sure to proceed calmly and carefully. A little impatience or carelessness during one of these relatively simple procedures can ruin your whole day's work and cost you a bundle if you wreck an expensive part.

Working facilities

Not to be overlooked when discussing tools is the workshop. If anything more than routine maintenance is to be carried out, some sort of suitable work area is essential.

It is understood, and appreciated, that many home mechanics do not have a good workshop or garage available, and end up removing an engine or doing major repairs outside. It is recommended, however, that the overhaul or repair be completed under the cover of a roof.

A clean, flat workbench or table of comfortable working height is an absolute necessity. The workbench should be equipped with a vise that has a jaw opening of at least four inches.

As mentioned previously, some clean, dry storage space is also required for tools, as well as the lubricants, fluids, cleaning solvents, etc. which soon become necessary.

Sometimes waste oil and fluids, drained from the engine or cooling system during normal maintenance or repairs, present a disposal problem. To avoid pouring them on the ground or into a sewage system, pour the used fluids into large containers, seal them with caps and take them to an authorized disposal site or recycling center. Plastic jugs, such as old antifreeze containers, are ideal for this purpose.

Always keep a supply of old newspapers and clean rags available. Old towels are excellent for mopping up spills. Many mechanics use rolls of paper towels for most work because they are readily available and disposable. To help keep the area under the vehicle clean, a large cardboard box can be cut open and flattened to protect the garage or shop floor.

Whenever working over a painted surface, such as when leaning over a fender to service something under the hood, always cover it with an old blanket or bedspread to protect the finish. Vinyl covered pads, made especially for this purpose, are available at auto parts stores.

Jacking and towing

Jacking

Warning: *The jack supplied with the vehicle should only be used for changing a tire or placing jackstands under the frame. Never work under the vehicle or start the engine while this jack is being used as the only means of support.*

The vehicle should be on level ground. Place the shift lever in Park, if you have an automatic, or Reverse if you have a manual transmission. Block the wheel diagonally opposite the wheel being changed. Set the parking brake. **Warning:** *When one rear wheel is lifted off the ground, neither the automatic nor the manual transmission will prevent the vehicle from moving and possibly slipping off the jack, even if it has been placed in Reverse or Park as described above. To prevent movement of the vehicle while changing a tire, always set the parking brake and block the wheel diagonally opposite the wheel being changed.*

Remove the spare tire and jack from stowage. If equipped with anti-theft wire wheel covers, pry off the emblem and remove the lock bolt with the special wrench **(see illustration).** Remove the wheel cover (if so equipped) with the tapered end of the lug nut wrench by inserting it and twisting the handle and then prying against the inner wheel cover flange. Loosen, but do not remove, the lug nuts (one-half turn is sufficient). If equipped with aluminum wheels, one of the lug nuts will be an anti-theft type (see Anti-theft wheel lug nuts below) **Note:** *Some models have ornamental lug nuts; do not attempt to remove them - they are decorative items only! The entire ornament assembly must be removed.*

Place the scissors-type jack under the side of the vehicle and adjust the jack height with the jack handle so it fits into the notch in the vertical rocker panel flange nearest the wheel to be changed. There is a front and rear jacking notch on each side of the vehicle. When lifting the vehicle in any other way, special care must be exercised to avoid damage to the fuel tank, filler neck, exhaust system and underbody. **Caution:** *Do not raise the vehicle with a bumper jack. The bumper could be damaged. Also, jack slippage may occur, causing personal injury.*

Turn the jack handle clockwise until the tire clears the ground. Remove the lug nuts and the wheel. Pull the wheel off and replace it with the spare.

Replace the lug nuts with the beveled edges facing in. Tighten them snugly. Don't attempt to tighten them completely until the vehicle is lowered or it could slip off the jack.

Turn the jack handle counterclockwise to lower the vehicle. Remove the jack and tighten the lug nuts in a criss-cross pattern.

Align the wheel cover (if so equipped) with the valve stem extension matching the hole in the cover. Install the cover and be sure that it's snapped in place all the way around. Stow the tire, jack and wrench. Unblock the wheels.

Anti-theft wheel lug nuts

If your vehicle is equipped with aluminum wheels, they have anti-theft wheel lug nuts (one per wheel). The key and your registration card are attached to the lug wrench stowed with the spare tire. Don't lose the registration card. You must send it to the manufacturer, not the dealer, to get a replacement key if yours is lost. To remove or install the anti-theft lug nut, insert the key into the slot in the lug nut. Place the lug nut wrench on the key and, while applying pressure on the key, remove or install the lug nut. Mark the anti-theft lug nut location on the wheel before removing it. This will allow you to install it in the same location.

Towing

As a general rule, the vehicle should be towed with the rear (drive) wheels off the ground. If they can't be raised, either place them on a dolly or disconnect the driveshaft from the differential. When a vehicle is towed with the rear wheels raised, the steering wheel must be clamped in the straight ahead position with a special device designed for use during towing. **Warning:** *Don't use the steering column lock to keep the front wheels pointed straight ahead. It's not strong enough for this purpose.*

Vehicles can be towed with all four wheels on the ground, provided that speeds don't exceed 35 mph and the distance is not over 50 miles. When the rear wheels are off the ground there's no distance limitation, but don't exceed 50 mph.

Equipment specifically designed for towing should be used. It should be attached to the main structural members of the vehicle, not the bumpers or brackets.

Safety is a major consideration when towing and all applicable state and local laws must be obeyed. A safety chain system must be used at all times.

While towing, the parking brake should be released and the transmission must be in Neutral. The steering must be unlocked (ignition switch in the Off position). Remember that power steering and power brakes will not work with the engine off.

Booster battery (jump) starting

Observe these precautions when using a booster battery to start a vehicle:

a) *Before connecting the booster battery, make sure the ignition switch is in the Off position.*

b) *Turn off the lights, heater and other electrical loads.*

c) *Your eyes should be shielded. Safety goggles are a good idea.*

d) *Make sure the booster battery is the same voltage as the dead one in the vehicle.*

e) *The two vehicles MUST NOT TOUCH each other!*

f) *Make sure the transaxle is in Neutral (manual) or Park (automatic).*

g) *If the booster battery is not a maintenance-free type, remove the vent caps and lay a cloth over the vent holes.*

Connect the red jumper cable to the positive (+) terminals of each battery **(see illustration)**.

Connect one end of the black jumper cable to the negative (-) terminal of the booster battery. The other end of this cable should be connected to a good ground on the vehicle to be started, such as a bolt or bracket on the body.

Start the engine using the booster battery, then, with the engine running at idle speed, disconnect the jumper cables in the reverse order of connection.

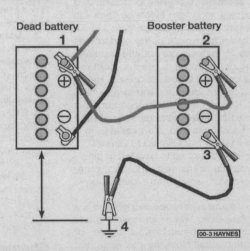

Make the booster battery cable connections in the numerical order shown (note that the negative cable of the booster battery is NOT attached to the negative terminal of the dead battery)

Automotive chemicals and lubricants

A number of automotive chemicals and lubricants are available for use during vehicle maintenance and repair. They include a wide variety of products ranging from cleaning solvents and degreasers to lubricants and protective sprays for rubber, plastic and vinyl.

Cleaners

Carburetor cleaner and choke cleaner is a strong solvent for gum, varnish and carbon. Most carburetor cleaners leave a dry-type lubricant film which will not harden or gum up. Because of this film it is not recommended for use on electrical components.

Brake system cleaner is used to remove brake dust, grease and brake fluid from the brake system, where clean surfaces are absolutely necessary. It leaves no residue and often eliminates brake squeal caused by contaminants.

Electrical cleaner removes oxidation, corrosion and carbon deposits from electrical contacts, restoring full current flow. It can also be used to clean spark plugs, carburetor jets, voltage regulators and other parts where an oil-free surface is desired.

Demoisturants remove water and moisture from electrical components such as alternators, voltage regulators, electrical connectors and fuse blocks. They are non-conductive and non-corrosive.

Degreasers are heavy-duty solvents used to remove grease from the outside of the engine and from chassis components. They can be sprayed or brushed on and, depending on the type, are rinsed off either with water or solvent.

Lubricants

Motor oil is the lubricant formulated for use in engines. It normally contains a wide variety of additives to prevent corrosion and reduce foaming and wear. Motor oil comes in various weights (viscosity ratings) from 0 to 50. The recommended weight of the oil depends on the season, temperature and the demands on the engine. Light oil is used in cold climates and under light load conditions. Heavy oil is used in hot climates and where high loads are encountered. Multi-viscosity oils are designed to have characteristics of both light and heavy oils and are available in a number of weights from 5W-20 to 20W-50.

Gear oil is designed to be used in differentials, manual transmissions and other areas where high-temperature lubrication is required.

Chassis and wheel bearing grease is a heavy grease used where increased loads and friction are encountered, such as for wheel bearings, balljoints, tie-rod ends and universal joints.

High-temperature wheel bearing grease is designed to withstand the extreme temperatures encountered by wheel bearings

in disc brake equipped vehicles. It usually contains molybdenum disulfide (moly), which is a dry-type lubricant.

White grease is a heavy grease for metal-to-metal applications where water is a problem. White grease stays soft under both low and high temperatures (usually from -100 to +190-degrees F), and will not wash off or dilute in the presence of water.

Assembly lube is a special extreme pressure lubricant, usually containing moly, used to lubricate high-load parts (such as main and rod bearings and cam lobes) for initial start-up of a new engine. The assembly lube lubricates the parts without being squeezed out or washed away until the engine oiling system begins to function.

Silicone lubricants are used to protect rubber, plastic, vinyl and nylon parts.

Graphite lubricants are used where oils cannot be used due to contamination problems, such as in locks. The dry graphite will lubricate metal parts while remaining uncontaminated by dirt, water, oil or acids. It is electrically conductive and will not foul electrical contacts in locks such as the ignition switch.

Moly penetrants loosen and lubricate frozen, rusted and corroded fasteners and prevent future rusting or freezing.

Heat-sink grease is a special electrically non-conductive grease that is used for mounting electronic ignition modules where it is essential that heat is transferred away from the module.

Sealants

RTV sealant is one of the most widely used gasket compounds. Made from silicone, RTV is air curing, it seals, bonds, waterproofs, fills surface irregularities, remains flexible, doesn't shrink, is relatively easy to remove, and is used as a supplementary sealer with almost all low and medium temperature gaskets.

Anaerobic sealant is much like RTV in that it can be used either to seal gaskets or to form gaskets by itself. It remains flexible, is solvent resistant and fills surface imperfections. The difference between an anaerobic sealant and an RTV-type sealant is in the curing. RTV cures when exposed to air, while an anaerobic sealant cures only in the absence of air. This means that an anaerobic sealant cures only after the assembly of parts, sealing them together.

Thread and pipe sealant is used for sealing hydraulic and pneumatic fittings and vacuum lines. It is usually made from a Teflon compound, and comes in a spray, a paint-on liquid and as a wrap-around tape.

Chemicals

Anti-seize compound prevents seizing, galling, cold welding, rust and corrosion in fasteners. High-temperature ant-seize, usu-

ally made with copper and graphite lubricants, is used for exhaust system and exhaust manifold bolts.

Anaerobic locking compounds are used to keep fasteners from vibrating or working loose and cure only after installation, in the absence of air. Medium strength locking compound is used for small nuts, bolts and screws that may be removed later. High-strength locking compound is for large nuts, bolts and studs which aren't removed on a regular basis.

Oil additives range from viscosity index improvers to chemical treatments that claim to reduce internal engine friction. It should be noted that most oil manufacturers caution against using additives with their oils.

Gas additives perform several functions, depending on their chemical makeup. They usually contain solvents that help dissolve gum and varnish that build up on carburetor, fuel injection and intake parts. They also serve to break down carbon deposits that form on the inside surfaces of the combustion chambers. Some additives contain upper cylinder lubricants for valves and piston rings, and others contain chemicals to remove condensation from the gas tank.

Miscellaneous

Brake fluid is specially formulated hydraulic fluid that can withstand the heat and pressure encountered in brake systems. Care must be taken so this fluid does not come in contact with painted surfaces or plastics. An opened container should always be resealed to prevent contamination by water or dirt.

Weatherstrip adhesive is used to bond weatherstripping around doors, windows and trunk lids. It is sometimes used to attach trim pieces.

Undercoating is a petroleum-based, tar-like substance that is designed to protect metal surfaces on the underside of the vehicle from corrosion. It also acts as a sound-deadening agent by insulating the bottom of the vehicle.

Waxes and polishes are used to help protect painted and plated surfaces from the weather. Different types of paint may require the use of different types of wax and polish. Some polishes utilize a chemical or abrasive cleaner to help remove the top layer of oxidized (dull) paint on older vehicles. In recent years many non-wax polishes that contain a wide variety of chemicals such as polymers and silicones have been introduced. These non-wax polishes are usually easier to apply and last longer than conventional waxes and polishes.

Conversion factors

Length (distance)
Inches (in)	X	25.4	= Millimeters (mm)	X	0.0394	= Inches (in)
Feet (ft)	X	0.305	= Meters (m)	X	3.281	= Feet (ft)
Miles	X	1.609	= Kilometers (km)	X	0.621	= Miles

Length (distance)
Inches (in) X 25.4 = Millimeters (mm) X 0.0394 = Inches (in)
Feet (ft) X 0.305 = Meters (m) X 3.281 = Feet (ft)
Miles X 1.609 = Kilometers (km) X 0.621 = Miles

Volume (capacity)
Cubic inches (cu in; in³) X 16.387 = Cubic centimeters (cc; cm³) X 0.061 = Cubic inches (cu in; in³)
Imperial pints (Imp pt) X 0.568 = Liters (l) X 1.76 = Imperial pints (Imp pt)
Imperial quarts (Imp qt) X 1.137 = Liters (l) X 0.88 = Imperial quarts (Imp qt)
Imperial quarts (Imp qt) X 1.201 = US quarts (US qt) X 0.833 = Imperial quarts (Imp qt)
US quarts (US qt) X 0.946 = Liters (l) X 1.057 = US quarts (US qt)
Imperial gallons (Imp gal) X 4.546 = Liters (l) X 0.22 = Imperial gallons (Imp gal)
Imperial gallons (Imp gal) X 1.201 = US gallons (US gal) X 0.833 = Imperial gallons (Imp gal)
US gallons (US gal) X 3.785 = Liters (l) X 0.264 = US gallons (US gal)

Mass (weight)
Ounces (oz) X 28.35 = Grams (g) X 0.035 = Ounces (oz)
Pounds (lb) X 0.454 = Kilograms (kg) X 2.205 = Pounds (lb)

Force
Ounces-force (ozf; oz) X 0.278 = Newtons (N) X 3.6 = Ounces-force (ozf; oz)
Pounds-force (lbf; lb) X 4.448 = Newtons (N) X 0.225 = Pounds-force (lbf; lb)
Newtons (N) X 0.1 = Kilograms-force (kgf; kg) X 9.81 = Newtons (N)

Pressure
Pounds-force per square inch (psi; lbf/in²; lb/in²) X 0.070 = Kilograms-force per square centimeter (kgf/cm²; kg/cm²) X 14.223 = Pounds-force per square inch (psi; lbf/in²; lb/in²)
Pounds-force per square inch (psi; lbf/in²; lb/in²) X 0.068 = Atmospheres (atm) X 14.696 = Pounds-force per square inch (psi; lbf/in²; lb/in²)
Pounds-force per square inch (psi; lbf/in²; lb/in²) X 0.069 = Bars X 14.5 = Pounds-force per square inch (psi; lbf/in²; lb/in²)
Pounds-force per square inch (psi; lbf/in²; lb/in²) X 6.895 = Kilopascals (kPa) X 0.145 = Pounds-force per square inch (psi; lbf/in²; lb/in²)
Kilopascals (kPa) X 0.01 = Kilograms-force per square centimeter (kgf/cm²; kg/cm²) X 98.1 = Kilopascals (kPa)

Torque (moment of force)
Pounds-force inches (lbf in; lb in) X 1.152 = Kilograms-force centimeter (kgf cm; kg cm) X 0.868 = Pounds-force inches (lbf in; lb in)
Pounds-force inches (lbf in; lb in) X 0.113 = Newton meters (Nm) X 8.85 = Pounds-force inches (lbf in; lb in)
Pounds-force inches (lbf in; lb in) X 0.083 = Pounds-force feet (lbf ft; lb ft) X 12 = Pounds-force inches (lbf in; lb in)
Pounds-force feet (lbf ft; lb ft) X 0.138 = Kilograms-force meters (kgf m; kg m) X 7.233 = Pounds-force feet (lbf ft; lb ft)
Pounds-force feet (lbf ft; lb ft) X 1.356 = Newton meters (Nm) X 0.738 = Pounds-force feet (lbf ft; lb ft)
Newton meters (Nm) X 0.102 = Kilograms-force meters (kgf m; kg m) X 9.804 = Newton meters (Nm)

Vacuum
Inches mercury (in. Hg) X 3.377 = Kilopascals (kPa) X 0.2961 = Inches mercury
Inches mercury (in. Hg) X 25.4 = Millimeters mercury (mm Hg) X 0.0394 = Inches mercury

Power
Horsepower (hp) X 745.7 = Watts (W) X 0.0013 = Horsepower (hp)

Velocity (speed)
Miles per hour (miles/hr; mph) X 1.609 = Kilometers per hour (km/hr; kph) X 0.621 = Miles per hour (miles/hr; mph)

Fuel consumption*
Miles per gallon, Imperial (mpg) X 0.354 = Kilometers per liter (km/l) X 2.825 = Miles per gallon, Imperial (mpg)
Miles per gallon, US (mpg) X 0.425 = Kilometers per liter (km/l) X 2.352 = Miles per gallon, US (mpg)

Temperature
Degrees Fahrenheit = (°C x 1.8) + 32   Degrees Celsius (Degrees Centigrade; °C) = (°F - 32) x 0.56

It is common practice to convert from miles per gallon (mpg) to liters/100 kilometers (l/100km), where mpg (Imperial) x l/100 km = 282 and mpg (US) x l/100 km = 235

Safety first!

Regardless of how enthusiastic you may be about getting on with the job at hand, take the time to ensure that your safety is not jeopardized. A moment's lack of attention can result in an accident, as can failure to observe certain simple safety precautions. The possibility of an accident will always exist, and the following points should not be considered a comprehensive list of all dangers. Rather, they are intended to make you aware of the risks and to encourage a safety conscious approach to all work you carry out on your vehicle.

Essential DOs and DON'Ts

DON'T rely on a jack when working under the vehicle. Always use approved jackstands to support the weight of the vehicle and place them under the recommended lift or support points.

DON'T attempt to loosen extremely tight fasteners (i.e. wheel lug nuts) while the vehicle is on a jack - it may fall.

DON'T start the engine without first making sure that the transmission is in Neutral (or Park where applicable) and the parking brake is set.

DON'T remove the radiator cap from a hot cooling system - let it cool or cover it with a cloth and release the pressure gradually.

DON'T attempt to drain the engine oil until you are sure it has cooled to the point that it will not burn you.

DON'T touch any part of the engine or exhaust system until it has cooled sufficiently to avoid burns.

DON'T siphon toxic liquids such as gasoline, antifreeze and brake fluid by mouth, or allow them to remain on your skin.

DON'T inhale brake lining dust - it is potentially hazardous (see *Asbestos* below).

DON'T allow spilled oil or grease to remain on the floor - wipe it up before someone slips on it.

DON'T use loose fitting wrenches or other tools which may slip and cause injury.

DON'T push on wrenches when loosening or tightening nuts or bolts. Always try to pull the wrench toward you. If the situation calls for pushing the wrench away, push with an open hand to avoid scraped knuckles if the wrench should slip.

DON'T attempt to lift a heavy component alone - get someone to help you.

DON'T rush or take unsafe shortcuts to finish a job.

DON'T allow children or animals in or around the vehicle while you are working on it.

DO wear eye protection when using power tools such as a drill, sander, bench grinder, etc. and when working under a vehicle.

DO keep loose clothing and long hair well out of the way of moving parts.

DO make sure that any hoist used has a safe working load rating adequate for the job.

DO get someone to check on you periodically when working alone on a vehicle.

DO carry out work in a logical sequence and make sure that everything is correctly assembled and tightened.

DO keep chemicals and fluids tightly capped and out of the reach of children and pets.

DO remember that your vehicle's safety affects that of yourself and others. If in doubt on any point, get professional advice.

Asbestos

Certain friction, insulating, sealing, and other products - such as brake linings, brake bands, clutch linings, torque converters, gaskets, etc. - may contain asbestos. Extreme care must be taken to avoid inhalation of dust from such products, since it is hazardous to health. If in doubt, assume that they do contain asbestos.

Fire

Remember at all times that gasoline is highly flammable. Never smoke or have any kind of open flame around when working on a vehicle. But the risk does not end there. A spark caused by an electrical short circuit, by two metal surfaces contacting each other, or even by static electricity built up in your body under certain conditions, can ignite gasoline vapors, which in a confined space are highly explosive. Do not, under any circumstances, use gasoline for cleaning parts. Use an approved safety solvent.

Always disconnect the battery ground (-) cable at the battery before working on any part of the fuel system or electrical system. Never risk spilling fuel on a hot engine or exhaust component. It is strongly recommended that a fire extinguisher suitable for use on fuel and electrical fires be kept handy in the garage or workshop at all times. Never try to extinguish a fuel or electrical fire with water.

Fumes

Certain fumes are highly toxic and can quickly cause unconsciousness and even death if inhaled to any extent. Gasoline vapor falls into this category, as do the vapors from some cleaning solvents. Any draining or pouring of such volatile fluids should be done in a well ventilated area.

When using cleaning fluids and solvents, read the instructions on the container carefully. Never use materials from unmarked containers.

Never run the engine in an enclosed space, such as a garage. Exhaust fumes contain carbon monoxide, which is extremely poisonous. If you need to run the engine, always do so in the open air, or at least have the rear of the vehicle outside the work area.

If you are fortunate enough to have the use of an inspection pit, never drain or pour gasoline and never run the engine while the vehicle is over the pit. The fumes, being heavier than air, will concentrate in the pit with possibly lethal results.

The battery

Never create a spark or allow a bare light bulb near a battery. They normally give off a certain amount of hydrogen gas, which is highly explosive.

Always disconnect the battery ground (-) cable at the battery before working on the fuel or electrical systems.

If possible, loosen the filler caps or cover when charging the battery from an external source (this does not apply to sealed or maintenance-free batteries). Do not charge at an excessive rate or the battery may burst.

Take care when adding water to a non maintenance-free battery and when carrying a battery. The electrolyte, even when diluted, is very corrosive and should not be allowed to contact clothing or skin.

Always wear eye protection when cleaning the battery to prevent the caustic deposits from entering your eyes.

Household current

When using an electric power tool, inspection light, etc., which operates on household current, always make sure that the tool is correctly connected to its plug and that, where necessary, it is properly grounded. Do not use such items in damp conditions and, again, do not create a spark or apply excessive heat in the vicinity of fuel or fuel vapor.

Secondary ignition system voltage

A severe electric shock can result from touching certain parts of the ignition system (such as the spark plug wires) when the engine is running or being cranked, particularly if components are damp or the insulation is defective. In the case of an electronic ignition system, the secondary system voltage is much higher and could prove fatal.

Troubleshooting

Contents

This section provides an easy reference guide to the more common problems which may occur during the operation of your vehicle. These problems and possible causes are grouped under various components or systems, such as Engine, Cooling system, etc., and also refer to the Chapter and/or Section which deals with the problem.

Remember that successful troubleshooting is not a mysterious black art practiced only by professional mechanics.

It's simply the result of a bit of knowledge combined with an intelligent, systematic approach to the problem. Always work by a process of elimination, starting with the simplest solution and working through to the most complex - and never overlook the obvious. Anyone can forget to fill the gas tank or leave the lights on overnight, so don't assume that you are above such oversights.

Finally, always get clear in your mind why a problem has occurred and take steps to ensure that it doesn't happen again. If the electrical system fails because of a poor connection, check all other connections in the system to make sure they don't fail as well. If a particular fuse continues to blow, find out why - don't just go on replacing fuses. Remember, failure of a small component can often be indicative of potential failure or incorrect functioning of a more important component or system.

Engine and performance

1 Engine will not rotate when attempting to start

1   Battery terminal connections are loose or corroded. Check the cable terminals at the battery. Tighten the cable or remove corrosion as necessary.
2   Battery discharged or faulty. It the cable connections are clean and tight on the battery posts, turn the key to the On position and switch on the headlights and/or windshield wipers. If they fail to function, the battery is discharged.
3   Automatic transmission not completely engaged in Park or clutch not completely depressed (1984 and later models).
4   Broken, loose or disconnected wiring in the starting circuit. Inspect all wiring and connectors at the battery, starter solenoid, ignition switch and neutral start switch (automatic transmission) or clutch interlock switch (1984 and later manual transmission models).
5   Starter motor pinion jammed in flywheel ring gear. If equipped with a manual transmission, place the transmission in gear and rock the vehicle to manually turn the engine. Remove the starter and inspect the pinion and flywheel at earliest convenience.
6   Starter solenoid faulty (see Chapter 5).
7   Starter motor faulty (see Chapter 5).
8   Ignition switch faulty (see Chapter 12).
9   Neutral start switch (automatic transmission) faulty (see Chapter 7B)
10   Clutch interlock switch faulty (see Chapter 8)

2 Engine rotates but will not start

1   Fuel tank empty.
2   Battery discharged (engine rotates slowly). Check the operation of electrical components as described in previous Section.
3   Battery terminal connections loose or corroded. See previous Section.
4   Carburetor flooded and/or fuel level in carburetor incorrect. This will usually be accompanied by a strong fuel odor from under the engine cover. Wait a few minutes, depress the accelerator pedal all the way to the floor and hold the pedal down while attempting to start the engine.
5   Choke control inoperative (see Chapter 4).
6   Fuel not reaching carburetor or fuel injector (s). On carbureted vehicles, with the ignition switch in the Off position, remove the top plate of the air cleaner assembly and observe the top of the carburetor (manually move the choke plate back it necessary). Depress the accelerator pedal and check that fuel spurts into the carburetor. If not, check the fuel filter (see Chapter 1), fuel lines and fuel pump (see Chapter 4).
7   Fuel injector (s) or fuel pump faulty (fuel injected vehicles) (see Chapter 4).

8   No power to fuel pump (see Chapter 4).
9   Worn, faulty or incorrectly gapped spark plugs (see Chapter 1).
10   Broken, loose or disconnected wiring in the starting circuit (see previous Section).
11   Distributor loose, causing ignition timing to change. Turn the distributor as necessary to start the engine, then set the ignition timing as soon as possible (see Chapter 1).
12   Broken, loose or disconnected wires at the ignition coil or faulty coil (see Chapter 5).
13   Fuel pump shut-off switch triggered (models with electric fuel pump). Locate the switch in the trunk and push the reset button (see Chapter 4).

3 Starter motor operates without rotating engine

1   Starter pinion sticking. Remove the starter (see Chapter 5) and inspect.
2   Starter pinion or flywheel teeth worn or broken. Remove the cover at the rear of the engine and inspect.

4 Engine hard to start when cold

1   Battery discharged or low. Check as described in Section 1.
2   Choke control inoperative or out of adjustment (see Chapter 4).
3   Carburetor flooded (see Section 2).
4   Fuel supply not reaching the carburetor or fuel injection system (see Section 2).
5   Carburetor/fuel injection system in need of overhaul (see Chapter 4).
6   Distributor rotor carbon tracked and/or damaged (see Chapter 1).
7   Fuel injection malfunction (see Chapter 4).

5 Engine hard to start when hot

1   Choke sticking in the closed position (see Chapter 4).
2   Carburetor flooded (see Section 2).
3   Air filter clogged (see Chapter 1).
4   Fuel not reaching the carburetor or fuel injector (s) (see Section 2).
5   Corroded electrical leads at the battery (see Chapter 1).
6   Bad engine ground (see Chapter 12).
7   Starter worn (see Chapter 5).
8   Corroded electrical leads at the fuel injector (see Chapter 4).

6 Starter motor noisy or excessively rough in engagement

1   Pinion or flywheel gear teeth worn or broken. Remove the cover at the rear of the engine (if so equipped) and inspect.
2   Starter motor mounting bolts loose or missing.

7 Engine starts but stops immediately

1   Loose or faulty electrical connections at distributor, coil or alternator.
2   Insufficient fuel reaching the carburetor or fuel injector (s). **Caution:** *On fuel-injected models, relieve fuel system pressure (see Chapter 4) before performing this test. Disconnect the fuel line. Place a container under the disconnected fuel line and observe the flow of fuel from the line. If little or none at all, check for blockage in the lines and/or replace the fuel pump (see Chapter 4).*
3   Vacuum leak at the gasket surfaces of the carburetor or fuel injection unit (CF I models) Make sure that all mounting bolts/nuts are tightened securely and that all vacuum hoses connected to the carburetor or fuel injection unit and manifold are positioned properly and in good condition.

8 Engine lopes while idling or Idles erratically

1   Vacuum leakage. Check mounting bolts/nuts at the carburetor or fuel injection unit (CFI models) and intake manifold for tightness. Make sure that all vacuum hoses are connected and in good condition. Check undersides of vacuum hoses; an apparently good hose may have a concealed hole or crack. Use a stethoscope or a length of fuel hose held against your ear to listen for vacuum leaks while the engine is running. A hissing sound will be heard. Check the carburetor/fuel injector and intake manifold gasket surface.
2   Leaking EAGER valve or plugged PCV valve (see Chapters 1 and 6).
3   Air filter clogged (see Chapter 1).
4   Fuel pump not delivering sufficient fuel to the carburetor/fuel injector (see Section 7).
5   Carburetor out of adjustment (see Chapters 1 and 4).
6   Leaking head gasket. It this is suspected, take the vehicle to a repair shop or dealer where the engine can be pressure checked.
7   Timing chain and/or gears worn (see Chapter 2).
8   Camshaft lobes worn (see Chapter 2).

9 Engine misses at idle speed

1   Spark plugs worn or not gapped properly (see Chapter 1).
2   Faulty spark plug wires (see Chapter 1).
3   Choke not operating properly (see Chapter 1).
4   Sticking or faulty emission system components (see Chapter 6).
5   Clogged fuel filter and/or foreign matter in fuel. Remove the fuel filter (see Chapter 1) and inspect.

6   Vacuum leaks at the intake manifold or at hose connections. Check as described in Section 8.
7   Incorrect idle speed or idle mixture (see Chapter 1).
8   Incorrect ignition timing (see Chapter 5).
9   Uneven or low cylinder compression. Check compression as described in Chapter 2.

10   Engine misses throughout driving speed range

1   Fuel filter clogged and/or impurities in the fuel system (see Chapter 1). Also check fuel output at the carburetor/fuel injector (see Section 7).
2   Faulty or incorrectly gapped spark plugs (see Chapter 1).
3   Incorrect ignition timing (see Chapter 5).
4   Check f or cracked distributor cap, disconnected distributor wires and damaged distributor components (see Chapter 1).
5   Leaking spark plug wires (see Chapter 1).
6   Faulty emissions system components (see Chapter 6).
7   Low or uneven cylinder compression pressures. Remove the spark plugs and test the compression with gauge (see Chapter 2).
8   Weak or faulty ignition system (see Chapter 5).
9   Vacuum leaks at the carburetor/fuel injection unit or vacuum hoses (see Section 8).

11   Engine stalls

1   Idle speed incorrect (see Chapter 1).
2   Fuel filter clogged and/or water and impurities in the fuel system (see ,Chapter 1).
3   Choke improperly adjusted or sticking (see Chapter 4).
4   Distributor components damp or damaged (see Chapter 5).
5   Faulty emissions system components (see Chapter 6).
6   Faulty or incorrectly gapped spark plugs (see Chapter 1). Also check spark plug wires (see Chapter 1).
7   Vacuum leak at the carburetor/ fuel injection unit or vacuum hoses. Check as described in Section 8.

12   Engine lacks power

1   Incorrect ignition timing (see Chapter 5).
2   Excessive play in distributor shaft. At the same time, cheek for worn rotor, faulty distributor cap, wires, etc. (see Chapter 1 and 5).
3   Faulty or incorrectly gapped spark plugs (see Chapter 1).
4   Fuel injection unit not adjusted properly or excessively worn (see Chapter 4).
5   Faulty coil (see Chapter 5).
6   Brakes binding (see Chapter 1).

7   Automatic transmission fluid level incorrect (see Chapter 1).
8   Clutch slipping (see Chapter 8).
9   Fuel filter clogged or impurities in the fuel system (see Chapter 1).
10   Emissions control system not functioning properly (see Chapter 6).
11   Use of substandard fuel. Fill tank with proper octane fuel.
12   Low or uneven cylinder compression pressures. Test with compression tester, which will detect leaking valves and/or blown head gasket (see Chapter 2).

13   Engine backfires

1   Emissions system not functioning properly (see Chapter 6).
2   Ignition timing incorrect (see Chapter 1).
3   Faulty secondary ignition system (cracked spark plug insulator, faulty plug wires, distributor cap and/or rotor (see Chapters 1 and 5).
4   Carburetor/ fuel injection unit in need of adjustment or worn excessively (see Chapter 4).
5   Vacuum leak at the carburetor/ fuel injection unit or vacuum hoses. Check as described in Section 8.
6   Valves sticking (see Chapter 2).
7   Firing order incorrect (see Chapter 1).

14   Pinging or knocking engine sounds during acceleration or uphill

1   Incorrect grade of fuel. Fill tank with fuel of the proper octane rating.
2   Ignition timing incorrect (see Chapter 5).
3   Carburetor/ fuel injection unit in need of adjustment (see Chapter 4).
4   Improper spark plugs. Check plug type against Emission Control Information label located under hood. Also check plugs and wires for damage (see Chapter 1).
5   Worn or damaged distributor components (see Chapter 5).
6   Faulty emissions system (see Chapter 6).
7   Vacuum leak. Check as described in Section 8.

15   Engine diesels (continues to run) after switching off

1   Idle speed too high (see Chapter 1).
2   Electrical solenoid at side of carburetor not functioning properly (not all models, see Chapter 4).
3   Ignition timing incorrectly adjusted (see Chapter 5).
4   Thermo-controlled air cleaner heat valve not operating properly (see Chapter 1).
5   Excessive engine operating temperature. Probable causes of this are malfunctioning thermostat, clogged radiator, faulty water pump (see Chapter 3).

Engine electrical system

16   Battery will not hold a charge

1   Alternator drivebelt defective or not adjusted properly (see Chapter 1).
2   Electrolyte level low or battery discharged (see Chapter 1).
3   Battery terminals loose or corroded (see Chapter 1).
4   Alternator not charging properly (see Chapter 5).
5   Loose, broken or faulty wiring in the charging circuit (see Chapter 5).
6   Short in vehicle wiring causing a continual drain on battery.
7   Battery defective internally.

17   Alternator light stays on

1   Fault in alternator or charging circuit (see Chapter 5).
2   Alternator drivebelt defective or not properly adjusted (see Chapter 1).

18   Alternator light falls to come on when key is turned on

1   Warning light bulb defective (see Chapter 12).
2   Alternator faulty (see Chapter 5).
3   Fault in the printed circuit, dash wiring or bulb holder (see Chapter 12).

Fuel system

19   Excessive fuel consumption

1   Dirty or clogged air filter element (see Chapter 1).
2   Incorrectly set ignition timing (see Chapter 5).
3   Choke sticking or improperly adjusted (see Chapter 1).
4   Emission system not functioning properly (not all vehicles, see Chapter 6).
5   Carburetor idle speed and/or mixture not adjusted properly (see Chapter 1).
6   Carburetor/fuel injection parts excessively worn or damaged (see Chapter 4).
7   Low tire pressure or incorrect tire size (see Chapter 1).

20   Fuel leakage and/or fuel odor

1   Leak in a fuel feed or vent line (see Chapter 4).
2   Tank overfilled. Fill only to automatic shut-off.
3   Emissions system clogged or damaged (see Chapter 6).
4   Vapor leaks from system lines (see Chapter 4).
5   Carburetor/fuel injection internal parts excessively worn or out of adjustment (see Chapter 4).

Cooling system

21 Overheating

1   Insufficient coolant in system (see Chapter 1).
2   Water pump drivebelt defective or not adjusted properly (see Chapter 1).
3   Radiator core blocked or radiator grille dirty and restricted (see Chapter 3).
4   Thermostat faulty (see Chapter 3).
5   Fan blades broken or cracked (see Chapter 3).
6   Radiator cap not maintaining proper pressure. Have cap pressure tested by gas station or repair shop.
7   Ignition timing incorrect (see Chapter 5).

22 Overcooling

1   Thermostat faulty (see Chapter 3).
2   Inaccurate temperature gauge or sender (see Chapter 3).

23 External coolant leakage

1   Deteriorated or damaged hoses or loose clamps. Replace hoses and/ or tighten clamps at hose connections (see Chapter 1).
2   Water pump seals defective. If this is the case, water will drip from the weep hole in the water pump body (see Chapter 3).
3   Leakage from radiator core or header tank. This will require the radiator to be professionally repaired (see Chapter 3 for removal procedures).

24 Internal coolant leakage

Note: *Internal coolant leaks can usually be detected by examining the oil. Check the dipstick and inside of the rocker arm cover (s) for water deposits and an oil consistency like that of a milkshake.*
1   Leaking cylinder head gasket. Have the cooling system pressure tested.
2   Cracked cylinder bore or cylinder head. Dismantle engine and inspect (see Chapter 2).

25 Coolant loss

1   Too much coolant in system (see Chapter 1).
2   Coolant boiling away due to overheating (see Section 21).
3   Internal or external leakage (see Sections 23 and 24).
4   Faulty radiator cap. Have the cap pressure tested.

26 Poor coolant circulation

1   Inoperative water pump. A quick test is to pinch the top radiator hose closed with your hand while the engine is idling, then let it loose. You should feel the surge of coolant if the pump is working properly (see Chapter 3).
2   Restriction in cooling system. Drain, flush and refill the system (see Chapter 1). If necessary, remove the radiator (see Chapter 3) and have it reverse flushed.
3   Water pump drivebelt defective or not adjusted properly (see Chapter 1).
4   Thermostat sticking (see Chapter 3).

Clutch

27 Fails to release (pedal pressed to the floor - shift lever does not move freely in and out of Reverse)

1   Clutch fork off ball stud. Look under the vehicle, on the left side of transmission.
2   Clutch cable out of adjustment or broken (mechanical release system) (see Chapter 8).
3   Master or slave cylinder faulty, faulty hydraulic line, low fluid level or air in system (hydraulic release system).
4   Clutch self-adjuster quadrant faulty (1981 and later models) (see Chapter 8).
5   Clutch plate warped or damaged (see Chapter 8).
6   If the pedal makes a ratcheting noise while traveling to the floor, the self-adjuster quadrant is probably faulty (see Chapter 8).

28 Clutch slips (engine speed increases with no increase in vehicle speed)

1   Clutch plate oil soaked or lining worn. Remove clutch (see Chapter 8) and inspect.
2   Clutch plate not seated. It may take 30 or 40 normal starts for a new one to seat.
3   Pressure plate worn (see Chapter 8).

29 Grabbing (chattering) as clutch is engaged

1   Oil on clutch plate lining. Remove (see Chapter 8) and inspect. Correct any leakage source.
2   Worn or loose engine or transmission mounts. These units move slightly when clutch is released. Inspect mounts and bolts.
3   Worn splines on clutch plate hub. Remove clutch components (see Chapter 8) and inspect.
4   Warped pressure plate or flywheel. Remove clutch components and inspect.

30 Squeal or rumble with clutch fully engaged (pedal released)

1   Worn, defective or broken release bearing (release bearing is constantly engaged on all models) (see Chapter 8).
2   Release bearing binding on transmission bearing retainer. Remove clutch components (see chapter 8) and check bearing. Remove any burrs or nicks, clean and relubricate before reinstallation.

31 Squeal or rumble with clutch fully disengaged (pedal depressed)

1   Worn, defective or broken release bearing (see Chapter 8).
2   Worn or broken pressure plate springs (or diaphragm fingers) (see Chapter 8).
3   Air in hydraulic line (see Chapter 8).

32 Clutch pedal stays on floor when disengaged

1   Bind in clutch cable. Inspect cable as necessary.
2   Binding release bearing. Remove clutch housing (see chapter 8) and inspect.
3   Faulty self-adjusting system (1981 and later models) (see chapters 8).

Manual transmission

Note; *All the following references are to Chapter 7, unless otherwise noted.*

33 Noisy in Neutral with engine running

1   Worn clutch release bearing (see Chapter 8) (release bearing is constantly engaged). To determine whether noise is from release bearing or transmission, disconnect clutch cable from release lever and pull release lever away from cable. If the noise stops, it is the release bearing; if it continues, it is from the transmission.
2   Damaged main drive gear bearing.
3   Worn countershaft bearings.
4   Worn or damaged countershaft end play shims.

34 Noisy in all gears

1   Any of the above causes, and/or:
2   Insufficient lubricant (see checking procedures in Chapter 1).

35 Noisy in one particular gear

1   Worn, damaged or chipped gear teeth for that particular gear.
2   Worn or damaged synchronizer for that particular gear.

36 Slips out of high gear

1   Transmission mounting bolts loose.
2   Shift rods not working freely.
3   Damaged mainshaft pilot bearing.
4   Dirt between transmission case and engine or misalignment of transmission.

37 Difficulty in engaging gears

1   Loose, damaged or out-of -adjustment shift linkage. Make a thorough inspection, replacing parts as necessary.

2 Clutch cable out of adjustment (1979-1980) or self-adjusting mechanism worn or damaged (1981 and later) (see Chapter 8).

38 Lubricant leakage

1 Excessive amount of lubricant in transmission (see Chapter 1 for correct checking procedures). Drain lubricant as required.
2 Side cover loose or gasket damaged.
3 Rear oil seal or speedometer oil seal in need of replacement.

Automatic transmission

Note: *Due to the complexity of the automatic transmission, it is difficult for the home mechanic to properly diagnose and service this component. For problems other than the following, the vehicle should be taken to a dealer or reputable repair shop.*

39 General shift mechanism problems

1 Chapter 7 deals with checking and adjusting the shift linkage on automatic transmissions. Common problems which may be attributed to poorly adjusted linkage are:
  Engine starting in gears other than Park or Neutral
  Indicator on shifter pointing to a gear other than the one actually being used
  Vehicle moves when in Park
2 Refer to Chapter 7 to adjust the linkage.

40 Transmission will not downshift with accelerator pedal pressed to floor

Chapter 7 deals with adjusting the downshift cable, downshift switch or TV cable to enable the transmission to downshift properly.

41 Transmission slips, shifts rough, is noisy or has no drive in forward or reverse gears

1 There are many probable causes for the above problems, but the home mechanic should be concerned with only one possibility- fluid level.
2 Before taking the vehicle to a repair shop, check the level and condition of the fluid as described in Chapter 1. Correct fluid level as necessary or change the fluid and filter if needed. If the problem persists, have a professional diagnose the probable cause.

42 Fluid leakage

1 Automatic transmission fluid is a deep red color. Fluid leaks should not be confused with engine oil, which can easily be blown by air flow to the transmission.
2 To pinpoint a leak, first remove all built-up dirt and grime from around the transmission.

Degreasing agents and/or steam cleaning will achieve this. With the underside clean, drive the vehicle at low speeds so air flow will not blow the leak far from its source. Raise the vehicle and determine where the leak is coming from. Common areas of leakage are:

a) **Pan:** *Tighten mounting bolts and/or replace pan gasket as necessary (see Chapters 1 and 7).*
b) **Filler pipe:** *Replace the rubber seal where pipe enters the transmission case,*
c) **Transmission oil lines:** *Tighten connectors where lines enter transmission case and/or replace lines.*
d) **Vent pipe:** *Transmission overfilled and/or water in fluid (see checking procedures, Chapter 1).*
e) **Speedometer connector:** *Replace the O-ring where speedometer cable enters transmission case (see Chapter 7).*

Driveshaft

43 Oil leak at front of driveshaft

Defective transmission rear oil seal. See Chapter 7 for replacement procedures. While this is done, check the splined yoke for burrs or a rough condition which may be damaging the seal. Burrs can be removed with crocus cloth or a fine whetstone.

44 Knock or clunk when the transmission is under Initial load oust after transmission is put into gear)

1 Loose or disconnected rear suspension components. Check all mounting bolts, nuts and bushings (see Chapter 10).
2 Loose driveshaft bolts. Inspect all bolts and nuts and tighten them to the specified torque.
3 Worn or damaged universal joint bearings. Check for wear (see Chapter 8).

45 Metallic grinding sound consistent with vehicle speed

Pronounced wear in the universal joint bearings. Check as described in Chapter 8.

46 Vibration

Note: *Before assuming that the driveshaft is at fault, make sure the tires are perfectly balanced and perform the following test.*
1 Install a tachometer inside the vehicle to monitor engine speed as the vehicle is driven. Drive the vehicle and note the engine speed at which the vibration (roughness) is most pronounced. Now shift the transmission to a different gear and bring the engine speed to the same point.
2 If the vibration occurs at the same engine speed (rpm) regardless of which gear the transmission is in, the driveshaft is NOT at fault since the driveshaft speed varies.

3 If the vibration decreases or is eliminated when the transmission is in a different gear at the same engine speed, refer to the following probable causes.
4 Bent or dented driveshaft. Inspect and replace as necessary (see Chapter 8).
5 Undercoating or built-up dirt, etc. on the driveshaft. Clean the shaft thoroughly and recheck.
6 Worn universal joint bearings. Remove and inspect (see Chapter 8).
7 Driveshaft and/or companion flange out-of-balance. Check for missing weights on the shaft. Remove the driveshaft (see Chapter 8) and reinstall 180-degrees from original position, then retest. Have the driveshaft professionally balanced if the problem persists.

Axles

47 Noise

1 Road noise. No corrective procedures available.
2 Tire noise. Inspect the tires and check tire pressures (see Chapter 1).
3 Rear wheel bearings loose, worn or damaged (see Chapter 8).

48 Vibration

See probable causes under Driveshaft. Proceed under the guidelines listed for the driveshaft. If the problem persists, check the rear wheel bearings by raising the rear of the vehicle and spinning the rear wheels by hand. Listen for evidence of rough (noisy) bearings. Remove and inspect (see Chapter 8).

49 Oil leakage

1 Pinion seal damaged (see Chapter 8).
2 Axleshaft oil seals damaged (see Chapter 8).
3 Differential inspection cover leaking. Tighten the bolts or replace the gasket as required (see Chapters 1 and 8).

Brakes

Note: *Before assuming that a brake problem exists, make sure that the tires are in good condition and inflated properly (see Chapter 1), that the front end alignment is correct and that the vehicle is not loaded with weight in an unequal manner.*

50 Vehicle pulls to one side during braking

1 Detective, damaged, or oil contaminated brake pads or shoes on one side. Inspect as described in Chapter 9.
2 Excessive wear of brake shoe or pad material or drum/disc on one side. Inspect and correct as necessary.
3 Loose or disconnected front suspension components. Inspect and tighten all bolts to the specified torque (see Chapter 10).

4   Defective drum brake or caliper assembly. Remove the drum or caliper and inspect for a stuck piston or other damage (see Chapter 9).

51   Noise (high-pitched squeal with the brakes applied)

Note. *Occasional squeal is normal. Severe conditions such as snow, rain, salt. mud, extreme cold or extreme heat may make the condition worse. An occasional squeal does not necessarily indicate loss of braking effectiveness or a need for corrective action.*

1   Disc brake pads worn out. The noise comes from the wear sensor rubbing against the disc. Replace the pads with new ones immediately (see Chapter 9).
2   Missing or damaged brake pad insulators (disc brakes). replace pad insulators (see Chapter 9).
3   Linings contaminated with dirt or grease. Replace pads or shoes.
4   Incorrect linings. Replace with correct linings.

52   Excessive brake pedal travel

1   Partial brake system failure. Inspect the entire system (see Chapter 9) and correct as required.
2   Insufficient fluid in the master cylinder. Check (see Chapter 1), add fluid and bleed the system if necessary (see Chapter 9).
3   Rear brakes not adjusting properly (drum brakes). On models with rear drum brakes (all except Mustang SVO), make a series of starts and stops with the vehicle in Reverse. If this does not correct the situation, remove the drums and inspect the self-adjusters (see Chapter 9).

53   Brake pedal feels spongy when depressed

1   Air in the hydraulic lines. Bleed the brake system (see Chapter 9).
2   Faulty flexible hoses. Inspect all system hoses and lines. Replace parts as necessary.
3   Master cylinder mounting bolts/nuts loose.
4   Master cylinder defective (see Chapter 9).

54   Excessive effort required to stop vehicle

1   Power brake booster not operating properly (see Chapter 9).
2   Excessively worn linings or pads. Inspect and replace if necessary (see Chapters 1 and 9).
3   One or more caliper pistons or wheel cylinders seized or sticking. Inspect and rebuild as required (see Chapter 9).
4   Brake linings or pads contaminated with oil or grease. Inspect and replace as required

(see Chapters 1 and 9).
5   New pads or shoes installed and not yet seated. It will take a while for the new material to seat against the drum (or rotor).

55   Pedal travels to the floor with little resistance

1   Little or no fluid in the master cylinder reservoir caused by leaking wheel cylinder (s), leaking caliper piston (s), loose, damaged or disconnected brake lines. Inspect the entire system and correct as necessary.
2   Worn master cylinder fluid seals (the problem can occur even when the master cylinder is full of fluid) (see Chapter 9).

56   Brake pedal pulsates during brake application

1   Wheel bearings not adjusted properly or in need of replacement (see Chapter 1).
2   Caliper not sliding properly due to improper installation or obstructions. Remove and inspect (see Chapter 9).
3   Rotor or drum defective. Remove the rotor or drum (see Chapter 9) and check for excessive lateral runout, out-of-round and parallelism. Have the drum or rotor resurfaced or replace it with a new one.

Suspension and steering systems

57   Vehicle pulls to one side

1   Tire pressures uneven (see Chapter 1).
2   Defective tire (see Chapter 1).
3   Excessive wear in suspension or steering components (see Chapter 10).
4   Front end out of alignment.
5   Front brakes dragging. Inspect the brakes as described in Chapter 9.

58   Shimmy, shake or vibration

1   Tire or wheel out-of -balance or out-of -round. Have professionally balanced.
2   Loose, worn or out-of -adjustment wheel bearings (see Chapters 1 and 8).
3   Shock absorbers and/or suspension components worn or damaged (see Chapter 10).

59   Excessive pitching and/or rolling around corners or during braking

1   Defective shock absorbers. Replace as a set (see Chapter 10).
2   Broken or weak springs and/or suspension components. Inspect as described in Chapter 10.

60   Excessively stiff steering

1   Lack of fluid in power steering reservoir

(see Chapter 1).
2   Incorrect tire pressures (see. Chapter 1).
3   Lack of lubrication at steering joints (see Chapter 1).
4   Front end out of alignment.
5   See Section 62.

61   Excessive play in steering

1   Loose front wheel bearings (see Chapter 1).
2   Excessive wear in suspension or steering components (see Chapter 10).
3   Steering gearbox out of adjustment (see Chapter 10).

62   Lack of power assistance

1   Steering pump drivebelt faulty or not adjusted properly (see Chapter 1).
2   Fluid level low (see Chapter 1).
3   Hoses or lines restricted. Inspect and replace parts as necessary.
4   Air in power steering system. Bleed the system (see Chapter 10).

63   Excessive tire wear (not specific to one area)

1   Incorrect tire pressures (see Chapter 1).
2   Tires out-of-balance. Have professionally balanced.
3   Wheels damaged. Inspect and replace as necessary.
4   Suspension or steering components excessively worn (see Chapter 10).

64   Excessive tire wear on outside edge

1   Inflation pressures incorrect (see Chapter 1).
2   Excessive speed in turns
3   Front end alignment incorrect (excessive toe- in). Have professionally aligned.
4   Suspension arm bent or twisted (see Chapter 10).

65   Excessive tire wear on Inside edge

1   Inflation pressures incorrect (see Chapter 1).
2   Front end alignment incorrect (toe-out). Have professionally aligned.
3   Loose or damaged steering components (see Chapter 10).

66   Tire tread worn in one place

1   Tires out-of-balance.
2   Damaged or buckled wheel. Inspect and replace if necessary.
3   Defective tire (see Chapter 1).

Chapter 1
Tune-up and routine maintenance

Contents

Specifications

Recommended lubricants and fluids

Note: Listed here are manufacturer recommendations at the time this manual was written. Manufacturers occasionally upgrade their fluid and lubricant specifications, so check with your local auto parts store for current recommendations.

Engine oil
    Type .... API "certified for gasoline engines"
    Viscosity .... See accompanying chart

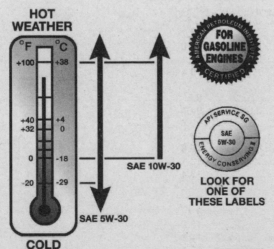

Engine oil viscosity chart

For best fuel economy and cold starting, select the lowest SAE viscosity grade oil for the expected temperature range

1-a3 HAYNES

Recommended lubricants and fluids (continued)

Power steering fluid type	Motorcraft Type F automatic transmission fluid
Brake fluid type	DOT 3 heavy duty brake fluid
Clutch fluid type	DOT 3 heavy duty brake fluid
Automatic transmission fluid type	
C5 transmission	
Through 1982	DEXRON II automatic transmission fluid
1983 on	Motorcraft Type H automatic transmission fluid
C3, C4, AOD and A4LD transmissions	
Through 1987	DEXRON II automatic transmission fluid
1988 on	MERCON automatic transmission fluid
Manual transmission lubricant type	
T50-D	MERCON automatic transmission fluid
All others	80W gear oil
Coolant type	Ethylene glycol-based antifreeze and water
Front wheel bearing grease	NLGI No. 2 grease
Chassis grease	Motorcraft multi-purpose grease
Differential lubricant*	Hypoid lubricant

* For Trak-Lok axles add 4 oz. of friction modifier (part C8AZ-19B546-A) when the lubricant is changed.

Capacities

Engine oil*	
All except four-cylinder turbo	
Without filter change	4 qts
With filter change	5 qts
Four-cylinder Turbo	
Without filter change	4.5 qts
With filter change	5.5 qts
Cooling system**	
1979	
Four-cylinder S/C	8.6
Four-cylinder non-turbo A/C	10.0
Four-cylinder turbo A/C	8.6
2.8L V6 M/T S/C	9.2
2.8L V6 (all others)	9.4
5.0L V8 S/C	14.0
5.0L V8 A/C	14.6
1980	
Four-cylinder non-turbo S/C	8.6
Four-cylinder non-turbo A/C	9.0
Four-cylinder turbo (all)	9.2
3.3L	8.1
4.2L V8 S/C	13.4
4.2L V8 A/C	13.5
1981 and 1982	
Four-cylinder non-turbo S/C	8.6
Four-cylinder non-turbo A/C	9.0
Four-cylinder turbo	9.4
3.3L	8.4
4.2L V8 S/C	14.7
4.2L V8 A/C	15.0
5.0L V8 S/C	13.1
5.0L V8 A/C	13.4
1983 and 1984	
Four-cylinder non-turbo S/C	8.6
Four-cylinder non-turbo A/C	9.0
Four-cylinder turbo	10.5
3.8L V6 S/C	10.7
3.8L V6 A/C	10.8
5.0L V8 S/C	13.1
5.0L V8 A/C	13.4
1985	
Four-cylinder non-turbo S/C	8.7
Four-cylinder non-turbo A/C	9.4
Four-cylinder turbo	10.2
3.8L V6	11.1
5.0L V8 HO (carbureted)	13.5
5.0L V8 HO (CFI)	13.4

1986 and 1987
    Four-cylinder non-turbo M/T, S/C 9.4
    Four-cylinder non-turbo M/T, A/C 9.2
    Four-cylinder non-turbo A/T 9.4
    Four-cylinder turbo S/C 9.8
    Four-cylinder turbo A/C 9.6
    3.8L V6 .... 10.9
    5.0L V8 .... 13.3
1988
    Four-cylinder 9.9
    5.0L V8 .... 14.1
1989 on
    Four-cylinder M/T, S/C 10.0
    Four-cylinder M/T A/C 9.7
    Four-cylinder A/T 10.0
    5.0L V8 .... 14.1

Use dipstick to determine exact fill level.

** *Capacity may vary +/- 15% due to equipment variations. Most service refills take only 80% of listed capacity because some coolant remains in the engine. All capacities expressed in quarts. S/C indicates standard cooling (no air conditioning). A/C indicates air conditioning. M/T indicates manual transmission. A/T indicates automatic transmission.*

Drivebelt tension (with special tool)
1979 and 1980
    1/4-inch V-belt
        New belt 50-80
        Used belt 40-60
    All other V-belts (including cogged)
        New belt 120-160
        Used belt 75-120
    V-ribbed belt
        New belt 140-170
        Used belt 110-130
1981
    1/4-inch V-belt
        New belt 50-80
        Used belt 40-60
    All other V-belts
        New belt 120-160
        Used belt 90-120
    4K V-ribbed belt
        New belt 90-120
        Used belt 90-110
    5K V-ribbed belt
        Fixed
            New belt 110-140
            Used belt 110-130
        With tensioner
            New belt 75-140
            Used belt 75-130
    6K V-ribbed belt
        Fixed
            New belt 140-170
            Used belt 140-160
        With tensioner (new or used belt) 85-140
1982
    1/4-inch V-belt
        New belt 50-80
        Used belt 40-60
    Air pump V-belt
        New belt 90-130
        Used belt 90-120
    All other V-belts
        New belt 120-160
        Used belt 90-120
    5K V-ribbed belt
        New belt 130-170
        Used belt 120-150

Drivebelt tension (with special tool) - (continued)

1982 (continued)
  6K V-ribbed belt
    Fixed
      New belt 140-180
      Used belt 130-160
    With tensioner
      New belt 85-140
      Used belt 80-140
1983 through 1987
  1/4-inch V-belt
    New belt.. 50-90
    Used belt... 40-60
  3/8-inch V-belt
    New belt.. 90-130
    Used belt... 80-100
  5K V-ribbed belt
    New belt.. 120-160
    Used belt... 110-130
  6K V-ribbed belt
    New belt.. 150-190
    Used belt... 140-160
1988 on (all) .... Refer to the wear indicator (see Section 14)

Radiator cap pressure (psi)

1979 through 1984
  All except four-cylinder without air conditioning
    Standard 16
    Lower limit (must hold pressure)................................. 13
    Upper limit (must relieve pressure) 19
  Four-cylinder without air conditioning
    Standard 13
    Lower limit (must hold pressure)................................. 11
    Upper limit (must relieve pressure) 17
1985 on
  Standard.. 16
  Lower limit (must hold pressure) 13
  Upper limit (must relieve pressure).................................. 18

Brakes

Disc brake pad thickness (minimum)...................................... 1/8 in.
Drum brake shoe lining thickness (minimum)............................ 1/16 in.

Ignition system

Spark plug type and gap*
  2.3L engine (except Turbo charged) .... Motorcraft AWSF42C or equivalent @ 0.044 inch
  2.3L Turbo charged engine .... Motorcraft AWSF32C or equivalent @ 0.034 inch
  3.3L Inline six-cylinder engine.. Motorcraft BSF82C or equivalent @ 0.050 inch
  2.8L V6 engine.. Motorcraft AWSF42C or equivalent @ 0.034 inch
  3.8L V6 engines .... Motorcraft AWSF54C or equivalent @ 0.054 inch
  All V8 engines... Motorcraft ASF42C or equivalent @ 0.050 inch
Firing order
  Four-cylinder engine 1-3-4-2
  3.3L inline six-cylinder engine.. 1-5-3-6-4-2
  V6 engines... 1-4-2-5-3-6
  V8 engines
    5.0L HO engine 1-3-7-2-6-5-4-8
    All others.. 1-5-4-2-6-3-7-8

Refer to the Vehicle Emission Control Information label in the engine compartment; use the information there if it differs from that listed here.

Valve clearances (2.8L V6 engine only) - engine cold

Intake .... 0.016 in
Exhaust .... 0.018 in

Torque specifications

	Ft-lbs (unless otherwise noted)
Wheel lug nuts	80 to 105
Front hub adjusting nut	
Step 1	17 to 25
Step 2	Back off 1/2 turn
Step 3	10 to 15 in-lbs
Spark plugs	
Four cylinder	5-10
2.8L V6	10-15
In-line six-cylinder	10-15
3.8L V6	5-11
V8 engines	
1979 through 1987	10-15
1988-on	5-10
Oil pan drain plug	
2.3L four-cylinder	15-25
2.8L V6	21-38
in-line six-cylinder	15-25
3.8L V6	15-25
Engine block coolant drain plug(s)	
2.3L four-cylinder	23-38
2.8L V6	14-18
in-line six-cylinder	not specified
All others	5-8
Automatic transmission pan bolts	
C3	12-17
C4	12-16
C5	12-16
A4LD	8-10
AOD	6-10

1

1 Introduction

This Chapter is designed to help the home mechanic maintain the Ford Mustang/Mercury Capri with the goals of maximum performance, economy, safety and reliability in mind.

Included is a master maintenance schedule, followed by procedures dealing specifically with each item on the schedule. Visual checks, adjustments, component replacement and other helpful items are included. Refer to the accompanying illustrations of the engine compartment and the underside of the vehicle for the locations of various components.

Servicing the vehicle in accordance with the mileage/time maintenance schedule and the step-by-step procedures will result in a planned maintenance program that should produce a long and reliable service life. Keep in mind that it is a comprehensive plan, so maintaining some items but not others at specified intervals will not produce the same results.

As you service the vehicle, you will discover that many of the procedures can - and should - be grouped together because of the nature of the particular procedure you're performing or because of the close proximity of two otherwise unrelated components to one another.

For example, if the vehicle is raised for chassis lubrication, you should inspect the exhaust, suspension, steering and fuel systems while you're under the vehicle. When you're rotating the tires, it makes good sense to check the brakes since the wheels are already removed. Finally, let's suppose you have to borrow or rent a torque wrench. Even if you only need it to tighten the spark plugs, you might as well check the torque of as many critical fasteners as time allows.

The first step in this maintenance program is to prepare yourself before the actual work begins. Read through all the procedures you're planning to do, then gather up all the parts and tools needed. If it looks like you might run into problems during a particular job, seek advice from a mechanic or an experienced do-it-yourselfer.

Maintenance schedule

The following maintenance intervals are based on the assumption that the vehicle owner will be doing the maintenance or service work, as opposed to having a dealer service department do the work. Although the time/mileage intervals are loosely based on factory recommendations, most have been shortened to ensure, for example, that such items as lubricants and fluids are checked/changed at intervals that promote maximum engine/driveline service life. Also, subject to the preference of the individual owner interested in keeping his or her vehicle in peak condition at all times, and with the vehicle's ultimate resale in mind, many of the maintenance procedures may be performed more often than recommended in the following schedule. We encourage such owner initiative.

When the vehicle is new it should be serviced initially by a factory authorized dealer service department to protect the factory warranty. In many cases the initial maintenance check is done at no cost to the owner (check with your dealer service department for more information).

Every 250 miles or weekly, whichever comes first

Check the engine oil level (Section 3)
Check the engine coolant level (Section 3)
Check the brake fluid level (Section 3)
Check the windshield washer fluid level (Section 3)
Check the tires and tire pressures (Section 8)
Perform owner safety checks (Section 35)

Every 3,000 miles or 3 months, whichever comes first

All items listed above, plus . . .
Check the power steering fluid level (Section 4)
Check the automatic transmission fluid level (Section 6)
Change the engine oil and oil filter (Section 10)
Check/adjust the clutch pedal freeplay and lubricate the linkage (Section 27)

Every 6,000 miles or 6 months, whichever comes first

All the items listed above, plus . . .
Inspect/replace the underhood hoses (Section 13)
Check/adjust the drivebelts (Section 14)
Check/service the battery (Section 15)
Check/regap the spark plugs (Section 30)

Every 12,000 miles or 12 months, whichever comes first

All items listed above, plus . . .
Check/replenish the manual transmission lubricant (Section 5)
Check the rear axle (differential) lubricant level (Section 7)
Rotate the tires (Section 9)
Lubricate the parking brake cable (Section 11)
Replace the air filter (Section 16)
Check/replace the crankcase vent filter (Section 17)
Check/replace the PCV valve (Section 18)
Check the fuel system (Section 19)

Replace the fuel filter (Section 20)
Inspect the cooling system (Section 21)
Inspect the exhaust system (Section 23)
Inspect the steering and suspension components (Section 24)
Inspect the brakes (Section 25)
Lubricate the automatic transmission control linkage (Section 26)
Check the front wheel bearings (Section 28)
Adjust valve clearances (2.8L V6 engine only) (Section 29)
Replace the spark plugs (Section 30)
Inspect/replace the windshield wiper blades (Section 34)
Check the exhaust heat control valve (3.8L V6 and V8) (Chapter 4)

Every 24,000 miles or 24 months, whichever comes first

All items listed above plus . . .
Change the automatic transmission fluid and filter (Section 12)*
Adjust automatic transmission bands (Chapter 7)*
Service the cooling system (drain, flush and refill) (Section 22)
Check/replace the spark plug wires, distributor cap and rotor (Section 31)
Check the choke and lubricate the linkage (Section 32)
Check the idle speed (carbureted models) (Section 33)

Every 30,000 miles or 30 months, whichever comes first

Change the rear axle (differential) lubricant (Section 7)
Lubricate the chassis components (Section 11)
Replace the EGR vacuum solenoid filter (3.8L V6 engine only) (Chapter 6)

* If operated under one or more of the following conditions, change the automatic transmission fluid and adjust the bands every 12,000 miles:

In heavy city traffic where the outside temperature regularly reaches 90-degrees F or higher
In hilly or mountainous terrain
Frequent trailer pulling

2 Tune-up general information

The term *tune-up* is used in this manual to represent a combination of individual operations rather than one specific procedure.

If, from the time the vehicle is new, the routine maintenance schedule is followed closely and frequent checks are made of fluid levels and high wear items, as suggested throughout this manual, the engine will be kept in relatively good running condition and the need for additional work will be minimized.

More likely than not, however, there will be times when the engine is running poorly due to a lack of regular maintenance. This is even more likely if a used vehicle, which has not received regular and frequent maintenance checks, is purchased. In such cases, an engine tune-up will be needed outside of the regular maintenance intervals.

The first step in any tune-up or diagnostic procedure to help correct a poor running engine is a cylinder compression check. A compression check (see Chapter 2) will help determine the condition of internal engine components and should be used as a guide for tune-up and repair procedures. If, for instance, a compression check indicates serious internal engine wear, a conventional tune-up will not improve the performance of the engine and would be a waste of time and money. Because of its importance, the compression check should be done by someone with the right equipment and the knowledge to use it properly.

The following procedures are those most often needed to bring as generally poor running engine back into a proper state of tune.

Minor tune-up

Clean, inspect and test the battery (see Section 15)
Check all engine related fluids (see Section 3)
Check and adjust the drivebelts (see Section 14)
Replace the spark plugs (see Section 30)
Inspect the distributor cap and rotor (see Section 31)
Inspect the spark plug and coil wires (see Section 31)
Check and adjust the idle speed (see Section 33)
Check the PCV valve (see Section 18)
Check the air filter (see Section 16)
Check the cooling system (see Section 21)
Check all underhood hoses (see Section 13)

Major tune-up

All items listed under minor tune-up, plus . . .

Check the EGR system (see Chapter 6)
Check the ignition system (see Chapter 5)
Check the charging system (see Chapter 5)
Check the fuel system (see Chapter 4)
Replace the distributor cap and rotor (see Section 31)
Replace the spark plug wires (see Section 31)

3 Fluid level checks

Refer to illustrations 3.4, 3.16a, 3.16b and 3.17

Note: *The following are fluid level checks to be done on a 250 mile or weekly basis. Additional fluid level checks can be found in specific maintenance procedures which follow. Regardless of intervals, be alert to fluid leaks under the vehicle which would indicate a fault to be corrected immediately.*

1   Fluids are an essential part of the lubrication, cooling, brake and windshield washer systems. Because the fluids gradually become depleted and/or contaminated during normal operation of the vehicle, they must be periodically replenished. See Recommended lubricants and fluids at the beginning of this Chapter before adding fluid to any of the following components. **Note:** *The vehicle must be on level ground when fluid levels are checked.*

Engine oil

2   Engine oil is checked with a dipstick, which is located on the side of the engine (refer to the underhood illustrations at the front of this Chapter for dipstick locations). The dipstick extends through a metal tube down into the oil pan.

3   The engine oil should be checked before the vehicle has been driven, or about 15 minutes after the engine has been shut off. If the oil is checked immediately after driving the vehicle, some of the oil will remain in the upper part of the engine, resulting in an inaccurate reading on the dipstick.

4   Pull the dipstick out of the tube and wipe all of the oil away from the end with a clean rag or paper towel. Insert the clean dipstick all the way back into the tube and pull it out again. Note the oil at the end of the dipstick. At its highest point, the oil should be above the ADD mark, in the SAFE range **(see illustration)**.

5   It takes one quart of oil to raise the level from the ADD mark to the FULL or MAX mark on the dipstick. Do not allow the level to drop below the ADD mark or oil starvation may cause engine damage. Conversely, overfilling the engine (adding oil above the FULL or MAX mark) may cause oil fouled spark plugs, oil leaks or oil seal failures.

6   To add oil, remove the filler cap located on the valve cover (see the illustrations at the front of this Chapter). After adding oil, wait a few minutes to allow the level to stabilize, then pull the dipstick out and check the level again. Add more oil if required. Install the filler cap and tighten it by hand only.

7   Checking the oil level is an important

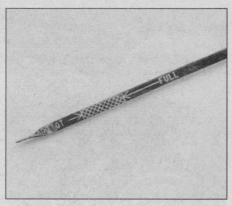

3.4 The engine oil level should be in the cross-hatched range - if it's below the ADD line, add enough oil to bring the level into the safe range (DO NOT add more oil if the level is at the FULL line)

preventive maintenance step. A consistently low oil level indicates oil leakage through damaged seals, defective gaskets or past worn rings or valve guides. The condition of the oil should also be noted. If the oil looks milky in color or has water droplets in it, the cylinder head gasket(s) may be blown or the head(s) or block may be cracked. The engine should be repaired immediately. Whenever you check the oil level, slide your thumb and index finger up the dipstick before wiping off the oil. If you see small dirt or metal particles clinging to the dipstick, the oil should be changed (see Section 10).

Engine coolant

Warning: *Do not allow antifreeze to come in contact with your skin or painted surfaces of the vehicle. Flush contaminated areas immediately with plenty of water. Do not store new coolant or leave old coolant lying around where it's accessible to children or pets - they are attracted by its sweet taste. Ingestion of even a small amount of coolant can be fatal! Wipe up garage floor and drip pan coolant spills. Keep antifreeze containers covered and repair leaks in your cooling system immediately.*

8   All vehicles covered by this manual are equipped with a pressurized coolant recovery system. A white plastic coolant reservoir located at the front of the engine compartment is connected by a hose to the radiator filler neck. If the engine overheats, coolant escapes through a valve in the radiator cap and travels through the hose into the reservoir. As the engine cools, the coolant is automatically drawn back into the cooling system to maintain the correct level.

9   The coolant level in the reservoir should be checked regularly. **Warning:** *Do not remove the radiator cap to check the coolant level when the engine is warm! The level in the reservoir varies with the temperature of the engine. When the engine is cold, the coolant level should be at or slightly above the COLD FULL mark on the reservoir. Once the engine has warmed up, the level should*

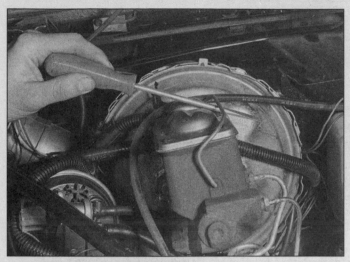

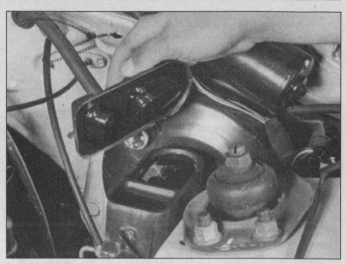

3.16a Prying loose the retainer on the master cylinder cover (early models)

3.16b Checking the brake fluid level (early models)

be at or near the FULL HOT mark. If it isn't, allow the engine to cool, then remove the cap from the reservoir and add a 50/50 mixture of ethylene glycol-based antifreeze and water.

10   Drive the vehicle and recheck the coolant level. Don't use rust inhibitors or additives. If only a small amount of coolant is required to bring the system up to the proper level, water can be used. However, repeated additions of water will dilute the antifreeze and water solution. In order to maintain the proper ratio of antifreeze and water, always top up the coolant level with the correct mixture. An empty plastic milk jug or bleach bottle makes an excellent container for mixing coolant.

11   If the coolant level drops consistently, there may be a leak in the system. Inspect the radiator, hoses, filler cap, drain plugs and water pump (see Section 21). If no leaks are noted, have the radiator cap pressure tested by a service station.

12   If you have to remove the radiator cap, wait until the engine has cooled completely, then wrap a thick cloth around the cap and turn it to the first stop. If coolant or steam escapes, let the engine cool down longer, then remove the cap.

13   Check the condition of the coolant as well. It should be relatively clear. If it's brown or rust colored, the system should be drained, flushed and refilled. Even if the coolant appears to be normal, the corrosion inhibitors wear out, so it must be replaced at the specified intervals.

Brake and clutch fluid

Warning: *Brake fluid can harm your eyes and damage painted surfaces, so use extreme caution when handling or pouring it. Do not use brake fluid that has been standing open or is more than one year old. Brake fluid absorbs moisture from the air, which can cause a dangerous loss of brake effectiveness. Use only the specified type of brake fluid. Mixing different types (such as DOT 3 or 4 and DOT 5) can cause brake failure.*

14   The brake master cylinder is mounted at the left (driver's side) rear corner of the engine compartment. The clutch fluid reservoir (used on some later models with manual transmissions) is mounted adjacent to it.

15   To check the clutch fluid level, observe the level through the translucent reservoir. The level should be at or near the step molded into the reservoir. If the level is low, remove the reservoir cap to add the specified fluid.

16   On 1979 through 1986 models, the brake fluid level is checked by removing the master cylinder cover. Clean the area around the master cylinder so dirt doesn't fall into the brake fluid. Pry back the cover retainer with a screwdriver **(see illustration)**, lift off the cover **(see illustration)** and check the level in both reservoir compartments. It should be 1/4 inch below the top edge of the reservoir. Top up the level, if necessary, with the recommended brake fluid, but do not overfill.

17   On 1987 and later models, the brake fluid level is checked by looking through the translucent plastic reservoir mounted on the master cylinder. The fluid level should be between the MAX and MIN lines on the reser-

voir **(see illustration)**. If the fluid level is low, wipe the top of the reservoir and the cap with a clean rag to prevent contamination of the system as the cap is unscrewed. Top up the level with the recommended brake fluid, but do not overfill.

18   While the reservoir cap is off, check the clutch or brake fluid for contamination. If rust deposits, dirt particles or water droplets are present, the system should be drained and refilled by a dealer service department or repair shop.

19   After filling the reservoir to the proper level, make sure the cap is seated to prevent fluid leakage and/or contamination. On 1979 through 1986 models, make sure the rubber diaphragm inside the brake fluid reservoir cover is seated properly.

20   The fluid level in the brake master cylinder will drop slightly as the disc brake pads wear. A very low level may indicate worn brake pads. Check for wear (see Section 25).

21   If the brake fluid level drops consistently, check the entire system for leaks immediately. Examine brake lines, hoses and connections, along with the calipers, wheel cylinders and master cylinder (see Section 25).

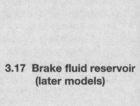

3.17 Brake fluid reservoir (later models)

MAX

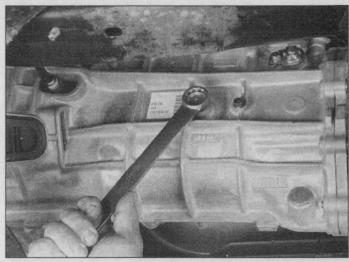

4.5 Once the engine is properly warmed up and the wheel has been turned back-and-forth a few times to rid the system of bubbles, pull the dipstick out and wipe it off, reinsert it and verify the power steering fluid level is in the FULL HOT range (be sure to use the proper range; one side is for checking the fluid cold) - if it isn't, add enough fluid to bring the level between the two lines

5.1 The manual transmission lubricant check till plug is located on the right side of the transmission case (which is the passenger's side of the vehicle) - a 3.8-inch drive ratchet or breaker bar will fit into the square hole to unscrew the plug

22   When checking the fluid level, if you discover one or both reservoirs to be empty or nearly empty, the brake or clutch release system should be checked for leaks (see Section 25) and bled (see Chapters 8 and 9).

Windshield washer fluid

23   Fluid for the windshield washer system is stored in a plastic reservoir in the engine compartment. On early models, the windshield washer reservoir is combined with the coolant reservoir (there are separate compartments for the two different fluids). On later models, the windshield washer reservoir is mounted inside the fender, and its filler neck protrudes through a hole in the fender into the engine compartment.

24   In milder climates, plain water can be used in the reservoir, but it should be kept no more than 2/3 full to allow for expansion if the water freezes. In colder climates, use windshield washer system antifreeze, available at any auto parts store, to lower the freezing point of the fluid. This comes in concentrated or pre-mixed form. If you purchase concentrated antifreeze, mix the antifreeze with water in accordance with the manufacturer's directions on the container. **Caution:** *Do not use cooling system antifreeze - it will damage the vehicle's paint.*

4   Power steering fluid level check

Refer to illustration 4.5

1   Check the power steering fluid level periodically to avoid steering system problems, such as damage to the pump. **Caution:** *DO NOT hold the steering wheel against either stop (extreme left or right turn) for more than five seconds. If you do, the power steering pump could be damaged.*

2   The power steering pump, located at the left front corner of the engine on all models, is equipped with a twist-off cap with an integral fluid level dipstick.

3   Park the vehicle on level ground and apply the parking brake.

4   Run the engine until it has reached normal operating temperature. With the engine at idle, turn the steering wheel back-and-forth several times to get any air out of the steering system. Shut the engine off, remove the cap by turning it counterclockwise, wipe the dipstick clean and reinstall the cap (make sure it is seated).

5   Remove the cap again and note the fluid level. It must be between the two lines designating the FULL HOT range **(see illustration)** (be sure to use the proper temperature range on the dipstick when checking the fluid level - the FULL COLD lines on the reverse side of the dipstick are only usable when the engine is cold).

6   If necessary, add small amounts of fluid until the level is correct. **Caution:** *Do not overfill the pump. If too much fluid is added, remove the excess with a clean syringe or suction pump.*

7   Check the power steering hoses and connections for leaks and wear (see Section 13).

8   Check the condition and tension of the power steering pump drivebelt (see Section 14).

5   Manual transmission lubricant level check and change

Refer to illustration 5.1

Note: *The transmission lubricant level and quality should not deteriorate under normal driving conditions. However, it's recommended that you check the level occasionally. The most convenient time would be when the vehicle is raised for another reason,* such as an engine oil change.

1   The transmission has a check/fill plug which must be removed to check the lubricant level **(see illustration)**. **Warning:** *The check/fill plug is the upper one - DO NOT remove the drain plug by mistake! Also, some early models have a reverse fork pivot bolt mounted on the side of the transmission near the check/fill plug. DO NOT remove the pivot bolt! If the vehicle is raised to gain access to the plug, be sure to support it safely on jackstands - DO NOT crawl under a vehicle which is supported only by a jack!*

2   Remove the plug from the transmission and use your little finger to reach inside the housing and feel the lubricant level. It should be at or very near the bottom of the plug hole.

3   If it isn't, add the recommended lubricant through the plug hole with a syringe or squeeze bottle.

4   Install and tighten the plug securely and check for leaks after the first few miles of driving.

5   Manual transmission lubricant does not normally need changing during the life of the vehicle, but if you wish to do so, place a drain pan beneath the drain plug. Remove the check/fill plug, then remove the drain plug and let the lubricant drain into a pan. Let it drain for 10 minutes or more, then reinstall the drain plug and tighten it securely.

6   Fill the transmission to the bottom of the filler plug hole with recommended lubricant.

7   Install and tighten the check/fill plug securely and check for leaks after the first few miles of driving.

6   Automatic transmission fluid level check

1   The automatic transmission fluid level should be carefully maintained. Low fluid

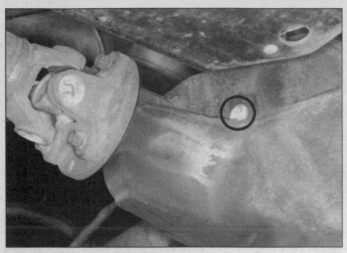

7.2 Remove the fill plug

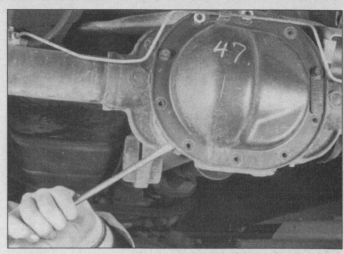

7.9 With the differential cover retained by two loosened bolts at the top, carefully pry it loose and allow the lubricant to drain

level can lead to slipping or loss of drive, while overfilling can cause foaming and loss of fluid. Either condition can cause transmission damage.

2   Since transmission fluid expands as it heats up, the fluid level should only be checked when the transmission is warm (at normal operating temperature). If the vehicle has just been driven over 20 miles (32 km), the transmission can be considered warm. **Caution:** *If the vehicle has just been driven for a long time at high speed or in city traffic, in hot weather, or if it has been pulling a trailer, an accurate fluid level reading cannot be obtained. Allow the transmission to cool down for about 30 minutes.* You can also check the transmission fluid level when the transmission is cold. If the vehicle has not been driven for over five hours and the fluid is about room temperature (70 to 95-degrees F), the transmission is cold. However, the fluid level is normally checked with the transmission warm to ensure accurate results.

3   Immediately after driving the vehicle, park it on a level surface, set the parking brake and start the engine. While the engine is idling, depress the brake pedal and move the selector lever through all the gear ranges, beginning and ending in Park.

4   Locate the automatic transmission dipstick tube in the engine compartment (see the illustrations at the front of this Chapter for dipstick location).

5   With the engine still idling, pull the dipstick away from the tube, wipe it off with a clean rag, push it all the way back into the tube and withdraw it again, then note the fluid level.

6   If the transmission is cold, the level should be in the room temperature range on the dipstick (between the two circles); if it's warm, the fluid level should be in the operating temperature range (between the two lines). If the level is low, add the specified automatic transmission fluid through the dipstick tube - use a clean funnel to prevent spills.

7   Add just enough of the recommended fluid to fill the transmission to the proper level. It takes about one pint to raise the level from the lower line to the upper line when the fluid is hot, so add the fluid a little at a time and keep checking the level until it's correct.

8   The condition of the fluid should also be checked along with the level. If the fluid is a dark reddish-brown color, or if it smells burned, it should be changed (see Section 12). If you are in doubt about its condition, purchase some new fluid and compare the two for color and smell.

7   Differential (rear axle) lubricant level check and change

Refer to illustrations 7.2, 7.9 and 7.12

1   The differential has a fill plug which must be removed to check the lubricant level. If the vehicle is raised to gain access to the plug,

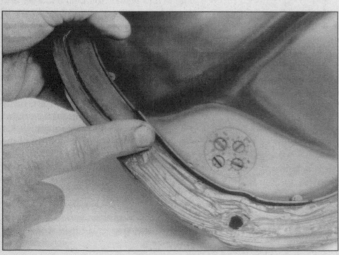

7.12 Apply RTV sealant to the differential housing just before installation

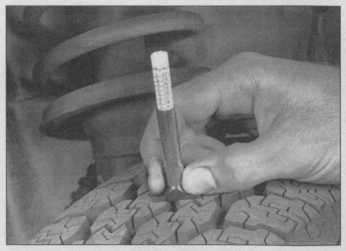

8.2 A tire tread depth indicator should be used to monitor tire wear - they're available at auto parts stores and service stations and cost very little

UNDERINFLATION

CUPPING

Cupping may be caused by:
- Underinflation and/or mechanical irregularities such as out-of-balance condition of wheel and/or tire, and bent or damaged wheel.
- Loose or worn steering tie-rod or steering idler arm.
- Loose, damaged or worn front suspension parts.

OVERINFLATION

1

INCORRECT TOE-IN OR EXTREME CAMBER

FEATHERING DUE TO MISALIGNMENT

8.3 This chart will help you determine the condition of your tires, the probable cause(s) of abnormal wear and the corrective action necessary

be sure to support it safely on jackstands - DO NOT crawl under the vehicle when it's supported only by the jack!

2   Remove the fill plug from the differential **(see illustration)**.

3   Use your little finger as a dipstick to make sure the lubricant level is even with the bottom of the plug hole. If not, use a syringe to add the recommended lubricant until it just starts to run out of the opening. On some models a tag is located in the area of the plug which gives information regarding lubricant type, particularly on models equipped with a limited slip differential.

4   Install the plug and tighten it securely.

5   If it is necessary to change the differential lubricant, remove the fill plug **(see illustration 7.2)**, then drain the differential. Some differentials can be drained by removing the drain plug, while on others it's necessary to remove the cover plate on the differential housing. As an alternative, a hand suction pump can be used to remove the differential lubricant through the fill plug hole. If there is no drain plug and a suction pump isn't available, obtain a tube of silicone sealant to be used when reinstalling the differential cover.

6   Raise the vehicle and support it securely on jackstands. Move a drain pan, rags, newspapers and the tools you will need under the vehicle.

7   If equipped with a drain plug, remove the plug and allow the differential lubricant to

drain completely. After it has drained, install the plug and tighten it securely.

8   If a suction pump is being used, insert the flexible hose. Work the hose down to the bottom of the differential housing and pump the oil out.

9   If the differential is being drained by removing the cover plate, remove all of the bolts except the two near the top. Loosen the remaining two bolts and use them to keep the cover loosely attached **(see illustration)**. Allow the lubricant to drain into the pan, then completely remove the cover.

10   Using a lint-free rag, clean the inside of the cover and the accessible areas of the differential housing. As this is done, check for chipped gears and metal particles in the lubricant, indicating that the differential should be more thoroughly inspected and/or repaired.

11   Clean all old gasket material from the cover and differential housing.

12   Apply a bead of sealant to the housing cover. Run the bead inside the housing bolt holes **(see illustration)**.

13   Place the cover on the differential housing and install the bolts. Tighten the bolts securely in a criss-cross pattern. Don't overtighten them or the cover may be distorted and leaks may develop.

14   On all models, use a hand pump, syringe, squeeze bottle or funnel to fill the differential housing with the specified lubricant

until it's level with the bottom of the plug hole.

15   Install the fill plug and tighten it securely.

8   Tire and tire pressure checks

Refer to illustrations 8.2, 8.3, 8.4a, 8.4b and 8.8

1   Periodic inspection of the tires may save you the inconvenience of being stranded with a flat tire. It can also provide you with vital information regarding possible problems in the steering and suspension systems before major damage occurs.

2   Tires are equipped with 1/2-inch wide bands that will appear when tread depth reaches 1/16-inch, at which point the tire can be considered worn out. Tread wear can be monitored with a simple, inexpensive device known as a tread depth indicator **(see illustration)**.

3   Note any abnormal tire wear **(see illustration)**. Tread pattern irregularities such as cupping, flat spots and more wear on one side than the other are indications of front end alignment and/or balance problems. If any of these conditions are noted, take the vehicle to a tire shop or service station to correct the problem.

4   Look closely for cuts, punctures and embedded nails or tacks. Sometimes a tire will hold air pressure for a short time or leak down very slowly after a nail has embedded

8.4a If a tire loses air on a steady basis, check the valve core first to make sure it's snug (special inexpensive wrenches are commonly available at auto parts stores)

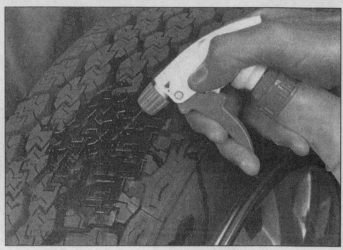

8.4b If the valve core is tight, raise the corner of the vehicle with the low tire and spray a soapy water solution onto the tread as the tire is rotated - slow leaks will cause small bubbles to appear

itself in the tread. If a slow leak persists, check the valve stem core to make sure it is tight **(see illustration)**. Examine the tread for an object that may have embedded itself in the tire or for a "plug" that may have begun to leak (radial tire punctures are repaired with a plug that is installed in the puncture). If a puncture is suspected, it can be easily verified by spraying a solution of soapy water onto the puncture **(see illustration)**. The soapy solution will bubble if there is a leak. Unless the puncture is unusually large, a tire shop or service station can usually repair the tire.

5   Carefully inspect the inner sidewall of each tire for evidence of brake fluid leakage. If you see any, inspect the brakes immediately.

6   Correct air pressure adds miles to the lifespan of the tires, improves mileage and enhances overall ride quality. Tire pressure cannot be accurately estimated by looking at a tire, especially if it's a radial. A tire pressure gauge is essential. Keep an accurate gauge in the glove compartment. The pressure gauges attached to the nozzles of air hoses at gas stations are often inaccurate.

7   Always check tire pressure when the tires are cold. Cold, in this case, means the vehicle has not been driven over a mile in the three hours preceding a tire pressure check. A pressure rise of four to eight pounds is not uncommon once the tires are warm.

8   Unscrew the valve cap protruding from the wheel or hubcap and push the gauge firmly onto the valve stem **(see illustration)**. Note the reading on the gauge and compare the figure to the recommended tire pressure shown in your owner's manual or on the tire placard on the passenger's side door or door pillar. Be sure to reinstall the valve cap to keep dirt an moisture out of the valve stem mechanism. Check all four tires and, if necessary, add enough air to bring them to the recommended pressure.

9   Don't forget to keep the spare tire inflated to the specified pressure (refer to your owner's manual or the placard attached to the door pillar). Note that the pressure recommended for temporary (mini) spare tires is higher than for the tires on the vehicle.

9   Tire rotation

Refer to illustration 9.2

1   The tires should be rotated at the specified intervals and whenever uneven wear is noticed. Since the vehicle will be raised and the tires checked anyway, check the brakes also (see Section 25).

2   Radial tires must be rotated in a specific pattern **(see illustration)**.

3   Refer to the information in jacking and towing at the front of this manual for the proper procedure to follow when raising the vehicle and changing a tire. If the brakes must be checked, don't apply the parking brake as stated.

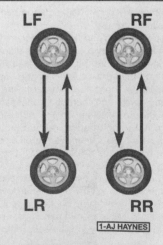

8.8 To extend the life of the tires, check the air pressure at least once a week with an accurate gauge (don't forget the spare!)

4   The vehicle must be raised on a hoist or supported on jackstands to get all four tires off the ground. Make sure the vehicle is safely supported!

5   After the rotation procedure is finished, check and adjust the tire pressures as necessary and be sure to check the lug nut tightness.

10   Engine oil and filter change

Refer to illustrations 10.2, 10.12 and 10.16

1   Frequent oil changes are the most important preventive maintenance procedures that can be done by the home mechanic. As engine oil ages, it becomes diluted and contaminated, which leads to premature engine wear.

2   Make sure that you have all the necessary tools before you begin this procedure **(see illustration)**. You should also have plenty of rags or newspapers handy for mop-

LF   RF

LR   RR

1-AJ HAYNES

9.2 Tire rotation diagram

ping up oil spills.

3   Access to the oil drain plug and filter will be improved if the vehicle can be lifted on a hoist, driven onto ramps or supported by jackstands. **Warning:** *Do not work under a vehicle supported only by a bumper, hydraulic or scissors-type jack - always use jackstands!*

4   If you haven't changed the oil on this vehicle before, get under it and locate the drain plug (both drain plugs on V8 engines) and the oil filter. The exhaust components will be warm as you work, so note how they are routed to avoid touching them when you are under the vehicle.

5   Start the engine and allow it to reach normal operating temperature - oil and sludge will flow more easily when warm. If new oil, a filter or tools are needed, use the vehicle to go get them and warm up the engine oil at the same time. Park on a level surface and shut off the engine when it's warmed up. Remove the oil filler cap from the rocker arm cover.

6   Raise the vehicle and support it on jackstands. Make sure it is safely supported!

7   Being careful not to touch the hot exhaust components, position a drain pan under the plug in the bottom of the engine. Clean the area around the plug (both plugs on V8 engines), then remove the plug(s). It's a good idea to wear a rubber glove while unscrewing the plug the final few turns to avoid being scalded by hot oil. It will also help to hold the drain plug against the threads as you unscrew it, then pull it away from the drain hole suddenly. This will place your arm out of the way of the hot oil, as well as reducing the chances of dropping the drain plug into the drain pan.

8   It may be necessary to move the drain pan slightly as oil flow slows to a trickle. Inspect the old oil for the presence of metal particles.

9   After all the oil has drained, wipe off the drain plug(s) with a clean rag. Any small metal particles clinging to the plug would immediately contaminate the new oil.

10   Reinstall the plug(s) and tighten securely, but don't strip the threads.

11   Move the drain pan into position under the oil filter.

12   Loosen the oil filter by turning it counterclockwise with a filter wrench **(see illustration)**. Any standard filter wrench will work.

13   Sometimes the oil filter is screwed on so tightly that it can't be loosened. If it is, punch a metal bar or long screwdriver directly through it, as close to the engine as possible, and use it as a T-bar to turn the filter. Be prepared for oil to spurt out of the canister as it's punctured.

14   Once the filter is loose, use your hands to unscrew it from the block. Just as the filter is detached from the block, immediately tilt the open end up to prevent oil inside the filter from spilling out.

15   Using a clean rag, wipe off the mounting surface on the block. Also, make sure that none of the old gasket remains stuck to the mounting surface. It can be removed with a scraper if necessary.

16   Compare the old filter with the new one to make sure they are the same type. Smear some engine oil on the rubber gasket of the new filter and screw it into place **(see illustration)**. Overtightening the filter will damage the gasket, so don't use a filter wrench. Most filter manufacturers recommend tightening the filter by hand only. Normally, they should be tightened 3/4-turn after the gasket contacts the block, but be sure to follow the directions on the filter or container.

17   Remove all tools and materials from under the vehicle, being careful not to spill the oil in the drain pan, then lower the vehicle.

18   Add new oil to the engine through the oil filler cap in the rocker arm cover. Use a funnel to prevent oil from spilling onto the top of the engine. Pour four quarts of fresh oil into the engine. Wait a few minutes to allow the oil to drain into the pan, then check the level on the dipstick (see Section 3 if necessary). If the oil level is in the SAFE range, install the filler cap.

19   Start the engine and run it for about a

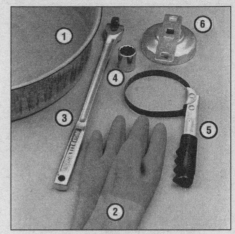

10.2 These tools are required when changing the engine oil and filter

1   **Drain pan** - *It should be fairly shallow in depth, but wide to prevent spills*

2   **Rubber gloves** - *When removing the drain plug and filter, you will get oil on your hands (the gloves will prevent burns)*

3   **Breaker bar** - *Sometimes the oil drain plug is tight and a long breaker bar is needed to loosen it*

4   **Socket** - *To be used with the breaker bar or a ratchet (must be the correct size to fit the drain plug - six-point preferred)*

5   **Filter wrench** - *This is a metal band-type wrench, which requires clearance around the filter to be effective*

6   **Filter wrench** - *This type fits on the bottom of the filter and can be turned with a ratchet or breaker bar (different size wrenches are available for different types of filters)*

minute. Check the oil pressure gauge or indicator light to make sure the engine develops normal oil pressure. While the engine is running, look under the vehicle and check for leaks at the oil pan drain plug and around the

10.12 Removing the oil filter

10.16 Lubricate the oil filter gasket with clean engine oil before installing the filter on the engine

11.1 Materials required for chassis and body lubrication

1 **Engine oil** - *Light engine oil in a can like this can be used for door and hood hinges*
2 **Graphite spray** - *Used to lubricate lock cylinders*
3 **Grease** - *Grease, in a variety of types and weights, is available for use in a grease gun. Check the Specifications for your requirements.*
4 **Grease gun** - *A common grease gun, shown here with a detachable hose and nozzle, is needed for chassis lubrication. After use, clean it thoroughly!*

11.2 If plugs are installed (arrow), they must be removed and grease fittings must be threaded into the holes

oil filter. If either one is leaking, stop the engine and tighten the plug or filter slightly.
20 Wait a few minutes, then recheck the level on the dipstick. Add oil as necessary to bring the level into the SAFE range.
21 During the first few trips after an oil change, make it a point to check frequently for leaks and proper oil level.
22 The old oil drained from the engine cannot be reused in its present state and should be discarded. Oil reclamation centers, auto repair shops and gas stations will normally accept the oil, which can be recycled. After the oil has cooled, it can be drained into a container (plastic jugs, bottles, milk cartons, etc.) for transport to a disposal site.

11 Chassis lubrication

Refer to illustrations 11.1 and 11.2

1 Refer to Recommended lubricants and fluids at the front of this chapter to obtain the necessary grease, etc. You'll also need a grease gun **(see illustration)**. Occasionally plugs will be installed rather than grease fittings. If so, grease fittings will have to be purchased and installed.
2 Look under the vehicle and see if grease fittings or plugs are installed in the tie-rod ends and balljoints **(see illustration)**. If there are plugs, remove them and buy grease fittings, which will thread into the component. A dealer or auto parts store will be able to sup-

ply the correct fittings. Straight, as well as angled, fittings are available.
3 For easier access under the vehicle, raise it with a jack and place jackstands under the frame. Make sure the vehicle is safely supported - DO NOT crawl under the vehicle when it is supported only by the jack! If the wheels are to be removed at this interval for tire rotation or brake inspection, loosen the lug nuts slightly while the vehicle is still on the ground.
4 Before beginning, force a little grease out of the nozzle to remove any dirt from the end of the gun. Wipe the nozzle clean with a rag.
5 With the grease gun and plenty of clean rags, crawl under the vehicle.
6 Wipe the tie-rod end grease fitting nipple clean and push the nozzle firmly over it. Squeeze the trigger on the grease gun to force grease into the component. They should be lubricated until the rubber seal is firm to the touch. Don't pump too much grease into the fitting as it could rupture the seal. If grease escapes around the grease gun nozzle, the nipple is clogged or the nozzle is not completely seated on the fitting. Resecure the gun nozzle to the fitting and try again. If necessary, replace the fitting with a new one.
7 Wipe the excess grease from the components and the grease fitting. Repeat the procedure for the remaining fitting(s).
8 On early models, the suspension balljoints can be lubricated. Original equipment balljoints on later models are sealed and cannot be lubricated. Lubricate non-sealed balljoints in the same manner as tie-rod ends.
9 All models are equipped with balljoint wear indicators. If the grease-fitting hex is flush with or below the surface of the balljoint cover, the balljoint is worn. Worn balljoints should be replaced (see Chapter 10).
10 Open the hood and smear a little chassis grease on the hood latch mechanism. Have an assistant pull the hood release lever from inside the vehicle as you lubricate the cable at the latch.
11 Lubricate all the hinges (door, hood, etc.) with engine oil to keep the in proper working order.
12 The key lock cylinders can be lubricated

with spray graphite or silicone lubricant, which is available at auto parts stores.
13 Lubricate the door weatherstripping with silicone spray. This will reduce chafing and retard wear.
14 Lubricate the parking brake linkage. Note that two different types of lubricant are required. Use multipurpose grease on the linkage, adjuster assembly and connectors; use speedometer cable lubricant on parts of the cable that touch other parts of the vehicle. Lubricate the cable twice: once with the parking brake set and once with it released.

12 Automatic transmission fluid and filter change

Refer to illustrations 12.9 and 12.12
Caution: *The use of transmission fluid other than the type listed in the Specifications could result in transmission malfunctions or failure.*

1 At the specified intervals, the transmission fluid should be drained and replaced. Since the fluid will remain hot long after driving, perform this procedure only after the engine has cooled down completely.
2 Before beginning work, purchase the specified transmission fluid (see *Recommended lubricants and fluids* at the front of this Chapter), a new filter and gasket. Never reuse the old filter or gasket!
3 Other tools necessary for this job include jackstands to support the vehicle in a raised position, a large, shallow drain pan capable of holding at least eight pints, newspapers and clean rags.
4 Raise the vehicle and support it securely on jackstands. DO NOT crawl under the vehicle when it is supported only by a jack!
5 Place the drain pan beneath the transmission.
6 On pan-filled C4 and C5 transmissions, disconnect the fluid filler tube from the pan to drain the transmission fluid.
7 On all other models, with the drain pan in place, remove the mounting bolts from the front and sides of the transmission pan.
8 Loosen the rear pan bolts approximately four turns. Let the pan hang down so the fluid can drain.

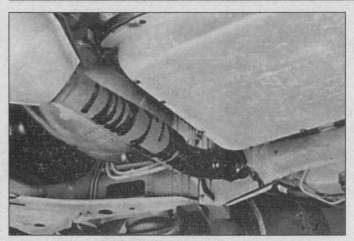

12.9 With the rear bolts loosened and holding it in place, lower the front of the transmission pan and allow the fluid to drain

12.12 The automatic transmission filter is held in place with small bolt(s)

9   Carefully pry the transmission pan loose with a screwdriver, allowing the fluid to drain **(see illustration)**. Don't damage the pan or transmission gasket surfaces or leaks could develop.

10   Remove the remaining bolts, pan and gasket. Carefully clean the gasket surface of the transmission to remove all traces of the old gasket and sealant.

11   Drain the fluid from the transmission pan, clean it with solvent and dry it with compressed air (if available).

12   Remove the filter from the mount inside the transmission **(see illustration)**.

13   Install a new filter and gasket. Tighten the mounting bolt(s) securely.

14   Make sure the gasket surface on the transmission pan is clean, then install a new gasket. Put the pan in place against the transmission and install the bolts. Working around the pan, tighten each bolt a little at a time until a final torque is reached. Don't overtighten the bolts! On pan-filled models, re-connect the filler tube to the pan.

15   Lower the vehicle and add automatic transmission fluid through the filler tube (see Section 7). **Caution:** *Refer to Specifications at the front of this Chapter for the correct amount and type of transmission fluid. Use of the wrong type or the wrong amount can cause transmission damage.*

16   With the transmission in Park and the parking brake set, run the engine at a fast idle, but don't race it.

17   Move the gear selector through each range and back to Park. Check the fluid level. Add fluid if needed to reach the correct level.

18   Check under the vehicle for leaks during the first few trips.

---

13   Underhood hose check and replacement

Caution: *Replacement of air conditioning hoses must be left to a dealer service department or air conditioning shop that has the* equipment to depressurize the system safely. Never remove air conditioning hoses or components until the system has been depressurized.

General

1   High temperatures under the hood can cause deterioration of the rubber and plastic hoses used for engine, accessory and emission systems operation. Periodic inspection should be made for cracks, loose clamps, material hardening and leaks.

2   Information specific to the cooling system can be found in Section 21.

3   Most (but not all) hoses are secured to the fitting with clamps. Where clamps are used, check to be sure they haven't lost their tension, allowing the hose to leak. If clamps aren't used, make sure the hose has not expanded and/or hardened where it slips over the fitting, allowing it to leak.

PCV system hose

4   To reduce hydrocarbon emissions, crankcase blow-by gas is vented through the PCV valve to the intake manifold via a rubber hose on most models. The blow-by gases mix with incoming air in the intake manifold before being burned in the combustion chambers.

5   Check the PCV hose for cracks, leaks and other damage. Disconnect it from the rocker arm cover and the intake manifold and check the inside for obstructions. If it's clogged, clean it out with solvent.

Vacuum hoses

6   It's quite common for vacuum hoses, especially those in the emissions system, to be color coded or identified by colored stripes molded into them. Various systems require hoses with different wall thicknesses, collapse resistance and temperature resistance. When replacing hoses, be sure the new ones are made of the same material.

7   Often the only effective way to check a hose is to remove it completely from the vehi- cle. If more than one hose is removed, be sure to label the hoses and fittings to ensure correct installation.

8   When checking vacuum hoses, be sure to include any plastic T-fittings in the check. Inspect the fittings for cracks and the hose where it fits over each fitting for distortion, which could cause leakage.

9   A small piece of vacuum hose (1/4-inch inside diameter) can be used as a stethoscope to detect vacuum leaks. Hold one end of the hose to your ear and probe around vacuum hoses and fittings, listening for the "hissing" sound characteristic of a vacuum leak. **Warning:** *When probing with the vacuum hose stethoscope, be careful not to come into contact with moving engine components such as drivebelts, the cooling fan, etc.*

Fuel hoses

Warning: *Gasoline is extremely flammable, so take extra precautions when you work on any part of the fuel system. Don't smoke or allow open flames or bare light bulbs near the work area, and don't work in a garage where a natural gas-type appliance (such as a water heater or clothes dryer) with a pilot light is present. If you spill any fuel on your skin, rinse it off immediately with soap and water. When you perform any kind of work on the fuel tank, wear safety glasses and have a Class B type fire extinguisher on hand.*

10   The fuel lines are usually under pressure, so if any fuel lines are to be disconnected be prepared to catch spilled fuel. **Warning:** *If your vehicle is equipped with fuel injection, you must relieve the fuel system pressure before servicing the fuel lines. Refer to Chapter 4 for the fuel system pressure relief procedure.*

11   Check all rubber fuel lines for deterioration and chafing. Check especially for cracks in areas where the hose bends and just before fittings, such as where a hose attaches to the fuel pump, fuel filter and carburetor or fuel injection unit.

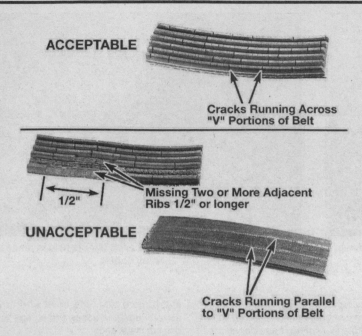

ACCEPTABLE

Cracks Running Across
"V" Portions of Belt

1/2"   Missing Two or More Adjacent
Ribs 1/2" or longer

UNACCEPTABLE

Cracks Running Parallel
to "V" Portions of Belt

14.3 Different types of drivebelts are used to power the various accessories mounted on the engine

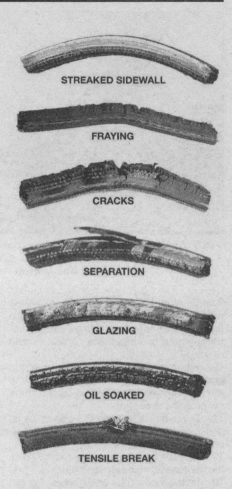

STREAKED SIDEWALL

FRAYING

CRACKS

SEPARATION

GLAZING

OIL SOAKED

TENSILE BREAK

14.4 Here are some of the more common problems associated with drivebelts (check the belts very carefully to prevent an untimely breakdown)

12   High quality fuel line, usually identified by the word Fluoroelastomer printed on the hose, should be used for fuel line replacement. Never, under any circumstances, use unreinforced vacuum line, clear plastic tubing or water hose for fuel lines.

13   Spring-type clamps are commonly used on fuel lines. These clamps often lose their tension over a period of time, and can be "sprung" during removal. Replace all spring-type clamps with screw clamps whenever a hose is replaced.

Metal lines

14   Sections of metal line are often used for fuel line between the fuel pump and carburetor or fuel injection system. Check carefully to make sure the line isn't bent, crimped or cracked.

15   If a section of metal fuel line must be replaced, use seamless steel tubing only, since copper and aluminum tubing do not have the strength necessary to withstand the vibration caused by the engine.

16   Check the metal brake lines where they enter the master cylinder and pressure control valve (if used) for cracks in the lines and loose fittings. Any sign of brake fluid leakage calls for an immediate thorough inspection of the brake system.

Nylon fuel lines

17   Nylon fuel lines are used at several points in fuel injection systems. These lines require special materials and methods for repair. Refer to Chapter 4 for details.

Power steering hoses

18   Check the power steering hoses for leaks, loose connections and worn clamps.

Tighten loose connections. Worn clamps or leaky hoses should be replaced.

14   Drivebelt check, adjustment and replacement

Refer to illustrations 14.3, 14.4, 14.6 and 14.11

1   The accessory drivebelts are located at the front of the engine. The belts drive the water pump, alternator, power steering pump, air conditioning compressor and Thermactor air pump. The condition and tension of the drivebelts are critical to the operation of the engine and accessories. Excessive tension causes bearing wear, while insufficient tension produces slippage, noise, component vibration and belt failure. Because of their composition and the high stress to which they are subjected, drivebelts stretch and continue to deteriorate as they get older. As a result, they must be periodically checked. Some belts require periodic tension adjustment; others have automatic tensioners and require no adjustment for the life of the belt.

Check

2   The number and type of belts used on a particular vehicle depends on the engine, model year and accessories installed.

3   Various types of drivebelts are used on these models **(see illustration)**. Some components are driven by V-belts, of either smooth or cogged design. Others are driven by V-ribbed belts. 3.8L V6 and V8 engines, as well as later four-cylinder engines, use a single V-ribbed belt to drive most or all of the accessories. This is known as a "serpentine" belt because of the winding path it follows

between various drive, accessory and idler pulleys.

4   With the engine off, open the hood and locate the drivebelt(s) at the front of the engine. With a flashlight, check each belt for separation of the rubber plies from each side of the core, a severed core, separation of the ribs from the rubber, cracks, torn or worn ribs and cracks in the inner ridges of the ribs. Also check for fraying and glazing, which gives the belt a shiny appearance **(see illustration)**. Cracks in the rib side of V-ribbed belts are acceptable, as are small chunks missing from the ribs. If a V-ribbed belt has lost chunks bigger than 1/2-inch (13 mm) from two adjacent ribs, or if the missing chunks cause belt noise, the belt should be replaced. Both sides of each belt should be inspected, which means you'll have to twist them to check the undersides. Use your fingers to feel a belt where you can't see it. If any of the above conditions are evident, replace the belt as described below.

5   To check the tension of V-belts and fixed (manually adjusted - used on earlier models) serpentine belts in accordance with factory recommendations, install a drivebelt

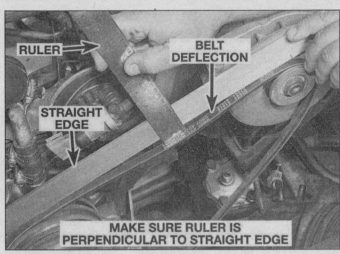

14.6 Measuring drivebelt deflection with a straightedge and ruler

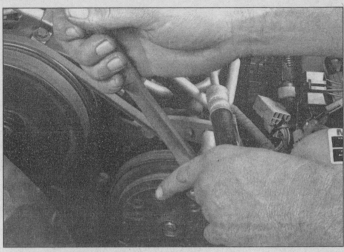

14.11 On some models a 1/2-inch drive breaker bar can be used to tension the A/C compressor drivebelt as the bolts are tightened

tension gauge, available at most auto parts stores that carry special tools. Measure the tension in accordance with the tension gauge instructions and compare your measurement to the specified drivebelt tension for either a used or a new belt. **Note:** *A "new" belt is defined as any belt which has not been run; a "used" belt is one that has been run for more than ten minutes.*

6   The special gauge is the most accurate way to check the tension of V-belts and manually adjusted serpentine belts. However, if you don't have a gauge, and cannot borrow one, the following "rule of thumb" method is recommended as an alternative (for smooth and cogged V-belts only; do not use this method on V-ribbed belts). Lay a straight-edge across the longest free span (the distance between two pulleys) of the belt. Push down firmly on the belt at a point half way between the pulleys and see how much the belt moves (deflects). Measure the deflection with a ruler **(see illustration)**. The belt should deflect 1/8 to 1/4-inch if the distance from pulley center-to-pulley center is less than 12 inches; it should deflect from 1/8 to 3/8-inch if the distance from pulley center-to-pulley center is over 12 inches.

7   Later models with V-ribbed belts use automatic tensioners and wear indicators. If the indicators show that the serpentine belt is worn beyond the maximum, the belt should be replaced.

Adjustment

8   Adjustment is necessary on smooth and cogged V-belts, as well as the serpentine belt on 1983 through 1986 3.8L V6 engines. All other engines, including V8 and later model four-cylinder engines, use V-ribbed belts which are adjusted by automatic tensioners. Manual adjustment is not required for these models.

9   To adjust V-belts, move the belt-driven accessory on the bracket.

10   For each accessory, there will be a lock-

ing bolt and a pivot bolt or nut. Both must be loosened slightly to enable you to move the component.

11   After the two bolts have been loosened, move the component away from the engine (to tighten the belt) or toward the engine (to loosen the belt). Many accessories are equipped with a square hole designed to accept a 1/2-inch square drive breaker bar **(see illustration)**. The bar can be used to lever the component and tension the drivebelt. Others have a cast lug which is designed to accept an open end wrench, which can be used to pry the accessory. **Caution:** *If it's necessary to pry against an accessory to tighten a drivebelt, be very careful not to damage the accessory or the point the prybar rests against.*

12   Hold the accessory in position and check the belt tension. If it's correct, tighten the two bolts until snug, then recheck the tension. If it's alright, tighten the two bolts completely.

13   To adjust the serpentine belt on 3.8L V6 engines, loosen the idler locking bolts and tighten the adjustment bolt.

14   When tension is correct, tighten the idler locking bolts.

Replacement

15   To replace a V-belt or the serpentine belt on 3.8L engines, follow the above procedures for drivebelt adjustment but loosen the belt until it will slip off the pulleys, then remove it. On some models, it may be necessary to remove forward belts to replace a rear belt. Since belts tend to wear out at the same time, it's a good idea to replace all of them at the same time. Mark each belt and the corresponding pulley grooves so the belt can be reinstalled properly.

16   To replace a serpentine belt on later four-cylinder engines 1979 through 1984 V8 engines, pry the tensioner away from the belt. Hold the tensioner in place and slip the belt off the pulleys. If the tensioner is removed and

disassembled, be sure the spring tang engages the hole in the tensioner bracket during reassembly.

17   Hold the tensioner away from the belt, install a new belt and make sure it is routed correctly. Be sure the ribs of the new belt engage the pulley ribs correctly **(see illustration)**. Release the tensioner once the belt is installed.

18   To replace a serpentine belt on 1985 and later V8 engines, rotate the tensioner with a breaker bar and socket. Hold the tensioner away from the belt and slip the belt off the pulleys. If the tensioner is removed and disassembled, be sure the locating pin engages the hole in the bracket during reassembly.

19   Hold the tensioner away from the belt, install a new belt and release the tensioner.

15   Battery check and maintenance

Refer to illustrations 15.1, 15.8a, 15.8b, 15.8c and 15.8d

Warning: *Certain precautions must be followed when checking and servicing the battery. Hydrogen gas, which is highly flammable, is always present in the battery cells, so keep lighted tobacco and all other flames and sparks away from it. The electrolyte inside the battery is actually dilute sulfuric acid, which will cause injury if splashed on your skin or in your eyes. It will also ruin clothes and painted surfaces. When removing the battery cables, always detach the negative cable first and hook it up last!*

Note: *On models equipped with the Distributorless (DIS) Ignition System, some precautions must be taken after disconnecting and reconnecting the battery cable(s). See Battery - removal and installation in Chapter 5, Section 2.*

1   Battery maintenance is an important procedure which will help ensure that you are not stranded because of a dead battery. Sev-

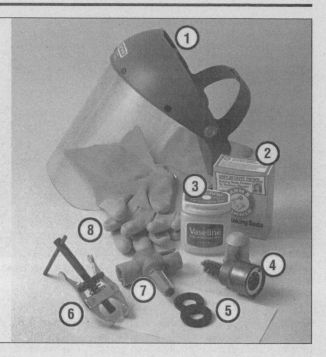

15.1 Tools and materials required for battery maintenance

1 **Face shield/safety goggles** - When removing corrosion with a brush, the acidic particles can easily fly up into your eyes
2 **Baking soda** - A solution of baking soda and water can be used to neutralize corrosion
3 **Petroleum jelly** - A later of this on the battery posts will help prevent corrosion
4 **Battery post/cable cleaner** - This wire brush cleaning tool will remove all traces of corrosion from the battery posts and cable clamps
5 **Treated felt washers** - Placing one of these on each post, directly under the cable clamps, will help prevent corrosion
6 **Puller** - Sometimes the cable clamps are very difficult to pull off the posts, even after the nut/bolt has been completely loosened. This tool pulls the clamp straight up and off the post without damage.
7 **Battery post/cable cleaner** - Here is another cleaning tool which is a slightly different version of number 4 above, but it does the same thing
8 **Rubber gloves** - Another safety item to consider when servicing the battery; remember that's acid inside the battery!

eral tools are required for this procedure **(see illustration)**.

2   Before servicing the battery, always turn the engine and all accessories off and disconnect the cable from the negative terminal of the battery.

3   A sealed (sometimes called maintenance free) battery is standard equipment on 1980 and later models. The cell caps cannot be removed, no electrolyte checks are required and water cannot be added to the cells. However, if an aftermarket battery has been installed and it is a type that requires regular maintenance, the following procedures can be used.

4   Check the electrolyte level in each of the battery cells. It must be above the plates. There's usually a split-ring indicator in each cell to indicate the correct level. If the level is low, add distilled water only, then install the cell caps. **Caution:** *Overfilling the cells may cause electrolyte to spill over during periods of heavy charging, causing corrosion and damage to nearby components.*

5   If the positive terminal and cable clamp on your vehicle's battery is equipped with a rubber protector, make sure that it's not torn or damaged. It should completely cover the terminal.

6   The external condition of the battery should be checked periodically. Look for damage such as a cracked case.

7   Check the tightness of the battery cable clamps to ensure good electrical connections and inspect the entire length of each cable, looking for cracked or abraded insulation and frayed conductors.

8   If corrosion (visible as white, fluffy deposits) is evident, remove the cables from the terminals, clean them with a battery brush and reinstall them **(see illustrations)**. Corrosion can be kept to a minimum by installing specially treated washers available at auto parts stores or by applying a layer of petroleum jelly or grease to the terminals and cable clamps after they are assembled.

9   Make sure that the battery carrier is in good condition and that the hold-down clamp bolt is tight. If the battery is removed (see Chapter 5 for the removal and installation procedure), make sure that no parts remain in the bottom of the carrier when it's reinstalled. When reinstalling the hold-down clamp, don't overtighten the bolt.

15.8a Battery terminal corrosion usually appears as light, fluffy powder

15.8b Removing the cable from a battery post with a wrench - sometimes a special battery pliers is required for this procedure if corrosion has caused deterioration of the nut hex (always remove the ground cable first and hook it up last!)

15.8c Regardless of the type of tool used on the battery posts, a clean, shiny surface should be the result

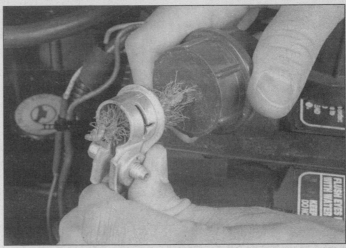

15.8d When cleaning the cable clamps, all corrosion must be removed (the inside of the clamp is tapered to match the taper on the post, do don't remove too much material)

1

10   Corrosion on the carrier, battery case and surrounding areas can be removed with a solution of water and baking soda. Apply the mixture with a small brush, let it work, then rinse it off with plenty of clean water.

11   Any metal parts of the vehicle damaged by corrosion should be coated with a zinc-based primer, then painted.

12   Additional information on the battery, charging and jump starting can be found in Chapter 5 and the front of this manual.

16   Air filter replacement

Refer to illustrations 16.2, 16.3 and 16.21

1   Purchase a new filter for your specific engine type. If the vehicle is equipped with Sequential Electronic Fuel Injection (later V0 engines), the filter is impregnated with charcoal. Be sure the replacement filter is the same type.

Carbureted and Central Fuel Injection (CFI)

2   Remove the wing nut from the top of the housing and lift the top plate off (see illustration).

3   Remove the filter (see illustration).

4   Wipe the inside of the air cleaner housing with a clean cloth.

5   Place the new air filter in the housing. If the filter is marked TOP be sure the marked side faces up.

6   Install the cover and wing nut. Don't overtighten the nut!

Four-cylinder EFI non-turbo

7   Disconnect the vacuum hose and outlet tube from the air cleaner cover. Remove the cover retaining screws and lift the cover off.

8   Remove the filter.

9   Wipe the inside of the air cleaner housing with a clean cloth.

10   Place the new air filter in the housing. If the filter is marked TOP, be sure the marked side faces up.

11   Reinstall the cover and retaining screws. Don't overtighten the screws!

12   Reconnect the vacuum hose and outlet tube.

Four-cylinder EFI turbo

13   Detach the air cleaner tube adapter.

14   Remove the cover wing nut and grommet. Lift the cover off.

15   Remove the filter.

16   Wipe the inside of the air cleaner housing with a clean cloth.

17   Place the new air filter in the housing. If the filter is marked TOP, be sure the marked side faces up.

18   Reinstall the cover and wing nut. Don't overtighten the wing nut!

16.2 On carbureted and CFI models, remove the air cleaner wing nut . . .

16.3 . . . and lift out the filter

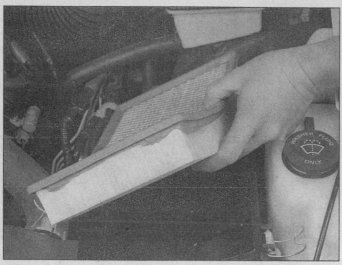

16.21 On later models, unclip the filter cover and lift out the filter

18.1 The PCV valve is in various locations, depending on engine type

V8 engines with Sequential Electronic Fuel Injection (SEFI)

19   Loosen the air cleaner outlet tube clamp.
20   Unfasten the cover clips and lift the cover off.
21   Lift out the filter **(see illustration)**.
22   Wipe the inside of the air cleaner housing with a clean cloth.
23   Place the new air filter in the housing. If the filter is marked TOP be sure the top side faces up.
24   Reinstall the cover and secure the clips.
25   Reconnect the outlet hose to the air cleaner.

---

17   Crankcase vent filter replacement

---

1   Obtain a new crankcase vent filter for your specific engine.

Through 1987, all except four-cylinder non-turbo and 3.8L V6 engines

2   Remove the air cleaner top plate (see Section 16) to expose the crankcase vent filter.
3   Remove the filter from its pocket in the side of the air cleaner housing.
4   Clean the filter pocket with a cloth or paper towel moistened with solvent.
5   Install the new filter.
6   Install the air cleaner top plate (see Section 16).

Through 1987, four-cylinder non-turbo and 3.8L V6 engines

7   The oil filler cap, filter and tube are replaced as an assembly.
8   Disconnect the tube.

9   Unscrew the oil filler cap from the valve cover and install a new one.

1988 on (V8 only)

10   Remove the PCV valve and grommet from the lower intake manifold.
11   Remove and discard the filter.
12   Install a new filter.
13   Install the grommet and PCV valve.

---

18   PCV valve check and replacement

Refer to illustration 18.1
Note: *To maintain the efficiency of the PCV system, clean the hoses and check the PCV valve at the intervals recommended in the maintenance schedule. For additional information on the PCV system, refer to Chapter 6.*
1   Locate the PCV valve **(see illustration)**. On four-cylinder EFI engines, the air cleaner assembly must be removed (see Chapter 4) to gain access to the PCV valve.
2   To check the valve, first pull it out of the grommet in the rocker arm cover or manifold, or out of the lower hose. Shake the valve. It should rattle, indicating that it is not clogged with deposits. If the valve does not rattle, replace it with a new one. If it does rattle, reinstall it.
3   Start the engine and allow it to idle, then disconnect the PCV hose (from the air cleaner on most models). If vacuum is felt, the PCV/valve system is working properly (see Chapter 6 for additional PCV system information).
4   If no vacuum is felt, the oil filler cap, hoses or rocker arm cover gasket may be leaking or the PCV valve may be bad. Check for vacuum leaks at the valve, filler cap and all hoses.
5   Pull straight up on the valve to remove

it. Check the rubber grommet for cracks and distortion (on four-cylinder models, check the hose where the PCV valve seats). If it's damaged, replace it.
6   If the valve is clogged, the hose is also probably plugged. Remove the hose and clean it with solvent.
7   After cleaning the hose, inspect it for damage, wear and deterioration. Make sure it fits snugly on the fittings.
8   If necessary, install a new PCV valve.
Note: *The elbow (models so equipped) is not part of the PCV valve. A new valve will not include the elbow. The original must be transferred to the new valve. If a new elbow is purchased, it may be necessary to soak it in warm water for up to an hour to slip it onto the new valve. Do not attempt to force the elbow onto the valve or it will break.*
9   Install the clean PCV system hose. Make sure the PCV valve and hose are secure.

---

19   Fuel system check

Warning: *Gasoline is extremely flammable, so take extra precautions when you work on any part of the fuel system. Don't smoke or allow open flames or bare light bulbs near the work area, and don't work in a garage where a natural gas-type appliance (such as a water heater or clothes dryer) with a pilot light is present. If you spill any fuel on your skin, rinse it off immediately with soap and water. When you perform any kind of work on the fuel tank, wear safety glasses and have a Class B type fire extinguisher on hand.*
1   If you smell gasoline while driving or after the vehicle has been sitting in the sun, inspect the fuel system immediately.
2   Remove the gas filler cap and inspect it for damage and corrosion. The gasket should have an unbroken sealing imprint. If the gasket is damaged or corroded, install a new cap.

3   Inspect the fuel feed and return lines for cracks. Make sure that the connections between the fuel lines and the carburetor or fuel injection system and between the fuel lines and the in-line fuel filter are tight. **Warning:** *If the vehicle is fuel injected, you must relieve the fuel system pressure before servicing fuel system components. The fuel system pressure relief procedure is in Chapter 4.*

4   Since some components of the fuel system - the fuel tank and part of the fuel feed and return lines, for example - are underneath the vehicle, they can be inspected more easily with the vehicle raised on a hoist. If that's not possible, raise the vehicle and support it on jackstands.

5   With the vehicle raised and safely supported, inspect the gas tank and filler neck for punctures, cracks or other damage. The connection between the filler neck and the tank is particularly critical. Sometimes a rubber filler neck will leak because of loose clamps or deteriorated rubber. Inspect all fuel tank mounting brackets and straps to be sure the tank is securely attached to the vehicle. **Warning:** *Do not, under any circumstances, try to repair a fuel tank (except rubber components). A welding torch or any open flame can easily cause fuel vapors inside the tank to explode.*

6   Carefully check all rubber hoses and metal or nylon lines leading away from the fuel tank. Check for loose connections, deteriorated hoses, crimped lines and other damage. Repair or replace damaged sections as necessary (see Chapter 4).

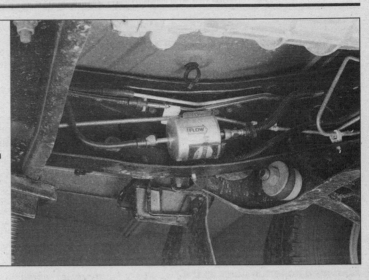

20.2 Here's the fuel filter used on later fuel-Injected models - be sure the arrow on the new filter points in the proper direction after the filter is installed

---

20   Fuel filter replacement

Warning: *Gasoline is extremely flammable, so take extra precautions when you work on any part of the fuel system. Don't smoke or allow open flames or bare light bulbs near the work area, and don't work in a garage where a natural gas-type appliance (such as a water heater or clothes dryer) with a pilot light is present. If you spill any fuel on your skin, rinse it off immediately with soap and water. When you perform any kind of work on the fuel tank, wear safety glasses and have a Class B type fire extinguisher on hand.*

Fuel-injected models

Refer to illustration 20.2

1   Obtain a new fuel filter before starting. **Warning:** *Be sure the new filter is specifically designed for the engine. Fuel injection system filters are built to withstand high pressure, and as a result, often cost more than filters meant for use in carbureted systems. Filters meant for carbureted systems may burst due to the high pressure. Also, be sure the new filter includes replacement hairpin clips.* **Warning:** *Before removing the fuel filter, the fuel system pressure must be relieved (see Chapter 4).*

2   Locate the fuel filter on the frame rail, near the fuel tank **(see illustration)**. Inspect the hose fittings at both ends of the filter to see if they're clean. If more than a light coating of dust is present, clean the fittings before proceeding.

3   Remove the hairpin clip from each fitting. To do this, first spread the two clip legs apart about 1/8-inch and detach the clip from the fitting.

4   Once both hairpin clips are released, grasp the fuel hoses, one at a time, and pull them straight off the filter.

5   Note which way the arrow on the filter is pointing - the new filter must be installed the same way. Loosen the clamp or two bolts and detach the filter from the bracket.

6   Install the new filter in the bracket with the arrow pointing in the right direction. Tighten the clamp or bolts securely.

7   Carefully push each hose onto the filter until it's seated against the collar on the fitting, then install the hairpin clips. The triangular side of each clip must point away from the filter. Make sure the clips are securely attached to the hose fittings - if they come off, the hoses could back off the filter and a fire could result!

8   Start the engine and check for fuel leaks.

Carbureted models

9   Remove the air cleaner housing from the top of the carburetor to gain access to the filter.

10   Place a rag under the filter, then remove the fuel line(s) from the filter. On hose connections, squeeze the clamps with pliers and slide them up the hose. On inverted flare connections, unscrew the fuel line from the filter while holding the filter hex with a back-up wrench. A flare-nut wrench should be used if available - it will prevent rounding off the fuel line fitting hex.

11   On models with an inline filter, discard the old filter. Install a new filter in the line and secure it with clamps. Spring-type clamps should be replaced with new ones.

12   If the vehicle has a carburetor-mounted filter, unscrew the filter or fuel inlet fitting from the carburetor. On models with a separate filter element, remove the element and spring from the housing in the carburetor body.

13   If the vehicle has a screw-in filter with an inverted flare-nut seat, apply a drop of Loctite hydraulic sealant No. 069 to the filter threads.

14   Screw the filter into the carburetor and it tighten securely. On Holley 1946 carburetors, hold the fuel inlet fitting with a back-up wrench so the carburetor body isn't damaged.

15   On models with a flare-nut fuel line connection, apply motor oil to the flare-nut fitting threads. Thread the flare nut into the filter, hold the filter with a back-up wrench and tighten the flare-nut securely.

16   On models with a fuel hose, slide new hose clamps down the metal fuel line. Install the fuel hose on the filter and metal line, then position the hose clamps on the hose.

17   Reinstall the air cleaner housing.

---

21   Cooling system check

Refer to illustration 21.4

1   Many major engine failures can be attributed to a faulty cooling system. If the vehicle is equipped with an automatic transmission, the cooling system also plays an important role in prolonging transmission life because it cools the fluid.

2   The engine should be cold for the cooling system check, so perform the following procedure before the vehicle is driven for the day or after it has been shut off for at least three hours.

3   Remove the radiator cap and clean it thoroughly, inside and out, with clean water. Also clean the filler neck on the radiator. The presence of rust or corrosion in the filler neck means the coolant should be changed (see Section 22). The coolant inside the radiator should be relatively clean and transparent. If it's rust colored, drain the system and refill with new coolant.

Check for a chafed area that could fail prematurely.

Check for a soft area indicating the hose has deteriorated inside.

Overtightening the clamp on a hardened hose will damage the hose and cause a leak.

Check each hose for swelling and oil-soaked ends. Cracks and breaks can be located by squeezing the hose.

21.4 hoses, like drivebelts, have a habit of failing at the worst possible time - to prevent the inconvenience of a blown radiator or heater hose, inspect them carefully as shown here

4   Carefully check the radiator hoses and smaller diameter heater hoses **(see illustration)**. Inspect each coolant hose along its entire length, replacing any hose which is cracked, swollen or deteriorated. Cracks will show up better if the hose is squeezed. Pay close attention to hose clamp that secure the hoses to cooling system components. Hose clamps can pinch and puncture hoses, resulting in coolant leaks.

5   Make sure all hose connections are tight. A leak in the cooling system will usually show up as white or rust-colored deposits on the area adjoining the leak. If wire-type clamps are used on the hoses, it may be a good idea to replace them with screw-type clamps.

6   Clean the front of the radiator and air conditioning condenser with compressed air, if available, or a soft brush. Remove all bugs, leaves, etc. embedded in the radiator fins. Be

extremely careful not to damage the cooling fins or cut your fingers on them.

7   If the coolant level has been dropping consistently and no leaks are detectable, have the radiator cap and cooling system pressure checked at a service station.

---

22   Cooling system servicing (draining, flushing and refilling)

Warning: *Do not allow antifreeze to come in contact with your skin or painted surfaces of the vehicle. Rinse off spills immediately with plenty of water. Antifreeze is highly toxic if ingested. Never leave antifreeze lying around in an open container or in puddles on the floor; children and pets are attracted by it's sweet smell and may drink it. Check with local authorities about disposing of used antifreeze. Many communities have collection centers which will see that antifreeze is disposed of safely.*

1   Periodically, the cooling system should be drained, flushed and refilled to replenish the antifreeze mixture and prevent formation of rust and corrosion, which can impair the performance of the cooling system and cause engine damage. When the cooling system is serviced, all hoses and the radiator cap should be checked and replaced if necessary.

Draining

2   Apply the parking brake and block the wheels. If the vehicle has just been driven, wait several hours to allow the engine to cool down before beginning this procedure.

3   Once the engine is completely cool, remove the radiator cap.

4   Move a large container under the radiator to catch the coolant. Attach a 3/8-inch diameter hose to the drain fitting to direct the coolant into the container, then open the drain fitting (a pair of pliers may be required to turn it). The drain fitting is normally at the lower right (passenger's side) corner of the radiator.

5   After the coolant stops flowing out of the radiator, move the container under the engine block drain plug. Remove the plug and allow the coolant in the block to drain.

6   While the coolant is draining, check the condition of the radiator hoses, heater hoses and clamps (see Section 21 if necessary).

7   Replace any damaged clamps or hoses (see Chapter 3 for detailed replacement procedures).

Flushing

8   Once the system is completely drained, flush the radiator with fresh water from a garden hose until the water runs clear at the drain. The flushing action of the water will remove sediments from the radiator but will not remove rust and scale from the engine and cooling tube surfaces.

9   These deposits can be removed by the chemical action of a cleaner, available at

most auto parts stores. Follow the procedure outlined in the manufacturer's instructions. If the radiator is severely corroded, damaged or leaking, it should be removed (see Chapter 3) and taken to a radiator repair shop.

10   The heater core should be backflushed whenever the cooling system is flushed. To do this, disconnect the heater return hose from the thermostat housing or engine. Slide a female garden hose fitting into the heater hose and secure it with a clamp. This will allow you to attach a garden hose securely.

11   Attach the end of a garden hose to the fitting you installed in the heater hose.

12   Disconnect the heater inlet hose and position it to act as a drain.

13   Turn the water on and off several times to create a surging action through the heater core. Then turn the water on full force and allow it to run for approximately five minutes.

14   Turn off the water and disconnect the garden hose from the female fitting. Remove the fitting from the heater return hose, then reconnect the hoses to the engine.

15   Remove the overflow hose from the coolant recovery reservoir. Drain the reservoir and flush it with clean water, then reconnect the hose.

Refilling

16   Close and tighten the radiator drain. Install and tighten the block drain plug(s).

17   Place the heater temperature control in the maximum heat position.

18   Slowly add new coolant (a 50/50 mixture of water and antifreeze) to the radiator until it is full. Add coolant to the reservoir up to the lower mark.

19   Leave the radiator cap off and run the engine in a well-ventilated area until the thermostat opens (coolant will begin flowing through the radiator and the upper radiator hose will become hot).

20   Turn the engine off and let it cool. Add more coolant mixture to bring the coolant level back up to the lip on the radiator filler neck.

21   Squeeze the upper radiator hose to expel air, then add more coolant mixture if necessary. Replace the radiator cap.

22   Start the engine, allow it to reach normal operating temperature and check for leaks.

---

23   Exhaust system check

1   With the engine cold (at least three hours after the vehicle has been driven), check the complete exhaust system from the engine to the end of the tailpipe. Ideally, the inspection should be done with the vehicle on a hoist to permit unrestricted access. If a hoist isn't available, raise the vehicle and support it securely on jackstands.

2   Check the exhaust pipes and connections for evidence of leaks, severe corrosion and damage. Make sure that all brackets and hangers are in good condition and are tight.

3   At the same time, inspect the underside

24.10 To check the suspension balljoints, try to move the lower edge of each front tire in-and-out while watching/feeling for movement at the top of the tire and balljoints

24.11 To check the steering gear mounts and tie-rod connections for play, grasp each front tire like this and try to move it back-and-forth - if play is noted, check the steering gear mounts and make sure that they're tight; if either tie-rod is worn or bent, replace it

of the body for holes, corrosion, open seams, etc. which may allow exhaust gases to enter the passenger compartment. Seal all body openings with silicone or body putty.

4   Rattles and other noises can often be traced to the exhaust system, especially the mounts and hangers. Try to move the pipes, muffler and catalytic converter. If the components can come in contact with the body or suspension parts, secure the exhaust system with new mounts.

5   Check the running condition of the engine by inspecting inside the end of the tailpipe. The exhaust deposits here are an indication of engine state-of-tune. If the pipe is black and sooty or coated with white deposits, the engine may need a tune-up, including a thorough fuel system inspection and adjustment.

24   Steering and suspension check

Refer to illustration 24.11
Note: *The steering linkage and suspension components should be checked periodically. Worn or damaged suspension and steering linkage components can result in excessive and abnormal tire wear, poor ride quality and vehicle handling and reduced fuel economy. For detailed illustrations of the steering and suspension components, refer to Chapter 10.*

Strut and shock absorber check

1   Park the car on level ground, turn the engine off and set the parking brake. Check the tire pressures.

2   Push down at one corner of the vehicle, then release it while noting the movement of the body. It should stop moving and come to rest in a level position with one or two bounces.

3   If the vehicle continues to move up-and-down or if it fails to return to its original position, a worn or weak strut or shock absorber is probably the reason.

4   Repeat the above check at each of the three remaining corners of the vehicle.

5   Raise the vehicle and support it on jack-stands.

6   Check the shock absorber and struts for evidence of fluid leakage. A light film of fluid is no cause for concern. Make sure that any fluid noted is from the shocks and not from any other source. If leakage is noted, replace the struts or shocks as a set.

7   Check the struts and shock absorbers to be sure that they are securely mounted and undamaged. Check the upper mounts for damage and wear. If damage or wear is noted, replace the struts or shock absorbers as a set.

8   If the struts or shock absorbers must be replaced, refer to Chapter 10 for the procedure.

Steering and suspension check

9   Visually inspect the steering system components for damage and distortion. Look for leaks and damaged seals, boots and fittings.

10   Clean the lower end of the steering knuckle. Have an assistant grasp the lower edge of the tire and move the wheel in-and-out while you look for movement at the steering knuckle-to-control arm balljoint. If there is any movement or the wear indicators are worn below the surface, the suspension balljoint must be replaced.

11   Grasp each front tire at the front and rear edges, push in at the front, pull out at the rear and feel for play in the steering system components **(see illustration)**. If any freeplay is noted, check the steering gear mounts and the tie-rod balljoints for looseness. If the steering gear mounts are loose, tighten them.

If the tie-rods are loose, the balljoints may be worn (check to make sure the nuts are tight). Make sure the steering gear rack and pinion boots are kept clean. Additional steering and suspension system illustrations can be found in Chapter 10.

Front wheel bearing check

12   Refer to Section 28 for the wheel bearing check, repack and adjustment procedure.

25   Brake system check

Refer to illustrations 25.11, 25.15 and 25.17
Note: *In addition to the specified intervals, the brake system should inspected each time the wheels are removed or a malfunction is indicated. Because of the obvious safety considerations, the following brake system checks are some of the most important maintenance procedures you can perform on the vehicle.*

Symptoms of brake system problems

1   The disc brakes have built-in wear indicators which should make a high-pitched squealing or scraping noise when they're worn to the replacement point. When you hear this noise, replace the pads immediately or expensive damage to the rotors could result.

2   Any of the following symptoms could indicate a potential brake system defect. The vehicle pulls to one side when the brake pedal is depressed, the brakes make squealing or dragging noises when applied, brake travel is excessive, the pedal pulsates and brake fluid leaks are noted (usually on the inner side of the tire or wheel). If any of these conditions are noted, inspect the brake system immediately.

25.11 The lining thickness of the front disc brake pad (arrow) can be checked through the caliper inspection hole

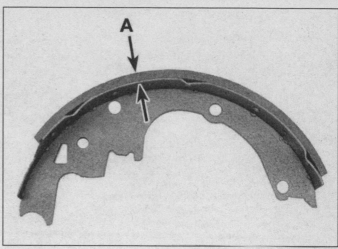

25.15 The rear brake shoe lining thickness (A) is measured from the outer surface of the lining to the metal shoe

Brake lines and hoses

Note: *Steel tubing is used throughout the brake system, with the exception of flexible, reinforced hoses at the front wheels and at connectors at the rear axle. Periodic inspection of these lines is very important.*

3   Park the vehicle on level ground and turn the engine off.

4   Remove the wheel covers. Loosen, but do not remove, the lug nuts on all four wheels.

5   Raise the vehicle and support it securely on jackstands.

6   Remove the wheels (see *Jacking and towing* at the front of this book, or refer to your owner's manual, if necessary).

7   Check all brake lines and hoses for cracks, chafing of the outer cover, leaks, blisters and distortion. Check the brake hoses at front and rear of the vehicle for softening, cracks, bulging, or wear from rubbing on other components. Check all threaded fittings for leaks and make sure the brake hose mounting bolts and clips are secure.

8   If leaks or damage are discovered, they must be fixed immediately. Refer to Chapter 9 for detailed brake system repair procedures.

Disc brakes

9   If it hasn't already been done, raise the vehicle and support it securely on jackstands. Remove the front wheels (also remove the rear wheels on Mustang SVO and Mustang Cobra).

10   The disc brake calipers, which contain the pads, are now visible. Each caliper has an outer and an inner pad - all pads should be checked.

11   Note the pad thickness by looking through the inspection hole in the caliper **(see illustration)**. If necessary, measure the thickness by placing a small ruler over the inspection hole. Compare your measurement with this Chapter's Specifications. Keep in mind that the lining material is riveted or bonded to a metal plate or shoe - the metal portion is not included in this measurement.

12   Check the condition of the brake disc. Look for score marks, deep scratches and overheated areas (they will appear blue or discolored). If damage or wear is noted, the disc can be removed and resurfaced buy an automotive machine shop or replaced with a new one. Refer to Chapter 9 for more detailed inspection and repair procedures.

Drum brakes

13   Refer to Chapter 9 and remove the rear brake drums.

14   **Warning:** *Dust produced by lining wear and deposited on brake components may contain asbestos, which is hazardous to your health. DO NOT blow it out with compressed air and DO NOT inhale it! DO NOT use gasoline or solvents to remove the dust. Brake system cleaner should be used to flush the dust into a drain pan. After the brake components are wiped with a damp rag, dispose of the contaminated rag(s) and brake cleaner in a covered and labeled container. Try to use non-asbestos replacement parts whenever possible.*

15   Note the thickness of the lining material on the rear brake shoes **(see illustration)** and look for signs of contamination by brake fluid or grease. If the lining material is within 1/16-inch of the recessed rivets or metal shoes, replace the brake shoes with new ones. The shoes should also be replaced if they are cracked, glazed (shiny lining surfaces), or contaminated with brake fluid or grease. See Chapter 9 for the replacement procedure.

16   Check the shoe return and hold-down springs and the adjusting mechanism to make sure they are installed correctly and in good condition. Deteriorated or distorted springs, if not replaced, could allow the linings to drag and wear prematurely.

17   Check the wheel cylinders for leakage by carefully peeling back the rubber boots **(see illustration)**. Slight moisture behind the boots is acceptable. If brake fluid is noted behind the boots or if it runs out of the wheel cylinder, the wheel cylinders must be overhauled or replaced (see Chapter 9).

18   Check the drums for cracks, score marks, deep scratches and hard spots, which will appear as small discolored areas. If imperfections cannot be removed with emery cloth, the drums must be resurfaced by an

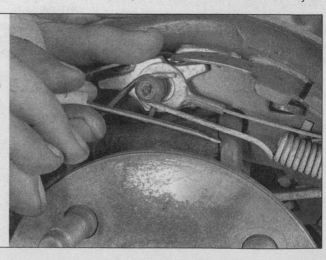

25.17 Carefully peel back the rubber boot on each end of the wheel cylinder - if the exposed area is covered with brake fluid, or if fluid runs out, the wheel cylinder must be overhauled or replaced

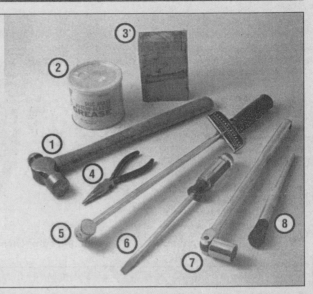

28.1 Tools and materials needed for front wheel bearing maintenance

1   **Hammer** - A common hammer will do just fine
2   **Grease** - High-temperature grease that is formulated specially for front wheel bearings should be used
3   **Wood block** - If you have a scrap piece of 2x4, it can be used to drive the new seal into the hub
4   **Needle-nose pliers** - Used to straighten and remove the cotter pin in the spindle
5   **Torque wrench** - This is very important in this procedure; if the bearing is too tight, the wheel won't turn freely - if it's too loose, the wheel will "wobble" on the spindle. Either way, it could mean extensive damage.
6   **Screwdriver** - Used to remove the seal from the hub (a long screwdriver would be preferred)
7   **Socket/breaker bar** - Needed to loosen the nut on the spindle if it's extremely tight
8   **Brush** - Together with some clean solvent, this will be used to remove old grease from the hub and spindle

automotive machine shop (see Chapter 9 for more detailed information).
19   Refer to Chapter 9 and install the brake drums.
20   Install the wheels, but don't lower the vehicle yet.

Parking brake

Note: The parking brake cable and linkage should be periodically lubricated (see Section 11). This maintenance procedure helps prevent the parking brake cable adjuster or the linkage from binding and adversely affecting the operation or adjustment of the parking brake.

21   The easiest, and perhaps most obvious, method of checking the parking brake is to park the vehicle on a steep hill with the parking brake set and the transmission in Neutral. If the parking brake doesn't prevent the vehicle from rolling, refer to Chapter 9 and adjust it.

26   Automatic transmission shift linkage lubrication

1   Raise the vehicle and support it securely on jackstands. Locate the shift cable or rod contact points.
2   Clean the linkage and pivot points.
3   Lubricate the shift linkage and pivot points with multi-purpose grease.

27   Clutch linkage lubrication and adjustment

Lubrication

1   On vehicles with a cable-actuated clutch, the clutch linkage should be lubricated with the specified grease whenever clutch movement becomes sluggish. DO NOT lubricate the clutch cable lining!

2   Raise the vehicle and support it securely on jackstands.
3   Lubricate the linkage friction points under the vehicle, on the transmission bellhousing.
4   Lower the vehicle and lubricate the friction points at the top of the clutch pedal.

Manual adjustment

5   Clutch pedal height on 1979 and 1980 models requires manual adjustment.
6   Measure and make a note of the following distances:
7   Steering wheel rim-to-clutch pedal, measuring to the flat of the pedal, off to the side of the ribbed contact patch.
8   Depress the clutch pedal to the floor and measure the distance between the steering wheel rim and the clutch pedal.
9   Subtract the two measurements (dimension X). The difference in measurements should be 6-1/2 in. If it's not, adjust the clutch cable.
10   Remove the dust shield covering the clutch cable-to-transmission bellhousing junction.
11   Loosen the cable locknut.
12   Adjust the cable by using the adjusting nut to lengthen or shorten the cable as required.
13   Tighten the locknut.
14   Depress the clutch pedal to the floor several times and then recheck the pedal travel. Readjust as necessary.
15   Reinstall the dust shield.

Automatic adjustment

16   An automatic adjusting mechanism is used on 1981 and later models. At the intervals specified in the maintenance schedule, the mechanism should be operated by foot.
17   Lift the clutch pedal to the top of its travel with your foot. This should take only about 10 lb. of effort.
18   Push the pedal all the way to the floor. If a click is heard, adjustment was necessary and has taken place.

28   Front wheel bearing check, repack and adjustment

Refer to illustrations 28.1, 28.3, 28.7, 28.9, 28.15 and 28.16
1   In most cases the front wheel bearings will not need servicing until the brake pads are changed. However, the bearings should be checked whenever the front of the vehicle is raised for any reason. Several items, including a torque wrench and special grease, are required for this procedure **(see illustration)**.
2   With the vehicle securely supported on jackstands, spin each wheel and check for noise, rolling resistance and freeplay.
3   Move the wheel in-and-out on the spindle **(see illustration)**. If there's any noticeable movement, the bearings should be checked and then repacked with grease or replaced if necessary.
4   Remove the wheel.

28.3 To check the wheel bearings, try to move the tire in-and-out if any play is noted, or if the bearings feel rough or sound noisy when the tire is rotated, maintenance is required

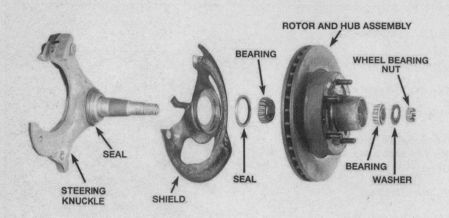

28.7 Front hub and wheel bearing components - exploded view

28.9 Pull out on the hub to dislodge the outer bearing

5   Remove the brake caliper (see Chapter 9) and hang it out of the way on a piece of wire. **Warning:** *DO NOT allow the brake caliper to hang by the rubber hose!*

6   Pry the grease cap out of the hub with a screwdriver or hammer and chisel.

7   Straighten the bent ends of the cotter pin, then pull the cotter pin out of the retaining nut and spindle **(see illustration)**. Discard the cotter pin and use a new one during reassembly.

8   Remove the retaining nut, adjusting nut and flat washer from the end of the spindle.

9   Pull the hub assembly out slightly, then push it back into its original position. This should force the outer bearing off the spindle enough so it can be removed **(see illustration)**.

10   Pull the hub off the spindle.

11   Use a screwdriver to pry the grease seal out of the rear of the hub. As this is done, note how the seal is installed.

12   Remove the inner wheel bearing from the hub.

13   Use solvent to remove all traces of old grease from the bearings, hub and spindle. A small brush may prove helpful; however make sure no bristles from the brush embed themselves inside the bearing rollers. Allow the parts to air dry.

14   Carefully inspect the bearings for cracks, heat discoloration, worn rollers, etc. Check the bearing races inside the hub for wear and damage. If the bearing races are defective, the hubs should be taken to a machine shop with the facilities to remove the old races and press new ones in. Note that the bearings and races come as matched sets and old bearings should never be installed on new races.

15   Use high-temperature front wheel bearing grease to pack the bearings. Work the grease completely into the bearings, forcing it between the rollers, cone and cage from the back side **(see illustration)**.

16   Apply a thin coat of grease to the spindle at the outer bearing seat, inner bearing seat, shoulder and seal seat **(see illustration)**.

17   Put a small quantity of grease inboard of each bearing race inside the hub. Using your finger, form a dam at these points to provide extra grease availability and to keep thinned grease from flowing out of the bearing.

18   Place the grease-packed inner bearing into the rear of the hub and put a little more grease outboard of the bearing.

19   Place a new seal over the inner bearing and tap the seal evenly into place with a hammer and block of wood until it's flush with the hub.

20   Carefully place the hub assembly onto the spindle and push the grease-packed outer bearing into position.

21   Install the flat washer and adjusting nut. Tighten the nut only slightly.

22   Spin the hub in a forward direction to seat the bearings and remove any grease or burrs which could cause excessive bearing play later.

23   While spinning the wheel, tighten the adjusting nut to the specified torque (Step 1 in this Chapter's Specifications).

24   Loosen the nut 1/2 turn, no more.

25   Tighten the nut to the specified torque (Step 3 in the Specifications). Install the retaining nut and a new cotter pin through the hole in the spindle and retaining nut. If the nut slots don't line up, remove the retaining nut, turn it slightly and reinstall it. Repeat until the slots line up.

26   Bend the ends of the cotter pin until they're flat against the nut. Cut off any extra

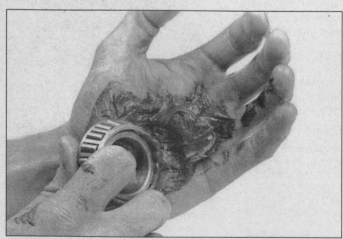

28.15 Pack each wheel baring by working the grease into the rollers from the back side

28.16 Apply a thin coat of grease to the spindle, particularly where the seal rides

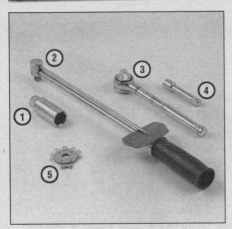

30.2 Tools required for changing spark plugs

1 *Spark plug socket - This will have special padding inside to protect the spark plug's porcelain insulator.*
2 *Torque wrench - Although not mandatory, using this tool is the best way to ensure the plugs are tightened properly*
3 *Ratchet - Standard hand tool to fit the spark plug socket*
4 *Extension - Depending on model and accessories, you may need special extensions and universal joints to reach one or more of the plugs*
5 *Spark plug gap gauge - This gauge for checking the tap comes in a variety of styles. Make sure the gap for your engine is included.*

length which could interfere with the grease cap.
27 Install the grease cap, tapping into place with a hammer.
28 Install the caliper (see Chapter 9).
29 Install the tire/wheel assembly on the hub and tighten the lug nuts.
30 Check the bearings in the manner described earlier in this Section.
31 Lower the vehicle.

29 Valve clearance check and adjustment (2.8L V6 engines only)

1 The valve stem-to-rocker arm clearance is adjusted mechanically on the 2.8L V6 engine. On all other models, it is adjusted automatically by hydraulic lifters.
2 The valve clearances are checked and adjusted with the engine cold.
3 Remove the rocker arm covers (see Chapter 2)
4 Disconnect the coil (high tension) wire from the distributor and ground it on the engine block.
5 Place your finger on the adjustment screw for the No. 5 cylinder intake valve (if you're not sure about cylinder locations). Have an assistant operate the starter, a little at a time, until you can feel the rocker arm just start to move to open the valve.

30.5a Spark plug manufacturers recommend using a wire type gauge when checking the gap - if the wire does not slide between the electrodes with a slight drag, adjustment is required

6 With the engine in this position, you can adjust the valves for the number one cylinder.
7 Start with the intake valve clearance. Insert a feeler gauge of the thickness listed in this Chapter's Specifications between the intake valve stem and the rocker arm. Withdraw it; you should feel a slight drag. If there's no drag or a heavy drag, loosen or tighten the adjuster screw until the correct clearance is obtained.
8 Adjust the number one exhaust valve using the same procedure you used for the intake valve(s). Be sure to use a feeler gauge of the thickness specified for exhaust valves.
9 Adjust the remaining valves by repeating the above procedure for the remaining cylinders. The following table shows which valves can be adjusted when a particular intake valve is just starting to open.

Intake valve opening on cylinder no.	Adjust the valves for cylinder no.
5	1
3	4
6	2
1	5
4	3
2	6

10 Reconnect the coil wire to the distributor and install the valve covers.

30 Spark plug replacement

Refer to illustrations 30.2, 30.5a, 30.5b, 30.6 and 30.10

1 The spark plugs are located on the side(s) of the engine.
2 In most cases, the tools necessary for spark plug replacement include a spark plug socket which fits into a ratchet (spark plug sockets are padded inside to prevent damage to the porcelain insulators on the new plugs and to hold the plugs in the socket dur-

30.5b To change the gap, bend the *side* electrode only, as indicated by the arrows, and be very careful not to crack or chip the porcelain insulator surrounding the center electrode

ing removal and installation), various extensions and a gap gauge to check and adjust the gaps on the new plugs **(see illustration)**. A special plug wire removal tool is available for separating the wire boots from the spark plugs, but it isn't absolutely necessary. A torque wrench should be used to tighten the new plugs.
3 The best approach when replacing the spark plugs is to purchase the new ones in advance, adjust them to the proper gap and replace the plugs one at a time. When buying the new spark plugs, be sure to obtain the correct type for your particular engine. This information can be found on the Emission Control Information label located under the hood and in the factory owner's manual. If differences exist between the plug specified on the emissions label and in the owner's manual, assume the emissions label is correct.
4 Allow the engine to cool completely before attempting to remove any of the plugs. Some models have aluminum cylinder heads, which can be damaged if the spark plugs are removed when the engine is hot. While you are waiting for the engine to cool, check the new plugs for defects and adjust the gaps.
5 The gap is checked by inserting the proper thickness gauge between the electrodes at the tip of the plug **(see illustration)**. The gap between the plugs should be the same as the one specified on the Emissions Control Information label. The gauge wire should just slide between the electrodes with a slight amount of drag. If the gap is incorrect, use the adjuster on the gauge body to bend the curved side electrode slightly until the specified gap is obtained **(see illustration)**. If the side electrode is not exactly over the center electrode, bend it with the adjuster until it is. Check for cracks in the porcelain insulator (if any are found, the plug should not be used).
6 With the engine cool, remove the spark

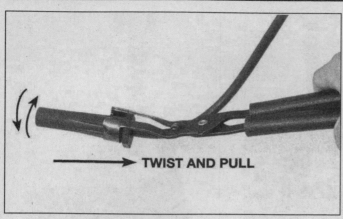

30.6 When removing the spark plug wires, pull only on the boot and twist it back-and-forth

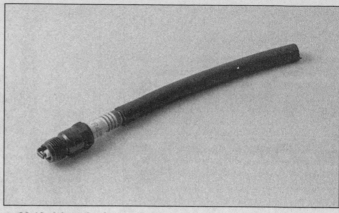

30.10 A length of snug-fitting rubber hose will save time and prevent damaged threads when installing the spark plugs

plug wire from one spark plug. Pull only on the boot at the end of the wire - do not pull on the wire. A plug wire removal tool should be used if available **(see illustration)**.

7   If compressed air is available, use it to blow any dirt or foreign material away from the spark plug hole. A common bicycle pump will also work. The idea here is to eliminate the possibility of debris falling into the cylinder as the spark plug is removed.

8   Place the spark plug socket over the plug and remove it from the engine by turning it counterclockwise.

9   Compare the spark plug to those shown on the inside back cover of this manual to get an indication of the general running condition of the engine.

10   Thread one of the new plugs into the hole until you can no longer turn it with your fingers, then tighten it with a torque wrench (if available) or the ratchet. It is a good idea to slip a short length of rubber hose over the end of the plug to use as a tool to thread it into place, particularly if the cylinder head is made of aluminum **(see illustration)**. The hose will grip the plug well enough to turn it, but will start to slip if the plug begins to cross-thread in the hole - this will prevent damaged threads and the accompanying repair costs.

11   Before pushing the spark plug wire onto the end of the plug, inspect it following the procedures outlined in Section 31.

12   Attach the plug wire to the new spark plug, again using a twisting motion on the boot until it is seated on the spark plug.

13   Repeat the procedure for the remaining spark plugs, replacing them one at a time to prevent mixing up the spark plug wires.

---

31 Spark plug wire, distributor cap and rotor check and replacement

Refer to illustrations 31.11 and 31.12

Spark plug wires

Note: *Every time a spark plug wire is detached from a spark plug, the distributor*

cap or the coil, silicone dielectric compound (a white grease available at auto parts stores) must be applied to the inside of each boot before reconnection. Use a small standard screwdriver to coat the entire inside surface of each boot with a thin layer of the compound.

1   The spark plug wires should be checked and, if necessary, replaced at the same time new spark plugs are installed.

2   The easiest way to identify bad wires is to make a visual check while the engine is running. In a dark, well-ventilated garage, start the engine and look at each plug wire. Be careful not to come into contact with any moving engine parts. If there is a break in the wire, you will see arcing or a small spark at the damaged area. If arcing is noticed, make a note to obtain new wires.

3   The spark plug wires should be inspected one at a time, beginning with the spark plug for the number one cylinder (on four-cylinder engines, the number one cylinder is at the front of the engine; on V6 and V8 engines it's the cylinder closest to the radiator on the right bank), to prevent confusion. Clearly label each original plug wire with a piece of tape marked with the correct number. The plug wires must be reinstalled in the correct order to ensure proper engine operation.

4   Disconnect the spark plug wire from the first spark plug. A removal tool can be used **(see illustration 30.6)**, or you can grab the wire boot, twist it slightly and pull the wire free. Do not pull on the wire itself, only on the rubber boot.

5   Push the wire and boot back onto the end of the spark plug. It should fit snugly. If it doesn't, detach the wire and boot once more and use a pair of pliers to carefully crimp the metal connector inside the wire boot until it does.

6   Using a clean rag, wipe the entire length of the wire to remove built-up dirt and grease.

7   Once the wire is clean, check for burns, cracks and other damage. Do not bend the wire sharply or you might break the conductor.

8   Disconnect the wire from the distributor.

Again, pull only on the rubber boot. Check for corrosion and a tight fit. Replace the wire in the distributor.

9   Inspect each of the remaining spark plug wires, making sure that each one is securely fastened at the distributor and spark plug when the check is complete.

10   If new spark plug wires are required, purchase a set for your specific engine model. Pre-cut wire sets with the boots already installed are available. Remove and replace the wires one at a time to avoid mix-ups in the firing order.

Distributor cap and rotor

Note: *It's common practice to install a new distributor cap and rotor each time new spark plug wires are installed. If you're planning to install new wires, install a new cap and rotor also. But if you're planning to reuse the existing wires, be sure to inspect the cap and rotor to make sure that they are in good condition.*

11   Pry back the cap clips or loosen the cap screws and detach the cap from the distributor. Check it for cracks, carbon track and worn, burned or loose terminals **(see illustration)**.

12   Check the rotor for cracks and carbon tracks. Make sure the center terminal spring tension is adequate and look for corrosion and wear on the rotor tip **(see illustration)**. **Note:** *The silicone dielectric compound used on single-point rotors darkens with age and may look like dirt or corrosion. Do not replace a rotor just because of the dielectric compound's appearance.*

13   Replace the cap and rotor if damage or defects are found. Note that the rotor is held on the shaft by two screws (some models) and on some models is indexed so it can only be installed one way. Before installing the cap, apply silicone dielectric compound to the rotor tip of single-point rotors.

14   When installing a new cap, remove the wires from the old cap one at a time and attach them to the new cap in the exact same location - do not simultaneously remove all the wires from the old cap or firing order mix-ups may occur.

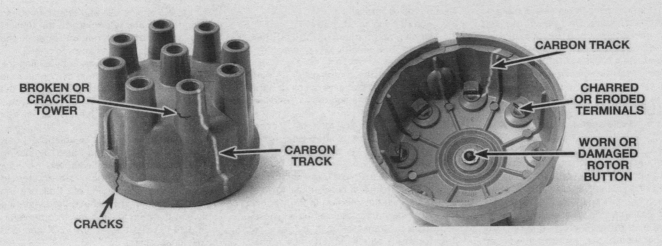

31.11 Shown here are some of the common defects to look for when inspecting the distributor cap (if in doubt about its condition, install a new one)

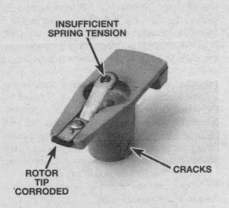

31.12 The ignition rotor should be checked for wear and corrosion as indicated here (if in doubt about its condition, buy a new one)

32   Carburetor choke check

1   The choke only operates when the engine is cold, so this check should be performed before the engine has been started for the day.

2   Open the hood and remove the air cleaner cover and filter from the top of the carburetor.

3   Locate the choke plate (the flat plate attached by small screws to pivot shaft) in the carburetor throat.

4   Operate the throttle linkage and make sure the plate closes completely. Start the engine and watch the plate - when the engine starts, the choke plate should open slightly.

5   Allow the engine to continue running at idle speed. As the engine warms up to operating temperature, the plate should slowly open.

6   After a few minutes, the choke plate should be fully open to the vertical position.

7   Note that the engine speed corresponds to the plate opening angle. With the plate closed, the engine should run at a fast idle speed. As the plate opens, the engine speed will decrease. The fast idle speed is controlled by the fast idle cam, and even though the choke plate is open completely, the idle speed will remain high until the throttle plate is opened, releasing the fast idle cam. Check the drop in idle speed as the choke plate opens by occasionally "blipping" the throttle.

8   If the choke doesn't work as described, shut off the engine and check the shaft and linkage for deposits which could cause binding. Use a spray-on choke cleaning solvent to remove the deposits as you operate the linkage. This should loosen up the linkage and the shaft and allow the choke to work properly. If the choke still fails to function correctly, the choke bimetal assembly is malfunctioning and the carburetor may have to be overhauled. Refer to Chapter 4 for carburetor overhaul information.

9   At regular intervals, clean and lubricate the choke shaft, the fast idle cam and linkage and the vacuum diaphragm pulldown rod to ensure good choke performance.

33   Idle speed check and adjustment (carbureted models)

Note: *The following adjustments are for carbureted models only. Idle speed does not require periodic adjustment on fuel-injected models. If the procedure below conflicts with the procedure listed on the Vehicle Emission Control Information label in the engine compartment, the procedure on the label is correct.*

1   Connect an accurate tune-up tachometer to the engine, following the manufacturer's instructions. On models so equipped, connect the tachometer pickup to the TACH TEST terminal on the ignition coil. Block the vehicle's wheels so it cannot move while adjustments are being made.

Model 5200/6500 carburetor

2   The Holley/Weber Model 5200 carburetor is used on early (through 1982) four-cylinder models first sold outside California. The Model 6500, a feedback version of the same carburetor design, is used on California four-cylinder models through 1982.

3   Remove the air cleaner and plug all vacuum lines that were attached to the air cleaner at the vacuum source end.

4   Apply the parking brake and block the wheels so the vehicle will not roll.

5   Check and adjust, if necessary, the choke and throttle linkage for freedom of movement.

6   Start the engine and run it up to normal operating temperature.

7   Disconnect the EGR vacuum line at the valve, and plug the line.

8   Where applicable, set the air conditioning to OFF.

9   Where applicable, remove the spark delay valve and route the primary advance vacuum signal line directly to the distributor vacuum diaphragm unit (advance side).

10 Place the transmission in Park (automatic) or Neutral (manual), then run the engine at normal operating temperature. Check that the choke plates are closed, then set the throttle so that the fast idle adjusting screw contacts the kick-down step of the choke cam; adjust the fast idle adjusting screw to obtain the specified fast idle rpm.

11 Set the throttle to the high step of the choke cam and allow the engine to run for approximately five seconds.

12 Rotate the choke cam until the fast idle adjusting screw contacts the choke cam kick-down step. Allow the engine speed to stabilize, then recheck the fast idle rpm, as described in Steps 10 and 11; readjust if necessary, then repeat the procedure given in the first sentence of this paragraph to ensure the same, consistent result.

13 Allow the engine to return to the normal

idle, then, for automatic transmission models, select Drive. **Warning:** *Be sure the parking brake is set securely and the wheels are blocked before selecting Drive. Do not accelerate the engine while it's in Drive, and stand to the side of the vehicle, not in front of it, while making the following adjustments.*

14   Where no TSP assembly is fitted, adjust the curb idle screw in or out to obtain the specified curb idle speed, then proceed to Step 18.

15   Where a TSP assembly is fitted, adjust the curb idle screw which contacts the solenoid plunger to obtain the specified curb idle speed (the solenoid is energized and the plunger extended when the ignition is On).

16   Now collapse the solenoid plunger by forcing the throttle linkage against the plunger, grasping the throttle lever and solenoid housing between the thumb and index finger to alleviate movement of the solenoid assembly position.

17   Adjust the TSP-off adjusting screw to obtain the specified TSP-off idle speed.

18   Open the throttle slightly to allow the solenoid plunger to extend.

19   Provided that all adjustments are now satisfactory, stop the engine, then install the air cleaner and its associated vacuum lines.

20   Restart the engine and, if necessary, run it up to normal operating temperature. With the engine running at 2000 rpm (approximately), select Park (automatic transmission) or Neutral (manual transmission). Allow five seconds (approximately) for the speed to stabilize, then let the engine return to idle; set automatic transmission models to Drive. Recheck the curb idle speed, and, if necessary readjust as described beginning at Step 12.

21   Reconnect all vacuum lines as they were originally.

YFA 1V carburetor

22   This carburetor, in feedback and non-feedback versions, was used on 1983 through 1986 non-turbocharged versions of the four-cylinder engine. The adjustments that follow apply to both versions.

23   Warm the engine to normal operating temperature.

24   Place the transmission in Park (automatic) or Neutral (manual), then shut the engine off.

25   Leave the key in the Off position and make sure the air conditioner (if so equipped) is also in the Off position.

26   Disconnect the vacuum line from the EGR valve, then plug the disconnected end of the line.

27   If equipped with an electric ported vacuum switch (PVS), disconnect its wire.

28   Refer to the Vehicle Emission Information label for the correct fast idle cam setting. Place the fast idle adjusting screw on the specified cam step.

29   Without touching the accelerator, start the engine and let it idle. Check fast idle speed and adjust if necessary by turning the fast idle adjusting screw.

30   "Blip" the throttle and let the engine

speed drop to normal idle.

31   Turn the engine off.

32   Unplug and reconnect the EGR hose. Reconnect the electric PVS wire (if so equipped).

33   Check that the transmission is still in Park or Neutral, the engine is still at normal operating temperature and the air conditioner is off.

34   Start the engine and let it idle. Place the transmission in the specified gear for idle adjustment (refer to Vehicle Emission Control Information label).

35   Check curb idle speed. Adjust if necessary by turning the hex-head adjusting screw.

36   Place the transmission in Park or Neutral. "Blip" the throttle, then let the engine idle.

37   Place the transmission in the gear specified for checking idle speed, then recheck idle speed. Readjust as needed, then turn the engine off. Reconnect all vacuum hoses and the PVS wire, if equipped.

1946/1946C carburetor

38   The model 1946C carburetor **(see illustration)** was used on California models equipped with the 3.3L inline six-cylinder engine. The Model 1946 carburetor was used on 49-state 3.3L models.

1980 models

39   Disconnect the vacuum hose from the EGR valve and plug the disconnected end of the hose. Disconnect and plug the fuel evaporative purge hose. To do this, trace the hose from the purge valve (on or near the evaporative emissions "charcoal" canister) to the first place where it can be disconnected from the underhood routing; e.g., a vacuum tee connection. Disconnect the hose and plug both the hose and the open connection.

40   Warm the engine to normal operating temperature.

41   Remove the air cleaner top plate and make sure the choke is off (see Section 32). Reinstall the air cleaner top plate.

42   With the engine at normal operating temperature, raise engine speed to 2500 rpm for 15 seconds.

43   Refer to the Vehicle Emission Information label for the correct fast idle cam setting. Place the fast idle screw on the specified cam step.

44   Let the engine speed stabilize, then measure the engine speed (rpm). Depending on the engine and the state of tune, it may require anywhere from 15 seconds to two minutes for the engine speed to stabilize. This will be indicated by a steady reading on the tachometer.

45   Repeat Step 44 three times to ensure accuracy.

46   If necessary, adjust the fast idle speed adjusting screw.

47   Repeat the rpm check if an adjustment has been made.

48   Turn the engine off. Unplug and reconnect the EGR hose.

49   Make sure the engine is at normal operating temperature and the air conditioner is off.

50   Let the engine idle and check its speed on the tachometer. Compare to the Vehicle Emission Control Information label. If the speed fluctuates, use the average speed.

51   Recheck each rpm range by raising the rpm to 2500 for 15 seconds, then letting the engine speed drop back to idle. Measure the engine speed between 15 seconds and two minutes of returning to idle. Readjust idle speed if necessary.

52   On models without a solenoid positioner, turn the curb idle speed adjusting screw to obtain the specified speed.

53   On models equipped with a solenoid positioner, turn the engine off. Collapse the solenoid plunger, then check the clearance between the plunger and the throttle lever. Compare the clearance to the VECI label and adjust if necessary.

54   On models with an anti-dieseling solenoid positioner (blue plastic connector), set curb idle (TSP-on) speed by turning the TSP-on adjusting screw. Then push the throttle lever against the TSP plunger to collapse the plunger. Adjust the TSP-off speed by turning the curb idle speed adjusting screw.

55   On models with an air conditioning solenoid positioner (black rubber connector), set curb idle speed by turning the curb idle speed adjusting screw.

56   On models with an air conditioning solenoid positioner (black rubber connector), set the A/C-on rpm. Turn on the air conditioner. Move the throttle linkage so the TSP plunger can extend, then release the throttle linkage. Disconnect the A/C compressor wire at the compressor, then adjust A/C-on speed by turning the TSP-on adjusting screw.

57   Turn off the air conditioner and reconnect the compressor wire.

58   Unplug and reconnect the fuel evaporative purge hose.

1981 and 1982 models

59   Warm the engine to normal operating temperature, then place the transmission in Neutral or Park.

60   Disconnect the vacuum hoses from the EGR valve and canister purge valve. Plug the disconnected ends of the hoses.

61   Place the fast idle rpm adjustment screw on the second step of the fast idle cam.

62   Check the engine speed on the tachometer. If necessary, use the fast idle adjustment screw to adjust the speed to the fast idle speed specified on the Vehicle Emission Control Information label in the engine compartment.

63   Unplug and reconnect the EGR and canister hoses.

64   Make sure the engine is still at normal operating temperature and the transmission is still in Neutral or Park.

65   On 1981 models, turn the air conditioner and heater off.

66   On 1982 models, set the heater to Heat, set the blower on High and turn on the high beam headlights.

67   Place the transmission in the gear spec-

ified on the Vehicle Emission Control Information label. Set the parking brake.
68 Check the curb idle speed and adjust if necessary.
69 On 1982 models, measure the dashpot clearance. It should be 0.100-inch. Adjust if necessary.
70 Turn off the headlights, blower and heater.
71 On 1982 models, place the transmission in Park or Neutral.
72 Make sure the engine is still at normal operating temperature.
73 Unplug the TSP electrical connector.
74 Place the transmission in the gear specified on the Vehicle Emission Control label.
75 Check the TSP-off idle speed and compare it to the Vehicle Emission Control label. Adjust as needed with the TSP-off adjustment screw.
76 Place the transmission in Park or Neutral and "blip" the throttle. Let the engine idle, place the transmission in the specified gear and recheck the curb idle speed. Readjust if necessary.
77 Connect the electrical connector to the TSP.
78 On all air conditioned 1981 models and 1982 air conditioned Canadian models, set the air conditioner for maximum cooling.
79 Disconnect the air conditioning compressor clutch wire.
80 Place the transmission in the specified position and check A/C-on speed. Adjust as needed.
81 Reconnect the compressor wire and turn off the air conditioner. Connect the hoses to the canister purge valve and EGR valve.

2150-2V carburetor

82 Warm the engine to normal operating temperature. Shut the engine off and remove the air cleaner. The air cleaner assembly must be in position when engine speeds are measured.
83 Apply the parking brake and block the rear wheels.
84 Check and adjust, if necessary, the choke and throttle linkage for freedom of movement.
85 Where applicable, turn the air conditioner to Off.
86 Disconnect the evaporative purge line from the carburetor and plug it.
87 Disconnect the EGR vacuum hose and plug it. If the vehicle is equipped with a ported vacuum switch (PVS), do not disconnect the EGR hose.
88 Disconnect the distributor vacuum hose from the advance side of the distributor and plug the hose.
89 Follow the vacuum hose from the Thermactor (air pump) dump valve to the carburetor and disconnect the dump valve vacuum hose nearest the carburetor. Plug the original vacuum source and connect the dump valve directly to manifold vacuum.
90 With the transmission in Park (automatic) or Neutral (manual) and the choke

plate fully open, run the engine at 2500 rpm for 15 seconds. Place the fast idle lever on the fast idle cam step specified on the Vehicle Emission Information label. Allow the engine speed to stabilize (10 to 15 seconds) and measure the fast idle rpm.
91 Repeat the procedure three times and adjust the fast idle rpm if not as specified.
92 Before adjusting the curb idle, it is necessary to determine which of the various throttle positioners and engine speed control devices the carburetor is equipped with.
93 Make all adjustments after adjusting the fast idle speed by following the procedure described in steps 82 through 91.
94 On vehicles without air conditioning or other solenoid devices, the curb idle is adjusted by turning the curb idle speed adjusting screw.
95 If the carburetor is equipped with a dashpot to control the throttle closing, the dashpot plunger must be collapsed with the engine off. Check the clearance between the plunger and the throttle lever pad and adjust, if necessary, to the specifications on the Vehicle Emission Control label. Each time the curb idle is adjusted, the dashpot clearance must also be adjusted.
96 On anti-dieseling solenoid (TSP) equipped vehicles, the curb idle speed is adjusted by collapsing the TSP plunger by forcing the throttle lever pad against the plunger. The curb idle speed is then adjusted by turning the curb idle speed adjusting screw.
97 If equipped with air conditioning, dashpot and TSP, turn the air conditioning off and measure the curb idle speed. Adjust to the curb idle speed listed on the Emissions Control Information label by turning the curb idle speed adjusting screw. Turn the engine off, collapse the TSP plunger and check the clearance between the plunger and the throttle lever pad. To adjust, turn the long screw which is part of the assembly mounting bracket.
98 Reconnect all vacuum lines and Thermactor hoses to their proper locations and reinstall the air cleaner.

4180C-4V carburetor

99 Place the transmission in Neutral or Park.
100 Warm the engine to normal operating temperature.
101 Disconnect the vacuum hose from the EGR valve. Plug the disconnected end of the hose.
102 Place the fast idle adjusting screw on the specified step of the fast idle cam. Refer to the Vehicle Emission Control Information label for the specified step and fast idle speed. Using the screw, adjust the fast idle speed if necessary.
103 Rev the engine momentarily, place the fast idle adjusting screw back on the specified step of the fast idle cam and recheck fast idle speed. Readjust if necessary.
104 Unplug and reconnect the EGR vacuum hose.

105 Make sure the transmission is still in Neutral or Park and that the engine is still at normal operating temperature.
106 Place the air conditioning/heat selector in the Off position.
107 Disconnect the vacuum hose from the throttle kicker on the carburetor and plug the disconnected end of the hose.
108 Place the transmission in the specified gear (see the Vehicle Emission Control Information label).
109 Check curb idle speed on the tachometer. Adjust if necessary to the speed listed on the Vehicle Emission Control label by turning the curb idle speed adjusting screw.
110 Place the transmission in Neutral or Park and "blip" the throttle momentarily.
111 Place the transmission back in the specified gear and recheck curb idle speed. Readjust if necessary.
112 Unplug and reconnect the throttle kicker vacuum hose.
113 Whenever engine idle speed must be changed by more than 50 rpm, readjust the AOD lever at the carburetor (see Chapter 7).

2700VV/7200VV carburetor

114 Disconnect the vacuum hose from the EGR valve and plug the disconnected end of the hose.
115 With the choke off and the engine at normal operating temperature, raise engine speed to 2500 rpm for 15 seconds. Place the fast idle adjusting screw on the specified step of the fast idle lever. Refer to the Vehicle Emission Control Information label for the specified step and fast idle speed.
116 Let engine speed stabilize, then measure the engine speed (rpm). Depending upon the engine and the state of tune, it may require anywhere from 15 seconds to 2 minutes for the engine speed (number of rpm) to stabilize.
117 Repeat the above step three times to ensure accuracy.
118 Adjust fast idle speed, if necessary, by turning the fast idle screw.
119 Repeat the rpm check if an adjustment has been made.
120 Turn the engine off.
121 Disconnect and plug the fuel evaporative purge hose. To do this, trace the hose from the purge valve (located on or near the evaporative emissions "charcoal" canister) to the first place where it can be disconnected from the underhood routing, eg: vacuum tee connection. Disconnect the hose and plug both the hose and the open connection.
122 Check the engine fast idle speed as described in Steps 115 through 117.
123 The method of curb idle adjustment is determined by the type of throttle positioning device installed on the carburetor. The adjustment procedures are as follows:
a) 2700VV carburetors with solenoid positioners must be in Drive when the curb idle rpm is checked. The curb idle is adjusted by turning the adjustment screw in the bracket

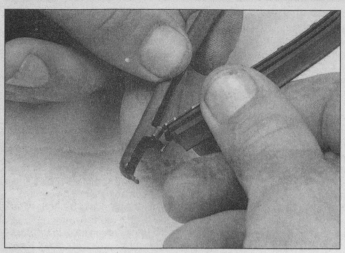

34.18 Twist the blade element when working it into the last retaining tabs (Trico type)

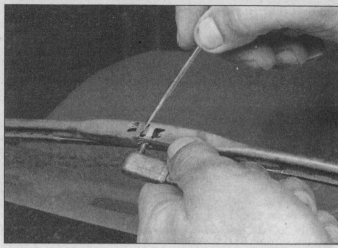

34.22 To remove the Trico-type blade assembly, push a small, flat-bladed screwdriver into the release hole

b) On vehicles with no solenoids or positioners, turn the throttle stop adjustment screw to obtain the specified curb idle rpm

c) On dashpot equipped carburetors, adjust the curb idle speed with the throttle stop adjustment screw. Turn the engine off, collapse the dashpot plunger and measure the distance between the throttle lever pad. Adjust to the specifications on the Emissions Control Information label if necessary. Start the engine and check the curb idle speed, repeating the procedure until the proper curb idle speed is obtained

d) On 7200VV carburetors equipped with vacuum-operated throttle modulator (VOTM), turn the throttle stop screw counterclockwise and recheck. If the curb idle rpm is below specifications, shut off the engine and turn the throttle stop screw a full turn clockwise. Start the engine and recheck the curb idle, repeating the procedure until the idle is within specifications.

124 Reconnect all vacuum hoses.

34   Windshield wiper blade check and replacement

Refer to illustrations 34.18 and 34.22

1   Road film can build up on the wiper blades and effect their efficiency, so they should be washed regularly with a mild detergent solution.

Check

2   The windshield wiper and blade assembly should be inspected periodically. Even if you don't use your wipers, the sun and elements will dry out the rubber portions, causing them to crack and break apart. If inspection reveals hardened or cracked rubber, replace the wiper blades. If inspection reveals nothing unusual, wet the windshield, turn the wipers on, allow them to cycle several times, then shut them off. An uneven wiper pattern across the glass or streaks over clean glass indicate that the blades should be replaced.

3   The operation of the wiper mechanism can loosen the fasteners, so they should be checked and tightened, as necessary, at the same time the wiper blades are checked (see Chapter 12 for further information regarding the wiper mechanism).

Blade assembly replacement (Tridon blades)

4   Park the wiper blades in a convenient position to be worked on. To do this, run the wipers, then turn the ignition key to Off when the wiper blades reach the desired position.

5   Lift the blade slightly from the windshield. Pull up on the spring lock to release the blade and take the blade off. **Caution:** *Do not pull too hard on the spring lock or it will be distorted.*

6   Push the new blade assembly onto the arm pivot pin. Make sure the spring lock secures the blade to the pin.

Blade element replacement (Tridon blades)

7   Remove the wiper blade from the arm.

8   Locate one of the 7/16-inch removal notches in the blade assembly. There is a notch at each end of the blade, approximately one inch from the end.

9   Stand the blade on a non-slippery surface, then press down on the upper end of the blade enough to bow it slightly. **Caution:** *Do not press down hard enough to break the blade.*

10   Take firm hold of the blade element's plastic backing strip. Pull up on the element and twist it counterclockwise at the same time, so the plastic backing strip snaps out of the retaining tab on the end of the blade.

11   Lift the blade off the surface and let it hang slack.

12   Slide the plastic backing strip down the blade until the removal notch aligns with the next retaining tab. Twist the element slightly to pop it out of the blade.

13   Repeat Step 12 with the remaining tabs to remove the blade.

14   To install, reverse steps 12 and 13. Be sure the element engages all six retaining tabs in the wiper blade.

Blade element replacement (Trico blades)

15   Remove the wiper blade from the arm (see Step 20 below).

16   Insert a flat-bladed screwdriver 1/8-inch or less into the space between the element and rubber backing strip. While pressing the screwdriver down and inward, twist it clockwise to separate the element from the retaining tab.

17   Slide the element out of the other retaining tabs.

18   Slide the new element into four of the five retaining tabs. Twist the element into the fifth retaining tab to secure it **(see illustration)**.

19   Make sure the new element is secured by all five tabs, then install the wiper blade on the arm.

Blade assembly replacement (Trico blades)

20   Trico metal blades have a rectangular release hole above the wiper arm mounting pin.

21   Park the wiper blades in a convenient position to be worked on. To do this, run the wipers, then turn the ignition key to Off when the wiper blades reach the desired position.

22   Let the blade assembly rest on the windshield and insert a small flat-bladed screwdriver into the release hole **(see illustration)**. Push down on the coil spring inside the hole and pull the wiper blade from the arm.

23   Push the new blade onto the pivot pin until it locks.

35 Owner safety checks

1   Most of these checks can be easily done while the vehicle is being driven, simply by paying attention to the specified items. The checks are intended to make the vehicle owner aware of potential safety problems before they occur.

2   Check the seatbelts for wear, fraying and cuts. Make sure the buckles latch securely and that the automatic retractors function correctly. Do not try to repair seatbelts; always replace them if any problems are found.

3   Make sure the ignition key cannot be removed when the transmission is in any gear other than Park (automatic) or Reverse (manual). Make sure the steering column locks when the key is removed from the ignition. It may be necessary to rotate the steering wheel slightly to lock the steering column.

4   Check the parking brake. The easiest way to do this is to park on a steep hill, set the parking brake and note whether it keeps the vehicle from rolling.

5   If equipped with automatic transmission, also check the Park mechanism. Place the transmission in Park, release the parking brake and note whether the transmission holds the vehicle from rolling. If the vehicle rolls while in Park, the transmission should be taken to a qualified shop for repairs.

6   If equipped with an automatic transmission, note whether the shift indicator shows the proper gear. If it doesn't, refer to Chapter 7 for linkage adjustment procedures.

7   If equipped with automatic transmission, make sure the vehicle starts only in Park or Neutral. If it starts in any other gear, refer to Chapter 7 for switch adjustment procedures.

8   On 1985 and later models equipped with a manual transmission, the starter should operate only when the clutch pedal is pressed to the floor. If the starter operates when it shouldn't, refer to Chapter 8 for clutch safety switch service.

9   Make sure the brakes do not pull to one side while stopping. The brake pedal should feel firm, but excessive effort should not be required to stop the vehicle. If the pedal sinks too low, if you have to pump it more than once to get a firm pedal, or if pedal effort is too high, refer to Chapter 9 for repair procedures. A squealing sound from the front brakes may be caused by the pad wear indicators. Refer to Chapter 9 for pad replacement procedures.

10   Rearview mirrors should be clean and undamaged. They should hold their position when adjusted.

11   Sun visors should hold their position when adjusted. They should remain securely out of the way when lifted off the windshield.

12   Make sure the defroster blows heated air onto the windshield. If it doesn't, refer to Chapter 3 for heating system service.

13   The horn should sound with a clearly audible tone every time it is operated. If not, refer to Chapter 12.

14   Make sure windows are clean and undamaged.

15   Turn on the lights, then walk around the vehicle and make sure they work. Check headlights in both the high beam and low beam positions. Check the turn indicators for one side of the vehicle, then for the other side. If possible, have an assistant watch the brake lights while you push the pedal. If no assistant is available, the brake lights can be checked by backing up to a wall or garage door, then pressing the pedal. There should be two distinct patches of red light (three for models equipped with a high mount brake light) when the brake pedal is pressed.

16   Make sure locks operate smoothly when the key is turned. Lubricate locks if necessary with lock lubricant available at most auto parts stores. Make sure all latches hold securely.

1

Notes

Chapter 2 Part A
Four-cylinder engine

Contents

2A

Specifications

General

Cylinder numbers (front-to-rear)	1-2-3-4
Firing order	1-3-4-2

Camshaft

Lobe lift (intake and exhaust)	
1979 through 1982	0.2437 in
1983, 1984 and 1991 on	0.2381 in
1985 through 1990	0.400 in
Allowable lobe lift loss	0.005 in max
Endplay	
Standard	0.001 to 0.007 in
Service limit	0.009 in
Journal diameter	1.7713 to 1.7720 in
Runout limit	0.005 in (total indicator reading)
Out-of-round limit	0.0005 in
Journal-to-bearing (oil) clearance	
Standard	0.001 to 0.003 in
Service limit	0.006 in
Front bearing location	0.000 to 0.010 in below front face of bearing tower

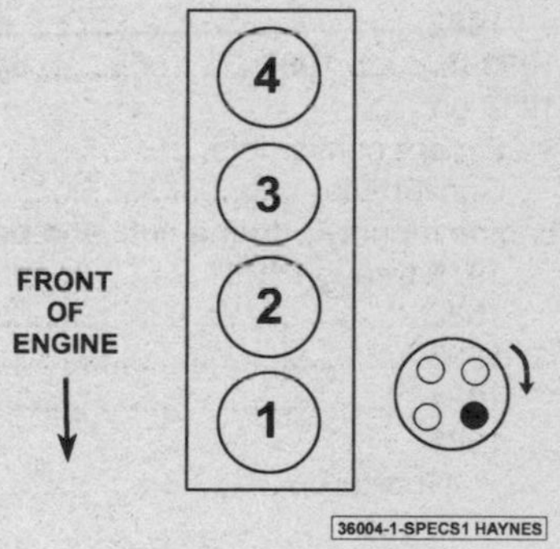

FRONT OF ENGINE

Cylinder location and distributor rotation
The blackened terminal on the distributor cap indicates the number one spark plug wire position

Torque specifications

	Ft-lbs (unless otherwise indicated)
Camshaft sprocket bolt	50 to 71
Crankshaft pulley/sprocket bolt	
1979 through 1986	100-120
1987 through 1990	103-133
1991 on	114-151
Camshaft retaining plate bolt	6 to 9
Auxiliary shaft sprocket bolt	28 to 40
Auxiliary shaft retaining plate screws	6 to 9
Timing belt outer cover bolts	6 to 9
Timing belt tensioner adjustment bolt	14 to 21
Timing belt tensioner pivot bolt	28 to 40
Camshaft cover bolts	6 to 8
Camshaft cover shield bolt (if equipped)	28 to 40
Cylinder head bolts	
Step 1	50 to 60
Step 2	80 to 90
Flywheel bolts	56 to 64

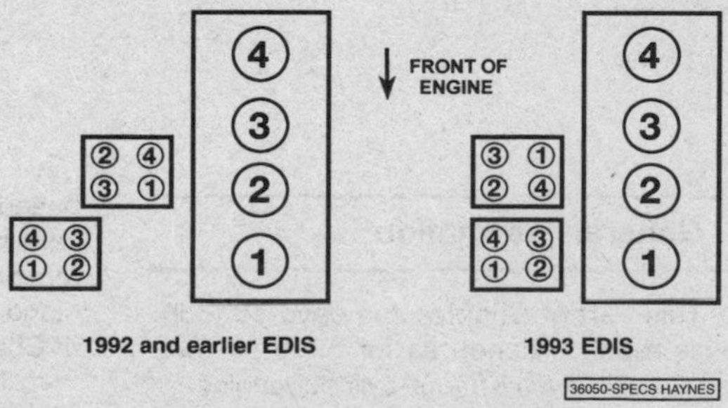

FRONT OF ENGINE

1992 and earlier EDIS   **1993 EDIS**

Cylinder location and coil terminal numbering

Torque specifications (continued)   Ft-lbs (unless otherwise indicated)

Intake manifold bolts	
1979 through 1986	
Step 1..	5 to 7
Step 2..	14 to 21
1987 through 1988..	15 to 22
1989 on	20 to 29
Exhaust manifold bolts	
1979 through 1986	
Step 1..	60 to 84 in-lbs
Step 2..	16 to 23
1987 on (except 1991 on 2.3L four-cylinder engines)	
Step 1..	178 to 204 in-lbs
Step 2..	20 to 30
1991 and later 2.3L four-cylinder engines	
Regular bolts	
Step 1..	15 to 17
Step 2..	20 to 30
Stud type bolts	20 to 33
Heat shield nuts (1991 on 2.3L four-cylinder engines)	20 to 29
Oil pan-to-engine block bolts	
1979 through 1986	
Small bolts	72 to 96 in-lbs
Large bolts	96 to 120 in-lbs
1987 on (except 1991 on 2.3L four-cylinder engines)....................	120 to 162 in-lbs
1991 on 2.3L four-cylinder engines...	120 to 144 in-lbs
Oil pan-to-transmission bolts (1991 on 2.3L four-cylinder engines)	
Step 1..	30 to 36
Step 2..	30 to 39
Oil pump bolts	14 to 21
Oil pump pick-up tube nut..	14 to 21
Engine mount-to-block bolts	
1979 through 1981	35 to 60
1982	40 to 55
1983 through 1987	33 to 45
1988 on	
Except convertible...	33 to 45
Convertible	25 to 35
Engine mount-to-frame nuts and bolts	
1979 through 1981	40 to 60
1982	70 to 90
1983	57 to 65
1984	50 to 65
1985	
Non-turbo	80 to 106
Turbo	
Bolt	33 to 45
Nut...	50 to 65
1986	45 to 55
1987 on	
Bolt...	45 to 63
Nut	80 to 106
Engine mount-to-bracket bolt	65 to 85

1   General information

This Part of Chapter 2 is devoted to in-vehicle repair procedures for the 2.3L Over Head Camshaft (OHC) four-cylinder engine. Information concerning engine removal and installation, as well as engine block and cylinder head overhaul, is in Part E of this Chapter.

The following repair procedures are based on the assumption that the engine is installed in the vehicle. If the engine has been removed from the vehicle and mounted on a stand, many of the steps included in this Part of Chapter 2 will not apply.

The specifications included in this Part of Chapter 2 apply only to the engine and procedures in this Part. The specifications necessary for rebuilding the block and cylinder head are found in Part E.

2   Repair operations possible with the engine in the vehicle

Many major repair operations can be accomplished without removing the engine from the vehicle.

Clean the engine compartment and the exterior of the engine with some type of pressure washer before any work is done. A clean engine will make the job easier and will help keep dirt out of the internal areas of the engine.

Depending on the components involved, it may be a good idea to remove the hood to improve access to the engine as repairs are performed (refer to Chapter 11 if necessary).

If vacuum, exhaust, oil or coolant leaks develop, indicating a need for gasket or seal replacement, the repairs can generally be made with the engine in the vehicle. The intake and exhaust manifold gaskets, oil pan gasket, camshaft cover gasket and cylinder head gasket are all accessible with the engine in place. The crankshaft oil seals can also be replaced without removing the engine.

Engine components such as the intake and exhaust manifolds, the oil pan, the oil pump, the auxiliary shaft, the water pump, the starter motor, the alternator, the distributor and the fuel system components can be removed for repair with the engine in place.

Since the cylinder head can be removed without pulling the engine, camshaft and valve component servicing can also be accomplished with the engine in the vehicle.

In extreme cases caused by a lack of necessary equipment, repair or replacement of piston rings, pistons, connecting rods and rod bearings is possible with the engine in the vehicle. However, this practice is not recommended because of the cleaning and preparation work that must be done to the components involved.

3 Top Dead Center (TDC) for number one piston - locating

1 Top Dead Center (TDC) is the highest point in the cylinder that each piston reaches as it travels up-and-down when the crankshaft turns. Each piston reaches TDC on the compression stroke and again on the exhaust stroke, but TDC generally refers to piston position on the compression stroke. The timing marks are referenced to the number one piston at TDC on the compression stroke.

2 Positioning the piston(s) at TDC is an essential part of many procedures such as in-vehicle valve train service, timing belt replacement and distributor removal.

3 In order to bring any piston to TDC, the crankshaft must be turned using one of the methods outlined below. When looking at the front of the engine, normal crankshaft rotation is clockwise. **Caution:** *Turning the crankshaft backwards may cause the timing belt to jump teeth.*

a) *The preferred method is to turn the crankshaft with a large socket and breaker bar attached to the large bolt that's threaded into the front of the crankshaft.*

b) *A remote starter switch, which may save some time, can also be used. Attach the switch leads to the switch and battery terminals on the solenoid. Once the pis-*

ton is close to TDC, use a socket and breaker bar as described in the previous paragraph.

c) *If an assistant is available to turn the ignition switch to the Start position in short bursts, you can get the piston close to TDC without a remote starter switch. Use a socket and breaker bar as described in Paragraph a) to complete the procedure.*

4 Locate the number one spark plug wire terminal in the distributor cap, then mark the distributor base directly under the terminal.

5 Remove the distributor cap as described in Chapter 1.

6 Turn the crankshaft (see Paragraph 3 above) until the ignition timing mark for TDC on the crankshaft pulley is aligned with the timing pointer on the belt cover.

7 The rotor should now be pointing directly at the mark you made earlier on the distributor. If it isn't, the piston is at TC on the exhaust stroke.

8 To get the piston to TDC on the compression stroke, turn the crankshaft one complete turn (360-degrees) clockwise. The rotor should now be pointing at the mark. When the rotor is pointing at the number one spark plug wire terminal in the distributor cap (which is indicated by the mark on the distributor) and the ignition timing marks are aligned, the number one piston is at TDC on the compression stroke.

9 After the number one piston has been positioned at TDC on the compression stroke, TDC for any of the remaining cylinders can be located by turning the crankshaft and following the firing order (refer to the Specifications).

4 Camshaft cover - removal and Installation

1 Disconnect the negative cable from the battery.

2 Non-Turbo - remove the air cleaner (see Chapter 4).

3 Turbo - detach the air duct from the turbocharger and throttle body (Chapter 4).

4 Remove the PCV tube from the camshaft cover (Chapter 6).

5 On EFI-equipped models, remove the throttle body (Chapter 4).

6 Remove the plug wires from the plugs and detach the wire holder from the camshaft cover.

7 Remove the bolts and studs and separate the cover from the engine. It may be necessary to break the gasket seal by tapping the cover with a soft-face hammer. If it's really stuck, use a knife, gasket scraper or chisel to remove it, but be very careful not to damage the gasket sealing surfaces of the cover or head. Don't lose the sealing grommets.

8 Place clean rags in the camshaft gallery to keep foreign material out of the engine.

9 Remove all traces of gasket material

from the cover and head. Be careful not to nick or gouge the surfaces. Clean the mating surfaces with lacquer thinner or acetone.

10 Reinstall the cover with a new gasket - apply gasket cement to the mating surfaces of the cover and head. The tabs on the gasket must fit into the slots in the cover. Install the bolts and tighten them to the specified torque in a criss-cross pattern.

11 Reinstall the throttle body (Chapter 4) and the remaining components previously removed or disconnected.

12 Run the engine and check for vacuum and oil leaks.

5 Valve seals and springs - replacement

Note: *Broken valve springs and defective valve stem seals can be replaced without removing the cylinder head. Two special tools and a compressed air source are normally required to perform this operation, so read through this Section carefully and rent or buy the tools before beginning the job. If compressed air isn't available, a length of nylon rope can be used to keep the valves from falling into the cylinder during this procedure.*

1 Refer to Section 4 and remove the camshaft cover.

2 Remove the spark plug from the cylinder which has the defective component. If all of the valve stem seals are being replaced, all of the spark plugs should be removed (Chapter 1).

3 Turn the crankshaft until the piston in the affected cylinder is at top dead center on the compression stroke (refer to Section 3 for instructions). If you're replacing all of the valve stem seals, begin with cylinder number one and work on the valves for one cylinder at a time. Move from cylinder-to-cylinder following the firing order sequence (1-3-4-2).

4 Thread an adapter into the spark plug hole and connect an air hose from a compressed air source to it. Most auto parts stores can supply the air hose adapter. **Note:** *Many cylinder compression gauges utilize a screw-in fitting that may work with your air hose quick-disconnect fitting.*

5 Apply compressed air to the cylinder. The valves for that cylinder should be held in place by the air pressure. If the valve faces or seats are in poor condition, leaks may prevent the air pressure from retaining the valves - refer to the alternative procedure below.

6 If you don't have access to compressed air, an alternative method can be used. Position the piston at a point just before TDC on the compression stroke, then feed a long piece of nylon rope through the spark plug hole until it fills the combustion chamber. Be sure to leave the end of the rope hanging out of the engine so it can be removed easily. Use a large breaker bar and socket to rotate the crankshaft in the normal direction of rotation until slight resistance is felt.

7 Stuff shop rags into the cylinder head

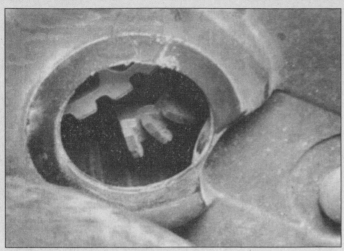

6.24 Before starting the engine, remove the plug from the belt cover and recheck the timing marks

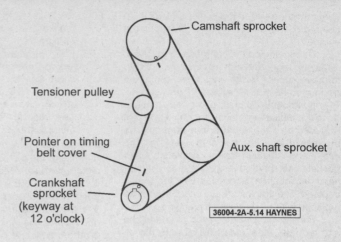

6.27 If the marks are aligned as shown here, the valve timing is correct (which means the timing belt has been installed correctly)

holes near the valves to prevent parts and tools from falling into the engine, then use a valve spring compressor to compress the spring. There are specialized compressors available that use the camshaft as a fulcrum so the camshaft does not have to be removed.

8   With the spring compressed, slide the cam follower over the lash adjuster to remove it. Also remove the lash adjuster.

9   Still compressing the spring, remove the keepers. Release the valve spring tool and remove the spring retainer, damper assembly and valve spring.

10   Remove and discard the valve stem seal. **Note:** *If air pressure fails to hold the valve in the closed position during this operation, the valve face or seat is probably damaged. If so, the cylinder head will have to be removed for additional repair operations.*

11   Wrap a rubber band or tape around the top of the valve stem so the valve will not fall into the cylinder, then release the air pressure.

12   Inspect the valve stem for damage. Rotate the valve in the guide and check the end for eccentric movement, which would indicate that the valve is bent.

13   Move the valve up-and-down in the guide and make sure it doesn't bind. If the valve stem binds, either the valve is bent or the guide is damaged. In either case, the head will have to be removed for repair.

14   Reapply air pressure to the cylinder to retain the valve in the closed position, then remove the tape or rubber band from the valve stem. Lubricate the valve stem with engine oil and install a new umbrella type guide seal, if used.

15   Place the plastic installation cap over the end of the valve stem.

16   Start the valve stem seal carefully over the cap and push the seal down until the jacket touches the top of the guide.

17   Remove the plastic cap and use a special installation tool, if available, or two screwdrivers to bottom the seal on the valve guide.

18   Install the valve spring, damper and retainer, compress the spring and install the keepers.

19   Install the lash adjuster and cam follower.

20   Disconnect the air hose and remove the adapter from the spark plug hole. If a rope was used in place of air pressure, pull it out of the cylinder. **Caution:** *Do not turn the crankshaft backwards to release the rope. Turning the crankshaft backwards will cause the timing belt to jump teeth.*

21   Reinstall the various components removed.

22   Start and run the engine, then check for oil leaks and unusual sounds coming from the camshaft cover area.

6   Timing belt - removal, installation and adjustment

Refer to illustrations 6.24 and 6.27

1   Disconnect the negative cable from the battery.

2   Remove the fan shroud (Chapter 3).

3   Remove the fan and the water pump pulley (Chapter 3).

4   Remove the drivebelts (Chapter 1).

5   Drain the cooling system (Chapter 1) and remove the upper radiator hose (Chapter 3).

6   Remove the thermostat housing and gasket (Chapter 3).

7   Position the number one piston at top dead center on the compression stroke (Section 3). **Caution:** *Always turn the crankshaft in the direction of normal rotation (clockwise, viewed from the front). Backward rotation may cause the timing belt to jump teeth. DO NOT turn the crankshaft during this procedure, after the number one piston is at TDC, until after the timing belt is reinstalled!*

8   Make sure the distributor rotor is pointing at the number one plug wire terminal.

9   Remove the crankshaft drivebelt pulley and belt guide.

10   On 1979 through 1990 models, remove the four bolts and one screw and detach the outer timing belt cover. On 1991 and later models, remove the one bolt, then carefully release the eight cover interlocking tabs and detach the outer timing belt cover.

11   Loosen the belt tensioner adjustment bolt, then position spreader tool on the tensioner pin and retract the belt tensioner. If the special tool is not available, a prybar wedged between the roll pin and tensioner may work. Tighten the adjustment bolt to hold the tensioner in the retracted position.

12   Remove the timing belt and inspect it for wear and damage. If it's worn or damaged, replace the belt. **Caution:** *If in doubt about the belt condition, install a new one. If the belt breaks during engine operation, extensive damage may occur!*

13   Check the sprockets for wear, cracks and burrs on the teeth. If the sprockets are worn or damaged, they can be detached after removing the mounting bolts. Make sure the new sprockets are installed correctly. Tighten the mounting bolts to the torque listed in this Chapter's Specifications. **Note:** *Install a new camshaft sprocket bolt or use Teflon sealing tape on the old bolt.*

14   Make sure the valve timing mark on the camshaft sprocket is aligned with the pointer on the engine case. Install the timing belt over the crankshaft sprocket, then over the auxiliary shaft sprocket.

15   Pull the belt up (pulling slack from between the auxiliary and camshaft sprockets) and install it on the camshaft sprocket in a counterclockwise direction so no slack will be between the two sprockets. Align the belt fore and aft on the sprockets.

16   Loosen the tensioner adjustment bolt to allow the tensioner to move against the belt. If the spring does not have enough tension to

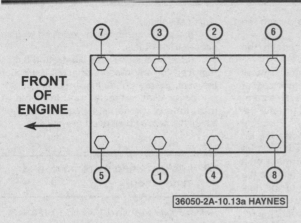

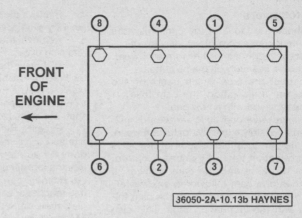

10.13a Intake manifold bolt TIGHTENING sequence - 1979 through 1985 models

10.13b Intake manifold TIGHTENING sequence - 1986 and later models

2A

move the roller against the belt (the belt hangs loose), it may be necessary to insert a special tool, available at most auto parts stores, or a prybar between the tensioner and pin and push the roller against the belt. Tighten the bolt to the torque listed in this Chapter's Specifications. **Note:** *The spring cannot be used to set belt tension. A wrench must be used on the tensioner assembly.*

17   Remove the spark plugs. Slowly rotate the crankshaft two complete turns in the direction of normal rotation to make sure the belt is seated and to remove any slack. While turning the crankshaft, feel and listen for valve-to-piston contact. Don't force the crankshaft - if binding is felt, recheck all work or seek professional advice!

18   Tighten the tensioner adjustment and pivot bolts to the specified torque. Recheck the alignment of the valve timing marks.

19   On 1979 through 1990 models, install the timing belt outer cover and tighten the bolts to the torque listed in this Chapter's Specifications. On 1991 and later models, snap the cover into place, making sure all interlocking tabs are engaged properly, then install the one bolt and tighten to the torque listed in this Chapter's Specifications.

20   The remaining installation steps are the reverse of removal. Be sure to tighten the crankshaft pulley/sprocket bolt to the specified torque.

21   Bring the number one piston to top dead center on the compression stroke (Section 3).

22   Remove the distributor cap and make sure the distributor rotor is pointing at the number one spark plug wire terminal.

23   Remove the access plug from the timing belt cover.

24   Look through the access hole in the belt cover to be sure that the timing mark on the camshaft sprocket is lined up with the pointer **(see illustration)**.

25   Make sure the timing mark on the crankshaft pulley aligns with the TDC mark on the belt cover.

26   Reinstall the belt cover access plug.

27   If the marks don't align as described, recheck the timing belt installation **(see illustration)**.

---

7 Camshaft and followers - removal, inspection and installation

---

Removal

1   Disconnect the negative cable from the battery.

2   Remove the camshaft cover, the timing belt cover and the timing belt (Sections 4 and 6). Unbolt the alternator bracket from the cylinder head and push it aside.

3   Remove the spring clip from the hydraulic valve lash adjuster end of each cam follower.

4   Using a valve spring compressor, compress the valve spring and slide out the cam follower (see Section 5 if necessary). Keep the cam followers in order so they can be reinstalled in their original locations.

5   Lift out the hydraulic lash adjusters, keeping each one with its respective cam follower.

6   Remove the camshaft sprocket mounting bolt and washer. A long screwdriver placed through one of the holes in the sprocket will prevent the camshaft from turning.

7   Draw off the sprocket with a puller, then remove the belt guide.

8   Remove the sprocket locating pin from the end of the camshaft.

9   Remove the camshaft retaining plate from the rear bearing pedestal.

10   Raise the vehicle and support it securely on jackstands.

11   Position a floor jack under the engine. Place a block of wood on the jack pad. Remove the left and right engine mount bolts and nuts. Raise the engine as high as it will go. Place blocks of wood between the engine mounts and frame brackets and remove the jack. **Warning:** *DO NOT place your hands under the engine where they would be crushed if the jack failed!*

12   Using a hammer and a brass or aluminum drift, drive the camshaft out toward the front of the engine, taking the front seal with it. Be very careful not to damage the camshaft bearings and journals as it's pushed out.

Inspection

Camshaft and bearings

13   After the camshaft has been removed from the engine, cleaned with solvent and dried, inspect the bearing journals for uneven wear, pits and galling. If the journals are damaged, the bearing inserts in the head are probably damaged as well. Both the camshaft and bearings will have to be replaced with new ones. Measure the inside diameter of each camshaft bearing and record the results (take two measurements, 90-degrees apart, at each bearing).

14   Measure the camshaft bearing journals with a micrometer to determine if they're excessively worn or out-of-round. If they're more than 0.005-inch out-of-round, the camshaft should be replaced with a new one. Subtract the bearing journal diameters from the corresponding bearing inside diameter measurements to obtain the oil clearance. If it's excessive, new bearings must be installed. **Note:** *Camshaft bearing replacement requires special tools and expertise that place it outside the scope of the do-it-yourselfer. Take the head to an automotive machine shop to ensure that the job is done correctly.*

15   Check the camshaft lobes for heat discoloration, score marks, chipped areas, pitting and uneven wear. If the lobes are in good condition the camshaft can be reused.

16   Make sure the camshaft oil passages are clear and clean.

17   To check the thrust plate for wear, install the camshaft in the cylinder head and position the thrust plate at the rear. Using a dial indicator, check the total end play by tapping the camshaft carefully back-and-forth. If the end play is outside the specified limit, replace the thrust plate with a new one.

Cam followers

18   Check the faces of the cam followers (which bear on the cam lobes) for signs of pitting, score marks and other forms of wear. They should fit snugly on the pivot bolt.

19   Inspect the face which bears on the valve stem. If it's pitted, the cam follower must be replaced with a new one.

20   If excessive cam follower wear is evident (and possibly excessive cam lobe wear), it may be due to a malfunction of the valve drive lubrication tube. If this has occurred, replace the tube and the cam follower. If more than one cam follower is excessively worn, replace the camshaft, all the cam followers and the lubrication tube. This also applies where excessive cam lobe wear is found.

21   During any operation which requires removal of the camshaft cover, make sure that oil is being discharged from the lubrication tube nozzles by cranking the engine with the starter motor.

Installation

22   Liberally coat the camshaft journals and bearings with engine assembly lube or moly-base grease, then carefully install the camshaft in the cylinder head.

23   Install the retaining plate and screws.

24   Lubricate the new camshaft oil seal with engine oil and carefully tap it into place at the front of the cylinder head with a large socket and a hammer. Make sure it enters the bore squarely and seats completely.

25   Install the belt guide and pin at the front end of the camshaft, then carefully tap on the sprocket.

26   Install a new sprocket bolt or use Teflon sealing tape on the threads of the old one.

27   Coat the hydraulic lash adjusters with engine assembly lube or moly-base grease, then install them in their original locations.

28   Coat the camshaft lobes and cam followers with engine assembly lube or moly-base grease.

29   Install the timing belt (Section 6).

30   Compress each valve spring and position each cam follower on its respective valve end and adjuster. Install the retaining spring clips.

31   Install the remaining components previously removed.

8   Auxiliary shaft - removal, inspection and installation

1   Detach the negative battery cable from the battery. Remove the large bolt from the front of the crankshaft and pull the drivebelt pulley off. Remove the bolts/screws and detach the outer timing belt cover.

2   Loosen the auxiliary shaft sprocket bolt. If the shaft turns, immobilize the sprocket by inserting a large screwdriver or 3/8-inch drive extension through one of the sprocket holes. Detach the timing belt (Section 6).

3   Pull off the sprocket (a puller may be required) and remove the pin from the shaft.

4   Remove the three bolts and detach the auxiliary shaft cover.

5   Remove the screws and detach the retaining plate.

6   Withdraw the shaft. If it's tight, reinstall the bolt and washer. Use a prybar and spacer block to pry out the shaft. Be extremely careful not to damage the bearings as you pull the shaft out of the block.

7   Examine the auxiliary shaft bearing for pits and score marks. Replacement must be done by a dealer service department or a repair shop (although it's easy to remove the old bearing, correct installation of the new one requires special tools). The auxiliary shaft may show signs of wear on the bearing journal or the eccentric. Score marks and damage to the bearing journals cannot be removed by grinding. If in doubt, ask a dealer service department to check the auxiliary shaft and offer advice on replacement. Examine the gear teeth for wear and damage. If either is evident, a replacement shaft must be obtained.

8   Dip the auxiliary shaft in engine oil before installing it in the block. Tap it in gently with a soft-face hammer to ensure that it's seated. Install the retaining plate and the auxiliary shaft cover.

9   The remainder of the procedure is the reverse of removal. Make sure that the auxiliary shaft pin is in place before installing the sprocket. Tighten the sprocket mounting bolt to the torque listed in this Chapter's Specifications.

9   Front oil seals - replacement

Note: *The camshaft, crankshaft and auxiliary shaft oil seals are all replaced the same way, using the same tools, after the appropriate sprocket has been removed. When replacing the sprocket(s), always use a new bolt or clean out the oil hole and use Teflon tape on the old bolt.*

1   Disconnect the negative battery cable from the battery.

2   To remove the camshaft or auxiliary shaft sprockets, referring to Section 7 or 8. A special puller designed for this purpose is available at some auto parts stores.

3   To remove the crankshaft sprocket, use a gear puller.

4   A special tool, available at most auto parts stores, may be used to remove all the seals. When using the tool, be sure the jaws are gripping the thin edge of the seal very tightly before operating the screw portion of the tool. If the tool isn't available, a hammer and chisel may be used to remove the seal(s) if care is exercised.

5   Clean the seal bore and shaft surface prior to installation of the new seal. Apply a thin layer of grease to the outer edge of the new seal(s).

6   Install the seal(s) with a seal driver. If a seal driver isn't available, you may be able to use a large deep socket and a hammer or a short piece of pipe, the sprocket bolt and a large flat washer.

7   Install the components removed to gain access to the seals.

8   If the front cover **(see illustration 8.4)** is removed for any reason, reinstall it without the seal. Before tightening the bolts, center the cover with a special tool, available at most auto parts stores, or equivalent, then install the seal as described previously.

10   Intake manifold - removal and installation

Refer to illustrations 10.13a and 10.13b

1   Relieve the fuel system pressure (Chapter 4).

2   Disconnect the negative battery cable from the battery.

3   Drain the cooling system (Chapter 1).

4   Remove the air cleaner and ducts (Chapter 4).

5   Label and disconnect the vacuum hoses from the throttle body and emissions devices attached to the intake manifold.

6   Remove the throttle body, fuel injection wiring harness, fuel rail and upper intake manifold (Chapter 4).

7   Remove the four bottom mounting bolts from the intake manifold.

8   Remove the four upper mounting bolts from the manifold. Note that the front two bolts also secure the engine lifting "eye".

9   Detach the manifold from the engine.

10   Clean the manifold and head mating surfaces and check the manifold for cracks. **Note:** *The mating surfaces of the head and manifold must be perfectly clean when the manifold is installed. Gasket removal solvents in aerosol cans are available at most auto parts stores and may be helpful when removing old gasket material that's stuck to the head and manifold. Be careful not to scrape or gouge the sealing surfaces.*

11   Clean and oil the manifold mounting bolts.

12   Position the new intake manifold gasket on the manifold.

13   Position the intake manifold and gasket, along with the lifting "eye", on the head, install the fasteners and tighten them in sequence, in two steps, to the torque listed in this Chapter's Specifications **(see illustrations)**.

14   The remainder of installation is the reverse of removal.

15   Reconnect the battery and refill the cooling system.

16   Start the engine and let it run while checking for coolant, fuel and vacuum leaks.

11   Exhaust manifold - removal and installation

Removal

1   Disconnect the negative battery cable from the battery.

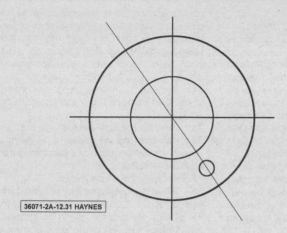

36071-2A-12.31 HAYNES

12.31 Be sure to turn the camshaft until the pin is in the five o'clock position as shown here before installing the head

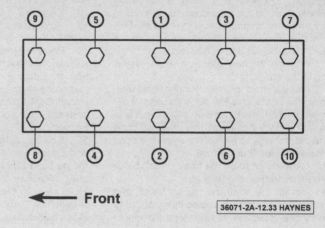

← **Front**

36071-2A-12.33 HAYNES

12.33 Cylinder head bolt TIGHTENING sequence

2   On 1991 and later models, remove the air cleaner and the air duct assembly (Chapter 4).

3   Remove the turbocharger (vehicles so equipped) (Chapter 4).

4   Disconnect the EGR tube at the exhaust manifold and loosen the EGR valve.

5   On vehicles so equipped, disconnect the EGO sensor from the exhaust manifold (see Chapter 6).

6   Remove the exhaust pipe-to-manifold bolts and carefully move the exhaust pipe out of the way.

7   Remove the mounting bolts and detach the exhaust manifold and lifting "eye" from the engine. On vehicles so equipped, remove the heat shield. **Note:** *Some vehicles are equipped with a combination of bolt types (regular and stud-type). Note the location of these different bolts as they must be reinstalled in the correct location during installation.*

8   Clean the manifold and cylinder head mating surfaces with a gasket scraper, them wipe them off with a cloth saturated with lacquer thinner or acetone. Clean the bolt threads with a wire brush.

Installation

9   Using a new gasket, install the manifold and the bolts attaching it to the cylinder head. Make sure the lifting "eye" is attached to the rear of the manifold. On vehicles with different types of bolts, make sure there installed in the correct location.

10   On 1979 through 1990 models, working from the center out, tighten the bolts (in two or three steps) to the torque listed in this Chapter's Specifications.

11   On 1991 and later models, tighten the regular bolts and then the stud bolts to the torque listed in this Chapter's Specifications.

12   Attach the exhaust pipe and tighten the bolts securely.

13   On vehicles so equipped, install the heat shield and tighten the nuts to the torque listed in this Chapter's Specifications.

14   The remainder of installation is the reverse of removal. Run the engine and check for exhaust leaks.

12   Cylinder head - removal and installation

Refer to illustrations 12.31 and 12.33

Removal

1   Begin the procedure by positioning the number one piston at top dead center (TDC) on the compression stroke (see Section 3).

2   Drain the cooling system (Chapter 1). Remove the air cleaner assembly and the air duct.

3   Remove the bolt retaining the heater hose to the camshaft cover.

4   Detach the distributor cap from the distributor.

5   Label and detach the spark plug wires from the spark plugs and remove the distributor cap and wires as an assembly. Remove the spark plugs.

6   Label and disconnect all vacuum hoses attached to the components on the head.

7   Remove the engine oil dipstick tube by pulling it straight out.

8   Remove the camshaft cover (Section 4).

9   Remove the intake manifold bolts (Section 10).

10   Loosen the alternator mounting bolts, remove the belt from the pulley and remove the bracket bolts.

11   Remove the upper radiator hose.

12   Remove the timing belt front cover.

13   Make sure the valve timing is correct (Section 6, Steps 21 through 25), then loosen the timing belt tensioner (Section 6).

14   Remove the timing belt from the camshaft and auxiliary shaft sprockets.

15   Remove the exhaust manifold mounting bolts (Section 11). The manifold itself can remain in place.

16   Remove the timing belt tensioner bolts.

17   Remove the timing belt tensioner spring stop from the cylinder head.

18   Disconnect the oil pressure sending unit lead wire at the left rear corner of the head.

19   Refer to Section 10 and remove the intake manifold.

20   Using a new head gasket, outline the cylinders and bolt pattern on a piece of cardboard. Be sure to indicate the front of the engine for reference. Punch holes at the bolt locations.

21   Loosen the cylinder head mounting bolts in 1/4-turn increments until they can be removed by hand.

22   Store the bolts in the cardboard holder as they're removed - this will ensure that they're reinstalled in their original locations.

23   Lift the head off the engine. If it's stuck, don't pry between the head and block. Instead, rap the head with a soft-face hammer or a block of wood and a hammer to break the gasket seal.

24   Place the head on a block of wood to prevent damage to the gasket surface. Refer to Part E for cylinder head disassembly and valve service procedures.

Installation

25   If a new cylinder head is being installed, transfer all external parts from the old cylinder head to the new one.

26   The mating surfaces of the cylinder head and block must be perfectly clean when the head is installed.

27   Use a gasket scraper to remove all traces of carbon and old gasket material, then clean the mating surfaces with lacquer thinner or acetone. If there's oil on the mating surfaces when the head is installed, the gasket may not seal correctly and leaks may develop. Use a vacuum cleaner to remove any debris that falls into the cylinders.

28   Check the block and head mating surfaces for nicks, deep scratches and other damage. If damage is slight, it can be removed with a file; if it's excessive, machining may be the only alternative.

29   Use a tap of the correct size to chase the

threads in the head bolt holes. Mount each bolt in a vise and run a die down the threads to remove corrosion and restore the threads. Dirt, corrosion, sealant and damaged threads will affect critical head bolt torque readings.

30   Position the new gasket over the dowel pins in the block.

31   Make a mark on the cylinder head indicating the position of the pin in the end of the camshaft. Turn the camshaft until the pin is in the five o'clock position - this must be done to avoid damage to the valves when the head is installed **(see illustration)**.

32   Carefully position the head on the block without disturbing the gasket.

33   Install the cylinder head bolts and tighten them in sequence **(see illustration)** to the torque listed in this Chapter's Specifications.

34   Return the camshaft to its original position (with the pin aligned with the mark you made on the head).

35   The remainder of installation is the reverse of the removal procedure.

36   Change the engine oil and filter (Chapter 1).

13 Oil pan - removal and installation

1978 through 1990 models

Note: *Some 1986 through 1990 models have a one-piece oil pan gasket. Others have a four-piece gasket. Be sure to obtain the correct type for your engine.*

Removal

1   Position number one piston at Top Dead Center (see Section 3). This will also position the number four piston at the top of its travel, so the oil pan will clear the rear part of the crankshaft during removal.

2   Disconnect the negative battery cable from the battery.

3   Raise the vehicle and support it securely on jackstands.

4   Drain the cooling system (Chapter 1). Remove the fan and shroud and disconnect both hoses from the radiator (Chapter 3).

5   Drain the oil and remove the oil filter (Chapter 1).

6   Disconnect the oil pan-mounted low oil level sensor, if equipped.

7   Refer to Section 17 and detach the engine mounts so the engine can be raised.

8   Using a block of wood to protect the oil pan, carefully raise the engine as far as it will safely go with a jack. Then place blocks of wood between the mounts and the subframe brackets. **Warning:** *Don't place any part of your body under the engine/transmission when it's supported only by a jack!*

9   Remove the bolt retaining the flex coupling to the steering gear. Unbolt the steering gear from the chassis and position it forward and down.

10   Remove the chassis stiffening brace (vehicles so equipped).

11   Unbolt the sway bar (see Chapter 10) and lower it out of the way.

12   Remove the starter motor (Chapter 5).

13   Remove the oil pan bolts and reinforcements.

14   Break the gasket seal by striking the pan with a rubber hammer, then detach the pan from the block. If the pan hangs up on the oil pump or pick-up tube and can't be removed, unbolt the pump and pick-up tube assembly from the engine and drop it into the pan (see Section 14).

15   Remove all traces of old gasket material and sealant with a gasket scraper, then clean the pan and block mating surfaces with lacquer thinner or acetone. They must be perfectly clean to prevent oil leaks after the pan is installed. Remove and clean the oil pump pick-up screen.

Installation

Models with a one-piece gasket

16   Attach the oil pan gasket to the pan with pan gasket adhesive. Use a dab of RTV sealant at the corners.

Models with a four-piece gasket

17   Apply sealer to the block-to-front cover and rear bearing cap-to-block joints. Position the end seals in place and press the tabs into the block.

All models

18   If the oil pump and pick-up tube were removed, install them. If they had to be removed for clearance to remove the pan, wait until the pan is lifted into place (Step 21).

19   Install two guide pins (supplied with the gasket set), as shown in the illustrations.

20   Install the oil pan and bolts (and reinforcement strips, if equipped). Remove the guide pins. Install the remaining bolts and tighten them to the torque listed in this Chapter's Specifications (follow a clockwise pattern).

21   The remaining Steps are the reverse of removal.

22   Replace the oil filter, oil and coolant.

23   Run the engine and check for leaks.

24   Remove the jackstands and lower the vehicle.

1991 and later models

Removal

25   Disconnect the negative battery cable from the battery.

26   Remove the air cleaner outlet tube at the throttle body (Chapter 4).

27   Drain the engine oil and remove the oil filter (Chapter 1).

28   Raise the vehicle and support it securely on jackstands.

29   Remove the engine oil dipstick.

30   Remove the starter (Chapter 5).

31   Disconnect the exhaust manifold tube to the inlet pipe bracket. Disconnect the catalytic converter at the inlet pipe (Chapter 4).

32   Refer to Section 17 and detach the engine mounts so the engine can be raised.

33   Using a block of wood to protect the oil pan carefully raise the engine as far as it will go with a jack. Then place blocks of wood between the mounts and the sub-frame brackets. **Warning:** *Don't place any part of your body under the engine/transmission when it's supported only by a jack!*

34   Remove the two oil pan-to-transmission bolts, then remove the transmission (Chapter 7).

35   Remove the flywheel (Section 15).

36   Remove the oil cooler lines from the retainer on the engine block (automatic transmission vehicles).

37   Remove the oil pan bolts.

38   Break the gasket seal by striking the pan with a rubber hammer, then detach it from the block and lower the pan in the chassis.

39   Remove the oil pump drive and pickup tube assembly from the engine and drop it into the pan (Section 14). Remove the oil pan.

40   Remove all traces of old gasket material and silicone sealant with a gasket scraper, then clean the pan and block mating surface with lacquer thinner or acetone. They must be perfectly clean to prevent oil leaks after the pan is installed. Remove the oil pump pick-up screen.

Installation

41   Apply silicone gasket sealant to the front cover-to-block joint, rear main bearing cap-to-block joints and the points where the flat portions of the front cover join the rounded surfaces.

42   Install the oil pan gasket onto the oil pan and press it into the groove. The gasket should be retained in the oil pan by press-fit only - not with the aid of an adhesive.

43   Place the oil pump drive and pickup tube assembly into the oil pan in its correct orientation to the engine.

44   Move the oil pan into position in the chassis. Install the oil pump drive and pickup tube assembly onto the engine (Section 14).

45   Install the oil pan and bolts. Tighten the oil pan bolts tight enough to compress the cork/rubber oil pan gasket to the block, but loose enough to allow movement of the oil pan relative to the cylinder block.

46   Install the flywheel (Section 15).

47   Install the transmission (Chapter 7).

48   Using a block of wood to protect the oil pan carefully raise the engine sufficiently until the wood blocks between the mounts and the sub-frame brackets can be removed, then remove them.

49   Lower the engine, refer to Section 17 and attach the engine mounts.

50   Install the two oil pan-to-transmission bolts and tighten to the Step 1 torque listed in this Chapter's Specifications. Loosen these two bolts one-half turn.

51   Tighten all other oil pan flange bolts to the torque listed in this Chapter's Specifications.

52   Tighten the two oil pan-to-transmission bolts to the Step 2 torque listed in this Chapter's Specifications.

53   Install the oil cooler lines onto the retainer on the engine block (automatic transmission vehicles).

54   The remaining Steps are the reverse of removal.

55   Replace the oil filter and add oil (Chapter 1).

56   Run the engine and check for leaks.

57   Remove the jackstands and lower the vehicle.

14 Oil pump - removal and installation

1   Remove the oil pan as described in Section 13.

2   Remove the nut securing the pick-up tube to the engine, then remove the bolts securing the pump to the engine. Remove the pump and pick-up tube as an assembly, then separate them when they're off the engine. The pump intermediate shaft should drop out of the bottom of the distributor shaft as the pump is removed.

3   If there is any possibility that the pump is faulty or if an engine overhaul is being performed, replace the pump. **Caution:** *A faulty pump can ruin an otherwise good engine.*

4   Prime the pump before installation. Hold it with the pick-up tube up and pour a few ounces of clean oil into the inlet screen. Turn the pump driveshaft by hand until oil comes out the outlet.

5   Install the pump intermediate shaft with the collar end in the engine block. Be sure the shaft seats in the distributor. Hold the shaft in place and install the pump and oil pan (see Section 12). Be sure to tighten the bolts to the torque listed in this Chapter's Specifications.

6   Add oil to the engine (Chapter 1), then start it and be sure the oil pressure comes up. If it doesn't come up within 10 or 15 seconds, shut off the engine immediately and find the cause of the problem. **Caution:** *Continued running of the engine without oil pressure will severely damage the moving parts!*

7   Check for oil leaks.

15 Flywheel - removal and installation

1   Raise the vehicle and support it securely on jackstands, then refer to Chapter 7 and remove the transmission. If it's leaking, now would be a very good time to replace the front pump seal/O-ring (automatic transmission only).

2   Remove the pressure plate and clutch disc (see Chapter 8) (manual transmission equipped vehicles). Now is a good time to check/replace the clutch components and pilot bearing.

3   Use a center-punch to make alignment marks on the flywheel and crankshaft to ensure correct alignment during reinstallation.

4   Remove the bolts that secure the flywheel to the crankshaft. If the crankshaft turns, wedge a screwdriver through the starter opening to jam the flywheel.

5   Remove the flywheel from the crankshaft. Since the flywheel is fairly heavy, be sure to support it while removing the last bolt.

6   Clean the flywheel to remove grease and oil. Inspect the surface for cracks, rivet grooves, burned areas and score marks. Light scoring can be removed with emery cloth. Check for cracked and broken ring gear teeth. Lay the flywheel on a flat surface and use a straightedge to check for warpage.

7   Clean and inspect the mating surfaces of the flywheel and the crankshaft. If the crankshaft rear seal is leaking, replace it before reinstalling the flywheel.

8   Position the flywheel against crankshaft. Be sure to align the marks made during removal. Note that some engines have an alignment dowel or staggered bolt holes to ensure correct installation. Before installing the bolts, apply thread locking compound to the threads.

9   Wedge a screwdriver through the starter motor opening to keep the flywheel from turning as you tighten the bolts to the torque listed in this Chapter's Specifications.

10   The remainder of installation is the reverse of the removal procedure.

16 Rear crankshaft oil seal - replacement

Refer to illustration 16.6

1   Remove the transmission and all other components necessary, such as the clutch and pressure plate, to get at the oil seal in the back of the engine (Chapters 7 and 8).

2   Remove the flywheel (Section 15).

3   Use a small punch to make two holes on opposite sides of the seal and install small sheet metal screws in the holes. Pry on the screws with two large screwdrivers until the seal is removed from the engine. It may be necessary to place small blocks of wood against the block to provide a fulcrum point for prying. **Caution:** *Be careful not to scratch or otherwise damage the crankshaft oil seal surface.*

4   Apply a thin film of engine oil to the outer edge of the new seal and the seal bore in the block, as well as the seal lips.

5   Position the seal on a special tool, available at most auto parts stores, then position the tool and seal at the rear of engine. Install the seal with the spring side toward the engine. Alternate tightening of the bolts to seat the seal in the block.

6   If the special seal installer is not available, work the seal into place and tap it gently into the bore with a hammer and the blunt end of a punch **(see illustration)**. Use the drive end of socket extension, or other blunt, smooth object, to ease the lip of the seal over the end of the crankshaft.

7   The remainder of installation is the reverse of the removal procedure.

16.6 After working the seal lip over the crankshaft, tap the seal into place

17 Engine mounts - check and replacement

1   Engine mounts seldom require attention, but broken or deteriorated mounts should be replaced immediately or the added strain placed on the driveline components may cause damage or wear.

Check

2   During the check, the engine must be raised slightly to remove the weight from the mounts.

3   Raise the vehicle and support it securely on jackstands, then position a jack under the engine oil pan. Place a large block of wood between the jack head and the oil pan, then carefully raise the engine just enough to take the weight off the mounts. **Warning:** *DO NOT place any part of your body under the engine when it's supported only by a jack!*

4   Check the mounts to see if the rubber is cracked, hardened or separated from the metal plates. Sometimes the rubber will split right down the center.

5   Check for relative movement between the mount plates and the engine or frame (use a large screwdriver or pry bar to attempt to move the mounts). If movement is noted, lower the engine and tighten the mount fasteners.

6   Rubber preservative should be applied to the mounts to slow deterioration.

Replacement

7   Disconnect the negative battery cable from the battery, then raise the vehicle and support it securely on jackstands (if not already done).

8   Remove the fasteners and detach the mount from the frame bracket.

9   Raise the engine slightly with a jack or hoist (make sure the fan doesn't hit the radiator or shroud). Remove the mount-to-block nuts/bolts and detach the mount.

10   Installation is the reverse of removal. Use thread locking compound on the mount bolts and be sure to tighten them securely.

Notes

Chapter 2 Part B
3.3 liter inline six-cylinder engine

Contents

Specifications

Camshaft endplay .... 0.009 in max

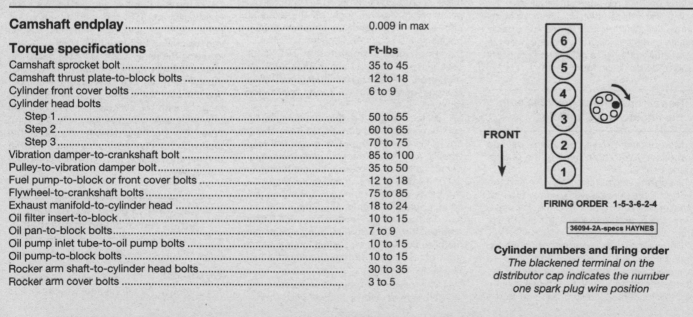

FIRING ORDER 1-5-3-6-2-4

36094-2A-specs HAYNES

Cylinder numbers and firing order
The blackened terminal on the distributor cap indicates the number one spark plug wire position

Torque specifications

	Ft-lbs
Camshaft sprocket bolt	35 to 45
Camshaft thrust plate-to-block bolts	12 to 18
Cylinder front cover bolts	6 to 9
Cylinder head bolts	
Step 1	50 to 55
Step 2	60 to 65
Step 3	70 to 75
Vibration damper-to-crankshaft bolt	85 to 100
Pulley-to-vibration damper bolt..	35 to 50
Fuel pump-to-block or front cover bolts	12 to 18
Flywheel-to-crankshaft bolts	75 to 85
Exhaust manifold-to-cylinder head	18 to 24
Oil filter insert-to-block...	10 to 15
Oil pan-to-block bolts	7 to 9
Oil pump inlet tube-to-oil pump bolts	10 to 15
Oil pump-to-block bolts	10 to 15
Rocker arm shaft-to-cylinder head bolts	30 to 35
Rocker arm cover bolts	3 to 5

1   General Information

This part of Chapter 2 is devoted to repair procedures for the inline six-cylinder engine. The latter Sections in this part of Chapter 2 cover the removal and installation procedures. All information concerning engine block and cylinder head servicing can be found in Part E of this Chapter.

Many repair procedures included in this part are based on the assumption the engine is still installed in the vehicle. Therefore, if this information is being used during a complete engine overhaul, with the engine already out of the vehicle and on a stand, many of the steps included here will not apply.

The specifications included in this part of Chapter 2 apply only to the engine and procedures found here. For specifications regarding engines other than the inline six-cylinder, see Part A, C or D, whichever applies. Part E of Chapter 2 contains the specifications necessary for engine block and cylinder head rebuilding procedures.

The 3.3 liter six-cylinder engine is an inline design, with overhead valves operated by hydraulic lifters and pushrods.

The camshaft is located to the right of the crankshaft and is driven by the crankshaft via a multi-link timing chain. The camshaft rides on four replaceable bearings.

The crankshaft is held in place by seven main bearings. Each main bearing consists of two replaceable sections.

The engine is lubricated by a pressurized oiling system. Oil is held in the oil pan where it's splashed on lower engine surfaces, as well as being pumped to the top of the engine (to the valve train), then forced down through the other components of the engine until it returns to the oil pan.

Because various components rub against one another, a certain amount of wear will take place. The rate of component wear depends on the cleanliness of the oil and filter and the replacement of all other filters at the specified intervals. Oversize components are available to prolong the operational life of the engine. They include oversize pistons, pushrods, valve guides and connecting rod and main bearings.

2   Repair operations possible with the engine in the vehicle

Many major repair operations can be accomplished without removing the engine from the vehicle.

Clean the engine compartment and the exterior of the engine with some type of degreaser before any work is done. It'll make the job easier and help keep dirt out of the internal areas of the engine.

Depending on the components involved, it may be helpful to remove the hood to improve access to the engine as repairs are performed (refer to Chapter 11 if necessary). Cover the fenders to prevent damage to the

paint. Special pads are available, but an old bedspread or blanket will also work.

If vacuum, exhaust, oil or coolant leaks develop, indicating a need for gasket or seal replacement, the repairs can generally be made with the engine in the vehicle. The intake and exhaust manifold gaskets, cylinder front (timing) cover gasket, oil pan gasket, crankshaft oil seals and cylinder head gasket are all accessible with the engine in place.

Exterior engine components, such as the intake and exhaust manifolds, the oil pan (and the oil pump), the water pump, the starter motor, the alternator, the distributor and the fuel system components can be removed for repair with the engine in place.

Since the cylinder head can be removed without pulling the engine, valve component servicing can also be accomplished with the engine in the vehicle. Replacement of the camshaft, timing chain and sprockets is also possible with the engine in the vehicle.

In extreme cases caused by a lack of necessary equipment, repair or replacement of piston rings, pistons, connecting rods and rod bearings is possible with the engine in the vehicle. However, this practice is not recommended because of the cleaning and preparation work that must be done to the components involved.

3   Top Dead Center (TDC) for number one piston - locating

Note: *The following procedure is based on the assumption the spark plug wires and distributor are correctly installed. If you are trying to locate TDC to install the distributor correctly, piston position must be determined by feeling for compression at the number one spark plug hole, then aligning the ignition timing marks as described in Step 8.*

1   Top Dead Center (TDC) is the highest point in the cylinder each piston reaches as it travels up-and-down when the crankshaft turns. Each piston reaches TDC on the compression stroke and again on the exhaust stroke, but TDC generally refers to piston position on the compression stroke.

2   Positioning the piston(s) at TDC is an essential part of many procedures such as rocker arm removal, camshaft and timing chain/sprocket removal and distributor removal.

3   Before beginning this procedure, be sure to place the transmission in Neutral and apply the parking brake or block the rear wheels. Also, disable the ignition system by detaching the coil wire from the center terminal of the distributor cap and grounding it on the block with a jumper wire. Remove the spark plugs (see Chapter 1).

4   To bring any piston to TDC, the crankshaft must be turned using one of the methods outlined below. When looking at the front of the engine, normal crankshaft rotation is clockwise.

a) *The preferred method is to turn the crankshaft with a socket and ratchet*

attached to the bolt threaded into the front of the crankshaft.

b) *A remote starter switch, which may save some time, can also be used. Follow the instructions included with the switch. Once the piston is close to TDC, use a socket and ratchet as described in the previous paragraph.*

c) *If an assistant is available to turn the ignition switch to the Start position in short bursts, you can get the piston close to TDC without a remote starter switch. Make sure the assistant is out of the vehicle, away from the ignition switch, then use a socket and ratchet as described in Paragraph a) to complete the procedure.*

5   Note the position of the terminal for the number one spark plug wire on the distributor cap. If the terminal isn't marked, follow the plug wire from the number one cylinder spark plug to the cap.

6   Use a felt-tip pen or chalk to make a mark on the distributor body directly under the terminal.

7   Detach the cap from the distributor and set it aside (see Chapter 1 if necessary).

8   Turn the crankshaft (see Paragraph 3 above) until the notch in the crankshaft pulley is aligned with the 0 on the timing plate (located at the front of the engine).

9   Look at the distributor rotor - it should be pointing directly at the mark you made on the distributor body.

10   If the rotor is 180-degrees off, the number one piston is at TDC on the exhaust stroke.

11   To get the piston to TDC on the compression stroke, turn the crankshaft one complete turn (360-degrees) clockwise. The rotor should now be pointing at the mark on the distributor. When the rotor is pointing at the number one spark plug wire terminal in the distributor cap and the ignition timing marks are aligned, the number one piston is at TDC on the compression stroke.

12   After the number one piston has been positioned at TDC on the compression stroke, TDC for any of the remaining pistons can be located by turning the crankshaft and following the firing order. Mark the remaining spark plug wire terminal locations on the distributor body just like you did for the number one terminal, then number the marks to correspond with the cylinder numbers. As you turn the crankshaft, the rotor will also turn. When it's pointing directly at one of the marks on the distributor, the piston for that particular cylinder is at TDC on the compression stroke.

4   Rocker arm cover and rocker arms - removal and installation

Refer to illustrations 4.8a, 4.8b, 4.10 and 4.14

Removal

1   Remove the air cleaner assembly and

4.8a Lubricate the pushrod ends with moly-base grease or engine assembly lube before installation

4.8b Make sure the pushrods are engaged in the rocker arms before installing the bolts

the crankcase ventilation system (Chapter 6).

2   Remove the accelerator cable bracket.

3   Remove the rocker arm cover bolts and separate the rocker arm cover from the engine. Discard the rocker arm cover gasket.

4   Loosen the rocker arm shaft bolts 1/2-turn at a time, starting from the front of the engine and working toward the rear.

5   Remove the rocker arm shaft assembly. Make sure the pushrods are identified before removal so they can be returned to the same location during installation.

6   Remove the pushrods.

Installation

7   Apply moly-base grease or engine assembly lube to both ends of the pushrods and to the valve stem tips.

8   Install the pushrods (see illustrations) and position the rocker arm shaft assembly on the cylinder head.

9   Install and tighten all the rocker arm support bolts 1/2-turn at a time, from front to rear, until the supports contact the cylinder head.

10   Tighten the bolts to the specified torque in the same sequence (see illustration).

11   Check the valve clearance following the procedure in Chapter 2, Part E.

12   Clean the rocker arm cover and cylinder head gasket surfaces.

13   Install a new gasket in the cover. Make sure all the gasket tangs are engaged in the notches provided in the cover.

14   Install the cover (see illustration) and tighten the bolts in two steps. First tighten the bolts to five ft-lbs, then retighten them to five ft-lbs again two minutes later.

15   Install the accelerator cable bracket.

16   Install the crankcase ventilation system and air cleaner assembly.

5   Valve spring, retainer and seal - replacement

Note: Broken valve springs and defective valve stem seals can be replaced without removing the cylinder head. Two special tools and a compressed air source are normally

required to perform this operation, so read through this Section carefully and rent or buy the tools before beginning the job. If compressed air isn't available, a length of nylon rope can be used to keep the valves from falling into the cylinder during this procedure.

1   Refer to Section 4 and remove the rocker arm cover from the cylinder head.

2   Remove the spark plug from the cylinder which has the defective component. If all of the valve stem seals are being replaced, all of the spark plugs should be removed.

3   Turn the crankshaft until the piston in the affected cylinder is at top dead center on the compression stroke (refer to Section 3 for instructions). If you're replacing all of the valve stem seals, begin with cylinder number one and work on the valves for one cylinder at a time. Move from cylinder-to-cylinder following the firing order sequence (see this Chapter's Specifications).

4   Thread an adapter into the spark plug hole and connect an air hose from a compressed air source to it. Most auto parts stores can supply the air hose adapter. Note: Many

4.10 Tighten the rocker arm shaft bolts to the specified torque

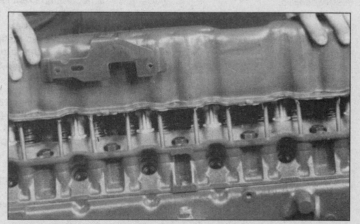

4.14 Make sure all gasket surfaces are clean before installing the rocker arm cover - if the cover flange is distorted (this usually happens around the bolt holes), use a hammer and block of wood to flatten and restore it

cylinder compression gauges utilize a screw-in fitting that may work with your air hose quick-disconnect fitting.

5   Loosen the rocker arm shaft support bolts until valve spring tension is relieved. Slide the rocker arms to the side and restrain them with pieces of wire, then remove both pushrods from the cylinder to be serviced. **Note:** *If all the valve stem seals must be replaced, remove the rocker arm assembly (refer to Section 4).*

6   Apply compressed air to the cylinder. **Warning:** *The piston may be forced down by compressed air, causing the crankshaft to turn suddenly. If the wrench used when positioning the number one piston at TDC is still attached to the bolt in the crankshaft nose, it could cause damage or injury when the crankshaft moves.*

7   The valves should be held in place by the air pressure. If the valve faces or seats are in poor condition, leaks may prevent air pressure from retaining the valves - refer to the alternative procedure below.

8   If you don't have access to compressed air, an alternative method can be used. Position the piston at a point just before TDC on the compression stroke, then feed a long piece of nylon rope through the spark plug hole until it fills the combustion chamber. Be sure to leave the end of the rope hanging out of the engine so it can be removed easily. Use a large ratchet and socket to turn the crankshaft in the normal direction of rotation until slight resistance is felt.

9   Stuff shop rags into the cylinder head holes above and below the valves to prevent parts and tools from falling into the engine, then use a valve spring compressor to compress the spring. Remove the keepers with small needle-nose pliers or a magnet. **Note:** *A couple of different types of tools are available for compressing the valve springs with the head in place. One type grips the lower spring coils and presses on the retainer as the knob is turned, while the other type utilizes the rocker arm shaft for leverage. Both types work very well, although the lever type is usually less expensive.*

10   Remove the spring retainer sleeve and valve spring, then remove the umbrella-type guide seal. **Note:** *If air pressure fails to hold the valve in the closed position during this operation, the valve face or seat is probably damaged. If so, the cylinder head will have to be removed for additional repair operations.*

11   Wrap a rubber band or tape around the top of the valve stem so the valve won't fall into the combustion chamber, then release the air pressure. **Note:** *If a rope was used instead of air pressure, turn the crankshaft slightly in the direction opposite normal rotation.*

12   Inspect the valve stem for damage. Rotate the valve in the guide and check the end for eccentric movement, which would indicate the valve is bent.

13   Move the valve up-and-down in the guide and make sure it doesn't bind. If the valve stem binds, either the valve is bent or

the guide is damaged. In either case, the head will have to be removed for repair.

14   Reapply air pressure to the cylinder to retain the valve in the closed position, then remove the tape or rubber band from the valve stem. If a rope was used instead of air pressure, turn the crankshaft in the normal direction of rotation until slight resistance is felt.

15   Lubricate the valve stem with engine oil and install a new seal.

16   Install the spring and sleeve in position over the valve.

17   Install the valve spring retainer. Compress the valve spring and carefully position the keepers in the groove. Apply a small dab of grease to the inside of each keeper to hold it in place.

18   Remove the pressure from the spring tool and make sure the keepers are seated.

19   Disconnect the air hose and remove the adapter from the spark plug hole. If a rope was used in place of air pressure, pull it out of the cylinder.

20   Refer to Section 4 and install the rocker arm assembly and pushrods.

21   Install the spark plug(s) and hook up the wire(s).

22   Refer to Section 4 and install the rocker arm cover.

23   Start and run the engine, then check for oil leaks and unusual sounds coming from the rocker arm cover area.

6   Cylinder head - removal and installation

Refer to illustration 6.30

Removal

Note: *If the engine has been removed from the vehicle, you can skip Steps 1 through 14.*

1   Drain the cooling system (Chapter 1).

2   Remove the air cleaner and hoses/ducts leading to the air cleaner.

3   Detach the PCV valve from the rocker arm cover and remove the valve.

4   Remove the vent hose from the intake manifold inlet tube.

5   Disconnect the fuel line leading from the fuel pump to the carburetor.

6   Detach all vacuum lines from the carburetor.

7   Disconnect the choke cable at the carburetor and position it out of the way.

8   Disconnect the accelerator cable or accelerator linkage from the carburetor. Remove the return spring.

9   Disconnect the kickdown link at the carburetor.

10   Remove the upper radiator hose from the thermostat outlet.

11   Remove the heater hose at the coolant outlet elbow.

12   Remove the nuts securing the exhaust pipe to the exhaust manifold and support the pipe out of the way.

13   Mark the wires leading to the coil and

disconnect them. Remove the coil bracket bolt and secure the coil and bracket out of the way.

14   Remove the rocker arm cover (Section 4).

15   Remove the rocker arm shaft assembly (Section 4).

16   Remove the pushrods. Label them so they can be reinstalled in their original locations - a numbered box or rack will keep them organized.

17   Disconnect the spark plug wires at the spark plugs.

18   Loosen the cylinder head bolts in 1/4-turn increments until they can be removed by hand. If you have an engine hoist or similar device handy, attach eyelet bolts at the ends of the head in the holes provided and lift the head off the engine block. If equipment of this nature isn't available, have a helper available and carefully pry the head up, off the block. **Caution:** *Do not wedge any tools between the cylinder head and block gasket mating surfaces.*

19   Turn the cylinder head upside-down and place it on a workbench. **Note:** *New and rebuilt cylinder heads are commonly available for engines at dealerships and auto parts stores. Due to the fact that some specialized tools are necessary for disassembly and inspection of the head, and replacement parts may not be readily available, it may be more practical and economical for the home mechanic to purchase a replacement head and install it.*

20   Another alternative at this point is to take the cylinder head to an automotive machine shop or shop specializing in cylinder heads and exchange it or leave it for an overhaul.

21   If the complete engine is being overhauled at this time, however, it may be wise to wait until the other components have been inspected.

22   If you're attempting to repair a part of the cylinder head assembly, or if you're going to inspect the components yourself, refer to Chapter 2, Part E.

Installation

23   The mating surfaces of the head and block must be perfectly clean when the head is installed.

24   Use a gasket scraper to remove all traces of carbon and old gasket material, then clean the mating surfaces with lacquer thinner or acetone. If there's oil on the mating surfaces when the head is installed, the gasket may not seal correctly and leaks may develop. When working on the block, it's a good idea to cover the lifters with shop rags to keep debris out of them. Use a shop rag or vacuum cleaner to remove any debris that falls into the cylinders.

25   Check the block and head mating surfaces for nicks, deep scratches and other damage. If damage is slight, it can be removed with a file; if it's excessive, machining may be the only alternative.

26 Use a tap of the correct size to chase the threads in the head bolt holes. Dirt, corrosion, sealant and damaged threads will affect torque readings.

27 Position the new gasket over the dowel pins in the block. Some gaskets are marked TOP or THIS SIDE UP to ensure correct installation.

28 Carefully position the head on the block without disturbing the gasket.

29 Using the previously installed lifting hooks (or a helper), carefully lower the cylinder head into place on the block. Don't move the head sideways or scrape it across the block, as it can dislodge the gasket and/or damage the mating surfaces.

30 Coat the cylinder head bolt threads with light engine oil and thread the bolts into the block. Tighten them in the recommended sequence **(see illustration)**. Work up to the final torque in three steps to avoid warping the head.

31 Install the pushrods, the rocker arm assembly and the rocker arm cover (Section 4).

32 The remaining steps are the reverse of the removal procedure.

33 Start the engine and allow it to reach operating temperature. Shut it off, allow it to cool completely, then retorque the head bolts. **Note:** *Be sure to read the instructions with the new head gasket. Some gaskets do not require retorquing - the instructions with the gasket should be followed if they differ from the instructions here.*

7 Manifolds - removal and installation

Removal

1 Remove the air cleaner assembly and related parts.

2 Tag all wires and vacuum hoses to simplify installation. On later models, a light-off catalyst is bolted directly to the outlet of the exhaust manifold and must be disconnected from the manifold flange.

3 Remove or disconnect the EGR tube and all other emission components which would interfere with the removal of the manifold.

4 Remove the manifold mounting bolts/nuts. It may be necessary to apply penetrating oil to the threads. **Note:** *Be sure to note the locations of the bolts, since they are different lengths.*

5 Detach the manifold.

Installation

6 Clean the mating surfaces of the manifold and cylinder head.

7 Install a new gasket, if applicable. Position the manifold on the cylinder head and install the bolts/nuts. Tighten the bolts/nuts to the specified torque, working from the rear to the front in an alternating pattern.

8 Position the light-off catalyst unit on the exhaust manifold.

9 Install and tighten the mounting nuts.

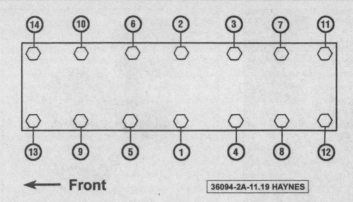

6.30 Cylinder head bolt TIGHTENING sequence (reverse the sequence when loosening the bolts)

Front

36094-2A-11.19 HAYNES

10 Install or connect the emission component vacuum hoses and wires previously disconnected.

11 Install the air cleaner assembly and related parts.

12 Start the engine and check for leaks at the manifold(s).

8 Cylinder front cover and timing chain - removal and installation

Refer to illustration 8.5

Removal

1 Drain the cooling system and disconnect the hoses. Remove the cooling fan, drivebelts and the crankshaft and water pump drive pulleys.

2 Remove the front cover-to-engine block and oil pan bolts. Carefully pry the cover away from the engine block at the top. Do not nick or gouge the mating surface of the engine block.

3 Scrape all gasket material and sealant off the engine block and cover mating surfaces, then clean them with lacquer thinner or acetone.

4 Before removing the timing chain and sprockets, the chain deflection must be checked as follows:

a) Turn the crankshaft counterclockwise and take up the slack on the left side of the chain.

b) Establish a reference point to the left of the timing chain. Measure the distance from the reference point to the center of the left run of the chain.

c) Turn the crankshaft clockwise and take up the slack in the right run of the timing chain.

d) Press the slack chain in the left run toward the center with your thumb and measure the distance from the reference point to the center of the slack chain on the left run.

e) Subtract the smaller figure from the larger and the difference will be the total deflection. **Note:** *If timing chain deflection is greater than 1/4-inch, the timing chain and sprockets must be replaced. Never replace just the chain or sprockets, replace them as a set.*

5 Rotate the crankshaft until the two timing marks on the sprockets are aligned **(see illustration)**.

6 Remove the camshaft sprocket bolt and pull both sprockets away from the front of the engine.

7 Clean the chain and sprockets in solvent if you have decided to reuse them. Inspect the sprocket teeth for damage and wear and the chain for a distinctive wear pattern. If a wear pattern exists on the chain or the sprockets, we recommend that you install new parts.

Installation

8 Position the camshaft and crankshaft

8.5 The camshaft and crankshaft sprocket timing marks (arrows) must be aligned with each other during installation

2B

9.4 Special tools are available for removing lifters, but they aren't always necessary

9.8a If the bottom of any lifter is worn concave, scratched or galled, replace the entire set with new ones

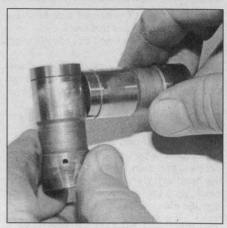

9.8b The foot of each lifter should be slightly convex - the side of another lifter can be used as a straightedge to check it; if it appears flat, it's worn and must not be reused

sprockets in the chain with the timing marks on the sprockets aligned.

9   Slide the two sprockets, complete with the timing chain, onto the ends of the crankshaft and camshaft.

10   Install the camshaft sprocket bolt and tighten it to the specified torque.

11   Before installing the front cover, check the condition of the oil seal. If the seal is dried out or been leaking, it must be replaced (see Section 13).

12   Apply RTV-sealant to the new front cover gasket and position the gasket on the cover. Coat all exposed portions of the gasket with sealant.

13   Install the cover. To prevent damage to the seal as it passes over the Woodruff key on the crankshaft, place a thin-wall socket over the crankshaft end. Make sure the outside diameter of the socket is less than the inside diameter of the seal.

14   Tighten all mounting bolts to the specified torque in three or four equal steps. Follow a criss-cross pattern to avoid warping the cover.

9   Lifters and camshaft - removal, inspection and installation

Lifters

Refer to illustrations 9.4, 9.8a, 9.8b and 9.8c

1   A noisy valve lifter can be isolated when the engine is idling. Hold a mechanic's stethoscope or a length of hose near the location of each valve while listening at the other end. Another method is to remove the rocker arm cover and, with the engine idling, touch each of the valve spring retainers, one at a time. If a valve lifter is defective, it'll be evident from the shock felt at the retainer each time the valve seats.

2   The most likely causes of noisy valve lifters are dirt trapped inside the lifter and lack of oil flow, viscosity or pressure. Before condemning the lifters, check the oil for fuel contamination, correct level, cleanliness and correct viscosity.

Removal

3   Remove the cylinder head and gasket as described in Section 6.

4   There are several ways to extract the lifters from the bores in the block. A special tool designed to grip and remove lifters **(see illustration)** is manufactured by many tool companies and is widely available, but it may not be required in every case. On newer engines without a lot of varnish buildup, the lifters can often be removed with a small magnet or even with your fingers. A machinist's scribe with a bent end can be used to pull the lifters out by positioning the point under the retainer ring in the top o each lifter. **Caution:** *Don't use pliers to remove the lifters unless you intend to replace them with new ones (along with the camshaft). The pliers may damage the precision machined and hardened lifters, rendering them useless.*

5   Before removing the lifters, arrange to store them in a clearly labeled box to ensure they're reinstalled in their original locations. Remove the lifters and store them where they won't get dirty.

Inspection and installation

6   Parts for valve lifters are not available separately. The work required to remove them from the engine again if cleaning is unsuccessful outweighs any potential savings from repairing them.

7   Clean the lifters with solvent and dry them thoroughly without mixing them up.

8   Check each lifter wall, pushrod seat and foot for scuffing, score marks and uneven wear **(see illustration)**. Each lifter foot (the surface that rides on the cam lobe) must be slightly convex, although this can be difficult t determine by eye **(see illustration)**. If the base of the lifter is concave, the lifters and camshaft must be replaced. If the lifter walls are damaged o worn (which isn't very likely), inspect the lifter bores in the engine block as well. If the pushrod seats **(see illustration)** are worn, check the pushrod ends.

9   If new lifters are being installed, a new camshaft must also be installed. If the

camshaft is replaced, then install new lifters as well. Never install used lifters unless the original camshaft is used and the lifters can be installed in their original locations! When installing lifters, make sure they're coated with moly-base grease or engine assembly lube. Soak new lifters in oil to remove trapped air.

Camshaft

Refer to illustration 9.21

Removal

10   Remove the front cover, but leave the timing chain and sprockets in place.

11   Check the camshaft endplay before removing the camshaft. Install a dial indicator on the front of the engine so the plunger of the indicator rests on the end of the camshaft. Push the camshaft as far to the rear of the engine block as it will go and zero the indicator. Push the camshaft to the front of the block as far as it will go and record the movement indicated on the dial indicator. This is the endplay. If the endplay exceeds the service limit given in the specifications, the thrust plate will have to be replaced.

12   Remove the timing chain and sprockets (Section 8).

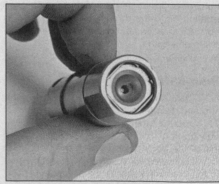

9.8c Check the pushrod seat (arrow) in the top of each lifter for wear

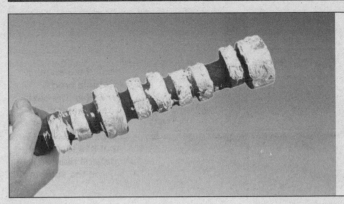

9.21 Apply moly-base grease or engine assembly lube to the lobes and journals on the camshaft prior to installation

13   Remove the bolts and detach the camshaft thrust plate.

14   Carefully pull the camshaft out of the block. Don't damage the bearings with the cam lobes.

Inspection

15   After the camshaft has been removed from the engine, cleaned with solvent and dried, inspect the bearing journals for uneven wear, pitting and evidence of seizure. If the journals are damaged, the bearing inserts in the block are probably damaged as well. Both the camshaft and bearings will have to be replaced.

16   Measure the bearing journals with a micrometer to determine if they're excessively worn or out-of-round.

17   Check the camshaft lobes and bearing journals for heat discoloration, score marks, chipped areas, pitting and uneven wear. If the lobes and journals are in good condition, the camshaft can be reused.

18   Check the bearings in the block for wear and damage. Look for galling, pitting and discolored areas.

19   The inside diameter of each bearing can be determined with a small hole gauge and outside micrometer or an inside micrometer. Subtract the camshaft bearing journal diameter(s) from the corresponding bearing inside diameter(s) to obtain the bearing oil clearance. If it's excessive, new bearings will be required regardless of the condition of the originals.

20   Camshaft bearing replacement requires special tools and expertise that place it outside the scope of the home mechanic. Remove the engine and take the block to an automotive machine shop to ensure the job is done correctly.

Installation

21   Camshaft installation is the reverse of removal. Coat the cam bearings and journals with a thick, even layer of moly-base grease or engine assembly lube **(see illustration)**.

10   Oil pan and oil pump - removal and installation

Note: *This procedure is for removal and installation of the oil pan with the engine in*

the vehicle only. If the engine has been removed for an overhaul, follow Step 11 and Steps 13 through 27.

Removal

1   Drain the engine oil and disconnect the negative cable at the battery. Remove the oil dipstick.

2   Drain the cooling system.

3   Remove the radiator as described in Chapter 3.

4   Raise the vehicle and support it securely on jackstands. Disconnect the starter cable at the starter.

5   Remove the starter from the bellhousing.

6   Remove the four nuts and bolts attaching the sway bar to the chassis and allow the sway bar to hang down.

7   Remove the K-brace.

8   Remove the bolt retaining the flex coupling to the steering gear. Unbolt the steering gear from the chassis and position it forward and down.

9   Remove the engine front insulator-to-support bracket retaining nuts. Loosen the two rear engine support bolts.

10   Raise the front of the engine with a jack. Place a thick wooden block between the jack and the oil pan.

11   Place 1-1/4-inch wood blocks between the front support insulators and the supporting brackets.

12   Place a jack beneath the transmission and raise it just enough to provide removal clearance for the oil pan.

13   Lower the engine onto the spacer blocks and remove the jack.

14   Remove the oil pan bolts.

15   Lower the pan to the crossmember.

16   Remove the two oil pump inlet tube-to-oil pump retaining bolts.

17   Remove the oil pump inlet assembly and allow it to rest in the oil pan.

18   Remove the oil pan from the vehicle. It may be necessary to rotate the crankshaft for the counterweights to clear the pan.

19   Clean all old gasket material from the mating surfaces of the block and the pan.

Installation

20   Remove the rear main bearing cap oil pan seal.

21   Remove the timing cover oil pan seal.

22   Clean all mating surfaces and seal grooves.

23   Install a new oil pan-to-front cover oil seal.

24   Install a new rear main bearing cap seal.

25   Install new oil pan side gaskets on the block. Apply a thin coat of RTV-sealant to both sides of the gaskets.

26   Make sure the tabs on the front and rear seals fit properly into the mating slots in the oil pan side seals. A small amount of RTV-sealant at each joint will help prevent leaks at these critical spots.

27   Clean the inlet tube and screen assembly and place it in the oil pan.

28   Position the oil pan underneath the engine.

29   Lift the inlet tube and screen assembly from the oil pan and secure it to the oil pump with a new gasket. Tighten the two retaining bolts to the specified torque.

30   Attach the oil pan to the engine block and install the bolts. Tighten the bolts to the specified torque, starting from the center and working out in each direction.

31   Raise the engine with a jack and a block of wood underneath the oil pan and remove the wood spacers previously installed under the support brackets.

32   Lower the engine to the correct installed position and install the front and rear engine mount bolts/nuts.

33   The remainder of installation is the reverse of the removal procedure.

34   Start the engine and check carefully for leaks at the oil pan gasket surfaces.

11   Flywheel/driveplate - removal, inspection and installation

This procedure is essentially the same for all engines. Refer to Part A and follow the procedure outlined there.

12   Engine mounts - check and replacement

This procedure is essentially the same for all engines. Refer to Part A and follow the procedure outlined there.

13   Crankshaft oil seals - replacement

Front seal

Refer to illustration 13.6

Note: *The factory recommends special tools for proper seal installation.*

1   Drain the coolant and engine oil (Chapter 1).

2   Remove the radiator.

3   Remove the crankshaft pulley and the timing cover (Section 6).

4   Drive out the oil seal with a pin punch.

2B

5   Clean out the recess in the cover.
6   Coat the outer edge of the new seal with grease and install it using the special tools designed for this operation. As an alternative, a large piece of pipe or a socket can be used to push the new seal in **(see illustration)**. However, use extreme caution as the seal can be damaged easily. Drive in the seal until it's completely seated in the recess. Make sure the spring is properly positioned within the seal.
7   The rest of installation is the reverse of the removal procedure.

Rear seal

Note: *If rear crankshaft oil seal replacement is the only operation being performed, it can be accomplished with the engine in the vehicle. If, however, the oil seal is being replaced along with the rear main bearing, the engine must be removed.*
8   Disconnect the negative battery cable from the battery, then remove the starter.
9   Remove the transmission (Chapter 7).
10   On manual transmission equipped vehicles, remove the pressure plate, disc and clutch assembly. On automatic transmission equipped vehicles, remove the driveplate.
11   Remove the flywheel and engine rear cover plate. **Note:** *Some models incorporate a two-piece, split-lip seal which requires removal of the rear main bearing cap. If this is the case with your vehicle, refer to the procedure in Chapter 2, Part E. One-piece seals*

13.6 If the special tools aren't available, the seal can be installed with a section of pipe or a socket that has the same outside diameter as the seal

can be serviced as follows:
12   Use an awl to punch two holes in the seal. Punch the holes on opposite sides of the crankshaft, just above the bearing cap-to-engine block junction.
13   Thread a sheet metal screw into each punched hole.
14   Use two large screwdrivers or small pry bars to pry against both screws at the same time, removing the seal. Blocks of wood placed against the engine will provide additional leverage.
15   Be very careful when performing this operation - do not damage the seal contact surfaces.
16   Clean the seal recess in the rear of the

engine block and the main bearing cap.
17   Inspect and clean the oil seal contact surface of the crankshaft.
18   Coat the new oil seal with engine oil.
19   Coat the crankshaft with engine oil.
20   Start the seal into the cavity in the back of the engine with the seal lip facing forward, using the special drive tool. Make sure the tool stays in alignment with the crankshaft until the tool contacts the block. See Step 6 for seal installation alternatives.
21   Install the engine rear cover plate.
22   Attach the flywheel (or driveplate) to the crankshaft.
23   The remainder of installation is the reverse of the removal procedure.

Chapter 2 Part C
2.8 liter V6 engine

Contents

Specifications

General

Displacement	2.8 liters
Cylinder numbers (front-to-rear)	
Left (driver's) side	4-5-6
Right side	1-2-3
Firing order	1-4-2-5-3-6

Camshaft

Lobe lift (intake and exhaust)	0.255 in
Allowable lobe lift loss	0.005 in
Theoretical valve lift @ zero lash (intake and exhaust)	0.3730 in
Endplay	
Standard	0.0008 to 0.004 in
Service limit	0.006 in
Journal-to-bearing (oil) clearance	
Standard	0.001 to 0.0026 in
Service limit	0.006 in
Journal diameter	
No. 1	1.6497 to 1.6505 in
No. 2	1.6347 to 1.6355 in
No. 3	1.6197 to 1.6205 in
No. 4	1.6047 to 1.6055 in
Journal runout, maximum (total indicator reading)	0.005 in
Journal out-of-round, maximum (total indicator reading)	0.0003 in
Bearing inside diameter	
No. 1	1.6515 to 1.6523 in
No. 2	1.6365 to 1.6373 in
No. 3	1.6215 to 1.6223 in
No. 4	1.6065 to 1.6073 in
Camshaft gear backlash	0.006 to 0.010 in

Torque specifications

	Ft-lbs
Camshaft gear bolt	30 to 36
Camshaft thrust plate bolts	12 to 15
Crankshaft damper bolt	92 to 103
Cylinder head bolts	
Step 1	29 to 40
Step 2	40 to 51
Step 3	65 to 80

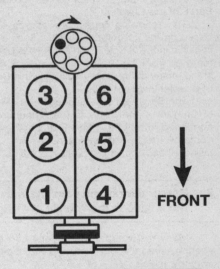

36004-1-SPECS2a HAYNES

Cylinder location and distributor rotation
The blackened terminal on the distributor cap indicates the number one spark plug wire position

Torque specifications (continued)

	Ft-lbs
Exhaust manifold mounting bolts	27 to 49
Exhaust pipe-to-manifold nuts	25 to 35
Flywheel/driveplate bolts	47 to 51
Front cover plate bolts	12 to 15
Front cover bolts	12 to 15
Intake manifold bolts/nuts	
Step 1	3 to 6
Step 2	6 to 11
Step 3	11 to 15
Step 4	15 to 18*
Oil pump inlet tube-to-pump bolt	7 to 9
Oil pump inlet tube-to-main bearing cap bolt	12 to 15
Oil pan bolts	7 to 10
Rocker arm cover bolts	3 to 5
Rocker arm shaft support bolts	43 to 49

Retighten in sequence to 15 to 18 ft-lbs after engine has been run.

1   General information

This Part of Chapter 2 is devoted to in-vehicle repair procedures for the 2.8 liter V6 engine. All information concerning engine removal and installation and engine block and cylinder head overhaul can be found in Part E of this Chapter.

The following repair procedures are based on the assumption that the engine is installed in the vehicle. If the engine has been removed from the vehicle and mounted on a stand, many of the steps outlined in this Part of Chapter 2 will not apply.

The Specifications included in this Part of Chapter 2 apply only to the procedures contained in this Part. Part E of Chapter 2 contains the Specifications necessary for cylinder head and engine block rebuilding.

2   Repair operations possible with the engine in the vehicle

Many major repair operations can be accomplished without removing the engine from the vehicle.

Clean the engine compartment and the exterior of the engine with some type of degreaser before any work is done. It will make the job easier and help keep dirt out of the internal areas of the engine.

Depending on the components involved, it may be helpful to remove the hood to improve access to the engine as repairs are performed (refer to Chapter 11 if necessary). Cover the fenders to prevent damage to the paint. Special pads are available, but an old bedspread or blanket will also work.

If vacuum, exhaust, oil or coolant leaks develop, indicating a need for gasket or seal replacement, the repairs can generally be made with the engine in the vehicle. The intake and exhaust manifold gaskets, timing cover gaskets, oil pan gasket, crankshaft oil seals and cylinder head gaskets are all accessible with the engine in place.

Exterior engine components, such as the intake and exhaust manifolds, the oil pan (and the oil pump), the water pump, the starter motor, the alternator, the distributor and the fuel system components can be removed for repair with the engine in place.

Since the cylinder heads can be removed without pulling the engine, valve component servicing can also be accomplished with the engine in the vehicle. Replacement of the camshaft and timing gears is also possible with the engine in the vehicle.

In extreme cases caused by a lack of necessary equipment, repair or replacement of piston rings, pistons, connecting rods and rod bearings is possible with the engine in the vehicle. However, this practice is not recommended because of the cleaning and preparation work that must be done to the components involved.

3   Top Dead Center (TDC) for number one piston - locating

Note: *The following procedure is based on the assumption that the spark plug wires and distributor are correctly installed. If you are trying to locate TDC to install the distributor correctly, piston position must be determined by feeling for compression at the number one spark plug hole, then aligning the ignition timing marks as described in step 8.*

1   Top Dead Center (TDC) is the highest point in the cylinder that each piston reaches as it travels up-and-down when the crankshaft turns. Each piston reaches TDC on the compression stroke and again on the exhaust stroke, but TDC generally refers to piston position on the compression stroke.

2   Positioning the piston(s) at TDC is an essential part of many procedures such as rocker arm removal, camshaft and timing gear removal and distributor removal.

3   Before beginning this procedure, be sure to place the transmission in Neutral and apply the parking brake or block the rear wheels. Also, disable the ignition system by detaching the coil wire from the center terminal of the distributor cap and grounding it on the block with a jumper wire. Remove the spark plugs (see Chapter 1).

4   In order to bring any piston to TDC, the crankshaft must be turned using one of the methods outlined below. When looking at the front of the engine, normal crankshaft rotation is clockwise.

a)   *The preferred method is to turn the crankshaft with a socket and ratchet attached to the bolt threaded into the front of the crankshaft.*

b)   *A remote starter switch, which may save some time, can also be used. Follow the instructions included with the switch. Once the piston is close to TDC, use a socket and ratchet as described in the previous paragraph.*

c)   *If an assistant is available to turn the ignition switch to the Start position in short bursts, you can get the piston close to TDC without a remote starter switch. Make sure your assistant is out of the vehicle, away from the ignition switch, then use a socket and ratchet as described in Paragraph a) to complete the procedure.*

5   Note the position of the terminal for the number one spark plug wire on the distributor cap. If the terminal isn't marked, follow the plug wire from the number one cylinder spark plug to the cap.

6   Use a felt-tip pen or chalk to make a mark on the distributor body directly under the terminal.

7   Detach the cap from the distributor and set it aside (see Chapter 1 if necessary).

8   Turn the crankshaft (see Paragraph 3 above) until the notch in the crankshaft pulley is aligned with the "TC" mark pointer on the engine front cover.

9   Look at the distributor rotor - it should

be pointing directly at the mark you made on the distributor body.

10   If the rotor is 180-degrees off, the number one piston is at TDC on the exhaust stroke.

11   To get the piston to TDC on the compression stroke, turn the crankshaft one complete turn (360-degrees) clockwise. The rotor should now be pointing at the mark on the distributor. When the rotor is pointing at the number one spark plug wire terminal in the distributor cap and the ignition timing marks are aligned, the number one piston is at TDC on the compression stroke.

12   After the number one piston has been positioned at TDC on the compression stroke, TDC for any of the remaining pistons can be located by turning the crankshaft and following the firing order. Mark the remaining spark plug wire terminal locations on the distributor body just like you did for the number one terminal, then number the marks to correspond with the cylinder numbers. As you turn the crankshaft, the rotor will also turn. When it's pointing directly at one of the marks on the distributor, the piston for that particular cylinder is at TDC on the compression stroke.

4   Rocker arm cover(s) - removal and installation

1   Remove any emission control components that obstruct access to the cover (see Chapter 6).

2   Mark the spark plug wires, then disconnect them from the spark plugs and lay them back out of the way (see Chapter 1).

3   Detach the throttle linkage from the carburetor, if necessary.

4   Remove the rocker arm cover screws and lift the cover off. If it won't come off easily, don't pry it loose. Make sure all screws are removed, then tap lightly on the end of the cover with a rubber mallet or a block of wood and a hammer to break the gasket seal.

5   Clean all traces of gasket and sealer from the cover and cylinder head. Aerosol gasket removers, available from auto parts stores, can be used to ease gasket removal.

6   Coat the rocker cover side of a new gasket with RTV sealer, then stick the gasket to the cover.

7   Install the cover and tighten the screws evenly to the torque listed in this Chapter's Specifications.

8   The remainder of installation is the reverse of the removal steps.

9   Run the engine and check for oil leaks.

5   Rocker arms and pushrods - removal, inspection and installation

Removal

1   Refer to Section 4 and detach the rocker

arm cover(s) from the cylinder head(s).

2   Loosen the rocker arm shaft support bolts two turns at a time, working from the center out, until the bolts can be removed by hand.

3   Lift the rocker assembly and oil baffle off of the cylinder head. The pins will hold the components together.

4   Lift the pushrods out of the engine. Place the pushrods in order in a holder so they can be returned to their original positions.

Inspection

5   Remove the pins and disassemble the rocker arm assembly. Place the parts in order on a clean workbench.

6   Check each rocker arm for wear, cracks and other damage, especially where the pushrods and valve stems contact the rocker arm faces.

7   Make sure the hole at the pushrod end of each rocker arm is open. Plugging can be cleared with a piece of wire.

8   Check each rocker arm bore, and its corresponding position on the rocker shaft, for wear, cracks and galling. If the rocker arms or shaft are damaged, replace them with new ones.

9   Inspect the pushrods for cracks and excessive wear at the ends. Roll each pushrod across a piece of plate glass to see if it's bent (if it wobbles, it's bent).

10   If necessary, remove the plug from each end of the rocker shaft. Drill into one plug and insert a long steel rod through it to knock out the other plug. Knock out the first plug in the same manner.

11   If the rocker shaft plugs were removed, tap in new ones with a hammer and suitable drift.

12   Assemble the rocker assembly. Lubricate all friction points with engine oil or assembly lube.

13   Install new cotter pins in the ends of the rocker shaft. Be sure the rocker shaft notches face down when the shaft is installed.

Installation

14   Coat each end of each pushrod with assembly lube, then install them in the engine. If you are reinstalling the original pushrods, be sure to return them to their original positions.

15   Coat the rocker arm pads with Lubriplate or equivalent.

16   Loosen the valve adjusting screws several turns.

17   Install the oil baffle and rocker assembly on the engine. The notch on the shaft should face down.

18   Position the rocker arm ball ends in the pushrods.

19   Tighten the rocker shaft support bolts two turns at a time, from the center out, to the torque listed in this Chapter's Specifications.

20   The remainder of installation is the reverse of removal.

21   Adjust the valve clearances (see Chapter 1).

22   Run the engine and check for leaks.

6   Valve springs, retainers and seals - replacement

Refer to illustrations 6.9a, 6.9b and 6.15

Note: *Broken valve springs and defective valve stem seals can be replaced without removing the cylinder heads. Two special tools and a compressed air source are normally required to perform this operation, so read through this Section carefully and rent or buy the tools before beginning the job. If compressed air isn't available, a length of nylon rope can be used to keep the valves from falling into the cylinder during this procedure.*

1   Refer to Section 4 and remove the rocker arm cover from the affected cylinder head. If all of the valve stem seals are being replaced, remove both rocker arm covers.

2   Remove the spark plug from the cylinder which has the defective component. If all of the valve stem seals are being replaced, all of the spark plugs should be removed.

3   Turn the crankshaft until the piston in the affected cylinder is at top dead center on the compression stroke (refer to Section 3 for instructions). If you're replacing all of the valve stem seals, begin with cylinder number one and work on the valves for one cylinder at a time. Move from cylinder-to-cylinder following the firing order sequence (see this Chapter's Specifications).

4   Thread an adapter into the spark plug hole and connect an air hose from a compressed air source to it. Most auto parts stores can supply the air hose adapter. **Note:** *Many cylinder compression gauges utilize a screw-in fitting that may work with your air hose quick-disconnect fitting.*

5   Remove the rocker arm assembly(ies) and pull out the pushrod(s) for the cylinder(s) being serviced. If all of the valve stem seals are being replaced, all of the rocker arms and pushrods should be removed (refer to Section 5).

6   Apply compressed air to the cylinder. **Warning:** *The piston may be forced down by compressed air, causing the crankshaft to turn suddenly. If the wrench used when positioning the number one piston at TDC is still attached to the bolt in the crankshaft nose, it could cause damage or injury when the crankshaft moves.*

7   The valves should be held in place by the air pressure. If the valve faces or seats are in poor condition, leaks may prevent air pressure from retaining the valves - refer to the alternative procedure below.

8   If you don't have access to compressed air, an alternative method can be used. Position the piston at a point just before TDC on the compression stroke, then feed a long piece of nylon rope through the spark plug hole until it fills the combustion chamber. Be

2C

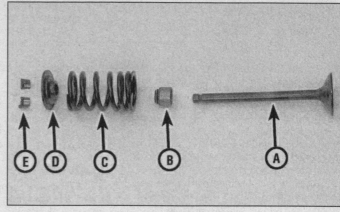

6.9b Valve and related components

A Valve   C Spring   E Keepers
B Stem seal   D Retainer

6.9a After compressing the spring, remove the keepers with a magnet

sure to leave the end of the rope hanging out of the engine so it can be removed easily. Use a large ratchet and socket to rotate the crankshaft in the normal direction of rotation until slight resistance is felt.

9   Stuff shop rags into the cylinder head holes above and below the valves to prevent parts and tools from falling into the engine, then use a valve spring compressor to compress the spring. Remove the locks with small needle-nose pliers or a magnet **(see illustrations)**. **Note:** *A couple of different types of tools are available for compressing the valve springs with the head in place. One type grips the lower spring coils and presses on the retainer as the knob is turned, while the other type, shown in illustration 6.4, utilizes the rocker shaft for leverage. Both types work very well, although the lever type is usually less expensive.*

10   Remove the spring retainer and valve spring, then remove the stem seal with a seal removal tool or pliers. **Note:** *If air pressure fails to hold the valve in the closed position during this operation, the valve face or seat is probably damaged. If so, the cylinder head will have to be removed for additional repair operations.*

11   Wrap a rubber band or tape around the top of the valve stem so the valve won't fall into the combustion chamber, then release the air pressure. **Note:** *If a rope was used instead of air pressure, turn the crankshaft slightly in the direction opposite normal rotation.*

12   Inspect the valve stem for damage. Rotate the valve in the guide and check the end for eccentric movement, which would indicate that the valve is bent.

13   Move the valve up-and-down in the guide and make sure it doesn't bind. If the valve stem binds, either the valve is bent or the guide is damaged. In either case, the head will have to be removed for repair.

14   Reapply air pressure to the cylinder to retain the valve in the closed position, then remove the tape or rubber band from the

6.15 An appropriately sized socket can be used as a seal installer

valve stem. If a rope was used instead of air pressure, rotate the crankshaft in the normal direction of rotation until slight resistance is felt.

15   Lubricate the valve stem with engine oil and install a new seal **(see illustration)**.

16   Install the spring in position over the valve.

17   Install the valve spring retainer. Compress the valve spring and care
fully position the locks in the groove. Apply a small dab of grease to the inside of each keeper to hold it in place.

18   Remove the pressure from the spring tool and make sure the locks are seated.

19   Disconnect the air hose and remove the adapter from the spark plug hole. If a rope was used in place of air pressure, pull it out of the cylinder.

20   Refer to Section 5 and install the rocker arm(s) and pushrod(s).

21   Install the spark plug(s) and hook up the wire(s).

22   Refer to Section 4 and install the rocker arm cover(s).

23   Start and run the engine, then check for oil leaks and unusual sounds coming from the rocker arm cover area.

7   Intake manifold - removal and installation

Refer to illustration 7.7

Removal

1   Disconnect the negative battery cable from the battery.

2   Remove the air cleaner (see Chapter 4) and disconnect the accelerator cable.

3   Drain the cooling system (see Chapter 1). Disconnect the radiator hose from the thermostat housing and the by-pass hose from the intake manifold (see Chapter 3).

4   Remove the distributor (see Chapter 5).

5   Remove the fuel filter (see Chapter 1) and fuel line.

6   Remove the rocker arm covers (see Section 4).

7   Remove the intake manifold bolts and nuts **(see illustration)**. **Note:** *A special crows-foot wrench (available at most auto parts stores) is required to loosen or tighten bolt number six when the carburetor is installed. If you don't have the special tool, remove the carburetor (see Chapter 4).*

8   Remove any wires, hoses or other com-

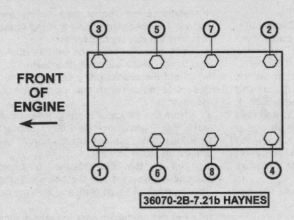

FRONT OF ENGINE ←

36070-2B-7.21b HAYNES

7.7 Intake manifold bolt locations and tightening sequence

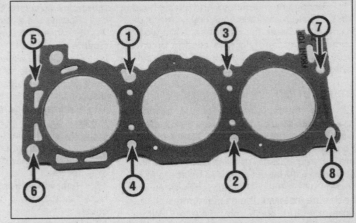

9.10 Cylinder head bolt loosening and tightening sequence

2C

ponents that would interfere with removal, then lift the manifold off. If the manifold is stuck, tap it lightly with a plastic mallet to break the gasket seal. If absolutely necessary, pry the manifold off, but pry against a casting protrusion, not against any gasket mating surfaces, or vacuum and oil leaks may occur.

Installation

Note: *The mating surfaces of the cylinder heads, block and manifold must be perfectly clean when the manifold is installed. Gasket removal solvents in aerosol cans are available at most auto parts stores and may be helpful when removing old gasket material that's stuck to the heads and manifold. Be sure to follow the directions printed on the container.*

9   Use a gasket scraper to remove all traces of sealant and old gasket material, then clean the mating surfaces with lacquer thinner or acetone. If there's old sealant or oil on the mating surfaces when the manifold is installed, oil or vacuum leaks may develop. When working on the heads and block, cover the lifter valley with shop rags to keep dirt out of the engine. Use a vacuum cleaner to remove any gasket material that falls into the intake ports in the heads.

10   Use a tap of the correct size to chase the threads in the bolt holes, then use compressed air (if available) to remove the debris from the holes. **Warning:** *Wear safety glasses or a face shield to protect your eyes when using compressed air! Remove excess carbon deposits and corrosion from the exhaust and coolant passages in the heads and manifold.*

11   Coat the gasket mating surfaces with a thin layer of sealant.

12   Install the gasket. Be sure to place the tab on the right head gasket into the cutout in the intake manifold gasket.

13   Carefully set the manifold in place while the sealant is still wet. **Caution:** *Don't disturb the gasket and don't move the manifold fore-and-aft after it contacts the gasket.*

14   Coat the manifold bolt bosses with sealant. Install the bolts and nuts, then tighten them to the torque listed in this Chap-

ter's Specifications in four steps, following the sequence in illustration 7.7. **Note:** *If the carburetor is on the manifold, the same special tool noted in Section 7 paragraph 7 will be necessary to torque bolt number six accurately.*

15   The remainder of installation is the reverse of removal.

16   Start the engine and check carefully for leaks at the intake manifold joints.

17   Recheck the mounting bolt and nut torque.

8   Exhaust manifolds - removal and installation

Warning: *The engine must be completely cool (allow it to cool for several hours) before attempting this procedure - the exhaust manifolds remain very hot after the engine is shut down and can cause severe burns.*

Removal

1   Remove the air cleaner (see Chapter 4).

2   On the right manifold, remove the heat shroud.

3   Raise the vehicle and support it securely on jackstands, then detach the exhaust pipe from the manifold. Discard the exhaust pipe gasket.

4   Remove the thermactor components as necessary to provide removal access (see Chapter 6).

5   Disconnect the choke heat tubes from the carburetor.

6   Remove the manifold fasteners, then take the manifold off the engine.

Installation

7   Check the manifold for cracks and make sure the fastener threads are clean and undamaged. The manifold and cylinder head mating surfaces must be clean before the manifolds are installed - use a gasket scraper to remove all carbon deposits and/or gasket material.

8   Place a new gasket on the manifold

(using two bolts to hold it in position), then position the manifold on the head and install the remainder of the fasteners. Tighten them to the torque listed in this Chapter's Specifications, working from the center out.

9   Install a new exhaust pipe-to-manifold gasket, then tighten the pipe-to-manifold fasteners to the torque listed in this Chapter's Specifications.

10   The remaining installation steps are the reverse of removal.

11   Start the engine and check for exhaust leaks.

9   Cylinder heads - removal and installation

Refer to illustration 9.10

Caution: *The engine must be completely cool when the heads are removed. Failure to allow the engine to cool off could result in head warpage.* **Note:** *Guide studs are recommended when installing the cylinder heads. These can be made by cutting the heads off of a pair of extra cylinder head bolts, grinding a taper and cutting a screwdriver slot in the cut ends.*

Removal

1   Disconnect the negative battery cable from the battery.

2   Remove the air cleaner (see Chapter 4) and disconnect the accelerator linkage.

3   Drain the cooling system (see Chapter 1).

4   Remove the distributor (see Chapter 5).

5   Disconnect the radiator hose from the thermostat housing and the coolant by-pass hose from the intake manifold (see Chapter 3).

6   Remove the rocker arm covers (see Section 4).

7   Remove the rocker arms and pushrods (see Section 5).

8   Remove the intake manifold (see Section 7).

9   Remove the exhaust manifold(s) (see Section 8).

10   Loosen the cylinder head bolts in several stages, following the specified sequence **(see illustration)**.

11   Remove the head bolts and lift the head off. If it is stuck, try tapping lightly with a plastic mallet to break the gasket seal. If it won't come off, pry carefully at a casting protrusion, but do not pry against any gasket surfaces or leaks may develop.

Installation

12   The mating surfaces of the cylinder heads and block must be perfectly clean when the heads are installed. Use a gasket scraper to remove all traces of carbon and old gasket material, then clean the mating surfaces with lacquer thinner or acetone. If there's oil on the mating surfaces when the heads are installed, the gaskets may not seal correctly and leaks may develop. When working on the block, cover the lifter valley with shop rags to keep debris out of the engine. Use a vacuum cleaner to remove any debris that falls into the cylinders.

13   Check the block and head mating surfaces for nicks, deep scratches and other damage. If damage is slight, it can be removed with a file - if it's excessive, machining (must be done by an automotive machine shop) may be the only alternative.

14   Use a tap of the correct size to chase the threads in the head bolt holes. Mount each bolt in a vise and run a die down the threads to remove corrosion and restore the threads. Dirt, corrosion, sealant and damaged threads will affect torque readings.

15   Install the new gaskets on the block. The gaskets are marked FRONT and TOP to indicate correct position. Gaskets are not interchangeable between left and right sides.

16   Install guide studs in two of the cylinder head bolt holes (see the Note at the beginning of this Section for instructions on fabricating these studs).

17   Install the head over the guide studs.

18   Install head bolts in the unoccupied holes and tighten them, using just your fingers. Remove the guide studs, then install bolts in their holes and tighten them with fingers.

19   Tighten the head bolts in three stages to the correct torque (see this Chapter's Specifications). Tighten them in the order shown in illustration 9.10.

20   The remaining installation steps are the reverse of removal.

21   Run the engine and check for coolant and oil leaks.

10   Engine front cover - removal and installation

Removal

1   Remove the oil pan (see Section 14).
2   Drain the cooling system (see Chapter 1).
3   Remove the fan and radiator (see Chapter 3).
4   Remove the air conditioning compressor (if equipped) and set it aside. DO NOT disconnect any refrigerant lines!
5   Remove the alternator and thermactor

pump drivebelts (see Chapter 1).
6   Remove the alternator (see Chapter 5).
7   Remove the thermactor pump (see Chapter 6).
8   Remove the water pump (see Chapter 3).
9   Remove the small outer bolts at the front of the crankshaft drivebelt pulley and disconnect the pulley from the crankshaft.
10   Remove the front cover bolts and take the front cover off the engine. If it's stuck, tap it gently with a plastic mallet to break the gasket seal. Do not pry between the gasket surfaces or you may damage them and leaks may develop.
11   Remove the front cover guide sleeves. Note that the sleeve chamfers face the front cover.
12   Remove two bolts that secure the front cover plate. Remove the plate and gasket.

Installation

13   The mating surfaces of the cylinder block, front cover plate and front cover must be perfectly clean when the plate and cover are installed. Use a gasket scraper to remove all traces of carbon and old gasket material, then clean the mating surfaces with lacquer thinner or acetone.

14   Apply a thin, even layer of sealant to the mating surfaces on the engine and the rear side of the front cover plate.

15   Place the cover plate gasket on the engine, then install the cover plate (**see illustration 10.12**). Temporarily install four of the front cover screws to position the cover plate accurately. Install both cover plate bolts, tighten the bolts to the torque listed in this Chapter's Specifications and remove the four screws.

16   Install new seal rings on the guide sleeves.

17   Install the guide sleeves, without sealant, in the cylinder block. The sleeve chamfers face the front cover.

18   Apply a thin, even coat of sealant to the gasket surface on the front cover. Stick the gasket to the cover.

19   Place the front cover on the engine. Install all of the cover screws and tighten them two or three turns.

20   Place a centering tool (available at most auto parts stores) in the front cover oil seal hole.

21   Tighten the front cover screws to the torque listed in this Chapter's Specifications.

22   Remove the centering tool. The remaining installation steps are the reverse of removal.

23   Run the engine and check for coolant and oil leaks.

11   Timing gears - check, removal and installation

Backlash and endplay check

1   Drain the cooling system (see Chapter 1).
2   Remove the oil pan (see Section 14).
3   Remove the front cover (see Section 10).

4   Remove the rocker arm covers (see Section 4). Loosen the valve adjusting screws to relieve the valve spring tension.
5   Set up a dial indicator with its pointer against one of the camshaft gear teeth.
6   Hold the crankshaft gear from turning and rotate the camshaft gear against the dial indicator.
7   Note the indicator reading (gear backlash). If it is excessive (see this Chapter's Specifications), replace the camshaft and crankshaft gears as a set.
8   Set up the dial indicator to check camshaft endplay. Push the camshaft gear back against the thrust plate and zero the dial indicator.
9   Pry the camshaft gear forward against the dial indicator and note the reading (camshaft endplay). If it is excessive (see this Chapter's Specifications), replace the camshaft thrust plate or spacer ring (see Section 13). These are available in two thicknesses.

Removal

10   Remove the camshaft timing gear bolt. Tap the timing gear lightly with a plastic mallet to separate it from the camshaft.
11   Remove the crankshaft timing gear with a gear puller.
12   If necessary, remove the timing gear Woodruff keys.

Installation

Refer to illustration 11.15

13   Install the Woodruff keys (if removed).
14   Install the camshaft gear and make sure it seats securely against the spacer. Tighten the camshaft gear bolt to the correct torque

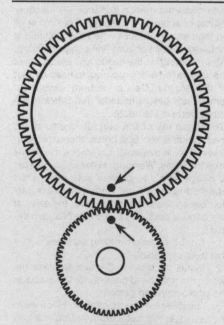

36060-2c-12.27 HAYNES

11.15 Timing marks on the gears must be directly opposite each other after the gears are installed

(see the torque listed in this Chapter's Specifications).

15 Install the crankshaft gear. Be sure the alignment marks on crankshaft and camshaft gears are positioned directly opposite each other **(see illustration)**.

16 The remaining installation steps are the reverse of removal.

17 Run the engine and check for leaks.

12 Valve lifters - removal, inspection and installation

Removal

Refer to illustration 12.2

1 Remove the cylinder head(s) (see Section 9).

2 There are several ways to extract the lifters from their bores. Special tools designed to grip and remove lifters are manufactured by many tool companies and are widely available, but may not be needed in every case. On engines without a lot of varnish buildup, the lifters can often be removed with a small magnet **(see illustration)** or even with your fingers. A machinist's scribe with a bent end can be used to pull the lifters out by positioning the point under the retainer ring in the top of each lifter. **Caution:** *Don't use pliers to remove the lifters unless you intend to replace them with new ones (along with the camshaft). The pliers may damage the precision machined and hardened lifters, rendering them useless. On engines with a lot of sludge and varnish, work the lifters up and down, using carburetor cleaner spray to loosen the deposits.*

3 Before removing the lifters, arrange to store them in a clearly labeled box to ensure that they're reinstalled in their original locations.

4 Remove the lifters and store them where they won't get dirty.

Inspection

5 Clean the lifters with solvent and dry them thoroughly without mixing them up.

6 Check each lifter wall, pushrod seat and foot for scuffing, score marks and uneven wear. Each lifter foot (the surface that rides on the cam lobe) must be slightly convex, although this can be difficult to determine by eye. **Note:** *Placing the foot of one lifter against the side of another may help you determine if the foot is convex. If the base of the lifter is concave, the lifters and camshaft must be replaced. If the lifter walls are damaged or worn (which isn't very likely), inspect the lifter bores in the engine block as well.*

7 If new lifters are being installed, a new camshaft must also be installed. If a new camshaft is installed, then use new lifters as well. Never install used lifters unless the original camshaft is used and the lifters can be reinstalled in their original locations!

Installation

8 The original lifters, if they're being reinstalled, must be returned to their original locations. Coat them with moly-base grease or engine assembly lube.

9 Install the lifters in the bores.

10 The remaining installation steps are the reverse of removal.

11 Adjust the valve clearances (see Chapter 1).

13 Camshaft - removal, inspection and installation

Camshaft lobe lift check

1 In order to determine the extent of cam lobe wear, the lobe lift should be checked prior to camshaft removal. Refer to Section 4 and remove the rocker arm covers. The rocker arm assembly must also be removed (Section 5), but leave the pushrods in place.

2 Position the number one piston at TDC on the compression stroke (see Section 3).

3 Beginning with the number one cylinder, mount a dial indicator on the engine and position the plunger in-line with and resting on the first pushrod.

4 Zero the dial indicator, then very slowly turn the crankshaft in the normal direction of rotation until the indicator needle stops and begins to move in the opposite direction. The point at which it stops indicates maximum cam lobe lift.

5 Record this figure for future reference, then reposition the piston at TDC on the compression stroke.

6 Move the dial indicator to the remaining number one cylinder pushrod and repeat the check. Be sure to record the results for each valve.

7 Repeat the check for the remaining valves. Since each piston must be at TDC on the compression stroke for this procedure, work from cylinder-to-cylinder following the firing order sequence.

8 After the check is complete, compare the results to this Chapter's Specifications. If camshaft lobe lift is less than specified, cam lobe wear has occurred and a new camshaft should be installed.

Removal

9 Remove the rocker arm covers (see Section 4).

10 Remove the rocker arms and pushrods (see Section 5).

11 Remove the intake manifold (see Section 7).

12 Remove the cylinder heads (see Section 9).

13 Remove the lifters (see Section 12).

14 Remove the oil pan (see Section 14).

15 Remove the engine front cover (see Section 10).

16 Remove the camshaft timing gear bolt **(see illustration 11.12)**.

17 Remove the camshaft thrust plate screws and take off the thrust plate.

18 Carefully pull the camshaft from the block, rotating it as you pull. Thread a long bolt into the timing gear bolt hole to act as a handle. Use both hands and carefully support the camshaft near the block. Work slowly and carefully to prevent damaging the camshaft bearing surfaces during removal.

19 Remove the Woodruff key and spacer ring from the camshaft.

Inspection

20 Refer to Part A, Section 7, for the camshaft and bearing inspection procedure. Lifter inspection procedures are covered in Section 12.

Bearing replacement

21 Camshaft bearing replacement requires special tools and expertise that place it outside the scope of the home mechanic. Take the block to an automotive machine shop to ensure that the job is done correctly.

Installation

22 Lubricate the camshaft bearing journals and cam lobes with moly-base grease or engine assembly lube.

23 Slide the camshaft into the engine. Support the cam near the block and be careful not to scrape or nick the bearings.

24 Install the spacer ring with its chamfered

12.2 If the lifters are not heavily coated with varnish, it may be possible to remove them with a magnet

2C

side toward the camshaft.

25   Install the camshaft Woodruff key.

26   Apply moly-base grease or engine assembly lube to the friction surfaces on both sides of the thrust plate. Install the thrust plate so it covers the oil gallery, then tighten the attaching bolts to the torque listed in this Chapter's Specifications.

27   The remaining installation steps are the reverse of removal.

28   Before starting the engine, refill it with oil and install a new oil filter (see Chapter 1).

14   Oil pan and pump - removal and installation

Removal

1   Disconnect the negative battery cable from the battery.

2   Remove the fan shroud bolts and place the shroud over the fan (see Chapter 3).

3   If necessary for access, jack up the vehicle and place it securely on jackstands. DO NOT get under a vehicle that is supported only by a jack!

4   Drain the engine oil and replace the drain plug (see Chapter 1).

5   Unbolt the steering gear from the crossmember (see Chapter 10). Move the steering gear so it rests on the frame and provides removal access for the oil pan.

6   Remove the engine mount nuts (see Section 18).

7   Place a jack beneath the engine oil pan. Use a block of wood between the jack and engine to prevent damage. Raise the engine, place 2 X 4 wooden blocks beneath the engine mounts and lower the jack.

8   Remove the four bolts securing the rear K-braces.

9   Remove the oil pan mounting bolts. Lower the pan to the frame. If it is stuck, tap it lightly with a rubber mallet to break the gasket seal. Reach into the oil pan and remove the oil pump and pick-up screen attaching bolts. Lower the oil pump, intermediate shaft and pick-up tube into the oil pan.

10   Take the oil pan out. If necessary, rotate the crankshaft so the oil pan clears the crankshaft throws.

Installation

11   Use a gasket scraper or putty knife to remove all traces of gasket material and sealant from the pan, block and front cover.

12   Clean the mating surfaces with lacquer thinner or acetone. Make sure the block and front cover bolt holes are clean.

13   Check the oil pan flange for distortion, particularly around the bolt holes. If necessary, place the pan on a block of wood and use a hammer to flatten and restore the gasket surface.

14   Remove the old rubber seals from the rear main bearing cap and engine front cover, then clean the grooves.

15   Install new seals. Use gasket contact

adhesive to hold the seals in place, then apply a bead of RTV sealant to the block-to-seal junctions.

16   Stick new gaskets to the engine with gasket contact adhesive.

17   Position the oil pump and inlet tube in the oil pan. **Caution:** *Be sure the intermediate shaft is installed in the oil pump, or the pump won't turn when the engine is run.*

18   Install the oil pump, then the oil pan. Tighten the bolts to the torque listed in this Chapter's Specifications, in stages, starting from the front and working clockwise.

19   The remaining installation steps are the reverse of removal.

20   Install a new oil filter (see Chapter 1). Fill the engine with oil.

21   Run the engine and check for leaks.

15   Crankshaft oil seals - replacement

Front seal - engine front cover in place

1   Drain the cooling system and remove the drivebelts (see Chapter 1).

2   Remove the radiator (Chapter 3).

3   Remove the crankshaft drivebelt pulley.

4   Remove the seal with a slide hammer and seal puller. Tools are available from rental outlets.

5   Check the seal bore and crankshaft, as well as the seal contact surface on the crankshaft pulley, for nicks or burrs. Position the new seal in the bore with the open end of the seal facing IN.

6   A small amount of oil applied to the outer edge of the seal will make installation easier - don't overdo it!

7   Carefully drive the seal into the bore until it seats against the front cover. Special tools are available, but if you don't have them, use a hammer and a socket the same diameter as the seal to drive the seal in. **Note:** *A piece of pipe can be used if a socket isn't available.*

8   Reinstall the crankshaft pulley and tighten its bolt (see the torque listed in this Chapter's Specifications).

9   The remaining installation steps are the reverse of removal.

10   Run the engine and check for leaks.

Front seal - front cover removed

11   Support the front cover on wooden blocks, then drive out the seal with a punch and hammer.

12   Check the seal bore in the front cover for nicks or burrs.

13   Apply a thin coat of clean engine oil to the outer circumference of the seal.

14   Position the new seal with its lip facing IN. Drive in the new seal with a seal driver. If a seal driver isn't available, use a socket or piece of pipe the same diameter as the seal.

Rear seal

15   Remove the transmission (see Chapter 7).

16   Remove the clutch (if equipped) (see Chapter 8).

17   Remove the flywheel (see Section 16).

18   Remove the engine rear plate.

19   With a sharp awl or similar tool, punch two holes in the seal on opposite sides just above the point where the main bearing cap meets the cylinder block.

20   Thread a sheet metal screw into each hole. Pry against the sheet metal screws with two large screwdrivers or small pry bars to remove the seal. **Note:** *If you need a fulcrum to pry against, use small blocks of wood.* **Caution:** *Don't scratch or gouge the crankshaft seal surface.*

21   Clean the oil seal bore in the block and main bearing cap. Check the seal bore and crankshaft sealing surface for nicks or burrs.

22   Apply a thin coat of clean engine oil to the outer diameter of the seal. Apply a thin coat of Lubriplate or equivalent to the contact surfaces of the seal and crankshaft.

23   Position the seal in the bore with its open end facing IN.

24   Drive the seal in with a seal driver until it is securely seated. Use a socket or piece of pipe the same diameter as the seal if a seal driver isn't available.

16   Flywheel/driveplate - removal and installation

1   Raise the vehicle and support it securely on jackstands, then refer to Chapter 7 and remove the transmission. If it's leaking, now would be a very good time to replace the front pump seal/O-ring (automatic transmission only).

2   Remove the pressure plate and clutch disc (see Chapter 8) (manual transmission equipped vehicles). Now is a good time to check/replace the clutch components and pilot bearing.

3   Use a center-punch to make alignment marks on the flywheel/driveplate and crankshaft to ensure correct alignment during reinstallation.

4   Remove the bolts that secure the flywheel/driveplate to the crankshaft. If the crankshaft turns, wedge a screwdriver through the starter opening to jam the flywheel.

5   Remove the flywheel/driveplate from the crankshaft. Since the flywheel is fairly heavy, be sure to support it while removing the last bolt.

6   Clean the flywheel to remove grease and oil. Inspect the surface for cracks, rivet grooves, burned areas and score marks. Light scoring can be removed with emery cloth. Check for cracked and broken ring gear teeth. Lay the flywheel on a flat surface and use a straightedge to check for warpage.

7   Clean and inspect the mating surfaces of the flywheel/driveplate and the crankshaft. If the crankshaft rear seal is leaking, replace it

before reinstalling the flywheel/driveplate.

8   Position the flywheel/driveplate against the crankshaft. Be sure to align the marks made during removal. Note that some engines have an alignment dowel or staggered bolt holes to ensure correct installation. Before installing the bolts, apply thread locking compound to the threads.

9   Wedge a screwdriver through the starter motor opening to keep the flywheel/driveplate from turning as you tighten the bolts to the torque listed in this Chapter's the torque listed in this Chapter's Specifications.

10   The remainder of installation is the reverse of the removal procedure.

17 Engine mounts - check and replacement

1   Engine mounts seldom require attention, but broken or deteriorated mounts should be replaced immediately or the added strain placed on the driveline components may cause damage or wear.

Check

2   During the check, the engine must be raised slightly to remove the weight from the mounts.

3   Raise the vehicle and support it securely on jackstands, then position a jack under the engine oil pan. Place a large block of wood between the jack head and the oil pan, then carefully raise the engine just enough to take the weight off the mounts. **Warning:** *DO NOT place any part of your body under the engine when it's supported only by a jack!*

4   Check the mounts to see if the rubber is cracked, hardened or separated from the metal plates. Sometimes the rubber will split right down the center.

5   Check for relative movement between the mount plates and the engine or frame (use a large screwdriver or pry bar to attempt to move the mounts). If movement is noted, lower the engine and tighten the mount fasteners.

6   Rubber preservative should be applied to the mounts to slow deterioration.

Replacement

7   Disconnect the negative battery cable from the battery, then raise the vehicle and support it securely on jackstands (if not already done).

8   Remove the fasteners and detach the mount from the frame.

9   Raise the engine slightly with a jack or hoist (make sure the fan doesn't hit the radiator or shroud). Remove the mount-to-block bolts and detach the mount.

10   Installation is the reverse of removal. Use thread locking compound on the mount bolts and be sure to tighten them securely.

2C

Notes

Camshaft

Lobe lift
  1979
     Intake .... 0.2373 in
     Exhaust .... 0.2474 in
  1980 through 1982 (intake and exhaust).. 0.2375 in
  1983 on (except HO)
     Intake .... 0.2375 in
     Exhaust .... 0.2474 in
  1983 through 1985 (HO)
     Intake .... 0.2600 in
     Exhaust .... 0.2780 in
  1986 on (HO) (intake and exhaust) .... 0.2780 in
  1993 (HO Cobra) .... 0.2822 in

Theoretical valve lift @ zero lash
  1979
     Intake .... 0.3823 in
     Exhaust .... 0.3980 in
  1980 through 1982 (intake and exhaust).. 0.3753 in
  1983 on (except HO)
     Intake .... 0.3753 in
     Exhaust .... 0.3909 in
  1983 through 1985 (HO)
     Intake .... 0.4130 in
     Exhaust .... 0.4420 in
  1986 on (HO) (intake and exhaust) .... 0.4420 in
  1993 (HO Cobra) .... 0.4797 in

Endplay
  1984 through 1987
     Standard .... 0.001 to 0.007 in
     Service limit... 0.009 in
  1988 on
     Standard .... 0.0005 to 0.0055 in
     Service limit... 0.009 in

Journal diameter
  No. 1 .... 2.0805 to 2.0815 in
  No. 2 .... 2.0655 to 2.0665 in
  No. 3 .... 2.0505 to 2.0515 in
  No. 4 .... 2.0355 to 2.0365 in
  No. 5 .... 2.0205 to 2.0215 in

Bearing inside diameter
  No. 1 .... 2.0825 to 2.0835 in
  No. 2 .... 2.0675 to 2.0685 in
  No. 3 .... 2.0525 to 2.0535 in
  No. 4 .... 2.0375 to 2.0385 in
  No. 5 .... 2.0225 to 2.0235 in

Journal-to-bearing (oil) clearance
  Standard.. 0.001 to 0.003 in
  Service limit .... 0.006 in
Runout limit.. 0.005 in (total indicator reading)
Out-of-round limit .... 0.0005 in (total indicator reading)
Camshaft gear backlash.. 0.006 to 0.011 in
Front bearing location.. 0.005 to 0.020 in below front face of block

Torque specifications

                                                             Ft-lbs

Camshaft sprocket bolt... 40 to 45
Camshaft thrust plate-to-engine block bolts............................ 9 to 12
Timing chain cover bolts... 12 to 18
Cylinder head bolts
  All except 1993 flanged bolts
     Step 1.. 55 to 65
     Step 2.. 65 to 72
  1993 flanged bolts
     Step 1.. 25 to 35
     Step 2.. 45 to 55
     Step 3.. Tighten all bolts an additional 1/4 turn
Vibration damper-to-crankshaft bolt .... 70 to 90
Exhaust manifold bolts
  All except 1993 HO Cobra .... 18 to 24
  1993 HO Cobra .... 26 to 32

Torque specifications

	Ft-lbs
Upper intake manifold bolts	12 to 18
Intake manifold-to-cylinder head bolts	23 to 25*
Oil filter insert-to-engine block adapter bolt	20 to 30
Oil pan mounting bolts	
1979	
First step	
Large bolts	11 to 13
Small bolts	7 to 9
Second step	
Large bolts	15 to 17
Small bolts	10 to 12
1980 through 1987	9 to 11
1988 on	6 to 9
Oil pump mounting bolts	22 to 32
Oil pick-up tube-to-oil pump bolts	
1979 through 1987	10 to 15
1988 on	12 to 18
Oil pick-up tube-to-main bearing cap nut	22 to 32
Drivebelt pulley-to-vibration damper bolts	35 to 50
Rocker cover-to-cylinder head bolts	10 to 13
Rocker arm fulcrum bolts	18 to 25
Flywheel/driveplate mounting bolts	75 to 85

After assembly, retorque with the engine hot

1   General information

This Part of Chapter 2 is devoted to in-vehicle repair procedures for the 3.8L V6 and V8 engines. All information concerning engine removal and installation and engine block and cylinder head overhaul can be found in Part E of this Chapter.

The following repair procedures are based on the assumption that the engine is installed in the vehicle. If the engine has been removed from the vehicle and mounted on a stand, many of the steps outlined in this Part of Chapter 2 will not apply.

The Specifications included in this Part of Chapter 2 apply only to the procedures contained in this Part. Part E of Chapter 2 contains the Specifications necessary for cylinder head and engine block rebuilding.

2   Repair operations possible with the engine in the vehicle

Many major repair operations can be accomplished without removing the engine from the vehicle.

Clean the engine compartment and the exterior of the engine with some type of pressure washer before any work is done. It will make the job easier and help keep dirt out of the internal areas of the engine.

It may help to remove the hood to improve access to the engine as repairs are performed (refer to Chapter 11 if necessary).

If vacuum, exhaust, oil or coolant leaks develop, indicating a need for gasket or seal replacement, the repairs can generally be made with the engine in the vehicle. The intake and exhaust manifold gaskets, timing cover gasket, oil pan gasket, crankshaft oil seals and cylinder head gaskets are all accessible with the engine in place.

Exterior engine components, such as the intake and exhaust manifolds, the oil pan (and the oil pump), the water pump, the starter motor, the alternator, the distributor and the fuel system components can be removed for repair with the engine in place.

Since the cylinder heads can be removed without pulling the engine, valve component servicing can also be accomplished with the engine in the vehicle. Replacement of the timing chain and sprockets is also possible with the engine in the vehicle.

In extreme cases caused by a lack of necessary equipment, repair or replacement of piston rings, pistons, connecting rods and rod bearings is possible with the engine in the vehicle. However, this practice is not recommended because of the cleaning and preparation work that must be done to the components involved.

3   Top Dead Center (TDC) for number one piston - locating

Refer to illustration 3.6

1   Top Dead Center (TDC) is the highest point in the cylinder that each piston reaches as it travels up-and-down when the crankshaft turns. Each piston reaches TDC on the compression stroke and again on the exhaust stroke, but TDC generally refers to piston position on the compression stroke. The timing marks on the vibration damper installed on the front of the crankshaft are referenced to the number one piston at TDC on the compression stroke.

2   Positioning the piston(s) at TDC is an essential part of many procedures such as rocker arm removal, valve adjustment, timing chain and sprocket replacement and distributor removal.

3   In order to bring any piston to TDC, the crankshaft must be turned using one of the methods outlined below. When looking at the front of the engine, normal crankshaft rotation is clockwise. **Warning:** *Before beginning this procedure, be sure to place the transmission in Neutral and ground the coil wire attached to the center terminal of the distributor cap to disable the ignition system.*

a) *The preferred method is to turn the crankshaft with a large socket and breaker bar attached to the vibration damper bolt threaded into the front of the crankshaft.*

b) *A remote starter switch, which may save some time, can also be used. Attach the switch leads to the S (switch) and B (battery) terminals on the starter motor. Once the piston is close to TDC, use a socket and breaker bar as described in the previous paragraph.*

c) *If an assistant is available to turn the ignition switch to the Start position in short bursts, you can get the piston close to TDC without a remote starter switch. Use a socket and breaker bar as described in Paragraph a) to complete the procedure.*

4   Using a felt pen, make a mark on the distributor housing directly below the number one spark plug wire terminal on the distributor cap. **Note:** *The terminal numbers are marked on the spark plug wires near the distributor.*

5   Remove the distributor cap as des-

3.6 Turn the crankshaft until the zero on the vibration damper scale Is directly opposite the pointer

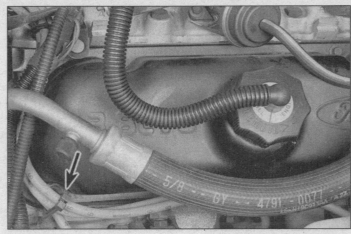

4.2 The spark plug wire routing clips (arrow) pull off the studs

cribed in Chapter 1.

6   Turn the crankshaft (see Paragraph 3 above) until the zero or groove on the vibration damper is aligned with the pointer or TDC mark **(see illustration)**. The pointer or TDC mark and vibration damper are located low on the front of the engine, near the pulley that turns the drivebelt.

7   The rotor should now be pointing directly at the mark on the distributor housing. If it isn't, the piston is at TDC on the exhaust stroke.

8   To get the piston to TDC on the compression stroke, turn the crankshaft one complete turn (360-degrees) clockwise. The rotor should no be pointing at the mark. When the rotor is pointing at the number one spar plug wire terminal in the distributor cap (which is indicated by the mark on the housing) and the ignition timing marks are aligned, the number one piston is at TDC on the compression stroke.

9   After the number one piston has been positioned at TDC on the compression stroke, TDC for any of the remaining cylinders can be located by turning the crankshaft and following the firing order (refer to the Specifications).

4   Rocker arm covers - removal and installation

Removal

Refer to illustrations 4.2, 4.11 and 4.12

1   Disconnect the negative cable from the battery.

2   Note their locations, then detach the spark plug wire clips from the rocker arm cover studs **(see illustration)**.

3   Refer to Chapter 1 and detach the spark plug wires from the plugs. Position the wires out of the way.

4   If so equipped, detach the diverter valve and hoses from the rocker arm cover.

5   On vehicles with cruise control, disconnect the servo linkage at the carburetor or throttle body and remove the servo bracket.

Right side

V6 engine

6   Position the air cleaner out of the way (Chapter 4) and remove the PCV valve. Remove the automatic choke heat tube (carburetor equipped vehicles only).

V8 engine

7   Remove the air cleaner assembly (Chapter 4) and disconnect the PCV tube.

8   Remove any solenoids attached to the rocker arm cover.

9   Remove the automatic choke heat tube (carbureted models only).

10   Disconnect the EGR vacuum amplifier hoses (models so equipped).

Left side

V6 engine

11   Remove the oil filler cap and the exhaust heat control valve vacuum hose **(see illustration)** (if equipped).

12   Remove the bolts and swivel the exhaust heat control valve out of the way **(see illustration)**.

13   On carbureted models equipped with cruise control, detach the air cleaner and move it out of the way. Detach the cruise control servo chain from the carburetor, detach the servo bracket and place the bracket and servo out of the way.

V8 engine

14   On 1983 through 1985 models, remove

4.11 Remove the oil filler cap and, after disconnecting the exhaust heat control valve vacuum , vacuum hose (arrow), push it aside

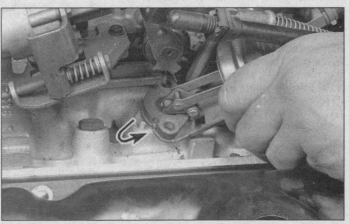

4.12 Remove the bolts and swivel the exhaust heat control valve 90-degrees counterclockwise

2D

5.2 The rocker arm fulcrum bolts (arrow) may not have to be completely removed - loosen them several turns and see if the rocker arms can be pivoted out of the way to allow pushrod removal

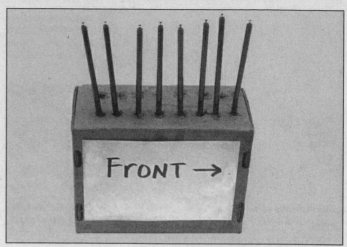

5.4 A perforated cardboard box can be used to store the pushrods to ensure that they are reinstalled in their original locations - note the label indicating the front of the engine

the air cleaner assembly (Chapter 4) and the solenoids attached to the rocker arm cover.

Both sides

15   Remove the rocker arm cover bolts/nuts, then detach the cover from the head. **Note:** *If the cover is stuck to the head, bump one end with a block of wood and a hammer to jar it loose. If that doesn't work, try to slip a flexible putty knife between the head and cover to break the gasket seal. Don't pry at the cover-to-head joint or damage to the sealing surfaces may occur (leading to oil leaks in the future). Some rocker arm covers are made of plastic - be extra careful when tapping or pulling on them.*

Installation

16   The mating surfaces of each cylinder head and rocker arm cover must be perfectly clean when the covers are installed. Use a gasket scraper to remove all traces of sealant and old gasket material, then clean the mating surfaces with lacquer thinner or acetone. If there's sealant or oil on the mating surfaces when the cover is installed, oil leaks may develop.

17   Clean the mounting bolt threads with a die to remove any corrosion and restore damaged threads. Make sure the threaded holes in the head are clean - run a tap into them to remove corrosion and restore damaged threads. Apply a small amount of light oil to the bolt threads.

18   The gaskets should be mated to the covers before the covers are installed. Make sure the tabs on the gaskets(s) engage in the slots in the cover(s). On engines that don't have gaskets, apply a 3/16-inch bead of RTV sealant to the cover flange, inside of the bolt holes.

19   Carefully position the cover on the head and install the bolts/nuts.

20   Tighten the bolts in three or four steps to the torque listed in this Chapter's Specifications. Plastic rocker arm covers are easily

damaged, so don't overtighten the bolts!

21   The remaining installation steps are the reverse of removal.

22   Start the engine and check carefully for oil leaks as the engine warms up.

---

5   Rocker arms and pushrods - removal, inspection and installation

Removal

Refer to illustrations 5.2 and 5.4

1   Refer to Section 4 and detach the rocker arm cover(s) from the cylinder head(s).

2   Beginning at the front of one cylinder head, remove the rocker arm fulcrum bolts **(see illustration)**. Store them separately in marked containers to ensure that they will be reinstalled in their original locations. **Note:** *If the pushrods are the only items being removed, loosen each bolt just enough to allow the rocker arms to be rotated to the side so the pushrods can be lifted out.*

3   On Mustang models, lift off the rocker arms, fulcrums and fulcrum guides (if used). On Cobra models, lift off the roller rocker arms and pedestal assembly. Store them in marked containers with the bolts (they must be reinstalled in their original positions).

4   Remove the pushrods and store them separately to make sure they don't get mixed up during installation **(see illustration)**.

Inspection

Refer to illustration 5.7

5   Check each rocker arm for wear, cracks and other damage, especially where the pushrods and valve stems contact the rocker arm faces.

6   Make sure the hole at the pushrod end of each rocker arm is open.

7   Inspect each rocker arm pivot area and fulcrum for wear, cracks and galling **(see illustration)**. If the rocker arms are worn or dam-

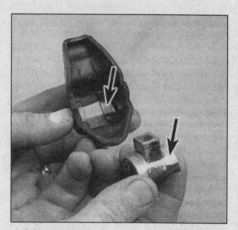

5.7 Inspect each rocker arm and fulcrum for wear

aged, replace them with new ones and use new fulcrums as well. On Cobra models, inspect the pivot portion of the rocker arms for roller bearing wear or noise. Make sure the bearing snap-rings are in place and are tight. Replace the rocker arms if necessary.

8   Inspect the pushrods for cracks and excessive wear at the ends. Roll each pushrod across a piece of plate glass to see if it's bent (if it wobbles, it's bent).

Installation

Caution: *Make sure that both lifters for each cylinder are on the base circle of the cam lobe (both valves closed) before tightening the rocker arm bolts.*

9   Lubricate the lower end of each pushrod with clean engine oil or moly-base grease and install them in their original locations. Make sure each pushrod seats completely in the lifter.

10   Apply moly-base grease to the ends of the valve stems and the upper ends of the pushrods before positioning the rocker arms, fulcrums and guides.

11   On Mustang models, apply moly-base

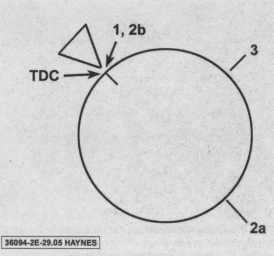

5.13 Crankshaft position for checking and adjusting valve clearances

5.20 Some very early 5.0L V8 engines have adjustable rocker arm nuts - check the valve clearance the same way as for positive stop rocker arms - if the clearance is not correct, adjust by turning the rocker arm nut, as shown here

2D

grease to the fulcrums to prevent damage to the mating surfaces before engine oil pressure builds up. Set the rocker arms and guides in place, then install the fulcrums and bolts.

Valve adjustment

Positive stop rocker arms

Refer to illustration 5.13

Caution: *5.0L HO (high output) V8 engines have a different firing order than 4.2L V8 and 5.0L non-HO V8 engines. For this reason, the valves are adjusted in a different sequence. The correct valve adjustment sequence for the vehicle's engine must be used to prevent possible valve train damage. 1979 through 1982 models are equipped with the non-HO 5.0L V8 or the 4.2L V8. Some later models may be equipped with the non-HO or HO 5.0L V8. If you are uncertain which type of engine the vehicle has, read the firing order cast into the intake manifold.*

Note: *Adjustment is normally only needed after valve train components have been replaced or the valves and/or seats have been ground a considerable amount.*

12 Using a lifter bleed-down tool available at most auto parts stores, press on the rocker arm until the lifter leaks down. Check the clearance between the valve stem and rocker arm with a feeler gauge. Compare the results to the Specifications and write it down for future reference. Repeat the procedure for each valve in the order shown below. **Note:** *The arrangement of intake and exhaust valves is as follows:*

V6 engine
Left side - E-I-E-I-E-I
Right side - I-E-I-E-I-E

V8 engine
Left side - E-I-E-I-E-I-E-I
Right side - I-E-I-E-I-E-I-E

13 Position the number one piston at TDC (Section 3). This is position 1 in the accompanying illustration.

14 Check the following valves:
V6 engine
Intake - no. 1, 3 and 6
Exhaust - no. 1, 2 and 4
V8 engine (except HO)
Intake - no. 1, 7 and 8
Exhaust - no. 1, 4 and 5
V8 engine (HO)
Intake - no. 1, 4 and 8
Exhaust - no. 1, 3 and 7

15 Rotate the crankshaft to position 2A (V8) or 2B (V6) and check the following valves:
V6 engine
Intake - no. 2, 4 and 5
Exhaust - no. 3, 5 and 6
(this completes V6)
V8 engine (except HO)
Intake - no. 4 and 5
Exhaust - no. 2 and 6
V8 engine (HO)
Intake - no. 3 and 7
Exhaust - no. 2 and 6

16 On V8 engines only, rotate the crankshaft to position 3 and check the following valves:
Except HO
Intake - no. 2, 3 and 6
Exhaust - no. 3, 7 and 8
HO
Intake - no. 2, 5 and 6
Exhaust - no. 4, 5 and 8

17 Clearance can be changed by using different length pushrods, available from your dealer. If there isn't enough clearance, use a shorter pushrod; too much clearance, use a longer one.

Adjustable rocker arms

Refer to illustration 5.20

18 Some very early 5.0L V8 engines are equipped with adjustable rocker arms.

19 Position the number one piston at Top Dead Center on the compression stroke (see Section 3). Check the valve clearance with a feeler gauge in the same manner as for positive stop rocker arms.

20 If the valve clearance is incorrect, adjust it by turning the rocker arm nut **(see illustration)**.

21 The valve adjustment sequence is the same as the firing order (1, 5, 4, 2, 6, 3, 7, 8). Place each piston in turn at Top Dead Center on the compression stroke. Check and adjust the valves for that cylinder, then proceed to the next cylinder.

6 Valve springs, retainers and seals - replacement

Refer to illustrations 6.4, 6.9 and 6.10

Note: *Broken valve springs and defective valve stem seals can be replaced without removing the cylinder heads. Two special tools and a compressed air source are normally required to perform this operation, so read through this Section carefully and rent or buy the tools before beginning the job. If compressed air isn't available, a length of nylon rope can be used to keep the valves from falling into the cylinder during this procedure.*

1 Refer to Section 4 and remove the rocker arm cover from the affected cylinder head. If all of the valve stem seals are being replaced, remove both rocker arm covers.

2 Remove the spark plug from the cylinder which has the defective component. If all of the valve stem seals are being replaced, all of the spark plugs should be removed.

3 Turn the crankshaft until the piston in the affected cylinder is at Top Dead Center on the compression stroke (refer to Section 3 for instructions). If you're replacing all of the valve stem seals, begin with cylinder number one and work on the valves for one cylinder at a time. Move from cylinder-to-cylinder following the firing order sequence (see this Chapter's Specifications).

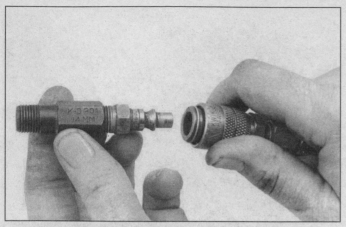

6.4 This is what the air hose adapter that threads into the spark plug hole looks like - they're commonly available from auto parts stores

6.9 Once the spring is depressed, the keepers can be removed with a small magnet or needle-nose pliers (a magnet is preferred to prevent dropping the keepers)

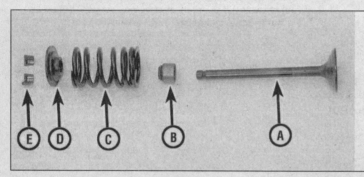

6.10a Valve and related components

A   *Valve*
B   *Valve stem seal*
C   *Valve spring*
D   *Retainer*
E   *Keepers*

6.10b The seal can be pulled off the guide with a pair of pliers

4   Thread an adapter into the spark plug hole **(see illustration)** and connect an air hose from a compressed air source to it. Most auto parts stores can supply the air hose adapter. **Note:** *Many cylinder compression gauges utilize a screw-in fitting that may work with your air hose quick-disconnect fitting.*

5   Remove the bolt, fulcrum and rocker arm for the valve with the defective part and pull out the pushrod. If all of the valve stem seals are being replaced, all of the rocker arms and pushrods should be removed (refer to Section 5).

6   Apply compressed air to the cylinder. **Warning:** *The piston may be forced down by compressed air, causing the crankshaft to turn suddenly. If the wrench used when positioning the number one piston at TDC is still attached to the bolt in the crankshaft nose, it could cause damage or injury when the crankshaft moves.*

7   The valves should be held in place by the air pressure. If the valve faces or seats are in poor condition, leaks may prevent air pressure from retaining the valves - refer to the alternative procedure below.

8   If you don't have access to compressed air, an alternative method can be used. Position the piston at a point just before TD on the compression stroke, then feed a long piece of nylon rope through the spark plug hole until it fills the combustion chamber. Be sure to leave the end of the rope hanging out of the engine so it can be removed easily. Use a large ratchet and socket to rotate the

crankshaft in the normal direction of rotation until slight resistance is felt.

9   Stuff shop rags into the cylinder head holes above and below the valves to prevent parts and tools from falling into the engine, then use a valve spring compressor to compress the spring. Remove the keepers with small needle-nose pliers or a magnet **(see illustration)**. **Note:** *A couple of different types of tools are available for compressing the valve springs with the head in place. One type, shown here, grips the lower spring coils and presses on the retainer as the knob is turned, while the other type utilizes the rocker arm bolt for leverage. Both types work very well, although the lever type is usually less expensive.*

10   Remove the spring retainer or rotator, sleeve (used on some intake valves) and valve spring assembly, then remove the umbrella-type guide seal **(see illustrations)**. **Note:** *If air pressure fails to hold the valve in the closed position during this operation, the valve face or seat is probably damaged. If so, the cylinder head will have to be removed for additional repair operations.*

11   Wrap a rubber band or tape around the top of the valve stem so the valve won't fall into the combustion chamber, then release the air pressure. **Note:** *If a rope was used instead of air pressure, turn the crankshaft slightly in the direction opposite normal rotation.*

12   Inspect the valve stem for damage. Rotate the valve in the guide and check the end for eccentric movement, which would

indicate that the valve is bent.

13   Move the valve up-and-down in the guide and make sure it doesn't bind. If the valve stem binds, either the valve is bent or the guide is damaged. In either case, the head will have to be removed for repair.

14   Reapply air pressure to the cylinder to retain the valve in the closed position, then remove the tape or rubber band from the valve stem. If a rope was used instead of air pressure, rotate the crankshaft in the normal direction of rotation until slight resistance is felt.

15   Lubricate the valve stem with engine oil and the valve stem tip with polyethylene grease, then install a new guide seal.

16   Install the spring in position over the valve.

17   Install the valve spring retainer or rotator. Some intake valves also have a sleeve that fits inside the retainer. Compress the valve spring and carefully position the keepers in the groove. Apply a small dab of grease to the inside of each keeper to hold it in place.

18   Remove the pressure from the spring tool and make sure the keepers are seated.

19   Disconnect the air hose and remove the adapter from the spark plug hole. If a rope was used in place of air pressure, pull it out of the cylinder.

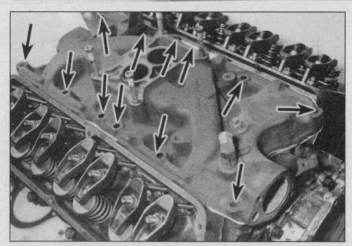

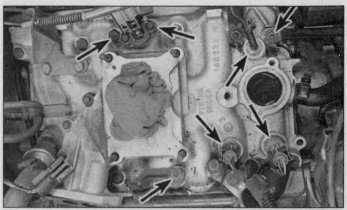

7.15 Stuff a rag into the intake manifold to prevent foreign matter from engineer, then unbolt the throttle cable bracket (arrows), the emission and electrical connectors (arrows), the compressor bracket (arrow) and the heater tube bracket (arrow).

7.10 Intake manifold bolt locations (arrows) - typical carbureted V8 engine

20 Refer to Section 5 and install the rocker arm(s) and pushrod(s).

21 Install the spark plug(s) and hook up the wire(s).

22 Refer to Section 4 and install the rocker arm cover(s).

23 Start and run the engine, then check for oil leaks and unusual sounds coming from the rocker arm cover area.

7 Intake manifold - removal and installation

Note: *It is recommended that guide pins be used when installing the manifold. To make these, buy four extra manifold bolts. Cut the heads off the bolts, then grind a taper and cut a screwdriver slot in the cut ends.*

Removal

Carbureted models

Refer to illustration 7.10

1 Drain the cooling system (see Chapter 1).

2 Remove the air cleaner, its duct and the crankcase ventilation hose.

3 Disconnect the crankcase ventilation hose from the rocker arm cover.

4 Disconnect the automatic choke heat tube, accelerator cable and speed control linkage (vehicles so equipped). Remove the accelerator cable bracket.

5 Label and disconnect the intake manifold vacuum lines.

6 Disconnect the ignition coil primary and high tension wires from the coil. Remove the distributor (see Chapter 5).

7 Disconnect the fuel line from the carburetor.

8 Disconnect the coolant hoses from the thermostat housing and intake manifold. Disconnect the coolant temperature sending unit (see Chapter 3). **Note:** *The heater outlet and coolant by-pass tubes are pressed in and cannot be removed.*

9 The carburetor may be removed now (see Chapter 4) or left on the intake manifold).

10 Remove the intake manifold mounting bolts **(see illustration)** and lift the manifold off. If necessary, carefully pry the manifold loose from the engine, but make sure all bolts and nuts have been removed first! **Caution:** *Don't pry between the block and manifold or between the heads and manifold or damage to the gasket sealing surfaces may occur, resulting in vacuum and oil leaks. Pry only at manifold casting protrusions.*

11 Disassemble the manifold as needed.

Fuel-injected 3.8L V6 models

Refer to illustrations 7.15, 7.25 and 7.26

12 Drain the cooling system (see Chapter 1).

13 Remove the air cleaner, intake duct and heat tube (see Chapter 4).

14 Disconnect the accelerator cable, automatic transmission cable and speed control cable (vehicles so equipped) at the throttle body assembly.

15 Remove the throttle cable bracket **(see illustration)**.

16 Disconnect the thermactor air supply hose from the check valve at the rear of the manifold.

17 Disconnect the fuel lines from the throttle body assembly.

Disconnect the radiator hose from the thermostat housing and the coolant bypass hose from the manifold (see Chapter 3).

18 Detach the heater tube and its bracket

from the intake manifold. Disconnect the heater hose from the rear of the tube. Loosen the hose clamp at the heater elbow, then remove the heater tube with the hose and the fuel lines still attached. Place the heater tube out of the way. **Note:** *The heater outlet and coolant by-pass tubes are pressed in, and cannot be removed.*

19 Label and disconnect the vacuum and emissions hoses and electrical connectors attached to the manifold and related components **(see illustration 7.15)**.

20 Air conditioned vehicles - remove the air conditioning compressor support bracket from the left front manifold bolt. Do not disconnect any refrigerant lines!

21 Remove the EGR tube bolts and three spacer mounting screws at the intake manifold (see Chapter 4).

22 With the EGR adapter and valve attached, work the EGR tube spacer loose from the manifold. Discard the old gasket.

23 Remove the wiring bracket at the left front corner of the intake manifold. Place the bracket and spark plug wires out of the way.

24 Remove the exhaust heat control valve vacuum tube mounting bolt located at the rear of the left cylinder head. Remove the nut located on the manifold and detach the tube.

25 Loosen the manifold mounting bolts **(see illustration)** in 1/4-turn increments until they can be removed by hand.

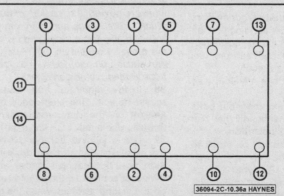

7.25 Intake manifold bolt tightening sequence - V6 engine

36094-2C-10.36a HAYNES

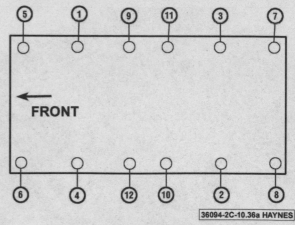

7.26 Carefully pry up on the manifold (arrow), but don't damage the gasket surfaces!

7.36 Intake manifold bolt tightening sequence - fuel-injected V8 engine (Mustang shown, Cobra similar)

26   The manifold will probably be stuck to the cylinder heads and force may be required to break the gasket seal. A prybar can be positioned under the cast-in lug near the thermostat housing **(see illustration)** to pry up the front end of the manifold, but make sure all bolts and nuts have been removed first! **Caution:** *Don't pry between the block and manifold or heads and manifold or damage to the gasket sealing surfaces may occur, leading to vacuum and oil leaks.*

Fuel-injected V8 models

Refer to illustration 7.36

27   Drain the cooling system (see Chapter 1.)
28   Remove the PCV and canister purge hoses.
29   Disconnect the accelerator cable, speed control linkage and automatic transmission cable (if so equipped). Remove the accelerator cable bracket.
30   Label and disconnect the intake manifold vacuum lines.
31   Remove the distributor (see Chapter 5).
32   Relieve the fuel system pressure (see Chapter 4) and disconnect the fuel supply and return lines.
33   Disconnect the radiator, heater and water pump bypass hoses from the water outlet (see Chapter 3). Disconnect the throttle body cooler hoses. **Note:** *The heater outlet and coolant bypass tubes are pressed in, and cannot be removed.*
34   Disconnect the electrical connectors from the coolant temperature sending unit, air charge temperature sensor, throttle positioner, idle speed control solenoid, EGR sensors, fuel injectors and fuel charging assembly.
35   Remove the upper intake manifold (see Chapter 4).
36   Loosen the lower intake manifold bolts and nuts in 1/4-turn increments until they can be removed by hand **(see illustration).**
37   The manifold will probably be stuck to the cylinder heads and force may be required to break the gasket seal. A prybar can be used to pry up the manifold, but make sure all bolts and nuts have been removed first!

7.39 After covering the lifter valley, use a gasket scraper to remove all traces of sealant and old gasket material from the head and manifold mating surfaces

Caution: *Don't pry between the block and manifold or the heads and manifold or damage to the gasket sealing surfaces may occur, leading to vacuum and oil leaks. Pry only at a manifold casting protrusion.*

Installation (all models)

Refer to illustration 7.39

Note: *The mating surfaces of the cylinder heads, block and manifold must be perfectly clean when the manifold is installed. Gasket removal solvents in aerosol cans are available at most auto parts stores and may be helpful when removing old gasket material that's stuck to the heads and manifold (since the manifold and some V6 engine cylinder heads are made of aluminum, aggressive scraping can cause damage! Be sure to follow directions printed on the container.*

38   If the manifold was disassembled, reassemble it. Use electrically conductive sealant on the temperature sending unit threads. Use a new EGR valve gasket.
39   Use a gasket scraper to remove all traces of sealant and old gasket material, then clean the mating surfaces with lacquer thinner or acetone. If there's old sealant or oil on the mating surfaces when the manifold is installed, oil or vacuum leaks may develop. When working on the heads and block, cover the lifter valley with shop rags to keep debris out of the engine **(see illustration)**. Use a vacuum cleaner to remove any gasket material that falls into the intake ports in the heads.
40   Use a tap of the correct size to chase the threads in the bolt holes, then use compressed air (if available) to remove the debris from the holes. **Warning:** *Wear safety glasses or a face shield to protect your eyes when using compressed air!* Remove excessive carbon deposits and corrosion from the exhaust and coolant passages in the heads and manifold.
41   Apply a 1/8-inch wide bead of RTV sealant to the four corners where the manifold, block and heads converge. **Note:** *This sealant sets up in 10 minutes. Do not take longer to install and tighten the manifold once the sealant is applied, or leaks may occur.*
42   Apply a small dab of contact adhesive or equivalent to the manifold gasket mating surface on each cylinder head. Position the gaskets on the cylinder heads. The upper side of each gasket will have a TOP or THIS SIDE UP label stamped into it to ensure correct installation.

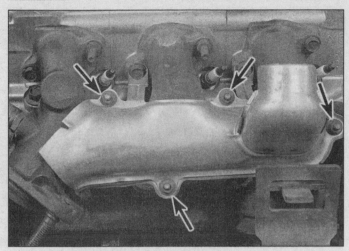

8.10 Remove the heat stove cover nuts (arrows) and lift the cover off (V6 engine shown)

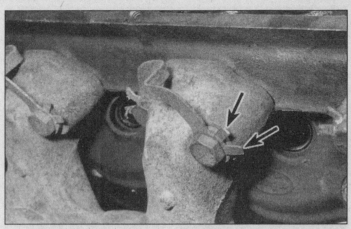

8.12 Some models are equipped with manifold bolt locking tabs - bend these down before removing the bolts - use new locking assemblies on installation, bending the tabs up to lock the bolts in place

43   Position the end seals on the block, then apply a 1/8-inch wide bead of RTV sealant to the four points where the end seals meet the heads.

44   Make sure all intake port openings, coolant passage holes and bolt holes are aligned correctly.

45   Carefully set the manifold in place while the sealant is still wet. **Caution:** *Don't disturb the gaskets and don't move the manifold fore-and-aft after it contacts the seals on the block. Make sure the end seals haven't been disturbed.*

46   Lightly oil the manifold bolts (V6 engine). Install the bolts and tighten them to the torque listed in this Chapter's Specifications, following the recommended sequence **(see illustrations 7.25 and 7.36)**. Work up to the final torque in three steps.

47   The remaining installation steps are the reverse of removal. Start the engine and check carefully for oil and coolant leaks at the intake manifold joints.

48   Recheck the mounting bolt torque.

8   Exhaust manifolds - removal and installation

Removal

Refer to illustrations 8.10 and 8.12

1   Disconnect the negative battery cable from the battery.

2   Unplug the exhaust gas oxygen sensor (EGO) wire (if equipped) and remove the spark plugs (Chapter 1).

3   Raise the vehicle and support it securely on jackstands.4

Working under the vehicle, apply penetrating oil to the exhaust pipe-to-manifold studs and nuts (they're usually rusty).

5   Remove the nuts holding the exhaust crossover pipe to the manifold(s). In extreme cases you may have to heat them with a propane or acetylene torch in order to loosen them.

6   Remove the air cleaner assembly (Chapter 4) and heat stove tube (if equipped) (Chapter 6).

7   Remove any cruise control brackets that are in the way.

Right side manifold

8   Remove the thermactor tube mounted between the air tube check valve and the crossover pipe (Chapter 6).

9   On some vehicles with an automatic transmission, the dipstick and tube must be removed.

10   Remove the outer heat stove cover (if equipped) **(see illustration)**.

Left side manifold

11   If it's in the way, remove the oil dipstick and tube. Also, remove the heat control valve (Chapter 6).

Both manifolds

12   Bend back the locking tabs (if equipped). Remove the mounting bolts and separate the manifold(s) from the head **(see illustration)**. Note the locations of the pilot bolts.

Installation

13   Check the manifold for cracks and make sure the bolt threads are clean and undamaged. The manifold and cylinder head mating surfaces must be clean before the manifolds are reinstalled - use a gasket scraper to remove all carbon deposits and old gasket material.

14   Position the manifold and gasket (if equipped) on the head and install the mounting bolts. **Note:** *Exhaust manifold warpage is common on the V6 engine. Although some were built without gaskets, we recommend installing them. If you're working on a V6 engine, install the pilot bolts first. Sometimes it's necessary to elongate the holes in the manifolds to start the bolts - never file out the pilot bolt holes!*

15   When tightening the mounting bolts, work from the center to the ends and be sure

to use a torque wrench. Tighten the bolts in three equal steps until the torque listed in this Chapter's Specifications is reached.

16   The remaining installation steps are the reverse of removal.

17   Start the engine and check for exhaust leaks.

9   Cylinder heads - removal and installation

Caution: *The engine must be completely cool when the heads are removed. Failure to allow the engine to cool off could result in head warpage.*

Removal

Refer to illustrations 9.11 and 9.13

Both cylinder heads

1   Remove the rocker arm cover (Section 4).

2   Remove the pushrods (Section 5).

3   Remove the intake manifold (Section 7).

4   Remove the drivebelts (Chapter 1) and idler pulley bracket.

Left (driver's side) cylinder head

5   Unbolt the power steering pump and tie it aside in an upright position. Leave the hoses connected (Chapter 10).

6   Remove the A/C compressor and position it out of the way (Chapter 3). DO NOT disconnect the hoses!

7   Remove the exhaust manifold (Section 8).

8   Proceed to Step 14.

Right cylinder head

9   Detach the fuel line from the clip at the front of the head (not all models).

10   Remove the thermactor diverter valve and pump and the crossover tube from the rear of the head (not all models).

2D

9.11 The alternator bracket bolts (arrows) must be removed to detach the V6 engine right cylinder head

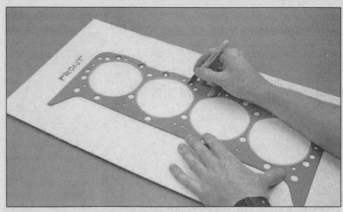

9.13 To avoid mixing up the V8 engine head bolts, use a new gasket to transfer the bolt hole, use a new gasket to transfer the bolt hole pattern to a piece of cardboard, then punch holes to accept the bolts

9.20 Locating dowels (arrows) are used to position the gaskets on the block - make sure the mark (circled) is correctly oriented

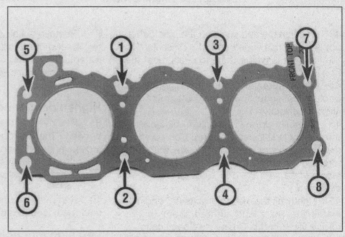

9.23a Cylinder head bolt tightening sequence - V6 engine

11 Remove the alternator bracket **(see illustration)**.

12 Remove the exhaust manifold (Section 7).

Both cylinder heads

13 Using a new head gasket, outline the cylinders and bolt pattern on a piece of cardboard (V8 engine only) **(see illustration)**. Be sure to indicate the front of the engine for reference. Punch holes at the bolt locations.

14 Loosen the head bolts in 1/4-turn increments until they can be removed by hand. Work from bolt-to-bolt in a pattern that's the reverse of the tightening sequence. Store the bolts in the cardboard holder as they're removed (V8 engine only); this will ensure that the bolts are reinstalled in their original holes. **Note:** *V6 engine head bolts should not be reused. Remove the bolts and discard them - NEW BOLTS MUST BE USED when installing the head(s).*

15 Lift the head(s) off the engine. If resistance is felt, DO NOT pry between the head and block as damage to the mating surfaces will result. To dislodge the head, place a block of wood against the end of it and strike the wood block with a hammer. Store the heads on blocks of wood to prevent damage to the gasket sealing surfaces.

16 Cylinder head disassembly and inspection procedures are covered in detail in Chapter 2, Part E.

Installation

Refer to illustrations 9.20, 9.23a and 9.23b

17 The mating surfaces of the cylinder heads and block must be perfectly clean when the heads are installed. Use a gasket scraper to remove all traces of carbon and old gasket material, then clean the mating surfaces with lacquer thinner or acetone. If there's oil on the mating surfaces when the heads are installed, the gaskets may not seal correctly and leaks may develop. When working on the block, cover the lifter valley with shop rags to keep debris out of the engine. Use a vacuum cleaner to remove any debris that falls into the cylinders.

18 Check the block and head mating surfaces for nicks, deep scratches and other damage. If damage is slight, it can be removed with a file - if it's excessive, machin-

ing may be the only alternative.

19 Use a tap of the correct size to chase the threads in the head bolt holes. Mount each bolt in a vise and run a die down the threads to remove corrosion and restore the threads (V8 engine only). Dirt, corrosion, sealant and damaged threads will affect torque readings.

20 Position the new gasket(s) over the dowel pins in the block **(see illustration)**. Make sure it's facing the right way.

21 Carefully position the head(s) on the block without disturbing the gasket(s).

22 Before installing the new V6 engine head bolts, coat the threads of the four short bolts with pipe sealant. Lightly oil the threads of the remaining V6 engine head bolts. If you're working on a V8 engine, lightly oil the threads on all of the bolts.

23 Install the bolts in their original locations and tighten them finger tight. Follow the recommended sequence and tighten the bolts, in two or four steps, to the torque listed in this Chapter's Specifications **(see illustrations)**. **Note 1:** *On V6 engines, after reaching the final torque, loosen all of the head bolts two or three turns, then repeat the tightening*

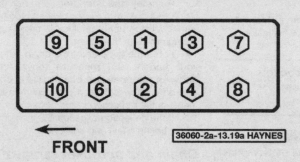

9.23b Cylinder head bolt tightening sequence - V8 engines

10.11 Gently tap the timing chain cover loose with a soft-face hammer (V6 engine shown)

sequence. **Note 2:** *On 1993 5.0L V8 engines, there are two different types of cylinder head bolts. Only one type is used on each engine (both types are not used on the same cylinder head). The non-flanged head bolts are tightened to the same torque as on prior years. If flanged bolts are used, they are to be tightened in three steps and to a different torque specification (listed in this Chapter's Specifications).*

24   The remaining installation steps are the reverse of removal.

25   Change the engine oil and filter (Chapter 1), then start the engine and check carefully for oil and coolant leaks.

10   Timing chain cover - removal and installation

Removal

Refer to illustrations 10.11

1   On V6 engines, refer to Chapter 3 and remove the water pump. On V8 engines, perform all water pump removal steps except actual removal of the pump. The pump may be removed or left attached to the timing chain cover.

2   Drain the engine oil and remove the oil filter (Chapter 1).

3   Remove the crankshaft vibration damper (Section 16).

4   Unbolt and remove all accessory brackets attached to the timing chain cover.

V6 engine only

5   Position the number one piston at TDC on the compression stroke (Section 3), then remove the distributor as described in Chapter 5.

6   On carburetor equipped models, remove the fuel pump (Chapter 4).

7   Remove the oil pan (Section 14).

8   Unbolt the ignition timing indicator or pointer.

V8 engine only

9   Remove the oil pan-to-timing chain cover bolts.

10   Use a razor knife (thin blade) or razor blade to cut the oil pan gasket flush with the engine block face.

All engines

11   Remove the bolts and separate the timing chain cover from the block. If it's stuck, tap it gently with a soft-face hammer. **Caution:** *DO NOT use excessive force or you may crack the cover.* If the cover is difficult to remove, double check to make sure all of the bolts are out. Be sure to mark each bolt as to its location - they are different lengths. On the V6 engine, the Allen head bolt under the oil filter housing is easy to miss **(see illustration)**.

V6 engine only

12   Remove the camshaft thrust button and spring assembly from the end of the camshaft.

13   To remove the intermediate shaft from the cover, remove the clip from the shaft and slide the shaft out.

Installation

14   If you're working on a V8 engine, remove the circular rubber seal from the front of the oil pan and stuff a shop rag into the oil pan opening to keep debris out of the engine. Use a gasket scraper to remove all traces of old gasket material and sealant from the cover, oil pan and engine block, then clean them with lacquer thinner or acetone.

V6 engine only

Refer to illustration 10.16

15   The oil pump is mounted in the timing chain cover. See Section 15 for oil pump information.

16   To install the intermediate shaft in the timing chain cover, make a mark one inch from the end. Insert the shaft until it seats in the oil pump and snap the clip onto the shaft with the top of the clip just below the mark on the shaft **(see illustration)**.

17   Be sure the camshaft thrust button and spring assembly is seated in the end of the camshaft **(see illustration 11.23)**. The small end of the spring must face the button. Lubricate the button end.

10.16 Install the clip with the top just below the mark (V6 engine only)

18   Lubricate the timing chain and front crankshaft oil seal lips with engine oil.

19   Apply a thin coat of RTV sealant to the block side of the new gasket, then position it on the engine. The dowel pins will hold it in place as the cover is installed.

20   Apply a thin coat of RTV sealant to the gasket surface of the cover and attach it to the engine. The dowel pins will position it correctly. Don't damage the seal and make sure the gasket remains in place. Make sure the thrust button is bottomed in the camshaft hole.

21   Install the bolts finger tight. Tighten them to the torque listed in this Chapter's Specifications only after the water pump has been installed (some of the water pump bolts also hold the timing chain cover in place). **Note:** *When installing the water pump, be sure to coat the threads with sealant (see Chapter 3).*

22   Install the oil pan (Section 14).

V8 engine only

23   Cut two sections out of a new oil pan gasket to install between the oil pan and timing chain cover.

24   Attach the gasket sections to the oil pan with contact cement.

2D

11.4 A dial indicator installed to measure timing chain deflection (V6 engine - a special cup-shaped adapter may be needed to keep the indicator plunger from sliding off the end of the pushrod)

25   Apply a 1/8-inch bead of RTV sealant to the oil pan-to-block joints.
26   Install a new circular rubber seal in the oil pan cutout (use contact cement to hold it in place).
27   Lubricate the timing chain and front crankshaft oil seal lips with engine oil.
28   Apply a thin coat of RTV sealant to the block side of the new cover gasket, then position it on the engine. The dowel pins will hold it in place as the cover is installed.
29   Apply a thin coat of RTV sealant to the gasket surface of the cover and attach it to the engine. Don't dislodge the circular rubber seal or the gaskets.
30   It may be necessary to compress the rubber seal by forcing the cover down before installing the bolts. Temporarily slip the vibration damper onto the crankshaft to align the cover.
31   Apply pipe sealant with Teflon to the threads, then install the bolts. Tighten the oil pan-to-cover bolts to the torque listed in this Chapter's Specifications while aligning the cover with the damper. Make sure the gaskets and seal stay in place.
32   Tighten the cover-to-block bolts to the torque listed in this Chapter's Specifications, then remove the vibration damper.

All engines

33   Install the remaining parts in the reverse order of removal.
34   Add engine oil and coolant (Chapter 1).
35   Run the engine and check for leaks.

11   Timing chain and sprockets - inspection, removal and installation

Timing chain inspection

1   Disconnect the negative battery cable from the battery.

V6 engine

Refer to illustration 11.4

2   Refer to Section 3 and position the number one piston several degrees before TDC on the compression stroke.
3   Remove the right rocker arm cover (Section 4).
4   Remove the number three cylinder exhaust rocker arm bolt, rocker arm and fulcrum. It's the last one on the right (passenger) side. Attach a dial indicator to the head with the plunger in-line with and resting on the pushrod **(see illustration)**.
5   Turn the crankshaft clockwise until the number one piston is at TDC (Section 3). This will take up the slack on the right side of the chain.
6   Zero the dial indicator.
7   Slowly turn the crankshaft counterclockwise until the slightest movement is seen on the dial indicator. Stop and note how far the number one piston has moved away from TDC by looking at the ignition timing marks.
8   If the mark has moved more than 6 degrees, install a new timing chain and sprockets.

V8 engine

9   Rotate the crankshaft in a counterclockwise direction to take up the slack in the left side of the chain.
10   Remove the timing chain cover (Section 10).

11   Establish a reference point on the block and measure from that point to the chain.
12   Reinstall the vibration damper bolt. Using this bolt, turn the crankshaft clockwise with a wrench until the slack is taken up on the right side of the chain.
13   Force the left side of the chain out with your fingers and measure the distance between the reference point and the chain. The difference between the two measurements is the deflection.
14   If the deflection exceeds 1/2-inch, install a new timing chain and sprockets.

Chain and sprocket removal and installation

Refer to illustrations 11.17, 11.22, 11.23 and 11.24

Removal

15   Make sure the number one piston is at TDC (Section 3).
16   Remove the timing chain cover (Section 10). Try to avoid turning the crankshaft during vibration damper removal.
17   Make sure the crankshaft and camshaft sprocket timing marks are aligned **(see illustration)**. If they aren't, install the vibration damper bolt and use it to turn the crankshaft clockwise until the two marks are aligned.
18   Remove the camshaft sprocket mounting bolt(s) and fuel pump eccentric (carburetor equipped models only).
19   Pull the sprocket/chain off the camshaft and detach the chain from the crankshaft sprocket. Don't lose the pin in the end of the camshaft (V8 engine only).
20   The crankshaft sprocket can be levered off with two large screwdrivers or a pry bar.

Installation

21   Align the keyway in the crankshaft sprocket with the Woodruff key in the end of the crankshaft. Press the sprocket onto the crankshaft with the vibration damper bolt, a large socket and some washers or tap it gently into place until it's completely seated. **Caution:** *If resistance is encountered, DO NOT hammer the sprocket onto the shaft. It may eventually move into place, but it may be*

11.17 Align the timing marks on the crankshaft and camshaft sprockets as shown here before removing the sprockets from the shafts

11.22 Position the crankshaft with the key facing up (12 o'clock), then . . .

11.23 . . . slip the chain over the crankshaft sprocket and attach the camshaft sprocket to the camshaft - note proper installation of the camshaft thrust button (arrow)

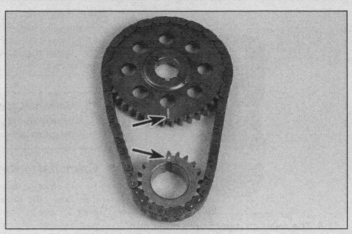

11.24 Correctly aligned timing marks

12.3a Stubborn lifters may be removed with a special slide hammer puller

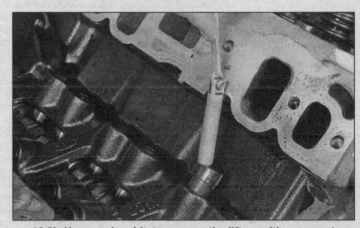

12.3b You may be able to remove the lifters with a magnet

2D

cracked in the process and fail later, causing extensive engine damage.

22   Turn the crankshaft until the key is facing up (12 o'clock position) **(see illustration)**.
23   Drape the chain over the camshaft sprocket and turn the sprocket until the timing mark faces down (6 o'clock position). Mesh the chain with the crankshaft sprocket and position the camshaft sprocket on the end of the cam **(see illustration)**. If necessary, turn the camshaft so the dowel pin fits into the sprocket hole (V8 engine) or the bolt holes in the sprocket are aligned with the off-set threaded holes in the camshaft flange (V6 engine).
24   When correctly installed, a straight line should pass through the center of the camshaft, the camshaft timing mark (in the 6 o'clock position), the crankshaft timing mark (in the 12 o'clock position) and the center of the crankshaft **(see illustration)**. DO NOT proceed until the valve timing is correct!
25   Install the fuel pump eccentric (carburetor equipped vehicles only).
26   Apply Loc-Tite to the threads and install the camshaft sprocket bolt(s). Tighten the bolt(s) to the torque listed in this Chapter's Specifications.
27   Reinstall the remaining parts in the reverse order of removal.

12   Valve lifters - removal, inspection and installation

Removal

Refer to illustrations 12.3a, 12.3b, and 12.4
1   Remove the intake manifold (Section 7).
2   Remove the rocker arms and pushrods (Section 5). On later models with roller lifters, unbolt and remove the lifter guide retainer from the valley between the lifters, then remove the guide plate from each pair of lifters.
3   There are several ways to extract the lifters from the bores. Special tools designed to grip and remove lifters are manufactured by many tool companies and are widely available **(see illustration)**, but may not be needed in every case. On newer engines without a lot of varnish buildup, the lifters can often be removed with a small magnet **(see illustration)** or even with your fingers. A machinist's scribe with a bent end can be used to pull the lifters out by positioning the point under the retainer ring in the top of each lifter. **Caution:** *Don't use pliers to remove the lifters unless you intend to replace them with new ones (along with the camshaft). The pliers may damage the precision machined and*

hardened lifters, rendering them useless. On engines with a lot of sludge and varnish, work the lifters up and down, using carburetor cleaner spray to loosen the deposits.
4   Before removing the lifters, arrange to store them in a clearly labeled box to ensure that they're reinstalled in their original locations. **Note:** *On engines equipped with roller lifters, the guide retainer and guide plates*

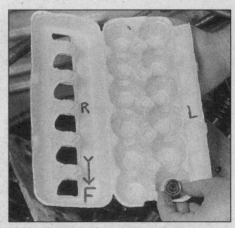

12.4 Be sure to store the lifters in an organized manner to make sure they're reinstalled in their original locations

12.6 The roller on roller lifters must turn freely - check for wear and excessive play as well

must be removed before the lifters are withdrawn. Remove the lifters and store them where they won't get dirty **(see illustration)**.

Inspection

Conventional lifters

5   The procedure for inspecting conventional lifters is in Chapter 2, part B, Section 9.

Roller lifters

Refer to illustration 12.6

6   Check the rollers carefully for wear and damage and make sure they turn freely without excessive play **(see illustration)**.

7   The inspection procedure for conventional lifters also applies to roller lifters (see Chapter 2, part B, Section 9).

8   Unlike conventional lifters, used roller lifters can be reinstalled with a new camshaft and the original camshaft can be used if new lifters are installed.

Installation

9   The original lifters, if they're being reinstalled, must be returned to their original locations. Coat them with moly-base grease or engine assembly lube.

10   Install the lifters in the bores.

11   Install the guide plates and retainer (roller lifters only).

12   Install the pushrods and rocker arms.

13   Install the intake manifold and rocker arm covers.

---

13   Camshaft and bearings - removal, inspection and installation

---

Camshaft lobe lift check

1   In order to determine the extent of cam lobe wear, the lobe lift should be checked prior to camshaft removal. Refer to Section 4 and remove the rocker arm covers. The rocker arms must also be removed (Section 5), but leave the pushrods in place.

2   Position the number one piston at TDC on the compression stroke (see Section 3).

3   Beginning with the number one cylinder, mount a dial indicator on the engine and position the plunger in-line with and resting on the first pushrod.

4   Zero the dial indicator, then very slowly turn the crankshaft in the normal direction of rotation until the indicator needle stops and begins to move in the opposite direction. The point at which it stops indicates maximum cam lobe lift.

5   Record this figure for future reference, then reposition the piston at TDC on the compression stroke.

6   Move the dial indicator to the remaining number one cylinder pushrod and repeat the check. Be sure to record the results for each valve.

7   Repeat the check for the remaining valves. Since each piston must be at TDC on the compression stroke for this procedure, work from cylinder-to-cylinder following the firing order sequence.

8   After the check is complete, compare the results to the Specifications. If camshaft lobe lift is less than specified, cam lobe wear has occurred and a new camshaft should be installed.

Removal

Refer to illustrations 13.11 and 13.12

9   Refer to the appropriate Sections and remove the pushrods, the valve lifters and the timing chain and camshaft sprocket. The radiator should be removed as well (Chapter 3). You also may have to remove the air conditioning condenser and the grille, but wait and see if the camshaft can be pulled out of the engine.

10   Check the V8 engine camshaft end play with a dial indicator. If it's greater than specified, replace the thrust plate with a new one when the camshaft is reinstalled.

11   Remove the camshaft thrust plate bolts. A T-30 Torx bit is required for the bolts on the V6 engine **(see illustration)**.

12   Carefully pull the camshaft out. Support the cam so the lobes don't nick or gouge the bearings as it's withdrawn **(see illustration)**.

Inspection

13   Refer to Part A, Section 7, for the camshaft and bearing inspection procedure. Lifter inspection procedures for roller lifters are covered in Section 12. Inspection procedures for conventional lifters are covered in Part B, Section 9 of this Chapter.

Bearing replacement

14   Camshaft bearing replacement requires special tools and expertise that place it outside the scope of the home mechanic. Take the block to an automotive machine shop to ensure that the job is done correctly.

Installation

Refer to illustration 13.15

15   Lubricate the camshaft bearing journals and cam lobes with moly-base grease or engine assembly lube **(see illustration)**.

16   Slide the camshaft into the engine. Support the cam near the block and be careful not to scrape or nick the bearings.

17   Apply moly-base grease or engine assembly lube to both sides of the thrust plate, then position it on the block with the oil grooves in (against the block). Install the bolts and tighten them to the torque listed in this

13.11 Some models use T-30 Torx screws to retain the camshaft thrust plate (arrows)

13.12 Carefully remove the camshaft to avoid damaging the bearings (note that in this case the lifters are not stored in a box because they will be discarded along with the camshaft)

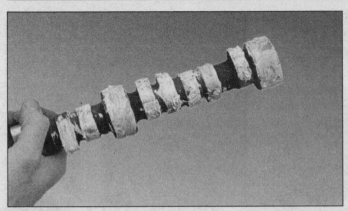

13.15 Apply moly-base grease or engine assembly lube to the camshaft lobes and journals prior to installation

14.15 Place a block of wood between the mount and subframe

Chapter's Specifications.

18   Refer to the appropriate Sections and install the lifters, pushrods, rocker arms, timing chain/sprocket, timing chain cover and rocker arm covers.

19   The remaining installation steps are the reverse of removal.

20   Before starting and running the engine, change the oil and install a new oil filter (see Chapter 1).

14   Oil pan - removal and installation

Removal

Refer to illustrations 14.15 and 14.19

1   Disconnect the negative battery cable from the battery.

2   Remove the air cleaner assembly (Chapter 4).

3   Remove the fan shroud mounting bolts and position the shroud back over the fan.

4   Remove the oil level dipstick and disconnect the oil level sensor switch on the side of the oil pan (if equipped).

5   If so equipped, remove the screws attaching the vacuum solenoids to the firewall behind the engine. Position the solenoids out of the way without disconnecting them.

6   If it will obstruct oil pan removal, disconnect the exhaust crossover pipe from the manifolds (Chapter 4).

7   Drain the engine oil and remove the oil filter (Chapter 1).

8   On models with an automatic transmission, disconnect the shift linkage where it goes from the body to the transmission (Chapter 7).

9   On models with an automatic transmission, disconnect the transmission cooler lines at the radiator (Chapter 3).

10   Remove the four torque converter cover retaining bolts and detach the cover.

11   Remove the starter motor (Chapter 5).

12   Disconnect the steering flex coupling and remove the two bolts attaching the steering gear to the subframe (Chapter 10). Let the steering gear rest on the subframe away from the oil pan.

13   Loosen the nuts holding the transmis-

14.19 Slip the oil pan out, turning it slightly to clear the oil pick-up (V6 engine)

sion mount to the crossmember, but don't remove them completely.

14   Remove the through bolts from the front engine mounts. Place a block of wood under the oil pan and lift the engine slightly with a jack. **Caution:** *When raising the engine on models with an automatic transmission, watch the clearance between the transmission dipstick tube and the Thermactor downstream air tube going to the catalytic converter. If the tubes contact before adequate mount-to-subframe clearance is achieved, lower the engine and remove the dipstick tube and downstream air tube. A clamp cutter and crimping tool, available at most auto parts stores, are recommended to disconnect the tube from the converter.*

15   Place wooden blocks between the mounts and subframe **(see illustration)**.

16   Remove the oil pan mounting bolts. Most models are equipped with a reinforcement strip on each side of the pan which may come loose as the bolts are removed.

17   Carefully separate the pan from the block. Don't pry between the block and pan or damage to the sealing surfaces may result and oil leaks could develop. Instead, dislodge the pan with a large rubber mallet or a block of wood and a hammer.

18   If you're working on a V8 engine, reach in and remove the oil pump and pick-up tube

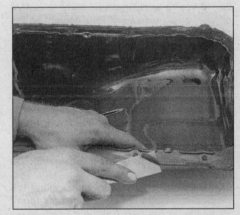

14.20 Scrape away all traces of gasket material and sealant, then clean the gasket surfaces with lacquer thinner or acetone

fasteners and allow them to drop into the oil pan (the pan can't be removed with them bolted to the block - there's not enough room).

19   Maneuver the pan out the rear, between the subframe and transmission **(see illustration)**.

Installation

Refer to illustration 14.20

Note: *Several different oil pan gasket configurations are found on engines covered by this manual. Most V6 engines have a half-round rubber seal in the rear main bearing cap groove and no gasket. RTV is used to seal the oil pan-to-block and timing chain cover joints. Later model V6's have one-piece rubber oil pan gaskets that incorporate the rear bearing cap seal. The V8 engine is equipped with rubber seals at the rear main bearing cap and timing chain cover, while conventional gaskets are used to seal the sides of the pan. Be sure to follow the installation instructions included with an OEM or aftermarket gasket set - they supersede the information included here.*

20   Use a gasket scraper or putty knife to remove all traces of old gasket material and sealant from the pan and block **(see illustration)**.

2D

21 Clean the mating surfaces with lacquer thinner or acetone. Make sure the bolt holes in the block are clean.
22 Check the oil pan flange for distortion, particularly around the bolt holes. If necessary, place the pan on a block of wood and use a hammer to flatten and restore the gasket surface.
23 Remove the old rubber seals from the rear main bearing cap and timing chain cover, then clean the grooves and install new seals (this doesn't apply to the later model V6 engine with a rubber gasket). Use RTV sealant or gasket contact adhesive to hold the new seals in place, then apply a bead of RTV sealant to the block-to-seal junctions. If you're working on a V8 engine, use the contact adhesive to attach the new gaskets to the block.
24 If you're working on an early model V6 engine, apply a bead of RTV sealant to the block mating surface. **Note:** *Aftermarket gasket sets may include a gasket for use on the early model V6 engine - be sure to follow the instructions included with the set.*
25 The rubber gasket used on the later model V6 engine should be positioned on the pan after the pan has been maneuvered back into place between the subframe and transmission.
26 If you're working on a V8 engine, don't forget to install the oil pump along with the pan.
27 Carefully position the pan against the block and install the bolts finger tight (don't forget the reinforcement strips, if used). Make sure the seal(s)/gasket(s) haven't shifted, then tighten the bolts in three steps to the torque listed in this Chapter's Specifications. Start at the center of the pan and work out toward the ends in a spiral pattern.
28 The remaining steps are the reverse of removal. **Caution:** *Don't forget to refill the engine with oil and replace the filter before starting it (see Chapter 1).*
29 Start the engine and check carefully for oil leaks at the oil pan.

15 Oil pump - removal and installation

V6 engine

Refer to illustrations 15.2 and 15.11

1 The oil pump is mounted externally on the timing chain cover.
2 Detach the oil filter (Chapter 1), then remove the oil pump cover bolts **(see illustration)**.
3 Detach the cover and gasket, then remove the gears from the cavity in the timing chain cover. Discard the gasket.
4 Clean and inspect the oil pump cavity. If the oil pump gear pocket in the timing chain cover is damaged or worn, replace the timing chain cover.
5 Remove all traces of gasket material from the oil pump cover, then check it for warpage with a straightedge and feeler

15.2 Remove the oil pump cover bolts

gauges. If it's warped more than 0.0016-inch, replace it with a new one.
6 To remove the pressure relief valve, first detach the timing chain cover from the engine (Section 10). Drill a hole in the plug **(see illustration 10.16)**, then pry it out or remove it with a slide hammer and screw adapter. Remove the spring and valve from the bore.
7 Remove all metal chips from the bore and the valve, then check them carefully for wear, score marks and galling. If the bore is worn or damaged,
a new timing chain cover will be required. The valve should fit in the bore with no noticeable side play or binding.
8 If the spring appears to be fatigued or collapsed, replace it with a new one. The tension can be measured and compared to the Specifications to determine its condition.
9 Apply clean engine oil to the valve and install it in the bore, small end first. Insert the spring, then install a new plug. Carefully tap it in until it's 0.010-inch below the machined surface of the cover.
10 Intermediate shaft removal and installation is covered in Section 10.
11 The oil pump pick-up is inside the oil pan. For access, remove the oil pan (Section 14). Remove the pick-up tube nut and the two mounting bolts **(see illustration)**.
12 Installation is the reverse of removal. **Caution:** *Be sure to pack the oil pump with petroleum jelly (NOT multi-purpose grease) before installing the cover. It must fill all voids between the gears, cavity and cover. If this isn't done, the pump may fail to prime when the engine is started. Install a new cover gasket and tighten the bolts to the torque listed in this Chapter's Specifications in a criss-cross pattern. Use a new pick-up tube gasket and tighten the mounting bolts securely.*

V8 engine

13 Unbolt and lower the oil pan as described in Section 14.
14 Remove the oil pick-up tube-to-main bearing cap nut.
15 Remove the oil pump mounting bolts.

15.11 Remove the nut and the two bolts (arrows) to detach the oil pick-up tube (V6 engine)

16 Lower the oil pump assembly into the oil pan and lift them both out together. If the pump is faulty, or you suspect that it's faulty, install a new one - do not attempt to repair the original.
17 Prime the oil pump prior to installation. Pour clean oil into the pickup and turn the pump shaft by hand.
18 If you separate the pump from the pick-up tube, use a new gasket and tighten the bolts securely when reattaching them.
19 Fit the oil pump driveshaft into the pump. It must seat all the way. DO NOT try to force it. If it doesn't align, turn the pump slightly and try again.
20 Install the mounting bolts/nut and tighten them to the torque listed in this Chapter's Specifications.

16 Crankshaft oil seals - replacement

Front seal - timing chain cover in place

Refer to illustrations 16.4, 16.5, 16.6, 16.8 and 16.10

1 Remove the bolts attaching the fan shroud to the radiator and position the shroud back over the fan.
2 Remove the fan/clutch assembly and the shroud (Chapter 3).
3 Remove the drivebelts (Chapter 1).
4 Mark the crankshaft pulley and vibration damper so they can be reassembled in the same relative position. This is important, since the damper and pulley are initially balanced as a unit. Unbolt and remove the pulley **(see illustration)**.
5 Remove the bolt from the front of the crankshaft, then use a puller to detach the vibration damper **(see illustration)**. **Caution:** *Don't use a puller with jaws that grip the outer edge of the damper. The puller must be the type shown in the illustration that utilizes bolts to apply force to the damper hub only. Clean*

16.4 Mark the pulley and vibration damper before removing the four bolts - the large vibration damper bolt (arrow) is usually very tight, so use a six-point socket and a breaker bar to loosen it

16.5 Use the recommended puller to remove the vibration damper - if a puller that applies force to the outer edge is used, the damper will be damaged!

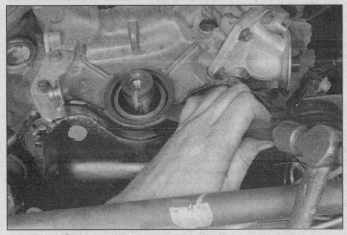

16.6 A chisel and hammer must be used to work the seal out of the timing chain cover - be very careful not to damage the cover or nick the crankshaft!

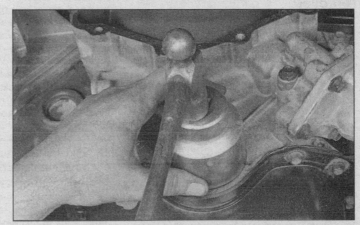

16.8 Clean the bore, then apply a small amount of oil to the outer edge of the new seal and drive it squarely into the opening with a large socket and a hammer - don't damage the seal in the process and make sure it's completely seated

2D

the crankshaft nose and the seal contact surface on the vibration damper with lacquer thinner or acetone. Leave the Woodruff key in place in the crankshaft keyway.

6   Carefully remove the seal from the cover with a small chisel and hammer (see illustration). Be careful not to damage the cover or scratch the wall of the seal bore. If the engine has accumulated a lot of miles, apply penetrating oil to the seal-to-cover joint and allow it to soak in before attempting to remove the seal.

7   Check the seal bore and crankshaft, as well as the seal contact surface on the vibration damper for nicks and burrs. Position the new seal in the bore with the open end of the seal facing IN. A small amount of oil applied to the outer edge of the new seal will make installation easier - don't overdo it!

8   Drive the seal into the bore with a large socket and hammer until it's completely seated (see illustration). Select a socket that's the same outside diameter as the seal (a section of pipe can be used if a socket isn't available).

9   Note: If a new vibration damper is being installed, balance pins must be located in the new damper in the same relative positions as the original. Also, the pulley must be attached to the damper with the same orientation to the pins as on the original. Apply moly-base grease or clean engine oil to the seal contact surface of the vibration damper and coat the keyway (groove) with a thin·layer of RTV sealant.

10   Install the damper on the end of the crankshaft. The keyway in the damper bore must be aligned with the Woodruff key in the crankshaft nose. If the damper can't be seated by hand, tap it into place with a soft-face hammer (see illustration) or slip a large washer over the bolt, install the bolt and tighten it to push the damper into place. Remove the large washer, then install the bolt and tighten it to the torque listed in this Chapter's Specifications.

11   Install the remaining parts removed for access to the seal.

12   Start the engine and check for leaks at the seal-to-cover joint.

16.10 A soft-face hammer can be used to tap the vibration damper onto the crankshaft - don't use a steel hammer!

16.17 If you're very careful not to damage the crankshaft or the seal bore, the rear seal can be pried out with a screwdriver - normally a special puller is used for this procedure

Front seal - timing chain cover removed

13   Use a punch or screwdriver and hammer to drive the seal out of the cover from the back side. Support the cover as close to the seal bore as possible. Be careful not to distort the cover or scratch the wall of the seal bore. If the engine has accumulated a lot of miles, apply penetrating oil to the seal-to-cover joint on each side and allow it to soak in before attempting to drive the seal out.

14   Clean the bore to remove any old seal material and corrosion. Support the cover on blocks of wood and position the new seal in the bore with the open end of the seal facing IN. A small amount of oil applied to the outer edge of the new seal will make installation easier - don't overdo it!

15   Drive the seal into the bore with a large socket and hammer until it's completely seated. Select a socket that's the same outside diameter as the seal (a section of pipe can be used if a socket isn't available).

Rear seal

Refer to illustration 16.17

16   Refer to Chapter 7 and remove the transmission, then detach the flywheel or driveplate and the rear cover plate from the engine (Section 17).

17   The old seal can be removed by prying it out with a screwdriver **(see illustration)**. Be sure to note how far it's recessed into the bore before removing it; the new seal will have to be recessed an equal amount. **Caution:** *Be very careful not to scratch or otherwise damage the crankshaft or the bore in the housing or oil leaks could develop!*

18   Clean the crankshaft and seal bore with lacquer thinner or acetone. Check the seal contact surface very carefully for scratches and nicks that could damage the new seal lip and cause oil leaks. If the crankshaft is damaged, the only alternative is a new or different crankshaft.

19   Make sure the bore is clean, then apply a thin coat of engine oil to the outer edge of the new seal. Apply moly-based grease to the seal lips. The seal must be pressed squarely

into the bore, so hammering it into place is not recommended. If you don't have access to a seal driver, you may be able to tap the seal in with a large section of pipe and a hammer. If you must use this method, be very careful not to damage the seal or crankshaft! And work the seal lip carefully over the end of the crankshaft with a blunt tool such as the rounded end of a socket extension.

20   Reinstall the engine rear cover plate, the flywheel or driveplate and the transmission.

17   Flywheel/driveplate - removal and installation

1   Raise the vehicle and support it securely on jackstands, then refer to Chapter 7 and remove the transmission. If it's leaking, now would be a very good time to replace the front pump seal/O-ring (automatic transmission only).

2   Remove the pressure plate and clutch disc (see Chapter 8) (manual transmission equipped vehicles). Now is a good time to check/replace the clutch components and pilot bearing.

3   Look for factory paint marks that indicate flywheel-to-crankshaft alignment. If they aren't there, use a center-punch to make alignment marks on the flywheel/driveplate and crankshaft to ensure correct alignment during reinstallation.

4   Remove the bolts that secure the flywheel/driveplate to the crankshaft. If the crankshaft turns, wedge a screwdriver through the starter opening to jam the flywheel.

5   Remove the flywheel/driveplate from the crankshaft. Since the flywheel is fairly heavy, be sure to support it while removing the last bolt.

6   Clean the flywheel to remove grease and oil. Inspect the surface for cracks, rivet grooves, burned areas and score marks. Light scoring can be removed with emery cloth. Check for cracked and broken ring gear teeth. Lay the flywheel on a flat surface and use a straightedge to check for warpage.

7   Clean and inspect the mating surfaces of the flywheel/driveplate and the crankshaft. If the crankshaft rear seal is leaking, replace it before reinstalling the flywheel/driveplate.

8   Position the flywheel/driveplate against the crankshaft. Be sure to align the marks made during removal. Note that some engines have a alignment dowel or staggered bolt holes to ensure correct installation. Before installing the bolts, apply Teflon pipe sealant to the threads.

9   Wedge a screwdriver through the starter motor opening to keep the flywheel/driveplate from turning as you tighten the bolts to the torque listed in this Chapter's Specifications.

10   The remainder of installation is the reverse of the removal procedure.

18   Engine mounts - check and replacement

1   Engine mounts seldom require attention, but broken or deteriorated mounts should be replaced immediately or the added strain placed on the driveline components may cause damage or wear.

Check

2   During the check, the engine must be raised slightly to remove the weight from the mounts.

3   Raise the vehicle and support it securely on jackstands, then position a jack under the engine oil pan. Place a large block of wood between the jack head and the oil pan, then carefully raise the engine just enough to take the weight off the mounts. **Warning:** *DO NOT place any part of your body under the engine when it's supported only by a jack!*

4   Check the mounts to see if the rubber is cracked, hardened or separated from the metal plates. Sometimes the rubber will split right down the center.

5   Check for relative movement between the mount plates and the engine or frame (use a large screwdriver or pry bar to attempt to move the mounts). If movement is noted, lower the engine and tighten the mount fasteners.

6   Rubber preservative should be applied to the mounts to slow deterioration.

Replacement

7   Disconnect the negative battery cable from the battery, then raise the vehicle and support it securely on jackstands (if not already done).

8   Remove the nut to disconnect the mount from the frame. On automatic transmission models, disconnect the shift linkage (see Chapter 7).

9   Raise the engine slightly with a jack or hoist (make sure the fan doesn't hit the radiator or shroud). Remove the mount-to-block bolts and detach the mount.

10   Installation is the reverse of removal. Use thread locking compound on the mount bolts and be sure to tighten them securely.

Chapter 2 Part E
General engine overhaul procedures

Contents

2E

Specifications

Four-cylinder engine

General

Displacement	2.3 liters
Cylinder compression pressure	Lowest cylinder must be within 75 percent of highest cylinder
Oil pressure (engine warm)	40 to 60 psi at 2000 rpm

Cylinder head warpage limit ... 0.003 in (in any 6 inches); 0.006 in overall

Valves and related components

Minimum valve margin width	1/32 in
Intake valve	
Seat angle	45-degrees
Seat width	0.060 to 0.080 in
Seat runout limit	0.0016 in (total indicator reading)
Stem diameter	
Standard	0.3416 to 0.3423 in
0.015 oversize	0.3566 to 0.3573 in
0.030 oversize	0.3716 to 0.3723 in
Valve stem-to-guide clearance	
Standard	0.0010 to 0.0027 in
Service limit	0.0055 in
Valve face runout limit	0.002 in

Valves and related components (Four-cylinder engine continued)

Exhaust valve
  Seat angle 45-degrees
  Seat width .... 0.070 to 0.090 in
  Seat runout limit .... 0.0016 in (total indicator reading)
  Stem diameter
    Standard .... 0.3411 to 0.3418 in
    0.015 oversize .... 0.3561 to 0.3568 in
    0.030 oversize .... 0.3711 to 0.3718 in
  Valve stem-to-guide clearance
    Standard .... 0.0015 to 0.0032 in
    Service limit .... 0.0055 in
  Valve face runout limit .... 0.002 in
Valve spring
  Out-of-square limit .... 5/64 in
  Pressure
    Standard
      1979 through 1983 .... 71 to 79 lbs at 1.56 in
      1984 on .... 71 to 79 lbs at 1.52 in
    Service limit
      1979 through 1982 .... 10-percent pressure loss at specified length
      1983 on .... 5-percent pressure loss at specified length
  Installed height .... 1-17/32 to 1-19/32 in
  Hydraulic valve lash adjuster
    Diameter (standard) .... 0.8422 to 0.8427 in
    Clearance in bore
      Standard .... 0.0007 to 0.0027 in
      Service limit .... 0.005 in

Crankshaft and connecting rods

Connecting rod journal
  Diameter
    1979 .... 2.0464 to 2.0472 in
    1980 through 1982 .... 2.0462 to 2.0472 in
    1983 on .... 2.0465 to 2.0472 in
  Out-of-round limit .... 0.0006 in
  Taper limit .... 0.0006 in per in
  Bearing oil clearance
    Desired .... 0.0008 to 0.0015 in
    Allowable .... 0.0008 to 0.0026 in
Connecting rod side clearance (endplay)
  Standard .... 0.0035 to 0.0105 in
  Service limit .... 0.014 in
Main bearing journal
  Diameter
    1979 through 1990 .... 2.399 to 2.3982 in
    1991 on .... 2.2059 to 2.2051 in
  Taper limit .... 0.0006 in per in
  Runout limit
    1979 through 1990 .... 0.005 in
    1991 on .... 0.002 in
  Bearing oil clearance
    Desired .... 0.0008 to 0.0015 in
    Allowable .... 0.0008 to 0.0026 in
Crankshaft endplay
  Standard .... 0.004 to 0.008 in
  Service limit .... 0.012 in

Cylinder bore

Diameter	3.7795 to 3.7825 in
Out-of-round limit	0.005 in
Taper limit	0.010 in

Pistons and rings

Piston diameter
  1979
    Coded red .... 3.7780 to 3.7786 in
    Coded blue .... 3.7792 to 3.7798 in
  1980 through 1982
    Turbo
      Coded red .... 3.7760 to 3.7766 in
      Coded blue .... 3.7772 to 3.7778 in
    Non-turbo
      Coded red .... 3.7780 to 3.7786 in
      Coded blue .... 3.7792 to 3.7798 in
  1983 on
    Coded red .... 3.7764 to 3.7770 in
    Coded blue .... 3.7776 to 3.7782 in
Piston-to-bore clearance limit (select fit)
  1979 through 1982
    Turbo .... 0.0034 to 0.0042 in
    Non-turbo .... 0.0014 to 0.0022 in
  1983 through 1990 .... 0.0030 to 0.0038 in
  1991 .... 0.0024 to 0.00338 in
  1992 on .... 0.0018 to 0.0029 in
Piston ring end gap
  Compression rings
    1979 through 1991 top and bottom .... 0.010 to 0.020 in
    1992
      Top ring .... 0.010 to 0.020 in
      Bottom ring .... 0.015 to 0.025 in
  Oil ring (steel rail) .... 0.015 to 0.055 in
Piston ring side clearance
  Compression rings
    Standard
      1979 through 1990 .... 0.002 to 0.004 in
      1991 on .... 0.016 to 0.0033 in
    Service limit .... 0.006 in
  Oil ring (steel rail) .... snug fit

Auxiliary shaft

Endplay	0.001 to 0.007 in
Bearing oil clearance	0.0006 to 0.0026 in

Torque specifications*

Ft-lbs

Main bearing cap bolts
  1979 through 1986
    Step 1 .... 50 to 60
    Step 2 .... 80 to 90
  1987 on
    Step 1 .... 50 to 60
    Step 2 .... 75 to 85
Connecting rod cap nuts
  Step 1 .... 25 to 30
  Step 2 .... 30 to 36

* **Note:** *Refer to Part A for additional torque specifications.*

3.3L inline six-cylinder engine

General

Displacement	3.3 liters (200 cu in)
Cylinder compression pressure	Lowest cylinder must be within 75 percent of highest cylinder
Oil pressure (engine warm at 2000 rpm)	30 to 50 psi

Cylinder head warpage limit	0.003 in per 6 in; 0.006 in overall

2E

Valves and related components (3.3L inline six-cylinder engine continued)

Minimum valve margin width	1/32 in

Intake valve
Seat angle	45-degrees
Seat width	0.060 to 0.080 in
Seat runout limit	0.002 in (total indicator reading)
Stem diameter	0.3100 to 0.3107 in
Stem-to-guide clearance	0.0008 to 0.0025 in
Valve face runout limit	0.002 in
Valve face angle	44-degrees

Exhaust valve
Seat angle	45-degrees
Seat width	0.070 to 0.090 in
Seat runout limit	0.002 in (total indicator reading)
Stem diameter	0.3098 to 0.3105 in
Stem-to-guide clearance	0.0010 to 0.0027 in
Valve face runout limit	0.002 in
Valve face angle	44-degrees

Valve spring
Pressure
Intake	51 at 57 lbs at 1.59 in
Exhaust	142 to 158 lbs at 1.222 in
Service limit (both valves)	10-percent pressure loss at specified length
Free length (approximate)	1.79 in
Installed height	1-9/16 to 1-19/32 in

Valve lifter
Diameter (standard)	0.8740 to 0.8745 in

Lifter-to-bore clearance
Standard	0.0007 to 0.0027 in
Service limit	0.005 in

Crankshaft and connecting rods

Connecting rod journal
Diameter (standard)	2.1232 to 2.1240 in
Out-of-round limit	0.0006 in
Taper limit	0.0006 in per inch

Bearing oil clearance
Desired	0.0008 to 0.0015 in
Allowable	0.0008 to 0.0024 in

Connecting rod side clearance (endplay)
Standard	0.0035 to 0.0105 in
Service limit	0.014 in

Main bearing journal
Diameter	2.2482 to 2.2490 in
Out-of-round limit	0.0006 in
Taper limit	0.0006 in per inch

Bearing oil clearance
Desired	0.0008 to 0.0015 in
Allowable	0.0008 to 0.0024 in

Crankshaft endplay
Standard	0.004 to 0.008 in
Service limit	0.012 in

Cylinder bore
Diameter	3.6800 to 3.6848 in
Out-of-round service limit	0.005 in
Taper service limit	0.010 in

Pistons and rings

Piston diameter*
Coded red	3.6784 to 3.6790 in
Coded blue	3.6796 to 3.6802 in
Piston-to-bore clearance	0.0013 to 0.0021 in

Piston ring end gap
Compression rings	0.008 to 0.016 in
Oil ring rails	0.015 to 0.055 in

Piston ring side clearance
Compression rings
Standard	0.002 to 0.004 in
Service limit	0.006 in
Oil ring	Snug fit

Chapter 2 Part E General engine overhaul procedures

Chapter 2 Part E General engine overhaul procedures

Torque specifications**

	Ft-lbs
Main bearing cap bolts	60 to 70
Connecting rod cap nuts	21 to 26

* *Measured at the pin bore centerline, at 90-degrees to the pin.*
** *Refer to Part B for additional torque specifications.*

2.8L V6 engine

General

Displacement	2.8 liters (2800 cc)
Cylinder compression pressure	Lowest cylinder must be within 75 percent of highest cylinder
Oil pressure (engine warm at 2000 rpm)	40 to 60 psi
Cylinder head warpage limit	0.003 in per 6 in; 0.006 in overall

Valves and related components

Minimum valve margin width	1/32 in
Intake valve	
Seat angle	45-degrees
Seat width	0.060 to 0.079 in
Seat runout limit	0.0015 in (total indicator reading)
Stem diameter	0.3159 to 0.3167
Stem-to-guide clearance	0.0008 to 0.0025 in
Valve face runout limit	0.002 in
Valve face angle	44-degrees
Exhaust valve	
Seat angle	45-degrees
Seat width	0.060 to 0.079 in
Seat runout limit	0.002 in (total indicator reading)
Stem diameter	0.3149 to 0.3156 in
Stem-to-guide clearance	0.0018 to 0.0035 in
Valve face runout limit	0.002 in
Valve face angle	44-degrees
Valve spring	
Pressure	
Standard	60.0 to 68.0 lbs at 1.585 in
Service limit	10-percent pressure loss at specified length
Free length (approximate)	1.91 in
Installed height	1-37/64 to 1-39/64 in
Valve lifter	
Diameter (standard)	0.8736 to 0.8741 in
Lifter-to-bore clearance	
Standard	0.0009 to 0.0024 in
Service limit	0.005 in

Crankshaft and connecting rods

Connecting rod journal	
Diameter (standard)	2.1252 to 2.1260 in
Out-of-round limit	0.0006 in
Taper limit	0.0006 in per inch
Bearing oil clearance	
Desired	0.0006 to 0.0016 in
Allowable	0.0005 to 0.0022 in
Connecting rod side clearance (endplay)	
Standard	0.004 to 0.011 in
Service limit	0.014 in
Main bearing journal	
Diameter	2.2433 to 2.2441 in
Out-of-round limit	0.0006 in
Taper limit	0.0006 in per inch
Bearing oil clearance	
Desired	0.0008 to 0.0015 in
Allowable	0.0005 to 0.0019 in
Crankshaft endplay	
Standard	0.004 to 0.008 in
Service limit	0.012 in

Cylinder bore

Diameter	3.6614 to 3.6630 in
Out-of-round service limit	0.005 in
Taper service limit	0.010 in

2.8L V6 engine (continued)

Pistons and rings

Piston diameter*
  Coded red .... 3.6605 to 3.6615 in
  0.020 in oversize .... 3.6802 to 3.6812 in
Piston-to-bore clearance .... 0.001 to 0.0019 in
Piston ring end gap
  Compression rings .... 0.015 to 0.023 in
  Oil ring rails.. 0.015 to 0.055 in
Piston ring side clearance
  Compression rings
    Standard .... 0.0020 to 0.0033 in
    Service limit... 0.006 in
  Oil ring .... Snug fit

Torque specifications**   **Ft-lbs**

Main bearing cap bolts .... 65 to 75
Connecting rod cap nuts .... 21 to 25

Measured at the pin bore centerline, at 90-degrees to the pin.
**Refer to Part C for additional torque specifications.*

3.8L V6 engine

General

Displacement... 3.8 liters (231 cu in)
Cylinder compression pressure.. Lowest cylinder must be within 75 percent of highest cylinder
Oil pressure (engine warm at 2500 rpm)
  1983 and 1984 .... 54 to 59 psi
  1985 on .... 40 to 60 psi
Cylinder head warpage limit.. 0.007 in

Valves and related components

Minimum valve margin width... 1/32 in
Intake valve
  Seat angle 45-degrees
  Seat width .... 0.060 to 0.080 in
  Seat runout limit .... 0.003 in (total indicator reading)
  Stem diameter.. 0.3423 to 0.3716 in
  Valve stem-to-guide clearance .... 0.001 to 0.0027 in
  Valve face runout limit .... 0.002 in
  Valve face angle 44-degrees
Exhaust valve
  Seat angle 45-degrees
  Seat width .... 0.060 to 0.080 in
  Seat runout limit .... 0.003 in (total indicator reading)
  Stem diameter.. 0.3418 to 0.3411 in
  Valve stem-to-guide clearance .... 0.0015 to 0.0032 in
  Valve face runout limit .... 0.002 in
  Valve face angle 44-degrees
Valve spring
  Pressure (not including dampener)
    1983 through 1985
      Valve open.. 215 lbs at 1.29 in
      Valve closed .... 75 lbs at 1.70 in
    1986
      Valve open.. 190 lbs 1.28 in
      Valve closed .... 73 lbs at 1.70 in
    Service limit... 10 lbs pressure loss at specified length
  Installed height .... 1.70 to 1.78 in
Valve lifter
  Diameter (standard).. 0.874 in
  Lifter-to-bore clearance
    Standard .... 0.0007 to 0.0027 in
    Service limit... 0.005 in

Crankshaft and connecting rods

Connecting rod journal
  Diameter.. 2.3103 to 2.3111 in
  Out-of-round limit... 0.0003 in
  Taper limit.. 0.0003 in per in

Bearing oil clearance
    Desired .... 0.001 to 0.0014 in
    Allowable .... 0.00086 to 0.0027 in
Connecting rod side clearance (endplay)
    Standard... 0.0047 to 0.0114 in
    Service limit .... 0.014 in
Main bearing journal
    Diameter .... 2.5190 to 2.5198 in
    Out-of-round limit.. 0.0003 in
    Taper limit.. 0.0003 in per in
    Bearing oil clearance
        Desired .... 0.001 to 0.0014 in
        Allowable .... 0.0005 to 0.0023 in
Crankshaft endplay.. 0.004 to 0.008 in

Cylinder bore

Diameter .... 3.810 in
Out-of-round limit .... 0.002 in
Taper limit.. 0.002 in

Pistons and rings

Piston diameter
    Coded red .... 3.8095 to 3.8101 in
    Coded blue.. 3.8107 to 3.8113 in
    Coded yellow .... 3.8119 to 3.8125 in
Piston-to-bore clearance limit
    1983 .... 0.0014 to 0.0022 in
    1984 on .... 0.0014 to 0.0032 in
Piston ring end gap
    Compression rings .... 0.010 to 0.020 in
    Oil ring .... 0.015 to 0.0583 in
Piston ring side clearance .... 0.0016 to 0.0037 in

Torque specifications*   Ft-lbs

Main bearing cap bolts .... 65 to 81
Connecting rod cap nuts .... 31 to 36

* Note: *Refer to Part D for additional torque specifications.*

V8 engines

Gonoral

Displacement
    1979 and 1983 on .... 5.0 liters (302 cu in)
    1980 through 1982 .... 4.2 liters (255 cu in)
Cylinder compression pressure.. Lowest cylinder must be within 75 percent of highest cylinder
Oil pressure (engine warm).. 40 to 65 psi at 2000 rpm
Cylinder head warpage limit .... 0.003 in (in any 6 inches)/0.006 in overall

Valves and related components

Minimum valve margin width.. 1/32 in
Intake valve
    Seat angle 45-degrees
    Seat width .... 0.060 to 0.080 in
    Seat runout limit .... 0.002 in (total indicator reading)
    Stem diameter
        Standard .... 0.3416 to 0.3423 in
        0.015 oversize... 0.3566 to 0.3573 in
        0.030 oversize... 0.3716 to 0.3723 in
    Valve stem-to-guide clearance
        Standard .... 0.0010 to 0.0027 in
        Service limit.. 0.005 in
    Valve face angle 44-degrees
    Valve face runout limit .... 0.002 in
Exhaust valve
    Seat angle 45-degrees
    Seat width .... 0.060 to 0.080 in
    Seat runout limit .... 0.002 in (total indicator reading)
    Stem diameter
        Standard .... 0.3411 to 0.3418 in
        0.015 oversize... 0.3561 to 0.3568 in
        0.030 oversize... 0.3711 to 0.3718 in

2E

V8 engines (continued)

Valve stem-to-guide clearance
  Standard .... 0.0015 to 0.0032 in
  Service limit.. 0.0055 in
Valve face angle 44-degrees
Valve face runout limit .... 0.002 in
Valve spring
  Pressure (not including dampener)
    Intake
      1979 and 1980
        Valve open.. 190 to 212 lbs at 1.36 in
        Valve closed .... 74 to 82 lbs at 1.78 in
      1981 and 1982
        Valve open.. 196 to 214 lbs at 1.36 in
        Valve closed .... 74 to 82 lbs at 1.78 in
      1983
        Valve open
          Except HO .... 196 to 214 lbs at 1.36 in
          HO .... 194 to 214 lbs at 1.33 in
        Valve closed .... 74 to 82 lbs at 1.78 in
      1984 through 1987
        Valve open
          Except HO .... 196 to 214 lbs at 1.36 in
          HO .... 215 to 235 lbs at 1.33 in
        Valve closed
          Except HO .... 74 to 82 lbs at 1.78 in
          HO .... 76 to 84 lbs at 1.79 in
      1988 on
        Valve open.. 211 to 230 lbs at 1.36 in
        Valve closed .... 74 to 82 lbs at 1.78 in
    Exhaust
      1979 through 1981
        Valve open.. 190 to 210 lbs at 1.20 in
        Valve closed .... 76 to 84 lbs at 1.60 in
      1982 and 1983
        Valve open.. 195 to 215 lbs at 1.05 in
        Valve closed .... 71 to 79 lbs at 1.60 in
      1984 through 1987
        Valve open
          Except HO .... 195 to 215 lbs at 1.05 in
          HO .... 210 to 230 lbs at 1.15 in
        Valve closed
          Except HO .... 71 to 79 lbs at 1.60 in
          HO .... 79 to 87 lbs at 1.60 in
      1988 on
        Valve open.. 200 to 226 lbs at 1.15 in
        Valve closed .... 77 to 85 lbs at 1.60 in
Valve spring pressure service limit .... 10-percent pressure loss at specified length
Out-of-square limit .... 5/64 in
Installed height
  Intake
    1979 through 1987
      Except HO .... 1-43/64 to 1-45/64 in
      HO .... Not available
    1988 on.. 1-3/4 to 1-13/16 in
  Exhaust
    1979 through 1987
      Except HO .... 1-37/64 to 1-39/64 in
      HO .... Not available
    1988 on.. 1-37/64 to 1-41/64 in
Free length (approximate)
  Intake
    1979 through 1982... 2.04 in
    1983 through 1987... 2.05 in
    1988 on.. 2.02 in
  Exhaust
    1979 through 1982... 1.85 in
    1983 through 1987... 1.87 in
    1988 on.. 1.79 in
    1993 HO Cobra.. 1.389 in

Valve lifter
    Diameter (standard)... 0.8740 to 0.8745 in
    Lifter-to-bore clearance
        Standard .... 0.0007 to 0.0027 in
        Service limit.. 0.005 in

Crankshaft and connecting rods

Connecting rod journal
    Diameter .... 2.1228 to 2.1236 in
    Out-of-round/taper limit .... 0.0006 in per in
    Bearing oil clearance
        Desired... 0.0008 to 0.0015 in
        Allowable.. 0.0008 to 0.0024 in
Connecting rod side clearance (endplay)
    Standard... 0.010 to 0.020 in
    Service limit... 0.023 in
Main bearing journal
    Diameter .... 2.2490 to 2.2482 in
    Out-of-round limit... 0.0006 in
    Taper limit.. 0.0004 in per in
    Runout
        Standard .... 0.002 in
        Service limit.. 0.005 in
    Bearing oil clearance
        1979 through 1981 (desired)
            No. 1 journal .... 0.0001 to 0.0015 in
            All others.. 0.0004 to 0.0015 in
        1979 through 1981 (allowable)
            No. 1 journal .... 0.0001 to 0.0017 in
            All others.. 0.0004 to 0.0021 in
        1982 through 1984 (desired)
            No. 1 journal .... 0.0004 to 0.0025 in
            All others.. 0.0004 to 0.0015 in
        1982 through 1984 (allowable)
            No. 1 journal .... 0.0001 to 0.0030 in
            All others.. 0.0004 to 0.0021 in
        1985 on
            Desired .... 0.0004 to 0.0015 in
            Allowable.. 0.0004 to 0.0021 in
Crankshaft endplay
    Standard... 0.004 to 0.008 in
    Service limit... 0.012 in

Cylinder bore

Diameter
    4.2L (255 cu in) .... 3.6800 to 3.6845 in
    5.0L (302 cu in)
        1979 through 1986.. 4.0004 to 4.0052 in
        1987 on .... 4.0004 to 4.0048 in
Out-of-round limit .... 0.005 in
Taper limit .... 0.010 in

Pistons and rings

Piston diameter
    Coded red
        1979 through 1987.. 3.9984 to 3.9990 in
        1988 on .... 3.9972 to 3.9980 in
    Coded blue
        1979 through 1987.. 3.9996 to 4.0002 in
        1988 on (non-HO) .... 3.9984 to 4.9992 in
        1993 HO.. 4.0009 to 4.0030 in
    Coded yellow
        1979 through 1987.. 4.0020 to 4.0026 in
        1988 through 1993 (non-HO) .... 3.9996 to 4.0004 in
        1993 HO.. 4.0015 to 4.0021 in
    0.003 in oversize (through 1987) .... 4.0008 to 4.0014 in
Piston-to-bore clearance limit
    1979 through 1987 .... 0.0018 to 0.0026 in
    1988 on .... 0.0030 to 0.0038 in

2E

V8 engines (continued)

Piston ring end gap
   1987 through 1992
      Compression rings... 0.010 to 0.020 in
      Oil ring.. 0.015 to 0.055 in
   1993 HO
   Compression rings
   Top .... 0.010 to 0.020 in
   Second .... 0.018 to 0.028 in
   Oil ring .... 0.010 to 0.040 in
Piston ring side clearance
   Compression rings
      Standard .... 0.002 to 0.004 in
      Service limit... 0.006 in
   Oil ring .... Snug fit

Torque specifications*   Ft-lbs

Main bearing cap bolts... 60 to 70
Connecting rod cap nuts... 19 to 24

* **Note:** *Refer to Part D for additional torque specifications.*

1 General information

Included in this portion of Chapter 2 are the general overhaul procedures for the cylinder head(s) and internal engine components.

The information ranges from advice concerning preparation for an overhaul and the purchase of replacement parts to detailed, step-by-step procedures covering removal and installation of internal engine components and the inspection of parts.

The following Sections have been written based on the assumption that the engine has been removed from the vehicle. For information concerning in-vehicle engine repair, as well as removal and installation of the external components necessary for the overhaul, see Parts A through D of this Chapter and Section 7 of this Part.

The Specifications included in this Part are only those necessary for the inspection and overhaul procedures which follow. Refer to Parts A through D for additional Specifications.

2 Engine overhaul - general information

Refer to illustration 2.4

It's not always easy to determine when, or if, an engine should be completely overhauled, as a number of factors must be considered.

High mileage is not necessarily an indication that an overhaul is needed, while low mileage doesn't preclude the need for an overhaul. Frequency of servicing is probably the most important consideration. An engine that's had regular and frequent oil and filter changes, as well as other required maintenance, will most likely give many thousands of miles of reliable service. Conversely, a neglected engine may require an overhaul very early in its life.

Excessive oil consumption is an indication that piston rings, valve seals and/or valve guides are in need of attention. Make sure that oil leaks aren't responsible before deciding that the rings and/or guides are bad. Perform a cylinder compression check to determine the extent of the work required (see Section 3).

Check the oil pressure with a gauge installed in place of the oil pressure sending unit. If it's extremely low, the bearings and/or oil pump are probably worn out. The accompanying illustration shows the sending unit location on 3.8L V6 engines. On four-cylinder engines, the sending unit is on the left rear side of the cylinder head. On 2.8L V6 engines, it's at the lower left front corner of the engine. On inline six-cylinder and V8 engines, it's near the oil filter.

Loss of power, rough running, knocking or metallic engine noises, excessive valve train noise and high fuel consumption rates may also point to the need for an overhaul, especially if they're all present at the same time. If a complete tune-up doesn't remedy the situation, major mechanical work is the only solution.

An engine overhaul involves restoring the internal parts to the specifications of a new engine. During an overhaul, the piston rings are replaced and the cylinder walls are reconditioned (rebored and/or honed). If a rebore is done by an automotive machine shop, new oversize pistons will also be installed. The main bearings, connecting rod bearings and camshaft bearings are generally replaced with new ones and, if necessary, the crankshaft may be reground to restore the journals. Generally, the valves are serviced as well, since they're usually in less-than-perfect condition at this point.

While the engine is being overhauled, other components, such as the distributor, starter and alternator, can be rebuilt as well. The end result should be a like-new engine that will give many trouble-free miles. **Note:** *Critical cooling system components such as*

2.4 On the 3.8L V6 engine, the oil pressure sending unit (arrow) is below the power steering pump and air conditioning compressor, which have been removed for this photo - see the text for the location on other engines

the hoses, drivebelts, thermostat and water pump MUST be replaced with new parts when an engine is overhauled. The radiator should be checked carefully to ensure that it isn't clogged or leaking (see Chapter 3). Also, we don't recommend overhauling the oil pump - always install a new one when an engine is rebuilt.

Before beginning the engine overhaul, read through the entire procedure to familiarize yourself with the scope and requirements of the job.

Overhauling an engine isn't difficult if you follow all of the instructions carefully, have the necessary tools and equipment and pay close attention to all specifications; however, it can be time consuming. Plan on the vehicle being tied up for a minimum of two weeks, especially if parts must be taken to an automotive machine shop for repair or reconditioning. Check on availability of parts and make sure that any necessary special tools and equipment are obtained in advance.

Most work can be done with typical hand tools, although a number of precision measuring tools are required for inspecting parts to determine if they must be replaced. Often an automotive machine shop will handle the inspection of parts and offer advice concerning reconditioning and replacement. **Note:** *Always wait until the engine has been completely disassembled and all components, especially the engine block, have been inspected before deciding what service and repair operations must be performed by an automotive machine shop. Since the block's condition will be the major factor to consider when determining whether to overhaul the original engine or buy a rebuilt one, never purchase parts or have machine work done on other components until the block has been thoroughly inspected. As a general rule, time is the primary cost of an overhaul, so it doesn't pay to install worn or substandard parts.*

As a final note, to ensure maximum life and minimum trouble from a rebuilt engine, everything must be assembled with care in a spotlessly clean environment.

3 Compression check

Refer to illustration 3.6

1 A compression check will tell you what mechanical condition the upper end (pistons, rings, valves, head gaskets) of your engine is in. Specifically, it can tell you if the compression is down due to leakage caused by worn piston rings, defective valves and seats or a blown head gasket. **Note:** *The engine must be at normal operating temperature and the battery must be fully charged for this check. Also, if the engine is equipped with a carburetor, the choke valve must be all the way open to get an accurate compression reading (if the engine's warm, the choke should be open).*

2 Begin by cleaning the area around the spark plugs before you remove them (compressed air should be used, if available, otherwise a small
brush or even a bicycle tire pump will work). The idea is to prevent dirt from getting into the cylinders as the compression check is being done.

3 Remove all of the spark plugs from the engine (see Chapter 1).

4 Block the throttle wide open.

5 Detach the coil wire from the center of the distributor cap and ground it on the engine block. Use a jumper wire with alligator clips on each end to ensure a good ground.

6 Install the compression gauge in the number one spark plug hole (**see illustration**).

7 Crank the engine over at least seven compression strokes and watch the gauge. The compression should build up quickly in a healthy engine. Low compression on the first stroke, followed by gradually increasing pressure on successive strokes, indicates worn piston rings. A low compression reading on

the first stroke, which doesn't build up during successive strokes, indicates leaking valves or a blown head gasket (a cracked head could also be the cause). Deposits on the undersides of the valve heads can also cause low compression. Record the highest gauge reading obtained.

8 Repeat the procedure for the remaining cylinders and compare the results to this Chapter's Specifications.

9 Add some engine oil (about three squirts from a plunger-type oil can) to each cylinder, through the spark plug hole, and repeat the test.

10 If the compression increases after the oil is added, the piston rings are definitely worn. If the compression doesn't increase significantly, the leakage is occurring at the valves or head gasket. Leakage past the valves may be caused by burned valve seats and/or faces or warped, cracked or bent valves.

11 If two adjacent cylinders have equally low compression, there's a strong possibility that the head gasket between them is blown. The appearance of coolant in the combustion chambers or the crankcase would verify this condition.

12 If one cylinder is 20 percent lower than the others, and the engine has a slightly rough idle, a worn exhaust lobe on the camshaft could be the cause.

13 If the compression is unusually high, the combustion chambers are probably coated with carbon deposits. If that's the case, the cylinder head(s) should be removed and decarbonized.

14 If compression is way down or varies greatly between cylinders, it would be a good idea to have a leak-down test performed by an automotive repair shop. This test will pinpoint exactly where the leakage is occurring and how severe it is.

4 Engine rebuilding alternatives

The do-it-yourselfer is faced with a number of options when performing an engine overhaul. The decision to replace the engine block, piston/connecting rod assemblies and crankshaft depends on a number of factors, with the number one consideration being the condition of the block. Other considerations are cost, access to machine shop facilities, parts availability, time required to complete the project and the extent of prior mechanical experience on the part of the do-it-yourselfer.

Some of the rebuilding alternatives include:

Individual parts - If the inspection procedures reveal that the engine block and most engine components are in reusable condition, purchasing individual parts may be the most economical alternative. The block, crankshaft and piston/connecting rod assemblies should all be inspected carefully. Even if the block shows little wear, the cylinder bores should be surface honed.

Crankshaft kit - This rebuild package

3.6 A gauge with a threaded fitting for the spark plug hole is preferred over the type that requires hand pressure to maintain the seal during the compression check

consists of a reground crankshaft and a matched set of pistons and connecting rods. The pistons will already be installed on the connecting rods. Piston rings and the necessary bearings will be included in the kit. These kits are commonly available for standard cylinder bores, as well as for engine blocks which have been bored to a regular oversize.

Short block - A short block consists of an engine block with a crankshaft and piston/connecting rod assemblies already installed. All new bearings are incorporated and all clearances will be correct. The existing camshaft, valve train components, cylinder head(s) and external parts can be bolted to the short block with little or no machine shop work necessary.

Long block - A long block consists of a short block plus an oil pump, oil pan, cylinder head(s), rocker arm cover(s), camshaft and valve train components, timing sprockets and chain or gears and timing cover. All components are installed with new bearings, seals and gaskets incorporated throughout. The installation of manifolds and external parts is all that's necessary.

Give careful thought to which alternative is best for you and discuss the situation with local automotive machine shops, auto parts dealers and experienced rebuilders before ordering or purchasing replacement parts.

5 Engine removal - methods and precautions

If you've decided that the engine must be removed for overhaul or major repair work, several preliminary steps should be taken.

Locating a place to work is extremely important. Adequate work space, along with storage space for the vehicle, will be needed. If a shop or garage isn't available, at the very least a flat, level, clean work surface made of concrete or asphalt is required.

2E

Cleaning the engine compartment and engine before beginning the removal procedure will help keep tools clean and organized.

An engine hoist or A-frame will also be necessary. Make sure the equipment is rated in excess of the combined weight of the engine and accessories. Safety is of primary importance, considering the potential hazards involved in lifting the engine out of the vehicle.

If the engine is being removed by a novice, a helper should be available. Advice and aid from someone more experienced would also be helpful. There are many instances when one person cannot simultaneously perform all of the operations required when lifting the engine out of the vehicle.

Plan the operation ahead of time. Arrange for or obtain all of the tools and equipment you'll need prior to beginning the job. Some of the equipment necessary to perform engine removal and installation safely and with relative ease are (in addition to an engine hoist) a heavy duty floor jack, complete sets of wrenches and sockets as described at the front of this manual, wooden blocks and plenty of rags and cleaning solvent for mopping up spilled oil, coolant and gasoline. If the hoist must be rented, make sure you arrange for it in advance and perform all of the operations possible without it ahead of time. This will save you money and time.

Plan for the vehicle to be out of use for quite a while. A machine shop will be required to perform some of the work the do-it-yourselfer can't accomplish without special equipment. They often have a busy schedule, so it would be a good idea to consult them before removing the engine in order to accurately estimate the amount of time required to rebuild or repair components that may need work.

Always be extremely careful when removing and installing the engine. Serious injury can result from careless actions. Plan ahead, take your
time and a job of this nature, although major, can be accomplished success- fully.

6   Engine - removal and installation

Refer to illustration 6.5 and 6.26
Warning: *The air conditioning system is under high pressure! Have a dealer service department or service station discharge the system before disconnecting any air conditioning system hoses or fittings.*

Removal

1   Refer to Chapter 4 and relieve the fuel system pressure (EFI equipped vehicles only), then disconnect the negative cable from the battery.
2   Cover the fenders and cowl and remove the hood (see Chapter 11). Special pads are available to protect the fenders, but an old bedspread or blanket will also work.

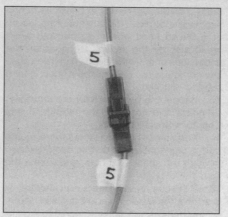

6.5 Label each wire before unplugging the connector

3   Remove the air cleaner assembly.
4   Drain the cooling system (see Chapter 1).
5   Label the vacuum lines, emissions system hoses, wiring connectors, ground straps and fuel lines, to ensure correct reinstallation, then detach them. Pieces of masking tape with numbers or letters written on them work well **(see illustration)**. If there's any possibility of confusion, make a sketch of the engine compartment and clearly label the lines, hoses and wires.
6   Label and detach all coolant hoses from the engine.
7   Remove the cooling fan, shroud and radiator (see Chapter 3).
8   Remove the drivebelts (see Chapter 1).
9   **Warning:** *Gasoline is extremely flammable, so extra precautions must be taken when working on any part of the fuel system. DO NOT smoke or allow open flames or bare light bulbs near the vehicle. Also, don't work in a garage if a natural gas appliance with a pilot light is present.* Disconnect the fuel lines running from the engine to the chassis (see Chapter 4). Plug or cap all open fittings/lines.
10   Disconnect the throttle linkage (and TV linkage/speed control cable, if equipped) from the engine (see Chapter 4).
11   On power steering equipped vehicles, unbolt the power steering pump (see Chapter 10). Leave the lines/hoses attached and make sure the pump is kept in an upright position in the engine compartment (use wire or rope to restrain it out of the way).
12   On air conditioned models, unbolt the compressor (see Chapter 3) and set it aside. Do not disconnect the hoses.
13   Drain the engine oil (Chapter 1) and remove the filter.
14   Remove the starter motor (see Chapter 5).
15   Remove the alternator (see Chapter 5).
16   Unbolt the exhaust system from the engine (see Chapter 4).
17   If you're working on a vehicle with an automatic transmission, refer to Chapter 7 and remove the torque converter-to-driveplate fasteners.
18   Support the transmission with a jack.

6.26 Support the transmission after engine removal by slipping a pipe through the frame holes and threading two bolts into the transmission (arrows)

Position a block of wood between them to prevent damage to the transmission. Special transmission jacks with safety chains are available - use one if possible.
19   Attach an engine sling or a length of chain to the lifting brackets on the engine.
20   Roll the hoist into position and connect the sling to it. Take up the slack in the sling or chain, but don't lift the engine. **Warning:** *DO NOT place any part of your body under the engine when it's supported only by a hoist or other lifting device.*
21   Remove the transmission-to-engine block bolts.
22   Remove the engine mount-to-frame bolts.
23   Recheck to be sure nothing is still connecting the engine to the transmission or vehicle. Disconnect anything still remaining.
24   Raise the engine slightly. Carefully work it forward to separate it from the transmission. If you're working on a vehicle with an automatic transmission, be sure the torque converter stays in the transmission (clamp a pair of vise-grips to the housing to keep the converter from sliding out). If you're working on a vehicle with a manual transmission, the input shaft must be completely disengaged from the clutch. Slowly raise the engine out of the engine compartment. Check carefully to make sure nothing is hanging up.
25   Remove the flywheel/driveplate and mount the engine on an engine stand.
26   Following engine removal, place a pipe across the frame and support the transmission with bolts **(see illustration)**.

Installation

27   Check the engine and transmission mounts. If they're worn or damaged, replace them.
28   If you're working on a manual transmission equipped vehicle, install the clutch and pressure plate (see Chapter 7). Now is a good time to install a new clutch.
29   Carefully lower the engine into the engine compartment - make sure the engine mounts line up.

30 If you're working on an automatic transmission equipped vehicle, guide the torque converter into the crankshaft following the procedure outlined in Chapter 7.

31 If you're working on a manual transmission equipped vehicle, apply a dab of high-temperature grease to the input shaft and guide it into the crankshaft pilot bearing until the bellhousing is flush with the engine block.

32 Install the transmission-to-engine bolts and tighten them securely. **Caution:** *DO NOT use the bolts to force the transmission and engine together!*

33 Reinstall the remaining components in the reverse order of removal.

34 Add coolant, oil, power steering and transmission fluid as needed.

35 Run the engine and check for leaks and proper operation of all accessories, then install the hood and test drive the vehicle.

36 Have the air conditioning system recharged and leak tested.

7 Engine overhaul - disassembly sequence

1 It's much easier to disassemble and work on the engine if it's mounted on a portable engine stand. A stand can often be rented quite cheaply from an equipment rental yard. Before the engine is mounted on a stand, the flywheel/driveplate should be removed from the engine.

2 If a stand isn't available, it's possible to disassemble the engine with it blocked up on the floor. Be extra careful not to tip or drop the engine when working without a stand.

3 If you're going to obtain a rebuilt engine, all external components must come off first, to be transferred to the replacement engine, just as they will if you're doing a complete engine overhaul yourself. These include:

Alternator and brackets
Emissions control components
Distributor, spark plug wires and spark plugs
Thermostat and housing cover
Water pump
Turbocharger (some four-cylinder engines)
EFI components or carburetor
Intake/exhaust manifolds
Oil filter
Engine mounts
Clutch and flywheel/driveplate
Engine rear plate

Note: *When removing the external components from the engine, pay close attention to details that may be helpful or important during installation. Note the installed position of gaskets, seals, spacers, pins, brackets, washers, bolts and other small items.*

4 If you're obtaining a short block, which consists of the engine block, crankshaft, pistons and connecting rods all assembled, then the cylinder head(s), oil pan and oil pump will have to be removed as well. See Engine rebuilding alternatives for additional informa-

tion regarding the different possibilities to be considered.

5 If you're planning a complete overhaul, the engine must be disassembled and the internal components removed in the following order:

Four-cylinder engine

Clutch and flywheel or driveplate
Camshaft cover
Intake and exhaust manifolds
Timing belt/sprockets and covers
Cylinder head
Camshaft and related components
Auxiliary shaft
Oil pan
Cylinder front cover (front crankshaft oil seal housing)
Oil pump
Piston/connecting rod assemblies
Crankshaft and main bearings

Inline six-cylinder engine

Clutch and flywheel or driveplate
Intake and exhaust manifolds
Rocker arm cover
Rocker assembly and pushrods
Timing chain cover
Timing chain and sprockets
Lifters
Camshaft
Oil pan
Oil pump
Piston/connecting rod assemblies
Crankshaft and main bearings

2.8L V6 engine

Clutch and flywheel or driveplate
Rocker arm covers
Rocker assemblies and pushrods
Intake and exhaust manifolds
Cylinder heads
Oil pan
Oil pump
Engine front cover and front plate
Timing gears
Lifters
Camshaft
Pistons and connecting rods
Crankshaft and main bearings

8.3 Use a valve spring compressor to compress the spring, then remove the keepers from the valve stem

3.8L V6 and all V8 engines

Clutch and flywheel or driveplate
Rocker arm covers
Intake and exhaust manifolds
Rocker arms and pushrods
Valve lifters
Cylinder heads
Timing chain cover
Timing chain and sprockets
Camshaft
Oil pan
Oil pump (V8 engine only)
Piston/connecting rod assemblies
Crankshaft and main bearings

6 Before beginning the disassembly and overhaul procedures, make sure the following items are available. Also, refer to Engine overhaul - reassembly sequence for a list of tools and materials needed for engine reassembly.

Common hand tools
Small cardboard boxes or plastic bags for storing parts
Gasket scraper
Ridge reamer
Vibration damper puller
Micrometers
Telescoping gauges
Dial indicator set
Valve spring compressor
Cylinder surfacing hone
Piston ring groove cleaning tool
Electric drill motor
Tap and die set
Wire brushes
Oil gallery brushes
Cleaning solvent

8 Cylinder head - disassembly

Refer to illustrations 8.3, 8.4 and 8.5
Note: *New and rebuilt cylinder heads are commonly available for most engines at dealerships and auto parts stores. Due to the fact that some specialized tools are necessary for the disassembly and inspection procedures, and replacement parts may not be readily available, it may be more practical and economical for the home mechanic to purchase replacement head(s) rather than taking the time to disassemble, inspect and recondition the original(s).*

1 Cylinder head disassembly involves removal of the intake and exhaust valves and related components. If they're still in place, remove the rocker arm nuts, pivot balls and rocker arms from the cylinder head studs (3.8L V6 and V8 engines only). Label the parts or store them separately so they can be reinstalled in their original locations.

2 Before the valves are removed, arrange to label and store them, along with their related components, so they can be kept separate and reinstalled in the same valve guides they are removed from.

3 Compress the springs on the first valve with a spring compressor and remove the keepers **(see illustration).** Carefully release the valve spring compressor and remove the

8.4 If the valve won't pull through the guide, deburr the edge of the stem end and the area around the top of the keeper groove with a file or whetstone

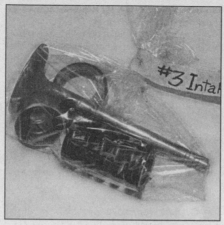

8.5 A small plastic bag, with an appropriate label, can be used to store the valve train components so they can be kept together and reinstalled in the original location

9.12a Check the cylinder head gasket surface for warpage by trying to slip a feeler gauge under the straightedge (see this Chapter's Specifications for the maximum warpage allowed and use a feeler gauge of that thickness)

retainer, sleeve (if used), the spring and the spring seat (if used).

4   Pull the valve out of the head, then remove the oil seal from the guide. If the valve binds in the guide (won't pull through), push it back into the head and deburr the area around the keeper groove with a fine file or whetstone **(see illustration)**.

5   Repeat the procedure for the remaining valves. Remember to keep all the parts for each valve together so they can be reinstalled in the same locations **(see illustration)**.

6   Once the valves and related components have been removed and stored in an organized manner, the head should be thoroughly cleaned and inspected. If a complete engine overhaul is being done, finish the engine disassembly procedures before beginning the cylinder head cleaning and inspection process.

9   Cylinder head - cleaning and inspection

Refer to illustrations 9.12a, 9.12b, 9.14, 9.15, 9.16, 9.17, 9.18 and 9.19

1   Thorough cleaning of the cylinder head(s) and related valve train components, followed by a detailed inspection, will enable you to decide how much valve service work must be done during the engine overhaul. **Note:** *If the engine was severely overheated, the cylinder head is probably warped (see Step 12).*

Cleaning

2   Scrape all traces of old gasket material and sealing compound off the head gasket, intake manifold and exhaust manifold sealing surfaces. Be very careful not to gouge the cylinder head. Special gasket removal solvents that soften gaskets and make removal

much easier are available at auto parts stores.

3   Remove all built up scale from the coolant passages.

4   Run a stiff wire brush through the various holes to remove deposits that may have formed in them.

5   Run an appropriate size tap into each of the threaded holes to remove corrosion and thread sealant that may be present. If compressed air is available, use it to clear the holes of debris produced by this operation. **Warning:** *Wear eye protection when using compressed air!*

6   Clean the exhaust manifold stud threads (V8 engine). Clean the rocker arm pivot stud threads (if applicable) with a wire brush.

7   Clean the cylinder head with solvent and dry it thoroughly. Compressed air will speed the drying process and ensure that all holes and recessed areas are clean. **Note:** *Decarbonizing chemicals are available and may prove very useful when cleaning cylinder heads and valve train components. They are very caustic and should be used with caution. Be sure to follow the instructions on the container.*

8   Clean the rocker arms, fulcrums and bolts (3.8L V6 and V8 engines only) and pushrods with solvent and dry them thoroughly (don't mix them up during the cleaning process). **Note:** *Some very early V8 engines may use nuts rather than bolts. Compressed air will speed the drying process and can be used to clean out the oil passages.*

9   Clean all the valve springs, spring seats, keepers and retainers (or rotators) with solvent and dry them thoroughly. Do the components from one valve at a time to avoid mixing up the parts.

10   Scrape off any heavy deposits that may have formed on the valves, then use a motorized wire brush to remove deposits from the valve heads and stems. Again, make sure the valves don't get mixed up.

Inspection

Note: *Be sure to perform all of the following inspection procedures before concluding that machine shop work is required. Make a list of the items that need attention.*

Cylinder head

11   Inspect the head very carefully for cracks, evidence of coolant leakage and other damage. If cracks are found, check with an automotive machine shop concerning repair. If repair isn't possible, a new cylinder head should be obtained.

12   Using a straightedge and feeler gauge, check the head gasket mating surface for warpage **(see illustrations)**. If the warpage exceeds the limit listed in this Chapter's Specifications, it can be resurfaced at an automotive machine shop. **Note:** *If the V6 or V8 engine heads are resurfaced, the intake manifold flanges will also require machining.*

13   Examine the valve seats in each of the combustion chambers. If they're pitted, cracked or burned, the head will require valve service that's beyond the scope of the home mechanic.

14   Check the valve stem-to-guide clearance by measuring the lateral movement of the valve stem with a dial indicator attached securely to the head **(see illustration)**. The valve must be in the guide and approximately 1/16-inch off the seat. The total valve stem movement indicated by the gauge needle must be divided by two to obtain the actual clearance. After this is done, if there's still some doubt regarding the condition of the valve guides they should be checked by an automotive machine shop (the cost should be minimal).

Valves

15   Carefully inspect each valve face for uneven wear, deformation, cracks, pits and burned areas **(see illustration)**. Check the valve stem for scuffing and galling and the

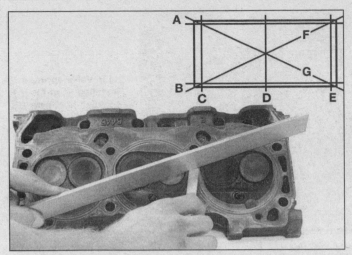

9.12b Check for both "twist" and "bulge" warpage by positioning the straightedge diagonally as well as straight across the gasket surface

9.14 A dial indicator can be used to determine the valve stem-to-guide clearance (move the valve stem as indicted by the arrows)

neck for cracks. Rotate the valve and check for any obvious indication that it's bent. Look for pits and excessive wear on the end of the stem. The presence of any of these conditions indicates the need for valve service by an automotive machine shop.

16   Measure the margin width on each valve **(see illustration)**. Any valve with a margin narrower than specified will have to be replaced with a new one.

Valve components

17   Check each valve spring for wear (on the ends) and pits. Measure the free length and compare it to the Specifications **(see illustration)**. Any springs that are shorter than specified have sagged and should not be reused. The tension of all springs should be checked with a special fixture before deciding that they're suitable for use in a rebuilt engine (take the springs to an automotive machine shop for this check).

18   Stand each spring on a flat surface and check it for squareness **(see illustration)**. If any of the springs are distorted or sagged, replace all of them with new parts.

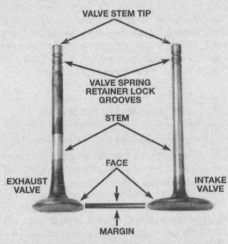

9.15 Check for valve wear at the points shown here

19   Check the spring retainers (or rotators) and keepers for obvious wear and cracks. Any questionable parts should be replaced with new ones, as extensive damage will

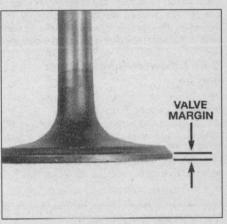

9.16 The margin width on each valve must be as specified (if no margin exists, the valve cannot be reused)

occur if they fail during engine operation. Make sure the rotators operate smoothly with no binding or excessive play **(see illustration)**.

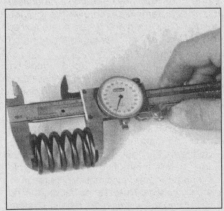

9.17 Measure the free length of each valve spring with a dial or vernier caliper

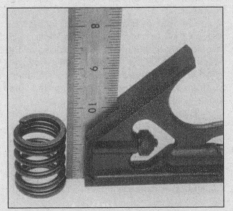

9.18 Check each valve spring for squareness

9.19 The exhaust valve rotators can be checked by turning the inner and outer sections in opposite directions - feel for smooth movement and excessive play

2E

Rocker arm components

20   Check the rocker arm faces (the areas that contact the pushrod ends and valve stems) for pits, wear, galling, score marks and rough spots.

Check the rocker arm pivot contact areas and fulcrums (3.8L V6 and V8 engines) or shafts (3.3L and 2.8L) as well. Look for cracks in each rocker arm and bolt (or nut on some very early V8 engines).

21   Inspect the pushrod ends for scuffing and excessive wear. Roll each pushrod on a flat surface, like a piece of plate glass, to determine if it's bent.

22   Check the rocker arm studs in the cylinder heads (if applicable) for damaged threads and secure installation.

23   Any damaged or excessively worn parts must be replaced with new ones.

24   If the inspection process indicates that the valve components are in generally poor condition and worn beyond the limits specified, which is usually the case in an engine that's being overhauled, reassemble the valves in the cylinder head and refer to Section 10 for valve servicing recommendations.

Cam followers (four-cylinder engine)

25   Clean all the parts thoroughly. Make sure all oil passages are open.

26   Inspect the pad at the valve end of the follower and the camshaft end pad for indications of scuffing or abnormal wear. If the pad is grooved, replace the follower. Do not attempt to true the surface by grinding.

10   Valves - servicing

1   Because of the complex nature of the job and the special tools and equipment needed, servicing of the valves, the valve seats and the valve guides, commonly known as a valve job, should be done by a professional.

2   The home mechanic can remove and disassemble the head, do the initial cleaning and inspection, then reassemble and deliver it to a dealer service department or an automotive machine shop for the actual service work. Doing the inspection will enable you to see what condition the head and valve train components are in and will ensure that you know what work and new parts are required when dealing with an automotive machine shop.

3   The dealer service department, or automotive machine shop, will remove the valves and springs, recondition or replace the valves and valve

seats, recondition the valve guides, check and replace the valve springs, spring retainers or rotators and keepers (as necessary), replace the valve

seals with new ones, reassemble the valve components and make sure the installed spring height is correct. The cylinder head

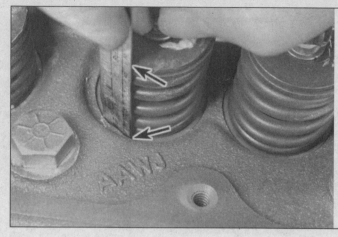

11.9 Valve spring installed height is the distance from the spring seat on the head to the bottom of the spring retainer

gasket surface will also be resurfaced if it's warped.

4   After the valve job has been performed by a professional, the head will be in like-new condition. When the head is returned, be sure to clean it again before installation on the engine to remove any metal particles and abrasive grit that may still be present from the valve service or head resurfacing operations. Use compressed air, if available, to blow out all the oil holes and passages.

11   Cylinder head - reassembly

Refer to illustration 11.9

1   Regardless of whether or not the head was sent to an automotive repair shop for valve servicing, make sure it's clean before beginning reassembly.

2   If the head was sent out for valve servicing, the valves and related components will already be in place. Begin the reassembly procedure with Step 9.

3   On all except four-cylinder engines, lubricate and install the valves, then install new seals on each of the valve guides. Using a hammer and deep socket, gently tap each seal into place until it's seated on the guide. Don't twist or cock the seals during installation or they will not seat properly on the valve stems.

4   On four-cylinder engines, install the valves, then install the valve stem seals. Slip a plastic installation cap over the end of the valve stem to allow the seal to pass over the grooves in the valve stem. After installation, remove the plastic cap and push the seal down until it's fully seated.

5   Beginning at one end of the head, lubricate and install the first valve. Apply moly-base grease or clean engine oil to the valve stem.

6   Drop the spring seat or shim(s) over the valve guide and set the valve spring, retainer (or rotator) and sleeve (if used) in place.

7   Compress the springs with a valve spring compressor and carefully install the keepers in the upper groove, then slowly release the compressor and make sure the keepers seat properly. Apply a small dab of

grease to each keeper to hold it in place if necessary.

8   Repeat the procedure for the remaining valves. Be sure to return the components to their original locations - don't mix them up!

9   Check the installed valve spring height with a ruler graduated in 1/32-inch increments or a dial caliper. If the head was sent out for service

work, the installed height should be correct (but don't automatically assume that it is). The measurement is taken from the top of each spring seat or shim(s) to the bottom of the retainer **(see illustration)**. If the height is greater than the figure listed in this Chapter's Specifications, shims can be

added under the springs to correct it. **Caution:** *Don't, under any circumstances, shim the springs to the point where the installed height is less than specified.*

10   On 3.8L V6 and V8 engines, apply moly-base grease to the rocker arm faces and the fulcrums, then install the rocker arms and fulcrums on the cylinder head studs.

12   Pistons/connecting rods - removal

Refer to illustrations 12.1, 12.3 and 12.6

Note: *Prior to removing the piston/connecting rod assemblies, remove the cylinder head(s), the oil pan and the oil pump (except 3.8L V6 models) by referring to the appropriate Sections in Chapter 2.*

1   Use your fingernail to feel if a ridge has formed at the upper limit of ring travel (about 1/4-inch down from the top of each cylinder). If carbon deposits or cylinder wear have produced ridges, they must be completely removed with a special tool **(see illustration)**. Follow the manufacturer's instructions provided with the tool. Failure to remove the ridges before attempting to remove the piston/connecting rod assemblies may result in piston breakage. **Note:** *Do not let the tool cut into the ring travel area more than 1/32-inch.*

2   After the cylinder ridges have been removed, turn the engine upside-down so the crankshaft is facing up.

3   Before   the   connecting   rods   are

12.1 A ridge reamer is required to remove the ridge from the top of each cylinder - do this before removing the pistons!

12.3 Check the connecting rod side clearance with a feeler gauge as shown

removed, check the endplay with feeler gauges. Slide them between the first connecting rod and the crankshaft throw until the play is removed (see illustration). The endplay is equal to the thickness of the feeler gauge(s). If the endplay exceeds the service limit, new connecting rods will be required. If new rods (or a new crankshaft) are installed, the endplay may fall under the specified minimum (if it does, the rods will have to be machined to restore it - consult an automotive machine shop for advice if necessary). Repeat the procedure for the remaining connecting rods.

4   Check the connecting rods and caps for identification marks. If they aren't plainly marked, use a small center-punch to make the appropriate number of indentations on each rod and cap (1, 2, 3, etc., depending on the engine type and cylinder they're associated with).

5   Loosen each of the connecting rod cap nuts 1/2-turn at a time until they can be removed by hand. Remove the number one connecting rod cap and bearing insert. Don't

drop the bearing insert out of the cap.

6   Slip a short length of plastic or rubber hose over each connecting rod cap bolt to protect the crankshaft journal and cylinder wall as the piston is removed (see illustration).

7   Remove the bearing insert and push the connecting rod/piston assembly out through the top of the engine. Use a wooden hammer handle to push on the upper bearing surface in the connecting rod. If resistance is felt, double-check to make sure that all of the ridge was removed from the cylinder.

8   Repeat the procedure for the remaining cylinders.

9   After removal, reassemble the connecting rod caps and bearing inserts in their respective connecting rods and install the cap nuts finger tight. Leaving the old bearing inserts in place until reassembly will help prevent the connecting rod bearing surfaces from being accidentally nicked or gouged.

10   Don't separate the pistons from the connecting rods (see Section 17 for additional information).

13 Crankshaft - removal

Refer to illustrations 13.1, 13.3, 13.4a and 13.4b

Note: *The crankshaft can be removed only after the engine has been removed from the vehicle. It's assumed that the flywheel or driveplate, vibration damper, timing chain or gears, oil pan, oil pump and piston/connecting rod assemblies have already been removed. The cylinder front cover (oil seal housing) on four-cylinder engines must also be removed.*

1   Before the crankshaft is removed, check the endplay. Mount a dial indicator with the stem in line with the crankshaft and just touching one of the crank throws (see illustration).

2   Push the crankshaft all the way to the rear and zero the dial indicator. Next, pry the crankshaft to the front as far as possible and check the reading on the dial indicator. The distance that it moves is the endplay. If it's greater than limit listed in this Chapter's Specifications, check the crankshaft thrust

2E

12.6 To prevent damage to the crankshaft journals and cylinder walls, slip sections of rubber or plastic hose over the rod bolts before removing the pistons

13.1 Checking crankshaft endplay with a dial indicator

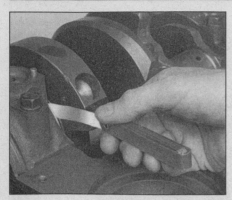

13.3 Checking crankshaft endplay with a feeler gauge

13.4a Use a center punch or number stamping dies to mark the main bearing caps to ensure installation in their original locations on the block (make the punch marks near one of the bolt heads)

13.4b The arrow on the main bearing cap indicates the front of the engine

surfaces for wear. If no wear is evident, new main bearings should correct the endplay.

3   If a dial indicator isn't available, feeler gauges can be used. Gently pry or push the crankshaft all the way to the front of the engine. Slip feeler gauges between the crankshaft and the front face of the thrust main bearing to determine the clearance **(see illustration)**.

4   Check the main bearing caps to see if they're marked to indicate their locations. They should be numbered consecutively from the front of the engine to the rear. If they aren't, mark them with number stamping dies or a center-punch **(see illustration)**. Main bearing caps generally have a cast-in arrow, which points to the front of the engine **(see illustration)**. Loosen the main bearing cap bolts 1/4-turn at a time each, until they can be removed by hand. Note if any stud bolts are used and make sure they're returned to their original locations when the crankshaft is reinstalled.

5   Gently tap the caps with a soft-face hammer, then separate them from the engine block. If necessary, use the bolts as levers to remove the caps. Try not to drop the bearing inserts if they come out with the caps.

6   Carefully lift the crankshaft out of the engine. It may be a good idea to have an assistant available, since the crankshaft is quite heavy. With the bearing inserts in place in the engine block and main bearing caps, return the caps to their respective locations on the engine block and tighten the bolts finger tight.

14 Engine block - cleaning

Refer to illustrations 14.1, 14.8 and 14.10
Caution: *The core plugs (also known as freeze plugs or soft plugs) may be difficult or impossible to retrieve if they're driven into the block coolant passages.* **Note:** *If you're working on a four-cylinder engine, remove the auxiliary shaft before cleaning the block (see Chapter 2A).*

1   Drill a small hole in the center of each core plug and pull them out with an auto body type dent puller **(see illustration)**.

2   Using a gasket scraper, remove all traces of gasket material from the engine block. Be very careful not to nick or gouge the gasket sealing surfaces.

3   Remove the main bearing caps and separate the bearing inserts from the caps and the engine block. Tag the bearings, indicating which cylinder they were removed from and whether they were in the cap or the block, then set them aside.

4   Remove all of the threaded oil gallery plugs from the block. The plugs are usually very tight - they may have to be drilled out and the holes retapped. Use new plugs when the engine is reassembled.

5   If the engine is extremely dirty it should be taken to an automotive machine shop to be steam cleaned or hot tanked.

6   After the block is returned, clean all oil holes and oil galleries one more time. Brushes specifically designed for this purpose are available at most auto parts stores. Flush the passages with warm water until the water runs clear, dry the block thoroughly and wipe all machined surfaces with a light, rust preventive oil. If you have access to compressed air, use it to speed the drying process and to blow out all the oil holes and galleries. **Warning:** *Wear eye protection when using compressed air!*

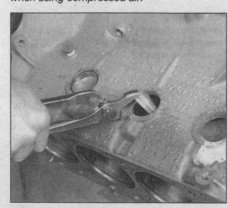

14.1 The core plugs should be removed with a puller - if they're driven into the block, they may be impossible to retrieve

7   If the block isn't extremely dirty or sludged up, you can do an adequate cleaning job with hot soapy water and a stiff brush. Take plenty of time and do a thorough job. Regardless of the cleaning method used, be sure to clean all oil holes and galleries very thoroughly, dry the block completely and coat all machined surfaces with light oil.

8   The threaded holes in the block must be clean to ensure accurate torque readings during reassembly. Run the proper size tap into each of the holes to remove rust, corrosion, thread sealant or sludge and restore damaged threads **(see illustration)**. If possible, use compressed air to clear the holes of debris produced by this operation. Now is a good time to clean the threads on the head bolts and the main bearing cap bolts as well.

9   Reinstall the main bearing caps and tighten the bolts finger tight.

10   After coating the sealing surfaces of the new core plugs with Permatex no. 2 sealant, install them in the engine block **(see illustration)**. Make sure they're driven in straight and seated properly or leakage could result. Special tools are available for this purpose, but a large socket, with an outside diameter that will just slip into the core plug, a 1/2-inch drive extension and a hammer will work just as well.

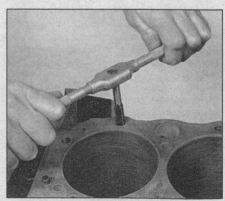

14.8 All bolt holes in the block - particularly the main bearing cap and head bolt holes - should be cleaned and restored with tap (be sure to remove debris from the holes after this is done)

14.10 A large socket on an extension can be used to drive the new core plugs into the bores

11   Apply non-hardening sealant (such as Permatex no. 2 or Teflon pipe sealant) to the new oil gallery plugs and thread them into the holes in the block. Make sure they're tightened securely.

12   If the engine isn't going to be reassembled right away, cover it with a large plastic trash bag to keep it clean.

15   Engine block - inspection

Refer to illustrations 15.4a, 15.4b and 15.4c

1   Before the block is inspected, it should be cleaned as described in Section 14.

2   Visually check the block for cracks, rust and corrosion. Look for stripped threads in the threaded holes. It's also a good idea to have the block checked for hidden cracks by an automotive machine shop that has the special equipment to do this type of work. If defects are found, have the block repaired, if possible, or replaced.

3   Check the cylinder bores for scuffing and scoring.

4   Measure the diameter of each cylinder at the top (just under the ridge area), center and bottom of the cylinder bore, parallel to

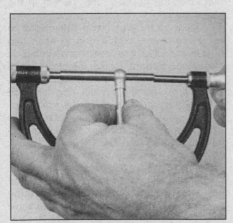

15.4c The gauge is then measured with a micrometer to determine the bore size

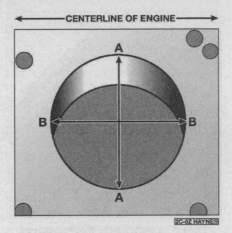

15.4a Measure the diameter of each cylinder at a right angle to the engine centerline (A), and parallel to engine centerline (B) - out-of-round is the difference between A and B; taper is the difference between A and B at the top of the cylinder and A and B at the top of the cylinder

the crankshaft axis **(see illustrations)**.

5   Next, measure each cylinder's diameter at the same three locations across the crankshaft axis. Compare the results to this Chapter's Specifications.

6   If the required precision measuring tools aren't available, the piston-to-cylinder clearances can be obtained, though not quite as accurately, using feeler gauge stock. Feeler gauge stock comes in 12-inch lengths and various thicknesses and is generally available at auto parts stores.

7   To check the clearance, select a feeler gauge and slip it into the cylinder along with the matching piston. The piston must be positioned exactly as it normally would be. The feeler gauge must be between the piston and cylinder on one of the thrust faces (90-degrees to the piston pin bore).

8   The piston should slip through the cylinder (with the feeler gauge in place) with moderate pressure.

9   If it falls through or slides through easily,

16.3a A "bottle brush" hone will produce better results if you've never honed cylinders before

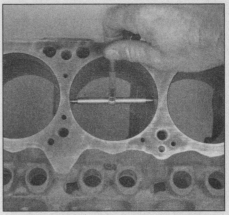

15.4b The ability to "feel" when the telescoping gauge is at the correct point will be developed over time, so work slowly and repeat the check until you're satisfied the bore measurement is accurate

the clearance is excessive and a new piston will be required. If the piston binds at the lower end of the cylinder and is loose toward the top, the cylinder is tapered. If tight spots are encountered as the piston/feeler gauge is rotated in the cylinder, the cylinder is out-of-round.

10   Repeat the procedure for the remaining pistons and cylinders.

11   If the cylinder walls are badly scuffed or scored, or if they're out-of-round or tapered beyond the limits given in this Chapter's Specifications, have the engine block rebored and honed at an automotive machine shop. If a rebore is done, oversize pistons and rings will be required.

12   If the cylinders are in reasonably good condition and not worn to the outside of the limits, and if the piston-to-cylinder clearances can be maintained properly, then they don't have to be rebored. Honing is all that's necessary (see Section 16).

16   Cylinder honing

Refer to illustrations 16.3a and 16.3b

1   Prior to engine reassembly, the cylinder bores must be honed so the new piston rings will seat correctly and provide the best possible combustion chamber seal. **Note:** *If you don't have the tools or don't want to tackle the honing operation, most automotive machine shops will do it for a reasonable fee.*

2   Before honing the cylinders, install the main bearing caps and tighten the bolts to the torque listed in this Chapter's Specifications.

3   Two types of cylinder hones are commonly available - the flex hone or "bottle brush" type and the more traditional surfacing hone with spring-loaded stones. Both will do the job, but for the less experienced mechanic the "bottle brush" hone will probably be easier to use. You'll also need some kerosene or honing oil, rags and an electric drill motor. Proceed as follows:

2E

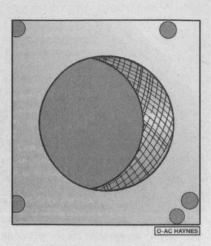

16.3b The cylinder hone should leave a smooth, crosshatch pattern with the lines intersecting at approximately a 60-degree angle

a) *Mount the hone in the drill motor, compress the stones and slip it into the first cylinder* **(see illustration)**. *Be sure to wear safety goggles or a face shield!*

b) *Lubricate the cylinder with plenty of honing oil, turn on the drill and move the hone up-and-down in the cylinder at a pace that will produce a fine crosshatch pattern on the cylinder walls. Ideally, the crosshatch lines should intersect at approximately a 60-degree angle* **(see illustration)**. *Be sure to use plenty of lubricant and don't take off any more material than is absolutely necessary to produce the desired finish.* **Note:** *Piston ring manufacturers may specify a smaller crosshatch angle than the traditional 60-degrees - read and follow any instructions included with the new rings.*

c) *Don't withdraw the hone from the cylinder while it's running. Instead, shut off the drill and continue moving the hone up-and-down in the cylinder until it comes to a complete stop, then compress the stones and withdraw the hone. If you're using a "bottle brush" type hone, stop the drill motor, then turn the chuck in the normal direction of rotation while withdrawing the hone from the cylinder.*

d) *Wipe the oil out of the cylinder and repeat the procedure for the remaining cylinders.*

4   After the honing job is complete, chamfer the top edges of the cylinder bores with a small file so the rings won't catch when the pistons are installed. Be very careful not to nick the cylinder walls with the end of the file.

5   The entire engine block must be washed again very thoroughly with warm, soapy water to remove all traces of the abrasive grit produced during the honing operation. **Note:** *The bores can be considered clean when a lint-free white cloth - dampened with clean engine oil - used to wipe them out doesn't pick up any more honing residue, which will show up as gray areas on the cloth. Be sure*

17.4a The piston ring grooves can be cleaned with a special tool, as shown here. . .

to run a brush through all oil holes and galleries and flush them with running water.

6   After rinsing, dry the block and apply a coat of light rust preventive oil to all machined surfaces. Wrap the block in a plastic trash bag to keep it clean and set it aside until reassembly.

17 Pistons/connecting rods - inspection

Refer to illustrations 17.4a, 17.4b, 17.10 and 17.11

1   Before the inspection process can be carried out, the piston/connecting rod assemblies must be cleaned and the original piston rings removed from the pistons. **Note:** *Always use new piston rings when the engine is reassembled.*

2   Using a piston ring installation tool, carefully remove the rings from the pistons. Be careful not to nick or gouge the pistons in the process.

3   Scrape all traces of carbon from the top of the piston. A handheld wire brush or a piece of fine emery cloth can be used once the majority of the deposits have been scraped away. Do not, under any circumstances, use a wire brush mounted in a drill motor to remove deposits from the pistons. The piston material is soft and may be eroded away by the wire brush.

4   Use a piston ring groove cleaning tool to remove carbon deposits from the ring grooves. If a tool isn't available, a piece broken off the old ring will do the job. Be very careful to remove only the carbon deposits - don't remove any metal and do not nick or scratch the sides of the ring grooves **(see illustrations)**.

5   Once the deposits have been removed, clean the piston/rod assemblies with solvent and dry them with compressed air (if available). Make sure the oil return holes in the back sides of the ring grooves are clear.

6   If the pistons and cylinder walls aren't damaged or worn excessively, and if the engine block is not rebored, new pistons won't

17.4b . . . or a section of a broken ring

be necessary. Normal piston wear appears as even vertical wear on the piston thrust surfaces and slight looseness of the top ring in its groove. New piston rings, however, should always be used when an engine is rebuilt.

7   Carefully inspect each piston for cracks around the skirt, at the pin bosses and at the ring lands.

8   Look for scoring and scuffing on the thrust faces of the skirt, holes in the piston crown and burned areas at the edge of the crown. If the skirt is scored or scuffed, the engine may have been suffering from overheating and/or abnormal combustion, which caused excessively high operating temperatures. The cooling and lubrication systems should be checked thoroughly. A hole in the piston crown is an indication that abnormal combustion (preignition) was occurring. Burned areas at the edge of the piston crown are usually evidence of spark knock (detonation). If any of the above problems exist, the causes must be corrected or the damage will occur again. The causes may include intake air leaks, incorrect fuel/air mixture, incorrect ignition timing and EGR system malfunctions.

9   Corrosion of the piston, in the form of small pits, indicates that coolant is leaking into the combustion chamber and/or the crankcase. Again, the cause must be corrected or the problem may persist in the rebuilt engine.

10   Measure the piston ring side clearance by laying a new piston ring in each ring groove and slipping a feeler gauge in beside it **(see illustration)**. Check the clearance at three or four locations around each groove. Be sure to use the correct ring for each groove- they are different. If the side clearance is greater than the figure listed in this Chapter's Specifications, new pistons will have to be used.

11   Check the piston-to-bore clearance by measuring the bore (see Section 15) and the piston diameter. Make sure the pistons and bores are correctly matched. Measure the piston across the skirt, at a 90-degree angle to and in line with the piston pin **(see illustration)**. Subtract the piston diameter from the bore diameter to obtain the clearance. If it's greater than specified, the block will have to

17.10 Check the ring side clearance with a feeler gauge at several points around the groove

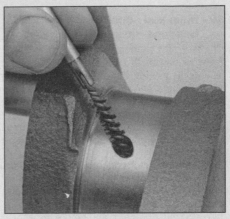

17.11 Measure the piston diameter at a 90-degree angle to the piston pin and in line with it

18.1 Use a wire or stiff plastic bristle brush to clean the oil passages in the crankshaft

be rebored and new pistons and rings installed.

12   Check the piston-to-rod clearance by twisting the piston and rod in opposite directions. Any noticeable play indicates excessive wear, which must be corrected. The piston/connecting rod assemblies should be taken to an automotive machine shop to have the pistons and rods resized and new pins installed.

13   If the pistons must be removed from the connecting rods for any reason, they should be taken to an automotive machine shop. While they are there have the connecting rods checked for bend and twist, since automotive machine shops have special equipment for this purpose. **Note:** *Unless new pistons and/or connecting rods must be installed, do not disassemble the pistons and connecting rods.*

14   Check the connecting rods for cracks and other damage. Temporarily remove the rod caps, lift out the old bearing inserts, wipe the rod and cap bearing surfaces clean and inspect them for nicks, gouges and scratches. After checking the rods, replace the old bearings, slip the caps into place and tighten the nuts finger tight. **Note:** *If the*

engine is being rebuilt because of a connecting rod knock, be sure to install new rods.

18   Crankshaft - inspection

Refer to illustrations 18.1, 18.3, 18.6 and 18.8

1   Clean the crankshaft with solvent and dry it with compressed air (if available). Be sure to clean the oil holes with a stiff brush **(see illustration)** and flush them with solvent.

2   Check the main and connecting rod bearing journals for uneven wear, scoring, pits and cracks.

3   Rub a penny across each journal several times **(see illustration)**. If a journal picks up copper from the penny, it's too rough and must be reground.

4   Remove all burrs from the crankshaft oil holes with a stone, file or scraper.

5   Check the rest of the crankshaft for cracks and other damage. It should be magnafluxed to reveal hidden cracks - an automotive machine shop will handle the procedure.

6   Using a micrometer, measure the diameter of the main and connecting rod journals

and compare the results to this Chapter's Specifications **(see illustration)**. By measuring the diameter at a number of points around each journal's circumference, you'll be able to determine whether or not the journal is out-of-round. Take the measurement at each end of the journal, near the crank throws, to determine if the journal is tapered.

7   If the crankshaft journals are damaged, tapered, out-of-round or worn beyond the limits given in the Specifications, have the crankshaft reground by an automotive machine shop. Be sure to use the correct size bearing inserts if the crankshaft is reconditioned.

8   Check the oil seal journals at each end of the crankshaft for wear and damage. If the seal has worn a groove in the journal, or if it's nicked or scratched **(see illustration)**, the new seal may leak when the engine is reassembled. In some cases, an automotive machine shop may be able to repair the journal by pressing on a thin sleeve. If repair isn't feasible, a new or different crankshaft should be installed.

9   Refer to Section 19 and examine the main and rod bearing inserts.

2E

18.3 Rubbing a penny lengthwise on each journal will reveal its condition - if copper rubs off and is embedded in the crankshaft, the journals should be reground

18.6 Measure the diameter of each crankshaft journal at several points to detect taper and out-of-round conditions

18.8 If the seals have worn grooves in the crankshaft journals, or if the seal contact surfaces are nicked or scratched, the new seals will leak

19 Main and connecting rod bearings - inspection

Refer to illustration 19.1

1   Even though the main and connecting rod bearings should be replaced with new ones during the engine overhaul, the old bearings should be retained for close examination, as they may reveal valuable information about the condition of the engine **(see illustration)**.

2   Bearing failure occurs because of lack of lubrication, the presence of dirt or other foreign particles, overloading the engine and corrosion. Regardless of the cause of bearing failure, it must be corrected before the engine is reassembled to prevent it from happening again.

3   When examining the bearings, remove them from the engine block, the main bearing caps, the connecting rods and the rod caps and lay them out on a clean surface in the same general position as their location in the engine. This will enable you to match any bearing problems with the corresponding crankshaft journal.

4   Dirt and other foreign particles get into the engine in a variety of ways. It may be left in the engine during assembly, or it may pass through filters or the PCV system. It may get into the oil, and from there into the bearings. Metal chips from machining operations and normal engine wear are often present. Abrasives are sometimes left in engine components after reconditioning, especially when parts are not thoroughly cleaned using the proper cleaning methods. Whatever the source, these foreign objects often end up embedded in the soft bearing material and are easily recognized. Large particles will not embed in the bearing and will score or gouge the bearing and journal. The best prevention for this cause of bearing failure is to clean all parts thoroughly and keep everything spotlessly clean during engine assembly. Frequent and regular engine oil and filter changes are also recommended.

5   Lack of lubrication (or lubrication breakdown) has a number of interrelated causes. Excessive heat (which thins the oil), overloading (which squeezes the oil from the bearing face) and oil leakage or throw off (from excessive bearing clearances, worn oil pump or high engine speeds) all contribute to lubrication breakdown. Blocked oil passages, which usually are the result of misaligned oil holes in a bearing shell, will also oil starve a bearing and destroy it. When lack of lubrication is the cause of bearing failure, the bearing material is wiped or extruded from the steel backing of the bearing. Temperatures may increase to the point where the steel backing turns blue from overheating.

6   Driving habits can have a definite effect on bearing life. Full throttle, low speed operation (lugging the engine) puts very high loads on bearings, which tends to squeeze out the oil film. These loads cause the bearings to flex, which produces fine cracks in the bear-

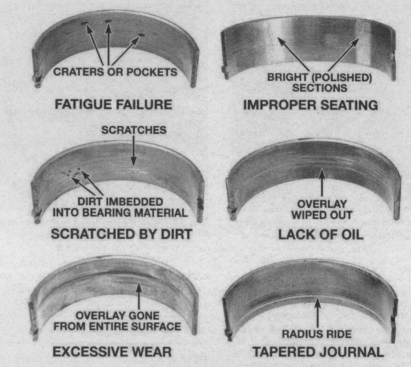

19.1 Typical bearing failures

ing face (fatigue failure). Eventually the bearing material will loosen in pieces and tear away from the steel backing. Short trip driving leads to corrosion of bearings because insufficient engine heat is produced to drive off the condensed water and corrosive gases. These products collect in the engine oil, forming acid and sludge. As the oil is carried to the engine bearings, the acid attacks and corrodes the bearing material.

7   Incorrect bearing installation during engine assembly will lead to bearing failure as well. Tight fitting bearings leave insufficient bearing oil clearance and will result in oil starvation. Dirt or foreign particles trapped behind a bearing insert result in high spots on the bearing which lead to failure.

20 Engine overhaul - reassembly sequence

1   Before beginning engine reassembly, make sure you have all the necessary new parts, gaskets and seals as well as the following items on hand:

Common hand tools
A 1/2-inch drive torque wrench
Piston ring installation tool
Piston ring compressor
Vibration damper installation tool
Short lengths of rubber or plastic hose to fit over connecting rod bolts
Plastigage
Feeler gauges
A fine-tooth file
New engine oil
Engine assembly lube or moly-base grease

Gasket sealant
Thread locking compound

2   In order to save time and avoid problems, engine reassembly must be done in the following general order:

Four-cylinder engine

Piston rings
Crankshaft and main bearings
Piston/connecting rod assemblies
Oil pump
Cylinder front cover (front crankshaft oil seal housing)
Oil pan
Auxiliary shaft
Camshaft and related components
Cylinder head
Timing belt/sprockets and covers
Intake and exhaust manifolds
Camshaft cover
Clutch and flywheel or driveplate

Inline six-cylinder engine

New camshaft bearings (must be done by an automotive machine shop)
Piston rings
Crankshaft and main bearings
Piston/connecting rod assemblies
Oil pump
Oil pan
Camshaft
Lifters
Timing chain and sprockets
Timing chain cover
Rocker assembly and pushrods
Rocker arm cover
Intake and exhaust manifolds
Clutch and flywheel or driveplate

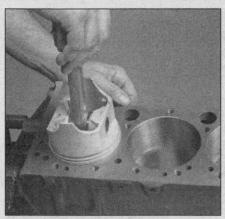

21.3 When checking piston ring end gap, the ring must be square in the cylinder bore (this is done by pushing the ring down with the top of a piston as shown)

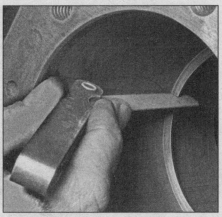

21.4 With the ring square in the cylinder, measure the end gap with a feeler gauge

21.5 If the end gap is too small, clamp a file in a vise and file the ring ends (from the outside in only) to enlarge the gap slightly

2.8L V6 engine

New camshaft bearings (must be done by an automotive machine shop)

Piston rings
Crankshaft and main bearings
Pistons and connecting rods
Camshaft
Lifters
Timing gears
Engine front plate and front cover
Oil pump
Oil pan
Cylinder heads
Intake and exhaust manifolds
Rocker assemblies and pushrods
Rocker arm covers
Clutch and flywheel or driveplate

3.8L V6 and all V8 engines

New camshaft bearings (must be done by an automotive machine shop)

Piston rings
Crankshaft and main bearings
Piston/connecting rod assemblies
Oil pump (V8 engine only)
Oil pan
Camshaft
Timing chain and sprockets
Timing chain cover
Cylinder heads
Valve lifters
Rocker arms and pushrods
Intake and exhaust manifolds
Rocker arm covers
Clutch and flywheel or driveplate

21 Piston rings - installation

Refer to illustrations 21.3, 21.4, 21.5, 21.9a, 21.9b and 21.12

1   Before installing the new piston rings, the ring end gaps must be checked. It's assumed that the piston ring side clearance has been checked and verified correct (see Section 17).

2   Lay out the piston/connecting rod assemblies and the new ring sets so the ring sets will be matched with the same piston and cylinder during the end gap measurement and engine assembly.

3   Insert the top (number one) ring into the first cylinder and square it up with the cylinder walls by pushing it in with the top of the piston **(see illustration)**. The ring should be near the bottom of the cylinder, at the lower limit of ring travel.

4   To measure the end gap, slip feeler gauges between the ends of the ring until a gauge equal to the gap width is found **(see illustration)**. The feeler gauge should slide between the ring ends with a slight amount of drag. Compare the measurement to this Chapter's Specifications. If the gap is larger or smaller than specified, double-check to make sure you have the correct rings before proceeding.

5   If the gap is too small, it must be enlarged or the ring ends may come in contact with each other during engine operation, which can cause serious damage to the engine. The end gap can be increased by filing the ring ends very carefully with a fine file. Mount the file in a vise equipped with soft jaws, slip the ring over the file with the ends contacting the file face and slowly move the

ring to remove material from the ends. When performing this operation, file only from the outside in **(see illustration)**.

6   Excess end gap isn't critical unless it's greater than 0.040-inch. Again, double-check to make sure you have the correct rings for your engine.

7   Repeat the procedure for each ring that will be installed in the first cylinder and for each ring in the remaining cylinders. Remember to keep rings, pistons and cylinders matched up.

8   Once the ring end gaps have been checked/corrected, the rings can be installed on the pistons.

9   The oil control ring (lowest one on the piston) is usually installed first. It's composed of three separate components. Slip the spacer/expander into the groove **(see illustration)**. If an anti-rotation tang is used, make sure it's inserted into the drilled hole in the ring groove. Next, install the lower side rail. Don't use a piston ring installation tool on the oil ring side rails, as they may be damaged. Instead, place one end of the side rail into the groove between the spacer/expander and the ring land, hold it firmly in place and slide a fin-

2E

21.9a Installing the spacer/expander in the oil control ring groove

21.9b DO NOT use a piston ring installation tool when installing the oil ring side rails

21.12 Installing the compression rings with a ring expander - the mark (arrow) must face up

22.5 Upper main bearing in position (flanged thrust bearing shown) - the oil hole in the bearing must align with the oil hole(s) in the block

ger around the piston while pushing the rail into the groove **(see illustration)**. Next, install the upper side rail in the same manner.

10   After the three oil ring components have been installed, check to make sure that both the upper and lower side rails can be turned smoothly in the ring groove.

11   The number two (middle) ring is installed next. It's usually stamped with a mark which must face up, toward the top of the piston. **Note:** *Always follow the instructions printed on the ring package or box - different manufacturers may require different approaches. Do not mix up the top and middle rings, as they have different cross sections.*

12   Use a piston ring installation tool and make sure the identification mark is facing the top of the piston, then slip the ring into the middle groove on the piston **(see illustration)**. Don't expand the ring any more than necessary to slide it over the piston.

13   Install the number one (top) ring in the same manner. Make sure the mark is facing up. Be careful not to confuse the number one and number two rings.

14   Repeat the procedure for the remaining pistons and rings.

22 Crankshaft - installation and main bearing oil clearance check

Refer to illustrations 22.5, 22.11 22.12a, 22.12b and 22.15

1   Crankshaft installation is the first step in engine reassembly. It's assumed at this point that the engine block and crankshaft have been cleaned, inspected and repaired or reconditioned.

2   Position the engine with the bottom facing up.

3   Remove the main bearing cap bolts and lift out the caps. Lay them out in the proper order to ensure correct installation.

4   If they're still in place, remove the original bearing inserts from the block and the main bearing caps. Wipe the bearing surfaces of the block and caps with a clean, lint-free cloth. They must be kept spotlessly clean.

Main bearing oil clearance check

5   Clean the back sides of the new main

bearing inserts and lay one in each main bearing saddle in the block. If one of the bearing inserts from each set has a large groove in it, make sure the grooved insert is installed in the block. Lay the other bearing from each set in the corresponding main bearing cap. Make sure the tab on the bearing insert fits into the recess in the block or cap.

Caution: *The oil holes in the block must line up with the oil holes in the bearing insert* **(see illustration)**. *Do not hammer the bearing into place and don't nick or gouge the bearing faces. No lubrication should be used at this time.*

6   The flanged thrust bearing **(see illustration 22.5)** must be installed in the third cap and saddle (all except 3.3L six-cylinder engine) or fifth cap and saddle (3.3L six-cylinder engine).

7   Clean the faces of the bearings in the block and the crankshaft main bearing journals with a clean, lint-free cloth.

8   Check or clean the oil holes in the crankshaft, as any dirt here can go only one way - straight through the new bearings.

9   Once you're certain the crankshaft is clean, carefully lay it in position in the

22.11 Lay the Plastigage strips (arrow) on the main bearing journals, parallel to the crankshaft centerline

22.12a Installing the center main bearing cap

22.12b Bearing cap numbers indicate cap position (counting from the front of the engine) - the arrow points to the front of the engine

22.15 Compare the width of the crushed Plastigage to the scale on the envelope to determine the main bearing oil clearance (always take the measurement at the widest point of the Plastigage); be sure to use the correct scale - standard and metric ones are included

main bearings.

10 Before the crankshaft can be permanently installed, the main bearing oil clearance must be checked.

11 Cut several pieces of the appropriate size Plastigage (they must be slightly shorter than the width of the main bearings) and place one piece on each crankshaft main bearing journal, parallel with the journal axis **(see illustration)**.

12 Clean the faces of the bearings in the caps and install the caps in their respective positions (don't mix them up) with the arrows pointing toward the front of the engine **(see illustrations)**. Don't disturb the Plastigage.

13 Starting with the center main and working out toward the ends, tighten the main bearing cap bolts, in three steps, to the torque listed in this Chapter's Specifications. Don't rotate the crankshaft at any time during this operation.

14 Remove the bolts and carefully lift off the main bearing caps. Keep them in order. Don't disturb the Plastigage or rotate the crankshaft. If any of the main bearing caps are difficult to remove, tap them gently from side-to-side with a soft-face hammer to loosen them.

15 Compare the width of the crushed Plastigage on each journal to the scale printed on the Plastigage envelope to obtain the main bearing oil clearance **(see illustration)**. Check the Specifications to make sure it's correct.

16 If the clearance is not as specified, the bearing inserts may be the wrong size (which means different ones will be required). Before deciding that different inserts are needed, make sure that no dirt or oil was between the bearing inserts and the caps or block when the clearance was measured. If the Plastigage was wider at one end than the other, the journal may be tapered (refer to Section 18).

17 Carefully scrape all traces of the Plastigage material off the main bearing journals and/or the bearing faces. Use your fingernail

or the edge of a credit card - don't nick or scratch the bearing faces.

Final crankshaft installation

18 Carefully lift the crankshaft out of the engine.

19 Clean the bearing faces in the block, then apply a thin, uniform layer of moly-base grease or engine assembly lube to each of the bearing surfaces. Be sure to coat the thrust faces as well as the journal face of the thrust bearing. On engines equipped with split-type (two-piece) rear main oil seals, install the seal together with the rear main bearing cap (see Section 23).

20 Make sure the crankshaft journals are clean, then lay the crankshaft back in place in the block.

21 Clean the faces of the bearings in the caps, then apply lubricant to them.

22 Install the caps in their respective positions with the arrows pointing toward the front of the engine.

23 Install the bolts.

24 Tighten all except the thrust bearing cap bolts to the specified torque (work from the center out and approach the final torque in three steps).

25 Tighten the thrust bearing cap bolts to 10-to-12 ft-lbs.

26 Tap the ends of the crankshaft forward and backward with a lead or brass hammer to line up the main bearing and crankshaft thrust surfaces.

27 Retighten all main bearing cap bolts to the specified torque, starting with the center main and working out toward the ends.

28 On manual transmission equipped models, install a new pilot bearing in the end of the crankshaft (see Chapter 8).

29 Rotate the crankshaft a number of times by hand to check for any obvious binding.

30 The final step is to check the crankshaft endplay with a feeler gauge or a dial indicator as described in Section 13. The endplay should be correct if the crankshaft thrust

faces aren't worn or damaged and new bearings have been installed.

31 If you are working on an engine with a one-piece rear main oil seal, refer to Section 23 and install the new seal.

23 Rear main oil seal installation

Block/main bearing cap counterbore

1 Clean the bore in the block/cap and the seal contact surface on the crankshaft. Check the crankshaft surface for scratches and nicks that could damage the new seal lip and cause oil leaks. If the crankshaft is damaged, the only alternative is a new or different crankshaft.

2 Apply a light coat of engine oil or multi-purpose grease to the outer edge of the new seal. Lubricate the seal lip with moly-base grease or engine assembly lube.

3 Press the new seal into place with the special tool (if available). The seal lip must face toward the front of the engine. If the special tool isn't available, carefully work the seal lip over the end of the crankshaft and tap the seal in with a hammer and punch until it's seated in the bore. On 2.8L V6 engines, drive in new wedge seals alongside the rear main bearing cap.

Split-type (two-piece) seal

4 Inspect the rear main bearing cap and engine block mating surfaces, as well as the seal grooves, for nicks, burrs and scratches. Remove any defects with a fine file or deburring tool.

5 Install one seal section in the block with the lip facing the front of the engine. On V8 engines, leave one end protruding from the block approximately 1/4 to 3/8-inch and make sure it's completely seated. On 2.3L and 3.8L engines, position both ends of the seal flush with the block, and the locating tabs to the

2E

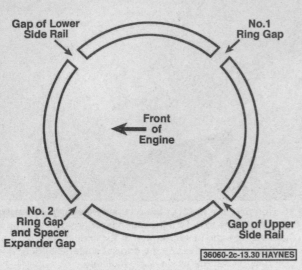

24.5 Ring gap positioning

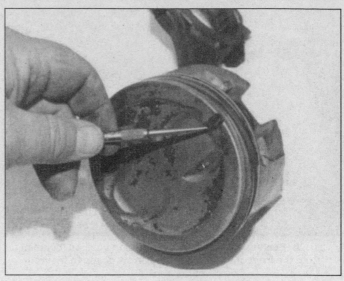

24.9 The notch or arrow in the top of each piston must face the FRONT of the engine as the pistons are installed

rear. On 3.8L engines, remove the locating tabs.

6   Repeat the procedure to install the remaining seal half in the rear main bearing cap. On V8 engines, leave the opposite end of the seal protruding from the cap the same distance the block seal is protruding from the block. On 2.3L and 3.8L engines, position both ends flush with the bearing cap.

7   During final installation of the crankshaft (after the main bearing oil clearances have been checked with Plastigage as described in Section 22), apply a thin, even coat of anaerobic-type gasket sealant to the main bearing cap. Don't get any sealant on the bearing face, crankshaft journal, seal ends or seal lips. Also, lubricate the seal lips with moly-base grease or engine assembly lube.

24   Pistons/connecting rods - installation and rod bearing oil clearance check

Refer to illustrations 24.5, 24.9, 24.11, 24.13 and 24.17

1   Before installing the piston/connecting rod assemblies, the cylinder walls must be perfectly clean, the top edge of each cylinder must be chamfered, and the crankshaft must be in place.

2   Remove the cap from the end of the number one connecting rod (refer to the marks made during removal). Remove the original bearing inserts and wipe the bearing surfaces of the connecting rod and cap with a clean, lint-free cloth. They must be kept spotlessly clean.

Connecting rod bearing oil clearance check

3   Clean the back side of the new upper bearing insert, then lay it in place in the con-

necting rod. Make sure the tab on the bearing fits into the recess

in the rod. Don't hammer the bearing insert into place and be very careful not to nick or gouge the bearing face. Don't lubricate the bearing at this time.

4   Clean the back side of the other bearing insert and install it in the rod cap. Again, make sure the tab on the bearing fits into the recess in the cap, and don't apply any lubricant. It's critically important that the mating surfaces of the bearing and connecting rod are perfectly clean and oil free when they're assembled.

5   Position the piston ring gaps at intervals around the piston **(see illustration)**.

6   Slip a section of plastic or rubber hose over each connecting rod cap bolt.

7   Lubricate the piston and rings with clean engine oil and attach a piston ring compressor to the piston. Leave the skirt protruding about 1/4-inch to guide the piston into the cylinder. The rings must be compressed until they're flush with the piston.

8   Rotate the crankshaft until the number one connecting rod journal is at BDC (bottom dead center) and apply a coat of engine oil to the cylinder walls.

9   With the arrow or notches on top of the piston **(see illustration)** facing the front of the engine, gently insert the piston/connecting rod assembly into the number one cylinder bore and rest the bottom edge of the ring compressor on the engine block.

10   Tap the top edge of the ring compressor to make sure it's contacting the block around its entire circumference.

11   Gently tap on the top of the piston with the end of a wooden hammer handle **(see illustration)** while guiding the end of the connecting rod into place on the crankshaft journal. The piston rings may try to pop out of the ring compressor just before entering the cylinder bore, so keep some downward pressure on the ring compressor. Work slowly,

and if any resistance is felt as the piston enters the cylinder, stop immediately. Find out what's hanging up and fix it before proceeding. Do not, for any reason, force the piston into the cylinder - you might break a ring and/or the piston.

12   Once the piston/connecting rod assembly is installed, the connecting rod bearing oil clearance must be checked before the rod cap is permanently bolted in place.

13   Cut a piece of the appropriate size Plastigage slightly shorter than the width of the connecting rod bearing and lay it in place on the number one connecting rod journal, parallel with the journal axis **(see illustration)**.

14   Clean the connecting rod cap bearing face, remove the protective hoses from the connecting rod bolts and install the rod cap. Make sure the mating mark on the cap is on the same side as the mark on the connecting rod.

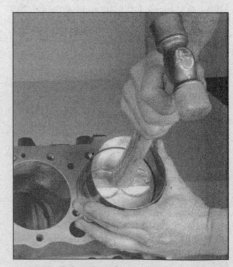

24.11 Drive the piston gently into the cylinder bore with the end of a wooden or plastic hammer handle

24.13 Lay the Plastigage strips on each rod bearing journal, parallel to the crankshaft centerline

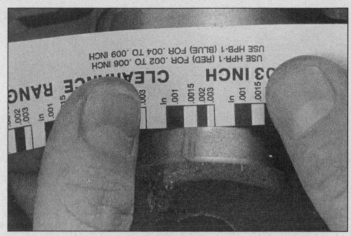

24.17 Measuring the width of the crushed Plastigage to determine the rod bearing oil clearance (be sure to use the correct scale - standard and metric ones are included)

15   Install the nuts and tighten them to the torque listed in this Chapter's Specifications, working up to it in three steps. **Note:** *Use a thin-wall socket to avoid erroneous torque readings that can result if the socket is wedged between the rod cap and nut. If the socket tends to wedge itself between the nut and the cap, lift up on it slightly until it no longer contacts the cap. Do not rotate the crankshaft at any time during this operation.*

16   Remove the nuts and detach the rod cap, being very careful not to disturb the Plastigage.

17   Compare the width of the crushed Plastigage to the scale printed on the Plastigage envelope to obtain the oil clearance **(see illustration)**. Compare it to the Specifications to make sure the clearance is correct.

18   If the clearance is not as specified, the bearing inserts may be the wrong size (which means different ones will be required). Before deciding that different inserts are needed, make sure that no dirt or oil was between the bearing inserts and the connecting rod or cap when the clearance was measured. Also, recheck the journal diameter. If the Plastigage was wider at one end than the other, the journal may be tapered (refer to Section 18).

Final connecting rod installation

19   Carefully scrape all traces of the Plastigage material off the rod journal and/or bearing face. Be very careful not to scratch the bearing - use your fingernail or the edge of a credit card.

20   Make sure the bearing faces are perfectly clean, then apply a uniform layer of clean moly-base grease or engine assembly lube to both of them. You'll have to push the piston into the cylinder to expose the face of the bearing insert in the connecting rod - be sure to slip the protective hoses over the rod bolts first.

21   Slide the connecting rod back into place on the journal, remove the protective hoses from the rod cap bolts, install the rod cap and tighten the nuts to the specified torque. Again, work up to the torque in three steps.

22   Repeat the entire procedure for the remaining pistons/connecting rods.

23   The important points to remember are:

a) *Keep the back sides of the bearing inserts and the insides of the connecting rods and caps perfectly clean when assembling them.*

b) *Make sure you have the correct piston/rod assembly for each cylinder.*

c) *The notches or mark on the piston must face the front of the engine.*

d) *Lubricate the cylinder walls with clean oil.*

e) *Lubricate the bearing faces when installing the rod caps after the oil clearance has been checked.*

24   After all the piston/connecting rod assemblies have been properly installed, rotate the crankshaft a number of times by hand to check for any obvious binding.

25   As a final step, the connecting rod endplay must be checked. Refer to Section 12 for this procedure.

26   Compare the measured endplay to the Specifications to make sure it's correct. If it was correct before disassembly and the original crankshaft and rods were reinstalled, it should still be right. If new rods or a new crankshaft were installed, the endplay may be inadequate. If so, the rods will have to be removed and taken to an automotive machine shop for resizing.

---

25   Initial start-up and break-in after overhaul

Warning: *Have a fire extinguisher handy when starting the engine for the first time.*

1   Once the engine has been installed in the vehicle, double-check the engine oil and coolant levels.

2   With the spark plugs out of the engine and the ignition system disabled (see Section 3), crank the engine until oil pressure registers on the gauge or the light goes out.

3   Install the spark plugs, hook up the plug wires and restore the ignition system functions (see Section 3).

4   Start the engine. It may take a few moments for the fuel system to build up pressure, but the engine should start without a great deal of effort. **Note:** *If backfiring occurs through the carburetor or throttle body, recheck the valve timing and ignition timing.*

5   After the engine starts, it should be allowed to warm up to normal operating temperature. While the engine is warming up, make a thorough check for fuel, oil and coolant leaks.

6   Shut the engine off and recheck the engine oil and coolant levels.

7   Drive the vehicle to an area with minimum traffic, accelerate at full throttle from 30 to 50 mph, then allow the vehicle to slow to 30 mph with the throttle closed. Repeat the procedure 10 or 12 times. This will load the piston rings and cause them to seat properly against the cylinder walls. Check again for oil and coolant leaks.

8   Drive the vehicle gently for the first 500 miles (no sustained high speeds) and keep a constant check on the oil level. It is not unusual for an engine to use oil during the break-in period.

9   At approximately 500 to 600 miles, change the oil and filter.

10   For the next few hundred miles, drive the vehicle normally. Do not pamper it or abuse it.

11   After 2000 miles, change the oil and filter again and consider the engine broken in.

2E

Notes

Chapter 3
Cooling, heating and air conditioning systems

Contents

Specifications

Thermostat opening temperature

3.3L six-cylinder engine
    Starts to open .... 193 to 200-degrees F
    Fully open .... 212-degrees F
2.8L V6 engine
    Starts to open .... 192 to 198-degrees F
    Fully open .... 226-degrees F
3.8L V6 engine
    Starts to open .... 193 to 200-degrees F
    Fully open .... 221-degrees F
4.2L V8 engine
    Starts to open .... 188 to 195-degrees F
    Fully open .... 221-degrees F
5.0L V8 engine (through 1988)
    Starts to open .... 193 to 200-degrees F
    Fully open .... 221-degrees F
5.0L V8 engine (1989 on)
    Starts to open .... 188 to 195-degrees F
    Fully open .... 221-degrees F

Blower motor current draw and voltage

1979

  Without air conditioning
    Low speed
      Amps 4
      Volts.. 7
    Medium speed
      Amps 5
      Volts.. 9
    High speed
      Amps 7
      Volts.. 12.8
  With air conditioning
    Low speed
      Amps 4
      Volts.. 3.9
    Medium low speed
      Amps 8
      Volts.. 6.2
    Medium high speed
      Amps 13
      Volts.. 8.9
    High speed
      Amps 23
      Volts.. 12.8

1980

  Without air conditioning
    Low speed
      Amps 3.6
      Volts.. 4.6
    Medium speed
      Amps 5.3
      Volts.. 7.4
    High speed
      Amps 8.5
      Volts.. 12.8
  With air conditioning
    Low speed
      Amps 4
      Volts.. 3.9
    Medium low speed
      Amps 8
      Volts.. 6.2
    Medium high speed
      Amps 13
      Volts.. 8.9
    High speed
      Amps 23
      Volts.. 12.8

1981

  Without air conditioning
    Low speed
      Amps 2.0
      Volts.. 5.5
    Medium speed
      Amps 5.3
      Volts.. 7.4
    High speed
      Amps 8.5
      Volts.. 12.8
  With air conditioning
    Low speed
      Amps 4
      Volts.. 3.9
    Medium low speed
      Amps 8
      Volts.. 6.2
    Medium high speed
      Amps 13
      Volts.. 8.9

High speed
    Amps 23
    Volts... 12.8
1982 through 1985
  Without air conditioning
    Low speed
      Amps 3.6
      Volts... 4.6
    Medium speed
      Amps 5.3
      Volts... 7.4
    High speed
      Amps 8.5
      Volts... 12.8
  With air conditioning
    Low speed
      Amps .... 3.5 to 5.0
      Volts... 3.5 to 4.5
    Medium low speed
      Amps .... 6 to 8
      Volts... 5.5 to 7.0
    Medium high speed
      Amps .... 10 to 14
      Volts... 7.5 to 10.5
    High speed
      Amps .... 15 to 22*
      Volts... 11 to 14
1986 on
  Without air conditioning
    Low speed
      Amps 2.2
      Volts... 5.1
    Medium speed
      Amps 3.7
      Volts... 7.3
    High speed
      Amps 9.2
      Volts... 12.8
  With air conditioning
    Low speed
      Amps .... 3.5 to 5.0
      Volts... 3.5 to 4.5
    Medium low speed
      Amps .... 6 to 8
      Volts... 5.5 to 7.0
    Medium high speed
      Amps .... 10 to 14
      Volts... 7.5 to 10.5
    High speed
      Amps .... 16 to 22
      Volts... 11 to 14

*16 to 22 on 1985 models

Torque specifications

	Ft-lbs
Fan pulley-to-hub bolts (through 1989)	12 to 18
Fan clutch-to-water pump bolts (1990 5.0L V8)	15 to 22
Thermostat housing bolts	
2.3L four-cylinder engine	14 to 21
2.8L V6 engine	12 to 15
3.3L six-cylinder engine	12 to 18
3.8L V6 engine	15 to 22
V8 engine	
Through 1987	9 to 12
1988 on	12 to 18
Water pump-to-block bolts	
2.3L four-cylinder engine	14 to 21
2.8L V6 engine	7 to 9
3.3L six-cylinder engine	12 to 18
3.8L V6 engine	15 to 22
V8 engine	12 to 18

3

1   General information

Engine cooling system

All vehicles covered by this manual employ a pressurized engine cooling system with thermostatically controlled coolant circulation. An impeller type water pump mounted on the front of the block pumps coolant through the engine. The coolant flows around each cylinder and toward the rear of the engine. Cast-in coolant passages direct coolant around the intake and exhaust ports, near the spark plug areas and in close proximity to the exhaust valve guides.

A wax pellet type thermostat is located in a housing near the front of the engine. During warm-up, the closed thermostat prevents coolant from circulating through the radiator. As the engine nears normal operating temperature, the thermostat opens and allows hot coolant to travel through the radiator, where it's cooled before returning to the engine.

The cooling system is sealed by a pressure type radiator cap, which raises the boiling point of the coolant and increases the cooling efficiency of the radiator. If the system pressure exceeds the cap pressure relief value, the excess pressure in the system forces the spring-loaded valve inside the cap off its seat and allows the coolant to escape through the overflow tube into a coolant reservoir. When the system cools, the excess coolant is automatically drawn from the reservoir back into the radiator. The coolant reservoir does double duty: As the point at which fresh coolant is added to the cooling system to maintain the proper fluid level and as a holding tank for coolant when it expands from the normal heat of engine operation.

This type of cooling system is known as a closed design because coolant that escapes past the pressure cap is saved and reused.

Heating system

The heating system consists of a blower fan and heater core located in the heater box, the hoses connecting the heater core to the engine cooling system and the heater/air conditioning control assembly on the dashboard. Hot engine coolant is circulated through the heater core. When the heater mode is activated, a flap door opens to expose the heater box to the passenger compartment. A fan switch on the control assembly activates the blower motor, which forces air through the core, heating the air.

Air conditioning system

The air conditioning system consists of a condenser mounted in front of the radiator, an evaporator mounted adjacent to the heater core, a compressor mounted on the engine, a receiver-drier (accumulator) which contains a high pressure relief valve and the plumbing connecting all of the above components.

A blower fan forces the warmer air of the passenger compartment through the evaporator core (sort of a radiator-in-reverse), transferring the heat from the air to the refrigerant. The liquid refrigerant boils off into low pressure vapor, taking the heat with it when it leaves the evaporator.

2   Antifreeze - general information

Warning: *Do not allow antifreeze to come in contact with your skin or painted surfaces of the vehicle. Rinse off spills immediately with plenty of water. Antifreeze is highly toxic if ingested. Never leave antifreeze lying around in an open container or in puddles on the floor; children and pets are attracted by it's sweet smell and may drink it. Check with local authorities about disposing of used antifreeze. Many communities have collection centers which will see that antifreeze is disposed of safely.*

The cooling system should be filed with a water/ethylene glycol based antifreeze solution, which will prevent freezing down to at least -20-degrees F, or lower if local climate requires it. It also provides protection against corrosion and increases the coolant boiling point.

The cooling system should be drained, flushed and refilled at least every other year (see Chapter 1). The use of antifreeze solutions for periods of longer then two years is likely to cause damage and encourage the formation of rust and scale in the system. If your tap water is "hard," use distilled water with the antifreeze.

Before adding antifreeze to the system, check all hose connections, because antifreeze tends to search out and leak through very minute openings. Engines do not normally consume coolant. Therefore, if the level goes down find the cause and correct it.

The exact mixture of antifreeze-to-water which you should use depends on the relative weather conditions. The mixture should contain at least 50-percent antifreeze, but should never contain more than 70 percent antifreeze. Consult the mixture ratio chart on the antifreeze container before adding coolant. Hydrometers are available at most auto parts stores to test the ratio of antifreeze to water. Use antifreeze which meets specification ESE-M97B44-A.

3   Thermostat - check and replacement

Warning: *Do not remove the radiator cap, drain the coolant or replace the thermostat until the engine has cooled completely.*

Check

1   Before assuming the thermostat is to blame for a cooling system problem, check the coolant level, drivebelt tension (see Chapter 1) and temperature gauge operation.
2   If the engine seems to be taking a long time to warm up (based on heater output or temperature gauge operation), the thermostat is probably stuck open. Replace the thermostat with a new one.
3   If the engine runs hot, use your hand to check the temperature of the upper radiator hose (lower radiator hose on 2.8L V6 models). If the hose isn't hot, but the engine is, the thermostat is probably stuck closed, preventing the coolant inside the engine from escaping to the radiator. Replace the thermostat. **Caution:** *Don't drive the vehicle without a thermostat. The computer may stay in open loop and emissions and fuel economy will suffer.*
4   If the upper radiator hose is hot, it means that the coolant is flowing and the thermostat is open. Consult the Troubleshooting Section at the front of this manual for cooling system diagnosis.

Replacement

Refer to illustrations 3.11a and 3.11b
5   Disconnect the negative battery cable from the battery.
6   Drain the cooling system (see Chapter 1). If the coolant is relatively new or in good condition (see Chapter 1), save it and reuse it. **Warning:** *Do not leave the drained coolant where it is accessible to children or pets - they are attracted by its sweet smell. Ingesting even a small amount of coolant can be fatal!*
7   Follow the appropriate radiator hose to the engine to locate the thermostat housing. On all except 2.8L V6 engines, this is the upper hose. On 2.8L V6 engines, follow the lower hose.
8   Loosen the hose clamp, then detach the hose from the fitting. If it's stuck, grasp it near the end with a pair of adjustable pliers and twist it to break the seal, then pull it off. If the hose is old or deteriorated, cut it off and install a new one. On inline engines, detach the small hose from the fitting in the same manner.
9   On V8 engines, the distributor vacuum diaphragm may block access to the thermostat. If so, remove the distributor cap and rotor, then remove the diaphragm retaining screws and take the diaphragm out.
10   If the outer surface of the large fitting that mates with the hose is deteriorated (corroded, pitted, etc.) it may be damaged further by hose removal. If it is, the thermostat housing will have to be replaced.
11   Remove the bolts and detach the housing **(see illustrations)**. If the cover is stuck, tap it with a soft-faced hammer to jar it loose. Be prepared for some coolant to spill as the gasket seal is broken. On most models, the thermostat will come away from the engine with the housing.
12   Note how it's installed (which end is facing away from the engine), then remove the thermostat. On most models, the thermostat

3.11a Location of the thermostat housing on four-cylinder engines

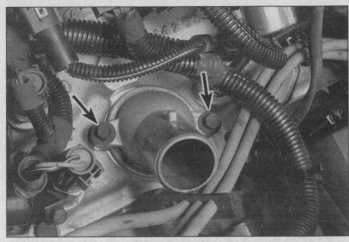

3.11b A top view of a V6 thermostat housing shows the locations of the bolts (arrows)

is secured by locking flats or locating ears. If this is the case, rotate the thermostat to release it from the housing. Do not pry the thermostat out or it will be damaged.

13 Stuff a rag into the engine opening, then remove all traces of old gasket material and sealant from the housing and engine with a gasket scraper. Remove the rag from the opening and clean the gasket mating surfaces with lacquer thinner or acetone.

14 On 2.3L four-cylinder engines, be sure to rotate the thermostat so the heater tube opening is unobstructed.

15 On models with locking flats or locking ears, install the thermostat in the housing, then rotate the thermostat to lock it in position.

16 On V8 models with a thermostat bleeder valve, the valve should be up.

17 Gaskets may be plain or precoated with adhesive. On precoated gaskets, peel the protective paper away from the adhesive. Coat plain gaskets on both sides with a thin, even layer of gasket sealant.

18 Install the thermostat gasket on the thermostat housing (2.8L V6) or on the engine (all others).

19 Install the thermostat housing evenly and tighten the bolts to the torque listed in this Chapter's Specifications.

20 Reattach the hose(s) to the thermostat housing and tighten the hose clamp(s) securely.

21 On V8 engines, install the distributor vacuum diaphragm, cap and rotor (if removed).

22 Refill the cooling system (see Chapter 1).

23 Start the engine and allow it to reach normal operating temperature, then check for leaks and proper thermostat operation (as described in steps 2 through 4).

4 Radiator - removal and installation

Refer to illustrations 4.6, 4.8 and 4.9
Warning 1: On models equipped with air-

bags, always disconnect the negative battery cable, then disconnect the positive battery cable and wait two minutes before working in the vicinity of the impact sensors, steering column or instrument panel to avoid the possibility of accidental deployment of the airbag, which could cause personal injury.

Warning 2: Wait until the engine is completely cool before beginning this procedure.

1 Disconnect the negative battery cable from the battery.

2 Drain the cooling system (see Chapter 1). If the coolant is relatively new or in good condition, save it and reuse it. Warning: Be sure to store coolant where children and pets can't get to it. It's sweet smell attracts them. Ingesting even a small amount can be fatal!

3 Loosen the hose clamps, then detach the radiator hoses from the fittings. If they're stuck, grasp each hose near the end with a pair of adjustable pliers and twist it to break the seal, then pull it off - be careful not to distort the radiator fittings! If the hoses are old or deteriorated, cut them off and install new ones.

4 Disconnect the reservoir hose from the radiator filler neck.

5 On vehicles equipped with a flex-blade or clutch-type fan, detach the shroud from the radiator and slide the shroud toward the engine.

6 If the vehicle is equipped with an automatic transmission, disconnect the cooler lines from the radiator (see illustration). Use a flare-nut wrench so the nut isn't rounded off and hold the fitting with a backup wrench so it isn't damaged. Use a drip pan to catch spilled fluid. On vehicles with quick-disconnect oil cooler line fittings, a special disconnecting tool is available from most auto parts stores. This inexpensive tool fits over the line and presses into the fitting to release the line.

7 Plug the lines and fittings. A very small amount of dirt can cause automatic transmission failure.

8 Remove the radiator mounting bolts (see illustration).

4.6 Use two wrenches when removing the transmission cooler lines to avoid damaging the fittings

4.8 Removing the upper radiator mounting bolts (inline six-cylinder model shown)

3

4.9 Lift the radiator up carefully to avoid damaging the radiator

6.10 Remove the four bolts (arrows) to separate the fan from the clutch (steel fan shown)

9   Carefully lift the radiator out (see illustration). Don't spill coolant on the vehicle or scratch the paint.
10   With the radiator removed, it can be inspected for leaks and damage. If it needs repair, have a radiator shop or dealer service department perform the work as special techniques are required.
11   Bugs and dirt can be removed from the radiator with compressed air and a soft brush. Don't bend the cooling fins as this is done.
12   Check the radiator mounts for deterioration and make sure there's nothing in them when the radiator is installed.
13   Installation is the reverse of the removal procedure.
14   After installation, fill the cooling system with the proper mixture of antifreeze and water. Refer to Chapter 1 if necessary.
15   Start the engine and check for leaks. Allow the engine to reach normal operating temperature, indicated by the upper radiator hose becoming hot (all except 2.8L V6) or by the lower radiator hose becoming hot (2.8L V6). Recheck the coolant level and add more if required.
16   If you're working on an automatic transmission equipped vehicle, check and add fluid as needed.

5   Electric cooling fan and motor - check, removal and installation

1   The Electrodrive cooling fan system is installed on 1980 and later turbocharged 2.3L engines, as well as on 1982 and later non-turbocharged 2.3L engines. It utilizes an electrically-driven fan motor which is triggered by a coolant temperature sensor. Turbocharged, carbureted vehicles also have a temperature sensor in the base of the carburetor which switches the fan on when carburetor temperature reaches 155-degrees F. On air conditioned vehicles, the fan operates whenever the A/C compressor is engaged, regardless of coolant temperature. **Warning:** *On some vehicles the fan may come on automatically, even with the ignition Off. DO NOT place your*

hands or tools where they may be struck by the fan if it starts moving suddenly! If possible, disconnect the negative cable from the battery when working near the fan.

Check

2   The fan controller (1981 and later models, except Fuel Economy Leader) is located under the instrument panel near the steering column.
3   To test the motor, unplug the electrical connector at the motor. Connect one jumper wire from the motor positive terminal to the battery positive terminal. Connect the other jumper wire from the motor negative terminal to ground. If the fan still does not work, replace the motor.
4   If the motor tested OK, the fault lies in the coolant temperature switch, the fan controller, the EEC system (see Chapter 6) or the wiring which connects these components. Carefully check all wiring and connections. If no obvious problems are found, further diagnosis should be done by a dealer service department or repair shop.

Removal and installation

5   Disconnect the negative cable from the battery.
6   Detach the fan wiring harness from its clip, then unplug the connector.
7   Remove the fan mounting screws and take the fan assembly out.
8   Remove the retainer clip and take the fan off the motor shaft. **Note:** *If the motor shaft is burred, remove the burr before attempting to remove the fan.*
9   Remove the fan motor-to-bracket nuts, then separate the motor from the bracket.
10   Installation is the reverse of the removal procedure.

6   Engine-mounted cooling fan - check and replacement

Warning: *DO NOT stand in line with an engine-mounted cooling fan while the engine is running!*

Flex-blade fan

1   A flex-blade fan is used on 1979 through 1981 models. Flexible blades are riveted to a central stamped hub. The blades flatten out at high engine speeds, reducing drag for lower noise and lower fuel consumption.
2   Check the fan carefully for cracks or separation of the blades from the hub. Replace the fan if any cracks or separation are found, no matter ho minor the problem may appear. A defective flex-blade fan can break apart in operation, creating a serious safety hazard.
3   To remove the fan, detach the fan shroud from the radiator and push the shroud over the fan. Unbolt the fan and spacer from the water pump pulley, then lift the fan, spacer and shroud out of the engine compartment.
4   To install the fan, reverse the removal procedure. Tighten the bolts to the torque listed in this Chapter's Specifications.

Clutch-type fan

Refer to illustrations 6.10 and 6.11
5   The clutch-type fan employs rigid blades with an aluminum fan clutch at the center (hub). Check the fan carefully for cracks, especially around the base of each blade. Replace a cracked fan immediately.
6   Check the clutch for fluid leakage. Replace the clutch if it has been leaking.
7   Try to move the fan blades in a front-to-rear direction. If the blades wobble, replace the fan clutch.
8   Spin the fan by hand. The fan should resist spinning (more when the engine is hot). If it spins freely or won't spin at all, replace the fan clutch.
9   To remove the fan, detach the fan shroud from the radiator and push it over the fan. Unbolt the fan and clutch from the water pump pulley, then lift the fan, clutch and shroud out of the engine compartment.
10   To separate the clutch from the fan, remove the attaching bolts (see illustration).
11   If the fan is stored, be sure to place the marked side down (see illustration).
12   To install the fan, reverse the removal

6.11 When the fan clutch is removed, store it with this side down (arrow)

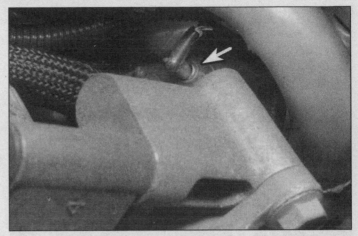

8.4 Location of a typical coolant temperature sending unit (arrow)

procedure. Tighten the bolts to the torque listed in this Chapter's Specifications.

7 Coolant reservoir - removal and installation

1   Disconnect the overflow hose at the radiator neck.
2   Detach the reservoir from the inner fender or bracket.
3   Lift the reservoir out.
4   Installation is the reverse of removal.

8 Coolant temperature sending unit - check and replacement

Warning: *The engine must be completely cool before removing the sending unit.*
Caution: *Do not ground the sending unit wire directly to the engine. This may damage the gauge or instrument voltage regulator.*

Check

Refer to illustration 8.4
1   If the coolant temperature gauge is inoperative, check the fuses first (see Chapter 12).
2   If all gauges have similar problems (high readings, low readings, erratic readings), the instrument voltage regulator may be at fault. This should be tested by a dealer service department or qualified electrical shop.
3   If the temperature indicator shows excessive temperature after running a while, see the Troubleshooting Section in the front of this manual.
4   If the temperature gauge indicates "Hot" shortly after the engine is started cold, or if it does not indicate any increase in temperature, disconnect the wire at the coolant temperature sending unit **(see illustration)**.
5   Turn the ignition key to On, but don't start the engine. Connect a 10-ohm resistor to the disconnected wire, then ground the resistor to the engine. The temperature gauge should indicate in the Hot range.
6   Repeat Step 4 using a 73-ohm resistor.

The gauge should indicate in the Cold range.
7   If the gauge indicated properly in Steps 5 and 6, the sending unit is bad. Replace it.
8   If the gauge did not indicate properly in Steps 5 and 6, the circuit may be open or the gauge may be faulty. See Chapter 12 for additional information.

Replacement

9   With the engine complete cool, remove the cap from the radiator to release any pressure, then replace the cap. This reduces coolant loss during sending unit replacement.
10   Disconnect the electrical connector from the sending unit.
11   Prepare the new sending unit for installation by applying electrically conductive sealant to the threads.
12   Unscrew the sending unit from the engine and quickly install the new one to prevent coolant loss.
13   Tighten the sending unit securely and reconnect the electrical connector.
14   Refill the cooling system and run the engine. Check for leaks and proper gauge operation.

9 Water pump - check and replacement

1   A failure in the water pump can cause overheating and serious engine damage due to overheating.

Check

2   There are three ways to check the operation of the water pump while it's installed on the engine. If the pump is defective, it should be replaced with a new or rebuilt unit.
3   With the engine running at normal operating temperature, squeeze the upper radiator hose. If the water pump is working properly, a pressure surge should be felt as the hose is released. **Warning:** *Keep your hands away from the fan blades!*
4   Water pumps are equipped with weep or vent holes. If a failure occurs in the pump seal, coolant will leak from the hole. In most

9.9 Once the fan is removed, the water pump pulley can be slipped off the shaft by hand (3.8L V6 engine shown, others similar)

cases you'll need a flashlight to find the hole on the water pump from underneath to check for leaks.
5   If the water pump shaft bearings fail there may be a howling sound at the front of the engine while it's running. Shaft wear can be felt if the water pump pulley is rocked up and down. Don't mistake drivebelt slippage, which causes a squealing sound, for water pump bearing failure.

Replacement

Refer to illustrations 9.9, 9.10, 9.13a, 9.13b, 9.13c and 9.19
Warning: *Wait until the engine is completely cool before beginning this procedure.*
6   Disconnect the negative battery cable from the battery.
7   Drain the cooling system (see Chapter 1). If the coolant is relatively new or in good condition, save it and reuse it.
8   Remove the cooling fan and shroud (see Section 5 or Section 6).
9   Remove the drivebelts (see Chapter 1) and the pulley at the end of the water pump shaft **(see illustration)**.

3

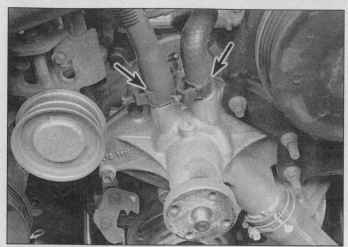

9.10 Loosen the clamps, then twist the hoses (arrows) to detach them from the pump fittings (3.8L V6 engine shown)

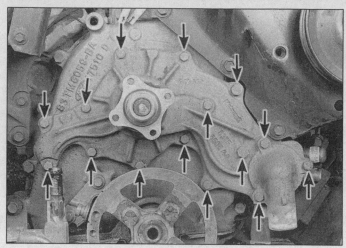

9.13a Water pump bolt locations - 2.8L V6 engine

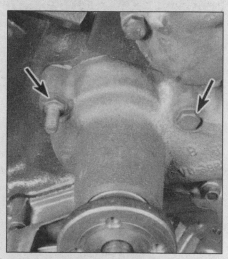

9.13b The water pump mounting bolts on a 3.3L six-cylinder engine (arrows) - one bolt on the bottom is obscured by the pump

10 Loosen the clamps and detach the hoses from the water pump (see illustration). If they're stuck, grasp each hose near the end with a pair of adjustable pliers and twist it to break the seal, then pull it off. If the hoses are deteriorated, cut them off and install new ones.

11 Remove all accessory brackets from the water pump. When removing the power steering pump and air conditioning compressor, don't disconnect the hoses. Tie the units aside with the hoses attached.

12 2.3L four-cylinder engine - remove the outer timing belt cover (see Chapter 2A).

13 Remove the bolts and detach the water pump from the engine (see illustrations). Note the locations of the various lengths and different types of bolts as they're removed to ensure correct installation.

14 Clean the bolt threads and the threaded holes in the engine to remove corrosion and sealant.

15 Compare the new pump to the old one to make sure they are identical.

16 Remove all traces of old gasket material from the engine with a gasket scraper.

17 Clean the engine and new water pump mating surfaces with lacquer thinner or acetone.

18 Apply a thin coat of RTV gasket sealant to the engine side of the water pump gasket. Position the new gasket on the engine.

19 Prior to installation, treat the water pump bolts as follows:

   2.3L four-cylinder engine - coat all bolts with Teflon sealant

   2.8L V6 and 3.3L six-cylinder engines - make sure the bolts are clean and free of corrosion

   3.8L V6 engine - coat only one bolt (see illustration) with Teflon sealant or equivalent. Lightly oil the remaining bolts.

   V8 engines - lightly oil all bolts.

20 Apply a thin layer of RTV sealant to the gasket mating surface of the new pump, then

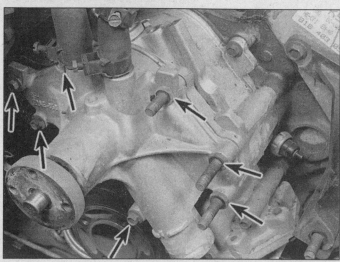

9.13c Note the locations of all bolts and studs during removal (3.8L V6 engine shown)

9.19 On 3.8L V6 models, apply sealant to the threads of this bolt (arrow)

carefully mate the gasket and pump. Slip a couple of bolts through the pump mounting holes to hold the gasket in place.

21 Install the remaining bolts (if they also hold an accessory bracket in place, be sure to reposition the bracket at this time). Tighten them to the torque listed in this Chapter's Specifications in 1/4-turn increments. Don't overtighten them or the pump may be distorted.

22 Reinstall all parts removed for access to the pump.

23 Refill the cooling system and check the drivebelt tension (see Chapter 1). Run the engine and check for leaks.

10 Heater - general information

The heater circulates engine coolant through a small radiator (heater core) in the passenger compartment. Air is drawn in through an opening in the cowl, then blown (by the blower motor) through the heater core to pick up heat. The heated air is blended with varying amounts of unheated air to regulate its temperature. The heated air is then blown into the passenger compartment. Various doors in the heater control the flow of air to the floor, instrument panel and defroster outlets.

11 Blower motor circuit - electrical testing

1979 through 1981 models

1 Make sure the battery is fully charged and the fuse is not blown (see Chapter 12). Also check the connections at the blower motor and resistor assembly to be sure they're tight and not corroded.

2 Connect the positive lead of a voltmeter to the blower motor electrical connector (orange/black wire) at the blower motor resistor assembly.

3 Connect the negative lead of the voltmeter to a good ground (bare metal) on the vehicle frame.

4 Place the temperature control lever in the middle of its travel.

5 Place the heater function control lever in the Heat position.

6 Place the ignition key in the On position.

7 Move the blower switch through each of its positions and note the voltage readings. Compare with the Specifications at the front of this Chapter. If the voltage readings are correct, but the blower motor won't work or doesn't work correctly, either the blower motor or the wiring to the blower motor is faulty. If there are no voltage readings, and the connections and fuse are good, the problem is probably in the wiring. If only one or two of the readings are too high or too low, and all connections in the circuit are tight and not corroded, the problem is probably in the resistor assembly. Remove the two screws,

pull it out of the blower case and check it visually.

8 Turn off the key and disconnect the voltmeter. Leave the temperature control and function control levers where they are.

9 Disconnect the blower motor electrical connector (orange/black wire) from the resistor assembly terminal.

10 Connect the positive lead of an ammeter to the male connector terminal on the resistor assembly.

11 Connect the negative lead of the ammeter to the electrical connector. If necessary, insert a male connector terminal into the connector so the ammeter clip will have something to attach to.

12 Turn the key to the On position.

13 Move the blower switch through each of its positions and note the ammeter readings. Current draw should be as shown in the Specifications in the front of this Chapter. If it's higher in all switch positions, and all connections are good, the problem is probably the blower motor. If the current draw is too high or too low in only one or two switch positions, the problem is likely in the resistor assembly.

1982 and later models

14 Check the fuse and all connections in the circuit for looseness and corrosion. Make sure the battery is fully charged. Move the temperature lever or knob to the Warm position. Move the function control lever or knob to the Floor position. **Note:** *On early production 1985 models, the function control lever may have a Heat position instead of a Floor position.*

15 With the transmission in Park, the parking brake securely set and the wheels blocked, start the engine.

16 Connect a voltmeter to the blower motor connector.

17 Move the blower switch through each of its positions and note the voltage readings. Compare with the Specifications at the front of this Chapter.
If there is voltage, but the blower motor does not operate or if all readings are higher than specified, the blower motor is probably faulty.

18 Disconnect the voltmeter and turn off the engine.

19 Leave the temperature lever or knob in the Warm position and move the function control lever or knob to the Heat position.

20 Disconnect the electrical connector from the blower motor resistor. Connect a jumper wire between the lower terminal of the resistor and the black wire's terminal in the electrical connector.

21 Connect an ammeter between the top terminal of the resistor and the orange wire's terminal in the electrical connector.

22 Start the engine.

23 Move the blower switch through each of its positions and note the ammeter reading. Compare with the Specifications at the front of this Chapter. If the readings are too high,

and all connections are good, the blower motor is probably faulty. If the readings are too high or too low in only one or two switch positions, the resistor assembly is probably faulty.

12 Heater control assembly - removal and installation

1979 through 1986 models

1 Remove three screws from the top edge of the instrument cluster trim panel. Lift the panel's lower locking tabs out of their slots, then remove the trim panel.

2 Remove four screws that secure the control assembly to the instrument panel. Pull the control assembly out from the panel.

3 Detach the function and temperature cables from the heater case. Disconnect the electrical connectors for the blower switch and control assembly illumination.

4 Pull the control assembly out, together with the function and temperature cables.

5 Remove the spring nut that secures the function cable end loop to the function control lever. Depress the white locking tang on the function cable housing, then detach the function cable from the control assembly.

6 Detach the temperature control cable in the same manner as the function control cable.

7 Install the control assembly by reversing Steps 1 through 7. Position the wire coils on the cable ends so they face away from the bases of the lever tangs.

1987 and later models

Warning: *On models equipped with airbags, always disconnect the negative battery cable, then disconnect the positive battery cable and wait two minutes before working in the vicinity of the impact sensors, steering column or instrument panel to avoid the possibility of accidental deployment of the airbag, which could cause personal injury.*

8 Disconnect the negative battery cable from the battery.

9 Unsnap the control assembly trim panel from the instrument panel.

10 Remove the control assembly mounting screws. Pull the control assembly out of the instrument panel.

11 Disconnect the electrical connectors, temperature control cable and vacuum harness from the control assembly.

12 If necessary, the control knobs can be pulled off.

13 Installation is the reverse of Steps 8 through 12. **Caution:** *Don't try to thread the vacuum harness retaining nuts onto their posts. Push the nuts on.*

13 Blower motor switch - replacement

1 Remove the control assembly (see Section 12).

3

2   Disconnect the blower switch electrical connectors.

3   On 1979 through 1986 models, detach the control lever tang from the knob with a screwdriver and remove the knob.

4   On 1987 and later models, pull the knob off.

5   Remove the switch attaching screw(s) and take the switch out.

6   Installation is the reverse of removal.

14 Heater control cables - adjustment

Warning: *On models equipped with airbags, always disconnect the negative battery cable, then disconnect the positive battery cable and wait two minutes before working in the vicinity of the impact sensors, steering column or instrument panel to avoid the possibility of accidental deployment of the airbag, which could cause personal injury.*

1   Before installing the cable:

  a) *Slip a small screwdriver blade into the wire coil on the end of the cable.*

  b) *Use pliers to slide the self-adjusting clip along the cable until it is about one inch from the wire loop.*

  c) *Install the cable (see Section 15).*

2   If the cable is already installed:

  a) *Move the control lever or knob to the Cool position.*

  b) *On vehicles equipped with control levers (not rotating knobs), move the function control lever to the Off position.*

3   If equipped with control levers, place the temperature control lever in the Warm position and the function control lever in the Def position to adjust the cable.

4   If equipped with rotating control knobs, quickly rotate the knob to the Warm position to adjust the cable.

15 Heater control cables - replacement

Warning: *On models equipped with airbags, always disconnect the negative battery cable, then disconnect the positive battery cable and wait two minutes before working in the vicinity of the impact sensors, steering column or instrument panel to avoid the possibility of accidental deployment of the airbag, which could cause personal injury.*

1   Detach the cable housing from the heater case. On 1979 through 1986 models, use the special tool or equivalent (see Section 12).

2   Slip the self-adjusting clip off the crank arm at the heater case.

3   Remove the heater control assembly (see Section 12).

4   Detach the cable from the control assembly and take it out.

5   Install the cable by reversing Steps 1 through 4. Adjust the cable as described in Section 13.

16 Blower motor - replacement (1979 through 1984 models)

Without air conditioning

1   Remove one screw to detach the right register duct from its mounting bracket.

2   Remove two screws and detach the ventilator control assembly from the lower edge of the instrument panel.

3   Remove the glovebox liner.

4   Remove the ventilator grille mounting pins, then take the grille out of the ventilator.

5   Remove the right register duct.

6   Remove the four ventilator assembly screws. One screw is easily accessible. Access to the other screws is as follows:

  a) *Upper left screw - through the glovebox opening*

  b) *Lower right screw - through the ventilator grille opening*

  c) *Upper right screw - through the register duct opening, using a long extension*

7   Remove the ventilator assembly to the right and down and take it out from under the instrument panel.

8   Remove the hub clamp spring and pull the blower wheel off its shaft.

9   Remove the blower motor mounting screws. Pull the motor out, disconnect its wiring connector and remove the motor.

10   Installation is the reverse of removal. Position the hub clamp spring in relation to the flat on the motor shaft as shown in illustration 16.8.

With air conditioning

11   Remove the glovebox liner. Reach through the opening and disconnect the vacuum hose from the outside-recirc door vacuum motor.

12   Remove the bolt securing the lower right side of the instrument panel to the cowl. Remove the trim panel from the right side of the passenger footwell.

13   Remove the screw that secures the top of the support brace to the air inlet nut.

14   Disconnect the blower motor wiring at the inline electrical connector.

15   Remove the nut that secures the blower housing lower support bracket to the evaporator case.

16   Remove the screw that secures the top of the air inlet duct to the evaporator case.

17   Pull the air inlet duct and blower housing assembly down to separate it from the evaporator case.

18   Remove the four screws that secure the blower mounting plate to the housing assembly. Lift the blower and wheel out of the housing. **Caution:** *Do not separate the mounting plate from the blower motor.*

19   If necessary, remove the spring clamp from the blower shaft and pull the blower wheel off.

20   If the blower wheel was removed from the shaft, slide it onto the shaft. Position the outer edge of the blower wheel 3 5/8-inches from the motor mounting plate. Secure the

blower wheel with a new spring clamp, positioned so its ends are 90-degrees from the flat on the motor shaft.

21   Place the blower motor on the housing. Position the flat side of the motor flange toward the blower outlet.

22   Install the blower motor attaching screws through the motor flange into the housing.

23   Tape the blower motor wiring to the air inlet duct so it won't be in the way when the motor is installed.

24   Place the air inlet duct and blower housing assembly in its installed position on the evaporator case. Slip the flange at the top of the blower outlet into its opening in the evaporator case.

25   Place the blower housing lower bracket on its stud, install the nut on the stud to secure the housing to the bracket. **Note:** *Route the blower motor wiring toward the passenger's side of the evaporator case.*

26   Connect a hand vacuum pump to the fitting on the outside-recirc door vacuum motor. Apply vacuum to hold the outside-recirc door open, then spin the blower wheel by hand. There should be no interference. If there is, correct the problem before continuing.

27   Connect the blower motor electrical connector.

28   Install the screw that secures the top of the air inlet duct to the evaporator case.

29   Connect the vacuum hose to the vacuum motor.

30   Install the glovebox liner.

31   Install the bolt securing the lower right side of the instrument panel to the cowl. Install the trim panel on the right side of the passenger's side footwell.

17 Blower motor - replacement (1985 and 1986 models)

Without air conditioning

1   Remove the glovebox.

2   Remove six screws that secure the lower duct to the upper duct an heater case.

3   Remove the hub clamp spring and pull the blower wheel off its shaft.

4   Remove the blower motor mounting screws. Pull the motor out, disconnect its wiring connector and remove the motor.

5   Installation is the reverse of removal. Position the hub clamp spring ends 90-degrees from the flat on the motor shaft.

With air conditioning

6   Replacement of the blower motor on 1985 and 1986 models with air conditioning is the same as for 1979 through 1984 models with air conditioning (see Section 16).

18 Blower motor - replacement (1987 and later models)

1   Open the glovebox door. Squeeze the

sides of the glovebox together to detach its retaining tabs from the instrument panel. Pull the glovebox out and let it hang down.

2   Disconnect the blower motor cooling hose and electrical connector.

3   Remove the four blower motor mounting screws and take the motor out.

4   If necessary, separate the blower wheel from the motor. Remove the spring clamp (1987 models) or push nut (1988 and later models).

5   If the blower wheel was removed from the motor, use a new spring clamp or push nut to secure it. On models with a spring clamp, position the spring clamp ends 90-degrees from the flat on the motor shaft.

6   Make sure both ends of the blower motor cooling hose are securely attached.

7   Connect the electrical connector. Reposition the blower motor and install the mounting screws.

8   Install the glovebox.

19   Heater core - replacement (1979 through 1986 models)

Warning: *On models equipped with airbags, always disconnect the negative battery cable, then disconnect the positive battery cable and wait two minutes before working in the vicinity of the impact sensors, steering column or instrument panel to avoid the possibility of accidental deployment of the airbag, which could cause personal injury.*

Without air conditioning

1   Partially drain the cooling system (see Chapter 1).

2   Loosen the clamps on the heater hoses at the engine compartment side of the firewall. Twist the hoses and carefully separate them from the heater core tubes.

3   Plug or cap the heater core tubes so coolant won't be spilled in the engine compartment when the heater core is removed.

4   Place a plastic sheet on the vehicle floor to prevent stains in case coolant spills.

5   Remove the glovebox liner.

6   Remove the instrument panel-to-cowl brace.

7   Place the temperature lever in the Warm position.

8   Remove four heater core cover screws, then remove the heater core cover through the glovebox opening.

9   Working in the engine compartment, loosen the three stud nuts that secure the heater case. Push the heater core tubes toward the passenger compartment to detach the heater core from the heater case.

10   Working in the passenger compartment, pull the heater core through the glovebox opening.

11   Position the heater core with the tubes on top, then slide it through the glovebox opening into the heater case.

12   Install the heater core cover and tighten its retaining screws.

13   Tighten the three stud nuts securely.

14   Install the instrument panel-to-cowl brace.

15   Install the glovebox liner.

16   Uncap or unplug the heater core tubes, then reconnect the hoses.

17   Fill the cooling system (see Chapter 1). Run the engine, check for leaks and test the heater.

With air conditioning

Warning: *The air conditioning system is under high pressure. Do not loosen any hose fittings or remove any components until after the system has been discharged by a dealer service department or service station. Always wear eye protection when disconnecting air conditioner system fittings.*

18   Remove the instrument panel (see Chapter 11).

19   After having the air conditioning system discharged, disconnect the high and low pressure hoses. Use backup wrenches on the hose fittings to prevent damage.

20   Cap or plug the disconnected hose ends and fittings to keep out dirt and moisture.

21   Partially drain the cooling system (see Chapter 1), then disconnect the heater hoses from the heater core. Cap or plug the heater core tubes so coolant won't spill into the passenger compartment during removal.

22   Disconnect the black vacuum hose at the inline check valve in the engine compartment.

23   The air inlet duct and blower housing assembly has a brace which is secured to the cowl top panel by a screw. Remove the screw.

24   Disconnect the electrical connectors from the blower motor and resistor.

25   In the engine compartment, remove two nuts that secure the evaporator case to the dash panel.

26   In the passenger compartment, remove the remaining evaporator case bracket screws, two at the cowl top panel and one below the evaporator case.

27   Carefully separate the evaporator case from the dash panel and withdraw it into the passenger compartment.

28   Remove the five screws and take off the heater core access cover **(see illustration)**.

29   Take the heater core out of the case. If necessary, remove the seals from the heater core.

20   Heater core - replacement (1987 and later models)

Warning 1: *On models equipped with airbags, always disconnect the negative battery cable, then disconnect the positive battery cable and wait two minutes before working in the vicinity of the impact sensors, steering column or instrument panel to avoid the possibility of accidental deployment of the airbag, which could cause personal injury.*

Warning 2: *The air conditioning system is under high pressure. Do not loosen any hose fittings or remove any components until after the system has been discharged by a dealer service department or service station. Always wear eye protection when disconnecting air conditioning system fittings.*

1   Remove the center console and instrument panel (see Chapter 11).

2   If the vehicle is air conditioned, disconnect the liquid line and accumulator/receiver-drier inlet tube from the evaporator core at the dash panel. Disconnect the high and low pressure hoses (be sure to use a backup wrench so the fittings aren't damaged during removal). Cap the hoses, line and tube to keep out dirt and moisture.

3   Drain the cooling system (see Chapter 1) and detach the heater hoses from the heater core at the firewall. Cap or plug the hoses.

4   Remove the screw that secures the air inlet duct/blower housing assembly to the cowl top panel.

5   Working in the engine compartment, disconnect the black heater vacuum supply hose from the inline check valve.

6   Remove the two heater case stud nuts from the engine compartment side of the firewall.

7   Working in the passenger compartment, disconnect the blower motor electrical connector from the motor and resistor block. Disconnect the blower motor ground wire.

8   On vehicles without air conditioning, remove the screw that secures the heater case support bracket to the cowl top panel.

9   On vehicles with air conditioning, remove the two screws that secure the evaporator case support brackets to the cowl top panel.

10   Remove the remaining screw that secures the lower part of the heater case to the dash panel. Carefully pull the heater case away from the dash panel and withdraw it into the passenger compartment.

11   Remove the screws from the heater core cover. Lift the cover off and remove the heater core and seal from the case.

12   If necessary, take the seal off of the heater core tubes.

13   Installation is the reverse of removal. Run the engine, check for leaks and test the heater.

21   Air conditioning system - check and maintenance

Warning: *The air conditioning system is under high pressure. Do not loosen any hose fittings or remove any components until after the system has been discharged by a dealer service department or service station. Always wear eye protection when disconnecting air conditioning system fittings.*

1   The following maintenance checks should be performed on a regular basis to ensure that the air conditioner continues to operate at peak efficiency.

3

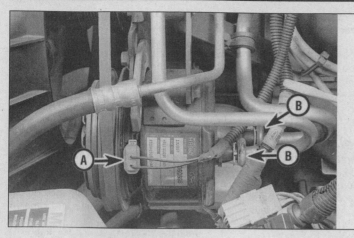

22.3 The air conditioning compressor on a V6 model (other models similar)

A Electrical connector
B Refrigerant line connections

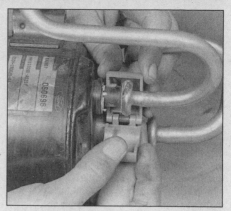

22.5a Slip the proper size tool over the fitting with the tang facing the spring lock . . .

a) Check the compressor drivebelt. If it's worn or deteriorated, replace it (see Chapter 1).
b) Check the drivebelt tension and, if necessary, adjust it (see Chapter 1).
c) Check the system hoses. Look for cracks, bubbles, hard spots and deterioration. Inspect the hoses and all fittings for oil bubbles and seepage. If there's any evidence of wear, damage or leaks, replace the hose(s).
d) Inspect the condenser fins for leaves, bugs and other debris. Use a "fin comb" or compressed air to clean the condenser.
e) Make sure the system has the correct refrigerant charge.

2   It's a good idea to operate the system for about ten minutes at least once a month, particularly during the winter. Long term non-use can cause hardening, and subsequent failure, of the seals.

3   Because of the complexity of the air conditioning system and the special equipment necessary to service it, in-depth troubleshooting and repairs are not included in this manual. However, simple checks and component replacement procedures are provided in this Chapter. For more complete information on the air conditioning system, refer to the Haynes automotive heating and air conditioning manual.

4   The most common cause of poor cooling is simply a low system refrigerant charge. If a noticeable drop in cool air output occurs, one of the following quick checks will help you determine if the refrigerant level is low.

Checking the refrigerant charge

5   Warm the engine up to normal operating temperature.

6   Place the air conditioning temperature selector at the coldest setting and put the blower at the highest setting. Open the doors (to make sure the air conditioning system doesn't cycle off as soon as it cools the passenger compartment).

7   With the compressor engaged - the clutch will make an audible click and the center of the clutch will rotate.

8   Feel for a temperature differential in the system, as described in Step 9 or 10 below.

9   On 1979 through 1981 models (receiver-drier system), feel the inlet and outlet pipes at the compressor. One side should be cold and one hot. If there's no perceptible difference between the two pipes, there's something wrong with the compressor or the system. It might be a low charge - it might be something else. Take the vehicle to a dealer service department or an automotive air conditioning shop.

10   On 1982 and later models (accumulator system), feel the evaporator inlet pipe between the orifice tube and the accumulator with one hand while placing your other hand on the surface of the accumulator housing. If both surfaces feel about the same temperature and if both feel a little cooler than the surrounding air, the refrigerant level is probably okay. If the inlet pipe has frost accumulation or feels cooler than the accumulator surface, the refrigerant charge is low. Add refrigerant. Further inspection of the system is beyond the scope of the home mechanic and should be left to a professional.

Adding refrigerant

11   Buy an automotive charging kit at an auto parts store. A charging kit includes a 14-ounce can of refrigerant, a tap valve and a short section o hose that can be attached between the tap valve and the system low side service valve. Because one can of refrigerant may not be sufficient to bring the system charge up to the proper level, it's a good idea to buy a few additional cans. Make sure that one of the cans contains red refrigerant dye. If the system is leaking, the red dye will leak out with the refrigerant and help you pinpoint the location of the leak. **Warning:** *Never add more than three cans of refrigerant to the system.*

12   Hook up the charging kit to the low side of the system by following the manufacturer's instructions. **Warning:** *DO NOT hook the charging kit hose to the system high side!*

13   Warm up the engine and turn on the air conditioner. Keep the charging kit hose away from the fan and other moving parts.

14   If the system in your vehicle is an accumulator type:

a) Add refrigerant to the low side of the system until both the accumulator surface and the evaporator inlet pipe feel about the same temperature. Allow stabilization time between each addition.
b) Once the accumulator surface and the evaporator inlet pipe feel about the same temperature, add the contents remaining in the can.

15   If the system in your vehicle is a receiver-drier type, place a thermometer in the dashboard vent nearest the evaporator and add refrigerant until the indicated temperature is around 40 to 45-degrees F.

22   Air conditioning system compressor - removal and installation

Refer to illustrations 22.3, 22.5a, 22.5b and 22.5c

Warning: *The air conditioning system is under high pressure. DO NOT disassemble any part of the system (hoses, compressor, line fittings, etc.) until after the system has been depressurized by a dealer service department or service station.*

Note: *The accumulator (see Section 24) should be replaced whenever the compressor is replaced.*

1   Have the air conditioning system discharged (see Warning above).

2   Disconnect the negative battery cable from the battery.

3   Disconnect the compressor clutch electrical connector **(see illustration)**.

4   Remove the drivebelt (see Chapter 1).

5   Disconnect the refrigerant lines from the rear of the compressor. Plug the open fittings to prevent entry of dirt and moisture. On vehicles having "spring lock" type couplings, slip the special tool of the proper size over the fitting, push the tool into the spring lock and pull the tubing out of the fitting **(see illustrations)**.

6   Unbolt the compressor from the mounting brackets and lift it out of the vehicle.

7   If a new compressor is being installed,

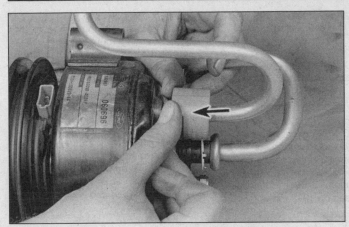

22.5b . . . close the tool and push it in . . .

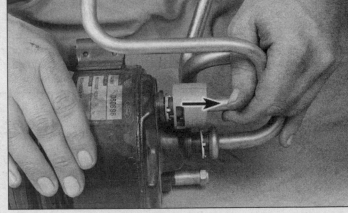

22.5c . . . then pull the line off

follow the directions with the compressor regarding the draining of excess oil prior to installation.

8   The clutch may have to be transferred from the original to the new compressor.

9   Installation is the reverse of removal. Replace all O-rings with new ones specifically made for air conditioning system use and lubricate them with refrigerant oil.

10   Have the system evacuated, recharged and leak tested by the shop that discharged it.

23   Air conditioning system condenser - removal and installation

Warning 1: *On models equipped with airbags, always disconnect the negative battery cable, then disconnect the positive battery cable and wait two minutes before working in the vicinity of the impact sensors, steering column or instrument panel to avoid the possibility of accidental deployment of the airbag, which could cause personal injury.*

Warning 2: *The air conditioning system is under high pressure. DO NOT disassemble any part of the system (hoses, compressor, line fittings, etc.) until after the system has been depressurized by a dealer service department or service station.*

Note: *The accumulator (see Section 24) or receiver/drier (see Section 25) should be replaced whenever the condenser is replaced.*

1979 through 1981 models (receiver/drier system)

1   Have the air conditioning system discharged (see Warning above).

2   Remove the battery (see Chapter 5).

3   Remove the radiator grille (see Chapter 11).

4   Position the ambient cutoff link out of the way.

5   Disconnect the refrigerant lines from the condenser.

6   Unbolt the condenser from the radiator

support and lift it out, together with the receiver/drier.

7   Installation is the reverse of removal. If the new condenser does not include a receiver/drier, install one. Use new O-rings, lubricated with air conditioning refrigerant oil, at the condenser line fittings and to install the new receiver/drier.

8   Take the vehicle back to the shop that discharged it. Have the air conditioning system evacuated, charged and leak tested.

1982 and later models (accumulator system)

Note: *Whenever the condenser is replaced, the accumulator/drier must be replaced also.*

9   Have the air conditioning system discharged (see Warning above).

10   Drain the radiator (see Chapter 1).

11   Remove the battery and its heat shield (see Chapter 5).

12   Disconnect the refrigerant lines from the condenser. The lines use spring-lock couplings, which require a special tool for connection and disconnection.

13   Detach the fan shroud and lay it back out of the way.

14   Disconnect the upper radiator hose. Remove the radiator retaining clamps and tilt the radiator back.

15   Remove both condenser mounting

screws and lift the condenser out.

16   Cap or plug the condenser and line openings to keep out dirt and moisture.

17   Installation is the reverse of removal. Transfer the rubber isolators from the old condenser to the new one. Add one fluid ounce of clean refrigerant oil to the condenser.

18   Take the vehicle back to the shop that discharged it. Have the air conditioning system evacuated, charged and leak tested.

24   Air conditioning system accumulator - removal and installation

Refer to illustration 24.3

Warning: *The air conditioning system is under high pressure. DO NOT disassemble any part of the system (hoses, compressor, line fittings, etc.) until after the system has been depressurized by a dealer service department or service station.*

1   Have the air conditioning system discharged (see Warning above).

2   Disconnect the negative battery cable from the battery.

3   Unplug the electrical connector from the pressure switch near the top of the accumulator **(see illustration)**.

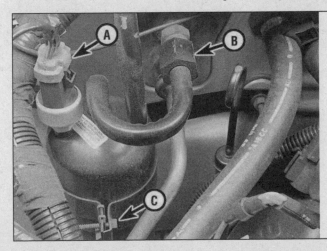

24.3 Details of the air conditioning accumulator

A   *Electrical connector*
B   *Refrigerant line connection*
C   *Holddown bracket pinch bolt*

3

4   Disconnect the refrigerant line from the accumulator. Use a back-up wrench to prevent twisting the tubing.

5   Plug the open fittings to prevent entry of dirt and moisture.

6   Loosen the holddown bracket pinch bolt and lift the accumulator out.

7   If a new accumulator is being installed, remove the Schrader valve and pour the oil out into a measuring cup, noting the amount. Add fresh refrigerant oil to the new accumulator equal to the amount removed from the old unit plus one ounce.

8   Installation is the reverse of removal.

9   Take the vehicle back to the shop that discharged it. Have the air conditioning system evacuated, charged and leak tested.

25   Air conditioning system receiver/drier - removal and installation

Warning: *The air conditioning system is under high pressure. DO NOT disassemble any part of the system (hoses, compressor, line fittings, etc.) until after the system has been depressurized by a dealer service department or service station.*

1   A receiver/drier is used on 1979 through 1981 models.

2   Have the air conditioning system discharged (see Warning above).

3   Remove the radiator grille (see Chapter 11).

4   Position the ambient cutoff switch out of the way.

5   Disconnect the refrigerant lines from the receiver/drier.

6   Remove the receiver/drier attaching screws and take it off the condenser.

7   Installation is the reverse of removal.

8   Take the vehicle back to the shop that discharged it. Have the air conditioning system evacuated, charged and leak tested.

Chapter 4
Fuel and exhaust systems

Contents

4

Specifications

Fuel pressure

Carbureted models	6 to 8 psi
Central Fuel Injection (CFI)	39 psi
EFI and SEFI fuel-injection systems	30 to 45 psi

Torque specifications

Ft-lbs

Carburetor-to-intake manifold nuts/bolts
Model 5200/6500	10 to 14
Model YFA 1V	13 to 14
Model 2150 2V	14 to 16
Model 7200-VV	12 to 15
Model 4180-C 4V	14 to 20

Mechanical fuel pump-to-block bolts
2.3L four-cylinder	14 to 21
3.3L six-cylinder	12 to 18
2.8L V6	12 to 15
V8	19 to 27

Fuel charging assembly-to-intake manifold nuts (CFI-equipped models)
1984 and 1985	10
1986	12 to 15

Torque specifications (continued)   Ft-lbs

V8 engines with SEFI

Upper intake manifold-to-lower intake manifold bolts

1987	15 to 22
1988 on	12 to 18
Lower intake manifold-to-cylinder head bolts..	23 to 25
Air intake throttle body mounting nuts	12 to 18
Fuel rail bolts	70 to 105 in-lbs

Four-cylinder engines with EFI

Lower intake manifold mounting bolts

1984 and 1985	12 to 15
1986	14 to 21
1987 on	15 to 22

Fuel supply manifold mounting bolts

1984 and 1985	12 to 15
1986 and 1987	15 to 22
1988 on	14 to 21
Upper intake manifold-to-lower intake manifold bolts	15 to 22

Turbocharger

Carbureted engines

Compressor housing bolts..	145 to 165 in-lbs
Turbine housing bolts...	164 to 181 in-lbs
Outlet elbow and wastegate assembly bolts	164 to 181 in-lbs

EFI engines

Exhaust pipe-to-exhaust manifold bolts	25 to 35
Turbocharger-to-exhaust manifold nuts	28 to 40
Outlet elbow-to-turbocharger housing...	14 to 15

---

1   General information

Fuel system

The fuel system consists of the fuel tank, the fuel pump, an air cleaner assembly, either a carburetor or a fuel injection system and the various steel, plastic and/or nylon lines and fittings connecting everything together.

Models covered by this manual are equipped with one of four general types of fuel systems: carburetor; Central Fuel Injection (CFI); Electronic Fuel Injection (EFI); and Sequential Electronic Fuel Injection (SEFI). To identify the system which applies to your vehicle, refer to Sections 8, 10, 11 and 13.

The fuel pump on carburetor equipped models is a mechanical type mounted on the engine block and driven off the camshaft. Early fuel-injected models have a low-pressure pump mounted inside the fuel tank and a high pressure pump mounted on the chassis. In later years, fuel-injected models have only a single high-pressure pump installed inside the fuel tank.

The turbocharger used on some early four-cylinder engines is a draw-through type which pulls air and fuel through a one-barrel carburetor. The later turbocharger blows air into an electronic fuel injection system. The turbocharger used with the Mustang SVO includes an intercooler and boost control system.

Exhaust system

All models are equipped with one (four and inline six-cylinder) or two (V6 and V8) exhaust manifolds, a catalytic converter, an exhaust pipe and a muffler. Any component of the exhaust system can be replaced. See Chapter 6 for further details regarding the catalytic converter.

2   Fuel pressure relief procedure (fuel-injected models)

1   The fuel pump switch - sometimes called the "inertia switch" - which shuts off fuel to the engine in the event of a collision, affords a simple and convenient means by which fuel pressure can be relieved before servicing fuel injection components. The switch is located in the luggage compartment, in a variety of locations and is usually covered by the carpet which comes up the sides of the trunk. In some cases the wiring from the fuel pump to the fuel pump switch can be traced to help locate the switch.
2   Unplug the inertia switch electrical connector.
3   Start the engine and allow it to run until it stops. This should take only a few seconds.
4   The fuel system pressure is now relieved. When you're finished working on the fuel system, simply plug the electrical connector back into the switch and push the reset button on the top of the switch.

3   Fuel lines and fittings - replacement

Refer to illustrations 3.5, 3.10, 3.14, 3.26a, 3.26b and 3.26c.

Warning: *The fuel system pressure must be relieved before disconnecting fuel lines and fittings on fuel-injected models (see Section 2). Gasoline is extremely flammable, so extra precautions must be taken when working on any part of the fuel system. DO NOT smoke or allow open flames or bare light bulbs near the work area. Also, don't work in a garage where a natural gas appliance such as a water heater or clothes dryer is present.*

Push connect fittings - disassembly and reassembly

1   There are two different push connect fitting designs. Fittings used with 3/8 and 5/16-inch diameter lines have a "hairpin" type clip; fittings used with 1/4-inch diameter lines have a "duck bill" type clip. The procedure used for releasing each type of fitting is different. The clips should be replaced whenever a connector is disassembled.
2   Disconnect all push connect fittings from fuel system components such as the fuel filter, the carburetor/fuel charging assembly, the fuel tank, etc. before removing the assembly.

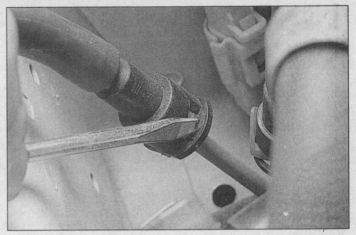

3.5 A hairpin clip-type push-connect fitting - the clip is being pointed to with a screwdriver

3.10 A push connect fitting with a duck bill clip

3/8 and 5/16-inch fittings (hairpin clip)

3   Inspect the internal portion of the fitting for accumulations of dirt. If more than a light coating of dust is present, clean the fitting before disassembly.

4   Some adhesion between the seals in the fitting and the line will occur over a period of time. Twist the fitting on the line, then push and pull the fitting until it moves freely.

5   Remove the hairpin clip from the fitting by bending the shipping tab down until it clears the body **(see illustration)**. Then, using nothing but your hands, spread each leg about 1/8-inch to disengage the body and push the legs through the fitting. Finally, pull lightly on the triangular end of the clip and work it clear of the line and fitting. Remember, don't use any tools to perform this part of the procedure.

6   Grasp the fitting and hose and pull it straight off the line.

7   Do not reuse the original clip in the fitting. A new clip must be used.

8   Before reinstalling the fitting on the line, wipe the line end with a clean cloth. Inspect the inside of the fitting to ensure that it's free of dirt and/or obstructions.

9   To reinstall the fitting on the line, align them and push the fitting into place. When the fitting is engaged, a definite click will be heard. Pull on the fitting to ensure that it's completely engaged. To install the new clip, insert it into any two adjacent openings in the fitting with the triangular portion of the clip pointing away from the fitting opening. Using your index finger, push the clip in until the legs are locked on the outside of the fitting.

1/4-inch fittings (duck bill clip)

10   The duck bill clip type fitting consists of a body, spacers, O-rings and the retaining clip **(see illustration)**. The clip holds the fitting securely in place on the line. One of the two following methods must be used to disconnect this type of fitting.

11   Before attempting to disconnect the fitting, check the visible internal portion of the

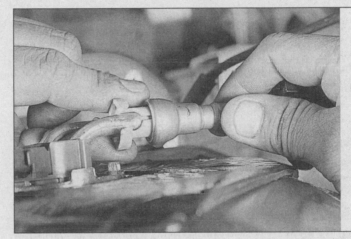

3.14 Disassembling a duck bill clip fitting using the special tool

fitting for accumulations of dirt. If more than a light coating of dust is evident, clean the fitting before disassembly.

12   Some adhesion between the seals in the fitting and line will occur over a period of time. Twist the fitting on the line, then push and pull the fitting until it moves freely.

13   The preferred method used to disconnect the fitting requires a special tool, available at most auto parts stores. To disengage the line from the fitting, align the slot in the push connect disassembly tool with either tab on the clip (90-degrees from the slots on the side of the fitting) and insert the tool. This disengages the duck bill from the line. **Note:** *Some fuel lines have a secondary bead which aligns with the outer surface of the clip. The bead can make tool insertion difficult. If necessary, use the alternative disassembly method described in Step 16.*

14   Holding the tool and the line with one hand, pull the fitting off **(see illustration)**. **Note:** *Only moderate effort is necessary if the clip is properly disengaged. The use of anything other than your hands should not be required.*

15   After disassembly, inspect and clean the line sealing surface. Also inspect the inside of the fitting and the line for any internal parts that may have been dislodged from the fitting.

Any loose internal parts should be immediately reinstalled (use the line to insert the parts).

16   The alternative disassembly procedure requires a pair of small adjustable pliers. The pliers must have a jaw width of 3/16-inch or less.

17   Align the jaws of the pliers with the openings in the side of the fitting and compress the portion of the retaining clip that engages the body. This disengages the retaining clip from the body (often one side of the clip will disengage before the other - both sides must be disengaged).

18   Pull the fitting off the line. **Note:** *Only moderate effort is required if the retaining clip has been properly disengaged. Do not use any tools for this procedure.*

19   Once the fitting is removed from the line end, check the fitting and line for any internal parts that may have been dislodged from the fitting. Any loose internal parts should be immediately reinstalled (use the line to insert the parts).

20   The retaining clip will remain on the line. Disengage the clip from the line bead to remove it. Do not reuse the retaining clip - install a new one!

21   Before reinstalling the fitting, wipe the line end with a clean cloth. Check the inside of the fitting to make sure that it's free of dirt

4

3.26a If the spring lock couplings are equipped with safety clips, pry them off with a small screwdriver

3.26b Open the spring-loaded halves of the spring lock coupling tool and place it in position around the coupling, then close it

and/or obstructions.

22   To reinstall the fitting, align it with the line and push it into place. When the fitting is engaged, a definite click will be heard. Pull on the fitting to ensure that it's fully engaged.

23   Install the new replacement clip by inserting one of the serrated edges on the duck bill portion into one of the openings. Push on the other side until the clip snaps into place.

Spring lock couplings - disassembly and reassembly

24   The fuel supply and return lines used on EFI engines utilize spring lock couplings at the engine fuel rail end instead of plastic push connect fittings. The male end of the spring lock coupling, which is girded by two O-rings, is inserted into a female flared end engine fitting. The coupling is secured by a garter spring which prevents disengagement by gripping the flared end of the female fitting. On later models, a cup-tether assembly provides additional security.

25   To disconnect the 1/2-inch (12.7mm) spring lock coupling supply fitting, you will need to obtain a spring lock coupling tool kit, available at most auto parts stores that carry specialty tools.

26   Study the accompanying illustrations carefully before detaching either spring lock coupling fitting **(see illustration)**.

---

4   Fuel pump - check

Mechanical fuel pump (carburetor equipped models)

1   If a problem occurs in the fuel pump itself, it will normally either deliver no fuel at all or not enough to sustain high engine speeds or loads.

2   When an engine develops a lean (fuel starved) condition, the fuel pump is often to blame, but the same symptoms will be evident if the carburetor float bowl filter is clogged. A lean condition will also occur if

the carburetor is malfunctioning, the fuel lines and hoses are leaking, kinked or restricted or the electrical system is shorting out or malfunctioning.

General check

3   If the fuel pump is noisy:

a) *Check for loose fuel pump mounting bolts and, if necessary, tighten them to the specified torque. Replace the gasket if necessary.*

b) *Check for loose or missing fuel line mounting clips. Loose or missing clips will sound louder when you are sitting inside the vehicle than when standing outside of it. Tighten the clips on the fuel lines if necessary.*

c) *Check for a worn, or sticking fuel pump pushrod.*

4   Before assuming a fuel pump is defective:

a) *Be sure the tank has fuel in it.*

b) *Be sure the fuel filter is not plugged. If it hasn't been changed recently, install a new one.*

c) *Inspect all rubber hoses from the fuel pump to the fuel tank for kinks and cracks. With the engine idling, check all fuel lines and rubber hoses and connections from the fuel pump to the fuel tank for fuel leaks. Tighten any loose connections and replace kinked, cracked or leaking fuel lines or hoses as required. Leaking or kinked lines or hoses will severely affect fuel pump performance.*

d) *Inspect the fuel pump inlet and outlet connections for fuel leaks. Tighten them if necessary.*

e) *Inspect the fuel pump diaphragm crimp (the area where the stamped steel section is attached to the casting) and the breather hole(s) in the casting for evidence of fuel or oil leakage. Replace the pump if it's leaking.*

Output (capacity) test

Warning: *Gasoline is extremely flammable so extra precautions must be taken when work-*

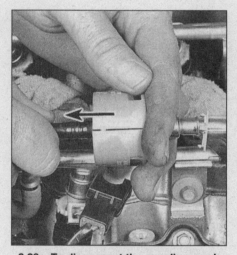

3.26c To disconnect the coupling, push the tool into the cage opening to expand the garter spring and release the female fitting, then pull the male and female fittings apart

ing on any part of the fuel system. DO NOT smoke or allow open flames or bare light bulbs in or near the work area. Also, don't work in a garage if a natural gas appliance such as a water heater or clothes dryer is present.

5   Remove the air cleaner assembly (see Section 8).

6   Carefully disconnect the fuel line at the fuel filter inlet (see Chapter 1).

7   Attach a section of rubber fuel hose to the end of the disconnected line with hose clamps and route the end of the hose into an approved gasoline container (1/2-liter or 1 pint minimum). **Note:** *It may be necessary to attach a section of hose to the disconnected fuel line in order to reach the container.* Disconnect the high tension wire from the coil and ground it on the engine with a jumper wire. Crank the engine over about 10 revolutions. The fuel pump should deliver at least 1/3-pint of fuel.

8   If the output is adequate, perform the pressure test below.

9   If the output is less than specified, repeat the test with a remote fuel supply. Detach the hose from the fuel pump inlet line and attach a separate section of fuel hose to the line with a hose clamp. Route the end of the hose into the remote fuel supply (an approved gasoline container at least half full of fuel) and repeat the procedure in Step 7. If the output is now as specified, the problem is either a plugged in-tank filter or a kinked or leaking fuel hose. Make the necessary repairs.

Pressure test

10   Connect a fuel pressure gauge (0 to 15 psi) to the fuel filter end of the line.

11   Start the engine - it should be able to run for over 30 seconds on the fuel in the carburetor bowl - and read the pressure after ten seconds. Compare your reading to the specified pressure.

12   If pump pressure is not as specified, install a new fuel pump (refer to Section 7).

13   Reconnect the fuel lines and install the air cleaner.

Electric fuel pump

14   An electric fuel pump malfunction will usually result in a loss of fuel flow and/or pressure that is often reflected by a corresponding drop in performance. If you suspect an electric fuel pump problem, disconnect the wire harness from the pump(s) (see Section 7), attach a fused jumper between the battery and the pump and carefully listen to the pump. If it's not running, replace it. If it is running, then the problem lies within the fuel pump circuit or elsewhere (see *Troubleshooting*). Diagnosis of this circuit is beyond the scope of the home mechanic. Take the vehicle to a dealer and have the fuel pump circuit checked by a professional.

5   Fuel tank - removal and installation

Note: *Don't begin this procedure until the gauge indicates that the tank is empty or nearly empty. If the tank must be removed when it's full (for example, if the fuel pump malfunctions), siphon any remaining fuel from the tank prior to removal.*

Warning: *Gasoline is extremely flammable so extra precautions must be taken when working on any part of the fuel system. DO NOT smoke or allow open flames or bare light bulbs in or near the work area. Also, don't work in a garage if a natural gas appliance such as a water heater or clothes dryer is present.*

1   On fuel-injected models, relieve the fuel pressure (refer to Section 2).

2   Detach the cable from the negative terminal of the battery.

3   Raise the vehicle and support it securely on jackstands.

4   Unless the vehicle has been driven far enough to completely empty the tank, it's a good idea to siphon the residual fuel out before removing the tank from the vehicle. Siphon or pump the fuel out through the fuel filler pipe. On US models, a small diameter hose may be necessary because of the small trap door installed in the fuel filler pipe to prevent vapors from escaping during refueling. fuel-injected models have reservoirs inside the tank to maintain fuel near the pump pick-up during vehicle cornering maneuvers and when the fuel level is low. The reservoirs could prevent siphon tubes or hoses from reaching the bottom of the fuel tank. This situation can be overcome by repositioning the siphon hose several times.

5   Remove the filler neck bracket bolt securing the fuel filler neck and the breather hose to the fuel tank.

6   If possible, disconnect the fuel and vapor lines (on some models, the fittings are on top of the tank and cannot be reached until the tank is partially lowered).

7   Remove the electric fuel pump (if equipped) and sending unit wire harness clips with a screwdriver. The harness connector is on top of the tank and inaccessible. Since no intermediate connection point is provided, the harness cannot be disconnected from the fuel sender until the tank is partially lowered.

8   Place a floor jack under the tank and position a block of wood between the jack pad and the tank. Raise the jack until it's supporting the tank.

9   Remove the bolts or nuts from the front ends of the fuel tank straps. The straps are hinged at the other end so you can swing them out of the way.

10   Lower the tank far enough to unplug the wiring harness.

11   Slowly lower the jack while steadying the tank. Remove the tank from the vehicle.

12   If you're replacing the tank, or having it cleaned or repaired, refer to Section 6.

13   Refer to Section 7 to remove and install the fuel pump/sending unit.

14   Installation is the reverse of removal. SAE 10W-40 engine oil can be used as an assembly aid when pushing the fuel filler neck back into the tank.

6   Fuel tank - cleaning and repair

1   Repairs to the fuel tank or filler neck should be performed by a professional with the proper training to carry out this critical and potentially dangerous work. Even after cleaning and flushing, explosive fumes can remain and could explode during repair of the tank.

2   If the fuel tank is removed from the vehicle, it should not be placed in an area where sparks or open flames could ignite the fumes coming out of the tank. **Warning:** *Be especially careful inside a garage where a natural gas appliance is located because the pilot light could cause an explosion!*

7   Fuel pump - removal and installation

Warning: *Gasoline is extremely flammable so extra precautions must be taken when working on any part of the fuel system. DO NOT smoke or allow open flames or bare light bulbs in or near the work area. Also, don't work in a garage if a natural gas appliance such as a water heater or clothes dryer is present.*

Mechanical fuel pump (carburetor equipped models)

Refer to illustrations 7.1 and 7.6

1   Loosen the threaded fuel line fittings (at the pump) with the proper size wrench (a flare nut wrench is recommended), then retighten them until they're just snug **(see illustration)**. Don't remove the lines at this time. The outlet line is pressurized, so protect your eyes with safety goggles or wrap the fitting with a shop rag, then loosen it carefully.

2   Loosen the mounting bolts two turns. Use your hands to loosen the fuel pump if it's stuck to the block (do not use a tool - you could damage the pump). If you cannot loosen the pump by hand, have an assistant operate the starter while you keep one hand on the pump. As the camshaft turns, it will operate the pump - when the pump feels loose, stop turning the engine over.

3   Disconnect the fuel lines from the pump. Be sure to use a backup wrench.

4   Remove the fuel pump bolts and detach the pump and gasket. Discard the old gasket.

5   Remove all old gasket material and sealant from the engine block. If you're installing the original pump, remove all the old gasket material from the pump mating surface as well. Wipe the mating surfaces of the block and pump with a cloth saturated with lacquer thinner or acetone.

6   Insert the bolts through the pump (to use as a guides for the new gasket) and place the gasket in position on the fuel pump

7.1 when disconnecting a metal fuel line from the pump, use a flare nut wrench and a backup wrench to prevent damage

7.6 When installing the fuel pump, apply white grease to the rocker arm; use RTV sealant to hold the gasket in place

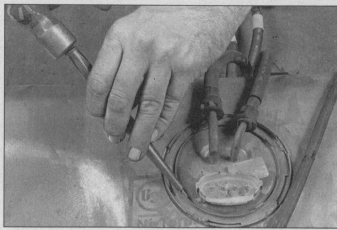

7.12 Be sure to use a brass punch or wood dowel when loosening the lock ring on the electric fuel pump/sending unit (a spark from a steel punch or hammer could cause an explosion)

mounting flange (use RTV sealant to hold the gasket in place). Position the fuel pump on the block (make sure the pump arm engages the camshaft properly) **(see illustration)**. Tighten the bolts a little at a time until they're at the specified torque.

7   Attach the fuel lines to the pump. Start the threaded fitting by hand to avoid cross-threading it. Tighten the outlet nut securely. If any of the hoses are cracked, hardened or otherwise deteriorated, replace them at this time.

8   Start the engine and check for fuel leaks for two minutes.

9   Stop the engine and check the fuel line connections for leaks by running a finger under each fitting. Check for oil leaks at the fuel pump mounting gasket.

Electric in-tank fuel pump (fuel-injected models)

Refer to illustrations 7.12 and 7.15

10   Relieve the fuel system pressure (refer to Section 2).

11   Remove the fuel tank (refer to Section 5).

12   Using a brass punch or wood dowel only, tap the lock ring counterclockwise until it's loose **(see illustration)**.

13   Carefully pull the fuel pump/sending unit assembly from the tank.

14   Remove the old lock ring gasket and discard it.

15   If you're planning to reinstall the original fuel pump/sending unit, remove the strainer by prying it off with a screwdriver **(see illustration),** wash it in clean solvent, then push it back onto the metal pipe on the end of the pump. If you're installing a new pump/sending unit, the assembly will include a new strainer.

16   Clean the fuel pump mounting flange and the tank mounting surface and seal ring groove.

17   Installation is the reverse of removal. Apply a thin coat of heavy grease to the new lock ring gasket to hold it in place during assembly.

Electric chassis-mount fuel pump (fuel-injected models)

18   Depressurize the fuel system as outlined in Section 2 and raise the vehicle with a hoist.

19   Disconnect the electrical connectors from the body harness and remove the inlet and outlet lines from the fuel pump.

20   The fuel pump may now be removed from the assembly by bending the tab out and sliding the pump out of the retaining ring.

21   Remove the electrical wiring harness from the assembly by inserting a screwdriver or knife between the connector and retaining clip and sliding the connector towards the pump inlet.

22   When installing, make sure the fittings on the pump have gaskets in place, that the gaskets are properly positioned and that the fittings have been tightened properly.

23   Check the wiring harness boots to make sure they are pushed into the pump terminals far enough to seal and check that the wire terminals are pushed onto the pump terminals all the way.

24   Wrap the fuel pump retaining ring around the fuel pump. Locate the slot in the ring so that it faces the bracket base and push the pump and ring assembly into the bracket. Make sure the tab on the ring contacts the tab of the bracket and that the bracket tabs do not contact the pump case. When the pump is inserted into the bracket as far as possible and the wiring harness comes out the bottom of the ring, bend the rear tab to prevent the pump from sliding out.

25   Connect the fuel lines to the pump assembly, then attach the electrical harness connector to the body electrical connector.

26   Start the vehicle, check for proper operation of the pump and look for leaks.

8   Air cleaner housing - removal and installation

Carburetor and CFI equipped models

Note: *The air cleaner housing assemblies used with carburetors and CFI are basically similar.*

1   Detach the cable from the negative terminal of the battery.

2   Detach the fresh air inlet tube from the mouth of the air cleaner housing assembly snorkel.

3   Clearly label and detach all vacuum hoses, lines and electrical connectors as nec-

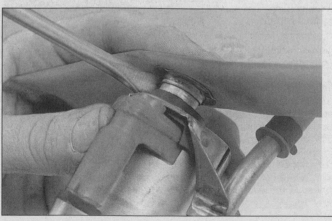

7.15 If you're replacing the pump, this step isn't necessary, but if you're going to reinstall the old pump, remove the strainer and clean it with solvent

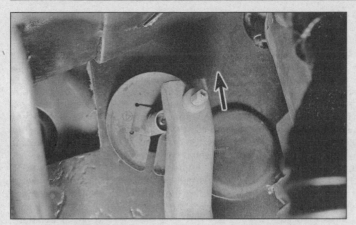

9.2 A typical throttle cable/accelerator pedal installation - to separate the cable from the pedal, pull back on the cable while pushing forward on the upper end of the pedal, then lift the cable up and out of the slot in the pedal arm

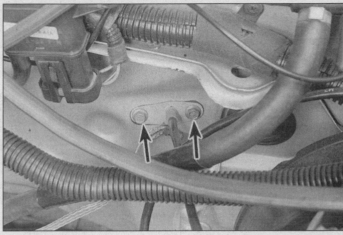

9.3 To detach the throttle cable from the firewall, simply remove the two bolts

essary from the air cleaner housing assembly.

4 Remove the wing nut and grommet (if equipped) from the air cleaner housing and remove the cover.

5 Remove the air cleaner filter element. Inspect it for signs of dust or dirt leaking through holes in the filter material or past the end seals (see Chapter 1).

6 Lift the air cleaner housing assembly off.

7 Installation is the reverse of removal.

EFI and SEFI equipped models

Note: *Because the air cleaner housing assemblies on EFI and SEFI fuel systems are virtually identical, the following procedure applies to both of them. However, it is a general guideline and small but insignificant differences may be noted.*

V8 engine

8 Detach the cable from the negative terminal of the battery.

9 Disconnect the air outlet tube from the air cleaner assembly (see Section 16 in Chapter 1).

10 Unclip the upper half of the air cleaner housing assembly and remove it.

11 Remove the air cleaner filter element.

12 Remove the air cleaner housing assembly mounting nuts and detach the assembly.

13 If you wish to remove or replace the resonator (which is located on the other side of the fender apron), simply remove the mounting nuts and detach it.

14 Installation is the reverse of removal.

Four-cylinder engine

15 Detach the cable from the negative terminal of the battery.

16 Remove the wing nut from the air cleaner housing cover (see Section 16 in Chapter 1).

17 Remove the air cleaner cover and the filter element.

18 Remove the air cleaner housing assembly mounting screws from the floor

of the assembly.

19 Slightly raise the housing assembly, loosen the hose clamp and remove the air cleaner outlet tube which connects to the vane air meter (electronic air control sensor).

20 Remove the air cleaner housing assembly.

21 Installation is the reverse of removal.

---

9 Throttle cable - replacement

Refer to illustrations 9.2 and 9.3

1 Remove the air intake duct and air cleaner housing assembly (see Section 8), if necessary.

2 Detach the cable snap-in nylon bushing from the accelerator pedal arm **(see illustration)**.

3 Remove the cable housing from the firewall by removing the two bolts **(see illustration)**.

4 Detach the cable from the bracket on the engine.

5 Detach the throttle cable and, if equipped, cruise control cable assembly from the throttle lever by inserting a screwdriver between the cable assembly and the throttle lever and twisting the screwdriver.

6 Separate the cruise control cable (if equipped) from the accelerator cable by removing the clip attaching them.

7 Installation is the reverse of removal.

---

10 Carburetor - diagnosis, removal, overhaul and installation

Warning: *Gasoline is extremely flammable, so extra precautions must be taken when working on any part of the fuel system. DO NOT smoke or allow open flames or bare light bulbs in or near the work area. Also, don't work in a garage if a natural gas appliance such as a water heater or clothes dryer is present.*

Diagnosis

1 A thorough road test and check of carburetor adjustments should be done before any major carburetor service work. Specifications for some adjustments are listed on the Vehicle Emissions Control Information label found in the engine compartment.

2 Some performance complaints directed at the carburetor are actually a result of loose, out-of-adjustment or malfunctioning engine or electrical components. Others develop when vacuum hoses leak, are disconnected or are incorrectly routed. The proper approach to analyzing carburetor problems should include a routine check of the following items:

a) *Inspect all vacuum hoses and actuators for leaks and correct installation (see Chapter 6).*

b) *Tighten the intake manifold nuts/bolts and carburetor mounting nuts evenly and securely.*

c) *Perform a cylinder compression test (see Chapter 2).*

d) *Clean or replace the spark plugs as necessary.*

e) *Check the spark plug wires.*

f) *Inspect the ignition primary wires and check the vacuum advance operation. Replace any defective parts.*

g) *Check the ignition timing according to the instructions printed on the Emissions Control Information label.*

h) *Check the fuel pump pressure.*

i) *Check the heat control valve in the air cleaner for proper operation (see Chapter 6).*

j) *Check/replace the air filter element.*

k) *Check the PCV system (see Chapter 6).*

3 Carburetor problems usually show up as flooding, hard starting, stalling, severe backfiring, poor acceleration and lack of response to idle mixture screw adjustments. A carburetor that is leaking fuel and/or covered with wet looking deposits definitely needs attention.

4

4   Diagnosing carburetor problems may require that the engine be started and run with the air cleaner off. While running the engine without the air cleaner, backfires are possible. This situation is likely to occur if the carburetor is malfunctioning, but just the removal of the air cleaner ca lean the fuel/air mixture enough to produce an engine back-fire. **Warning:** *Do not position any part of your body, especially your face, directly over the carburetor during inspection and servicing procedures!*

Removal

5   Remove the air cleaner housing assembly (see Section 8).
6   Disconnect the throttle cable from the throttle lever (see Section 9).
7   If your vehicle is equipped with an automatic transmission, disconnect the TV rod from the throttle lever (see Chapter 7).
8   **Note:** *To simplify installation, label all vacuum hoses and fittings before removing them. Disconnect all vacuum hoses and the fuel line from the carburetor. Use a backup wrench on the fuel inlet fitting when removing the fuel line to avoid changing the float level.*
9   Label the wires and terminals, then unplug all wire harness connectors at the carburetor.
10   Remove the mounting nuts and detach the carburetor from the intake manifold. Remove the carburetor mounting gasket and, if equipped, spacer. Place a rag inside the intake manifold cavity to prevent dirt and debris from falling down into the engine while the carburetor is removed.

Overhaul

11   Once it's determined that the carburetor needs adjustment or an overhaul, several options are available. If you're going to attempt to overhaul the carburetor yourself, first obtain a good quality carburetor rebuild kit (which will include all necessary gaskets, internal parts, instructions and a parts list). You'll also need some special solvent and a means of blowing out the internal passages of the carburetor with air.
12   Because carburetor designs are constantly modified by the manufacturer in order to meet increasingly more stringent emissions regulations, it isn't feasible for us to do a step-by-step overhaul of each type. You'll receive a detailed, well illustrated set of instructions with any carburetor overhaul kit; they will apply in a more specific manner to the carburetor on your vehicle.
13   Another alternative is to obtain a new or rebuilt carburetor. They are readily available from dealers and auto parts stores. Make absolutely sure the exchange carburetor is identical to the original. A tag is usually attached to the top of the carburetor. It will aid in determining the exact type of carburetor you have. When obtaining a rebuilt carburetor or a rebuild kit, take time to make sure that the kit or carburetor matches your application exactly. Seemingly insignificant differ-

ences can make a large difference in the performance of your engine.
14   If you choose to overhaul your own carburetor, allow enough time to disassemble the carburetor carefully, soak the necessary parts in the cleaning solvent (usually for at least one-half day or according to the instructions listed on the carburetor cleaner) and reassemble it, which will usually take much longer than disassembly. When disassembling the carburetor, match each part with the illustration in the carburetor kit and lay the parts out in order on a clean work surface. Overhauls by inexperienced mechanics can result in an engine which runs poorly or not at all. To avoid this, use care and patience when disassembling the carburetor so you can reassemble it correctly.

Installation

15   Clean the gasket mating surfaces of the intake manifold and the carburetor to remove all traces of the old gasket. Remove the rag from the manifold. Place the spacer, if equipped, and a new gasket on the intake manifold. Position the carburetor on the gasket and spacer and install the mounting nuts. To prevent distortion or damage to the carburetor body flange, tighten the nuts to the specified torque in several steps.
16   The remaining installation steps are the reverse of removal.

---

11   Fuel injection systems - general information

Central Fuel Injection (CFI) system

The Central Fuel Injection (CFI) system is a single point, pulse time modulated injection system. Fuel is metered into the air intake stream in accordance with engine demands by two solenoid injection valves mounted in a throttle body on the intake manifold.

Fuel is supplied from the fuel tank by a low pressure, electric fuel pump mounted in the fuel tank. The fuel is filtered and sent to the air throttle body, where a regulator maintains the fuel delivery pressure at a nominal value of 14.5 psi. A pair of injector nozzles are mounted vertically above the throttle plates and connected in series with the fuel pressure regulator. Excess fuel supplied by the pump but not needed by the engine is returned to the fuel tank by a steel fuel return line.

The fuel charging assembly consists of five individual components which perform the fuel and air metering function. The throttle body assembly is attached to the conventional carburetor mounting pad on the intake manifold and houses the air control system, fuel injector nozzle, fuel pressure regulator, fuel pressure diagnostic valve, cold engine speed control and throttle position sensor.

Air flow to the engine is controlled by a

single butterfly valve mounted in a two piece, die-cast aluminum housing called a throttle body. The butterfly valve is identical in configuration to the throttle plates of a conventional carburetor and is actuated by a similar pedal and linkage arrangement.

The fuel injector nozzle is mounted vertically above the throttle plate and is an electro-mechanical device which meters and atomizes the fuel delivered to the engine. The injector valve body consists of a solenoid actuated ball and seat valve assembly.

An electrical control signal from the EEC electronic processor activates the solenoid, causing the ball to move off the seat and allowing fuel to flow. The injector flow orifice is fixed and the fuel supply is constant. Therefore, fuel flow to the engine is controlled by how long the solenoid is energized.

The pressure regulator is integral to the fuel charging main body near the rear of the air horn surface. The regulator is located so as to nullify the effects of the supply line pressure drops. Its design is such that it is not sensitive to back pressure in the return line to the tank.

A second function of the pressure regulator is to maintain fuel supply pressure upon fuel pump shutdown. The regulator functions as a downstream check valve and traps the fuel between itself and the fuel pump. The constant fuel pressure level after engine shutdown precludes fuel line vapor formation and allows for rapid restarts and stable idle operation immediately thereafter.

The throttle actuator controls idle speed by modulating the throttle lever for the required air flow to maintain the desired engine rpm for any operating condition, from an idling cold engine to a warm engine at normal operating temperature. An idle tracking switch (ITS) determines when the throttle lever has contacted the actuator, signaling the need to control engine rpm. The DC motor extends or retracts a linear shaft through a gear reduction system. The motor direction is determined by the polarity of the applied voltage.

A throttle position sensor (non-adjustable) is mounted to the throttle shaft on the choke side of the fuel charging assembly and is used to supply a voltage output proportional to the change in the throttle position. The TP sensor is used by the computer (EEC) to determine the operation mode (closed throttle, part throttle and wide open throttle) for selection of the proper fuel mixture, spark and EGR at all engine speeds and loads.

Electronic Fuel Injection (EFI) and Sequential Electronic Fuel Injection (SEFI)

Two basically similar electronic fuel injection systems are used on many of the models covered by this manual.

The Sequential Electronic Fuel Injection (SEFI) system and the Electronic Fuel Injection (EFI) system are known as multi-point, pulse time, speed density control designs. On the SEFI system, fuel is metered into each intake port in sequence with the engine firing order in accordance with engine demand through eight injectors mounted on a tuned intake manifold. On the EFI system used with the 2.3L four-cylinder engine, fuel is metered into the intake air stream in accordance with engine demand through four injectors mounted on a tuned intake manifold. A blow-through turbocharger system is utilized on the Mustang SVO to reduce fuel delivery time, increase turbine energy available and eliminate compressor throttling.

On both systems, an on-board Electronic Engine Control (EEC-IV) computer accepts inputs from various engine sensors to compute the required fuel flow rate necessary to maintain a prescribed air/fuel ratio throughout the entire engine operational range. The computer then outputs a command to the fuel injectors to meter the approximate quantity of fuel.

The EEC-IV engine control system also determines and compensates for the age of the vehicle and its uniqueness. The system automatically senses and compensates for changes in altitude and, on models with a manual transmission, permits push-starting, should it become necessary.

The fuel delivery systems for both designs are similar. An electric in-tank fuel pump forces pressurized fuel through a series of metal and plastic lines and an inline fuel filter/reservoir to the fuel charging manifold assembly. The early SEFI system utilizes two pumps - a low pressure unit in the tank and a high pressure model mounted outside the tank. The later SEFI system uses a single high-pressure pump mounted inside the tank.

The fuel charging manifold assembly incorporates electrically actuated fuel injectors directly above each intake port. When energized, the injectors spray a metered quantity of fuel into the intake air stream.

A constant fuel pressure drop is maintained across the injector nozzles by a pressure regulator. The regulator is connected in series with the fuel injectors and is positioned downstream from them. Excess fuel passes through the regulator and returns to the fuel tank through a fuel return line.

On the SEFI, each injector is energized once every other crankshaft revolution in sequence with engine firing order. On the EFI, the injectors are energized every crankshaft revolution; on models through 1988, all four injectors are energized at once, while on 1989 and later models, the injectors are energized in pairs (1-4 and 2-3). The period of time that the injectors are energized (known as "on time" or "pulse width") is controlled by the EEC computer. Air entering the engine is sensed by speed, pressure and temperature sensors. The outputs of these sensors are processed by the EEC-IV computer. The computer determines the needed injector pulse width and outputs a command to the injector to meter the exact quantity of fuel.

On the turbocharged four-cylinder, all injectors are energized simultaneously, once every crankshaft revolution. Air entering the engine is measured by a vane airflow meter located between the air cleaner and the turbocharger. The airflow is then compressed by the turbocharger before introduction into an intercooler (only on SVO models) and then into the fuel charging manifold. This airflow information, combined with input from several other engine sensors, enables the computer to determine the required fuel flow rate necessary to maintain a prescribed air/fuel ratio for the given engine operation. The computer calculates the necessary injector pulse width and outputs a command to the injector to meter the right amount of fuel.

12 Fuel injection system - pressure check

Refer to illustration 12.1
Warning: *Gasoline is extremely flammable, so extra precautions must be taken when working on any part of the fuel system. DO NOT smoke or allow open flames or bare light bulbs in or near the work area. Also, don't work in a garage if a natural gas appliance such as a water heater or clothes dryer is present.*
1   With a fuel pressure gauge and adapter, available at most auto parts stores that carry specialty tools, the fuel pressure of any fuel-injected vehicle covered by this manual can be measured easily and quickly. All fuel-injected versions of this vehicle are equipped with Schrader valves. On CFI-equipped models, the Schrader valve is located on the fuel charging (throttle body) assembly **(see illustration)**. On EFI and SEFI models, the Schrader valve is on the fuel rail.
2   The special fuel pressure gauge/adapter assembly is designed to relieve fuel pressure, as well as measure it, through the Schrader valve. If you have this gauge, you can use this method as an alternative to the procedure for fuel pressure relief outlined in Section 2. **Warning:** *DO NOT attempt to relieve fuel pressure through the Schrader valve without this special setup!*

3   To attach the gauge, simply remove the valve cap, screw on the adapter and attach the gauge to the adapter.
4   Start the engine and allow it to reach a steady idle. Note the indicated fuel pressure reading and compare it to the pressure listed in this Chapter's Specifications.
5   If the indicated fuel pressure is lower than specified, the problem is probably either a leaking fuel line, a malfunctioning fuel pump or a leaking injector. If the pressure is higher than specified, the cause could be a blocked fuel line or a stuck fuel pressure regulator.

13 Central Fuel Injection (CFI) system - component replacement

Warning: *Gasoline is extremely flammable, so extra precautions must be taken when working on any part of the fuel system. DO NOT smoke or allow open flames or bare light bulbs in or near the work area. Also, don't work in a garage if a natural gas appliance such as a water heater or clothes dryer is present.*

CFI assembly

1   When buying replacement parts for the CFI assembly, always check the number on the identification tag on the side of the CFI assembly to make sure that you are getting the right parts.
2   Relieve the fuel system pressure (see Section 2). Detach the cable from the negative terminal of the battery.
3   Remove the air cleaner housing assembly (see Section 8).
4   Detach the throttle cable and, if equipped, cruise control cable fitting from the throttle lever (see Section 9).
5   If your vehicle is equipped with an automatic transmission, detach the downshift rod.
6   Unplug the electrical connectors to the fuel injectors, the Idle Speed Control (ISC) and the Throttle Position (TP) sensor.
7   Remove the fuel line bracket bolt.
8   Using a backup wrench, detach the fuel

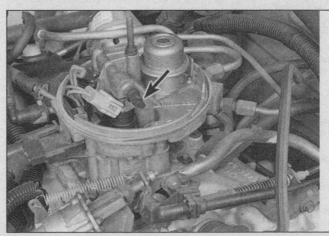

12.1 This Schrader valve fitting (arrow) on the fuel charging assembly of the Central Fuel Injection (CFI) system can be used to relieve fuel pressure if you have the special pressure gauge and adapter

13.27 Do not remove these a three screws (arrows) - they attach the pressure regulator to the fuel charging assembly

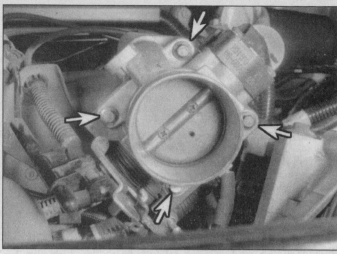

14.2 Disconnect the electrical connector and remove the throttle body mounting bolts

feed and return lines. **Note:** *If either line proves difficult to pull out, carefully wiggle it up and down - do not strike the lines with a tool or attempt to pry them loose or you may dent them.*

9   Detach the PCV hose.
10   Remove the four mounting nuts.
11   Installation is the reverse of removal.

Idle Speed Control (ISC) motor

12   Detach the cable from the negative terminal of the battery and unplug the electrical connector from the ISC motor.
13   Remove the downshift lever return spring.
14   Remove the two mounting bolts and detach the ISC motor.
15   Installation is the reverse of removal.

Throttle Position (TP) sensor

Note: *It is not necessary to remove the CFI assembly to replace the TP sensor.*

Removal

16   Detach the cable from the negative terminal of the battery.
17   Unplug the wire harness electrical connector from the TP sensor connector.
18   Remove the TP sensor electrical connector bracket retaining screw and detach the bracket and connector from the throttle body.
19   Remove the TP sensor retaining screws.
20   Slide the throttle position sensor off the throttle shaft.

Installation

21   Holding the throttle sensor with the wire harness facing up and to the left, slide it onto the throttle shaft.
22   Rotate the throttle position sensor clockwise until it's aligned with the screw holes on the throttle body. Install the retaining screws and tighten them securely.
23   Install the throttle position sensor wiring harness bracket bolt.

24   The remainder of installation is the reverse of removal.

Fuel injector

Refer to illustration 13.27

25   Remove the CFI assembly from the intake manifold (see above).
26   Remove the air cleaner stud.
27   Remove the four throttle body-to-main body screws and separate the throttle body and main body assemblies. **Caution:** *Do not remove the three screws which attach the pressure regulator to the main body assembly* **(see illustration)**.
28   Clearly mark the injectors with respect to their orientation to the throttle lever and TP sensor. **Caution:** *The injectors must not be mixed up during reassembly.*
29   Unplug the injector electrical connectors. Pull on the connector plugs, not on the wires.
30   Remove the fuel injector retainer screw and retainer.
31   Carefully pull up on the injector while using a twisting motion.
32   Discard the old O-rings and replace them with new ones. Use a light grade oil to lubricate the new O-rings before installing them.
33   Installation is the reverse of removal.

---

14   Sequential Electronic Fuel Injection (SEFI) and Electronic Fuel Injection (EFI) systems - component replacement

---

Upper intake manifold and air intake throttle body

Refer to illustrations 14.2 and 14.8

Removal

1   Detach the cable from the negative terminal of the battery.
2   Unplug the electrical connectors at the air bypass valve, throttle position sensor and

EGR position sensor **(see illustration)**.
3   Detach the throttle linkage (see Section 9) and transmission linkage (see Chapter 7) from the air intake throttle body.
4   Detach the throttle cable/downshift cable bracket from the intake manifold (see Section 9) and position the bracket and cables out of the way.
5   Clearly label, then detach, the vacuum lines to the upper intake manifold vacuum tree, the EGR valve and the fuel pressure regulator.
6   Detach the PCV system by disconnecting the hose from the fitting on the rear of the upper manifold.
7   If equipped, detach the canister purge line or lines from the throttle body and detach the EGR spacer coolant lines from the EGR spacer.
8   Remove the cover plate, then remove the six upper intake manifold retaining bolts **(see illustration)**.
9   Remove the upper intake manifold and throttle body as an assembly from the lower intake manifold.

Installation

10   Be sure to clean and inspect the mounting faces of the lower and upper intake manifolds before positioning the new gasket on the lower intake mounting face. The use of alignment studs may be helpful. Install the upper intake manifold and throttle body assembly on the lower manifold. Ensure that the gasket remains in place (if alignment studs are not used). Install the six upper intake manifold retaining bolts and tighten to the specified torque. Installation is otherwise the reverse of removal.

Air intake throttle body

Removal

11   Detach the cable from the negative terminal of the battery.
12   Detach the throttle position sensor and throttle air bypass valve connectors.

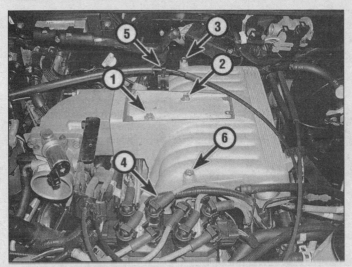

14.8 Upper intake manifold bolt locations and tightening sequence

14.26 Remove the two screws securing the air bypass valve assembly

13   If equipped, remove the PCV vent closure hose at the throttle body.
14   Remove the four throttle body mounting nuts **(see illustration 14.2)**.
15   Carefully separate the air throttle body from the EGR spacer.
16   Remove and discard the gasket between the throttle body and the EGR spacer.

Installation

17   Clean the gasket mating surfaces. If scraping is necessary, be careful not to damage the gasket surfaces or allow material to drop into the manifold. Installation is the reverse of removal. Be sure to tighten the throttle body mounting nuts to the specified torque.

Throttle Position (TP) sensor

18   The throttle position sensor is located on the throttle body. Detach the cable from the negative terminal of the battery.
19   Detach the throttle position sensor from the wiring harness.
20   Scribe a reference mark across the edge of the sensor and the throttle body to ensure correct position during installation.
21   Remove the two throttle position sensor mounting screws.
22   Remove the throttle position sensor.
23   Installation is the reverse of removal. Be sure to tighten the screws securely.

Air bypass valve assembly

Refer to illustration 14.26
24   Detach the cable from the negative terminal of the battery.
25   Detach the air bypass valve assembly from the wiring harness.
26   Remove the two air bypass valve retaining bolts **(see illustration)**.
27   Remove the air bypass valve and gasket.
28   Clean the gasket mating surface. If scraping is necessary, be careful not to damage the air bypass valve or throttle body gas-

ket surfaces or drop material into the throttle body.
29   Installation is essentially the reverse of removal. Be sure to tighten the bolts securely.

Fuel rail assembly

Removal

30   Relieve the fuel pressure (see Section 2).
31   Detach the cable from the negative terminal of the battery.
32   Remove the upper manifold assembly (see above).
33   Using a special spring lock coupler tool, available at most auto parts stores, disconnect the crossover fuel hose from the fuel rail assembly.
34   Remove the four fuel rail assembly retaining bolts (two on each side).
35   Carefully disengage the fuel rail from the fuel injectors and remove the fuel rail. **Note:** *It may be easier to remove the injectors with the fuel rail as an assembly.*
36   Use a rocking, side-to-side motion while lifting to remove the injectors from the fuel rail.

Installation

37   Ensure that the injector caps are clean and free of contamination.
38   Place the fuel injector fuel rail assembly over each of the injectors and seat the injectors into the fuel rail. Ensure that the injectors are well seated in the fuel rail assembly. **Note:** *It may be easier to seat the injectors in the fuel rail and then seat the entire assembly in the lower intake manifold.*
39   Secure the fuel rail assembly with the four retaining bolts and tighten them to the specified torque.
40   The remainder of installation is the reverse of removal.

Fuel pressure regulator

Removal

41   Relieve the system fuel pressure (see

Section 2).
42   Detach the cable from the negative terminal of the battery.
43   Remove the vacuum line at the pressure regulator.
44   Remove the three Allen retaining screws from the regulator housing.
45   Remove the pressure regulator assembly, gasket and O-ring. Discard the gasket and inspect the O-ring for signs of cracks or deterioration.
46   If scraping is necessary, be careful not to damage the fuel pressure regulator or fuel supply line gasket surfaces.

Installation

47   Lubricate the fuel pressure regulator O-ring with engine oil. **Note:** *Never use silicone grease. It will clog the injectors.*
48   Ensure that the gasket surfaces of the fuel pressure regulator and fuel rail assembly are clean.
49   Install the O-ring and new gasket on the regulator.
50   Install the fuel pressure regulator on the fuel rail assembly. Tighten the three screws securely.
51   The remainder of installation is the reverse of removal.

Fuel injector

Removal

Refer to illustration 14.56
52   Relieve the system fuel pressure (see Section 2).
53   Remove the upper intake manifold assembly (see above).
54   Remove the fuel rail assembly (see above).
55   Carefully remove the electrical harness connectors from the individual injectors as required.
56   Grasping the injector body, pull up while gently rocking the injector from side-to-side

4

(see illustration).

57 Inspect the injector O-rings (two per injector) for signs of deterioration. Replace as required.

58 Inspect the injector plastic "hat" (covering the injector pintle) and washer for signs of deterioration. Replace as required. If the hat is missing, look for it in the intake manifold.

Installation

59 Lubricate the new O-rings with light grade oil and install two on each injector. **Note:** *Do not use silicone grease. It will clog the injectors.*

60 Using a light, twisting motion, install the injector(s).

61 The remainder of installation is the reverse of removal.

---

15 Electronic Fuel Injection (EFI) system - component replacement (four-cylinder engine)

While the appearance and design of the various components of this system vary somewhat from those in the previous Section, the procedures there will apply to this system as well. Exploded and assembled views of the four-cylinder engine fuel system are included here to help identify and locate the components.

---

16 Turbocharger - removal and installation

EFI models

Removal

1 The turbocharger is mounted low on the right side of the engine. Make sure the engine has cooled overnight (or for several hours) before beginning work on the turbocharger.

2 Detach the cable from the negative terminal of the battery. Drain the engine coolant (see Chapter 1).

3 If the turbocharger is not equipped with an intercooler, remove the two bolts retaining the throttle body discharge tube to the turbocharger and loosen the hose clamp on the inlet hose.

4 If the turbocharger is equipped with an intercooler, loosen the upper and lower clamps securing the hoses to the intercooler. Detach the aspirator hoses at the intercooler and loosen the bolts securing the bracket to the intercooler housing. Pull the upper front bracket pins out of the lower bracket, rotate the housing clockwise to disengage the upper rear bracket, then remove the intercooler together with the upper brackets.

5 Clearly label, then disconnect, the vacuum hoses and tubes.

6 Detach the PCV tube from the turbocharger air inlet elbow.

7 If the turbocharger is not equipped with

14.56 The proper way to remove an injector from the intake manifold is to grasp the body and pull up while gently rocking the injector from side-to-side

an intercooler, remove the throttle body discharge tube and hose as an assembly.

8 If the turbocharger is equipped with an intercooler (Mustang SVO), loosen the clamp and detach the air inlet tube from the inlet elbow.

9 Disconnect the electrical ground wire and turbocharger air inlet elbow and remove the air inlet elbow. Discard the old gasket.

10 Remove the water connections and fittings from the turbo center housing. **Note:** *Some coolant will drain from the engine block.*

11 Remove the turbocharger oil supply.

12 Detach the oxygen sensor connector at the turbocharger.

13 Raise the vehicle and place it securely on jackstands.

14 Disconnect the exhaust pipe by removing the two exhaust pipe-to-turbocharger bolts.

15 Remove the two bolts from the oil return line located below the turbocharger. Do not kink or damage the line as it is removed.

16 Remove the lower turbocharger bracket-to-block stud.

17 Lower the vehicle.

18 Remove the front lower turbocharger retaining nut.

19 Simultaneously, remove the three remaining nuts while sliding the turbocharger off the studs.

20 Remove the turbocharger assembly from the vehicle.

Bearing clearance check

21 Manually move the turbocharger blade shaft assembly as far in one direction as possible. Spin the shaft by hand.

22 Manually move the shaft in the opposite direction as far as possible and spin the shaft again.

23 If neither the turbine blade nor the compressor blade contacts any portion of their respective housings, the bearings are still good.

24 If either blade comes in contact with the housing, the bearings are worn and the turbocharger should be replaced.

Installation

25 Apply Teflon pipe sealant to the water inlet 90-degree elbow fitting. Install the fitting in the turbocharger assembly center housing. Tighten it securely and rotate it clockwise so that the fitting is within 5 degrees of vertical, pointing down.

26 Position a new turbocharger gasket on the mounting studs. Make sure that the bead faces out.

27 Install the turbocharger assembly on the mounting studs. **Note:** *Use four new mounting studs.*

28 Install the turbocharger bracket on the two lower studs. Start the two lower retaining nuts followed by the two upper retaining nuts.

29 Raise the vehicle and place it securely on jackstands.

30 Install the lower bracket-to-block bolt. Tighten it securely.

31 Install a new oil return line gasket. Bolt the oil return line fitting to the turbocharger and tighten it securely.

32 Connect the water inlet tube assembly to the inlet fitting at the turbocharger assembly. Tighten the hose clamp securely.

33 Install the exhaust pipe and tighten the retaining nuts to the specified torque.

34 Lower the vehicle.

35 Using four new nuts, tighten the turbocharger-to-exhaust manifold nuts to the specified torque.

36 Apply pipe sealant with Teflon and install the water fittings in the turbocharger center housing. Tighten securely.

37 Connect the water tube assemblies to the fitting on the turbocharger and tighten it securely. Be sure to use a backup wrench to hold the water outlet fitting while tightening.

38 Use a new gasket and install the compressor inlet elbow.

39 Attach the air inlet tube to the turbocharger inlet elbow. Tighten the hose clamp securely.

40 Install the PCV tube fitting and tighten the clamp securely.

41 Attach all vacuum lines.

42   Connect the oxygen sensor.
43   Connect the electrical ground wire to the air inlet elbow.
44   Install the turbocharger oil supply line. Tighten the fitting securely.
45   Install the turbocharger intercooler assembly. Tighten the clamps and the nut securely.
46   Fill and bleed the cooling system (see Chapter 1).
47   Connect the cable to the negative terminal of the battery.
48   Start the engine and check for leaks.

Carbureted models

49   Disconnect the negative battery cable from the battery.
50   Remove the two nuts which hold the turbocharger heat shield to the turbine housing and remove the shield.
51   Raise the vehicle and position it securely on jackstands.
52   Remove the four bolts which attach the crossover pipes to the turbocharger. Remove the crossover pipe at that end.
53   Disconnect the exhaust pipe from the check valve located just above the catalytic converter.
54   Remove the bolts which attach the crossover pipes to the exhaust manifold. Loosen and lower the crossover pipe. Remove the exhaust pipe retaining bolts at the inlet of the rear catalytic converter.
55   Remove the rear turbocharger brace bolts and the brace.
56   Remove the jackstands and lower the vehicle. Remove the air cleaner and duct assembly. Place a shop rag over the carburetor mouth to prevent dirt and parts from falling in.
57   Disconnect the oil supply line from the turbocharger central housing.
58   Disconnect the two hoses from the wastegate actuator diaphragm.
59   Remove the accelerator cable and its two mounting bolts from the intake manifold.
60   Disconnect the turbocharger vacuum line at the intake manifold.
61   Remove the engine oil dipstick bracket bolt to provide removal access.
62   Loosen the flange nuts at both ends of the EGR tube, then remove the tube.
63   Remove three nuts and one bolt that secure the turbocharger to the intake manifold.
64   Label and detach any remaining vacuum hoses.
65   Lift the turbocharger out of the engine compartment.
66   Installation is the reverse of removal. Use new O-rings, lightly coated with clean engine oil, at the following points:

 a) *Compressor inlet-to-manifold joint*
 b) *Compressor outlet-to-manifold joint*
 c) *Oil drain line adapter-to-intake manifold joint*

17   Exhaust system servicing - general information

Warning: *Inspection and repair of exhaust system components should be done only after enough time has elapsed after driving the vehicle to allow the system components to cool completely. Also, when working under the vehicle, make sure it is securely supported on jackstands.*
1   The exhaust system consists of the exhaust manifold(s), the catalytic converter, the muffler, the tailpipe and all connecting pipes, brackets, hangers and clamps. The exhaust system is attached to the body with mounting brackets and rubber hangers. If any of the parts are improperly installed, excessive noise and vibration will be transmitted to the body.
2   Conduct regular inspections of the exhaust system to keep it safe and quiet.
Look for any damaged or bent parts, open seams, holes, loose connections, excessive corrosion or other defects which could allow exhaust fumes to enter the vehicle. Deteriorated exhaust system components should not be repaired; they should be replaced with new parts.
3   If the exhaust system components are extremely corroded or rusted together, welding equipment will probably be required to remove them.
The convenient way to accomplish this is to have a muffler repair shop remove the corroded sections with a cutting torch. If, however, you want to save money by doing it yourself (and you don't have a welding outfit with a cutting torch), simply cut off the old components with a hacksaw. If you have compressed air, special pneumatic cutting chisels can also be used. If you do decide to tackle the job at home, be sure to wear safety goggles to protect your eyes from metal chips and work gloves to protect your hands.
4   Here are some simple guidelines to follow when repairing the exhaust system:

 a) *Work from the back to the front when removing exhaust system components.*
 b) *Apply penetrating oil to the exhaust system component fasteners to make them easier to remove.*
 c) *Use new gaskets, hangers and clamps when installing exhaust systems components.*
 d) *Apply anti-seize compound to the threads of all exhaust system fasteners during reassembly.*
 e) *Be sure to allow sufficient clearance between newly installed parts and all points on the underbody to avoid overheating the floor pan and possibly damaging the interior carpet and insulation. Pay particularly close attention to the catalytic converter and heat shield.*

4

Notes

Chapter 5
Engine electrical systems

Contents

Specifications

Drivebelt deflection .... See Chapter 1

Battery voltage
Engine off 12-volts
Engine running .... 14-to-15 volts
Firing order .... See Chapter 2

Ignition coil-to-distributor cap wire resistance
Duraspark II systems .... 5000 ohms per inch
TFI-IV system .... 5000 ohms per foot

Ignition coil resistance
Duraspark II and III systems
  Primary resistance .... 0.8 to 1.6 ohms
  Secondary resistance .... 7.7 to 10.5 K-ohms
  Ballast resistor .... 0.8 to 1.6 ohms
TFI-IV system
  Primary resistance .... 0.3 to 1.0 ohms
  Secondary resistance .... 8.0 to 11.5 K-ohms
Ignition timing .... See the Vehicle Emissions Control Information label in the engine compartment

Alternator brush length
New .... 1/2 in
Minimum .... 1/4 in

1   General information

The engine electrical systems include all ignition, charging and starting components. Because of their engine-related functions, these components are considered separately from chassis electrical devices like the lights, instruments, etc.

Be very careful when working on the engine electrical components. They are easily damaged if checked, connected or handled improperly. The alternator is driven by an engine drivebelt which could cause serious injury if your hands, hair or clothes become entangled in it with the engine running. Both the starter and alternator are connected directly to the battery and could arc or even cause a fire if mishandled, overloaded or shorted out.

Never leave the ignition switch on for long periods of time with the engine off. Don't disconnect the battery cables while the engine is running. Correct polarity must be maintained when connecting battery cables from another source, such as another vehicle, during jump starting. Always disconnect the negative cable first and hook it up last or the battery may be shorted by the tool being used to loosen the cable clamps.

Additional safety related information on the engine electrical systems can be found in Safety first near the front of this manual. It should be referred to before beginning any operation included in this Chapter.

2   Battery - removal and installation

Refer to illustration 2.2

Note: *On models equipped with the Distributorless (DIS) Ignition System, some precautions must be taken after disconnecting the battery cable(s). When the battery cable(s) has been disconnected and reconnected, some abnormal drive symptoms may occur while the EEC processor within the ignition system relearns its adaptive strategy. The vehicle may need to be driven 10 miles or more to relearn the strategy. Caution should be taken during this period of time.*

1   *Disconnect both cables from the battery terminals.* **Caution:** *Always disconnect the negative cable first and hook it up last or the battery may be shorted by the tool being used to loosen the cable clamps.*

2   Locate the battery hold-down clamp at the base of the battery **(see illustration)**. Remove the bolt and the hold-down clamp.

3   Lift out the battery. Special straps that attach to the battery posts are available - lifting and moving the battery is much easier if you use one.

4   Installation is the reverse of removal.

3   Battery - emergency jump starting

Refer to the *Booster battery (jump) starting* procedure at the front of this manual.

4   Battery cables - check and replacement

1   Periodically inspect the entire length of each battery cable for damage, cracked or burned insulation and corrosion. Poor battery cable connections can cause starting problems and decreased engine performance.

2   Check the cable-to-terminal connections at the ends of the cables for cracks, loose wire strands and corrosion. The presence of white, fluffy deposits under the insulation at the cable terminal connection is a sign that the cable is corroded and should be replaced. Check the terminals for distortion, missing mounting bolts and corrosion.

3   When replacing the cables, always disconnect the negative cable first and hook it up last or the battery may be shorted by the tool used to loosen the cable clamps. Even if only the positive cable is being replaced, be sure to disconnect the negative cable from the battery first.

4   Disconnect and remove the cable. Make sure the replacement cable is the same length and diameter.

5   Clean the threads of the relay or ground connection with a wire brush to remove rust and corrosion. Apply a light coat of petroleum jelly to the threads to prevent future corrosion.

6   Attach the cable to the relay or ground connection and tighten the mounting nut/bolt securely.

7   Before connecting the new cable to the battery, make sure that it reaches the battery post without having to be stretched. Clean the battery posts thoroughly and apply a light coat of petroleum jelly to prevent corrosion.

8   Connect the positive cable first, followed by the negative cable.

5   Ignition system - general information

Distributor type (Duraspark II and TFI-IV)

The ignition system is a solid state electronic design consisting of an ignition module, coil, distributor, the spark plug wires and the spark plugs. Mechanically, the system is similar to a breaker point system, except that the distributor cam and ignition points are replaced by an armature and magnetic pickup unit. The coil primary circuit is controlled by an amplifier module.

When the ignition is switched on, the ignition primary circuit is energized. When the distributor armature "teeth" or "spokes" approach the magnetic coil assembly, a voltage is induced which signals the amplifier to turn off the coil primary current. A timing circuit in the amplifier module turns the coil current back on after the coil field has collapsed.

When it's on, current flows from the battery through the ignition switch, the coil pri-

2.2 To remove the battery, detach both cables (negative first) and remove the battery hold-down bolt and clamp (arrow)

mary winding, the amplifier module and then to ground. When the current is interrupted, the magnetic field in the ignition coil collapses, inducing a high voltage in the coil secondary windings. The voltage is conducted to the distributor where the rotor directs it to the appropriate spark plug. This process is repeated continuously.

All vehicles are equipped with a gear driven distributor with a die cast base housing a "Hall Effect" vane switch stator assembly and a device for fixed octane adjustment. However, there are a few differences between earlier Canadian and US distributors.

Duraspark distributors have a two piece cap. When removing the cap, the upper half is removed, then the rotor is removed, then the lower half of the cap is removed. TFI-IV distributors have a conventional one piece cap.

The distributors on earlier Canadian vehicles are equipped with centrifugal and vacuum advance mechanisms which control the actual point
of ignition based on engine speed and load. As engine speed increases, two weights move out and alter the position of the armature in relation to the distributor shaft, advancing the ignition timing. As engine load increases (when climbing hills or accelerating, for example), a drop in intake manifold vacuum causes the base plate to move slightly in the opposite direction (clockwise) under the action of the spring in the vacuum unit, retarding the timing and counteracting the centrifugal advance. Under light loads (moderate steady speeds, for example), the comparatively high intake manifold vacuum acting on the vacuum advance diaphragm causes the base plate assembly to move in a counterclockwise direction to provide a greater amount of timing advance.

Early models may be equipped with Duraspark I (DSI) or Duraspark II (DSII) ignition modules. Most 1983 and 1984 models are equipped with the standard Duraspark II

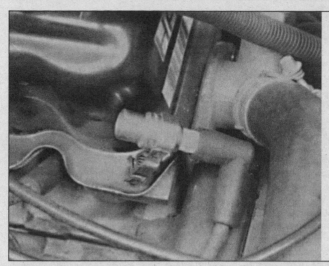

6.2 To use a calibrated ignition tester (available at most auto parts stores), simply disconnect a spark plug wire, attach the wire to the tester, clip the tester to a convenient ground (like a rocker arm cover bolt) and operate the starter - if there's enough power to fire the plug, sparks will be visible between the electrode tip and the tester body

ignition module. Later models use the Thick Film Integrated IV (TFI-IV) ignition module, which is housed in a molded thermoplastic box mounted on the base of the distributor. The important difference between the DSII and TFI-IV modules is that the TFI-IV module is controlled by the Electronic Engine Control IV (EEC-IV), while the Duraspark I and II modules are not.

The TFI-IV/EEC-IV type distributor is similar to the Duraspark II model but has neither a centrifugal nor a vacuum advance mechanism (advance is handled by the computer instead). The TFI-IV module does, however, include a "push start" mode that allows push starting of the vehicle if necessary.

Distributorless (DIS) type

The 1992 and later 2.3L four-cylinder engines are equipped with the Distributorless Ignition System (DIS) that is a solid state electronic design. It consists of a crankshaft timing sensor, EDIS module, one ignition coil pack, the spark angle portion of the EEC IV, the spark plug wires and the spark plugs. This engine features a twin spark plug cylinder head and is equipped with an ignition coil for each pair of spark plugs.

This ignition system does not have any moving parts (no distributor) and all engine timing and spark distribution is handled electronically. This system has fewer parts that require replacement and provide more accurate spark timing. During engine operation, the EDIS ignition module calculates spark angle and determines the turn-on and firing time of the ignition coil.

The crankshaft timing sensor is a variable reluctance-type sensor consisting of a 36-tooth trigger wheel with one missing tooth that is incorporated into the crankshaft front damper. The signal generated by this sensor is called a Variable Reluctance Sensor signal (VRS) and it provides the base timing and engine RPM information to the EDIS ignition modules. The main function of the EDIS module is to synchronize the ignition coils so they are turned on an off in the proper sequence for accurate spark control.

6   Ignition system - check

Refer to illustration 6.2
Warning: *Because of the very high secondary (spark plug) voltage generated by the ignition system, extreme care should be taken when this check is done.*

Distributor type ignition system (Duraspark II and TFI IV)
Calibrated ignition tester method

1   If the engine turns over but won't start, disconnect the spark plug lead from any spark plug and attach it to a calibrated ignition tester (available at most auto parts stores). Make sure the tester is designed for your ignition system if a universal tester isn't available.

2   Connect the clip on the tester to a bolt or metal bracket on the engine **(see illustration)**, crank the engine and watch the end of the tester to see if bright blue, well-defined sparks occur.

3   If sparks occur, sufficient voltage is reaching the plug to fire it (repeat the check at the remaining plug wires to verify that the distributor cap and rotor are OK). However, the plugs themselves may be fouled, so remove and check them as described in Chapter 1 or install new ones.

4   If no sparks or intermittent sparks occur, remove the distributor cap and check the cap and rotor as described in Chapter 1. If moisture is present, dry out the cap and rotor, then reinstall the cap and repeat the spark test.

5   If there's still no spark, detach the secondary coil wire from the distributor cap and hook it up to the tester (reattach the plug wire to the spark plug), then repeat the spark check.

6   If no sparks occur, check the primary (small) wire connections at the coil to make sure they're clean and tight. Refer to Section 7 and check the ignition coil supply voltage circuit. Make any necessary repairs, then repeat the check again.

7   If sparks now occur, the distributor cap, rotor, plug wire(s) or spark plug(s) (or all of them) may be defective.

8   If there's still no spark, the coil-to-cap wire may be bad (check the resistance with an ohmmeter and compare it to the Specifications). If a known good wire doesn't make any difference in the test results, the ignition coil, module or other internal components may be defective.

Alternative method
Note: *If you're unable to obtain a calibrated ignition tester, the following method will allow you to determine if the ignition system has spark, but it won't tell you if there's enough voltage produced to actually initiate combustion in the cylinders.*

9   Remove the wire from one of the spark plugs. Using an insulated tool, hold the wire about 1/4-inch from a good ground and have an assistant crank the engine.

10   If bright blue, well-defined sparks occur, sufficient voltage is reaching the plug to fire it. However, the plug(s) may be fouled, so remove and check them as described in Chapter 1 or install now ones.

11   If there's no spark, check the remaining wires in the same manner. A few sparks followed by no spark is the same condition as no spark at all.

12   If no sparks occur, remove the distributor cap and check the cap and rotor as described in Chapter 1. If moisture is present, dry out the cap and rotor, then reinstall the cap and repeat the spark test.

13   If there's still no spark, disconnect the secondary coil wire from the distributor cap, hold it about 1/4-inch from a good engine ground and crank the engine again.

14   If no sparks occur, check the primary (small) wire connections at the coil to make sure they're clean and tight.

15   If sparks now occur, the distributor cap, rotor, plug wire(s) or spark plug(s) (or all of them) may be defective.

16   If there's still no spark, the coil-to-cap wire may be bad (check the resistance with an ohmmeter and compare it to the Specifications). If a known good wire doesn't make any difference in the test results, the ignition coil, module or other internal components may be defective. Refer further testing to a qualified electrical specialist.

Distributorless (DIS) ignition system
Calibrated ignition tester method
Note: *Disconnect the spark plugs for this test from the exhaust side only.*

17   If the engine turns over but won't start, disconnect the spark plug lead from any spark plug and attach it to a calibrated ignition tester (available at most auto parts stores). Make sure the tester is designed for your ignition system if a universal tester isn't available.

18   Connect the clip on the tester to a bolt or metal bracket on the engine **(see illustra-**

5

tion 6.2), crank the engine and watch the end of the tester to see if bright blue, well-defined sparks occur.

19   If sparks occur, sufficient voltage is reaching the spark plug to fire it (repeat the check at the remaining plug wires to verify that all the ignition coils and wires are functioning). However, the plugs themselves may be fouled, so remove and check them as described in Chapter 1 or install new ones.

20   If no sparks or intermittent sparks occur, there's a problem in the ignition system. Check for a bad spark plug wire by swapping wires. Refer further testing to a qualified electrical specialist.

Alternative method

Note: *If you're unable to obtain a calibrated ignition tester, the following method will allow you to determine if the ignition system has spark, but i won't tell you if there's enough voltage produced to actually initiate combustion in the cylinders.*

Note: *Disconnect the spark plugs for this test from the exhaust side only.*

21   Remove the wire from one of the spark plugs. Using an insulated tool, hold the wire about 1/4-inch from a good ground and have an assistant crank the engine.

22   If bright blue, well-defined sparks occur, sufficient voltage is reaching the plug to fire it. However, the plug(s) may be fouled, so remove and check them as described in Chapter 1 or install new ones.

23   If there's no spark, check the remaining wires in the same manner. A few sparks followed by no spark is the same condition as no spark at all. If there's spark at some wires but not at others, bad spark plug wires may be the problem. Swap the wires and re-test to see if the wires are the problem.

24   If there's still no sparks or intermittent sparks, there's a problem in the ignition system. Refer further testing to a qualified electrical specialist.

7   Ignition coil - check and replacement

Distributor type ignition system (Duraspark II and TFI-IV)

Check

1   With the ignition off, disconnect the wires from the coil. Connect an ohmmeter across the coil primary (small wire) terminals. The resistance should be as listed in this Chapter's Specifications. If not, replace the coil.

2   Connect and ohmmeter between the negative primary terminal and the secondary terminal (the one that the distributor cap wire connects to). The resistance should be as listed in this Chapter's Specifications. If not, replace the coil.

Replacement

3   Detach the cable from the negative terminal of the battery.

4   Detach the wires from the primary termi-

nals on the coil (some coils have a single electrical connector for the primary wires).

5   Unplug the coil secondary lead.

6   Remove both bracket bolts and detach the coil.

7   Installation is the reverse of removal.

Distributorless (DIS) ignition system

Note: *Checking the DIS coil is beyond the scope of the home mechanic. Remove the coil as described below and take it to a dealer service department for diagnosis.*

8   Disconnect the negative cable from the battery.

9   Squeeze the locking tab of the ignition coil wire retainer by hand and remove the spark plug lead from the ignition coil assembly with a twisting and pulling motion. DO NOT just pull on the wires to disconnect them. Disconnect all spark plug leads.

10   Disconnect the engine wiring harness from the ignition coil assembly.

11   Remove the three bolts securing the ignition coil to the mounting bracket on the engine.

12   Installation is the reverse of the removal procedure with the following additions:

a) *Prior to installing the spark plug lead into the ignition coil, coat the entire interior of the rubber boot with silicone dielectric compound.*

b) *Insert each spark plug wire into the proper terminal of the ignition coil. Push the wire into the terminal and make sure the boots are fully seated and both locking tabs are engaged properly.*

8   Distributor - removal and installation

Removal

1   Unplug the primary lead from the coil.

2   Unplug the electrical connector for the module. Follow the wires as they exit the distributor to find the connector.

3   Note the raised "1" on the distributor cap. This marks the location for the number one cylinder spark plug wire terminal.

4   Remove the distributor cap (see Chapter 1) and turn the engine over until the rotor is pointing toward the number one spark plug terminal (see the locating TDC procedure in Chapter 2).

5   Make a mark on the edge of the distributor base directly below the rotor tip and in line with it (if the rotor on your engine has more than one tip, use the center one for reference). Also, mark the distributor base and the engine block to ensure that the distributor is installed correctly.

6   Remove the distributor hold-down bolt and clamp, then pull the distributor straight up to remove it. Be careful not to disturb the intermediate driveshaft. **Caution:** *DO NOT turn the engine while the distributor is removed, or the alignment marks will be useless.*

Installation

7   Insert the distributor into the engine in exactly the same relationship to the block that it was in when removed.

8   To mesh the helical gears on the camshaft and the distributor, it may be necessary to turn the rotor slightly. If the distributor doesn't seat completely, the hex shaped recess in the lower end of the distributor shaft is not mating properly with the oil pump shaft. Recheck the alignment marks between the distributor base and the block to verify that the distributor is i the same position it was in before removal. Also check the rotor to see if it's aligned with the mark you made on the edge of the distributor base. **Note:** *If the crankshaft has been moved while the distributor is out, locate Top Dead Center (TDC) for the number one piston (see Chapter 2) and position the distributor and rotor accordingly.*

9   Place the hold-down clamp in position and loosely install the bolt.

10   Install the distributor cap and tighten the cap screws securely.

11   Plug in the module electrical connector.

12   Reattach the spark plug wires to the plugs (if removed).

13   Connect the cable to the negative terminal of the battery.

14   Check the ignition timing (refer to Section 9) and tighten the distributor hold-down bolt securely.

9   Ignition timing - check and adjustment

Note 1: *Ignition timing on the distributorless (DIS) ignition system is preset and cannot be checked or adjusted.*

Note 2: *Always check the Vehicle Emission Control Information (VECI) label on your vehicle to see if a different procedure is specified. The VECI label contains detailed information which is specific to your vehicle.*

1   Apply the parking brake and block the wheels. Place the transmission in Park (automatic) or Neutral (manual). Turn off all accessories (heater, air conditioner, etc.).

2   Start the engine and warm it up. Once it has reached operating temperature, turn it off.

3   If you have a vehicle with a DSI or DSII ignition system (see Section 5), disconnect the vacuum hoses from the distributor vacuum advance unit and plug the hoses.

4   If you have a later model vehicle with an EEC-IV system, unplug the single wire connector located immediately above the harness connector for the module.

5   Connect an inductive timing light and a tachometer in accordance with the manufacturer's instructions. **Caution:** *Make sure that the timing light and tach wires don't hang anywhere near the electric cooling fan or they may become entangled in the fan blades when the fan begins to rotate.*

6   Locate the timing marks on the crankshaft pulley (see Chapter 2).

10.6 To remove the TFI-IV ignition module from the distributor base, remove the two screws (arrows) . . .

10.7 . . . then pull the module straight down to detach the spade terminals from the stator connector

7   Start the engine again.

8   Point the timing light at the pulley timing marks and note whether the specified timing mark (see the VECI label) is aligned with the timing pointer on the front of the timing chain/belt cover.

9   If the proper mark isn't aligned with the stationary pointer, loosen the distributor hold-down bolt. Turn the distributor clockwise (to retard timing) or counterclockwise (to advance timing) until the correct timing mark on the crankshaft pulley is aligned with the stationary pointer. Tighten the distributor hold-down bolt securely when the timing is correct and recheck it to make sure it didn't change when the bolt was tightened.

10   Turn off the engine.

11   Plug in the single wire connector (TFI-IV-equipped vehicles) or attach the vacuum hoses (DSI- or DSII-equipped vehicles).

12   Restart the engine and check the idle speed. The specified rpm for each vehicle is different (see your VECI Label). On vehicles with an adjustable idle speed, see Chapter 1 for adjustment procedure. On engines equipped with automatic idle speed control, idle rpm is not adjustable. If the idle rpm is not within the range specified on your VECI label, take the vehicle to a dealer service department or repair shop. Adjustment requires specialized test equipment and procedures that are beyond the scope of the home mechanic.

13   Turn off the engine.

14   Remove the timing light and tachometer.

10   Ignition module - replacement

Caution: *The ignition module is a delicate and relatively expensive electronic component. Failure to follow the step-by-step procedures could result in damage to the module and/or other electronic devices, including the EEC-IV microprocessor itself. Additionally, all devices under computer control are protected by a Federally mandated extended warranty. Check with your dealer before attempting to replace them yourself.*

Duraspark I and II ignition module

1   Detach the cable from the negative terminal of the battery.

2   Vehicles equipped with a Duraspark I or II system may have either the standard Duraspark I or II module or the universal ignition module. If your vehicle is equipped with the standard module, unplug both connectors; if your vehicle is equipped with the UIM module, unplug all three connectors.

3   Remove the mounting screws and detach the module.

4   Installation is the reverse of removal.

TFI-IV ignition module

Refer to illustrations 10.6, 10.7 and 10.8

5   Remove the distributor from the engine (refer to Section 8) if access to the module is blocked.

6   Remove the two module mounting screws with a 1/4-inch drive 7/32-inch deep socket **(see illustration)**.

7   Pull straight down on the module to disconnect the spade connectors from the stator connector **(see illustration)**.

8   Whether you are installing the old module or a new one, wipe the back side of the module clean with a soft, clean rag and apply a film of silicone dielectric grease to the back side of the module **(see illustration)**.

9   Installation is the reverse of removal. When plugging in the module, make sure that the three terminals are inserted all the way into the stator connector.

EDIS ignition module

10   Disconnect the negative cable from the battery.

11   Disconnect the electrical connector from the EDIS ignition module.

12   Remove the screws securing the EDIS module to the lower intake manifold.

13   Installation is the reverse of the removal procedure. Prior to installing the EDIS module onto the manifold, apply about a 1/32-inch of silicone dielectric compound to the mounting surface of the module.

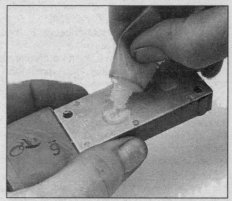

10.8 Be sure to wipe the back side of the module clean and apply a film of dielectric grease (essential for cool operation of the module) - DO NOT use any other type of grease!

11   Crankshaft timing sensor (DIS ignition systems) - removal and installation

Removal

1   Disconnect the negative cable from the battery.

2   Disconnect the crankshaft timing sensor electrical connector from the engine main wiring harness.

3   Pry out the red retaining clip and remove the four wires, then remove the large electrical connector from the crankshaft timing sensor assembly.

4   Remove the accessory drivebelts, the crankshaft pulley assembly and the timing belt outer cover (see Chapter 2A).

5   Rotate the crankshaft so the keyway is at the ten o'clock position. This will locate the vane window of both the inner and outer vane cups (part of the crankshaft pulley hub assembly) over the crankshaft timing sensor assembly.

6   Remove the two bolts securing the crankshaft timing sensor assembly to the

5

cylinder block.

7   Remove the bolt securing the wiring harness plastic retainer to the mounting bracket. Carefully slide the wiring harness out from behind the timing belt inner cover and remove the crankshaft timing sensor assembly.

Installation

8   If a new crankshaft timing sensor assembly is being installed, remove the large electrical connector from it. If installing the old assembly, the connector is already removed.

9   Slide the electrical wire harness behind the timing belt inner cover.

10   Install the crankshaft timing sensor assembly into place and install the two bolts finger tight at this time.

11   Install the large electrical connector onto the harness. **Caution:** *Ensure the four wires are installed in the proper location within the connector. If installed incorrectly the sensor will NOT operate correctly.*

12   Connect the electrical connector to the engine main wiring harness.

13   Rotate the crankshaft so the outer vane on the crankshaft pulley hub assembly engages both sides of a crankshaft hall-effect sensor positioner available at most auto parts stores. Tighten the crankshaft timing sensor assembly mounting bolts.

14   Rotate the crankshaft so the outer vane on the crankshaft pulley hub assembly no longer engages the positioner tool, then remove the tool.

15   Install the wire harness plastic retainer, install the bolt and tighten securely. If a new retainer was installed, trim off the excess.

16   Install the timing belt outer cover, the crankshaft pulley assembly and the accessory drive belts (see Chapter 2A).

17   Attach the negative cable to the battery.

---

12 Charging system - general information and precautions

The charging system includes the alternator, either an internal or an external voltage regulator, a charge indicator or warning light, the battery, a fusible link and the wiring between all the components. The charging system supplies electrical power for the ignition system, the lights, the radio, etc. The alternator is driven by a drivebelt at the front of the engine.

The purpose of the voltage regulator is to limit the alternator's voltage to a preset value. This prevents power surges, circuit overloads, etc., during peak voltage output. On EVR (external voltage regulator) systems, the regulator is mounted on the right fender apron of the vehicle. On IAR (integral alternator/regulator) systems, a solid state regulator is housed inside a plastic module mounted on the alternator itself.

The fusible link is a short length of insulated wire integral with the engine compartment wiring harness. The link is four wire gauges smaller in diameter than the circuit it

13.2 To measure battery voltage, attach the voltmeter leads to the battery terminals - to measure charging voltage, start the engine

protects. Production fusible links and their identification flags are identified by the flag color. Refer to Chapter 12 for additional information on fusible links.

The charging system doesn't ordinarily require periodic maintenance. However, the drivebelt, battery and wires and connections should be inspected at the intervals outlined in Chapter 1.

Be very careful when making electrical circuit connections to a vehicle equipped with an alternator and note the following:

a) *When reconnecting wires to the alternator from the battery, be sure to note the polarity.*

b) *Before using arc welding equipment to repair any part of the vehicle, disconnect the wires from the alternator and the battery terminals.*

c) *Never start the engine with a battery charger connected.*

d) *Always disconnect both battery leads before using a battery charger.*

---

13 Charging system - check

Refer to illustration 13.2

1   If a malfunction occurs in the charging circuit, do not immediately assume that the alternator is causing the problem. First check the following items:

a) *The battery cables where they connect to the battery. Make sure the connections are clean and tight.*

b) *The battery electrolyte specific gravity. If it is low, charge the battery.*

c) *Check the external alternator wiring and connections.*

d) *Check the drivebelt condition and tension (see Chapter 1).*

e) *Check the alternator mounting bolts for tightness.*

f) *Run the engine and check the alternator for abnormal noise.*

2   Using a voltmeter, check the battery voltage with the engine off. It should be approximately 12-volts **(see illustration)**.

3   Start the engine and check the battery voltage again. It should now be approximately 14 to 15-volts.

4   If the indicated voltage reading is less or more than the specified charging voltage, replace the voltage regulator. If replacing the regulator fails to restore the voltage to the specified range, the problem may be within the alternator.

5   Due to the special equipment necessary to test or service the alternator, it is recommended that if a fault is suspected the vehicle be taken to a dealer or a shop with the proper equipment. Because of this, the home mechanic should limit maintenance to checking connections and the inspection and replacement of the brushes.

6   The ammeter (1979 through 1986 models) on the instrument panel indicates charge or discharge - current passing into or out of the battery. With the electrical equipment switched on and the engine idling, the gauge needle may show a discharge condition. At fast idle or at normal driving speeds the needle should stay on the charge side of the gauge, with th charged state of the battery determining just how far over (the lower the battery state of charge, the farther the needle should swing toward the charge side).

7   The voltmeter on the instrument panel (1987 and later models) indicates battery voltage with the key on and engine off, and alternator output when the engine is running.

8   The charge light on the instrument panel illuminates with the key on and engine not running, and should go out when the engine runs.

9   If the gauge does not show a charge when it should or the alternator light (if equipped) remains on, there is a fault in the system. Before inspecting the brushes or replacing the alternator, the battery condition, alternator belt tension and electrical cable connections should be checked.

---

14 Alternator - removal and installation

Refer to illustrations 14.2 and 14.3

1   Detach the cable from the negative terminal of the battery.

2   Unplug the electrical connectors from the alternator and (if your charging system is equipped with an IAR type alternator) the voltage regulator **(see illustration)**.

3   Loosen the alternator bolts **(see illustration)** and detach the drivebelt.

4   Remove the adjustment and pivot bolts and separate the alternator from the engine.

5   Installation is the reverse of removal.

6   After the alternator is installed, adjust the drivebelt tension (refer to Chapter 1).

14.2 To remove the alternator, unplug the electrical connectors (arrows), . . .

14.3 . . . remove the drivebelt, remove the strut bolt (upper left arrow), swing the strut out of the way and remove both alternator mounting bolts (arrows)

15 Alternator brushes - replacement (EVR type alternator)

Note: *Internal replacement parts for alternators may not be readily available in your area. Check into availability before proceeding.*

Rear terminal alternator

Refer to illustrations 15.2, 15.5a, 15.5b and 15.7

1   Remove the alternator as described in Section 14.
2   Scribe a line across the length of the alternator housing to ensure correct reassembly **(see illustration)**.
3   Remove the housing through bolts and the nuts and insulators from the rear housing. Make a careful note of all insulator locations.
4   Withdraw the rear housing section from the stator, rotor and front housing assembly.
5   Remove the brushes and springs from the brush holder assembly, which is located inside the rear housing **(see illustrations)**.
6   Check the length of the brushes against the wear dimensions given in the Specifica-

15.2 Scribe a line across the alternator housing for alignment reference

tions and replace the brushes with new ones if necessary.
7   Install the springs and brushes in the holder assembly and retain them in place by inserting a piece of stiff wire through the rear

15.5a Remove the bolts and detach the brush holder and the brush in the holder

housing and brush terminal insulator **(see illustration)**. Make sure enough wire protrudes through the rear housing so it can be withdrawn at a later stage.
8   Attach the rear housing, rotor and front

5

15.5b Remove the rear field housing nut (orange) to detach the remaining brush

15.7 Insert a paper clip through the hole in the back to retain the brushes

17.3 To detach the voltage regulator/brush holder assembly, remove the four screws (arrows)

17.5 To remove the brushes from the voltage regulator/brush holder assembly, detach the rubber plugs from the two brush lead wire screws and remove both screws (arrows)

housing assembly to the stator, making sure the scribed marks are aligned.

9   Install the housing through bolts and rear end insulators and nuts but do not tighten the nuts at this time.

10   Carefully extract the piece of wire from the rear housing and make sure that the brushes are seated on the slip ring. Tighten the through bolts and rear housing nuts.

11   Install the alternator as described in Section 14.

Side terminal alternator

12   Remove the alternator as described in Section 14 and scribe a mark on both end housings and the stator for ease of reassembly.

13   Remove the through bolts and separate the front housing and rotor from the rear housing and stator. Be careful that you do not separate the rear housing and stator.

14   Use a soldering iron to unsolder and disengage the brush holder from the rear housing. Remove the brushes and springs from the brush holders.

15   Remove the two brush holder attaching screws and lift the brush holder from the rear housing.

16   Remove any sealing compound from the brush holder and rear housing.

17   Inspect the brushes for damage and check their dimensions against the Specifications. If they are worn, replace them with new ones.

18   To reassemble, install the springs and brushes in the brush holders, inserting a piece of stiff wire to hold them in place.

19   Place the brush holder in position in the rear housing, using the wire to retract the brushes through the hole in the rear housing.

20   Install the brush holder attaching screws and push the holder toward the shaft opening as you tighten the screws. **Caution:** *The rectifier can be overheated and damaged if the soldering is not done quickly. Press the brush holder lead onto the rectifier lead and solder them in place.*

21   Place the rotor and front housing in position in the stator and rear housing. After aligning the scribe marks, install the through bolts.

22   Turn the fan and pulley to check for binding in the alternator.

23   Withdraw the wire which is retracting the brushes and seal the hole with waterproof cement. **Caution:** *Do not use RTV-type sealer on the hole.*

16   External Voltage Regulator (EVR) - replacement

1   Detach the cable from the negative terminal of the battery.

2   Locate the voltage regulator on the right side of the engine compartment.

3   If necessary, remove the battery or air cleaner duct to gain access to the voltage regulator.

4   Unplug the electrical connector from the voltage regulator.

5   Remove the regulator mounting bolts.

6   Remove the regulator.

7   Installation is the reverse of removal.

17   Voltage regulator/alternator brushes - replacement (IAR-type alternator)

Refer to illustrations 17.3, 17.5 and 17.9

1   Remove the alternator (refer to Section 13).

2   Set the alternator on a clean workbench.

3   Remove the four voltage regulator mounting screws **(see illustration)**.

4   Detach the voltage regulator.

5   Detach the rubber plugs and remove the brush lead retaining screws and nuts to separate the brush leads from the holder **(see illustration)**. Note that the screws have Torx heads and require a special screwdriver.

6   After noting the relationship of the brushes to the brush holder assembly, remove both brushes. Don't lose the springs.

7   If you're installing a new voltage regulator, insert the old brushes into the brush holder of the new regulator. If you're installing new brushes, insert them into the brush holder of the old regulator. Make sure the springs are properly compressed and the

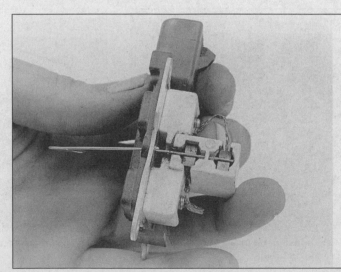

17.9 Before installing the voltage regulator/brush holder assembly, insert a paper clip as shown to hold the brushes in place during installation - after installation, simply pull the paper clip out

brushes are properly inserted into the recesses in the brush holder.

8   Install the brush lead retaining screws and nuts.

9   Insert a short section of wire, like a paper clip, through the hole in the voltage regulator **(see illustration)** to hold the brushes in the retracted position during regulator installation.

10   Carefully install the regulator. Make sure the brushes don't hang up on the rotor.

11   Install the voltage regulator screws and tighten them securely.

12   Remove the wire or paper clip.

13   Install the alternator (refer to Section 14).

18 Starting system - general information

The function of the starting system is to crank the engine to start it. The system is composed of the starter motor, starter relay, battery, switch and connecting wires.

Turning the ignition key to the Start position actuates the starter relay through the starter control circuit. The starter relay then connects the battery to the starter. The battery supplies the electrical energy to the starter motor, which does the actual work of cranking the engine.

Vehicles equipped with an automatic transmission have a Neutral start switch in the starter control circuit, which prevents operation of the starter unless the shift lever is in Neutral or Park. The circuit on vehicles with a manual transmission prevents operation of the starter motor unless the clutch pedal is depressed.

Never operate the starter motor for more than 30 seconds at a time without pausing to allow it to cool for at least two minutes. Excessive cranking can cause overheating, which can seriously damage the starter.

19 Starter motor and circuit - in-vehicle check

Note: *Before diagnosing starter problems, make sure the battery is fully charged.*

General check

1   If the starter motor doesn't turn at all when the switch is operated, make sure the shift lever is in Neutral or Park (automatic transmission) or the clutch pedal is depressed (manual transmission).

2   Make sure the battery is charged and that all cables at the battery and starter relay terminals are secure.

3   If the starter motor spins but the engine doesn't turn over, then the drive assembly in the starter motor is slipping and the starter motor must be replaced (see Section 20).

4   If, when the switch is actuated, the starter motor doesn't operate at all but the starter relay operates (clicks), then the prob-

lem lies with either the battery, the starter relay contacts or the starter motor connections.

5   If the starter relay doesn't click when the ignition switch is actuated, either the starter relay circuit is open or the relay itself is defective. Check the starter relay circuit (see the wiring diagrams at the end of this book) or replace the relay (see Section 21).

6   To check the starter relay circuit, remove the push-on connector from the relay wire. Make sure that the connection is clean and secure and the relay bracket is grounded. If the connections are good, check the operation of the relay with a jumper wire. To do this, place the transmission in Park (automatic) or Neutral (manual). Remove the push-on connector from the relay. Connect a jumper wire between the battery positive terminal and the exposed terminal on the relay. If the starter motor now operates, the starter relay is okay. The problem is in the ignition switch, Neutral start switch, starter/clutch switch, or in the starting circuit wiring (look for open or loose connections).

7   If the starter motor still doesn't operate, replace the starter relay (see Section 21).

8   If the starter motor cranks the engine at an abnormally slow speed, first make sure the battery is fully charged and all terminal connections are clean and tight. Also check the connections at the starter relay and battery ground. Eyelet terminals should not be easily rotated by hand. Also check for a short to ground. If the engine is partially seized, or has the wrong viscosity oil in it, it will crank slowly.

Starter cranking circuit test

Note: *To determine the location of excessive resistance in the starter circuit, perform the following simple series of tests.*

9   Disconnect the ignition coil wire from the distributor cap and ground it on the engine.

10   Connect a remote control starter switch from the battery terminal of the starter relay to the S terminal of the relay.

11   Connect a voltmeter positive lead to the starter motor terminal of the starter relay, then connect the negative lead to ground.

12   Actuate the ignition switch and take the voltmeter readings as soon as a steady figure

is indicated. Do not allow the starter motor to turn for more than 30 seconds at a time. A reading of 9-volts or more, with the starter motor turning at normal cranking speed, is normal. If the reading is 9-volts or more but the cranking speed is slow, the motor is faulty. If the reading is less than 9-volts and the cranking speed is slow, the relay contacts are probably burned.

13   The voltage drop in the circuit will be indicated by the voltmeter (put the voltmeter on the 0-to-20 volt range). The maximum allowable voltage drop should be:

a) *0.5-volt with the voltmeter negative lead connected to the starter terminal and the positive lead connected to the battery positive terminal.*

b) *0.1-volt with the voltmeter negative lead connected to the starter relay (battery side) and the positive lead connected to the positive terminal of the battery.*

c) *0.3-volt with the voltmeter negative lead connected to the starter relay (starter side) and the positive lead connected to the positive terminal of the battery.*

d) *0.3-volt with the voltmeter negative lead connected to the negative terminal of the battery and the positive lead connected to the engine ground.*

20 Starter motor - removal and installation

Refer to illustration 20.6

1   Detach the cable from the negative terminal of the battery.

2   Raise the vehicle and support it securely on jackstands.

3   Disconnect the large cable from the terminal on the starter motor.

4   1979 models - remove four bolts that secure the crossmember under the transmission bellhousing. Remove the screw that secures the flex coupling to the steering gear. Detach the flex coupling and pull the steering gear down.

5   4.2L V8 engines - remove the wishbone brace.

6   Remove the starter motor mounting bolts **(see illustration)** and detach the starter from the engine.

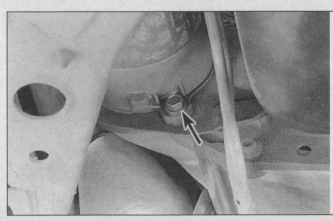

20.6 The starter motor lower mounting bolt (arrow) (upper bolt not visible)

7   If necessary, turn the wheels to one side
to provide removal access.
8   Installation is the reverse of removal.

21   Starter relay - removal and installation

Refer to illustration 21.2
1   Detach the cable from the negative terminal of the battery.
2   Label the wires and the terminals then
disconnect the Neutral safety switch wire
(automatics only), the battery cable, the
fusible link and the starter cable from the
relay terminals **(see illustration)**.
3   Remove the mounting bolts and detach
the relay.
4   Installation is the reverse of removal.

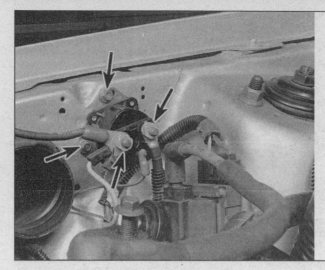

**21.2 To remove the
starter relay, detach
the Neutral safety
switch wire (if equipped
with an automatic), the
fusible link, the battery
positive lead and the
starter motor leads
(arrows), then remove
the relay mounting
bracket bolts (arrows)**

Chapter 6
Emissions control systems

Contents

Specifications

Torque specifications

	Ft-lbs
Air pump pulley bolts	10 to 12.5
Air pump mounting bolts	25

1   General information

Refer to illustration 1.7

To prevent pollution of the atmosphere from incompletely burned and evaporating gases, and to maintain good driveability and fuel economy, a number of emission control systems are incorporated. They include the:

Microprocessor Control Unit (MCU) system
Electronic Engine Control (EEC-IV) system
Exhaust Gas Recirculation (EGR) system
Managed Thermactor Air (MTA) system
Fuel evaporative emission control system
Positive Crankcase Ventilation (PCV) system
Inlet air temperature control system
Catalytic converter

On vehicles equipped with EEC-IV, all of these systems are linked, directly or indirectly, to the EEC-IV system.

The Sections in this Chapter include general descriptions, checking procedures within the scope of the home mechanic and component replacement procedures (when possible) for each of the systems listed above.

Before assuming that an emissions control system is malfunctioning, check the fuel and ignition systems carefully. The diagnosis of some emission control devices requires specialized tools, equipment and training. If checking and servicing become too difficult or if a procedure is beyond your ability, consult a dealer service department.

This doesn't mean, however, that emission control systems are particularly difficult to maintain and repair. You can quickly and easily perform many checks and do most (if not all) of the regular maintenance at home with common tune-up and hand tools. **Note:** *The most frequent cause of emissions problems is simply a loose or broken vacuum hose or wire, so always check the hose and wiring connections first.*

Pay close attention to any special precautions outlined in this Chapter. It should be noted that the illustrations of the various systems may not exactly match the system installed on your vehicle because of changes made by the manufacturer during production or from year-to-year.

A Vehicle Emissions Control Information label is located in the engine compartment **(see illustration)**. This label contains important emission specifications and adjustment information, as well as a vacuum hose schematic with emissions components identified. When servicing the engine or emissions systems, the VECI label in your particular vehicle should always be checked for up-to-date information.

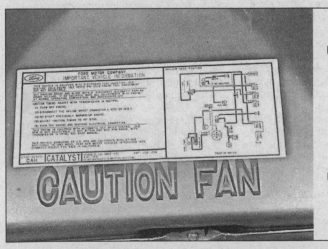

1.7 The Vehicle Emission Control Information (VECI) label, normally located on the top of the cooling fan shroud, contains essential and specific information (like spark plug type, the proper ignition timing procedure for your vehicle and a vacuum hose routing schematic) that applies to the emissions-related devices on your vehicle

6

2 Electronic Engine Control (EEC-IV) system and trouble codes

General description

1 All vehicles equipped with TFI-IV electronic ignition systems (see Chapter 5) are also equipped with the Electronic Engine Control (EEC-IV) system. The EEC-IV system consists of an onboard computer, known as the Electronic Control Assembly (ECA), and the information sensors, which monitor various functions of the engine and send data to the ECA. Based on the data and the information programmed into the computer's memory, the ECA generates output signals to control various engine functions.

2 The ECA, located inside the dashboard to the left of the steering column, is the "brain" of the EEC-IV system. It receives data from a number of sensors and other electronic components (switches, relays, etc.). Based on the information it receives, the ECA generates output signals to control various relays, solenoids and other actuators (see below). The ECA is specifically calibrated to optimize the emissions, fuel economy and driveability of your vehicle.

3 Because of a Federally-mandated extended warranty (five years or 50,000 miles at the time this manual was written) which covers the ECA, the information sensors and all components under its control, and because any owner-induced damage to the ECA, the sensors and/or the control devices may void the warranty, it isn't a good idea to attempt diagnosis or replacement of the ECA at home. Take your vehicle to a dealer service department if the ECA or a system component malfunctions.

Information input sensors

Note: *Not all of the following devices will be on your vehicle. Your VECI label is the most specific and accurate source of information for determining what sensors are on your vehicle.*

4 When battery voltage is applied to the compressor clutch, a signal is sent to the ECA, which interprets the signal as an added load created by the A/C compressor and increases engine idle speed accordingly to compensate.

5 The Air Charge Temperature sensor (ACT), threaded into a runner of the intake manifold, provides the ECA with fuel/air mixture temperature information. The ECA uses this information to correct fuel flow and control fuel flow during cold enrichment (cold starts).

6 The EGR Valve Position Sensor (EVP), located on the EGR valve, tells the ECA the position of the EGR valve.

7 The Engine Coolant Temperature (ECT) sensor, which is threaded into a coolant passage in the front of the intake manifold next to the thermostat housing, monitors engine coolant temperature. The ECT sends the ECA a constantly varying voltage signal which influences ECA control of the fuel mixture, ignition timing and EGR operation.

8 The Manifold Absolute Pressure (MAP) sensor, mounted on the firewall, measures the absolute pressure of the mixture in the intake manifold and sends a signal to the ECA that is proportional to absolute pressure.

9 The exhaust gas oxygen sensors (EGO), which are threaded into the exhaust manifolds, constantly monitor the oxygen content of the exhaust gases. A voltage signal which varies in accordance with the difference between the oxygen content of the exhaust gases and the surrounding atmosphere is sent to the ECA. The ECA converts this exhaust gas oxygen content signal to the fuel/air ratio, compares it to the ideal ratio for current engine operating conditions and alters the signal to the injectors accordingly.

10 The Profile Ignition Pick-up (PIP), integral with the distributor, informs the ECA of crankshaft position and speed. The PIP assembly consists of an armature with four windows and four metal tabs that rotate past a stator assembly (the Hall Effect switch).

11 The Throttle Position Sensor (TPS), which is mounted on the side of the throttle body (see Chapter 4) and connected directly to the throttle shaft, senses throttle movement and position, then transmits an electrical signal to the ECA. This signal enables the ECA to determine when the throttle is closed, in its normal cruise condition or wide open.

Output devices

Note: *Not all of the following devices will be on your vehicle. Also, the location and appearance of the following devices may differ somewhat on your vehicle from those illustrated and/or described below. Your VECI label is the most specific and accurate source of information for determining what devices are on your vehicle.*

12 The A/C and cooling fan controller module is operated by the ECA, the coolant temperature switch and the brake light switch. The controller module provides an output signal which controls operation of the A/C compressor clutch and the engine cooling fan.

13 The EEC power relay, which is activated by the ignition switch, supplies battery voltage to the ECA when the switch is on.

14 The canister purge solenoid (CANP), located in the left front corner of the engine compartment, switches manifold vacuum to operate the canister purge valve when a signal is received from the ECA. Vacuum opens the purge valve when the solenoid is energized.

15 The EGR control solenoid, located in the left front corner of the engine compartment, switches manifold vacuum to operate the EGR valve on command from the ECA. Vacuum opens the EGR valve when the solenoid is energized.

16 The EGR shut-off solenoid is an electrically operated vacuum valve located between the manifold vacuum source and the EGR valve. A controlled vacuum bleed is located between the solenoid and the EGR valve. This vacuum bleed is a Backpressure Variable Transducer (BVT). These two devices operate the EGR valve for optimum performance. Solenoid switch vacuum is also supplied to the canister purge valve.

17 The EGR vent solenoid opens the EGR control solenoid vacuum line. When the vent solenoid is energized, the control solenoid opens the EGR valve.

18 The feedback control solenoid regulates the idle, off idle and main system fuel/air ratios in accordance with signals from the ECA.

19 The solenoid operated fuel injectors are located in the throttle body on vehicles with Central Fuel Injection and in the intake ports of vehicles equipped with EFI or SEFI. The ECA controls the length of time the injector is open. The "open" time of the injector determines the amount of fuel delivered. For information regarding injector replacement, refer to Chapter 4.

20 The fuel pump relay (used on fuel injected vehicles) is activated by the ECA with the ignition switch in the On position. When the ignition switch is turned to the On position, the relay is activated to supply initial line pressure to the system. For information regarding fuel pump check and replacement, refer to Chapter 4.

21 The Idle Speed Control (ISC) motor changes idle speed in accordance with signals from the ECA. For information regarding ISC replacement, refer to Chapter 4.

22 The shift indicator light tells the driver when to shift gears for optimum fuel economy. The ECA signals it to light up in accordance with the information it receives regarding engine speed and manifold vacuum levels.

23 The Thermactor Air By-Pass (TAB) solenoid provides a vacuum signal to the by-pass valve in response to signals from the ECA. the TAB valve then by-passes the thermactor air pump to the atmosphere. For information regarding the thermactor system, refer to Section 4 in this Chapter.

24 The Thermactor Air Diverter (TAD) solenoid provides a vacuum signal to the diverter valve in response to signals from the ECA. The TAD valve then diverts thermactor pump air to either the exhaust manifold or the catalytic converter. For more information regarding the thermactor system, refer to Section 5 in this Chapter.

25 The TFI-IV ignition module (see Chapter 5), mounted on the side of the distributor base, triggers the ignition coil and determines dwell. The ECA uses a signal from the Profile Ignition Pick-Up to determine crankshaft position. Ignition timing is determined by the ECA, which then signals the module to fire the coil. For further information regarding the TFI-IV module, refer to the appropriate Section in Chapter 5.

26 The throttle kicker solenoid is a two-port valve with an atmospheric vent. A vacuum diaphragm is used to maintain nominal idle speed on command from the ECA. For fur-

ther information regarding the throttle kicker, refer to the appropriate Section in Chapter 4.

27   The Wide Open Throttle (WOT) A/C cut-out circuit is energized by the ECA when a WOT condition is detected. During WOT, power to the A/ compressor clutch is disconnected until sometime after partial throttle operation resumes. For further information regarding the WOT A/C cut-out, refer to Chapter 4.

28   The Mass Air Flow (MAF) sensor, used on 1988 and later California 5.0L engines, measures the mass of air flowing into the engine in grams per second. The MAF sensor uses a thermistor (an electrical resistor whose resistance changes with temperature). The ECU maintains a voltage signal across the thermistor. As air flows into the engine, it cools the thermistor and causes the voltage flowing through it to drop. The ECU measures this voltage drop and converts it into a measurement of air flow.

EEC-IV system trouble codes

Refer to illustration 2.31

29   The EEC-IV engine management system has a self-diagnosis capability that stores trouble codes in the PCM (computer) that identify problem areas in the system. You can retrieve these codes and use them as an aid to diagnosing problems in the engine management system. Often, when a code is stored in the PCM, the "SERVICE ENGINE SOON" light on the instrument panel will illuminate.

30   In the engine compartment, find the "Self-Test" connector. Usually, the connector has two parts: a large one with six output terminals and a single input terminal. The connector is located on the right (passenger's) side of the firewall, near the strut tower.

31   With the engine off, connect the positive probe of an analog voltmeter to the battery positive post. Unplug the "Self-Test" connector. Connect a jumper wire between the input

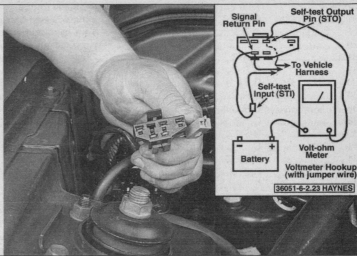

2.31 To output the trouble codes, connect a voltmeter as shown and, using a jumper wire, bridge the self-test input connector to the signal return pin (terminal number 2)

to pin 2 on the larger connector and connect the voltmeter negative probe to pin 4 **(see illustration)**. Set the voltmeter on a 15 or 20-volt scale, then connect a timing light to the engine. The three types of codes this test will provide are:

O - **Key On Engine Off (KOEO)** *(on-demand codes with the engine off)*

C - **Continuous Memory** *(codes stored when the engine was running)*

R - **Engine Running (ER)** *(codes produced as the engine is running)*

O (KOEO)

32   Turn on the ignition and watch the voltmeter needle. It will display the codes as sweeps of the needle. For example, two sweeps followed by three sweeps is code 23, with a four-second delay between codes. Write the codes down for reference. The codes will appear in numerical order, repeating once.

C (Continuous Memory)

33   After the KOEO codes are reported, there will be a short pause and any stored Continuous Memory codes will appear in order. Remember that the "Pass" code is 11, or sweep, two-second pause, sweep.

R (Engine Running)

34   Start the engine. The first part of this test makes sure the system can advance the ignition timing. Check the ignition timing. It should be advanced about 20-degrees above base timing (check the VECI label for the base timing specification).

35   Shut off the engine, restart it and run it for two minutes, then turn it off for ten seconds before restarting it. The voltmeter needle should make some quick sweeps, then show an engine code (two sweeps for a four-cylinder engine, three for a V6). After another pause will be one sweep, the signal to tap the accelerator so the system can check throttle component operation (this is called the "throttle goose test"). After this there will be a pause, followed by the Engine Running codes, which will appear in the same manner as before, repeating twice.

Trouble code chart

Code	Test condition	Probable cause
11	O,R,C	System OK, testing complete
12	R	Idle speed control out of specified range
13	O,R,C	Normal idle not within specified range
14	O,C	Ignition profile pickup erratic
15	O	ROM test failure
15	C	Power interrupt to computer memory
16	R	Erratic idle, oxygen sensor out of range or throttle not closing
17	R	Curb idle out of specified range
18	R	SPOUT circuit open
19	O	No power to processor
19	R	Erratic idle speed or signal
21	O,R,	Coolant temperature out of specified range
21	O,R,C	Coolant temperature sensor out of specified range
22	O,R,C	MAP sensor out of specified range
23	O,R,C	Throttle position signal out of specified range
24	O,R	Air charge temperature low
26	O,R	Mass Air Flow sensor or circuit

Code	Test condition	Probable cause
27	C	Vehicle Speed Sensor or circuit
28	O,R	Vane air temperature sensor or circuit
29	C	No continuity in Vehicle Speed Sensor circuit
31	O,R,C	Canister or EGR valve control system
32	O,R,C	Canister or EGR valve control system
33	R,C	Canister or EGR valve not operating properly
34	O,R,C	EVP voltage above closed unit
35	O,R,C	EGR pressure feedback, regulator circuit
38	C	Idle control circuit
39	C	Automatic overdrive circuit
41	C	Oxygen sensor signal
41	R	Lean fuel mixture
42	R,C	Fuel mixture rich
43	C	Lean fuel mixture at wide open throttle
43	R	Engine too warm for test
44	R	Air management system inoperative
45	R	Thermactor air diverter circuit
46	R	Thermactor air bypass circuit
47	R	Low flow of unmetered air at idle
48	R	High flow of unmetered air at idle
49	C	SPOUT signal defaulted to 10-degrees
51	O,C	Coolant temperature sensor out of specified range
52	O,R	Power steering pressure switch out of specified range
53	O,C	Throttle Position Sensor input out of specified range
54	O,C	Vane air flow sensor or air charge temperature sensor
55	R	Charging system under specified voltage (1984 through 1988)
55	R	Open ignition key power circuit (1984 through 1988)
56	O,R,C	Mass Air Flow sensor or circuit
57	C	Transmission neutral pressure switch circuit
58	O	CFI - idle control circuit; EFI - vane air flow circuit
58	R	Idle speed control motor or circuit
58	C	Vane air temperature sensor or circuit
59	O,C	Transmission throttle pressure switch circuit
61	O,C	Coolant temperature switch out of specified range
62	O	Transmission circuit fault
63	O,C	Throttle Position Sensor or circuit
64	O,C	Air Charge Temperature (ACT) sensor
65	C	Fuel control system not switching to closed loop
66	O,C	No Mass Air Flow sensor signal
67	O,R,C	Neutral drive switch or circuit
67	C	Air conditioner clutch switch circuit
69	O,C	Vehicle Speed Sensor or circuit
72	C	System power circuit, electrical interference
72	R	No Manifold Absolute Pressure or Mass Air Flow sensor signal fluctuation
73	O,R	Throttle Position Sensor or circuit
74	R	Brake on/off ground circuit fault
75	R	Brake on/off power circuit fault
76	R	No vane airflow change
77	R	Throttle "goose" test not performed
78	C	Power circuit
79	O	Air conditioner clutch circuit
81	O	Thermactor air circuit
82	O	Thermactor air circuit, integrated controller circuit
83	O	EGR control circuit (four-cylinder models only)
83	O	Cooling fan circuit (V6 models only)
83	O,C	Low speed fuel pump relay (1984 through 1988 models)
83	O,C	EGR solenoid or circuit (1989 and later models)
84	O,R	EGR control circuit
85	O,R	Canister purge circuit or transmission shift control circuit
85	C	Excessive fuel pressure or flow
85	O	Canister purge circuit
86	C	Low fuel pressure or flow
87	O,R, C	Fuel pump circuit
88	O	Integrated controller
89	O	Lock-up solenoid
91	R,C	Oxygen sensor problem, fuel pressure out of specified range or injectors out of balance
92	R	Fuel mixture rich, fuel pressure high
93	O	Throttle Position Sensor or circuit

Code	Test condition	Probable cause
94	R	Secondary air system inoperative
95	O,C	Fuel pump circuit problem
95	R	Thermactor air diverter circuit
96	O,C	Fuel pump circuit
96	R	Thermactor air bypass circuit
98	R	Repeat test sequence
99	R	Repeat test sequence
99	R	System hasn't learned to control idle speed

1991 and later codes

Code	Test condition	Probable cause
111	o,r,c	System Pass
112	q,o,c	Air Charge Temp (ACT) Sensor circuit below minimum voltage/ 254 F
113	o,c	Air Charge Temp (ACT) Sensor circuit above maximum voltage/ -40 F
114	o,r	Air Charge Temp (ACT) out of self test range
116	o,r	Coolant Temp (ECT) out of self test range
117	o,c	Coolant Temp (ECT) Sensor circuit below minimum voltage/ 254 F
118	o,c	Coolant Temp (ECT) Sensor circuit above maximum voltage/ -40 F
121	o,r,c	Closed Throttle Voltage higher or lower than expected
122	o,c	Throttle Position (TP) Sensor circuit below minimum voltage
123	o,c	Throttle Position (TP) Sensor circuit above maximum voltage
124	c	Throttle Position (TP) Sensor voltage higher than expected
125	c	Throttle Position (TP) Sensor voltage lower than expected
126	o,r,c	BP Sensor higher or lower than expected
129	r	Insufficient Mass Air Flow (MAF) change during Dynamic Response Test
144	c	No Oxygen Sensor (HEGO) Switches detected
157	c	Mass Air Flow (MAF) Sensor circuit below minimum voltage
158	o,c	Mass Air Flow (MAF) Sensor circuit above maximum voltage
159	o,r	Mass Air Flow (MAF) Sensor out of self test range
167	r	Insufficient Throttle Position change during Dynamic Response Test
171	c	Fuel system at adaptive limits, Oxygen Sensor (HEGO) unable to switch
172	r,c	Lack of Oxygen Sensor (HEGO) Switches, indicates lean
173	r,c	Lack of Oxygen Sensor (HEGO) Switches, indicates rich
179	c	Fuel system at lean adaptive limit at part throttle, system rich
181	c	Fuel system at rich adaptive limit at part throttle, system lean
182	c	Fuel system at lean adaptive limit at idle, system rich
183	c	Fuel system at rich adaptive limit at idle, system lean
184	c	Mass Air Flow (MAF) higher than expected
185	c	Mass Air Flow (MAF) lower than expected
186	c	Injector pulse width higher than expected
187	c	Injector pulse width lower than expected
211	c	Profile Ignition Pickup (PIP) circuit fault
212	c	Ignition module circuit failure - SPOUT circuit grounded
213	r	SPOUT circuit
214	c	Cylinder Identification (CID) circuit failure
215	c	EEC Processor detected Coil 1 primary circuit failure
216	c	EEC Processor detected Coil 2 primary circuit failure
218	c	Loss of Ignition Diagnostic Monitor (IDM) signal-left side
222	c	Loss of Ignition Diagnostic Monitor (IDM) signal-right side
223	c	Loss of Dual Plug Inhibit (DPI) control
224	c	Erratic Ignition Diagnostic Monitor (IDM) input to processor
225	r	Knock not sensed during Dynamic Response Test
327	o,r,c	EVP circuit below minimum voltage
328	o,r,c	EGR "closed valve" voltage lower than expected
332	r,c	Insufficient EGR flow detected
334	o,r,c	EGR "closed valve" voltage higher than expected
337	o,r,c	EVP circuit above maximum voltage
341	o	Octane Adjust Service Pin in use
411	r	Cannot control RPM during KOER low rpm check
412	r	Cannot control rpm during KOER high rpm check
452	c	Insufficient input from Vehicle Speed Sensor (VSS)
511	o	EEC Processor Read Only Memory (ROM) test failure
512	c	EEC Processor Keep Alive Memory (KAM) test failure
519	o	Power Steering Pressure Switch (PSPS) circuit open
521	r	Power Steering Pressure Switch (PSPS) circuit did not change states
522	o	Vehicle not in PARK or NEUTRAL during KOEO
528	c	Clutch Switch Circuit failure
536	r,c	Brake On/Off (BOO) circuit failure / not actuated during KOER
538	r	Insufficient RPM change during KOER Dynamic Response Test
539	o	AC On/Defrost ON during KOEO

6

Code	Test condition	Probable cause
542	o,c	Fuel Pump secondary circuit failure
543	o,c	Fuel Pump secondary circuit failure
556	o,c	Fuel Pump Relay primary circuit failure
558	o	EGR Vacuum Regulator (EVR) circuit failure
564	o	Electro-Drive FAN(EDF) circuit failure
565	o	Canister Purge (CANP) circuit failure
566	o	3-4 Shift Solenoid circuit failure
629	o	Converter Clutch Control circuit failure
998	o,r	Hard Fault present

KEY: o = Key On Engine Off (KOEO) r = Engine Running (ER) c = Continuous Memory

Component replacement

Note: *Because of the Federally-mandated extended warranty which covers the ECA, the information sensors and the devices it controls, check with your dealer about warranty coverage. Once the warranty has expired, you may wish to perform some of the following component replacement procedures yourself after having the problem diagnosed by a dealer service department or repair shop.*

Air Charge Temperature (ACT) sensor

36   Detach the cable from the negative terminal of the battery.
37   Locate the ACT sensor in the intake manifold.
38   Unplug the electrical connector from the sensor.
39   Remove the sensor with a wrench.
40   Wrap the threads of the new sensor with thread-sealing tape to prevent air leaks.
41   Installation is the reverse of removal.

EGR Valve Position (EVP) sensor

42   Detach the cable from the negative terminal of the battery.
43   Locate the EVP sensor on top of the EGR valve.
44   Unplug the electrical connector from the sensor.
45   Remove the three mounting bolts and detach the sensor.
46   Installation is the reverse of removal.

Engine Coolant Temperature (ECT) sensor

47   Detach the cable from the negative terminal of the battery.
48   Locate the ECT sensor on the intake manifold, next to the thermostat housing.
49   Unplug the electrical connector from the sensor.
50   Remove the sensor with a wrench.
51   Wrap the threads of the new sensor with thread-sealing tape to prevent coolant leakage.
52   Installation is the reverse of removal.

Manifold Absolute Pressure (MAP) sensor

53   Detach the cable from the negative terminal of the battery.
54   Locate the MAP sensor on the firewall.
55   Unplug the electrical connector from the sensor.
56   Detach the vacuum line from the sensor.
57   Remove the mounting screws and detach the sensor.
58   Installation is the reverse of removal.

Exhaust Gas Oxygen (EGO) sensor

59   Detach the cable from the negative terminal of the battery.
60   Locate the EGO sensor on the exhaust manifold.
61   If it's more convenient, raise the vehicle and support it securely on jackstands.
62   Unplug the electrical connector from the sensor.
63   Remove the sensor with a wrench.
64   Coat the threads of the new sensor with anti-seize compound to prevent the threads from welding themselves to the manifold.
65   Installation is the reverse of removal.

Throttle Position (TP) sensor

66   Don't attempt to replace the TP sensor! Specialized calibration equipment is necessary to adjust the switch once it's installed, making adjustment beyond the scope of the home mechanic.

Canister Purge Solenoid

67   Detach the cable from the negative terminal of the battery.
68   Locate the canister purge solenoid in the engine compartment.
69   Unplug the electrical connector from the solenoid.
70   Label the vacuum hoses and ports, then detach the hoses.
71   Remove the solenoid.
72   Installation is the reverse of removal.

Vacuum control solenoids

73   Detach the cable from the negative terminal of the battery.
74   If necessary, remove the coolant reservoir (see Chapter 3).
75   Locate the vacuum control solenoids to be replaced (refer to the VECI label).
76   Unplug the electrical connector from the solenoid.
77   Label the vacuum hoses and ports, then detach the hoses.
78   Remove the solenoid/bracket screws and detach the solenoid.
79   Installation is the reverse of removal.

Mass air flow (MAF) sensor

80   The mass air flow sensor is mounted in the air intake duct.
81   Disconnect the negative battery cable from the battery.
82   Disconnect the MAF sensor electrical connector.
83   Detach the air cleaner duct and MAF sensor from the air cleaner and from the throttle body. Remove the mounting screws and take the MAF sensor out of the engine compartment.
84   Installation is the reverse of removal.

3   Microprocessor Control Unit (MCU) system

General description

1   The MCU system is used on 1980 2.3L engines, as well as 1981 through 1983 2.3L, 4.2L and 5.0L engines. The MCU, which controls the system, is located in the left rear corner of the engine compartment.
2   Early MCU systems use four input sources: An exhaust gas oxygen (EGO) sensor, a wide-open throttle (WOT) vacuum switch, an idle tracking switch and an engine rpm signal. The early system controls the feedback carburetor (and thus the air-fuel ratio) and the Thermactor (air injection) system.
3   Later MCU systems include a knock sensor, coolant temperature switches and additional vacuum switches. The later systems control canister purge, spark retard and a throttle kicker solenoid, in addition to the earlier system's functions.
4   The MCU system is similar to the EEC-IV system, but doesn't control ignition timing.

Information input sensors

5   The oxygen sensor works in the same way as the EEC-IV oxygen sensor. It's a galvanic generator, mounted in the exhaust system near the engine, which produces a voltage signal in response to the oxygen content of the exhaust gas. It transmits the signal to the MCU, which uses it to regulate the feedback solenoid in the carburetor. A signal of approximately 0.4 volt or less indicates an excessive amount of oxygen (lean fuel mixture). A signal of approximately 0.6 volt or more indicates an insufficient amount of oxy-

gen (rich fuel mixture).

6 The wide open throttle vacuum switch is actuated by manifold vacuum. When the engine is idling at normal operating temperature, the coolant temperature sensing vacuum valve routes vacuum to the switch to keep it open. When the throttle opens past a certain point, the switch closes and sends an electrical signal to the MCU.

7 The idle tracking switch is mounted on the carburetor. It indicates prolonged idling or deceleration to the MCU.

8 The tach input signal is sent from the ignition coil's primary circuit to the MCU. It is used by the MCU to prevent over-correction or excessively sudden changes when it adjusts the air-fuel ratio.

9 Coolant temperature switches indicate engine temperature to the MCU.

10 Vacuum switches indicate throttle position to the MCU, as well as preventing the Thermactor system from causing backfires.

Output devices

11 The canister purge solenoid, which is similar to the EEC-IV solenoid, lets manifold vacuum purge fuel vapor from the evaporative emission canister.

12 The Thermactor air solenoids direct air flow from the Thermactor pump upstream, downstream or into the atmosphere.

13 The vacuum regulator solenoid regulates vacuum to the air-fuel mixture control diaphragm on the Model 6500 feedback carburetor used with early 2.3L four-cylinder engines.

14 The fuel control solenoid is mounted directly on the YFA carburetor used on later 2.3L engines. It uses an electrical signal, rather than vacuum, to control fuel mixture.

15 The feedback carburetor actuator is mounted on the Model 7200 VV (variable venturi) carburetor used with V8 engines. It controls the air bleed jet in the carburetor to regulate fuel mixture.

16 The throttle kicker solenoid and actuator are used to open the throttle slightly under specified conditions.

Checking

17 As with the EEC-IV system, MCU system diagnosis is beyond the scope of the home mechanic. If engine performance deteriorates, perform the basic electrical and mechanical checks: Compression, vacuum line condition and connections, ignition system condition and carburetor idle adjustment. If these checks don't find the cause, have the MCU system tested by a dealer service department or other qualified specialist.

Component replacement

18 Exhaust gas oxygen sensors, coolant temperature sensors and the canister purge solenoid are replaced in the same manner as EEC-IV system components (see Section 2).

Vacuum regulator solenoid

19 Disconnect the negative battery cable from the battery.

20 Disconnect the solenoid electrical connector.

21 Label and disconnect the solenoid vacuum lines. Check the lines to make sure they are in good condition; if not, replace them.

22 Detach the solenoid from the engine compartment wall and take it out.

23 Installation is the reverse of removal.

Fuel control solenoid

24 Disconnect the negative battery cable from the battery.

25 Disconnect the solenoid electrical connector.

26 Detach the solenoid from the carburetor.

27 Installation is the reverse of removal.

Feedback actuator (V8 engines)

28 This is part of the complicated 7200VV carburetor. Removal and installation are beyond the scope of the home mechanic.

Throttle kicker solenoid

29 Throttle kicker solenoids are mounted on the carburetor in a position where they can contact the throttle linkage.

30 Disconnect the negative battery cable from the battery.

31 If necessary, detach the solenoid bracket from the carburetor.

32 Loosen the solenoid locknut. Unscrew the solenoid, making sure to write down the number of turns required.

33 Install the solenoid, turning it the same number of turns required for removal.

34 The remainder of installation is the reverse of removal.

---

4 Exhaust Gas Recirculation (EGR) system

General description

1 The EGR system is designed to reintroduce small amounts of exhaust gas into the combustion cycle, thus reducing the generation of oxides of nitrogen (NOx) emissions. The amount of exhaust gas reintroduced and the timing of the cycle is controlled by various factors such as engine speed, altitude, manifold vacuum, exhaust system backpressure, coolant temperature and throttle angle. All EGR valves are vacuum actuated (the vacuum diagram for your particular vehicle is shown on the Vehicle Emissions Control Information [VECI] label in the engine compartment). Three types of EGR valves are used on these vehicles: the ported valve, the integral backpressure valve and the electronic type.

Ported valve (four-cylinder engine)

2 The ported EGR valve is operated by a vacuum signal from the EGR port, which actuates the valve diaphragm. As the vacuum increases sufficiently to overcome the spring, the valve is opened, allowing EGR flow. The amount of flow is contingent upon the tapered pintle or the poppet position, which is affected by the vacuum signal.

Integral backpressure transducer valve (1983 US and 1983 thru 1986 Canadian V6 engines)

3 The integral backpressure transducer EGR valve combines backpressure and EGR ported vacuum into one unit. The valve won't operate on vacuum alone - it requires both inputs to operate. There are two basic types of backpressure valves: poppet and tapered pintle.

Electronic valve

4 The electronic EGR valve used in EEC-IV systems controls EGR flow with an EGR valve position (EVP) sensor attached to the top of the valve. The valve is operated by a vacuum signal from the dual EGR solenoid valves or the electronic vacuum regulator which actuates the valve diaphragm. As supply vacuum overcomes the spring load, the diaphragm is actuated, lifting the pintle off the seat and allowing exhaust gas to recirculate. The amount of flow is proportional to the pintle position. The EVP sensor sends an electrical signal indicating its position to the ECA.

Checking

Ported valve

5 Make sure that all vacuum lines are properly routed (see your VECI label in the engine compartment), secure and in good condition (not cracked, kinked or broken off).

6 When the engine is cold, there should be no vacuum to operate the EGR valve. If there is vacuum, check the ported vacuum switch (PVS) or temperature vacuum switch (TVS) and replace them as required.

7 There should be no vacuum to the valve at curb idle (engine warm).

8 There should be vacuum to the valve at 3000 rpm. If there is no vacuum, check the TVS and PVS and replace them as required.

9 With the engine at idle, apply 8 in-Hg vacuum to the valve. The valve stem should move, opening the valve, and the engine should stall or run roughly. If the valve stem moves but the engine doesn't respond, remove and clean the inlet and outlet ports with a wire brush. **Caution:** *Do not sandblast or clean the valve with gasoline or damage will result!*

10 With the engine at idle, apply 4 in-Hg vacuum to the valve, using a hand vacuum pump. Vacuum shouldn't drop more than 1 in-Hg in 30 seconds. If it does, replace the valve.

11 When the valve is suspected of leaking (indicated by a rough idle or stalling) perform the following simple check:

a) *Insert a blocking gasket (no flow holes) between the valve and base and reinstall the valve.*

b) *If the engine idle improves, replace the valve and remove the blocking gasket. If the idle doesn't improve, take the vehicle to a dealer service department.*

6

Integral backpressure transducer valve

12   Make sure that all vacuum lines are properly routed (see your VECI label in the engine compartment), all connections are secure and no vacuum hoses are cracked, crimped or broken.

13   Detach the vacuum line to the EGR valve and plug it. Connect a vacuum pump to the EGR valve. Start the engine and let it idle. Apply six in-Hg vacuum to the valve. It should bleed off and the valve should not operate. If the vacuum holds and the valve opens and stays open, i.e. the valve does not bleed off the vacuum, replace the valve.

14   There should be no vacuum to the valve at idle under any conditions. If there is, check the hose routing.

15   There should be no vacuum to the valve nor should the valve operate when the engine is cold. If there is vacuum at the valve when the engine is cold, check the ported vacuum switch (PVS) or the thermal vacuum switch (TVS) and replace as required. (The PVS is a temperature actuated switch that changes vacuum connections when the coolant temperature changes; the TVS, which is used with some systems instead of the PVS, controls vacuum to the EGR valve by responding to the temperature of the inlet air heated by the exhaust manifold. Most PVS switches are mounted somewhere on the intake manifold; most TVS switches are located in the air cleaner housing. Refer to your VECI label to determine which kind of switch you have and where it is located.)

16   There should be vacuum to the valve at 3000 rpm with a normally warm engine. If there isn't, check back through the vacuum line from the EGR to the vacuum source; for example, the TVS and/or the PVS may not be opening. Check and replace as required.

17   If a valve is suspected of sticking, remove it from the engine and cycle the valve by pressing carefully with your fingers against the lower transducer plate. If the valve sticks open when you release your fingers, replace it.

Electronic valve

Note: *Aside from the following check and maintenance steps, the electronic EGR valve cannot be diagnosed or serviced by the home mechanic. Additional checks must be done by a dealer service department.*

18   Make sure the vacuum hoses are in good condition and hooked up correctly.

19   Clean the inlet and outlet ports with a wire brush or scraper. Do not sandblast the valve or clean it with gasoline or solvents as they will damage the valve.

20   To perform a leakage test, connect a vacuum pump to the EGR valve.

21   Apply 5-to-6 in-Hg of vacuum to the valve.

22   Trap the vacuum - it should not drop more than 1 in-Hg in 30 seconds.

23   If the specified conditions are not met, the EGR valve, O-ring or EVP must be replaced.

EGR valve replacement

24   Detach the cable from negative terminal of the battery.

25   On engines with an electronic valve, unplug the electrical connector from the EGR valve position sensor.

26   If your vehicle is powered by a four-cylinder engine, unscrew the threaded fitting that attaches the EGR pipe to the EGR valve.

27   Remove the EGR valve mounting nuts and detach the valve.

28   Remove the old gasket. Be sure to thoroughly clean the gasket surfaces of the intake manifold (and valve, if the same valve will be reinstalled).

29   If you're replacing an electronic type EGR valve but not the position sensor, remove the sensor from the old valve (see Section 2) and install it on the new valve.

30   Installation is the reverse of removal.

---

5   Managed air thermactor system

General description

1   The thermactor (air injection) exhaust emission control system reduces carbon monoxide and hydrocarbon content in the exhaust gases by injecting fresh air into the hot exhaust gases leaving the exhaust ports. When fresh air is mixed with hot exhaust gases, oxidation is increased, reducing the concentration of hydrocarbons and carbon monoxide and converting them into harmless carbon dioxide and water.

2   All of these models utilize either a conventional thermactor system (1983 through 1986 Canadian V6 engine) or a "managed air" thermactor system (all US models and other Canadian models). The two systems are basically the same. The managed air thermactor system diverts thermactor air either upstream to the exhaust manifold check valve or downstream to the rear section check valve and dual bed catalyst. An extended idle air bypass system in carburetor equipped vehicles also vents thermactor air to the atmosphere during extended idling.

3   On managed air systems, an air control valve directs the air upstream or downstream. An air bypass valve is used to dump air to the atmosphere. In some applications, the two valves are combined into a single air bypass/control valve.

Checking

Air supply pump

4   Check and adjust the drivebelt tension (see Chapter 1).

5   Disconnect the air supply hose at the air bypass valve inlet.

6   The pump is operating satisfactorily if air flow is felt at the pump outlet with the engine running at idle, increasing as the engine speed is increased.

7   If the air pump doesn't pass the above tests, replace it with a new or rebuilt unit.

Air bypass valve

8   With the engine running at idle, disconnect the hose from the valve outlet.

9   Remove the vacuum hose from the port and remove or bypass any restrictors or delay valves in the vacuum hose.

10   Verify that vacuum is present in the vacuum hose by putting your finger over the end.

11   Reconnect the vacuum hose to the port.

12   With the engine running at 1500 rpm, the air pump supply air should be felt or heard at the air bypass valve outlet.

13   With the engine running at 1500 rpm, disconnect the vacuum hose. Air at the valve outlet should be decreased or shut off and air pump supply air should be felt or heard at the silencer ports.

14   Reconnect all hoses.

15   If the normally closed air bypass valve doesn't successfully pass the above tests, check the air pump (refer to Steps 5 through 7).

16   If the air pump is operating satisfactorily, replace the air bypass valve with a new one.

Check valve

17   Disconnect the hoses from both ends of the check valve, carefully noting the installed position of the valve and the hoses.

18   Blow through both ends of the check valve, verifying that air flows in one direction only.

19   If air flows in both directions or not at all, replace the check valve with a new one.

20   When reconnecting the valve, make sure it is installed in the proper direction.

Thermactor system noise test

21   The thermactor system is not completely noiseless. Under normal conditions, noise rises in pitch as the engine speed increases. To determine if noise is the fault of the air injection system, detach the drivebelt (after verifying that the belt tension is correct) and operate the engine. If the noise disappears, proceed with the following diagnosis. **Caution:** *The pump must accumulate 500 miles (vehicle miles) before the following check is valid.*

22   If the belt noise is excessive:

a)   *Check for a loose belt and tighten as necessary (refer to Chapter 1).*

b)   *Check for a seized pump and replace it if necessary.*

c)   *Check for a loose pulley. Tighten the mounting bolts as required.*

d)   *Check for loose, broken or missing mounting brackets or bolts. Tighten or replace as necessary.*

23   If there is excessive mechanical noise:

a)   *Check for an overtightened mounting bolt.*

b)   *Check for an overtightened drivebelt (refer to Chapter 1).*

c)   *Check for excessive flash on the air pump adjusting arm boss and remove as necessary.*

d)   *Check for a distorted adjusting arm and, if necessary, replace the arm.*

5.26 To replace the combination air bypass/air control valve (3.8L V6 unit shown, others similar), label, then detach, the following:

1 *Vacuum line to control solenoid*
2 *Air pump-to-combination valve hose*
3 *Vacuum line to control solenoid*
4 *Combination valve-to-right exhaust manifold hose*
5 *Combination valve-to-left exhaust manifold hose*

5.27 To remove the air pump (unit for a 3.8L V6 engine shown, others similar) loosen the hose clamp (arrow) and detach the hose to the combination valve, then remove both mounting bolts (arrows)

24 If there is excessive thermactor system noise (whirring or hissing sounds):
a) *Check for a leak in the hoses (use a soap and water solution to find the leaks) and replace the hose(s) as necessary.*
b) *Check for a loose, pinched or kinked hose and reassemble, straighten or replace the hose and/or clamps as required.*
c) *Check for a hose touching other engine parts and adjust or reroute the hose to prevent further contact.*
d) *Check for an inoperative bypass valve (refer to Step 8) and replace if necessary.*
e) *Check for an inoperative check valve (refer to Step 17) and replace if necessary.*
f) *Check for loose pump or pulley mounting fasteners and tighten as necessary.*
g) *Check for a restricted or bent pump outlet fitting. Inspect the fitting and remove any casting flash blocking the air passageway. Replace bent fittings.*
h) *Check for air dumping through the bypass valve (only at idle). On many vehicles, the thermactor system has been designed to dump air at idle to prevent overheating the catalytic converter. This condition is normal. Determine that the noise persists at higher speeds before proceeding.*
i) *Check for air dumping through the bypass valve (the decel and idle dump). On many vehicles, the thermactor air is dumped into the air cleaner or the remote silencer. Make sure that the hoses are connected properly and not cracked.*

25 If there is excessive pump noise, make sure the pump has had sufficient break-in time (at least 500 miles). Check for a worn or damaged pump and replace as necessary.

Component replacement

Refer to illustrations 5.26 and 5.27

26 To replace the air bypass valve, air supply control valve, check valve, combination air bypass/air control valve **(see illustration)** or the silencer, clearly label, then disconnect, the hoses leading to them, replace the faulty component and reattach the hoses to the proper ports. Make sure the hoses are in good condition. If not, replace them with new ones.

27 To replace the air supply pump, first loosen the engine drivebelt (see Chapter 1), then remove the pump mounting bolts **(see illustration)** from the mounting bracket. Label all wires and hoses as they're removed to facilitate installation of the new unit.

28 If you're replacing either of the check valves on a Pulse Air System (Thermactor II), be sure to use a back-up wrench.

29 After the new pump is installed, adjust the drivebelts to the specified tension (see Chapter 1).

---

6 Fuel evaporative emissions control system

General description

1 This system is designed to prevent hydrocarbons from being released into the atmosphere by trapping and storing fuel vapor from the fuel tank, the carburetor or the fuel injection system.

2 The serviceable parts of the system include a charcoal filled canister and the connecting lines between the fuel tank, fuel tank filler cap and the carburetor or fuel injection system.

3 Vapor trapped in the gas tank is vented through a valve in the top of the tank. From the valve, the vapor is routed through a single line to a carbon canister located on the right lower front corner of the engine compartment, where it's stored until the next time the engine is started.

System checking

4 There are no moving parts and nothing to wear in the canister. Check for loose, missing, cracked or broken fittings and check for deteriorated o damaged hoses attached to the canister. Inspect the canister for cracks and other damage. If the canister is damaged, replace it (see below).

5 Check for fuel smells around the vehicle. Make sure the gas cap is in good condition and properly installed.

Component replacement

Charcoal canister

6 Locate the canister in the engine compartment.

7 Reach up above the canister, remove the single mounting bolt and remove the canister.

8 Clearly label the hoses and detach them from the canister.

9 Installation is the reverse of removal.

All other components

10 Referring to the VECI label of your vehicle, locate the component you intend to replace.

11 Label the hoses, then detach them and remove the component.

12 Installation is the reverse of removal.

---

7 Positive Crankcase Ventilation (PCV) system

General description

1 The Positive Crankcase Ventilation

6

8.4 A typical temperature vacuum switch (TVS) installed in the air cleaner housing cover

8.5 A typical cold weather modulator (CWM) installation in the air cleaner housing assembly

(PCV) system cycles crankcase vapors back through the engine where they are burned. The valve regulates the amount of ventilating air and blow-by gas to the intake manifold and prevents backfire from traveling into the crankcase.

2   The PCV system consists of a replaceable PCV valve, a crankcase ventilation filter and the connecting hoses.

3   The air source for the crankcase ventilation system is in the air cleaner. Air passes through the PCV filter (in the rocker arm cover or the oil filler cap) and through a hose connected to the air cleaner housing. On vehicles with a PCV filter integrated into the oil filler cap, the cap is sealed at the opening to prevent the entrance of outside air. From the oil filler cap, or separate PCV filter in the rocker arm cover, the air flows into the rocker arm chamber and the crankcase, from which it circulates up into another section of the rocker arm chamber and finally enters a spring loaded regulator valve (PCV valve) that controls the amount of flow as operating conditions vary. The vapors are routed to the intake manifold through the crankcase vent hose tube and fittings. This process goes on continuously while the engine is running.

Checking

4   Checking procedures for the PCV system components are included in Chapter 1.

Component replacement

5   Component replacement involves simply installing a new valve or hose in place of the one removed during the checking procedure.

8   Inlet air temperature control system

General description

Refer to illustrations 8.4 and 8.5

1   The inlet air temperature control system

(carburetor and CFI equipped vehicles) provides heated intake air during warm-up, then maintains the inlet air temperature within a 70-degrees F to 105-degrees F operating range by mixing warm and cool air. This allows leaner fuel/air mixture settings for the carburetor or CFI system, which reduces emissions and improves driveability.

2   Two fresh air inlets - one warm and one cold - are used. The balance between the two is controlled by intake manifold vacuum, a temperature vacuum switch and a time delay valve. A vacuum motor, which operates a heat duct valve in the air cleaner, is controlled by the vacuum switch.

3   When the underhood temperature is cold, warm air radiating off the exhaust manifold is routed by a shroud which fits over the manifold up through a hot air inlet tube and into the air cleaner. This provides warm air for the carburetor or CFI, resulting in better driveability and faster warm-up. As the underhood temperature rises, a heat duct valve is gradually closed by a vacuum motor and the air cleaner draws air through a cold air duct instead. The result is a consistent intake air temperature.

4   A temperature vacuum switch **(see illustration)** mounted on the air cleaner housing monitors the temperature of the inlet air heated by the exhaust manifold. A bimetal disc in the temperature vacuum switch orient itself in one of two positions, depending on the temperature. One position allows vacuum through a hose to the motor; the other position blocks vacuum.

5   The vacuum motor itself is regulated by a cold weather modulator (CWM), mounted in the side of the air cleaner housing assembly, between the temperature vacuum switch and the motor **(see illustration)**, which provides the motor with a range of graduated positions between fully open and fully closed.

Checking

Note: *Make sure that the engine is cold before beginning this test.*

6   Always check the vacuum source and the integrity of all vacuum hoses between the source and the vacuum motor before beginning the following test. Do not proceed until they're okay.

7   Apply the parking brake and block the wheels.

8   Detach, but do not remove, the air cleaner housing and element (see Chapter 4).

9   Turn the air cleaner housing upside down so the vacuum motor door is visible. The door should be open. If it isn't, it may be binding or sticking. Make sure that it's not rusted in an open or closed position by attempting to move it by hand. If it's rusted, it can usually be freed by cleaning and oiling the hinge. If it fails to work properly after servicing, replace it.

10   If the vacuum motor door is okay but the motor still fails to operate correctly, check carefully for a leak in the hose leading to it. Check the vacuum source to and from the bimetal sensor and the time delay valve as well. If no leak is found, replace the vacuum motor (see Step 26).

11   Start the engine. If the duct door has moved or moves to the "heat on" (closed to fresh air) position, go to Step 15.

12   If the door stays in the "heat off" (closed to warm air) position, place a finger over the bimetal sensor bleed. The duct door must move rapidly t the "heat on" position. If the door doesn't move to the "heat on" position, stop the engine and replace the vacuum motor (see Step 26). Repeat this Step with the new vacuum motor.

13   With the engine off, allow the bimetal sensor and the cold weather modulator to cool completely.

14   Restart the engine. The duct door should move to the "heat on" position. If the door doesn't move or moves only partially, replace the TVS (see Step 18).

15   Start and run the engine briefly (less than 15 seconds). The duct door should move to the "heat on" position.

16   Shut off the engine and watch the duct door. It should stay in the "heat on" position

8.20 To remove the TVS, label and detach the hoses, then pry off the retaining clip with a small screwdriver

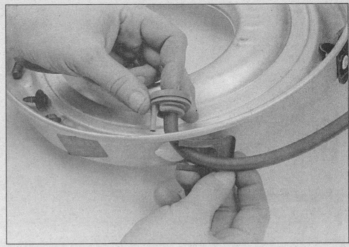

8.24 To remove the CWM, label and detach the hoses, then slide off the retaining clip and pull the CWM out of the mounting hole

for at least two minutes.

17 If it doesn't stay in the "heat on" position for at least two minutes, replace the CWM (see Step 23).

Component replacement

Refer to illustrations 8.20, 8.24 and 8.28

Temperature vacuum switch (TVS)

18 Clearly label, then detach both vacuum hoses from the TVS (one is coming from the vacuum source at the manifold and the other is going to the vacuum motor underneath the air cleaner housing).

19 Remove the air cleaner housing cover assembly (see Chapter 4).

20 Pry the TVS retaining clip off with a screwdriver **(see illustration)**.

21 Remove the TVS.

22 Installation is the reverse of removal.

Cold weather modulator (CWM)

23 Locate the CWM, then detach both vacuum hoses and remove the CWM.

24 Slide the CWM retaining clip off **(see illustration)** and remove the CWM.

25 Installation is the reverse of removal.

Vacuum motor

26 Remove the air cleaner housing assembly (see Chapter 4) and place it on a workbench.

27 Detach the vacuum hose from the motor.

28 Drill out the vacuum motor retaining strap rivet **(see illustration)**.

29 Remove the motor.

30 Installation is the reverse of removal. Use a sheet metal screw of the appropriate size to replace the rivet.

---

9 Catalytic converter

Note: *Because of a Federally mandated extended warranty which covers emissions-related components such as the catalytic*

converter, check with a dealer service department before replacing the converter at your own expense.

General description

1 The catalytic converter is an emission control device added to the exhaust system to reduce pollutants from the exhaust gas stream. There are two types of converters. The conventional oxidation catalyst reduces the levels of hydrocarbon (HC) and carbon monoxide (CO). The three-way catalyst lowers the levels of oxides of nitrogen (NOx) as well as hydrocarbons (HC) and carbon monoxide (CO).

Checking

2 The test equipment for a catalytic converter is expensive and highly sophisticated. If you suspect that the converter on your vehicle is malfunctioning, take it to a dealer or authorized emissions inspection facility for diagnosis and repair.

3 Whenever the vehicle is raised for servicing of underbody components, check the converter for leaks, corrosion, dents and other damage. Check the welds/flange bolts that attach the front and rear ends of the converter to the exhaust system. If damage is discov-

ered, the converter should be replaced.

4 Although catalytic converters don't break too often, they do become plugged. The easiest way to check for a restricted converter is to use a vacuum gauge to diagnose the effect of a blocked exhaust on intake vacuum.

a) *Open the throttle until the engine speed is about 2000 RPM.*

b) *Release the throttle quickly.*

c) *If there is no restriction, the gauge will quickly drop to not more than 2 in Hg or more above its normal reading.*

d) *If the gauge does not show 5 in Hg or more above its normal reading, or seems to momentarily hover around its highest reading for a moment before it returns, the exhaust system, or the converter, is plugged (or an exhaust pipe is bent or dented, or the core inside the muffler has shifted).*

Component replacement

5 Because the converter is welded to the exhaust system, converter replacement requires removal of the exhaust pipe assembly (see Chapter 4). Take the vehicle, or the exhaust pipe system, to a dealer service department or a muffler shop.

6

8.28 To remove the vacuum motor, label and detach the hoses, then drill out the rivet (arrow) and slide out the retaining strap

Notes

Chapter 7 Part A
Manual transmission

Contents

Specifications

Lubricant type... Soo Chapter 1

Torque specifications Ft-lbs
Shift lever attaching bolts
All except T50D transmission .... 17 to 25
T50D transmission... 23 to 32
Transmission-to-clutch housing or engine bolts 48

1 General information

All vehicles oovorod in this manual come equipped with a 4-speed or 5-speed manual transmission or an automatic transmission. All information on the manual transmission is included in this Part of Chapter 7. Information for the automatic transmission can be found in Part B of this Chapter.

Several different manual transmissions have been used in these models. Early models were equipped with SROD, RAD or ET 4-speed transmissions. The 1981 through 1983 five-speed transmission is similar to earlier four-speed designs, but incorporates an overdrive fifth gear. The T50D transmission, used on 1984 and later models, is an all-new design.

Due to the complexity, unavailability of replacement parts and the special tools necessary, internal transmission repair procedures are not recommended for the home mechanic. The information contained within this manual will be limited to general information and removal and installation of the transmission assembly.

Depending on the expense involved in having a faulty transmission overhauled, it may be an advantage to consider replacing the unit with either a new or rebuilt one. Your local dealer or transmission shop should be able to supply you with information concerning cost, availability and exchange policy.

Regardless of how you decide to remedy a transmission problem, you can still save considerable expense by removing and installing the unit yourself.

2 Shift lever - removal and installation

All models except T50D

1   Place the transmission in Neutral.
2   Remove the floor trim and carpeting as necessary to gain access to the shift lever boot retaining screws. Remove the screws and detach the shift lever boot from the floor.
3   Working through the shift lever boot hole, unbolt the shift lever from the transmission.
4   Lift the shift lever out of the transmission.
5   Installation is the reverse of the removal steps.

T50D

6   Remove the center console.
7   Remove the four shift boot-to-floor pan bolts.
8   Remove the two mounting bolts and detach the lever assembly from the transmission.
9   To install, place the shift lever in position and install the bolts. The bolts must be installed from the left side of the shifter only. Tighten the bolts securely.
10   Install the shift boot and console.

3 Manual transmission - removal and installation

Removal

1   Disconnect the negative cable at the battery. Place the cable out of the way so it cannot accidentally come in contact with the negative terminal of the battery, as this would once again allow power into the electrical system of the vehicle.
2   From inside the vehicle, remove the shift lever (Section 2).
3   Raise the vehicle and support it securely on jackstands.
4   Disconnect the speedometer cable and electrical connections from the transmission.
5   Remove the driveshaft (Chapter 8). Use a plastic bag to cover the end of the transmission to prevent fluid loss and contamination.
6   Remove the exhaust system components as necessary for clearance (Chapter 4).
7   Support the engine. This can be done from above by using an engine hoist, or by placing a jack (with a block of wood as an insulator) under the engine oil pan. The engine should remain supported at all times while the transmission is out of the vehicle.

8   Support the transmission with a jack - preferably a special jack made for this purpose. Safety chains will help steady the transmission on the jack.

9   Remove the rear transmission support-to-crossmember nuts and bolts.

10   Remove the nuts from the crossmember bolts. Raise the transmission slightly and remove the crossmember.

11   All except ET transmissions - remove the bolts securing the transmission to the clutch housing.

12   ET transmission - remove the bolts securing the clutch housing to the engine.

13   Make a final check that all wires and hoses have been disconnected from the transmission and then move the transmission and jack toward the rear of the vehicle until the transmission input shaft is clear of the clutch housing or engine. Keep the transmission level as this is done.

14   Once the input shaft is clear, lower the transmission and remove it from under the vehicle. **Caution:** *Do not depress the clutch pedal while the transmission is removed from the vehicle.*

15   The clutch components can be inspected while the transmission is removed. On all except ET transmissions, it will be necessary to remove the clutch housing from the engine (Chapter 8). In most cases, new clutch components should be installed as a matter of course if the transmission is removed.

Installation

16   If removed, install the clutch components (Chapter 8).

17   If removed, attach the clutch housing to the engine and tighten the bolts to the specified torque (Chapter 8).

18   With the transmission secured to the jack as on removal, raise the transmission into position behind the clutch housing and then carefully slide it forward, engaging the input shaft with the clutch splines. Do not use excessive force to install the transmission - if the input shaft does not slide into place, readjust the angle of the transmission so it is level and/or turn the input shaft so the splines engage properly with the clutch.

19   Install the transmission-to-clutch housing bolts. Tighten the bolts to the specified torque.

20   Install the crossmember and transmission support. Tighten all nuts and bolts securely.

21   Remove the jacks supporting the transmission and the engine.

22   Install the various items removed previously, referring to Chapter 8 for the installation of the driveshaft and Chapter 4 for information regarding the exhaust system components.

23   Make a final check that all wires, hoses and the speedometer cable have been connected and that the transmission has been filled with lubricant to the proper level (Chapter 1). Lower the vehicle.

24   From inside the vehicle connect the shift lever (see Section 2).

25   Connect the negative battery cable. Road test the vehicle for proper operation and check for leakage.

---

4   Manual transmission overhaul - general information

Overhauling a manual transmission is a difficult job for the do-it-yourselfer. It involves the disassembly and reassembly of many small parts. Numerous clearances must be precisely measured and, if necessary, changed with select fit spacers and snap-rings. As a result, if transmission problems arise, it can be removed and installed by a competent do-it-yourselfer, but overhaul should be left to a transmission repair shop. Rebuilt transmissions may be available - check with your dealer parts department and auto parts stores. At any rate, the time and money involved in an overhaul is almost sure to exceed the cost of a rebuilt unit.

Nevertheless, it's not impossible for an inexperienced mechanic to rebuild a transmission if the special tools are available and the job is done in a deliberate step-by-step manner so nothing is overlooked.

The tools necessary for an overhaul include internal and external snap-ring pliers, a bearing puller, a slide hammer, a set of pin punches, a dial indicator and possibly a hydraulic press. In addition, a large, sturdy workbench and a vise or transmission stand will be required.

During disassembly of the transmission, make careful notes of how each piece comes off, where it fits in relation to other pieces and what holds it in place.

Before taking the transmission apart for repair, it will help if you have some idea what area of the transmission is malfunctioning. Certain problems can be closely tied to specific areas in the transmission, which can make component examination and replacement easier. Refer to the Troubleshooting section at the front of this manual for information regarding possible sources of trouble.

Chapter 7 Part B
Automatic transmission

Contents

Specifications

Transmission types	C3, C4, C5, AOD and A4LD
Fluid type and capacity	See Chapter 1

Torque specifications	**Ft-lbs** (unless otherwise indicated)
Driveplate-to-torque converter nuts or bolts	30 to 35
Transmission-to-engine bolts	
C3, C5 and A4LD	28 to 38
C4	
Four and inline six-cylinder engines	28 to 38
V8 engines	40 to 50
AOD	40 to 50
Neutral start switch	
C3	
1979 through 1981	12 to 15
1982 on	7 to 10
C4	6.2 to 8.4
C5	55 to 75 in-lbs
A4LD	84 to 120 in-lbs
AOD	8 to 11

1 General information

All vehicles covered in this manual come equipped with either a 4-speed or 5-speed manual transmission or an automatic transmission. All information on the automatic transmission is included in this Part of Chapter 7. Information for the manual transmission can be found in Part A of this Chapter.

Due to the complexity of the automatic transmissions covered in this manual and to the specialized equipment necessary to perform most service operations, this Chapter addresses only those procedures concerning general diagnosis, routine maintenance, adjustment and removal and installation.

If the transmission requires major repair work, it should be left to a dealer service department or an automotive or transmission repair shop. You can, however, remove and install the transmission yourself and save the expense, even if the repair work is done by a transmission specialist.

Models covered in this manual may be equipped with any one of five automatic transmissions. They are the C3, C4, C5, AOD and A4LD, which are of the same fundamental design but with varying power handling capabilities. The A4LD and AOD use electronic controls integrated into the on-board EEC-IV system. These controls operate a piston/plate clutch in the torque converter that eliminates converter slip when applied.

On some models the manufacturer specifies a different grade transmission fluid than other vehicle manufacturers, and this must be used when refilling or adding fluid. The fluid specification for your vehicle can be found embossed on the transmission fluid dipstick.

2 Diagnosis - general

Note: *Automatic transmission malfunctions may be caused by five general conditions: poor engine performance, improper adjustments, hydraulic malfunctions, mechanical malfunctions or malfunctions in the computer or its signal network. Diagnosis of these problems should always begin with a check of the easily repaired items: fluid level and condition (Chapter 1), shift linkage adjustment and throttle linkage adjustment. Next, perform a road test to determine if the problem has been corrected or if more diagnosis is necessary. If the problem persists after the preliminary tests and corrections are completed, additional diagnosis should be done by a dealer service department or transmission repair shop.*

Preliminary checks

1   Drive the vehicle to warm the transmission to normal operating temperature.
2   Check the fluid level as described in Chapter 1:

 a) If the fluid level is unusually low, add enough fluid to bring the level within the designated area of the dipstick, then check for external leaks (see below).
 b) If the fluid level is abnormally high; drain off the excess, then check the drained fluid for contamination by coolant. The presence of engine coolant in the automatic transmission fluid indicates that a failure has occurred in the internal radiator walls that separate the coolant from the transmission fluid (see Chapter 3).
 c) If the fluid is foaming, drain it and refill the transmission, then check for coolant in the fluid or a high fluid level.

3   Check the engine idle speed. **Note:** If the engine is malfunctioning, do not proceed with the preliminary checks until it has been repaired and runs normally.
4   Check the throttle valve cable (AOD transmission) for freedom of movement. Adjust it if necessary (Section 3). **Note:** The throttle cable may function properly when the engine is shut off and cold, but it may malfunction once the engine is hot. Check it cold and at normal engine operating temperature.
5   Inspect the shift control linkage (Section 5). Make sure that it's properly adjusted and that the linkage operates smoothly.

Fluid leak diagnosis

6   Most fluid leaks are easy to locate visually. Repair usually consists of replacing a seal or gasket. If a leak is difficult to find, the following procedure may help.
7   Identify the fluid. Make sure it's transmission fluid and not engine oil or brake fluid.
8   Try to pinpoint the source of the leak. Drive the vehicle several miles, then park it over a large sheet of cardboard. After a minute or two, you should be able to locate the leak by determining the source of the fluid dripping onto the cardboard.
9   Make a careful visual inspection of the suspected component and the area immediately around it. Pay particular attention to gasket mating surfaces. A mirror is often helpful for finding leaks in areas that are hard to see.
10   If the leak still cannot be found, clean the suspected area thoroughly with a degreaser or solvent, then dry it.
11   Drive the vehicle for several miles at normal operating temperature and varying speeds. After driving the vehicle, visually inspect the suspected component again.
12   Once the leak has been located, the cause must be determined before it can be properly repaired. If a gasket is replaced but the sealing flange is bent, the new gasket will not stop the leak. The bent flange must be straightened.
13   Before attempting to repair a leak, check to make sure that the following conditions are corrected or they may cause

another leak. **Note:** Some of the following conditions (a leaking torque converter, for instance) cannot be fixed without highly specialized tools and expertise. Such problems must be referred to a transmission shop or a dealer service department.

Gasket leaks

14   Check the pan periodically. Make sure the bolts are tight, no bolts are missing, the gasket is in good condition and the pan is flat (dents in the pan may indicate damage to the valve body inside).
15   If the pan gasket is leaking, the fluid level or the fluid pressure may be too high, the vent may be plugged, the pan bolts may be too tight, the pan sealing flange may be warped, the sealing surface of the transmission housing may be damaged, the gasket may be damaged or the transmission casting may be cracked or porous. If sealant instead of gasket material has been used to form a seal between the pan and the transmission housing, it may be the wrong sealant.

Seal leaks

16   If a transmission seal is leaking, the fluid level or pressure may be too high, the vent may be plugged, the seal bore may be damaged, the seal itself may be damaged or improperly installed, the surface of the shaft protruding through the seal may be damaged or a loose bearing may be causing excessive shaft movement.
17   Make sure the dipstick tube seal is in good condition and the tube is properly seated. Periodically check the area around the speedometer gear or sensor for leakage. If transmission fluid is evident, check the O-ring for damage.

Case leaks

18   If the case itself appears to be leaking, the casting is porous and will have to be repaired or replaced.
19   Make sure the oil cooler hose fittings are tight and in good condition.

Fluid comes out vent pipe or fill tube

20   If this condition occurs, the transmission is overfilled, there is coolant in the fluid, the case is porous, the dipstick is incorrect, the vent is plugged or the drain back holes are plugged.

---

3   Throttle valve (TV) linkage - description, inspection and adjustment (AOD transmissions only)

Description

1   The throttle valve cable or rod used on AOD transmissions should not be thought of as merely a "downshift" device. The TV linkage controls line pressure, shift points, shift feel, part throttle downshifts and detent downshifts.
2   If the TV linkage is broken, sticky or misadjusted, the vehicle will experience a num-

ber of problems such as early and/or soft upshifts and no downshift or a harsh downshift function.

Inspection

3   Grasp the cable or rod a few inches behind where it attaches to the throttle linkage and pull forward. The cable should slide easily through the cable terminal.
4   When released the cable should return to its original position.
5   If the TV linkage does not operate as above, the cause is misadjusted or damaged components.

TV cable adjustment

6   Cable adjustment on 1984 through 1986 models requires special pressure testing equipment and should be done by a dealer service department or qualified transmission shop. The cable on 1987 and later models can be adjusted without special equipment.
7   The engine should not be running and the throttle lever must be at its minimum idle stop during this adjustment.
8   Remove the air cleaner cover and inlet tube from the throttle body to provide access.
9   Pry the grooved pin on the cable assembly out of the grommet on the throttle body lever with a wide bladed screwdriver.
10   Push the white locking tab out with a small screwdriver.
11   Make sure the plastic block with the pin and tab slides freely on the notched rod. If it doesn't, the white tab may not be pushed out far enough.
12   Hold the throttle lever firmly against the idle stop and push the grooved pin into the grommet on the throttle lever as far as it will go. Make sure not to move the throttle lever away from the idle stop during this procedure.
13   Install the air cleaner assembly.

---

4   Throttle Valve (TV) linkage - removal and installation

Cable type

1   Remove the air cleaner and disconnect the cable at the throttle lever.
2   Under the vehicle, disconnect the cable at the transmission.
3   Remove the cable from the vehicle.
4   Installation is the reverse of removal.

Rod type

Refer to illustration 4.5

5   Disconnect the rod at the throttle lever and transmission. Remove the rod.
6   Installation is the reverse of removal.

---

5   Shift linkage - adjustment

---

1   Place the selector lever in Drive (C3, C4 and C5 transmissions) or Overdrive (AOD and A4LD transmissions). The lever must be held

6.3 A chisel is used here to carefully tap around the flange of the oil seal and separate it from the transmission extension housing

6.7 A large socket or length of pipe of the proper diameter should be used to install the new oil seal (a blunt punch and hammer can also be used to tap the new seal into the bore)

against the rear Drive/Overdrive stop during the adjustment procedure.

2   Raise the vehicle and support it securely on jackstands.

3   Loosen the nut attaching the rod or cable to the lever on the transmission.

4   Move the transmission lever to the Drive or Overdrive position, which is the second (C3, C4 and C5) or third (AOD or A4LD) detent from the full counterclockwise position.

5   With both the selector and transmission levers now in the same positions, tighten the retaining nut securely.

6   After adjustment, check the shift selector for proper operation.

6   Extension housing oil seal - replacement

Refer to illustration 6.3 and 6.7

1   Raise the vehicle and support it securely on jackstands.

2   Remove the driveshaft (Chapter 8).

3   Remove the oil seal from the end of the extension housing with a seal removing tool, available at most auto parts stores. An alternative to these tools is to use a wide-bladed screwdriver or chisel to remove the seal.

4   Before installing the new seal inspect the sealing surface of the universal joint yoke for scoring. If scoring is found, replace the yoke.

5   Inspect the counterbore of the housing for burrs. Remove any burrs with emery cloth or medium grit wet-or-dry sandpaper.

6   Coat the outside (case) diameter of the seal with RTV sealant.

7   Install the new seal into the extension housing.

8   The remainder of the installation is the reverse of the removal procedures.

7   Automatic transmission - removal and installation

Removal

Refer to illustrations 7.5, 7.6 and 7.14

1   Disconnect the negative cable at the battery. Place the cable out of the way so it cannot accidentally come in contact with the negative terminal of the battery, as this would once again allow power into the electrical system of the vehicle.

2   Raise the vehicle and support it securely.

3   Drain the transmission fluid (Chapter 1).

4   Remove the torque converter cover.

5   Mark one of the torque converter studs and the torque converter with white paint so they can be installed in the same position **(see illustration)**.

6   On models equipped with a drain plug on the torque converter, rotate the engine until the drain plug is at its lowest point **(see illustration)**. Place a pan under the torque converter and remove the drain plug. Use a suitable large socket and breaker bar on the crankshaft bolt to manually turn the engine over.

7   Remove the torque converter-to-flywheel nuts. Turn the crankshaft bolt for access to each nut in turn. Turn the engine only in a clockwise direction (as viewed from the front).

8   Remove the starter motor (Chapter 5).

9   Remove the driveshaft (Chapter 8).

7B

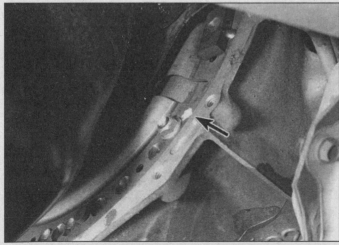

7.5 Mark the torque converter and stud with white paint so they can be reinstalled in the same position

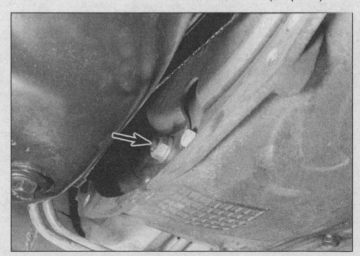

7.6 The torque converter plug (arrow) must be at the bottom prior to removal

10   Disconnect the speedometer cable.
11   Disconnect the electrical connectors from the transmission.
12   On models so equipped, disconnect the vacuum hose from the modulator.
13   Remove any exhaust components which will interfere with transmission removal (chapter 4).
14   Disconnect the TV or kickdown linkage rod or cable from the ballstud **(see illustration)**.
15   Disconnect the shift linkage.
16   Support the engine using a jack and a block of wood under the oil pan to spread the load.
17   Remove the rear mount to crossmember attaching bolts and the two crossmember-to-frame attaching bolts.
18   Remove the two engine rear support-to-transmission extension housing attaching bolts.
19   Raise the transmission sufficiently to allow removal of the crossmember.
20   Lower the transmission slightly and disconnect and plug the transmission cooler lines.
21   Remove the transmission fluid filler tube.
22   Move the transmission to the rear to disengage it from the engine block dowel pins and make sure the torque converter is detached from the flywheel. Lower the transmission from the vehicle.

Installation

23   On C3 and A4LD transmissions, make sure prior to installation that the torque converter hub is securely engaged in the pump. This can be checked by measuring the distance between the outer surface of the hub and a straightedge laid across the transmission mounting flange to make sure this dimension is 3/8-inch (C3) or 7/16-inch to 9/16-inch (A4LD).
24   Raise the transmission into position, making sure to keep it level so the torque converter does not slide forward. Connect the transmission cooler lines.
25   Turn the torque converter to line up the drive studs with the holes in the flywheel. The white paint mark on the torque converter and the stud made during Step 5 must line up.
26   Move the transmission carefully forward until the dowel pins are engaged and the torque converter is engaged.
27   Install the transmission housing-to-engine bolts and nuts. Tighten the bolts and nuts to the specified torque.
28   Install the torque converter-to-flywheel nuts. Tighten the nuts to the specified torque. On models so equipped, install the torque converter drain plug.
29   Install the transmission mount crossmember and through-bolts. Tighten the bolts and nuts securely.
30   Install the fluid filler tube.
31   Install the starter.
32   Connect the hose to the vacuum modulator (if equipped).

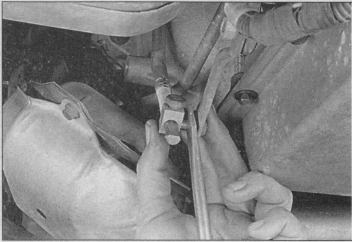

7.14 Use a large screwdriver to disconnect the TV linkage

33   Connect the shift and TV or kickdown linkage.
34   Plug in the transmission electrical connectors.
35   Install the torque converter cover.
36   Connect the driveshaft.
37   Connect the speedometer.
38   Adjust the shift linkage (Section 5).
39   Install any exhaust system components which were removed.
40   Lower the vehicle.
41   Fill the transmission (Chapter 1), run the vehicle and check for fluid leaks.

8   Neutral start switch - removal, installation and adjustment

C4 and C5 transmissions

1   Jack up the vehicle and support it securely on jackstands.
2   Disconnect the downshift linkage rod from the transmission downshift lever.
3   Apply penetrating oil to the downshift lever shaft and nut and allow it to soak for a few minutes. Remove the transmission downshift lever retaining nut and lift away the lever.
4   Remove the two neutral start switch securing bolts.
5   Disconnect the wire connector from the switch. Remove the switch.
6   To install, place the switch on the transmission and install the bolts finger tight. Move the selector lever to Neutral position. Rotate the switch and fit a No. 43 drill bit into the gauge pin hole The bit must be inserted a full 1/2 inch (12.3 mm). Tighten the switch securing bolts fully and remove the drill.
7   Check that the engine starts only when the selector is in the Neutral and Park positions.

C3, AOD and A4LD transmissions

8   Disconnect the ground cable at the battery.
9   Disconnect the electrical connector

from the neutral start switch.
10   Carefully remove the switch. **Caution:** *It is easy to crush or puncture the walls of the switch.*
11   Install the switch and tighten to the specified torque.
12   Install the electrical connector.
13   Connect the negative battery cable.
14   Check that the engine starts only when the selector is in the Neutral and Park positions.

9   Transmission mounts - check and replacement

Refer to illustration 9.2
1   Insert a large screwdriver or prybar into the space between the transmission extension and the crossmember and pry up.
2   The transmission should not spread excessively away from the insulator **(see illustration)**.
3   To replace, support the transmission with a jack and remove the two nuts attaching the insulator to the crossmember and the two bolts attaching the insulator to the transmission.
4   Raise the transmission and remove the insulator.
5   Installation is the reverse of the removal procedure.

10   Speedometer pinion gear and seal - replacement

1   Remove the bolt on the speedometer cable retaining bracket and remove the bracket and bolt as an assembly.
2   Pull the pinion gear assembly straight out of the extension housing.
3   Use a small screwdriver to remove the retaining clip from the pinion gear and slide the gear off the cable.
4   To replace the O-ring use a screwdriver to remove the O-ring from the retaining groove.
5   Lubricate the new O-ring and slide it onto the pinion shaft until it seats in the

9.2 Pry between the crossmember and the transmission to check for movement of the mount

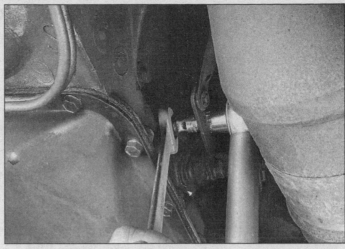

11.4 The front (intermediate) band is located at the left front of the transmission - when tightening, hold the adjustment screw so it can't move, then tighten the nut

retaining groove.

6　Install the new gear and secure with the retaining clip.

7　Install the pinion gear assembly and secure it with the retaining bracket and bolt.

11　Automatic transmission band adjustment (C-series transmissions)

Refer to illustration 11.4
Note: *AOD transmissions do not require band adjustments.*

1　Because of normal band wear, automatic transmission bands require adjustment at approximately 24,000 mile intervals. Bands should also be adjusted whenever performance-related symptoms are noted. Normal wear can cause sluggish shifts, delayed shifts, slipping and, in extreme cases, a loss of drive.

2　Raise the vehicle and support it securely on jackstands.

Intermediate (front) band

3　The intermediate or front band is used to hold the sun gear stationary to produce Second gear. If it is not correctly adjusted, there will be noticeable slip during the First-to-Second gear shift or on the downshift from the Third-to-Second gear. The first symptoms of these problems will be very sluggish shifts.

4　To adjust the intermediate band, loosen, remove and discard the locknut on the band adjustment screw (located on the left-hand side of the case). Tighten the adjusting screw to 120 in-lbs (10 ft-lbs), then loosen it exactly 1-1/2 turns (1980 and earlier C3), 2 turns (1981 and later C3), 1-3/4 turns (C4) or 4-1/4 turns (C5) **(see illustration)**. Install a new locknut

and tighten it to 40 ft-lbs while holding the adjustment screw to keep it from turning.

Low and Reverse band

5　The Low and Reverse band is operational when the selector lever is placed in the Low or Reverse positions. If it is not correctly adjusted, there will be no drive with the selector lever in Reverse (also associated with no engine braking with the selector lever in Low).

6　To adjust this band, remove the adjusting screw locknut from the screw (located on the right-hand side of the case, at the rear) and discard it. Tighten the adjusting screw to 120 in-lbs (10 ft-lbs), then loosen it exactly three turns. Install a new locknut and tighten it securely while holding the adjusting screw to keep it from turning.

Notes

Chapter 8
Clutch and driveline

Contents

Specifications

Clutch
Fluid type	See Chapter 1
Slave cylinder pushrod travel	33/64 in (13.5 mm)

Torque specifications
	Ft-lbs
Bellhousing-to-engine bolts	28 to 38
Pressure plate-to-flywheel bolts	12 to 24
Driveshaft flange bolts	70 to 95
Pedal support bracket bolt/nuts	13 to 25
Brake booster mounting nuts	See Chapter 9
Clutch self-adjuster quadrant nut	17 to 26

1 General information

The information in this Chapter deals with the components from the rear of the engine to the rear wheels, except for the transmission, which is dealt with in the previous Chapter. For the purposes of this Chapter, these components are grouped into three categories; clutch, driveshaft and rear axle. Separate Sections within this Chapter offer general descriptions and checking procedures for each of these three groups.

Since nearly all the procedures covered in this Chapter involve working under the vehicle, make sure it's securely supported on sturdy jackstands or on a hoist where the vehicle can be easily raised and lowered.

2 Clutch - description and check

1   All vehicles with a manual transmission use a single dry plate, diaphragm spring type clutch. The clutch disc has a splined hub which allows it to slide along the splines of the transmission input shaft. The clutch and pressure plate are held in contact by spring pressure exerted by the diaphragm in the pressure plate.
2   The clutch release system is operated by hydraulic pressure on some models, while on others a mechanical system is used. The hydraulic release system consists of the clutch pedal, a master cylinder and fluid reservoir, the hydraulic line, a slave cylinder which actuates the clutch release lever and

the clutch release (or throwout) bearing. The mechanical release system includes the clutch pedal with adjuster mechanism, a clutch cable which actuates the clutch release lever and the release bearing.
3   When pressure is applied to the clutch pedal to release the clutch, hydraulic or mechanical pressure is exerted against the outer end of the clutch release lever. As the lever pivots the shaft fingers push against the release bearing. The bearing pushes against the fingers of the diaphragm spring of the pressure plate assembly, which in turn releases the clutch plate.
4   Terminology can be a problem regarding the clutch components because common names have in some cases changed from that used by the manufacturer. For example,

3.7 After removal of the transmission, this will be the view of the clutch components - be sure to mark the relationship of the pressure plate to the flywheel, if marks don't already exist

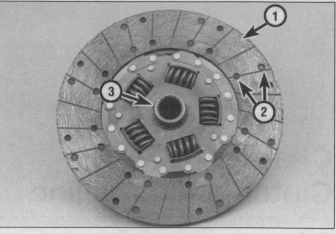

3.12 The clutch disc

1   *Lining* - this will wear down in use
2   *Rivets* - these secure the lining and will damage the flywheel or pressure plate if allowed to contact the surfaces
3   *Marks* - "Flywheel side" or something similar

the driven plate is also called the clutch plate or disc, the clutch release bearing is sometimes called a throwout bearing, the slave cylinder is sometimes called the operating cylinder.

5   Other than to replace components with obvious damage, some preliminary checks should be performed to diagnose a clutch system failure.

a) *On vehicles with hydraulic release systems, the first check should be of the fluid level in the clutch master cylinder. If the fluid level is low, add fluid as necessary and inspect the hydraulic clutch system for leaks. If the master cylinder reservoir has run dry, bleed the system as described in Section 7 and re-test the clutch operation.*

b) *To check "clutch spin down time," run the engine at normal idle speed with the transmission in Neutral (clutch pedal up - engaged). Disengage the clutch (pedal down), wait nine seconds and shift the transmission into Reverse. No grinding noise should be heard. A grinding noise would most likely indicate a problem in the pressure plate or the clutch disc.*

c) *To check for complete clutch release, run the engine (with the parking brake applied to prevent movement) and hold the clutch pedal approximately 1/2-inch from the floor. Shift the transmission between 1st gear and Reverse several times. If the shift is not smooth, component failure is indicated. On vehicles with a hydraulic release system, measure the slave cylinder pushrod travel (with the engine stopped and the vehicle supported securely on jackstands). With the clutch pedal depressed completely the slave cylinder pushrod should extend 13.5 mm (33/64 inch) minimum. If the pushrod doesn't meet this requirement, check the fluid level in the clutch master cylinder.*

d) *Visually inspect the clutch pedal bushing at the top of the clutch pedal to make sure there is no sticking or excessive wear.*

e) *On vehicles with mechanical release systems, a clutch pedal that is difficult to operate is most likely caused by a faulty clutch cable. Check the cable where it enters the casing for fraying, rust or other signs of corrosion. If it looks good, lubricate the cable with penetrating oil. If pedal operation improves, the cable is worn out and should be replaced. If the pedal makes a ratcheting noise while traveling to the floor, the self-adjusting mechanism (used on later models with mechanical release systems) is probably faulty. For more diagnosis information, see Troubleshooting at the beginning of this manual.*

3   Clutch components - removal, inspection and installation

Warning: *Dust produced by clutch wear and deposited on clutch components may contain asbestos, which is hazardous to your health. DO NOT blow it out with compressed air and DO NOT inhale it. DO NOT use gasoline or petroleum-based solvents to remove the dust. Brake system cleaner should be used to flush the dust into a drain pan. After the clutch components are wiped clean with a rag, dispose of the contaminated rags and cleaner in a covered container.*

Removal

Refer to illustration 3.7

1   Access to the clutch components is normally accomplished by removing the transmission, leaving the engine in the vehicle. If, of course, the engine is being removed for major overhaul, then the opportunity should always be taken to check the clutch for wear

and replace worn components as necessary. The following procedures assume that the engine will stay in place.

2   Referring to Chapter 7 Part A, remove the transmission from the vehicle. Support the engine while the transmission is out. Preferably, an engine hoist should be used to support it from above. However, if a jack is used underneath the engine, make sure a piece of wood is used between the jack and oil pan to spread the load. **Caution:** *The pickup for the oil pump is very close to the bottom of the oil pan. If the pan is bent or distorted in any way, engine oil starvation could occur.*

3   On models with a mechanical release system, remove the rubber dust cover and disconnect the clutch release cable from the bellhousing and release lever (see Section 6). On models with a hydraulic release system, remove the slave cylinder (see Section 9), but don't disconnect the hydraulic line or the hydraulic system will have to be bled (see Section 11).

4   On all models, remove the bellhousing-to-engine bolts and then detach the housing. It may have to be gently pried off the alignment dowels with a screwdriver or prybar.

5   The clutch fork and release bearing can remain attached to the housing for the time being.

6   To support the clutch disc during removal, install a clutch alignment tool through the clutch disc hub **(see illustration 3.16).**

7   Carefully inspect the flywheel and pressure plate for indexing marks. The marks are usually an X, an O or a white letter. If they cannot be found, scribe marks yourself so the pressure plate and the flywheel will be in the same alignment during installation **(see illustration).**

8   Turning each bolt only 1/2-turn at a time, slowly loosen the pressure plate-to-flywheel bolts. Work in a diagonal pattern and loosen each bolt a little at a time until all

NORMAL FINGER WEAR   **BROKEN OR BENT FINGERS**

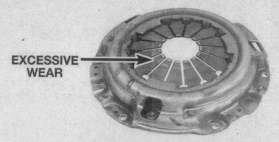

EXCESSIVE
WEAR

EXCESSIVE FINGER WEAR

3.14 Replace the pressure plate if excessive or abnormal wear is noted

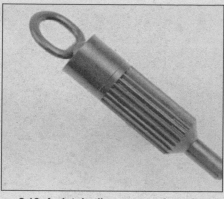

3.16 A clutch alignment tool can be purchased at most auto parts stores and eliminates all guesswork when centering the clutch disc in the pressure plate

spring pressure is relieved. Then hold the pressure plate securely and completely remove the bolts, followed by the pressure plate and clutch disc.

Inspection

Refer to illustrations 3.12 and 3.14

9   Ordinarily, when a problem occurs in the clutch, it can be attributed to wear of the clutch driven plate assembly (clutch disc). However, all components should be inspected at this time.
10   Inspect the flywheel for cracks, heat checking, grooves or other signs of obvious defects. If the imperfections are slight, a machine shop can machine the surface flat and smooth, which is highly recommended regardless of the surface appearance. Refer to Chapter 2 for the flywheel removal and installation procedure.
11   Inspect the pilot bearing (Section 5).
12   Inspect the lining on the clutch disc. There should be at least 1/16-inch of lining above the rivet heads. Check for loose rivets, distortion, cracks, broken springs and other obvious damage **(see illustration)**. As mentioned above, ordinarily the clutch disc is replaced as a matter of course, so if in doubt about the condition, replace it with a new one.
13   Ordinarily, the release bearing is also replaced along with the clutch disc (see Section 4).
14   Check the machined surfaces of the pressure plate **(see illustration)**. If the surface is grooved or otherwise damaged, take it to a machine shop for possible machining or replacement. Also check for obvious damage, distortion, cracking, etc. Light glazing can be removed with medium grit emery cloth. If a new pressure plate is indicated, new or factory-rebuilt units are available.

Installation

Refer to illustration 3.16

15   Before installation, carefully wipe the flywheel and pressure plate machined surfaces clean. It's important that no oil or grease is on these surfaces or the lining of the clutch disc. Handle these parts only with clean hands.
16   Position the clutch disc and pressure plate with the clutch held in place with an alignment tool **(see illustration)**. Make sure it's installed properly (most replacement clutch plates will be marked "flywheel side" or something similar - if not marked, install the clutch disc with the damper springs toward the transmission).
17   Tighten the pressure plate-to-flywheel bolts only finger tight, working around the pressure plate.
18   Center the clutch disc by inserting the alignment tool through the splined hub and into the pilot bearing in the crankshaft.

4.6 Lubricate the release bearing and lever at the points shown. Also fill the groove in the inside diameter of the bearing

Tighten the pressure plate-to-flywheel bolts a little at a time, working in a crisscross pattern to prevent distorting the cover. After all of the bolts are snug, tighten them to the specified torque. Remove the alignment tool.
19   Using high temperature grease, lubricate the inner groove of the release bearing (refer to Section 4). Also place grease on the release lever contact areas.
20   Install the clutch release bearing as described in Section 4.
21   Install the bellhousing and tighten the bolts to the proper torque specification.
22   Install the transmission, slave cylinder or release cable and all components removed previously, tightening all fasteners to the proper torque specifications.

4   Clutch release bearing - removal, inspection and installation

Removal

1   Disconnect the negative cable from the battery.
2   Remove the transmission (Chapter 7).
3   Remove the bellhousing (Section 3).
4   Remove the clutch release lever from the ball stud, then remove the bearing from the lever.

Inspection

5   Hold the center of the bearing and rotate the outer portion while applying pressure. If the bearing doesn't turn smoothly or if it's noisy, replace it with a new one. Wipe the bearing with a clean rag and inspect it for damage, wear and cracks. Don't immerse the bearing in solvent - it's sealed for life and to do so would ruin it.

Installation

Refer to illustration 4.6

6   Lightly lubricate with lithium base grease the clutch lever crown and spring retention crown where they contact the bearing. Fill the inner groove of the bearing with the same grease **(see illustration)**.

8

5.1   **The pilot bearing incorporates an O-ring seal which cannot be replaced separately. If there is any evidence that the seal has been leaking, or if the bearing is dry, replace it - the bearing must be installed with the seal towards the transmission.**

5.5   **One method of removing the pilot bearing requires an internal puller connected to a slide hammer**

7   Attach the release bearing to the clutch lever.

8   Lubricate the clutch release lever ball socket with high temperature grease and push the lever onto the ball stud until it's firmly seated.

9   Apply a light coat of high temperature grease to the face of the release bearing, where it contacts the pressure plate diaphragm fingers.

10   Install the bellhousing and tighten the bolts to the specified torque.

11   Prior to installing the transmission, apply a light coat of grease to the transmission front bearing retainer.

12   The remainder of the installation is the reverse of the removal procedure, tightening all bolts to the specified torque.

5   Pilot bearing - inspection and replacement

Refer to illustrations 5.1, 5.5 and 5.9

1   The clutch pilot bearing is a needle roller type bearing which is pressed into the rear of the crankshaft **(see illustration)**. It is greased at the factory and does not require additional lubrication. Its primary purpose is to support the front of the transmission input shaft. The pilot bearing should be inspected whenever the clutch components are removed fro the engine. Due to its inaccessibility, if you are in doubt as to its condition, replace it with a new one. **Note:** *If the engine has been removed from the vehicle, disregard the following steps which do not apply.*

2   Remove the transmission (refer to Chapter 7 Part A).

3   Remove the clutch components (Section 3).

4   Inspect for any excessive wear, scoring, lack of grease, dryness or obvious damage. If any of these conditions are noted, the bearing should be replaced. A flashlight will be

helpful to direct light into the recess.

5   Removal can be accomplished with a special puller and slide hammer available at most auto parts stores that carry special tools **(see illustration)**, but an alternative method also works very well.

6   Find a solid steel bar which is slightly smaller in diameter than the bearing. Alternatives to a solid bar would be a wood dowel or a socket with a bolt fixed in place to make it solid.

7   Check the bar for fit - it should just slip into the bearing with very little clearance.

8   Pack the bearing and the area behind it (in the crankshaft recess) with heavy grease. Pack it tightly to eliminate as much air as possible.

9   Insert the bar into the bearing bore and strike the bar sharply with a hammer which will force the grease to the backside of the bearing an push it out **(see illustration)**. Remove the bearing and clean all grease from the crankshaft recess.

10   To install the new bearing, lightly lubricate the outside surface with lithium-based grease, then drive it into the recess with a

soft-face hammer. The seal must face out **(see illustration 5.1)**.

11   Install the clutch components, transmission and all other components removed previously, tightening all fasteners properly.

6   Clutch cable - removal and installation

Manually adjusted cable (early models)

1   Disconnect the negative battery cable from the battery.

2   On all except 3.3L inline six-cylinder models, loosen the cable locknut and adjusting nut. Pull the clutch cable forward out of its bellhousing boss.

3   On 3.3L models, pull the adjusting nut forward out of the rubber insulator. Turn the adjusting nut and loosen the cable until it can be removed from the bellhousing. Don't try to turn the adjusting nut without pulling it clear of the rubber insulator.

5.9   **Pack the recess behind the pilot bearing with heavy grease and force it out hydraulically with a steel rod slightly smaller than the bore in the bearing - when the hammer strikes the rod, the bearing will pop out of the crankshaft**

4   Remove the cable retaining clip at the bellhousing.
5   Remove the retaining clip that secures the cable to the top of the clutch pedal. Detach the cable from the pedal, then take it out of the vehicle.
6   Installation is the reverse of the removal steps. Adjust the cable (see Chapter 1).

Self-adjusting cable (later models)

7   Lift the clutch pedal all the way up to disengage the pawl and quadrant. Push the quadrant forward and unhook the cable from the quadrant. Allow the quadrant to swing slowly to the rear. The quadrant is under spring pressure - don't allow it to snap back into position.
8   Open the hood and remove the retaining screw that holds the cable to the dash panel.
9   If equipped, remove the screw that secures the cable bracket to the front sidemember.
10   Raise the vehicle and support it securely on jackstands.
11   Remove the dust cover from the bellhousing.
12   Remove the retainer ring holding the cable to the bellhousing.
13   Disengage the clutch cable from the release lever:

  a) On all except 1987 and later four-cylinder engines, slide the ball on the end of the cable through the hole in the clutch release lever and remove the cable.
  b) On 1987 and later four-cylinder engines, remove the clip and clevis pin from the end of the cable.

14   Installation is the reverse of removal with the following notes:

  a) To install the cable into the adjusting assembly, lift the clutch pedal to disengage the pawl and quadrant. **Caution:** The clutch pedal must be lifted to prevent damage to the pawl and quadrant. While pushing the quadrant forward, hook the cable over the rear of the quadrant. Do not use any prying tool to attach the cable to the quadrant.
  b) After the cable is installed, depress the clutch pedal several times to adjust the cable.

7   Self-adjusting mechanism - removal and installation

1   Disconnect the negative battery cable from the battery.
2   Remove the steering wheel (see Chapter 10).
3   Remove the lower left instrument panel section (see Chapter 11), then remove the steering column shrouds.
4   Disconnect the hood release mechanism inside the vehicle.
5   Disconnect the master cylinder pushrod and stoplight switch from the brake pedal

(see Chapter 9).
6   Carefully rotate the quadrant forward until you can unhook the clutch cable from it. Hold the quadrant and allow it to move slowly rearward.
7   Move the interval wiper governor (if equipped) out of the way and disconnect all of the steering column electrical connectors.
8   Detach the steering column from the brake pedal bracket and let the column rest on the floor of the vehicle.
9   Unbolt the brake pedal bracket support brace from the left-hand side.
10   Remove the brake booster mounting nuts (see Chapter 9).
11   Unbolt the brake pedal support bracket from the instrument panel and take the bracket out.
12   Remove the clutch pedal (see Section 12). Take the self-adjusting mechanism out of the brake pedal support bracket.
13   Remove the self-adjusting mechanism shaft bushings from the brake pedal support bracket. Inspect the bushings and replace them if they are worn.
14   Apply engine oil to the self-adjusting mechanism shaft, then install the mechanism in the brake pedal support bracket.
15   Turn the quadrant toward the top of the vehicle. Align the flats on the self-adjusting shaft with the clutch pedal flats, then install the nut and tighten it securely.
16   Install the brake pedal support bracket and tighten its nuts loosely. Install the bolt. Tighten the bolt, then the nuts securely.
17   The remainder of installation is the reverse of the removal steps.
18   Press the clutch pedal several times to adjust the clutch.
19   Check steering column operation.

8   Self-adjusting mechanism quadrant pawl - replacement

1   Remove the self-adjusting mechanism (see Section 7).
2   Remove both hairpin clips, then remove the quadrant and spring.
3   Remove the pawl spring and pawl.
4   Apply multi-purpose grease to the pivot shafts of pawl and quadrant.
5   Install the pawl with its teeth toward the longer shaft. Position the spring hole in the end of the arm, not beneath the arm.
6   Place the straight end of the spring in the hole (coil upward), then turn the spring 1/2 turn to the left and place the coil over the boss.
7   Hook the spring under the arm and install the hairpin clip to secure the pawl.
8   Install the quadrant spring on the shaft. Its bent end goes in the hole in the arm.
9   Place the quadrant on the shaft with its bottom projection under the shaft arm. Mesh the bottom tooth of the pawl with the bottom tooth of the quadrant.
10   Install the hairpin clip that retains the quadrant.

11   Use pliers to hook the quadrant spring behind the quadrant ear.
12   Install the self-adjusting mechanism (see Section 7).
13   Install the clutch pedal (see Section 12).

9   Clutch slave cylinder - removal and installation

1   Disconnect the cable from the negative battery terminal.
2   Raise the vehicle and support it securely on jackstands.
3   Remove the slave cylinder dust cover self-tapping screw and detach the cover.
4   Detach the slave cylinder from the mounting bracket on the transmission. It may be necessary to pry it out with a screwdriver.
5   If the slave cylinder must be replaced, support the cylinder and, using a small punch, drive out the roll pin that retains the line to the cylinder. Pull the line off the cylinder.
6   To install the slave cylinder, reverse the removal procedure. Be sure to use a new O-ring and roll pin when reinstalling the line. If a new cylinder is being installed, do not remove the plastic retaining strap from the pushrod - it is designed to break off the first time the clutch pedal is depressed.

10   Clutch master cylinder - removal and installation

1   Remove the clutch slave cylinder following the procedure described in the preceding Section.
2   From inside the vehicle, remove the left side under dash panel and disconnect the pushrod from the clutch pedal.
3   Unscrew the two clutch fluid reservoir nuts and lower the reservoir, taking care not to spill any fluid.
4   Grasp the clutch master cylinder and turn it clockwise approximately 45-degrees, then pull the cylinder from the firewall.
5   Remove the line from the master cylinder by driving out the roll pin with a small punch.
6   Installation is the reverse of the removal procedure. Be sure to use a new roll pin and a new O-ring where the line enters the cylinder.

11   Clutch hydraulic system - bleeding

1   The hydraulic system should be bled of all air whenever any part of the system has been removed or if the fluid level has been allowed to fall so low that air has been drawn into the master cylinder. The procedure is very similar to bleeding a brake system.
2   Fill the master cylinder with new brake fluid conforming to DOT 3 specifications.

8

Caution: *Do not re-use any of the fluid coming from the system during the bleeding operation or use fluid which has been inside an open container for an extended period of time.*

3   Raise the vehicle and place it securely on jackstands to gain access to the slave cylinder, which is located on the left side of the clutch housing.

4   Remove the dust cap which fits over the bleeder valve and push a length of plastic hose over the valve. Place the other end of the hose into a clear container with about two inches of brake fluid. The hose end must be in the fluid at the bottom of the container.

5   Have an assistant depress the clutch pedal and hold it. Open the bleeder valve on the slave cylinder, allowing fluid to flow through the hose. Close the bleeder valve when your assistant signals that the clutch pedal is at the bottom of its travel. Once closed, have your assistant release the pedal.

6   Continue this process until all air is evacuated from the system, indicated by a full, solid stream of fluid being ejected from the bleeder valve each time and no air bubbles in the hose or container. Keep a close watch on the fluid level inside the clutch master cylinder reservoir; if the level drops too low, air will be sucked back into the system and the process will have to be started all over again.

7   Install the dust cap and lower the vehicle. Check carefully for proper operation before placing the vehicle in normal service.

12   Clutch pedal - removal and installation

1   Disconnect the cable from the negative terminal of the battery.
2   Remove the left side under dash panel.
3   If equipped, disconnect the starter/clutch interlock switch pushrod from the clutch pedal.
4   Remove the nut that retains the clutch pedal to the pivot shaft and wiggle the pedal off the shaft.
5   Installation is the reverse of the removal procedure.

13   Starter/clutch interlock switch - removal and installation

Removal

1   Detach the wire harness connector from the interlock switch.
2   Remove the retaining clip from the switch rod mounting pin on the clutch pedal.
3   Remove the interlock switch-to-bracket screws and detach the switch.

Installation

4   Position the adjuster clip approximately 1-inch from the end of the rod.
5   Attach the eyelet end of the rod to the pin on the clutch pedal. Install the retaining clip.

15.3 Before removing the bolts, mark the relationship of the driveshaft flange and the differential companion flange. To prevent the dfriveshaft from turning when loosening the flange bolts, insert a screwdriver through the yoke

6   With the clutch pedal all the way up, swing the switch up into place. Install the mounting screws and tighten them securely.
7   Push the clutch pedal to the floor to adjust the switch. Plug in the electrical connector.
8   Confirm that the engine starts only when the clutch pedal is depressed to the floor. If it doesn't, remove the adjusting clip from the rod and position it closer to the switch **(see illustration 13.4)**. Check the switch operation again. If the engine still doesn't crank over, or cranks over when the pedal is in the released position, replace the switch.

14   Driveshaft and universal joints - description and check

1   The driveshaft is a tube running between the transmission and the rear end. Universal joints are located at either end of the driveshaft and permit power to be transmitted to the rear wheels at varying angles.
2   The driveshaft features a splined yoke at the front, which slips into the extension housing of the transmission. This arrangement allows the driveshaft to slide back-and-forth within the transmission as the vehicle is in operation.
3   An oil seal is used to prevent leakage of fluid at this point and to keep dirt and contaminants from entering the transmission. If leakage is evident at the front of the driveshaft, replace the oil seal referring to the procedures in Chapter 7.
4   The driveshaft assembly requires very little service. The universal joints are lubricated for life and must be replaced if problems develop. The driveshaft must be removed from the vehicle for this procedure.
5   Since the driveshaft is a balanced unit, it's important that no undercoating, mud, etc. be allowed to stay on it. When the vehicle is raised for service it's a good idea to clean the driveshaft and inspect it for any obvious damage. Also check that the small weights used to originally balance the driveshaft are

in place and securely attached. Whenever the driveshaft is removed it's important that it be reinstalled in the same relative position to preserve this balance.
6   Problems with the driveshaft are usually indicated by a noise or vibration while driving the vehicle. A road test should verify if the problem is the driveshaft or another vehicle component:

a)   *On an open road, free of traffic, drive the vehicle and note the engine speed (rpm) at which the problem is most evident.*
b)   *With this noted, drive the vehicle again, this time manually keeping the transmission in 1st, then 2nd, then 3rd gear ranges and running the engine up to the engine speed noted.*
c)   *If the noise or vibration occurs at the same engine speed regardless of which gear the transmission is in, the driveshaft is not at fault because the speed of the driveshaft varies in each gear.*
d)   *If the noise or vibration decreased or was eliminated, visually inspect the driveshaft for damage, material on the shaft which would effect balance, missing weights and damaged universal joints. Another possibility for this condition would be tires which are out-of-balance.*

7   To check for worn universal joints:
a)   *On an open road, free of traffic, drive the vehicle slowly until the transmission is in High gear. Let off on the accelerator, allowing the vehicle to coast, then accelerate. A clunking or knocking noise will indicate worn universal joints.*
b)   *Drive the vehicle at a speed of about 10 to 15 mph and then place the transmission in Neutral, allowing the vehicle to coast. Listen for abnormal driveline noises.*
c)   *Raise the vehicle and support it securely on jackstands. With the transmission in Neutral, manually turn the driveshaft, watching the universal joints for excessive play.*

15 Driveshaft - removal and installation

Removal

Refer to illustration 15.3

1   Disconnect the cable from the negative battery terminal.

2   Block the front wheels. Raise the rear of the vehicle and support it securely on jackstands. Place the transmission in Neutral with the parking brake off.

3   Using white paint or a hammer and punch, place marks on the driveshaft flange and the differential companion flange in line with each other **(see illustration)**. This is to make sure the driveshaft is reinstalled in the same position to preserve the balance.

4   Remove the rear universal joint flange bolts. Turn the driveshaft (or rear wheels) as necessary to bring the bolts into the most accessible position.

5   Lower the rear of the driveshaft and then slide the front out of the transmission.

6   To prevent loss of fluid and contamination while the driveshaft is out, wrap a plastic bag over the transmission housing and hold it in place with a rubber band.

Installation

7   Remove the plastic bag on the transmission and wipe the area clean. Inspect the oil seal carefully. Procedures for replacement of this seal can be found in Chapter 7.

8   Slide the front of the driveshaft into the transmission.

9   Raise the rear of the driveshaft into position, checking to be sure that the marks are in alignment. If not, turn the rear wheels to match the pinion flange and the driveshaft flange.

10   Install the flange bolts, tightening them to the specified torque.

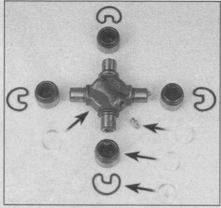

16.2a An exploded view of the universal joint compounds

16 Universal joints - replacement

Refer to illustrations 16.2a, 16.2b, 16.4 and 16.9

Note: *A press or large vise will be required for this procedure. It may be advisable to take the driveshaft to a local dealer or machine shop where the universal joints can be replaced for you, normally at a reasonable charge.*

1   Remove the driveshaft as outlined in the previous Section.

2   Using a small pair of pliers, remove the snap-rings from the spider **(see illustrations)**.

3   Supporting the driveshaft, place it in position on either an arbor press or on a workbench equipped with a vise.

4   Place a piece of pipe or a large socket with the same inside diameter over one of the bearing caps. Position a socket which is of slightly smaller diameter than the cap on the opposite bearing cap **(see illustration)** and use the vise or press to force the cap out (inside the pipe or large socket), stopping just

16.2b A pair of needle-nose pliers can be used to remove the universal joint snap-rings

before it comes completely out of the yoke. Use the vise or large pliers to work the cap the rest of the way out.

5   Transfer the sockets to the other side and press the opposite bearing cap out in the same manner.

6   Pack the new universal joint bearings with grease. Ordinarily, specific instructions for lubrication will be included with the universal joint servicing kit and should be followed carefully.

7   Position the spider in the yoke and partially install one bearing cap in the yoke.

8   Start the spider into the bearing cap and then partially install the other cap. Align the spider and press the bearing caps into position, being careful not to damage the dust seals.

9   Install the snap-rings. If difficulty is encountered in seating the snap-rings, strike the driveshaft yoke sharply with a hammer. This will spring the yoke ears slightly and allow the snap-rings to seat in the groove **(see illustration)**.

10   Install the grease fitting and fill the joint

16.4 To press the universal joint out of the driveshaft yoke, set it up in a vise with the small socket pushing the joint and bearing cap into the large socket

16.9 If the snap-ring will not seat in the groove, strike the yoke with a brass hammer. This will relieve the tension that has set up in the yoke, and slightly spring the yoke ears. This should also be done if the joint feels tight when assembled.

8

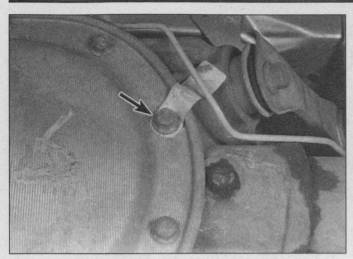

17.4 The axle identification tag is held in place with a differential cover bolt

18.5 The wheel bearing retainer plate nuts are accessible through the holes in the axle drive flange (brake shoes shown removed for clarity - normally, the shoes don't have to be removed)

with grease. Be careful not to overfill the joint, as this could blow out the grease seals.

11 Install the driveshaft, tightening the flange bolts to the specified torque.

17 Rear axle - description and check

Description

Refer to illustration 17.4

1 The rear axle assembly is a hypoid, semi-floating type (the centerline of the pinion gear is below the centerline of the ring gear, and the outer end of the axle shaft provides a support surface for the rear wheel bearing). The differential carrier is a casting with a pressed steel or plastic cover and the axle tubes are made of steel, pressed and welded into the carrier.

2 The rear wheel bearings on early models (equipped with a 6.75-inch ring gear) are pressed onto the axle shafts. The rear wheel bearings on later models (equipped with a 7.5-inch or 8.8-inch ring gear) are pressed into the axle housing.

3 An optional locking rear axle is also available. This differential allows for normal differential operation until one wheel loses traction. The unit utilizes multi-disc clutch packs or friction cones and a speed sensitive engagement mechanism which locks both axleshafts together, applying equal rotational power to both wheels.

4 In order to undertake certain operations, particularly replacement of the axleshafts, it's important to know the axle identification number. This information can be found on the Axle Identification Tag, which is located under a differential cover-to-carrier bolt in the 2 o'clock position **(see illustration)**.

Check

5 Many times a fault is suspected in the rear axle area when, in fact, the problem lies

elsewhere. For this reason, a thorough check should be performed before assuming a rear axle problem.

6 The following noises are those commonly associated with rear axle diagnosis procedures:

a) *Road noise is often mistaken for mechanical faults. Driving the vehicle on different surfaces will show whether the road surface is the cause of the noise. Road noise will remain the same if the vehicle is under power or coasting.*

b) *Tire noise is sometimes mistaken for mechanical problems. Tires which are worn or low on pressure are particularly susceptible to emitting vibrations and noises. Tire noise will remain about the same during varying driving situations, where rear axle noise will change during coasting, acceleration, etc.*

c) *Engine and transmission noise can be deceiving because it will travel along the driveline. To isolate engine and transmission noises, make a note of the engine speed at which the noise is most*

18.6 The axle shaft can be withdrawn once the retainer plate nuts are removed; during installation, take care not to damage the oil seal with the axle shaft

pronounced. Stop the vehicle and place the transmission in Neutral and run the engine to the same speed. If the noise is the same, the rear axle is not at fault.

7 Overhaul and general repair of the rear axle is beyond the scope of the home mechanic due to the many special tools and critical measurements required. Thus, the procedures listed here will involve axleshaft removal and installation, axleshaft oil seal replacement, axleshaft bearing replacement and removal of the entire unit for repair or replacement.

18 Axleshaft - removal and installation

Early models (6.75-inch ring gear)

Refer to illustrations 18.5 and 18.6

1 Park the vehicle on level ground.

2 Securely block the front wheels so the vehicle can't roll forward or backward.

3 Jack up the rear of the vehicle and place it securely on jackstands. DO NOT get under a vehicle that is supported only by a jack!

4 Make sure the parking brake is released, then remove the brake drum. If the drum is secured by speed nuts, remove the nuts and keep them for re-use.

5 Remove the nuts securing the wheel bearing retainer plate **(see illustration)**.

6 Pull the axleshaft out of the housing to clear the brake backing plate **(see illustration)**.

7 Take the axleshaft to a machine shop for bearing replacement.

8 Replace the axleshaft oil seal whenever the axleshaft is removed (see Section 18).

9 Check for nicks or gouges in the oil seal mounting surface.

10 Use a large socket or seal driver to tap in a new seal. The lip of the seal faces into the

18.17a Position a large screwdriver between the rear axle case and a ring gear bolt to keep the differential case from turning when removing the pinion shaft lock bolt

18.17b Rotate the differential case 180-degrees and slide the pinion shaft out of the case until the stepped part of the shaft contacts the ring gear

axle housing. Tap the new seal in squarely, making sure the seal does not tilt in its bore.

11 Carefully install the axleshaft without damaging the seal. Position the bearing retainer plate over the studs, then install the nuts and tighten them securely.

12 Install the brake drum and speed nuts (if used).

13 Install the wheel. Remove the jackstands, lower the vehicle to the ground and tighten the wheel nuts to specifications (see Chapter 1).

Later models (7.5-inch or 8.8-inch ring gear)

Refer to illustrations 18.17a, 18.17b, 18.18 and 18.19

14 Raise the rear of the vehicle, support it securely and remove the wheel.

15 Remove the brake drum or rear caliper and brake disc (refer to Chapter 9).

16 Remove the cover from the differential carrier and allow the oil to drain into a container.

17 Remove the lock bolt from the differen-

tial pinion shaft. Slide the notched end of the pinion shaft out of the differential case as far as it will go (see illustrations).

18 Push the outer (flanged) end of the axleshaft in and remove the C-lock from the inner end of the shaft (see illustration).

19 Withdraw the axleshaft, taking care not to damage the oil seal in the end of the axle housing as the splined end of the axleshaft passes through it (see illustration).

20 Installation is the reverse of removal. Tighten the lock bolt securely.

21 Refer to Chapter 1 for the proper cover installation procedure.

22 Refill the axle with the correct quantity and grade of lubricant (Chapter 1).

19 Axleshaft oil seal - replacement

Refer to illustrations 19.2 and 19.3

1 Remove the axleshaft as described in the preceding Section.

2 Pry the old oil seal out of the end of the axle housing. On later models, use a large

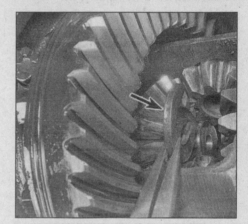

18.18 Push in on the axle flange and remove the C-lock(arrow) from the inner end of the axleshaft

screwdriver or the inner end of the axleshaft itself as a lever (see illustration). On early models, a special slide hammer puller may be required.

3 Using a large socket as a seal driver, tap

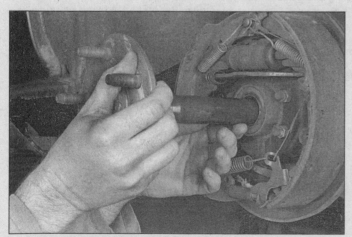

18.19 Pull the axle out of the housing, supporting it with one hand to prevent damage to the seal

19.2 If a seal removal tool isn't available, a prybar or even the end of the axle can be used to pop the seal out of the housing

the seal into position so that the lips are facing in and the metal face is visible from the end of the axle housing **(see illustration)**. When correctly installed, the face of the oil seal should be flush with the end of the axle housing. Lubricate the lips of the seal with gear oil.

4   Installation of the axleshaft is covered in the preceding Section.

20   Axleshaft bearing - replacement

Early models (bearing on axleshaft)

1   Bearing replacement on early models with the bearing pressed onto the axleshaft requires a hydraulic press and special tools. Remove the axleshaft (see Section 18) and have a dealer service department or automotive machine shop replace the bearing.

Later models (bearing in axle housing)

2   Remove the axleshaft (refer to Section 18) and the oil seal (refer to Section 19).
3   A bearing puller will be required or a tool which will engage behind the bearing will have to be fabricated.
4   Attach a slide hammer and pull the bearing out of the axle housing.
5   Clean out the bearing recess and drive in the new bearing with a bearing driver. Lubricate the new bearing with gear lubricant. Make sure that the bearing is tapped into the full depth of its recess.
6   Discard the old oil seal and install a new one (Section 19), then install the axleshaft.

21   Rear axle assembly - removal and installation

Removal

1   Disconnect the cable from the negative battery terminal.
2   Loosen, but do not remove the rear wheel lug nuts. Block the front wheels and raise the rear of the vehicle. Support it securely on jackstands. Remove the rear wheels.
3   Remove the brake drums or brake calipers, anchor plates and discs (see Chapter 9).
4   Remove the rear axle cover and allow the lubricant to drain (Chapter 1).

19.3 A large socket or a piece of pipe (as shown here) can be used to install the seal - the diameter of the tool should be slightly smaller than the outside diameter of the seal.

5   Remove both rear axleshafts following the procedure in Section 18.
6   Unbolt the brake line junction block from the rear axle cover.
7   Detach the brake lines from the axle housing.
8   Drum brake models - remove the four bolts that attach the brake backing plates to the axle housing. Detach the brake assemblies from the housing and wire them out of the way.
9   Disconnect the vent tube from the axle housing.
10   Unbolt the driveshaft from the differential flange (Section 15) and wire it out of the way.
11   Place a floor jack under the differential and raise the rear axle slightly.
12   Detach the traction bars or axle dampers (if equipped) from the axle housing (see Chapter 10).
13   Remove the coil springs following the procedure outlined in Chapter 10.
14   Remove the shock absorber lower mounting bolts.
15   Remove the upper control arm-to-rear axle housing nuts and bolts.
16   Remove the lower control arm-to-axle housing nuts and bolts.
17   Lower the axle housing and guide it out from underneath the vehicle.

Installation

18   Raise the rear axle assembly into place and install the upper control arm-to-axle housing bolts and nuts. Don't completely

tighten the nuts at this time.
19   Install the coil springs (See Chapter 10) and connect the lower control arms to the rear axle assembly.
20   Connect the traction bars or axle dampers (if equipped) to the axle housing.
21   Raise the axle housing to simulate normal ride height and tighten the upper and lower control arm-to-axle housing nuts securely.
22   Connect the lower ends of the shock absorbers to the rear axle housing and tighten the bolts securely.
23   Connect the driveshaft to the differential flange, aligning the matchmarks. Tighten the bolts to the specified torque.
24   Drum brake models - attach the brake backing plates to the axle housing, tightening the nuts securely.
25   Attach the brake lines to the axle housing.
26   Install the axleshafts (see Section 18).
27   Install the brake drums or rear caliper anchor plates, discs and calipers.
28   Connect the axle vent tube.
29   Install the rear axle cover and fill the differential with the recommended lubricant (see Chapter 1).
30   Attach the brake junction block to the rear axle cover (drum brake models) and tighten the bolt securely. If, in the course of removal, the brake fluid lines were disconnected, bleed the brake system (Chapter 9).
31   Install the wheels and lug nuts. Lower the vehicle and tighten the lug nuts to the specified torque (see Chapter 1).

Chapter 9   Brakes

Contents

Specifications

Brake fluid type .... See Chapter 1

Disc brakes

Minimum pad thickness	See Chapter 1
Front brake disc	
Standard thickness	0.870 in
Minimum thickness*	0.810 in
Runout limit	0.003 in
Thickness variation (parallelism)	
Steel wheels	0.0005 in
Aluminum wheels	0.0003 in
Rear brake disc	
Standard thickness	0.945 in
Minimum thickness*	0.895 in
Runout limit	0.003 in
Thickness variation (parallelism)	0.0005 in

Refer to marks stamped on the disc (they supersede information printed here)

Rear brake drum diameter

Standard	
Heavy-duty models	10.000 in
All others	9.000 in
Maximum*	
Heavy-duty models	10.060 in
All others	9.060 in

Refer to marks cast into the drum (they supersede information printed here)

9

Torque specifications

	Ft-lbs
Brake hose-to-caliper bolt	
Front disc brakes	
1979 through 1992	17 to 25
1993	26 to 44
Rear disc brakes	20 to 30
Brake hose to caliper (screw-in hose end)	20 to 30
Front disc brake caliper locating pins	
All except SVO and 1987 and later 5.0L V8	30 to 40
Mustang SVO and 1987 and later 5.0L V8	40 to 60
Brake hose to caliper (screw-in hose end)	20 to 30
Front disc brake caliper locating pins	
All except SVO and 1987 and later 5.0L V8	30 to 40
Mustang SVO and 1987 and later 5.0L V8	40 to 60
Rear disc brake (Mustang SVO)	
Caliper end retainer	75 to 96
Caliper end retaining screw	16 to 22
Rear disc brake (1993 Mustang Cobra)	
Pinch bolt	30 to 35
Master cylinder-to-booster nuts	13 to 25
Power brake booster nuts	13 to 25
Wheel cylinder bolts	9 to 13
Brake pedal pivot shaft nut	10 to 20
Wheel lug nuts	See Chapter 1

1   General information and precautions

General information

All vehicles covered by this manual are equipped with hydraulically operated power assisted brake systems. All front brake systems are disc type, while the rear brakes are either disc (Mustang SVO or 1993 Cobra) or drum type.

All brakes are self-adjusting. The front and rear disc brakes automatically compensate for pad wear, while the rear drum brakes incorporate an adjustment mechanism which is activated as the brakes are applied when the vehicle is driven in reverse.

The hydraulic system is a split design, meaning there are separate circuits for the front and rear brakes. If one circuit fails, the other circuit will remain functional and a warning indicator will light up on the dashboard, showing that a failure has occurred.

Master cylinder

The master cylinder is located under the hood, mounted to the power brake booster, and is best recognized by the large fluid reservoir on top. The fluid reservoir on pre-1987 models is integral with the master cylinder casting, while later models feature a removable plastic reservoir. In either case, the reservoir is partitioned to prevent total fluid loss in the event of a front or rear brake hydraulic system failure.

The master cylinder is designed for the "split system" mentioned earlier and has separate primary and secondary piston assemblies, the piston nearest the firewall being the primary piston, which applies hydraulic pressure to the front brakes.

Brake control valve

The brake control valve is located below the master cylinder and bolted to the strut tower. It is actually two separate valves - a pressure differential valve and a proportioning valve (pre-1987 models) or a proportioning valve and a shuttle valve (1987 and later models).

On pre-1987 models, the portion that contains the pressure differential valve consists of the brake light warning switch and a piston. This valve senses an unbalanced hydraulic condition between the front and rear brake systems in the event of a failure in either system. If there is a sudden pressure loss in one of the systems, the piston within the valve will move off center, activating the brake warning light switch. The warning lamp will go off when the problem is corrected, the brakes are bled and the pedal is depressed with considerable force to center the piston in the valve.

On 1987 and later models, the shuttle valve will allow full hydraulic pressure to the rear brakes in the event of a front hydraulic system failure. It operates in a similar way to the pressure control valve, except that there is no brake light warning switch.

The proportioning valve regulates the hydraulic pressure to the rear brakes during heavy braking to eliminate rear wheel lock-up. Under normal braking conditions it allows full pressure to the rear brake system until a predetermined pedal pressure is reached. Above that point, the pressure to the rear brakes will be limited.

The brake control valve is not serviceable - if a problem develops with the valve, it must be replaced as an assembly.

Parking brake

The parking brake mechanically operates the rear brakes only.

On drum brake models the parking brake cables pull on a lever attached to the brake shoe assembly, causing the shoes to expand against the drum. On models with rear disc brakes, the cables pull on levers that are attached to screw-type actuators in the caliper housings, which apply force to the caliper pistons, clamping the brake pads against the brake disc.

Precautions

There are some general cautions and warnings involving the brake system on this vehicle:

a) *Use only brake fluid conforming to DOT 3 specifications.*

b) *The brake pads and linings contain asbestos fibers which are hazardous to your health if inhaled. Whenever you work on brake system components, clean all parts with brake system cleaner or denatured alcohol. Do not allow the fine dust to become airborne.*

c) *Safety should be paramount whenever any servicing of the brake components is performed. Do not use parts or fasteners which are not in perfect condition, and be sure that all clearances and torque specifications are adhered to. If you are at all unsure about a certain procedure, seek professional advice. Upon completion of any brake system work, test the brakes carefully in a controlled area before putting the vehicle into normal service. If a problem is suspected in the brake system, don't drive the vehicle until it's fixed.*

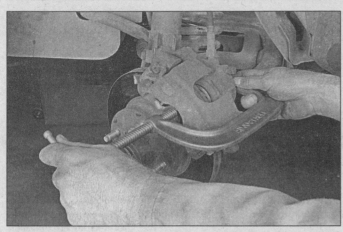

2.6 Using a large C-clamp, push the piston back into the caliper bore just enough to allow the caliper to slide off the brake disc easily - note that one end of the clamp is on the flat area of the inboard side of the caliper and the other end (screw end) is pressing on the outer pad. DO NOT press directly on the piston, as some models use phenolic pistons which will be damaged by direct contact with the clamp

2.7a Remove the two caliper locating pins that hold the caliper to the spindle; on some models, this will require a special TORX socket - DO NOT try to use an Allen wrench instead of a TORX socket!

2 Front brake pads - replacement

Refer to illustrations 2.6 and 2.7a through 2.7i

Warning: *Disc brake pads must be replaced on both front wheels at the same time - never replace the pads on only one wheel. Also, the dust created by the brake system is harmful to your health. Never blow it out with compressed air and don't inhale any of it. An approved filtering mask should be worn when working on the brakes. Do not, under any circumstances, use petroleum-based solvents to clean brake parts. Use brake cleaner or denatured alcohol only!*

Note: *When servicing the disc brakes, use only high quality, nationally recognized brand name pads.*

1   The caliper designs for all models are essentially the same.

2   Remove the covers from the brake fluid reservoir.

3   Loosen the wheel lug nuts, raise the front of the vehicle and support it securely on jackstands.

4   Remove the front wheels. Work on one brake assembly at a time, using the assembled brake for reference if necessary.

5   Inspect the brake disc carefully as outlined in Section 4. If machining is necessary, follow the information in that Section to remove the disc, at which time the pads can be removed from the caliper as well.

6   Push the piston back into its bore. If necessary, a C-clamp can be used, but a pry-bar will usually do the job **(see illustration)**. As the piston is depressed to the bottom of the caliper bore, the fluid in the master cylinder will rise. Make sure that it doesn't overflow. If necessary, siphon off some of the fluid.

7   Follow the accompanying photos,

beginning with illustration 2.7a, for the actual pad replacement procedure. Be sure to stay in order and read the caption under each illustration.

8   When reinstalling the caliper, be sure to tighten the locating pins to the specified torque. On Mustang SVO and 5.0L V8 models from 1987 on, the caliper pins may be reused. On all others, the caliper pins must be replaced with new ones. After the job has been completed, firmly depress the brake pedal a few times to bring the pads into contact with the disc.

3 Front brake caliper - removal, overhaul and installation

Warning: *Dust created by the brake system is harmful to your health. Never blow it out with compressed air and don't inhale any of it. An*

2.7b Pull the caliper straight up and off the disc

2.7c Slide the outer brake pad out of the caliper frame - note how it fits into the frame as this is done

2.7d Using a C-clamp and a block of wood, bottom the piston in the caliper bore

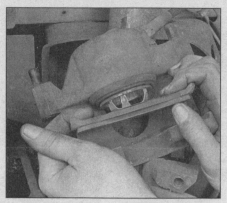

2.7e Pull the inner brake pad straight out of the caliper piston

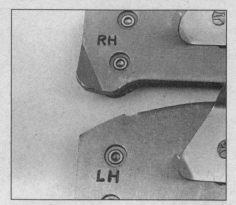

2.7f The brake pads are marked for left and right sides - be sure they are installed in the correct positions

2.7g To install the inner pad, hold each end of the pad, align the retaining clips with the caliper piston, then push the pad straight in until the backing plate contacts the piston face - don't let it cock, or the clips may bend

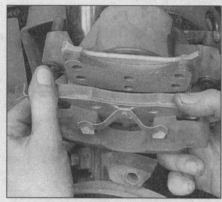

2.7h Slide the outer pad into the caliper frame as shown. If the outer pad is equipped with torque buttons (early models), be sure they are seated in the holes in the caliper, or temporary brake loss may occur

2.7i Place the caliper assembly over the brake disc and install the locating pins, tightening them to the torque listed in this Chapter's Specifications

approved filtering mask should be worn when working on the brakes. Do not, under any circumstances, use petroleum-based solvents to clean brake parts. Use brake cleaner or denatured alcohol only!

Note: *If an overhaul is indicated (usually because of fluid leakage) explore all options before beginning the job. New and factory-rebuilt calipers are available on an exchange basis, which makes this job quite easy. If it is decided to rebuild the calipers, make sure that a rebuild kit is available before proceeding. Always rebuild the calipers in pairs - never rebuild just one of them.*

Removal

1   Apply the parking brake and block the rear wheels. Loosen the wheel lug nuts, raise the front of the vehicle and support it securely on jackstands. Remove the wheel.

2   If the caliper brake hose screws directly into the caliper, loosen the hydraulic fitting at the frame bracket and remove the brake hose securing clip (see Section 10). The brake hose can now be unscrewed from the caliper. If the brake hose is secured to the caliper by a union bolt, remove the bolt and both sealing washers. Discard the washers and use

new ones on installation. Wrap a plastic bag around the end of the hose to prevent fluid loss and contamination. **Note:** *If the caliper will not be completely removed from the vehicle - as for pad inspection or disc removal - leave the hose connected and suspend the caliper with a length of wire. This will save the trouble of bleeding the brake system.*

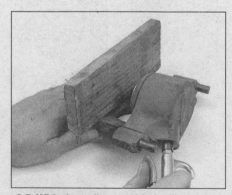

3.5 With the caliper padded with a wood block, use compressed air to force the piston out of its bore - make sure your hands or fingers are not caught between the piston and caliper!

3   Refer to the first few steps in Section 2 to separate the caliper from the spindle - it's part of the brake pad replacement procedure.

Overhaul

Refer to illustrations 3.5, 3.6, 3.7, 3.12, 3.17, 3.18, 3.19a, 3.19b, 3.20 and 3.21

4   Clean the exterior of the caliper with brake cleaner or denatured alcohol. Never use gasoline, kerosene or petroleum-based cleaning solvents. Place the caliper on a clean workbench.

5   Position a wooden block in the center of the caliper as a cushion, then use compressed air to remove the piston from the caliper **(see illustration)**. Use only enough air to ease the piston out of the bore. If the piston is blown out, even with the cushion in place, it may be damaged. **Warning:** *Never place your fingers in front of the piston in an attempt to catch or protect it when applying compressed air, as serious injury could occur.*

6   Pull the dust boot out of the caliper bore **(see illustration)**.

7   Using a wood or plastic tool, remove the piston seal from the caliper bore **(see illustration)**. Metal tools may cause bore damage.

8   Carefully examine the piston for nicks, burrs, cracks, loss of plating, corrosion or any signs of damage. If surface defects are pre-

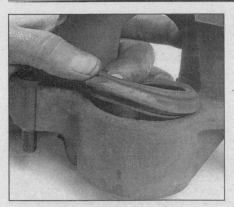

3.6 Remove the dust boot from the caliper bore groove

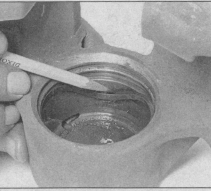

3.7 The piston seal should be removed with a plastic or wooden tool to avoid damage to the bore and seal groove (a pencil, as shown here, will do the job)

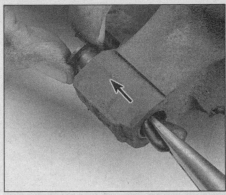

3.12 On models with plastic sleeves inside the insulators, remove the sleeves; grab the ends of the locating pin insulators and, using a twisting motion, push them through the caliper ears

sent, the parts must be replaced.

9 Check the caliper bore in a similar way. Light polishing with crocus cloth is permissible to remove light corrosion and stains.

10 Remove the bleeder valve and rubber cap.

11 Inspect the caliper locating pins for corrosion and damage. Replace them with new ones if necessary.

12 Remove the caliper locating pin insulators from the caliper ears **(see illustration)**.

13 Use clean brake fluid or denatured alcohol to clean all the parts. **Warning:** *Do not, under any circumstances, use petroleum-based solvents to clean brake parts. Allow all parts to dry, preferably using compressed air to blow out all passages. Make sure the compressed air is filtered, as a harmful lubricant residue or moisture may be present in unfiltered systems.*

14 Push the new locating pin insulators into place, making sure they are fully installed. On models with plastic sleeves, make sure they're also installed.

15 Check the fit of the piston in the bore by sliding it into the caliper. The piston should move easily.

16 Thread the bleeder valve into the caliper

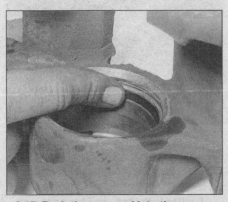

3.17 Push the new seal into the groove with you fingers, then check to see that it isn't twisted or kinked

and tighten it securely. Install the rubber cap.

17 Lubricate the new piston seal and caliper bore with clean brake fluid. Position the seal in the caliper bore groove, making sure it doesn't twist **(see illustration)**.

18 Fit the new dust boot in the caliper bore upper groove, making sure it's seated **(see illustration)**.

3.18 Install the dust boot in the upper groove in the caliper bore, making sure it's completely seated

19 Lubricate the caliper piston with clean brake fluid. Push the piston into the caliper, using a turning motion to roll the lip of the dust boot over the piston **(see illustrations)**. Push the piston into the caliper by hand as far as possible.

3.19a Lubricate the piston and bore with clean brake fluid, insert the piston into the dust boot (NOT the bore) at an angle, then, using a rotating motion, work the piston completely into the dust boot . . .

3.19b . . . and push it straight into the caliper as far as possible by hand

9

3.20 Use a C-clamp and a block of wood to bottom the piston in the caliper bore - make sure it goes in perfectly straight, or the sides of the piston may be damaged, rendering it useless

3.21 Install the lip of the dust boot in the groove in the caliper piston

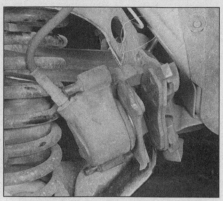

4.2 Suspend the caliper with a piece o wire after it's removed- don't let it hang by the brake hose!

20   Using a C-clamp and a block of wood, push the piston all the way to the bottom of the bore. Work slowly, keeping an eye on the side of the piston, making sure it enters the bore perfectly straight with no resistance **(see illustration)**.

21   Seat the lip of the dust boot in the groove on the piston **(see illustration)**.

Installation

22   Refer to Section 2 for the caliper installation procedure, as it is part of the brake pad replacement procedure.

23   If the brake hose is the thread-in type, thread it into the caliper. The hose is not designed to thread all the way in, so don't overtighten it. One or two threads should still be exposed when the brake hose is tightened to the correct torque.

24   If the brake hose is secured to the caliper by a union bolt, install a new sealing washer on each side of the fitting, then install the union bolt and tighten to the correct torque (see this Chapter's Specifications).

25   Bleed the brakes as outlined in Section 11. This is not necessary if the inlet fitting was not loosened or removed.

26   Install the wheel and lower the vehicle. Tighten the lug nuts to the torque specified in Chapter 1.

27   Test the brake operation before placing the vehicle into normal service.

---

4   Brake disc - inspection, removal and installation

Inspection

Refer to illustrations 4.2, 4.5a, 4.5b, 4.6a and 4.6b

Note: *This procedure applies to both front and rear disc brake assemblies.*

1   Loosen the wheel lug nuts, raise the vehicle and support it securely on jackstands. Remove the wheel.

2   Remove the brake caliper as outlined in Section 3 (front) or Section 6 (rear). It's not

4.5a Use a dial indicator to check disc runout - if the reading exceeds the maximum allowable runout limit, the rotor will have to be machined or replaced

necessary to disconnect the brake hose. After removing the caliper bolts, suspend the caliper out of the way with a piece of wire **(see illustration)**. Don't let the caliper hang by the hose and don't stretch or twist the hose.

3   If the rear disc is being inspected, reinstall two lug nuts to hold the disc against the axle flange.

4   Visually check the disc surface for score marks and other damage. Light scratches and shallow grooves are normal after use and may not always be detrimental to brake operation, but deep score marks - over 0.015-inch (0.38 mm) - require disc removal and refinishing by an automotive machine shop. Be sure to check both sides of the disc. If pulsating has been noticed during application of the brakes, suspect disc runout.

5   To check disc runout, place a dial indicator at a point about 1/2-inch from the outer edge of the disc **(see illustration)**. Set the indicator to zero and turn the disc. The indicator reading should not exceed the specified allowable runout limit. If it does, the disc should be refinished by an automotive machine shop. **Note:** *Professionals recommend resurfacing of brake discs regardless of the dial indicator reading (to produce a smooth, flat surface, that will eliminate brake pedal pulsations and other undesirable symp-*

4.5b Using a swirling motion, remove the glaze from the disc surface with medium-grit emery cloth

toms related to questionable discs). At the very least, if you elect not to have the discs resurfaced, deglaze the brake pad surface with medium-grit emery cloth (use a swirling motion to ensure a non-directional finish) **(see illustration)**.

6   The disc must not be machined to a thickness less than the specified minimum refinish thickness. The minimum wear (or discard) thickness is cast into the inside of the disc **(see illustration)**. It should not be confused with the minimum refinish thickness.

4.6a The minimum thickness limit is cast into the inside of the disc

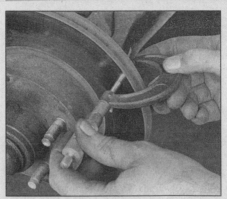

4.6b Use a micrometer to measure disc thickness at several points near the edge

The disc thickness can be checked with a micrometer (see illustration).

Removal

7   Refer to Chapter 1, Section 28, to remove the disc and hub assembly. To remove the rear disc, unscrew the two lug nuts that held the disc to the axle during the inspection procedure, then pull the disc off the axle flange.

Installation

8   Install the disc and hub assembly and adjust the wheel bearing (front discs only) (Chapter 1).
9   Install the caliper and brake pad assembly over the disc and position it on the spindle (front) or anchor plate (rear) (refer to Section 3 for the front caliper installation procedure, or Section 6 for the rear brake caliper installation procedure, if necessary). Tighten the caliper bolts to the specified torque.
10   Install the wheel, then lower the vehicle to the ground. Depress the brake pedal a few times to bring the brake pads into contact with the rotor. Bleeding of the system will not be necessary unless the brake hose was disconnected from the caliper. Check the operation of the brakes carefully before placing the vehicle into normal service.

5   Rear brake caliper - removal, installation and pad replacement

Warning: *Dust created by the brake system, which is harmful to your health. Never blow it out with compressed air and don' inhale any of it. An approved filtering mask should be worn when working on the brakes. Do not, under any circumstances, use petroleum-based solvents to clean brake parts. Use brake cleaner or denatured alcohol only!*
Note: *Due to the relatively complex design of the rear brake caliper/parking brake actuator assembly, all service procedures requiring disassembly and reassembly should be left to a professional mechanic. The home mechanic can, however, remove the caliper and take it to a repair shop or dealer service department or other qualified shop for repair, thereby sav-*

ing the cost of removal and installation.
1   Securely block the front wheels, then raise the vehicle and support it securely on jackstands. DO NOT get under a vehicle that's supported only by a jack.
2   Remove the rear wheels.
3   On Mustang SVO models, detach the parking brake cable from the lever. If you use pliers, be careful not to cut the cable or return spring. On 1993 Mustang Cobra models, pull down on the parking brake cable end with pliers, remove the retaining clip and remove the cable from the lever.
4   If you are removing the caliper only for pad replacement, it isn't necessary to disconnect the brake line. Get a piece of wire to tie the caliper up so it won't hang by the brake line once it is removed.
5   On Mustang SVO models, remove the caliper pins. Lift up on the top of the caliper, then rotate the bottom end out of the anchor plate. **Note:** *Discard the locating pin insulators. They must be replaced with new ones each time the locating pins are removed.* Remove the caliper from the disc. On 1993 Mustang Cobra models, hold the slider hex heads with an open-end wrench and unscrew the pinch bolts. Remove the screw securing the brake hose bracket to the shock absorber bracket. Remove the caliper from the disc.
6   On Mustang SVO models, if the caliper is difficult to remove because the pads are tight against the disc, loosen the caliper end retainer one-half turn (no more) so the piston can retract (Steps 7 through 9).
7   On Mustang SVO models, remove the parking brake lever (the one at the rear wheel, not the one in the passenger compartment.
8   On Mustang SVO models, make alignment marks on the parking brake end retainer and caliper housing so you don't loosen the end retainer too far.
9   On Mustang SVO models, loosen the end retainer one-half turn, then push the caliper piston into the bore. **Caution:** *Loosening the end retainer more than one-half turn may allow brake fluid to leak into the parking brake portion of the caliper. If this happens, the caliper will have to disassembled and overhauled.*
10   Remove the outer brake pad from the anchor plate. Mark the pad as an outer pad if you plan to reinstall it.
11   On Mustang SVO models, remove the brake disc retaining nuts and take the brake disc off.
12   Remove the inner pad from the anchor plate. Label it as an inner pad if you plan to reinstall it.
13   Remove the anti-rattle clip.
14   If the caliper is being removed just for pad replacement, hang it from the vehicle with wire so the brake hose isn't stretched. If the caliper is being removed from the vehicle, remove the hollow bolt to detach the brake line from the caliper. Use new sealing washers on each side of the bolt on reassembly.
15   Inspect the brake disc carefully as outlined in Section 4.
16   Check for signs of brake fluid leakage

from the caliper, at both the piston boot and the parking brake lever. If any wetness is found, have the caliper overhauled by a dealer service department or qualified brake specialist.
17   Thoroughly clean the caliper, anchor plate and surrounding area with spray brake cleaner. Check all parts for wear and damage.
18   On Mustang SVO models, temporarily reinstall the caliper in the anchor plate without the pads. Tighten the end retainer to the torque listed in this Chapter's Specifications.
19   On Mustang SVO models, install the parking brake lever so it points to the rear and down. Tighten the retainer screw to the torque listed in this Chapter's Specifications, then make sure the lever still moves freely.
20   If new pads are being installed, rotate the piston to bottom it in the bore. Use a special tool designed for this job, available at most auto parts stores that carry special tools, if it's available. Turn the piston clockwise until it bottoms completely in the bore (it will keep turning after it bottoms). If the special tool is not available, try rotating the piston with a pair of needle nose pliers, placing the tips of the pliers into the holes in the piston. On 1993 Mustang Cobra models, position the piston slots so the locating nib on the inboard brake pad will align correctly with one of the slots. **Note:** *This alignment is necessary for proper installation of the inboard pad.*
21   On Mustang SVO models, take the caliper out of the anchor plate.
22   On Mustang SVO models, install new locating pin insulators in the caliper.
23   Apply a thin coat of disc brake caliper slide grease to the caliper sliding surfaces on the anchor plate. Be sure to use the correct lubricant; the wrong type may melt and contaminate the brake pads.
24   If the anti-rattle clip was removed, install it.
25   Install the inner pad on the anchor plate (refer to the identification marks made during removal if the old pads are being reinstalled).
26   On Mustang SVO models, install the brake disc and its retaining nuts. Discs are not interchangeable from side to side of the vehicle. The disc fins must face rearward when the disc is installed.
27   Install the outer brake pad on the anchor plate with the wear indicator up.
28   If the brake hose was disconnected from the caliper, reconnect it. Use new sealing washers and tighten the bolt to the torque listed in this Chapter's Specifications.
29   Hook the upper end of the caliper into the anchor plate, then rotate the caliper down over the pads and disc. Take care not to damage the piston dust boot.
30   On Mustang SVO models, pull the caliper firmly out to seat the inner pad against the disc. Measure pad-to-caliper clearance. If not as specified in the illustration, remove the caliper and rotate the piston to adjust the clearance. Turn the piston counterclockwise to reduce the gap or clockwise to enlarge it.

9

One-quarter turn of the piston changes the gap by approximately 1/16-inch. **Caution:** *Don't skip this adjustment. If the gap is too small, the brakes may drag. If it is too large, the adjuster may fall out of the piston when the brakes are applied. It will then be necessary to overhaul the caliper and replace the adjuster/piston assembly.*

6.4b Before removing anything, clean the brake assembly with brake cleaner and allow it to dry - position a drain pan under the brake to catch the residue - DO NOT USE COMPRESSED AIR TO BLOW THE DUST FROM THE PARTS!

31   On Mustang SVO models, coat the caliper locating pins and the insides of their insulator with silicone grease. On 1993 Mustang Cobra models, coat the caliper slider pins and the insides of the slider pin boots with silicone grease (same as used on SVO models).

32   On Mustang SVO models, apply a single drop of thread locking agent to the threads of each locating pin. On 1993 Mustang Cobra models, apply the same thread locking agent to the pinch bolts. Install and start the locating pins (or pinch bolts) by hand only, then tighten them to the torque listed in this Chapter's Specifications.

33   Connect the parking brake cable. On 1993 Mustang Cobra models, install the screw securing the brake hose bracket to the shock absorber bracket.

34   If the brake hose was disconnected, bleed the brakes (see Section 11).

35   Recheck the brake fluid level (see Chapter 1) and correct it as needed.

36   To adjust the calipers, pump the brake pedal about 30 times, with at least one second between pumps. Apply light pedal pressure (about 87 lbs).

37   Pull the parking brake lever. If travel is excessive or the lever is extremely easy to pull, repeat the adjustment. If this doesn't work, check the parking brake (see Sections 12 through 15).

38   The remainder of installation is the reverse of the removal steps.

39   Make sure the brake pedal is firm, then carefully road test the foot brake and parking brake.

6   Rear brake shoes - replacement

Refer to illustrations 6.4b through 6.4y

Warning: *Drum brake shoes must be replaced on both wheels at the same time - never replace the shoes on only one wheel. Also, the dust created by the brake system is harmful to your health. Never blow it out with compressed air and don't inhale any of it. An approved filtering mask should be worn when working on the brakes. Do not, under any circumstances, use petroleum-based solvents to clean brake parts. Use brake cleaner or denatured alcohol only!*

Caution: *Whenever the brake shoes are replaced, the retractor and holddown springs should also be replaced. Due to the continuous heating/cooling cycle that the springs are subjected to, they lose their tension over a*

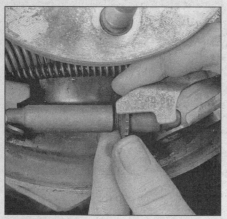

6.4c Pull back on the adjuster lever and turn the star wheel to retract the brake shoes

6.4d Using a brake spring tool, unhook the secondary shoe return spring . . .

6.4e . . . then remove the spring and cable guide from the secondary shoe

6.4f Unhook the primary shoe return spring from the anchor pin

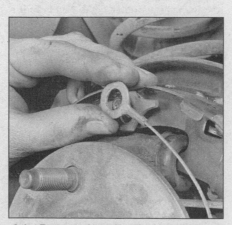

6.4g Remove the self-adjuster cable and shoe guide plate from the anchor pin

6.4h Remove the brake shoe hold-down springs and pins - a special tool, shown here, will make the job easier

6.4i Remove the parking brake link

6.4j Spread the brake shoes apart and lift them from the backing plate and over the axle flange

6.4k Unhook the parking brake lever from the secondary brake shoe

6.4l Lubricate the brake shoe contact areas with high-temperature grease

6.4m Insert the top of the parking brake lever into the notch at the top of the secondary brake shoe (the secondary shoe is the one with the longer lining area). Place the shoe against the backing plate and install the hold-down pin and spring

6.4n Install the parking brake strut, making sure that the slot in the strut seats in the notches in the brake shoe and the parking brake lever

period of time and may allow the shoes to drag on the drum and wear at a much faster rate than normal. When replacing the rear brake shoes, use only high quality nationally recognized brand-name parts.

1   Loosen the wheel lug nuts, raise the rear of the vehicle and support it securely on jackstands. Block the front wheels to keep the vehicle from rolling.

2   Release the parking brake.
3   Remove the wheel. **Note:** *All four rear brake shoes must be replaced at the same time, but to avoid mixing up parts, work on only one brake assembly at a time.*

4   Follow the accompanying photos (illustrations 6.4b through 6.4y) for the inspection and replacement of the brake shoes. Be sure to stay in order and read the caption under each illustration. **Note:** *If the brake drum cannot be easily pulled off the axle and shoe assembly, make sure that the parking brake is*

6.4o Place the primary shoe against the backing plate and install the hold-down pin and spring

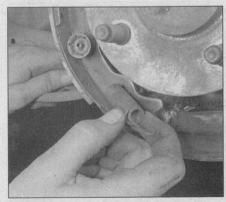

6.4p Hook, the automatic adjuster spring into the hole at the bottom of the primary brake shoe

6.4q Hook the other end of the spring into the adjuster lever and push the lever toward the secondary shoe, hooking it into the hole provided

9

6.4r   Place the shoe guide plate over the anchor pin

6.4s   Install the self adjuster cable over the anchor pin

6.4t   Using a brake spring installation tool, hook the primary shoe return spring over the anchor pin

6.4u   Install the secondary shoe return spring through the cable guide and into the hole in the shoe; hook the other end onto the anchor pin

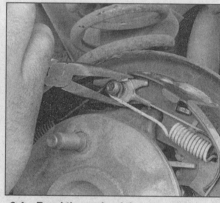

6.4v   Bend the ends of the return springs around the anchor pin

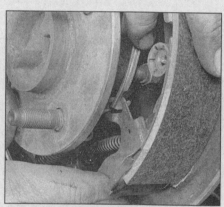

6.4w   Route the cable around the cable guide, push up on the adjuster lever and hook the cable into the hole in the lever. Check the cable again to ensure that it rests in the cable guide groove, not behind it

completely released, then squirt some penetrating oil around the center hub area. Allow the oil to soak in and try to pull the drum off. If the drum still cannot be pulled off, the brake shoes will have to be retracted. This is accomplished by first removing the plug from the backing plate. With the plug removed, pull the lever off the adjusting star wheel with one small screwdriver while turning the adjusting wheel with another small screwdriver, moving the shoes away from the drum. The drum should now come off.

5   Before reinstalling the drum it should be checked for cracks, score marks, deep scratches and hard spots, which will appear as small discolored areas. If the hard spots cannot be removed with fine emery cloth or if any of the other conditions listed above exist, the drum must be taken to an automotive machine shop to have it turned. **Note:** *Professionals recommend resurfacing the drums whenever a brake job is done. Resurfacing will eliminate the possibility of out-of-round drums. If the drums are worn so much that they can't be resurfaced without exceeding the maximum allowable diameter (stamped into the drum), then new ones will be required. At the very least, if you elect not to have the drums resurfaced, remove the glaz-*ing from the surface with medium-grit emery cloth using a swirling motion.

6   Install the brake drum on the axle flange.

7   Mount the wheel, install the lug nuts, then lower the vehicle.

8   Make a number of forward and reverse stops to adjust the brakes until satisfactory pedal action is obtained.

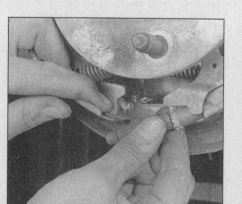

6.4x   Lubricate the adjuster screw threads, spread the shoes apart and install the screw between them

7   Wheel cylinder - removal, overhaul and installation

Note: *If an overhaul is indicated (usually because of fluid leakage or sticky operation) explore all options before beginning the job. New wheel cylinders are available, which*

6.4y   Wiggle the brake shoe assembly back and forth to make sure it's centered on the backing plate

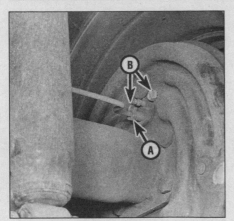

7.4 Disconnect the brake line fitting (A), then remove the two wheel cylinder bolts (B)

8.1a Disconnect the fluid lines at the master cylinder with a flare-nut wrench, being careful not to bend them

8.1b Lift the master cylinder from the engine compartment - note the newspaper to catch dripping brake fluid, which could damage paint

makes this job quite easy. If it's decided to rebuild the wheel cylinder, make sure that a rebuild kit is available before proceeding. Never overhaul only one wheel cylinder - always rebuild both of them at the same time.

Removal

Refer to illustration 7.4

1   Raise the rear of the vehicle and support it securely on jackstands. Block the front wheels to keep the vehicle from rolling.
2   Remove the brake shoe assembly (Section 6).
3   Remove all dirt and foreign material from around the wheel cylinder.
4   Disconnect the brake line (**see illustration**). Don't pull the brake line away from the wheel cylinder.
5   Remove the wheel cylinder mounting bolts.
6   Detach the wheel cylinder from the brake backing plate and place it on a clean workbench. Immediately plug the brake line to prevent fluid loss and contamination.

Overhaul

7   Remove the bleeder screw, cups, pis-

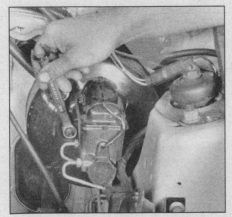

8.2 Remove the two nuts to detach the master cylinder from the brake booster or engine compartment firewall

tons, boots and spring assembly from the wheel cylinder body.
8   Clean the wheel cylinder with brake fluid, denatured alcohol or brake system cleaner. **Warning:** *Do not, under any circumstances, use petroleum based solvents to clean brake parts!*
9   Use compressed air to remove excess fluid from the wheel cylinder and to blow out the passages.
10   Check the cylinder bore for corrosion and score marks. Crocus cloth can be used to remove light corrosion and stains, but the cylinder must be replaced with a new one if the defects cannot be removed easily, or if the bore is scored.
11   Lubricate the new cups with brake fluid.
12   Assemble the brake cylinder components. Make sure the cup lips face in.

Installation

13   Place the wheel cylinder in position and install the bolts.
14   Connect the brake line and install the brake shoe assembly.
15   Bleed the brakes (Section 11).

---

8   Master cylinder (1979 through 1986 models) - removal, installation and overhaul

---

Removal and installation

Refer to illustrations 8.1a, 8.1b and 8.2

1   Unscrew the brake lines from the primary and secondary outlet ports of the master cylinder (**see illustration**). Plug the ends of the lines to prevent contamination. Place newspapers or rags under the connections to catch the brake fluid that will spill (**see illustration**).
2   Remove the two nuts securing the master cylinder to the firewall or power booster unit (**see illustration**).
3   Pull the master cylinder forward and lift it from the vehicle (**see illustration 8.1b**). Brake fluid will damage paint, so don't spill

any on the vehicle.
4   Installation is the reverse of the removal procedure.
5   **Note:** *Whenever the master cylinder is removed, the complete hydraulic system must be bled. The time required to bleed the system can be reduced if the master cylinder is filled with fluid and bench bled (refer to Steps 6 through 10) before the master cylinder is installed on the vehicle.*
6   Insert threaded plugs of the correct size into the cylinder outlet holes and fill the reservoirs with brake fluid. The master cylinder should be supported in such a manner that brake fluid will not spill during the bench bleeding procedure.
7   Loosen one plug at a time, starting with the rear outlet port first, and use a large Phillips screwdriver to push the piston assembly into the bore to force air from the master cylinder. To prevent air from being drawn back into the cylinder, the appropriate plug must be replaced before allowing the piston to return to its original position.
8   Stroke the piston three or four times for each outlet to ensure that all air has been expelled.
9   Since high pressure is not involved in the bench bleeding procedure, an alternative to the removal and replacement of the plugs with each stroke of the piston assembly is available. Before pushing in on the piston assembly, remove one of the plugs completely. Before releasing the piston, however, instead of replacing the plug, simply put your finger tightly over the hole to keep air from being drawn back into the master cylinder. Wait several seconds for the brake fluid to be drawn from the reservoir to the piston bore, then repeat the procedure. When you push down on the piston it will force your finger off the hole, allowing the air inside to be expelled. When only brake fluid is being ejected from the hole, replace the plug and go on to the other port.
10   Refill the master cylinder reservoirs and install the diaphragm and cap assembly.

9

8.14 Remove the snap-ring from the master cylinder bore

8.15 Remove the primary piston from the bore

8.17 Remove the secondary piston from the bore after removing the stop screw, if equipped

Overhaul

Refer to illustrations 8.14, 8.15, 8.17 and 8.19

Note: *Before deciding to overhaul the master cylinder, check on the availability and cost of a new or factory rebuilt unit and also the availability of a rebuild kit.*

11   Clean the exterior of the master cylinder and wipe dry with a lint free rag. Remove the cover and gasket from the top of the reservoir and pour out any remaining brake fluid.

12   Use a large Phillips screwdriver to depress the piston assembly, then remove the secondary piston stop bolt from the bottom of the master cylinder body, if equipped.

13   Remove the bleed screw, if equipped.

14   Depress the piston assembly again, then remove the snap-ring from the groove at the rear of the master cylinder bore as shown in the accompanying illustration.

15   Remove the primary piston assembly **(see illustration)**.

16   Do not remove the screw on the primary piston or disassemble the piston. The piston assembly is replaced as a unit.

17   Remove the secondary piston assembly **(see illustration)**.

18   Do not remove the tube seats, from the master cylinder body.

19   Examine the bore of the cylinder carefully for scoring or ridges. If the bore is smooth, the cylinder body can be reused. If there is any doubt of the condition of the bore, install a new or rebuilt master cylinder. If the cylinder is made of cast iron, minor scratches or scoring in the bore can be removed using a honing tool **(see illusrtration)**. **Caution:** *Do not hone the bore on aluminum master cylinders; the hardened surface in the bore will be removed.*

20   If the seals are swollen or very loose on the pistons, suspect oil contamination in the system. Oil will swell these rubber seals and if one is found to be swollen, others in the brake system may also be damaged.

Flush the system thoroughly (follow the bleeding procedure in section 11) with clean brake fluid after overhaul to remove the oil.

21   Thoroughly clean all parts in clean brake fluid or alcohol.

22   All components should be assembled wet after dipping them in fresh brake fluid.

23   Insert the complete secondary piston and return spring assembly into the master cylinder bore, easing the seals into the bore.

24   Insert the primary piston assembly into the master cylinder bore.

25   Depress the primary piston and install the snap-ring into the cylinder bore groove.

26   Fit the secondary piston stop bolt and O-ring into the bottom of the master cylinder body.

27   Reinstall the gasket onto the cover, making sure it is correctly seated, and replace the cover.

9   Master cylinder (1987 and later models) - removal, overhaul and installation

Note: *Before deciding to overhaul the master cylinder, check on the availability and cost of a new or factory rebuilt unit and also the availability of a rebuild kit.*

Removal

1   Place rags under the brake line fittings and prepare caps or plastic bags to cover the ends of the lines once they are disconnected. **Caution:** *Brake fluid will damage paint. Cover all body parts and be careful not to spill fluid during this procedure.*

2   Unscrew the tube nuts at the ends of the brake lines where they enter the master cylinder. To prevent rounding off the flats on these nuts, a flare-nut wrench, which wraps around the fitting, should be used. **Note:** *1987 and later models use metric tube nuts at the master cylinder connections.*

3   Pull the brake lines away from the master cylinder slightly and plug the ends to prevent contamination.

4   Disconnect the brake warning light electrical connector, remove the two master cylinder mounting nuts, and detach the master cylinder from the vehicle.

5   Remove the reservoir cap, then discard any fluid remaining in the reservoir.

8.19 If the master cylinder is made from cast iron, use a hone and drill motor to remove minor scratches from the bore - DO NOT hone the bore on aluminum cylinders

Overhaul

Refer to illustrations 9.7, 9.8, 9.9, 9.10 and 9.14

6   Mount the master cylinder in a vise with the vise jaws clamping on the mounting flange.

7   Remove the primary piston snap-ring by depressing the piston and extracting the ring with a pair of snap-ring pliers. **(see illustration)**.

8   Remove the primary piston assembly from the cylinder bore **(see illustration)**.

9   Remove the secondary piston assembly from the cylinder bore. It may be necessary to remove the master cylinder from the vise and invert it, carefully tapping it against a block of wood to expel the piston **(see illustration)**.

10   If fluid has been leaking past the reservoir grommets, pry the reservoir from the cylinder body with a screwdriver **(see illustration)**. Remove the grommets.

11   Inspect the cylinder bore for corrosion and damage. If any corrosion or damage is found, replace the master cylinder body with a new one, as abrasives cannot be used on the bore.

9.7 Use a Phillips head screwdriver to push the primary piston into the cylinder, then remove the snap-ring

9.8 Remove the primary piston assembly from the cylinder

9.9 Tap the master cylinder against a block of wood to eject the secondary piston assembly

12 Lubricate the new reservoir grommets with silicone lubricant and press them into the master cylinder body. Make sure they're properly seated.

13 Lay the reservoir on a hard surface and press the master cylinder body onto the reservoir, using a rocking motion.

14 Lubricate the cylinder bore and primary and secondary piston assemblies with clean brake fluid. Insert the secondary piston assembly into the cylinder **(see illustration)**.

15 Install the primary piston assembly in the cylinder bore, depress it and install the snap-ring.

16 Inspect the reservoir cap and diaphragm for cracks and deformation. Replace any damaged parts with new ones and attach the diaphragm to the cap.

17 **Note:** *Whenever the master cylinder is removed, the complete hydraulic system must be bled. The time required to bleed the system can be reduced if the master cylinder is filled with fluid and bench bled (refer to Steps 18 through 23) before the master cylinder is installed on the vehicle.*

18 Insert threaded plugs of the correct size into the cylinder outlet holes and fill the reservoirs with brake fluid. The master cylinder should be supported in such a manner that brake fluid will not spill during the bench bleeding procedure.

19 Loosen one plug at a time, starting with the rear outlet port first, and push the piston assembly into the bore to force air from the master cylinder To prevent air from being drawn back into the cylinder, the appropriate plug must be replaced before allowing the piston to return to its original position.

20 Stroke the piston three or four times for each outlet to ensure that all air has been expelled.

21 Since high pressure is not involved in the bench bleeding procedure, an alternative to the removal and replacement of the plugs with each stroke of the piston assembly is available. Before pushing in on the piston assembly, remove one of the plugs completely. Before releasing the piston, however, instead of replacing the plug, simply put your finger tightly over the hole to keep air from

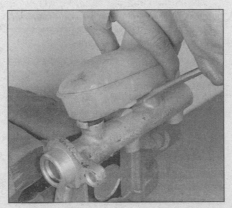

9.10 If you must remove the fluid reservoir (to replace leaking seals or a broken reservoir), gently pry it off with a screwdriver or prybar

being drawn back into the master cylinder. Wait several seconds for the brake fluid to be drawn from the reservoir to the piston bore, then repeat the procedure. When you push down on the piston it will force your finger off the hole, allowing the air inside to be expelled. When only brake fluid is being ejected from the hole, replace the plug and go on to the other port.

22 Refill the master cylinder reservoirs and install the diaphragm and cap assembly.

Installation

23 Carefully install the master cylinder by reversing the removal steps, then bleed the brakes (refer to Section 11).

10 Brake hoses and lines - inspection and replacement

Inspection

1 About every six months, with the vehicle raised and supported securely on jackstands, the rubber hoses which connect the steel brake lines with the front and rear brake assemblies should be inspected for cracks, chafing of the outer cover, leaks, blisters and other damage. These are important and vul-

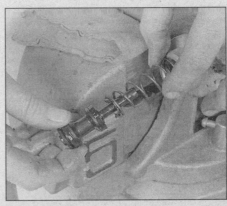

9.14 Coat the secondary piston with clean brake fluid and install it in the master cylinder, spring end first

nerable parts of the brake system and inspection should b complete. A light and mirror will be helpful for a thorough check. If a hose exhibits any of the above conditions, replace it with a new one.

Replacement

Front brake hose

2 Using a back-up wrench, disconnect the brake line from the hose fitting, being careful not to bend the frame bracket or brake line.

3 Use a pair of pliers to remove the U-clip from the female fitting at the bracket, then detach the hose from the bracket.

4 Unscrew the brake hose from the caliper or remove the union bolt and sealing washers (be sure to use new sealing washers on reassembly).

5 To install the hose, first thread it into the caliper, tightening it securely.

6 Without twisting the hose, install the female fitting in the hose bracket. It will fit the bracket in only one position.

7 Install the U-clip retaining the female fitting to the frame bracket.

8 Using a back-up wrench, attach the brake line to the hose fitting.

9 When the brake hose installation is complete, there should be no kinks in the hose. Make sure the hose doesn't contact

9

any part of the suspension. Check this by turning the wheels to the extreme left and right positions. If the hose makes contact, remove it and correct the installation as necessary. Bleed the system (see Section 11).

Rear brake hose (drum brake models)

10   Using a back-up wrench, disconnect the hose at the frame bracket, being careful not to bend the bracket or steel lines.
11   Remove the U-clip with a pair of pliers and separate the female fitting from the bracket.
12   Disconnect the two brake lines at the junction block, then unbolt and remove the hose.
13   Bolt the junction block to the axle housing and connect the lines, tightening them securely. Without twisting the hose, install the female end of the hose in the frame bracket.
14   Install the U-clips retaining the female end to the bracket.
15   Using a back-up wrench, attach the steel line fittings to the female fittings. Again, be careful not to bend the bracket or steel line.
16   Make sure the hose installation did not loosen the frame bracket. Tighten the bracket if necessary.
17   Fill the master cylinder reservoir and bleed the system (see Section 11).

Rear brake hoses (disc brake models)

18   Vehicles equipped with rear disc brakes use a brake hose at each wheel. The hose is permanently attached to a bracket bolted to the rear axle. The other end of the hose is secured to the caliper by a union bolt and sealing washers.
19   Using a back-up wrench, disconnect the steel line from the brake hose at the rear axle.
20   Remove the union bolt and sealing washers that secure the brake hose to the caliper.
21   Remove the bracket-to-axle bolt, then take the brake housing and bracket off the axle housing.
22   Loosely bolt the bracket and brake hose to the axle housing, then connect the steel line.
23   Using new sealing washers, connect the brake hose to the caliper. Tighten the union bolt to the correct torque (see this Chapter's Specifications).
24   Tighten the bracket-to-axle housing bolt and steel brake line securely. Bleed the brakes as described in Section 11.

Metal brake lines

25   When replacing brake lines be sure to use the correct parts.
Don't use copper tubing for any brake system components. Purchase steel brake lines from a dealer or auto parts store.
26   Prefabricated brake line, with the tube ends already flared and fittings installed, is available at auto parts stores and dealers. These lines are also bent to the proper shapes.
27   When installing the new line make sure

11.8 When bleeding the brakes, a hose is connected to the bleeder valve at the caliper or wheel cylinder and then submerged in brake fluid. Air will be seen as bubbles in the tube and container. All air must be expelled before moving to the next wheel

it's securely supported in the brackets and has plenty of clearance between moving or hot components.
28   After installation, check the master cylinder fluid level and add fluid as necessary. Bleed the brake system as outlined in the next Section and test the brakes carefully before driving the vehicle in traffic.

11   Brake hydraulic system - bleeding

Refer to illustration 11.8
Warning: *Wear eye protection when bleeding the brake system. If the fluid comes in contact with your eyes, immediately rinse them with water and seek medical attention.*
Note: *Bleeding the hydraulic system is necessary to remove any air that manages to find its way into the system when it's been opened during removal and installation of a hose, line, caliper or master cylinder.*
1   It will probably be necessary to bleed the system at all four brakes if air has entered the system due to low fluid level, or if the brake lines have been disconnected at the master cylinder.
2   If a brake line was disconnected only at a wheel, then only that caliper or wheel cylinder must be bled.
3   If a brake line is disconnected at a fitting located between the master cylinder and any of the brakes, that part of the system served by the disconnected line must be bled.
4   Remove any residual vacuum from the brake power booster by applying the brake several times with the engine off.
5   Remove the master cylinder reservoir cover and fill the reservoir with brake fluid. Reinstall the cover. **Note:** *Check the fluid level often during the bleeding operation and add fluid as necessary to prevent the fluid level from falling low enough to allow air bubbles into the master cylinder.*
6   Have an assistant on hand, as well as a supply of new brake fluid, a clear container

12.4 Parking brake equalizer locknut and adjusting nut - models with rear drum brakes (arrow)

partially filled with clean brake fluid, a length of 3/16-inch plastic, rubber or vinyl tubing to fit over the bleeder valve and a wrench to open and close the bleeder valve.
7   Beginning at the right rear wheel, loosen the bleeder valve slightly, then tighten it to a point where it is snug but can still be loosened quickly and easily.
8   Place one end of the tubing over the bleeder valve and submerge the other end in brake fluid in the container (**see illustration**).
9   Have the assistant pump the brakes slowly a few times to get pressure in the system, then hold the pedal firmly depressed.
10   While the pedal is held depressed, open the bleeder valve just enough to allow a flow of fluid to leave the valve. Watch for air bubbles to exit the submerged end of the tube. When the fluid flow slows after a couple of seconds, close the valve and have your assistant release the pedal.
11   Repeat Steps 9 and 10 until no more air is seen leaving the tube, then tighten the bleeder valve and proceed to the left rear wheel, the right front wheel and the left front wheel, in that order, and perform the same procedure. Be sure to check the fluid in the master cylinder reservoir frequently.
12   Never use old brake fluid. It contains moisture which will deteriorate the brake system components.
13   Refill the master cylinder with fluid at the end of the operation.
14   Check the operation of the brakes. The pedal should feel solid when depressed, with no sponginess. If necessary, repeat the entire process. **Warning:** *Do not operate the vehicle if you are in doubt about the effectiveness of the brake system.*

12   Parking brake - adjustment

Models with rear drum brakes
Refer to illustration 12.4
1   Block the front wheels so the vehicle can't roll in either direction.

2   Jack up the rear of the vehicle and support the axle securely on jackstands. DO NOT get under a vehicle that is supported only by a jack!

3   Release the parking brake and place the transmission in Neutral.

4   On early models, loosen the equalizer locknut **(see illustration)**. Slowly tighten the adjusting nut on the equalizer rod until the rear brakes just begin to drag.

5   On later models, tighten the adjusting nut against the cable equalizer until the rear brakes just begin to drag.

6   Loosen the equalizer adjusting nut just enough so the rear wheels turn freely, then secure the adjusting nut with the locknut.

7   Remove the jackstands and lower the vehicle. Unblock the front wheels and test parking brake operation.

Models with rear disc brakes

8   Because of the complexity of adjusting this system, we recommend it be done by a dealer service department or other qualified shop.

13   Parking brake - releasing cable tension (1987 and later models)

1   This procedure is necessary to remove parking brake system components on 1987 and later models, which use a ratchet wheel at the parking brake control lever. **Note:** *If this procedure is not done when required, the ratchet wheel spring will unwind and the control assembly will have to be removed to reset cable tension.*

2   Release the parking brake.

3   Remove the console (see Chapter 11).

4   Jack up the vehicle and support it securely on jackstands. DO NOT get under a vehicle that's supported only by a jack!

5   Have an assistant under the vehicle pull the equalizer approximately 1 to 2-1/2 inches rearward to unwind the ratchet wheel. At the same time, insert a steel pin through the holes in the lever and control assembly to lock the ratchet wheel in the released position. **Caution:** *Do not remove the steel pin unless all parts of the parking brake mechanism are installed and connected.*

14   Parking brake cables - replacement

1   Block both front wheels so the vehicle can't roll. Jack up the rear end of the vehicle and place it securely on jackstands. DO NOT get under a vehicle that's supported only by a jack!

2   Release the parking brake completely.

3   On 1979 through 1986 models, loosen the cable locknut and adjusting nut to completely release cable tension **(see illustration 12.4)**.

4   On 1987 and later models, release the cable tension (see Section 13).

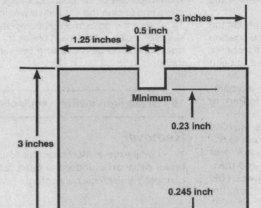

Gauge dimensions

3 inches

1.25 inches   0.5 inch

Minimum

0.23 inch

3 inches

0.245 inch

Maximum

15.11 Power brake push rod gauge template

36051-9-9.16 Haynes

5   Detach the cable(s) from the equalizer

6   Detach the cable snap fitting(s) and unbolt the cable brackets from the vehicle body.

Models with rear drum brakes

7   Remove the rear brake drum (see Section 6).

8   Remove the automatic adjuster spring from between the brake shoes.

9   Move the automatic adjuster lever and small cable as necessary to provide access to the end of the parking brake cable.

10   Disconnect the parking brake cable from the lever on the secondary shoe.

11   Squeeze the cable retainer prongs together so the retainer will fit through the hole in the backing plate (this can usually be done by sliding an appropriately-sized box-end wrench over the retainer). Pull the cable out through the hole in the backing plate and take it out from under the vehicle.

Models with rear disc brakes

12   Disconnect the cable(s) from the caliper(s).

All models

13   Installation is the reverse of the removal steps.

14   Adjust the parking brake (see Section 12).

15   Remove the jackstands and lower the vehicle. Unblock the front wheels and check parking brake operation.

15   Power brake booster - removal, installation and adjustment

Refer to illustration 15.11

1   The power brake booster unit requires no special maintenance apart from periodic inspection of the vacuum hose and the case.

2   Disassembling the brake booster requires special tools and is not ordinarily

done by the home mechanic. If a problem develops, install a new or factory rebuilt unit.

Removal

3   Remove the nuts attaching the master cylinder to the booster and carefully pull the master cylinder forward until it clears the mounting studs. Use caution so as not to bend or kink the brake lines.

4   Disconnect the vacuum hose where it attaches to the power brake booster.

5   Working in the passenger compartment under the steering column, unplug the wiring connector from the brake light switch, then remove the pushrod retaining clip and nylon washer from the brake pedal pin. Slide the pushrod off the pin.

6   Also remove the nuts attaching the brake booster to the firewall.

7   Carefully detach the booster from the firewall and lift it out of the engine compartment.

Installation

8   Place the booster into position on the firewall and tighten the mounting nuts. Connect the pushrod and brake light switch to the brake pedal. Install the retaining clip in the brake pedal pin.

9   Install the master cylinder to the booster, tightening the nuts to the torque listed in this Chapter's Specifications.

10   Carefully check the operation of the brakes before driving the vehicle in traffic.

Adjustment

11   Some boosters feature an adjustable pushrod. They are matched to the booster at the factory and most likely will not require adjustment, but if a misadjusted pushrod is suspected, a gauge can be fabricated out of heavy gauge sheet metal using the accompanying template **(see illustration)**.

12   Some common symptoms caused by a misadjusted pushrod include dragging brakes (if the pushrod is too long) or exces-

9

sive brake pedal travel accompanied by a groaning sound from the brake booster (if the pushrod is too short).

13   To check the pushrod length, unbolt the master cylinder from the booster and position it to one side. It isn't necessary to disconnect the hydraulic lines, but be careful not to bend them.

14   Block the front wheels, apply the parking brake and place the transaxle in Park or Neutral.

15   Start the engine and place the pushrod gauge against the end of the pushrod, exerting a force of approximately 5-pounds to seat the pushrod in the power unit. The rod measurement should fall somewhere between the minimum and maximum cutouts on the

gauge. If it doesn't, adjust it by holding the knurled portion of the pushrod with a pair of pliers and turning the end with a wrench.

16   When the adjustment is complete, reinstall the master cylinder and check for proper brake operation before driving the vehicle in traffic.

---

16   Brake light switch - replacement

Removal

1   Locate the switch near the top of the brake pedal arm, under the dash, and disconnect the electrical connector.

2   Remove the pushrod retaining clip and nylon washer from the brake pedal pin and slide the pushrod off far enough for the outer hole of the switch to clear the pin. Now pull up on the switch to remove it.

Installation

3   Position the switch so it straddles the pushrod and the slot on the inner side of the switch rests on the pedal pin. Slide the pushrod and switch back onto the pin, then install the nylon washer and retaining clip.

4   Reconnect the wiring harness.

5   Check the brake lights for proper operation.

Chapter 10
Suspension and steering systems

Contents

Specifications

Torque specifications

Front suspension

	Ft-lbs
Control arm-to-crossmember pivot bolts/nuts	
1979 through 1981	200 to 220
1982	215 to 260
1983 through 1985	150 to 180
1986 on	110 to 150
Control arm balljoint-to-spindle nut*	
1979 through 1982	80 to 120
1983 through 1986	100 to 120
1987 on	80 to 120
Strut/shock absorber upper mount-to-body nuts	
1979 through 1986 (three nuts)	62 to 75
1987 on (two nuts)	50 to 75
Strut/shock absorber-to-upper mount nut	
1979 through 1982	60 to 75
1983 through 1986	55 to 92
1987 on	50 to 75
Strut/shock absorber-to-spindle nuts/bolts	
1979 through 1985	150 to 180
1986 on	140 to 200

10

Rear suspension

Upper suspension arm-to-frame pivot bolt/nut

1979 and 1980	70 to 100
1981 and 1982	100 to 110
1983 through 1986	100 to 105
1987 on	80 to 105

Upper suspension arm-to-axle housing pivot bolt/nut

1979 and 1980	70 to 100
1981 through 1986	90 to 100
1987 on	70 to 100

Lower suspension arm-to-frame pivot bolt/nut

1979 and 1980	70 to 100
1981 and 1982	100 to 110
1983 through 1986	100 to 105
1987 on	80 to 105

Lower suspension arm-to-axle housing pivot bolt/nut

1979 and 1980	70 to 100
1981 through 1986	90 to 100
1987 on	70 to 100

Steering

Tie-rod end-to-spindle arm nuts*	35 to 47

Steering gear mounting bolts/nuts

1979 through 1985	80 to 100
1986 on	30 to 40

Intermediate shaft-to-steering gear input shaft pinch bolt

1979 through 1985	20 to 30
1986 on	20 to 37
Intermediate shaft flange-to-steering gear clamp nuts	20 to 30

Intermediate shaft-to-steering column shaft nut and bolt

1979 through 1989	35 to 45
1990	38 to 54

Steering wheel nut or bolt

1979 through 1986	30 to 35
1987 on	23 to 33
Air bag module nuts	3 to 4
Wheel lug nuts	See Chapter 1

Tighten to the minimum specified torque, then align the next castellation in the nut with the cotter pin hole.

1   General information

Refer to illustrations 1.1 and 1.2

Warning: *Whenever any of the suspension or steering fasteners are loosened or removed they must be inspected and, if necessary, replaced with new ones of the same part number or of original equipment quality and design. Torque specifications must be followed for proper reassembly and component retention. Never attempt to heat, straighten or weld any suspension or steering component. Instead, replace any bent or damaged part with a new one.*

Note: *These vehicles use a combination of standard and metric fasteners on the various suspension and steering components, so it would be a good idea to have both types of tools available when beginning work.*

The front suspension is independent, allowing each wheel to compensate for road surface changes without appreciably affecting the other **(see illustration)**. Each wheel is connected to the frame by a spindle, balljoint, control arm and a shock absorber/strut assembly positioned vertically between the spindle and frame. Each side uses a coil spring mounted between the control arm and the frame. Body side roll is controlled by a stabilizer bar.

The rear suspension consists of the axle, two coil springs, shock absorbers, two lower and two upper control arms **(see illustration)**. Some models use a rear stabilizer bar, traction bars and hydraulic axle dampers to control axle movement.

The steering system consists of the steering wheel, steering column, an articulated intermediate shaft, the steering gear, power steering pump (if equipped) and the tie-rods, which connect the steering gear to the spindles.

Frequently, when working on the suspension or steering system components, you may come across fasteners which seem impossible to loosen. These fasteners on the underside of the vehicle are continually subjected to water, road grime, mud, etc., and can become rusted or "frozen," making them extremely difficult to remove. In order to unscrew these stubborn fasteners without damaging them (or other components), be sure to use lots of penetrating oil and allow it to soak in for a while. Using a wire brush to clean exposed threads will also ease removal of the nut or bolt and prevent damage to the threads. Sometimes a sharp blow with a hammer and punch is effective in breaking the bond between a nut and bolt threads, but care must be taken to prevent the punch from slipping off the fastener and ruining the threads. Heating the stuck fastener and surrounding area with a torch sometimes helps too, but isn't recommended because of the obvious dangers associated with fire. Long breaker bars and extension, or "cheater," pipes will increase leverage, but never use an extension pipe on a ratchet - the ratcheting mechanism could be damaged. Sometimes, turning the nut or bolt in the tightening (clockwise) direction first will help to break it loose. Fasteners that require drastic measures to unscrew should always be replaced with new ones.

Since most of the procedures that are dealt with in this chapter involve jacking up the vehicle and working underneath it, a good pair of jackstands will be needed. A hydraulic floor jack is the preferred type of jack to lift the vehicle, and it can also be used to support certain components during various operation. **Warning:** *Never, under any circumstances, rely on a jack to support the vehicle while working on it.*

1.1 An underside view of a 1990 Mustang GT's front end, showing its steering and suspension components (other models similar)

1   Stabilizer bar
2   Tie-rod ends absorber assemblies
3   Strut and shock
4   Springs
5   Balljoints
6   Control arms
7   Steering gear

1.2 An underside view of a 1990 Mustang GT's rear end, showing its suspension and related components (other models similar)

1   Shock absorbers
2   Upper control arms
3   Axle assembly
4   Stabilizer bar
5   Coil springs
6   Lower control arms
7   Driveshaft

10

2   Front stabilizer bar - removal and installation

Removal

1   Raise the vehicle and support it securely on jackstands. Apply the parking brake.
2   Remove the stabilizer bar link nuts, noting how the washers and bushings are positioned. On early models which use a link bolt, hold the bolt head from turning with a wrench. On later models which use a link threaded on both ends, clamp a pair of locking pliers to the stabilizer bar link to prevent it from turning.
3   Remove the stabilizer bar bracket bolts and detach the bar from the vehicle.
4   Pull the brackets off the stabilizer bar and inspect the bushings for cracks, hardening and other signs of deterioration. If the bushings are damaged, cut them off the bar.

Installation

5   Lubricate the new stabilizer bar bushings with a rubber lubricant (such as a silicone spray) and slide the bushings onto the bar.
6   Push the brackets over the bushings and raise the bar up to the frame. Install the bracket bolts but don't tighten them completely at this time.
7   Install the stabilizer bar link washers and rubber bushings and tighten the nuts securely.
8   Tighten the bracket bolts.

3   Front strut/shock absorber assembly - removal and installation

Note: *The strut/shock absorbers are not serviceable and must be replaced as complete assemblies.*

Removal

1   Loosen the front wheel lug nuts, raise the vehicle and support it securely on jackstands. Remove the wheel.
2   Remove the disc brake caliper and hang it out of the way with a piece of wire (Chapter 9).
3   Place a floor jack under the control arm and raise it slightly. The jack must remain in this position throughout the entire procedure.
4   Unscrew the three upper mount-to-shock tower retaining nuts. If the upper mount is to be removed from the strut/shock absorber assembly, loosen (but do not remove) the center nut at this time.
5   Remove the strut-to-spindle nuts and bolts.
6   Separate the strut/shock absorber assembly from the spindle and remove it from the vehicle.
7   If the upper mount is to be replaced, remove the center retaining nut and slide the mount off of the assembly.

Installation

8   If the upper mount was removed, place it over the top of the strut/shock assembly and install the nut.
9   Guide the assembly into position in the wheel well, pushing the upper mount studs through the holes in the shock tower. Install the three nuts and tighten them to the specified torque. **Note:** *It is recommended that the nuts not be re-used - replace them with new ones.*
10   Insert the spindle into the lower mounting flange of the strut/shock assembly and install the two bolts. Again, it is recommended that new bolts and nuts be used. Install the nuts and tighten them to the torque listed in this Chapter's Specifications.
11   Tighten the upper mount-to-shock assembly retaining nut to the torque listed in this Chapter's Specifications.
12   Remove the jack from under the control arm and install the disc brake caliper as outlined in Chapter 9.
13   Install the wheel, lower the vehicle and tighten the lug nuts to the torque specified in Chapter 1.

4   Balljoints - check and replacement

The balljoints on this vehicle are not replaceable separately. The entire control arm must be replaced if the balljoints are worn out. Refer to the Steering and suspension check in Chapter 1 for the checking procedure. Refer to Section 7 in this Chapter for control arm removal and installation.

5   Spindle - removal and installation

Removal

1   Loosen the wheel lug nuts, apply the parking brake and raise the vehicle. Support it securely on jackstands placed under the frame. Remove the wheel.
2   Remove the brake caliper and place it on top of the upper control arm (see Chapter 9 if necessary).
3   Remove the brake disc and hub assembly (see Chapter 1).
4   Remove the splash shield from the spindle.
5   Separate the tie-rod end from the spindle arm (see Section 19).
6   Remove the cotter pin from the control arm balljoint stud and back off the nut two turns.
7   Break the balljoint loose from the spindle by rapping the spindle boss sharply with a hammer. If a hammer does not work, try using a puller, as shown in illustration 19.4. **Note:** *A pickle fork type balljoint separator may damage the balljoint seals.*
8   Position a floor jack under the control arm and raise it slightly to take the spring pressure off the shock absorber/strut assem-

bly. The jack must remain in this position throughout the entire procedure.
9   Remove the two large nuts and bolts that attach the spindle to the strut/shock absorber assembly (see Section 3).
10   Remove the nut from the control arm balljoint stud, separate the spindle from the strut/shock assembly and remove the spindle from the vehicle.

Installation

11   Place the spindle onto the control arm balljoint.
12   Insert the top of the spindle into the opening in the strut/shock absorber assembly and install the bolts. Tighten the nuts to the torque listed in this Chapter's Specifications. **Note:** *It is recommended that these bolts (and nuts) be replaced, not re-used.*
13   Tighten the control arm balljoint stud nut to the torque listed in this Chapter's Specifications.
14   Install the splash shield.
15   Connect the tie-rod end to the spindle arm and tighten the nuts to the torque listed in this Chapter's Specifications. Be sure to use a new cotter pin.
16   Install the brake disc and adjust the wheel bearings following the procedure outlined in Chapter 1.
17   Install the brake caliper.
18   Install the wheel and lug nuts. Lower the vehicle to the ground and tighten the nuts to the torque listed in this Chapter's Specifications.

6   Front coil spring - removal and installation

Warning: *The following procedure is potentially dangerous if the proper safety precautions are not taken. A coil spring compressor of the type discussed below must be obtained and positioned properly to safely perform this procedure.*

Removal

Refer to illustration 6.3

1   Loosen the wheel lug nuts on the side to be dismantled. Raise the vehicle, support it securely on jackstands and remove the wheel.
2   Disconnect the stabilizer bar link from the control arm (see Section 2).
3   Install a spring compressor, available at most auto parts stores that carry special tools, according to the directions **(see illustration)**.
4   Safely and carefully compress the spring, according to the tool manufacturers instructions. Tighten the compressor only enough to relieve pressure from the spring seats.
5   Remove the control arm-to-crossmember nuts and pivot bolts. It may be necessary to remove the steering gear mounting bolts and reposition the gear to allow bolt removal. Loosen the forcing nut on the compressor

tool until all of the spring pressure is relieved.
6   Remove the spring compressor compression rod, then maneuver the coil spring out from between the control arm and crossmember.

Installation

7   Install the coil spring insulator on the top of the spring.
8   Install the spring in between the control arm and the spring upper pocket in the crossmember.
9   Position the bottom of the spring so that the pigtail covers only one of the drain holes, but leaves the other one open.
10   Locate the spring in the upper seat in the crossmember. Install the spring compressor tool as described in Steps 3 and 4, then tighten the forcing nut until the control arm bushing holes line up with the pivot bolt holes in the crossmember.
11   Install the pivot bolts and nuts, but don't tighten them completely at this time.
12   Remove the spring compressor tool. Position a floor jack under the outboard side of the control arm and raise it to simulate a normal ride position. Now tighten the pivot bolt nuts to the torque listed in this Chapter's Specifications.
13   Reconnect the stabilizer bar link to the control arm.
14   Install the wheel and lug nuts. Lower the vehicle and tighten the nuts to the torque specified in Chapter 1.

7   Front control arms - removal and installation

Note: *The control arm bushings and balljoint are not serviceable.*
If they wear out, the entire control arm must be replaced.
1   Loosen the wheel lug nuts, raise the vehicle and support it securely on jackstands. Remove the wheel.
2   Separate the control arm balljoint from

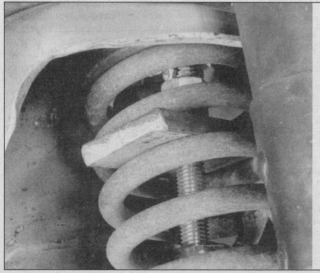

the spindle as described in Section 5. Do not remove the balljoint stud nut at this time.
3   Remove the coil spring as described in the previous Section, noting the Warning in that Section.
4   Unscrew the balljoint nut and remove the control arm from the vehicle.
5   Installation is the reverse of the removal procedure. Be sure to tighten all of the fasteners to the torque listed in this Chapter's Specifications.

8   Rear stabilizer bar - removal and installation

1   Raise the rear of the vehicle and support it securely on jackstands.
2   Support the stabilizer bar and remove the stabilizer bar-to-lower suspension arm bolts.
3   Remove the bar from the vehicle.
4   Installation is the reverse of the removal procedure. Be sure to install the bar with the paint mark on the right hand side of the vehicle.

9   Traction bars - removal and installation

1   Raise the rear of the vehicle and support it securely o jackstands.
2   Remove the two nuts that hold the traction bar to the axle U-bolt and remove the traction bar, U-bolt and adjusting shim(s).
3   Installation is the reverse of the removal procedure.

10   Rear shock absorbers - removal and installation

Note: *Some models use Torx bolts to secure the lower ends of the rear shock absorbers. If this is the case and you don't have the proper*

6.3 When using this type tool, make sure that the spring compressor plates are fully seated before applying pressure; mark the position of the spring plates on the spring coils with chalk for use during installation

size Torx driver, buy one before you start the job. Do not try to substitute an Allen wrench for a Torx driver - it may strip out the bolt head.

Removal

1   Raise the rear of the vehicle and support it securely on jackstands.
2   Support the rear axle with a floor jack to prevent it from dropping when the shock absorber is disconnected.
3   On two-door models, open the trunk. On 3-door models, open the rear compartment and remove the trim panel access door.
4   Remove the upper mounting nut from the shock absorber rod. It may be necessary to prevent the rod from turning by holding it with a wrench or locking pliers.
5   Remove the lower mounting bolt or nut, separate the bottom of the shock absorber from the mounting bracket and remove it from the vehicle.

Installation

6   Before installing a new hydraulic shock absorber, expel all air. Hold the shock right side up and extend it fully. Turn the shock upside down and compress it all the way. Extend and compress the shock absorber in this manner at least three times.
7   Place the inner washer and rubber insulator on the shock rod and insert the rod through the upper mounting hole. **Note:** *Gas shocks will extend by themselves unless they are equipped with a restraint strap.*
8   Models with lower mounting stud - slip the end of the shock absorber over the stud. Install the nut and tighten it securely.
9   Models with lower mounting bolt - Push up on the shock absorber to align the lower shock eye in the mounting bracket and install the bolt and nut. On models equipped with a self-wrenching nut, start the bolt into the nut by hand and let the nut turn by itself until it stops. Don't try to hold it any other way. Once the nut stops, tighten the bolt securely.
10   Install the upper mounting rubber insulator and the dished washer on the shock rod. Install the nut and tighten it securely.
11   Install the trim panel access door (three-door models).

11   Axle damper - removal and installation

Removal

1   Loosen the wheel lug nuts, raise the vehicle and support it on jackstands. Remove the wheel and place a floor jack under the rear axle to support it, just in case it shifts when the axle damper is removed.
2   Remove the axle damper front attaching nut and bolt from the axle bracket.
3   Remove the rear attaching nut. Remove the bolts that hold the rear mounting bracket to the frame sidemember and remove the damper from the vehicle.

10

Installation

4   Place the rear bracket onto the axle damper and install the nut (don't tighten it yet).

5   Position the rear bracket on the frame sidemember and install the bolts, tightening them securely.

6   Swing the axle damper into the mount on the rear axle and install the pivot bolt and attaching nut, tightening them securely.

7   Tighten the rear retaining nut securely.

8   Install the wheel and lug nuts and lower the vehicle. Tighten the lug nuts to the torque specified in Chapter 1.

12   Rear coil spring - removal and installation

Note: *Rear coil springs should always be replaced in pairs.*

Removal

1   Loosen the wheel lug nuts, raise the rear of the vehicle and support it securely on jackstands placed under the frame. Remove the wheel and block the front wheels.

2   Remove the rear stabilizer bar (see Section 8) if the vehicle is equipped with one.

3   Support the rear axle assembly with a jackstand placed under the axle tube on the side being dismantled. Position a safety chain through one of the spring coils and around a convenient frame member. This will prevent the spring from flying out before it's fully extended.

4   Place a floor jack under the lower suspension arm axle pivot bolt. Remove the nut and bolt.

5   Slowly lower the jack until the spring is fully extended.

6   Remove the safety chain, coil spring and insulators from between the suspension arm and the spring upper seat.

Installation

7   Set the upper insulator on top of the spring, using tape to hold it in place, if necessary.

8   Place the lower insulator on the lower suspension arm.

9   Install the internal damper in the spring.

10   Place the spring between the suspension arm and the frame, so that the pigtail (the end of the spring) on the lower suspension arm is pointing toward the left side of the vehicle.

11   Raise the lower suspension arm up into position and install the pivot bolt and nut, but don't fully tighten the nut yet.

12   Raise the axle to simulate a normal ride height and tighten the pivot bolt nut to the torque listed in this Chapter's Specifications.

13   If the vehicle is equipped with a rear stabilizer bar, install it, referring to Section 8 if necessary.

13   Rear suspension arms - removal and installation

Upper arm

Note: *If one upper arm requires replacement, replace the other upper arm as well. It is recommended that new fasteners be used when reassembling the rear suspension components.*

Removal

1   Raise the rear of the vehicle and support it securely on jackstands placed beneath the frame rails. Block the front wheels.

2   Position a jack under the differential and raise it slightly.

3   Remove the upper arm-to-rear axle pivot bolt and nut.

4   Remove the upper arm-to-frame pivot bolt and nut and remove the arm from the vehicle.

Installation

5   Position the leading end of the suspension arm in the frame bracket. Install a new pivot bolt and nut with the nut on the outboard side, but don't fully tighten the nut at this time.

6   Place the other end of the arm over the axle bushing ear. It may be necessary to jack up the rear axle to align the holes. Install a new pivot bolt and nut with the nut on the inboard side, but don't tighten it to the specified torque yet.

7   Raise the axle to normal ride height and tighten the fasteners to the torque listed in this Chapter's Specifications.

Lower arm

Note: *If one lower arm requires replacement, replace the other lower arm as well. Installing new fasteners when reassembling the rear suspension components is recommended.*

Removal

8   Loosen the wheel lug nuts, raise the rear of the vehicle and support it securely on jackstands placed beneath the frame rails. Block the front wheels and remove the rear wheel.

9   Remove the coil spring following the procedure outlined in Section 12.

10   Remove the lower arm-to-frame pivot bolt and nut, then remove the arm from the vehicle.

Installation

11   Position the lower arm in the frame mounting bracket and install a new pivot bolt and nut, with the nut facing out. Do not tighten the nut completely at this time.

12   Install the coil spring and connect the trailing end of the lower suspension arm to the rear axle bracket (Section 12). Raise the axle to simulate normal ride height, then tighten the pivot bolt nuts to the torque listed in this Chapter's Specifications.

13   Install the wheel and lug nuts. Lower the vehicle and tighten the lug nuts to the torque specified in Chapter 1.

14   Steering wheel - removal and installation

Warning: *On models equipped with airbags, Always disconnect the negative battery cable, then disconnect the positive battery cable and wait 2 minutes before working in the vicinity of the impact sensors, steering column or instrument panel to avoid the possibility of accidental deployment of the airbag, which could cause personal injury.*

1   Disconnect the cable from the negative terminal of the battery.

2   Expose the steering wheel nut or bolt as follows:

   a)   ***Round horn button*** - *pull the button off.* **Note:** *On some models, it is necessary to twist the button counterclockwise before pulling it off. Don't pry or force the button if it won't come easily.*

   b)   ***Square trim emblem*** - *from the back side of the steering wheel, insert a rod into the two removal holes and push the emblem out of the steering wheel. Push alternately and evenly against the emblem until it can be removed.*

   c)   ***Airbag-equipped models*** - *Remove the four nuts that secure the airbag module. Separate the air bag module from The steering wheel and disconnect its electrical connector.* **Warning:** *Be very careful when removing or installing the airbag module and don't allow its electrical connector to come into contact with any other wires or metal objects. The air bag could activate, possibly resulting in injury. When carrying the airbag module, hold it with the trim side (airbag opening) facing away from you. When storing the module, set it down in an isolated area with the trim side facing up.*

3   Remove the steering wheel retaining nut or bolt, then mark the relationship of the steering shaft to the hub (if marks don't already exist or don't line up) to simplify installation and ensure correct steering wheel alignment. **Note:** *Discard the hub nut or bolt. Use a new one during installation.*

4   Use a steering wheel puller to detach the steering wheel from the shaft. Don't use an impact puller and don't pound on the steering wheel or shaft. **Warning:** *On airbag-equipped models, don't allow the steering column to turn after the steering wheel has been removed; damage to the airbag clockspring could result.*

5   If equipped with cruise control, make sure the slip ring grease is not contaminated. Check the slip ring contacts for wear or damage and make sure they are properly seated.

6   To install the wheel, align the mark on the steering wheel hub with the mark on the shaft and slip the wheel onto the shaft. Install a new hub nut or bolt and tighten it to the torque listed in this Chapter's Specifications.

7   On airbag-equipped models, connect the air bag electrical connector and install the airbag module.

8   On other models, install the trim piece or horn button.
9   Connect the negative battery cable.

15   Intermediate shaft - removal and installation

Note: *It is recommended that new intermediate shaft fasteners be used once they have been removed.*
1   Turn the front wheels to the straight ahead position.
2   Using white paint, place alignment marks on the intermediate shaft-to-steering shaft and the lower flexible coupling-to-steering gear input shaft joints.
3   Remove the upper clamp bolt and lower flexible coupling pinch bolt.
4   Remove the steering gear-to-frame mounting bolts (Section 16) and lower the steering gear enough to allow intermediate shaft removal.
5   Pry the intermediate shaft off the steering gear input shaft with a large screwdriver, then pull the upper end of the shaft out of the steering column shaft.
6   Installation is the reverse of the removal procedure. Be sure to align the marks and tighten the pinch bolts to the torque listed in this Chapter's Specifications.

16   Steering gear - removal and installation

Warning: *On models equipped with air bags, make sure the steering shaft is not turned while the steering gear or box is removed or you could damage the air bag system. To prevent the shaft from turning, turn the ignition key to the lock position before beginning work or run the seat belt through the steering wheel and clip the seat belt into place. Due to the possible damage to the air bag system, we recommend only experienced mechanics attempt this procedure.*

Removal

1   Raise the front of the vehicle and support it securely on jackstands. Apply the parking brake.
2   Place a drain pan under the steering gear (power steering only). Remove the power steering pressure and return lines and cap the ends to prevent excessive fluid loss and contamination.
3   Mark the relationship of the intermediate shaft flexible coupling to the steering gear input shaft. Remove the pinch bolt.
4   Separate the tie-rod ends from the spindle arms (see Section 19).
5   Support the steering gear and remove the steering gear-to-frame mounting nuts and bolts. Lower the unit, separate the intermediate shaft from the steering gear input shaft and remove the steering gear from the vehicle.

19.2a Hold the tie-rod end with a wrench and loosen the jam nut

Installation

6   Raise the steering gear into position and connect the intermediate shaft, aligning the marks.
7   Install the mounting bolts and washers and tighten the nuts to the torque listed in this Chapter's Specifications.
8   Connect the tie-rod ends to the spindle arms (Section 19)
9   Install the intermediate shaft pinch bolt and tighten it to the torque listed in this Chapter's Specifications.
10   Connect the power steering pressure and return hoses to the steering gear and fill the power steering pump reservoir with the recommended fluid (Chapter 1).
11   Lower the vehicle and bleed the steering system as outlined in Section 18.

17   Power steering pump - removal and installation

Removal

1   Disconnect the cable from the negative terminal of the battery.
2   Place a drain pan under the power steering pump. Remove the drivebelt (Chapter 1).
3   Using a special power steering pump pulley remover, remove the pulley from the pump.
4   Remove the pressure and return hoses from the backside of the pump and allow the fluid to drain. Plug the hoses to prevent contaminants from entering.
5   Remove the pump mounting bolts and lift the pump from the vehicle, taking care not to spill fluid on the painted surfaces.
6   Position the pump in the mounting bracket and install the bolts. Tighten the bolts securely.
7   Connect the hoses to the pump. Tighten the fittings securely.

Installation

8   Press the pulley onto the pump shaft using a special pulley installer tool. Push the pulley onto the shaft until the front of the hub is flush with the end of the shaft, but no further.

9   Install the drivebelt.
10   Fill the power steering reservoir with the recommended fluid (see Chapter 1) and bleed the system following the procedure described in the next Section.

18   Power steering system - bleeding

1   Following any operation in which the power steering fluid lines have been disconnected, the power steering system must be bled to remove all air and obtain proper steering performance.
2   With the front wheels in the straight ahead position, check the power steering fluid level and, if low, add fluid until it reaches the Cold mark on the dipstick.
3   Start the engine and allow it to run at fast idle. Recheck the fluid level and add more if necessary to reach the Cold mark on the dipstick.
4   Bleed the system by turning the wheels from side-to-side, without hitting the stops. This will work the air out of the system. Keep the reservoir full of fluid as this is done.
5   When the air is worked out of the system, return the wheels to the straight ahead position and leave the vehicle running for several more minutes before shutting it off.
6   Road test the vehicle to be sure the steering system is functioning normally and noise free.
7   Recheck the fluid level to be sure it is up to the Hot mark on the dipstick while the engine is at normal operating temperature. Add fluid if necessary (see Chapter 1).

19   Tie-rod ends - removal and installation

Removal

Refer to illustrations 19.2a, 19.2b and 19.4
1   Loosen the wheel lug nuts. Block the rear wheels and set the parking brake. Raise the front of the vehicle and support it securely on jackstands. Remove the front wheel.
2   Hold the tie-rod end with a wrench and loosen the jam nut enough to mark the position of the tie-rod end in relation to the threads **(see illustrations)**.

10

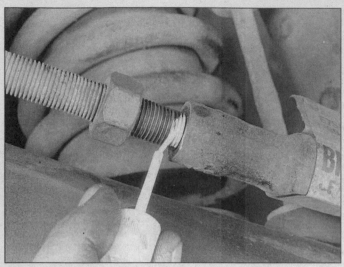

19.2b Use white paint to mark the position of the tie-rod end on the tie-rod

19.4 Use a two-jaw puller to disconnect the tie-rod end

3   Remove the cotter pin and loosen the nut on the tie-rod end stud.
4   Disconnect the tie-rod from the spindle arm with a puller **(see illustration)**. Remove the nut and separate the tie-rod.
5   Unscrew the tie-rod end from the tie-rod.

Installation

6   Thread the tie-rod end on to the marked position and insert the tie-rod stud into the spindle arm. Tighten the jam nut securely.
7   Install a new nut on the stud and tighten it to the torque listed in this Chapter's Specifications. Install a new cotter pin.
8   Install the wheel and lug nuts. Lower the vehicle and tighten the lug nuts to the torque specified in Chapter 1.
9   Have the alignment checked by a dealer service department or an alignment shop.

20   Steering gear boots - replacement

1   Loosen the lug nuts, raise the vehicle and support it securely on jackstands. Remove the wheel.
2   Referring to Section 19, loosen the tie-rod end jam nut and separate the tie-rod end from the spindle arm.
3   Remove the steering gear boot clamps and slide the boot (bellows) off **(see illustration 16.5)**.
4   Before installing the new boot, wrap the threads and serrations on the end of the steering rod with a layer of tape so the small end of the new boot isn't damaged.
5   Slide the new boot into position on the steering gear until it seats in the groove in the steering rod and install new clamps.
6   Remove the tape and install the tie-rod end (Section 19).
7   Install the wheel and lug nuts. Lower the vehicle and tighten the lug nuts to the torque

specified in Chapter 1.
8   Have the alignment checked by a dealer service department or an alignment shop.

21   Wheels and tires - general information

Refer to illustration 21.1

All vehicles covered by this manual are equipped with metric-sized fiberglass or steel belted radial tires **(see illustration)**. Use of other size or type of tires may affect the ride and handling of the vehicle. Don't mix different types of tires, such as radial and bias

belted, on the same vehicle as handling may be seriously affected. It's recommended that tires be replaced in pairs on the same axle, but if only one tire is being replaced, be sure it's the same size, structure and tread design as the other.

Because tire pressure has a substantial effect on handling and wear, the pressure on all tires should be checked at least once a month or before any extended trips (see Chapter 1).

Wheels must be replaced if they are bent, dented, leak air, have elongated bolt holes, are heavily rusted, out of vertical symmetry or if the lug nuts won't stay tight.

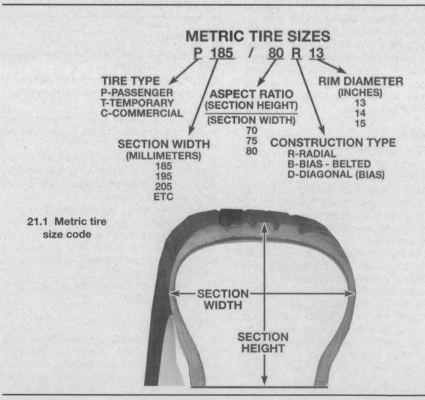

21.1 Metric tire size code

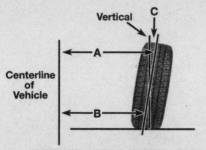

CAMBER ANGLE (FRONT VIEW)

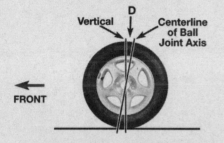

CASTER ANGLE (SIDE VIEW)

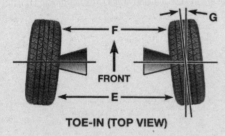

TOE-IN (TOP VIEW)

22.1 Front end alignment details

A minus B = C (degrees camber)
E minus F = toe-in (measured in inches)
G = toe-in (expressed in degrees)

Wheel repairs that use welding or peening are not recommended.

Tire and wheel balance affects the overall handling, braking and performance of the vehicle. Unbalanced wheels can adversely affect handling and ride characteristics as well as tire life. Whenever a tire is installed on a wheel, the tire and wheel should be balanced by a shop with the proper equipment.

22   Front end alignment - general information

Refer to illustration 22.1

A front end alignment refers to the adjustments made to the front wheels so they are in proper angular relationship to the suspension and the ground. Front wheels that are out of proper alignment not only affect steering control, but also increase tire wear. The only front end adjustments possible on this vehicle are camber and toe-in **(see illustration)**.

Getting the proper front wheel alignment is a very exacting process, one in which complicated and expensive machines are necessary to perform the job properly. Because of this, you should have a technician with the proper equipment perform these tasks. We will, however, use this space to give you a basic idea of what is involved with front end alignment so you can better understand the process and deal intelligently with the shop that does the work.

Toe-in is the turning in of the front wheels. The purpose of a toe specification is to ensure parallel rolling of the front wheels. In a vehicle with zero toe-in, the distance between the front edges of the wheels will be the same as the distance between the rear edges of the wheels. The actual amount of toe-in is normally only a fraction of an inch. Toe-in adjustment is controlled by the tie-rod end position on the inner tie-rod. Incorrect toe-in will cause the tires to wear improperly by making them scrub against the road surface.

Camber is the tilting of the front wheels from the vertical when viewed from the front of the vehicle. When the wheels tilt out at the top, the camber is said to be positive (+). When the wheels tilt in at the top the camber is negative (-). The amount of tilt is measured in degrees from the vertical and this measurement is called the camber angle. This angle affects the amount of tire tread which contacts the road and compensates for changes in the suspension geometry when the vehicle is cornering or traveling over an undulating surface.

Notes

Chapter 11 Body

Contents

1 General Information

These models feature a "unibody" layout, using a floor pan with front and rear side frame rails which support the body components, front and rear suspension systems and other mechanical components.

Certain components are particularly vulnerable to accident damage and can be unbolted and repaired or replaced. Among these parts are the body moldings, bumpers, the hood and trunk lid and all glass.

Only general body maintenance procedures and body panel repair procedures within the scope of the do-it-yourselfer are included in this Chapter.

2 Body - maintenance

1 The condition of your vehicle's body is very important, because the resale value depends a great deal on it. It's much more difficult to repair a damaged body than it is to repair mechanical components. The hidden areas of the body, such as the wheel wells, the frame and the engine compartment, are equally important, although they don't require as frequent attention as the rest of the body.

2 Once a year, or every 12,000 miles, it's a good idea to have the underside of the body steam cleaned. All traces of dirt and oil will be removed and the area can then be inspected carefully for rust, damaged brake lines, frayed electrical wires, damaged cables and other problems. The front suspension components should be greased after completion of this job.

3 At the same time, clean the engine and the engine compartment with a steam cleaner or water soluble degreaser.

4 The wheel wells should be given close attention, since undercoating can peel away and stones and dirt thrown up by the tires can cause the paint to chip and flake, allowing rust to set in. If rust is found, clean down to the bare metal and apply an anti-rust paint.

5 The body should be washed about once a week. Wet the vehicle thoroughly to soften the dirt, then wash it down with a soft sponge and plenty of clean soapy water. If the surplus dirt is not washed off very carefully, it can wear down the paint.

6 Spots of tar or asphalt thrown up from the road should be removed with a cloth soaked in solvent.

7 Once every six months, wax the body and chrome trim. If a chrome cleaner is used to remove rust from any of the vehicle's plated parts, remember that the cleaner also removes part of the chrome, so use it sparingly.

3 Vinyl trim - maintenance

Don't clean vinyl trim with detergents, caustic soap or petroleum-based cleaners. Plain soap and water works just fine, with a soft brush to clean dirt that may be ingrained. Wash the vinyl as frequently as the rest of the vehicle. After cleaning, application of a high quality rubber and vinyl protectant will help prevent oxidation and cracks. The protectant can also be applied to weatherstripping, vacuum lines and rubber hoses, which often fail as a result of chemical degradation, and to the tires.

4 Upholstery and carpets - maintenance

1 Every three months remove the carpets or mats and clean the interior of the vehicle (more frequently if necessary). Vacuum the upholstery and carpets to remove loose dirt and dust.

2 Leather upholstery requires special care. Stains should be removed with warm water and a very mild soap solution. Use a clean, damp cloth to remove the soap, the wipe again with a dry cloth. Never use alcohol, gasoline, nail polish remover or thinner to clean leather upholstery.

11

These photos illustrate a method of repairing simple dents. They are intended to supplement *Body repair - minor damage* in this Chapter and should not be used as the sole instructions for body repair on these vehicles.

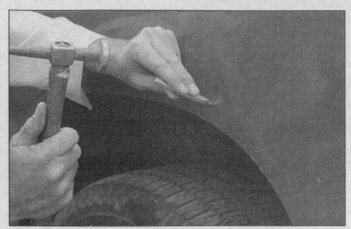

1 If you can't access the backside of the body panel to hammer out the dent, pull it out with a slide-hammer-type dent puller. In the deepest portion of the dent or along the crease line, drill or punch hole(s) at least one inch apart . . .

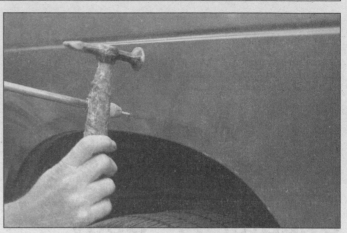

2 . . . then screw the slide-hammer into the hole and operate it. Tap with a hammer near the edge of the dent to help 'pop' the metal back to its original shape. When you're finished, the dent area should be close to its original contour and about 1/8-inch below the surface of the surrounding metal

3 Using coarse-grit sandpaper, remove the paint down to the bare metal. Hand sanding works fine, but the disc sander shown here makes the job faster. Use finer (about 320-grit) sandpaper to feather-edge the paint at least one inch around the dent area

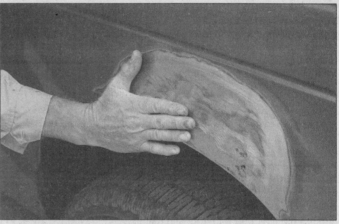

4 When the paint is removed, touch will probably be more helpful than sight for telling if the metal is straight. Hammer down the high spots or raise the low spots as necessary. Clean the repair area with wax/silicone remover

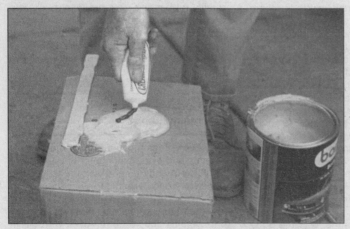

5 Following label instructions, mix up a batch of plastic filler and hardener. The ratio of filler to hardener is critical, and, if you mix it incorrectly, it will either not cure properly or cure too quickly (you won't have time to file and sand it into shape)

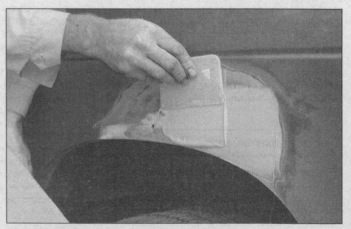

6 Working quickly so the filler doesn't harden, use a plastic applicator to press the body filler firmly into the metal, assuring it bonds completely. Work the filler until it matches the original contour and is slightly above the surrounding metal

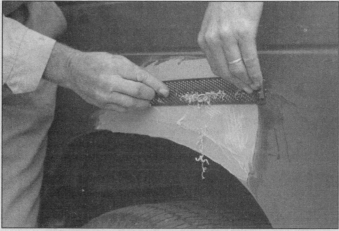

7 Let the filler harden until you can just dent it with your fingernail. Use a body file or Surform tool (shown here) to rough-shape the filler

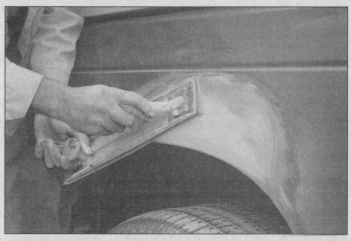

8 Use coarse-grit sandpaper and a sanding board or block to work the filler down until it's smooth and even. Work down to finer grits of sandpaper - always using a board or block - ending up with 360 or 400 grit

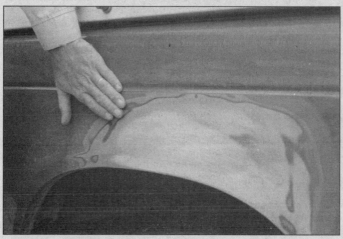

9 You shouldn't be able to feel any ridge at the transition from the filler to the bare metal or from the bare metal to the old paint. As soon as the repair is flat and uniform, remove the dust and mask off the adjacent panels or trim pieces

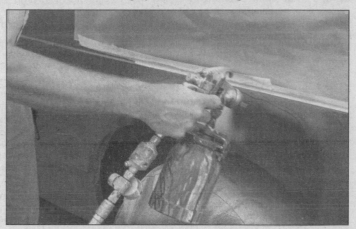

10 Apply several layers of primer to the area. Don't spray the primer on too heavy, so it sags or runs, and make sure each coat is dry before you spray on the next one. A professional-type spray gun is being used here, but aerosol spray primer is available inexpensively from auto parts stores

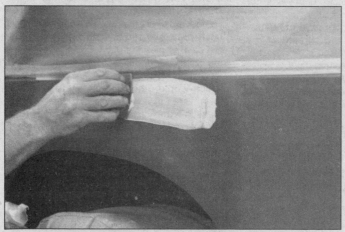

11 The primer will help reveal imperfections or scratches. Fill these with glazing compound. Follow the label instructions and sand it with 360 or 400-grit sandpaper until it's smooth. Repeat the glazing, sanding and respraying until the primer reveals a perfectly smooth surface

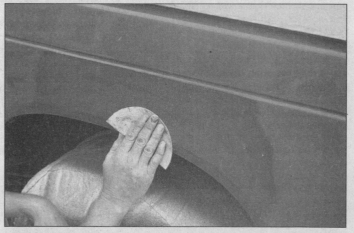

12 Finish sand the primer with very fine sandpaper (400 or 600-grit) to remove the primer overspray. Clean the area with water and allow it to dry. Use a tack rag to remove any dust, then apply the finish coat. Don't attempt to rub out or wax the repair area until the paint has dried completely (at least two weeks)

3 After cleaning, regularly treat leather upholstery with a leather wax. Never use car wax on leather upholstery.

4 In areas where the interior of the vehicle is subject to bright sunlight, cover leather seats with a sheet if the vehicle is to be left out for any length of time.

5 Body repair - minor damage

See photo sequence

Repair of minor scratches

1 If the scratch is superficial and does not penetrate to the metal of the body, repair is very simple. Lightly rub the scratched area with a fine rubbing compound to remove loose paint and built up wax. Rinse the area with clean water.

2 Apply touch-up paint to the scratch, using a small brush. Continue to apply thin layers of paint until the surface of the paint in the scratch is level with the surrounding paint. Allow the new paint at least two weeks to harden, then blend it into the surrounding paint by rubbing with a very fine rubbing compound. Finally, apply a coat of wax to the scratch area.

3 If the scratch has penetrated the paint and exposed the metal of the body, causing the metal to rust, a different repair technique is required. Remove all loose rust from the bottom of the scratch with a pocket knife, then apply rust inhibiting paint to prevent the formation of rust in the future. Using a rubber or nylon applicator, coat the scratched area with glaze-type filler. If required, the filler can be mixed with thinner to provide a very thin paste, which is ideal for filling narrow scratches. Before the glaze filler in the scratch hardens, wrap a piece of smooth cotton cloth around the tip of a finger. Dip the cloth in thinner and then quickly wipe it along the surface of the scratch. This will ensure that the surface of the filler is slightly hollow. The scratch can now be painted over as described earlier in this section.

Repair of dents

4 When repairing dents, the first job is to pull the dent out until the affected area is as close as possible to its original shape. There is no point in trying to restore the original shape completely as the metal in the damaged area will have stretched on impact and cannot be restored to its original contours. It is better to bring the level of the dent up to a point about 1/8-inch below the level of the surrounding metal. In cases where the dent is very shallow, it is not worth trying to pull it back out at all.

5 If the back side of the dent is accessible, it can be hammered out gently from behind using a soft-face hammer. While doing this, hold a block of wood firmly against the opposite side of the metal to absorb the hammer blows and prevent the metal from being stretched.

6 If the dent is in a section of the body which has double layers, or some other factor makes it inaccessible from behind, a different technique is required. Drill several small holes through the metal inside the damaged area, particularly in the deeper sections. Screw long, self tapping screws into the holes just enough for them to get a good grip in the metal. Now the dent can be pulled out by pulling on the protruding heads of the screws with locking pliers.

7 The next stage of repair is the removal of the paint from the damaged area and from an inch or so of the surrounding metal. This is easily done with a wire brush or sanding disk in a drill motor, although it can be done just as effectively by hand with sandpaper. To complete the preparation for filling, score the surface of the bare metal with a screwdriver or the tang of a file or drill small holes in the affected area. This will provide a good grip for the filler material. To complete the repair, see the Section on filling and painting.

Repair of rust holes or gashes

8 Remove all paint from the affected area and from an inch or so of the surrounding metal using a sanding disk or wire brush mounted in a drill motor. If these are not available, a few sheets of sandpaper will do the job just as effectively.

9 With the paint removed, you will be able to determine the severity of the corrosion and decide whether to replace the whole panel, if possible, or repair the affected area. New body panels are not as expensive as most people think and it is often quicker to install a new panel than to repair large areas of rust.

10 Remove all trim pieces from the affected area except those which will act as a guide to the original shape of the damaged body, such as headlight shells, etc. Using metal snips or a hacksaw blade, remove all loose metal and any other metal that is badly affected by rust. Hammer the edges of the hole inward to create a slight depression for the filler material.

11 Wire brush the affected area to remove the powdery rust from the surface of the metal. If the back of the rusted area is accessible, treat it with rust inhibiting paint.

12 Before filling is done, block the hole in some way. This can be done with sheet metal riveted or screwed into place, or by stuffing the hole with wire mesh.

13 Once the hole is blocked off, the affected area can be filled and painted. See the following subsection on filling and painting.

Filling and painting

14 Many types of body fillers are available, but generally speaking, body repair kits which contain filler paste and a tube of resin hardener are best for this type of repair work. A wide, flexible plastic or nylon applicator will be necessary for imparting a smooth and contoured finish to the surface of the filler material. Mix up a small amount of filler on a clean piece of wood or cardboard (use the hardener sparingly). Follow the manufacturer's instructions on the package, otherwise the filler will set incorrectly.

15 Using the applicator, apply the filler paste to the prepared area. Draw the applicator across the surface of the filler to achieve the desired contour and to level the filler surface. As soon as a contour that approximates the original one is achieved, stop working the paste. If you continue, the paste will begin to stick to the applicator. Continue to add thin layers of paste at 20-minute intervals until the level of the filler is just above the surrounding metal.

16 Once the filler has hardened, the excess can be removed with a body file. From then on, progressively finer grades of sandpaper should be used, starting with a 180-grit paper and finishing with 600-grit wet-or-dry paper. Always wrap the sandpaper around a flat rubber or wooden block, otherwise the surface of the filler will not be completely flat. During the sanding of the filler surface, the wet-or-dry paper should be periodically rinsed in water. This will ensure that a very smooth finish is produced in the final stage.

17 At this point, the repair area should be surrounded by a ring of bare metal, which in turn should be encircled by the finely feathered edge of good paint. Rinse the repair area with clean water until all of the dust produced by the sanding operation is gone.

18 Spray the entire area with a light coat of primer. This will reveal any imperfections in the surface of the filler. Repair the imperfections with fresh filler paste or glaze filler and once more smooth the surface with sandpaper. Repeat this spray-and-repair procedure until you are satisfied that the surface of the filler and the feathered edge of the paint are perfect. Rinse the area with clean water and allow it to dry completely.

19 The repair area is now ready for painting. Spray painting must be carried out in a warm, dry, windless and dust free atmosphere. These conditions can be created if you have access to a large indoor work area, but if you are forced to work in the open, you will have to pick the day very carefully. If you are working indoors, dousing the floor in the work area with water will help settle the dust which would otherwise be in the air. If the repair area is confined to one body panel, mask off the surrounding panels. This will help minimize the effects of a slight mismatch in paint color. Trim pieces such as chrome strips, door handles, etc. will also need to be masked off or removed. Use masking tape and several thicknesses of newspaper for the masking operations.

20 Before spraying, shake the paint can thoroughly, then spray a test area until the spray painting technique is mastered. Cover the repair area with a thick coat of primer. The thickness should be built up using several thin layers of primer rather than one thick one. Using 600-grit wet-or-dry sandpaper, rub down the surface of the primer until it is very smooth. While doing this, the work area

should be thoroughly rinsed with water and the wet-or-dry sandpaper periodically rinsed as well. Allow the primer to dry before spraying additional coats.

21   Spray on the top coat, again building up the thickness by using several layers of paint. Begin spraying in the center of the repair area and then, using a circular motion, work outward until the whole repair area and about two inches of the surrounding original paint is covered. Remove all masking material 10 to 15 minutes after spraying on the final coat of paint. Allow the new paint at least two weeks to harden, then use a very fine rubbing compound to bend the edges of the new paint into the existing paint, Finally, apply a coat of wax.

6   Body repair - major damage

1   Major damage must be repaired by an auto body shop specifically equipped to perform unibody repairs. These shops have the specialized equipment required to do the job properly.
2   If the damage is extensive, the body must be checked for proper alignment or the vehicle's handling characteristics may be adversely affected and other components may wear at an accelerated rate.
3   Due to the fact that all of the major body components (hood, fenders, etc.) are separate and replaceable units, any seriously damaged components should be replaced rather than repaired. Sometimes the components can be found in a wrecking yard that specializes is used vehicle components, often at a considerable savings over the cost of new parts.

7   Hinges and locks - maintenance

Once every 3,000 miles, or every three months, the hinges and latch assemblies on the doors, hood and trunk should be given a few drops of light oil or lock lubricant. The door latch strikers should also be lubricated with a thin coat of grease to reduce wear and ensure free movement. Lubricate the door and trunk locks with spray-on graphite lubricant.

8   Hood - removal, installation and adjustment

Refer to illustration 8.3
Note: *The hood is heavy and somewhat awkward to remove and install - at least two people should perform this procedure.*
1   Open the hood.
2   Scribe or paint alignment marks around the bolt heads to ensure proper alignment on reinstallation.
3   Place cloths or pads at the rear corners of the hood to prevent damage during

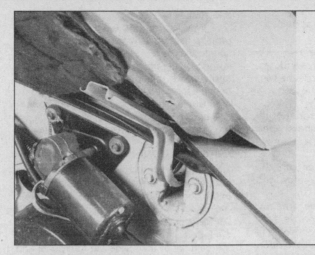

8.3 Pad the hood to protect the windshield when lifting the hood from the vehicle

removal **(see illustration)**.
4   Remove the hinge assembly-to-hood mounting bolts.
5   Remove the hood.
6   Installation is the reverse of removal.
7   The hood can be adjusted fore-and-aft and side-to-side by loosening the hood-to-hinge bolts at each hinge. Reposition the hood and tighten the bolts.
8   To raise or lower the rear of the hood, loosen the hinge-to-body bolts. Raise or lower the hinge as necessary to make the hood flush with the surrounding panels. Then tighten the hinge-to-body bolts.

9   Grille opening panel, front fender and front bumper - removal and installation

Warning: *On models equipped with airbags, always disconnect the negative battery cable, then disconnect the positive battery cable and wait two minutes before working in the vicinity of the impact sensors, steering column or instrument panel to avoid the possibility of accidental deployment of the airbag, which could cause personal injury.*
1   Disconnect the negative cable from the battery.
2   Remove the grille opening panel.
3   Detach the radiator support brace from the front fender and radiator support.
4   Remove the fender fasteners (nuts, bolts and splash shield push pins). Lift the fender off.
5   If bumper removal is necessary, remove the bumper fasteners and take it off.
6   Installation is the reverse of removal.

10   Trunk lid - removal, installation and adjustment

1   Open the trunk lid.
2   Scribe or paint alignment marks around the trunk lid hinge bolt flanges.
3   Remove the hinge bolts and lift off the trunk lid.

4   Installation is the reverse of removal.
5   The trunk lid can be adjusted fore-and-aft and from side-to-side. The up-and-down adjustment is made by loosening the hinge-to-body bolts and raising or lowering the trunk lid.
6   The trunk lid should be adjusted for an even and parallel fit in the opening. It should also be adjusted up-and-down and for a flush fit with the surrounding panels. Care should be taken not to distort or mar the trunk lid or surrounding body panels.

11   Rear hatch - removal, installation and adjustment

1   Open the rear hatch.
2   Scribe alignment marks around the hinge-to-roof panel attaching bolts.
3   Have an assistant support the rear hatch, then detach the lift struts from the lid by popping them off the ballstud retainers with a screwdriver.
4   Unbolt the hinges from the roof panel and lift the hatch off.
5   Installation is the reverse of removal.
6   To adjust the hatch side-to-side or fore-and-aft, loosen the hinge-to-roof bolts. Make the adjustment, then tighten the bolts.
7   To adjust the front of the hatch up or down, add or remove shims at the hinge-to-roof panel.
8   To adjust the bottom of the hatch up or down, screw the bumpers in or out.

12   Rear bumper - removal and installation

1   Remove the bumper cover fasteners and detach the cover from the bumper.
2   Unbolt the bumper from the isolator and lift the bumper off.
3   To install, place the bumper in position and attach it to the isolator. Install the bumper cover.

11

13 Door trim panel - removal and installation

1 On models with manual windows, remove the screw from the center of the window crank arm and remove the window crank.
2 Disconnect the manual mirror knob (if equipped) by unscrewing the cone-shaped sleeve surrounding the control knob. Remove the mirror trim panel.
3 Remove the trim plate beneath the inside door latch by lifting the latch and removing the screw.
4 Pry the trim plugs from the armrest. Remove the armrest retaining screws. Disconnect the armrest electrical connector (if equipped) and take the armrest off the door. Pull it forward until it disengages from the lock button.
5 Remove the speaker grille screw (if equipped).
6 Using a special tool (available at many auto parts stores) or a putty knife, carefully pry between the trim panel and the door to separate the trim clips from the door.
7 Lift the trim panel to unhook its top edge from the door, then take the trim panel out.
8 Installation is the reverse of removal. Install the retaining clips in the trim panel before installing the trim panel on the door.

14 Door and lock mechanism - removal, installation and adjustment

1 The door hinges are welded to the door and bolted to the body. For this reason, all door adjustment is done at the hinge-to-body bolts.
2 Open the door. Place thick padding on top of a jack, then place the jack beneath the door to support it.
3 Remove the hinge-to-body bolts and take the door off.
4 To remove the lock mechanism, remove the trim panel (see Section 13).
5 Installation is the reverse of removal. Loosen the hinge-to-body bolts to adjust the door, then tighten the bolts.

15 Center console - removal and installation

Warning: *On models equipped with airbags, always disconnect the negative battery cable, then disconnect the positive battery cable and wait two minutes before working in the vicinity of the impact sensors, steering column or instrument panel to avoid the possibility of accidental deployment of the airbag, which could cause personal injury.*

Early models

1 Pry up the front edge of the shift lever trim plate, then lift the plate out.
2 Remove the console panel trim plate and ashtray.
3 Working through the ashtray opening, remove the two screws that secure the console to the floor.
4 Open the console storage compartment and remove the four screws securing the console to the floor.
5 Unplug the console electrical connectors and lift the console out.
6 Installation is the reverse of removal.

Later models

7 If equipped with a center armrest, pry out the armrest bolt access covers at the rear of the console. Unbolt the armrest and take it out.
8 Pry out the shift lever trim panel. If equipped with manual transmission, remove the shift knob, then slide the trim panel and shift boot off the shift lever.
9 Set the parking brake to position the lever out of the way. Remove the four screws that secure the top panel, lift the panel and disconnect the electrical connectors.
10 Carefully pry out the front upper trim panel by inserting a small screwdriver into the two notches at the bottom.
11 If the vehicle doesn't have a radio, pry the radio opening cover panel out of the opening.
12 If the vehicle has a radio, remove it (see Chapter 12).
13 Open the glove compartment door. If the vehicle has a remote fuel filler switch, detach it. Lower the glove compartment, then remove two screws that secure the console to the instrument panel.
14 Remove the four screws that secure the console to its bracket, then remove the console from the vehicle.
15 Installation is the reverse of removal.

16 Seats - removal and installation

Front seats

1 Remove the seat track retaining bolts and nuts, disconnect any electrical or other connectors and lift the seat and track assembly from the vehicle.
2 Installation is the reverse of removal. Tighten the retaining nuts and bolts securely.

Conventional rear seats (early models)

3 Early models - remove the screws that secure the seat cushion to the floor, then lift the seat cushion out.
4 Lift the seatback up and out.
5 Installation is the reverse of removal.

Conventional rear seats (later models)

6 Kneel on the seat cushion to push it downward, then push it rearward to unhook it from its supports. Lift the cushion out.
7 Remove one of the quarter armrests (if equipped).
8 Remove the seatback lower retaining screws, then lift the seatback up and out.
9 Installation is the reverse of removal.

Fold-down rear seats

10 Fold the seat down, then carefully pry out five push pins that secure the carpet to the seat back.
11 Remove the three screws that secure the folding arm to the seat back. Slide the seat outboard, off its center pivot and take it out.
12 Installation is the reverse of removal.

17 Instrument panel - removal and installation

Warning: *On models equipped with airbags, always disconnect the negative battery cable, then disconnect the positive battery cable and wait two minutes before working in the vicinity of the impact sensors, steering column or instrument panel to avoid the possibility of accidental deployment of the airbag, which could cause personal injury.*
1 Disconnect the cable from the negative terminal of the battery.
2 On early models, remove the instrument panel pad from the top of the instrument panel.
3 On later models, remove the floor console (see Section 15).
4 Remove the steering column trim shrouds and covers.
5 Remove the steering column nuts and carefully lower and support the steering column. On early models, reach between the steering column and instrument panel and lift the selector cable off the shift lever. Remove the cable clamp from the steering column tube.
6 Remove the screws and/or nuts attaching the instrument panel to the brake pedal support and to any braces below the radio or glove compartment.
7 On later models, remove the defroster grille and the speaker grilles.
8 Remove the attaching screws at each end of the instrument panel.
9 Remove the screws along the top edge of the cowl and support the instrument panel. **Note:** *On early models, it will be necessary to use an angle Phillips screwdriver to remove the top screws.*
10 Pull the instrument panel to the rear and disconnect the speedometer cable and any electrical connectors, vacuum lines, or control cables that are attached to the instrument panel. **Note:** *On later models it may be necessary to disconnect the electrical connectors from the main wiring harness under the hood, then push the wiring harness through the grommet in the firewall to create some slack.*
11 Remove the instrument panel. If you're replacing the instrument panel, transfer all components, wiring and hardware to the new panel.
12 Installation is the reverse of removal.

Chapter 12
Chassis electrical system

Contents

1   General information

Warning: *To prevent electrical shorts, fires and injury, always disconnect the cable from the negative terminal of the battery before checking, repairing or replacing electrical components.*

The chassis electrical system of this vehicle is a 12-volt, negative ground type. Power for the lights and all electrical accessories is supplied by a lead/acid-type battery which is charged by the alternator.

This chapter covers repair and service procedures for various chassis (non-engine related) electrical components. For information regarding the engine electrical system components (battery, alternator, distributor and starter motor), see Chapter 5.

2   Electrical troubleshooting - general information

A typical electrical circuit consists of an electrical component, any switches, relays, motors, fuses, fusible links or circuit breakers, etc. related to that component and the wiring and connectors that link the components to both the battery and the chassis. To help you pinpoint an electrical circuit problem, wiring diagrams are included at the end of this book.

Before tackling any troublesome electrical circuit, first study the appropriate wiring diagrams to get a complete understanding of what makes up that individual circuit. Trouble spots, for instance, can often be isolated by noting if other components related to that cir-

cuit are routed through the same fuse and ground connections.

Electrical problems usually stem from simple causes such as loose or corroded connectors, a blown fuse, a melted fusible link or a bad relay. Visually inspect the condition of all fuses, wires and connectors in a problem circuit before troubleshooting it.

The basic tools needed for electrical troubleshooting include a circuit tester, a high impedance (10 K-ohm) digital voltmeter, a continuity tester and a jumper wire with an inline circuit breaker for bypassing electrical components. Before attempting to locate or define a problem with electrical test instruments, use the wiring diagrams to decide where to make the necessary connections.

Voltage checks

Perform a voltage check first when a circuit is not functioning properly. Connect one lead of a circuit tester to either the negative battery terminal or a known good ground.

Connect the other lead to a connector in the circuit being tested, preferably nearest to the battery or fuse. If the bulb of the tester lights up. voltage is present, which means that the part of the circuit between the connector and the battery is problem free. Continue checking the rest of the circuit in the same fashion.

When you reach a point at which no voltage is present, the problem lies between that point and the last test point with voltage. Most of the time the problem can be traced to a loose connection. **Note:** *Keep in mind that some circuits receive voltage only when the ignition key is in the Accessory or Run position.*

Finding a short circuit

One method of finding shorts in a circuit is to remove the fuse and connect a test light or voltmeter in its place. There should be no voltage present in the circuit. Move the wiring harness from side-to-side while watching the test light. If the bulb goes on, there is a short to ground somewhere in that area, probably where the insulation has been rubbed through. The same test can be performed on each component in a circuit, even a switch.

Ground check

Perform a ground test to check whether a component is properly grounded. Disconnect the battery and connect one lead of a self-powered test light, known as a continuity tester, to a known good ground. Connect the other lead to the wire or ground connection being tested. If the bulb goes on, the ground is good. If the bulb does not go on, the ground is not good.

Continuity check

A continuity check determines if there are any breaks in a circuit - if it is conducting electricity properly. With the circuit off (no power in the circuit), a self-powered continuity tester can be used to check the circuit. Connect the test leads to both ends of the circuit, and if the test light comes on the circuit is passing current properly. If the light doesn't come on, there is a break somewhere in the circuit. The same procedure can be used to test a switch, by connecting the continuity tester to the power in and power out sides of the switch. With the switch turned on, the test light should come on.

12

Finding an open circuit

When diagnosing for possible open circuits it is often difficult to locate them by sight because oxidation or terminal misalignment are hidden by the connectors. Merely wiggling a connector on a sensor or in the wiring harness may correct the open circuit condition. Remember this if an open circuit is indicated when troubleshooting a circuit. Intermittent problems may also be caused by oxidized or loose connections.

Electrical troubleshooting is simple if you keep in mind that all electrical circuits are basically electricity running from the battery, through the wires, switches, relays, fuses and fusible links to each electrical component (light bulb, motor, etc.) and then to ground, from which it is passed back to the battery. Any electrical problem is an interruption in the flow of electricity to and from the battery.

3   Connectors - general information

Always release the lock lever(s) before attempting to unplug inline type connectors. There are a variety of lock lever configurations. Although nothing more than a finger is usually necessary to pry lock levers open, a small pocket screwdriver is effective for hard-to-release levers. Once the lock levers are released, try to pull on the connectors themselves, not the wires, when unplugging two connector halves (there are times, however, when this is not possible - use good judgment).

It is usually necessary to know which side, male or female, of the connector you're checking. Male connectors are easily distinguished from females by the shape of their internal pins.

When checking continuity or voltage with a circuit tester, insertion of the test probe into the receptacle may open the fitting to the connector and result in poor contact. Instead, insert the test probe from the wire harness side of the connector (known as "backprobing").

4   Fuses - general information

Refer to illustration 4.2

The electrical circuits are protected by a combination of fuses, fusible links and circuit breakers. The fuse panel is located under the left end of the dashboard.

Two types of fuses are used, depending on date of manufacture. Early models use a glass tube design where the metal element inside can be readily seen for checking. Miniaturized fuses are used on later models. These compact fuses, with blade terminal design, allow fingertip removal and replacement. If an electrical component fails, always check the fuse first **(see illustration)**. To check the fuses, turn the ignition key to the ON position. Connect one lead of a test light to a good ground and connect the other lead

to each of the fuse's exposed terminal ends. The test light should light when connected to each end. If it doesn't light when connected to one of the terminal ends, the fuse is open and should be replaced.

Be sure to replace blown fuses with the correct type and amp rating. Fuses of different ratings are physically interchangeable, but replacing a fuse with one of a higher or lower value than specified is not recommended. Each electrical circuit needs a specific amount of protection. The amperage value of each fuse is usually molded into the fuse body. Different colors are also used to denote fuses of different amperage types. **Caution:** *Always turn off all electrical components and the ignition switch before replacing a fuse. Never bypass a fuse with pieces of metal or foil. Fire and/or serious damage to the electrical system could result.*

If the replacement fuse immediately fails, do not replace it again until the cause of the problem (a short circuit) is isolated and corrected.

5   Fusible links - general information

Some circuits are protected by fusible links. The links are used in circuits which are not ordinarily fused, such as the ignition circuit.

Although the fusible links appear to be a heavier gauge than the wire they are protecting, the appearance is due to the thick insulation. All fusible links are four wire gauges smaller than the wire they are designed to protect.

Fusible links cannot be repaired, but a new link of the same size wire can be put in its place. The procedure is as follows:

a) *Disconnect the negative cable from the battery.*
b) *Disconnect the fusible link from the wiring harness.*
c) *Cut the damaged fusible link out of the wiring just behind the connector.*
d) *Strip the insulation back approximately 1/2-inch.*
e) *Position the connector on the new fusible link and crimp it into place.*

f) *Use rosin core solder at each end of the new link to obtain a good solder joint.*
g) *Use plenty of electrical tape around the soldered joint. No wires should be exposed.*
h) *Connect the battery ground cable. Test the circuit for proper operation.*

6   Circuit breakers - general information

Circuit breakers protect accessories such as power windows, power door locks, the windshield wipers, windshield washer pump, interval wiper, low washer fluid, etc. Circuit breakers are located in the fuse box. Refer to the fuse panel guide in your owner's manual for the location of the circuit breakers used in your vehicle.

Because a circuit breaker resets itself automatically, an electrical overload in a circuit breaker protected system will cause the circuit to fail momentarily, then come back on. If the circuit does not come back on, check it immediately.

a) *Remove the circuit breaker from the fuse panel.*
b) *Using an ohmmeter, verify that there is continuity between both terminals of the circuit breaker. If there is no continuity, replace the circuit breaker.*
c) *Install the old or new circuit breaker. If it continues to cut out, a short circuit is indicated. Troubleshoot the appropriate circuit (see the wiring diagrams at the back of this book) or have the system checked by a professional mechanic.*

7   Turn signal/hazard flasher/dimmer (multi-function) switch - replacement

Warning: *On models equipped with airbags, always disconnect the negative battery cable, then disconnect the positive battery cable and wait two minutes before working in the vicinity of the impact sensors, steering column or instrument panel to avoid the possibility of accidental deployment of the airbag,*

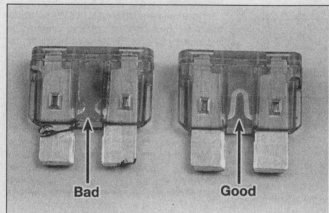

4.2 When a fuse blows, the element between the terminals melts - the fuse on the left is blown, the fuse on the right is good

Bad   Good

which could cause personal injury.

1   Disconnect the negative cable from the battery.

2   Remove the steering column cover.

3   Unplug the switch electrical connectors.

4   Remove the switch mounting screws and take the switch off the steering column.

5   Installation is the reverse of removal.

8   Ignition switch - replacement

Refer to illustration 8.5

Warning: *On models equipped with airbags, always disconnect the negative battery cable, then disconnect the positive battery cable and wait two minutes before working in the vicinity of the impact sensors, steering column or instrument panel to avoid the possibility of accidental deployment of the airbag, which could cause personal injury.*

1   Disconnect the negative cable from the battery.

2   Remove the steering column covers.

3   Turn the ignition key lock cylinder to the On (Run) position.

4   Unplug the ignition switch electrical connector.

5   Use a 1/8-inch drill bit to drill out the break-off head bolts that connect the switch to the lock cylinder housing **(see illustration)**.

6   Remove both bolts with an easy-out tool.

7   Disengage the ignition switch from the actuator pin.

8   Make sure the actuator pin slot in the new ignition switch is in the Run position. **Note:** *A new replacement switch assembly will be set in the On (Run) position.*

9   Place the new switch in position and install the break-off head bolts. Tighten the bolts until the heads break off.

10   Plug the electrical connector into the switch.

11   Install the steering column cover.

12   Connect the negative battery cable.

9   Ignition key lock cylinder - replacement

Warning: *On models equipped with airbags, always disconnect the negative battery cable, then disconnect the positive battery cable and wait two minutes before working in the vicinity of the impact sensors, steering column or instrument panel to avoid the possibility of accidental deployment of the airbag, which could cause personal injury.*

1   Disconnect the negative cable from the battery.

2   If your vehicle is equipped with a tilt column, remove the upper extension shroud by snapping it loose from its retaining clip.

3   Remove the steering column cover.

4   Locate the single key warning buzzer wire and disconnect it.

5   Turn the ignition switch to the Run position.

8.5 An easy-out tool is required to remove the two break-off head bolts (arrows) retaining the ignition switch to the lock cylinder housing

6   Place a 1/8-inch punch in the hole in the casting surrounding the lock cylinder. Depress the punch while pulling out on the lock cylinder to remove it from the column housing.

7   Install the lock cylinder by turning it to the Run position and depressing the retaining pin. Insert the lock cylinder into the lock cylinder housing. Make sure the cylinder is completely seated and aligned in the interlocking washer before turning the key to the Off position. This will permit the retaining pin to extend into the hole.

8   Turn the lock to ensure that operation is correct in all positions.

9   The remainder of installation is the reverse of removal.

10   Windshield wiper/washer switch and motor - removal and installation

Warning: *On models equipped with airbags, always disconnect the negative battery cable, then disconnect the positive battery cable and wait two minutes before working in the vicinity of the impact sensors, steering column or instrument panel to avoid the possibility of accidental deployment of the airbag, which could cause personal injury.*

Wiper switch

1   Disconnect the negative cable from the battery.

2   Remove the steering column shroud.

3   Unplug the switch electrical connector. **Note:** *On some models, it may be easier to remove the switch from the steering column first, then unplug the electrical connector.*

4   Remove the switch mounting screws and take the switch off the steering column. **Note:** *Later models use Torx screws to secure the switch. Be sure to use the proper size Torx driver.*

5   Installation is the reverse of removal.

Front wiper motor

6   Remove the cowl top grille.

7   Remove the link retaining clip and detach the wiper linkage from the motor.

8   Remove the motor mounting screws and take the motor out.

9   Installation is the reverse of removal. Make sure the wiper blades are in the parked position before attaching the linkage to the motor.

Rear wiper motor

10   Raise the wiper arm off the rear window. Pull the slide latch and lift away the wiper arm.

11   Remove the pivot shaft nuts and washers.

12   Remove the liftgate trim screws and panel.

13   Disconnect the motor electrical connector.

14   Remove the screws that secure the motor and linkage to the liftgate.

15   Remove the motor and linkage as an assembly.

16   Installation is the reverse of removal.

11   Hazard/turn signal flashers - replacement

1   When a flasher unit is functioning properly, an audible click can be heard during its operation. If the turn signals fail on one side or the other and the flasher unit does not make its characteristic clicking sound, a faulty turn signal bulb is indicated. A burned-out bulb affects the hazard flasher by causing it to flash slower than normal.

2   If the turn signals fail to blink on either side of the vehicle, the problem may be due to a blown fuse, a faulty flasher unit, a broken switch or a loose or open connection. If the turn signal fuse has blown, check the wiring for a short before installing a new fuse.

3   If the hazard flashers do not work (either the bulbs light up but do not flash, or none of the lights come on), the most likely cause is a faulty flasher unit.

4   The flasher units, which look like small plastic or metal canister-shaped devices, are located in various places depending on the year of the vehicle:

12

Turn signal flasher

1986 and earlier models:
    Front side of fuse box
1987 and later models:
    Attached to instrument panel reinforcement above fuse box OR behind radio

Hazard flasher

1986 and earlier models:
    Behind right side of instrument panel, above glove box
1987 and later models:
    Back side of fuse box

Note: *On some models, both flashers may be plugged into the fuse box.*

5   If you are replacing a fuse box mounted flasher, unplug it from the fuse box. On some models the flasher pulls straight out. On later models, remove the flasher by turning it 90-degrees counterclockwise and pulling straight out. Install the new flasher by reversing the removal procedure.

6   If you are replacing a flasher fastened to an instrument panel reinforcement bracket, detach the flasher from the bracket and unplug its electrical connector. Installation is the reverse of removal.

12   Headlight switch - replacement

Early models

1   Disconnect the negative battery cable from the battery.
2   Pull the headlamp switch to the On position.
3   Reach under the instrument panel and press the knob release button. Remove the knob.
4   Remove the switch retaining nut and take the switch out.
5   Disconnect the electrical connector from the switch.
6   Installation is the reverse of removal.

Later models

7   Disconnect the negative battery cable from the battery.
8   Locate the two lock tabs that secure the switch. These are behind the switch levers. Use a small screwdriver to disengage the lock tabs.
9   Pull the switch out and disconnect the electrical connectors.
10   To install, connect the wiring connectors to the switch. Push it into the instrument panel until the lock tabs engage.

13   Headlights - removal and installation

1   Disconnect the negative battery cable from the battery.

Sealed beam headlights

2   Remove the headlight bezel screws and remove the bezel.

3   Remove the headlight retaining screws. Pull the headlight out of the frame, disconnect the electrical connector and take the headlight out. **Caution:** *Do not disturb the (usually larger) adjusting screws or the headlight aim will be altered.*
4   Installation is the reverse of removal. Have the headlights adjusted by a properly equipped shop.

Aero headlights

5   Open the hood.
6   Disconnect the electrical connector from the back of the bulb.
7   Rotate the retaining ring about 1/8-turn counterclockwise (viewed from the rear) and slide it off the base.
8   Carefully pull the bulb straight out of the socket.
9   Insert the bulb into the socket. Position the flat on the plastic base upward.
10   Align the socket locating tabs with the grooves in the forward part of the plastic base, then push the socket firmly into the base. Make sure the base mounting flange contacts the socket.
11   Slide the retaining ring on. Turn it clockwise until it hits the stop.
12   Connect the electrical connector. Test headlight operation, then close the hood.
13   Have headlight aim checked by a properly equipped shop.

14   Bulb replacement

1   The lenses of many lights are held in place by screws, which makes it a simple procedure to gain access to the bulbs.
2   On some lights the lenses are held in place by clips. The lenses can be removed either by unsnapping them or by using a small screwdriver to pry them off.
3   Several types of bulbs are used. Some are removed by pushing in and turning them counterclockwise. Others can simply be unclipped from the terminals or pulled straight out of the socket.
4   To gain access to the instrument panel lights, the instrument cluster will have to be removed first.

15   Radio - removal and installation

1979 through 1986 models

1   Disconnect the negative battery cable from the battery.
2   Disconnect the power, speaker and antenna wires from the radio.
3   Pull off the knobs and discs, then remove the radio retaining nuts (if equipped).
4   Remove the upper support screws (if equipped).
5   Remove the rear support nut or screw.
6   Take the radio out.
7   Installation is the reverse of removal.

1987 and later models

Refer to illustrations 15.10a and 15.10b
Warning: *On models equipped with airbags, always disconnect the negative battery cable, then disconnect the positive battery cable and wait two minutes before working in the vicinity of the impact sensors, steering column or instrument panel to avoid the possibility of accidental deployment of the airbag, which could cause personal injury.*
8   The radio receiver is retained in the instrument panel by internal, concealed clips. Releasing these clips requires the use of two special removal tools (available at most auto parts stores), or you can fabricate a substitute out of two lengths of coathanger bent into "U" shapes.
9   Insert the removal tools into the holes at the corners of the radio faceplate until you feel the internal clips release.
10   With the clips released, push outward simultaneously on both tools and pull the radio out of the instrument panel, disconnect the antenna lead and electrical connectors and remove the unit from the vehicle **(see illustrations)**.
11   To install the radio, reconnect the antenna lead and electrical connectors, then push the radio back into place along its track until the clips snap into place.

16   Instrument cluster - removal and installation

Warning: *On models equipped with airbags, always disconnect the negative battery cable, then disconnect the positive battery cable and wait two minutes before working in the vicinity of the impact sensors, steering column or instrument panel to avoid the possibility of accidental deployment of the airbag, which could cause personal injury.*
1   Disconnect the negative battery cable from the battery (and, on models with an airbag, the positive cable).
2   On 1988 and later models, remove the switch assemblies from either side of the instrument panel (see Section 12).
3   Remove the screws securing the trim panel to the cluster. Remove the trim panel.
4   Remove four cluster retaining screws.
5   Pull the cluster out. Reach behind it and disconnect the speedometer cable.
6   Pull the cluster the rest of the way out and disconnect its wiring connectors.
7   Apply a 3/16-inch diameter ball of silicone damping grease to the drive hole in the speedometer head.
8   The remainder of installation is the reverse of removal.

17   Airbag, general information

Some later models are equipped with a Supplemental Restraint System (SRS), more commonly known as an airbag. This system

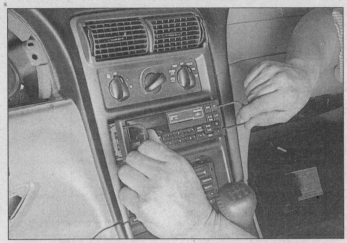

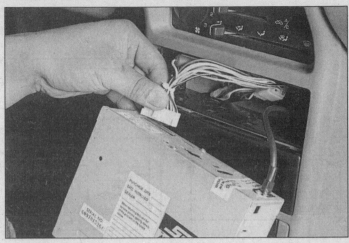

15.10a On 1987 and later models, insert the removal tools until they seat, then push outward simultaneously on both tools to release the clips and withdraw the radio from the dash

15.10b Disconnect the electrical connectors and the antenna lead, then remove the unit

is designed to protect the driver from serious injury in the event of a head-on or frontal collision. It consists of an airbag module in the center of the steering wheel, three crash sensors mounted at the front of the vehicle, one crash sensor mounted in the passenger compartment and a diagnostic module located in the center of the instrument panel.

Airbag module

The airbag inflator module contains a housing incorporating the cushion (airbag) and inflator unit, mounted in the center of the steering wheel. The inflator assembly is mounted on the back of the housing over a hole through which gas is expelled, inflating the bag almost instantaneously when an electrical signal is sent from the system. A coil assembly, or "clockspring," on the steering column under the steering wheel carries this signal to the module.

This coil assembly can transmit an electrical signal regardless of steering wheel position. The igniter in the airbag converts the electrical signal to heat and ignites the charge, which inflates the bag.

Sensors

The system has four sensors: three forward crash sensors at the front of the vehicle and one inside the passenger compartment. The left-side and right-side sensors are located behind the headlights; the center sensor is located behind the grille, bolted to the radiator support; the other sensor is mounted behind the trim panel in the left-side B-pillar.

The forward and passenger compartment sensors are basically pressure sensitive switches that complete an electrical circuit during an impact of sufficient G force. The electrical signal from these sensors is sent to the electronic diagnostic monitor which then completes the circuit and inflates the airbag(s).

Electronic diagnostic monitor

The electronic diagnostic monitor, mounted in the instrument panel behind the heater/air conditioner control panel, supplies the current to the airbag system in the event of the collision, even if battery power is cut off. It checks this system every time the vehicle is started, causing the "AIRBAG" light to go on then off, if the system is operating properly. If there is a fault in the system, the light will go on and stay on, flash, or the dash will make a beeping sound. If this happens, the vehicle should be taken to your dealer or other qualified repair shop immediately for service.

Disabling the system

Whenever working in the vicinity of the steering wheel, steering column or near other components of the airbag system, the system should be disarmed. To do this, perform the following steps:

a) Turn the ignition switch to Off.
b) Detach the cable from the negative battery terminal then detach the positive cable. Wait two minutes for the electronic module backup power supply to be depleted.

Enabling the system

a) Turn the ignition switch to the Off position.
b) Connect the positive battery cable first, then connect the negative cable.

---

18 Wiring diagrams and color codes - general information

Since it isn't possible to include all wiring diagrams for every year covered by this manual, the following diagrams are those that are typical and most commonly needed.

Prior to troubleshooting any circuits, check the fuse and circuit breakers (if equipped) to make sure they're in good condition. Make sure the battery is properly charged and check the cable connections (see Chapter 1).

When checking a circuit, make sure that all connectors are clean, with no broken or loose terminals. When unplugging a connector, do not pull on the wires. Pull only on the connector housings themselves.

Color codes

Wire colors in wiring diagrams are identified by one or two-character alphabetical codes. The following list tells the color indicated by each of these codes.

B = Black	P = Purple
BR = Brown	PK = Pink
DB = Dark blue	R = Red
DG = Dark green	T = Tan
GY = Gray	W = White
LB = Light blue	Y = Yellow
LG = Light green	(H) = Hash*
N = Natural	(D) = Dot*
O = Orange	

Note: The presence of a tracer on the wire is indicated by a secondary color followed by an "H" for hash or "D" for dot. A stripe is understood if no letter follows.

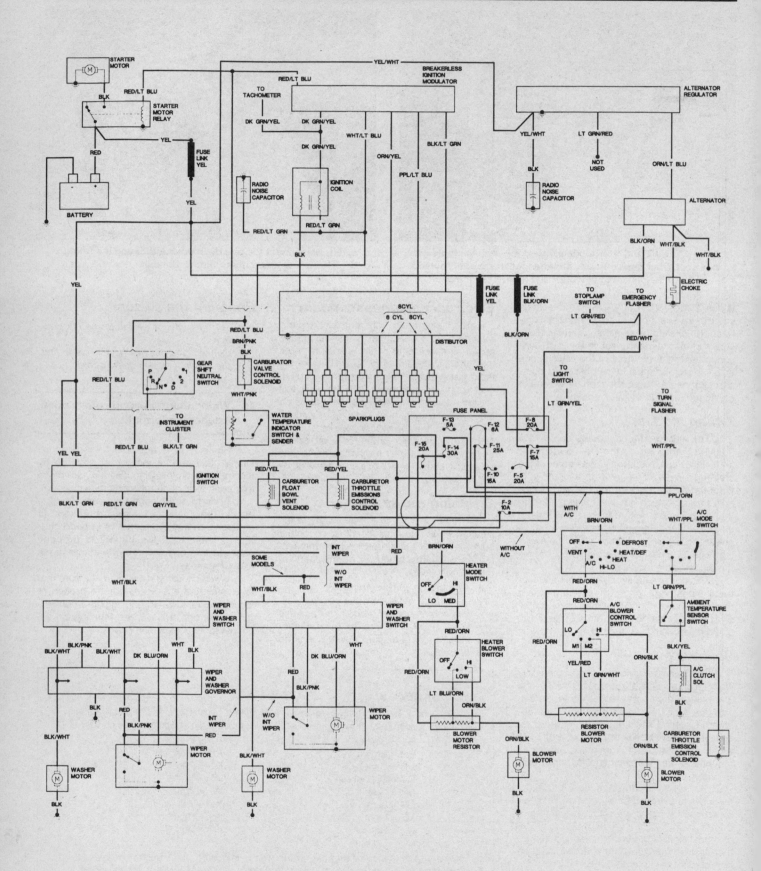

Wiring diagram for 1979 models (1 of 2)

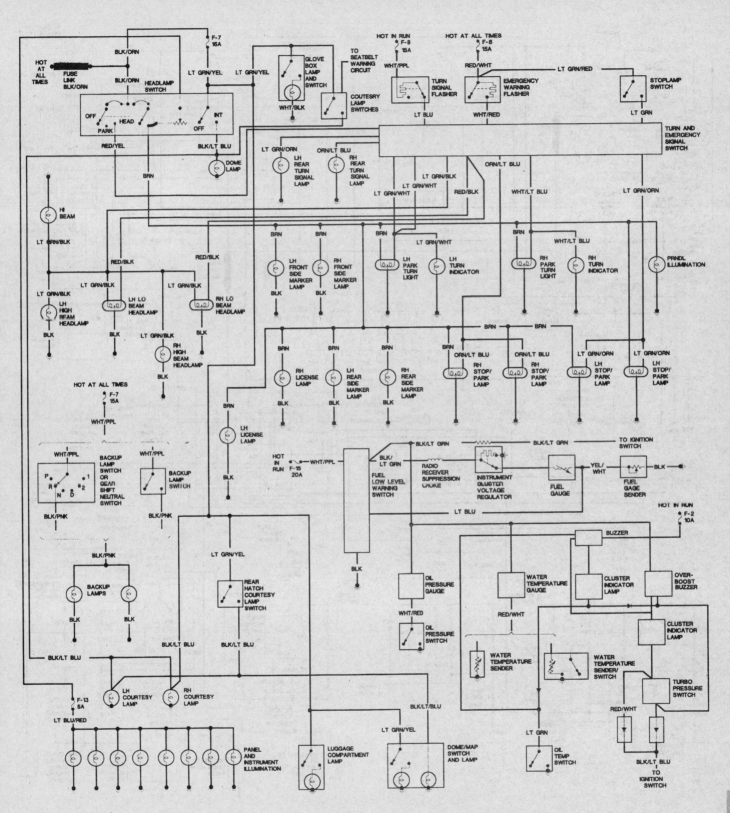

Wiring diagram for 1979 models (2 of 2)

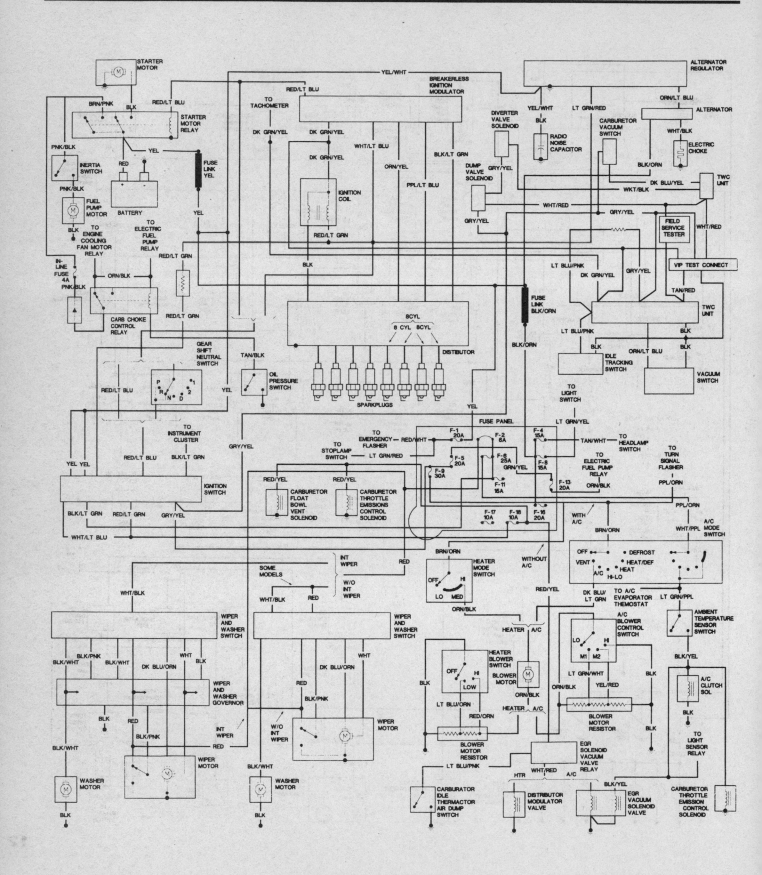

Wiring diagram for 1980 models (1 of 2)

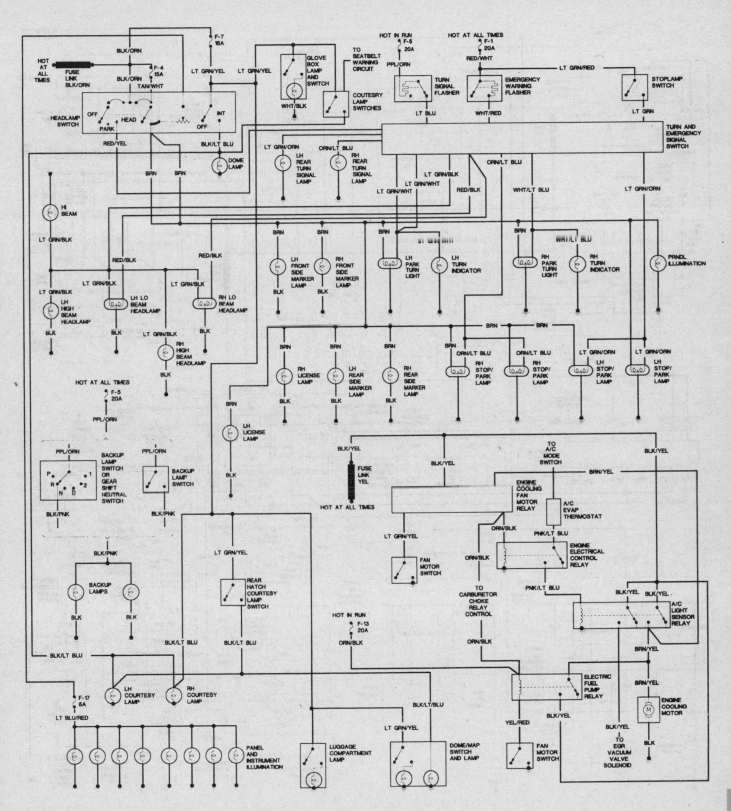

Wiring diagram for 1980 models (2 of 2)

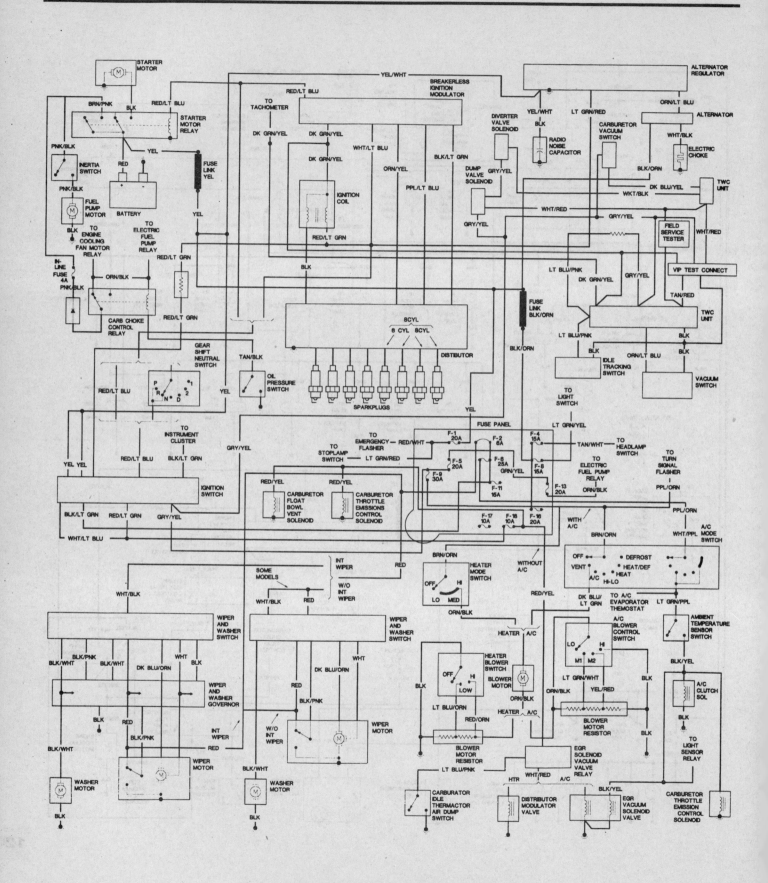

Wiring diagram for 1981 models (1 of 2)

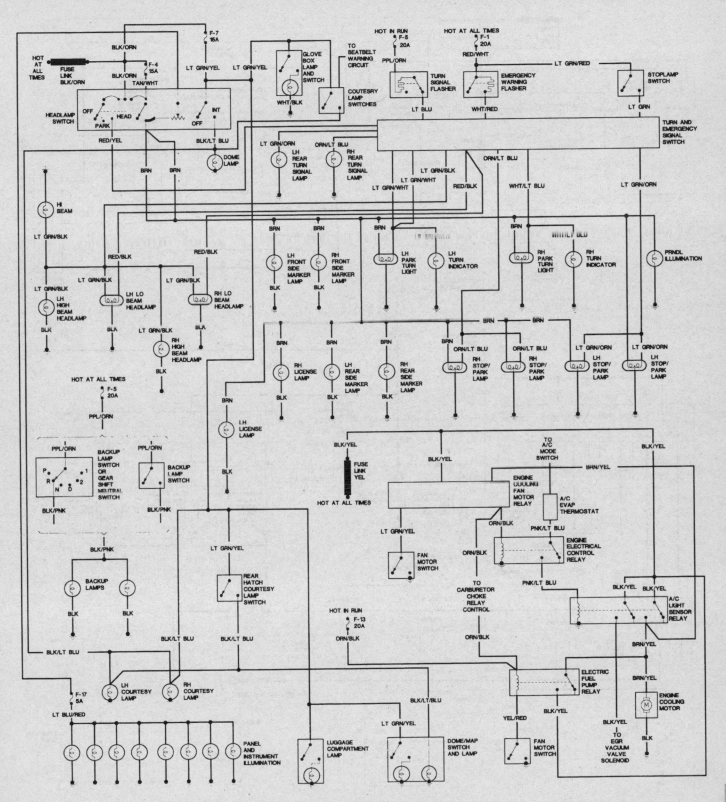

Wiring diagram for 1981 models (2 of 2)

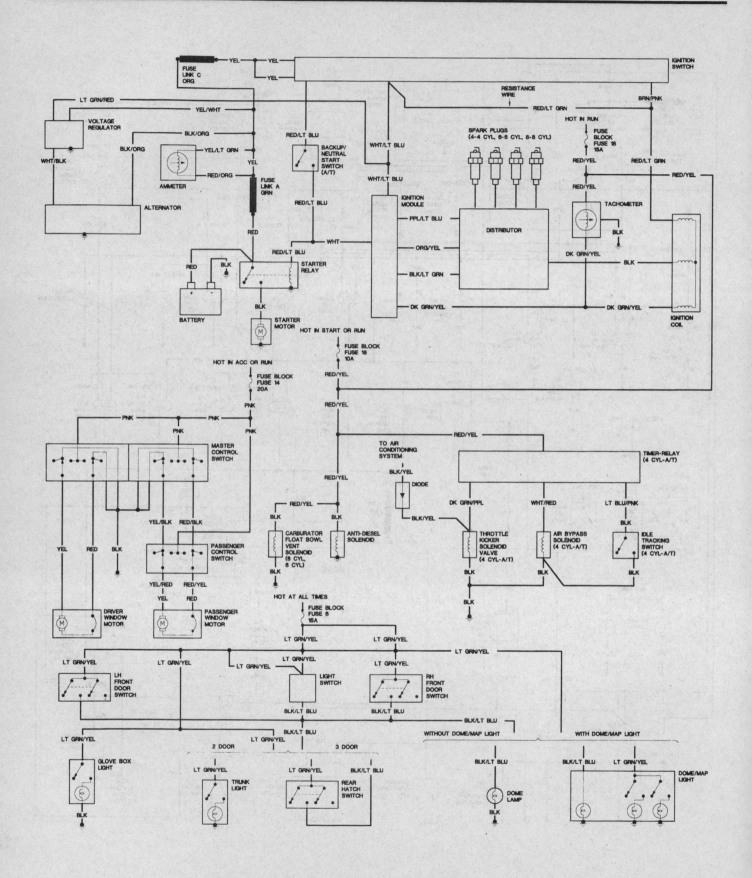

Wiring diagram for 1982 models, except California/Turbo (1 of 4)

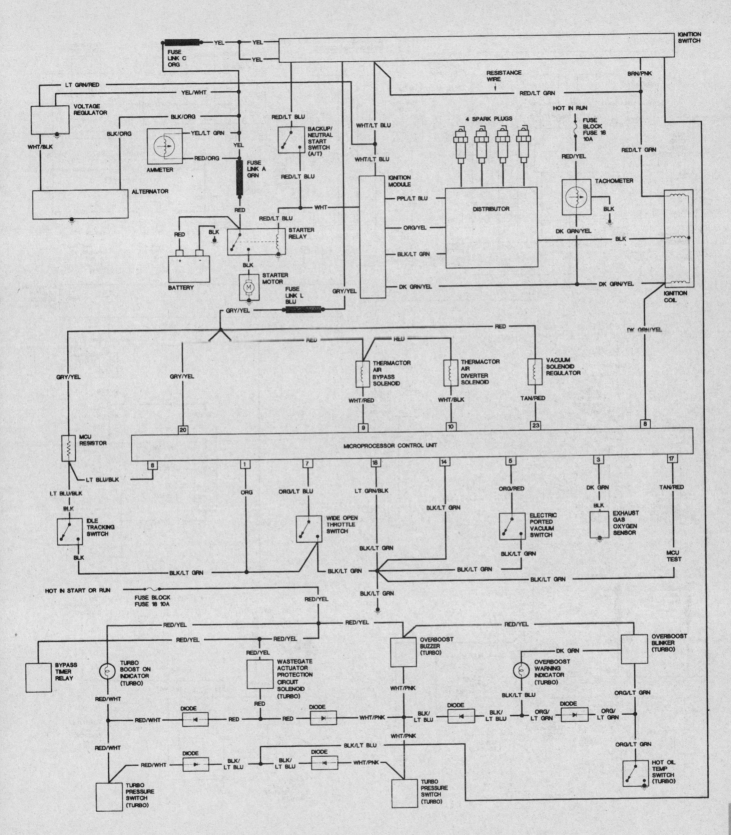

Wiring diagram for 1982 models, California/Turbo (2 of 4)

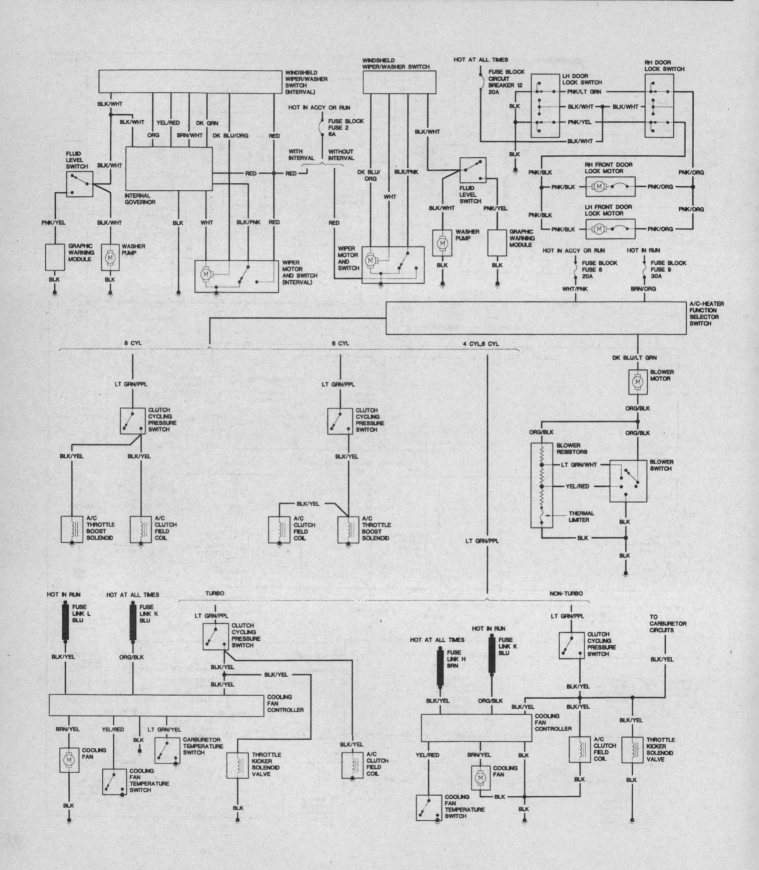

Wiring diagram for 1982 models (3 of 4)

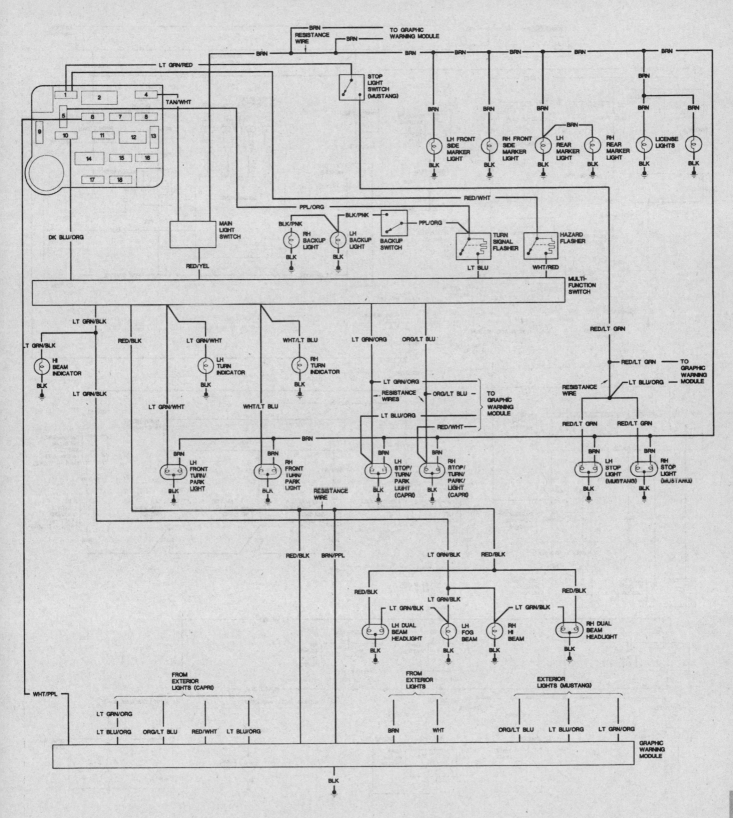

Wiring diagram for 1982 models (4 of 4)

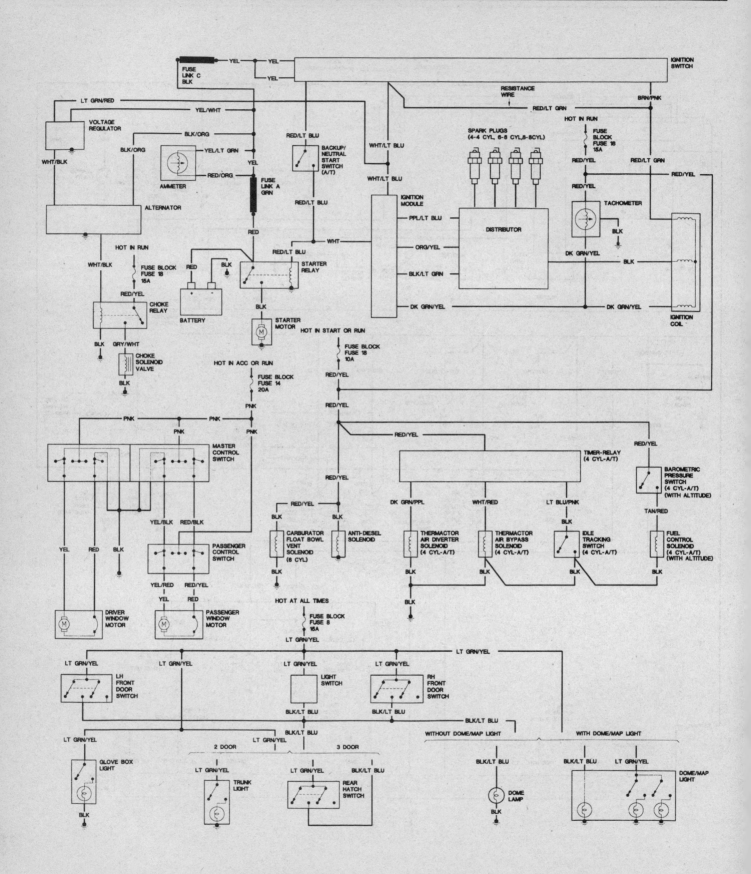

Wiring diagram for 1983 models, except four-cylinder manual transmission and California (1 of 4)

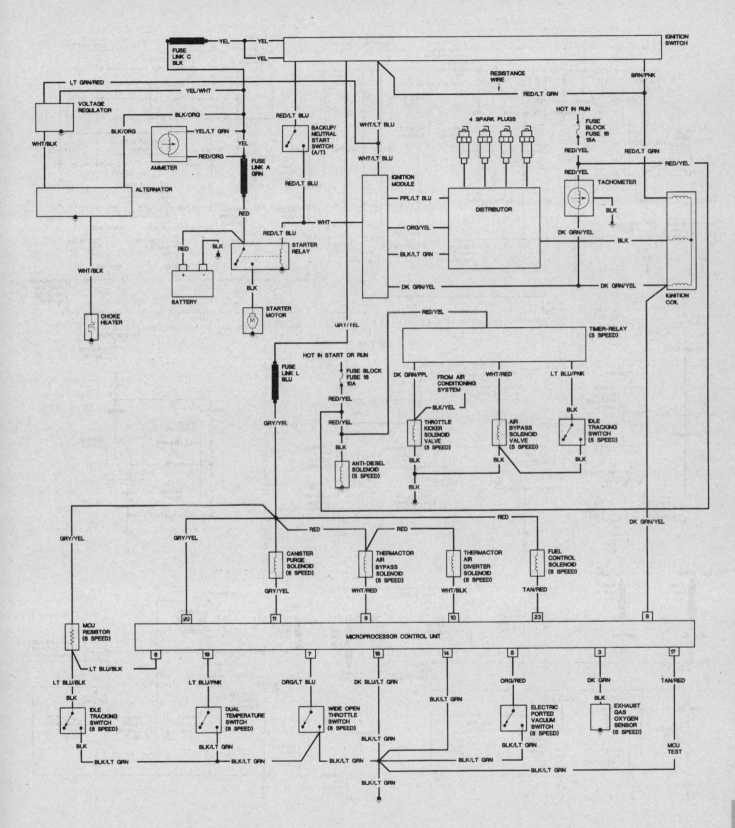

Wiring diagram for 1983 models, four-cylinder manual transmission and California (2 of 4)

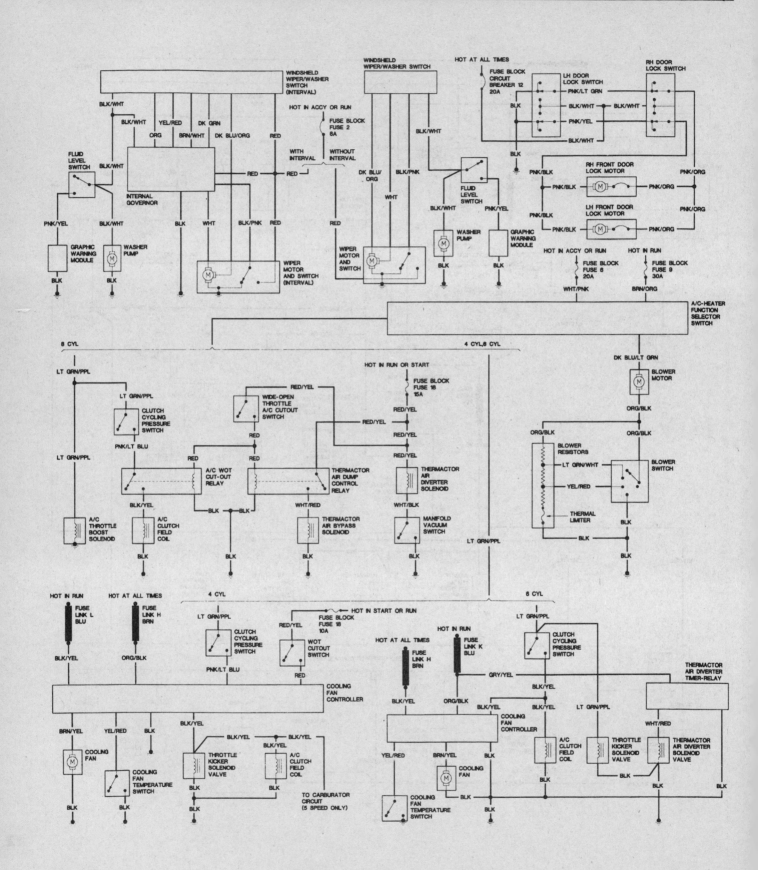

Wiring diagram for 1983 models (3 of 4)

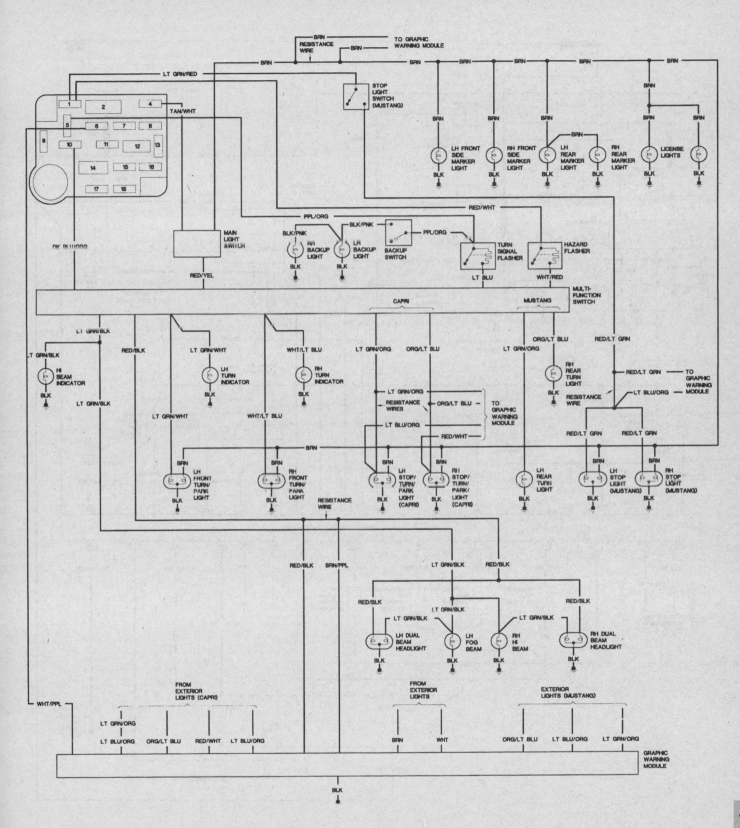

Wiring diagram for 1983 models (4 of 4)

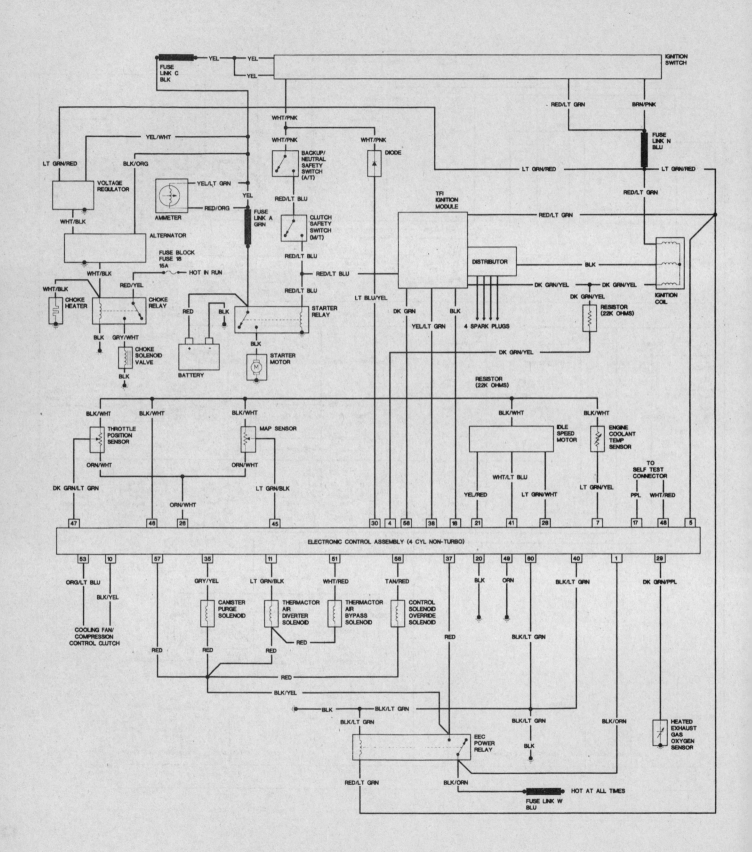

Wiring diagram for 1984 models, four-cylinder non-turbo (1 of 6)

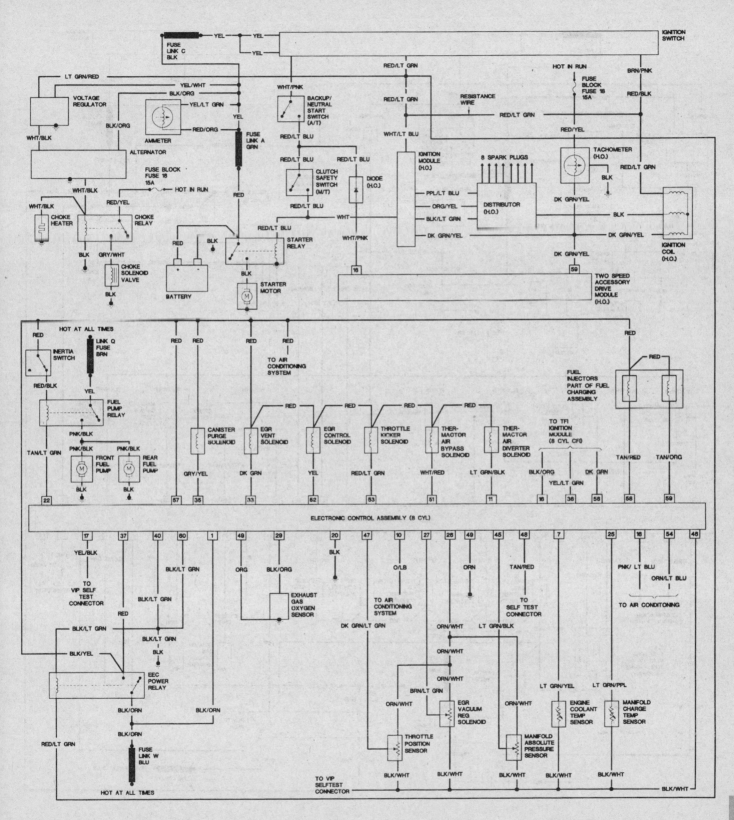

Wiring diagram for 1984 models, V8 with High-Output Ignition (2 of 6)

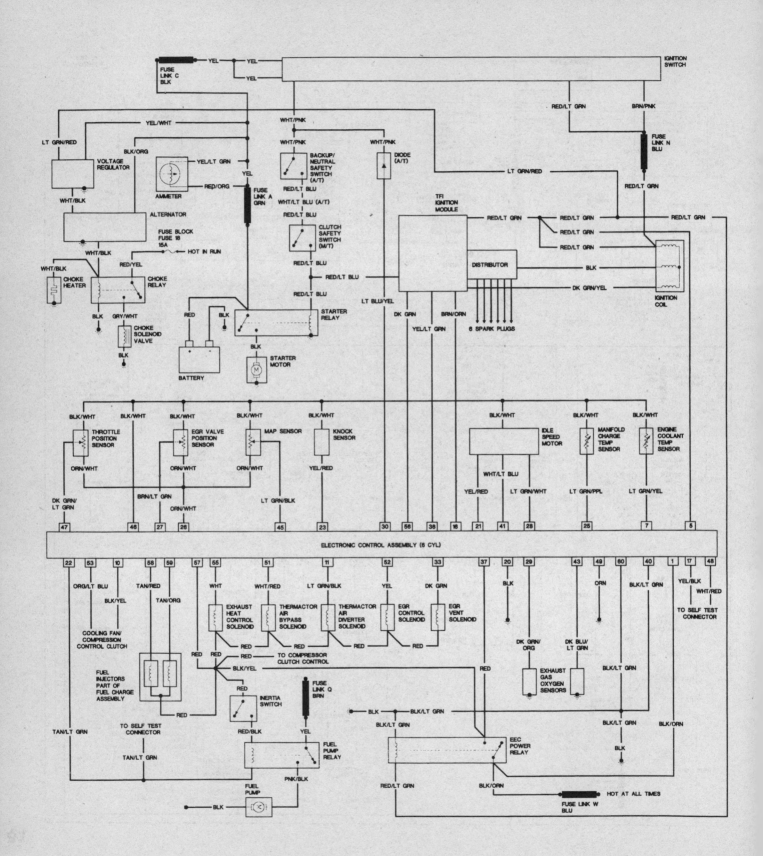

Wiring diagram for 1984 V6 models (3 of 6)

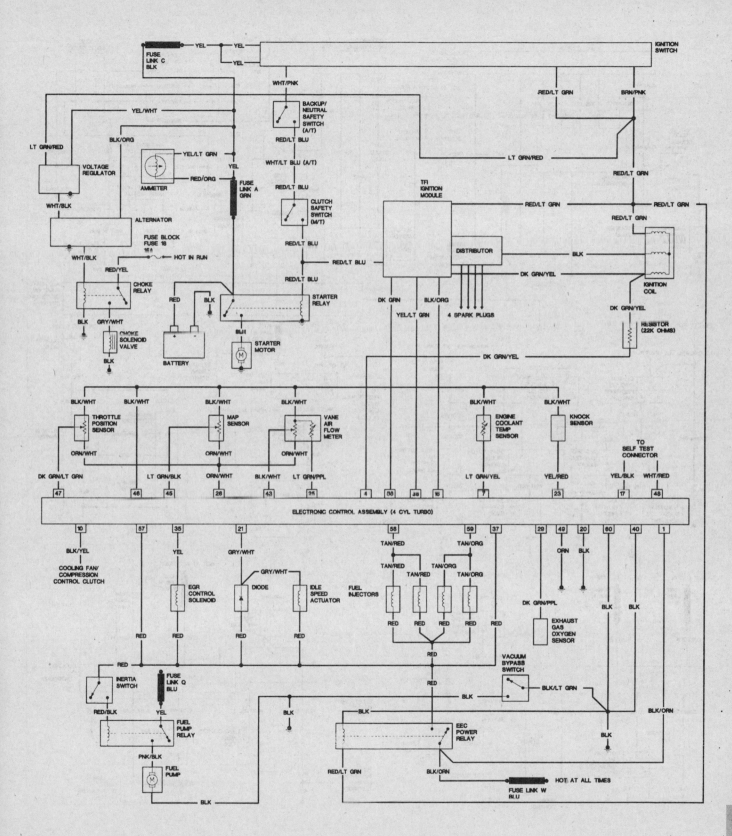

Wiring diagram for all 1984 models (4 of 6)

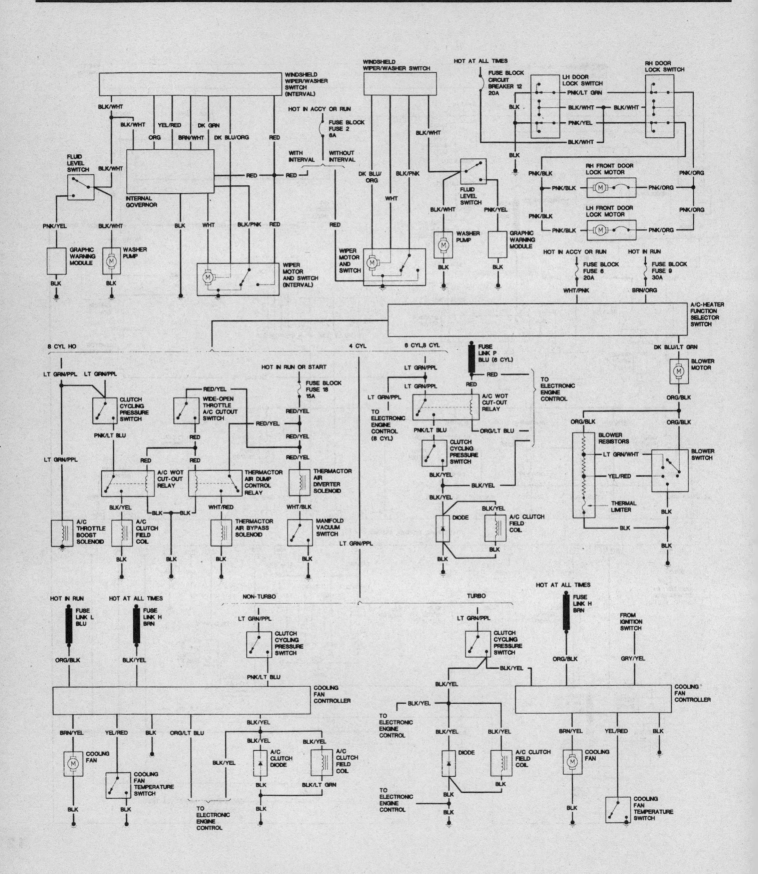

Wiring diagram for all 1984 models (5 of 6)

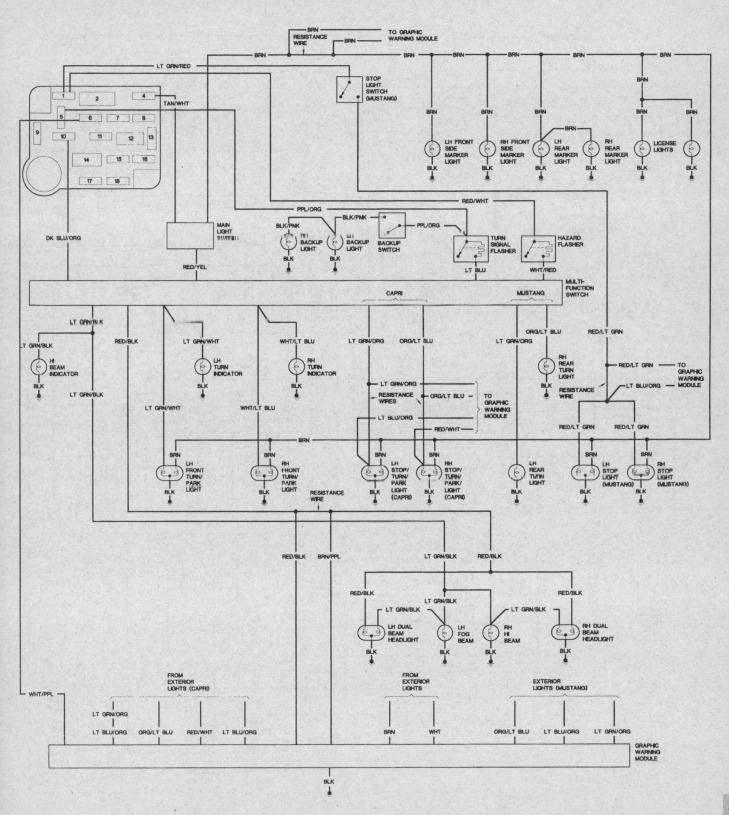

Wiring diagram for all 1984 models (6 of 6)

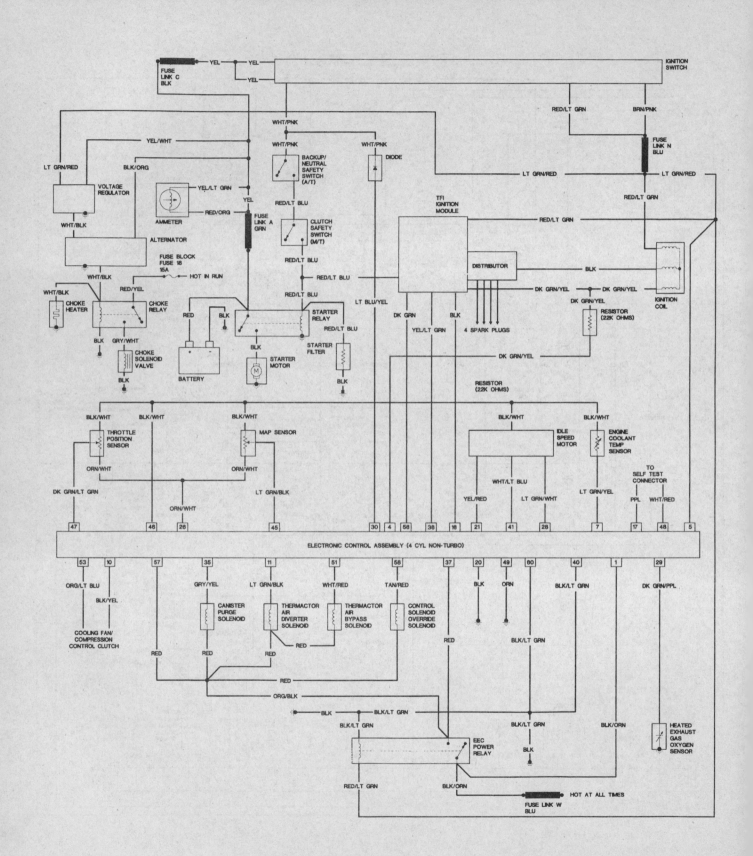

Wiring diagram for 1985 models, four-cylinder non-turbo (1 of 6)

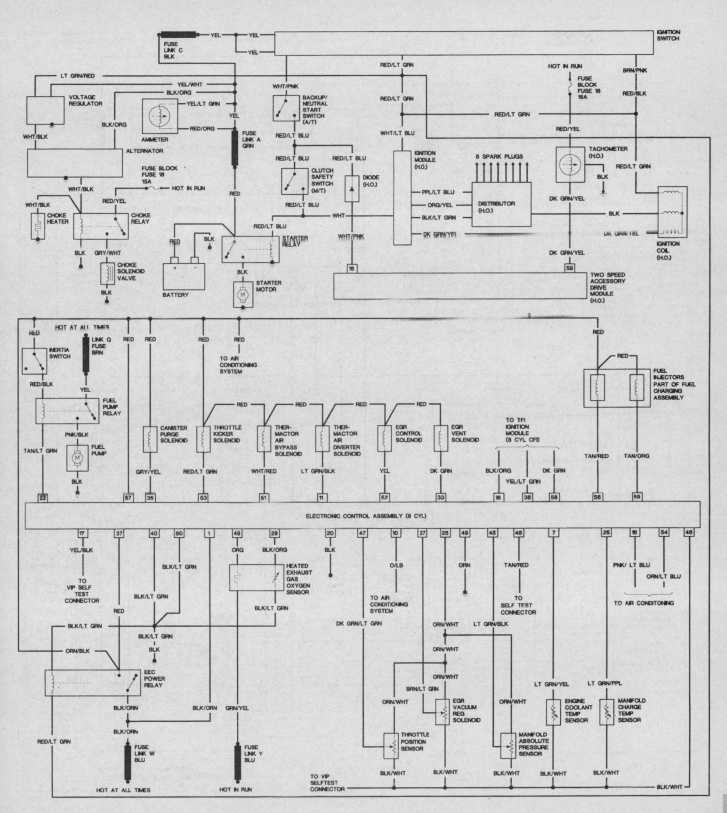

Wiring diagram for 1985 models, V8 with High-Output Ignition (2 of 6)

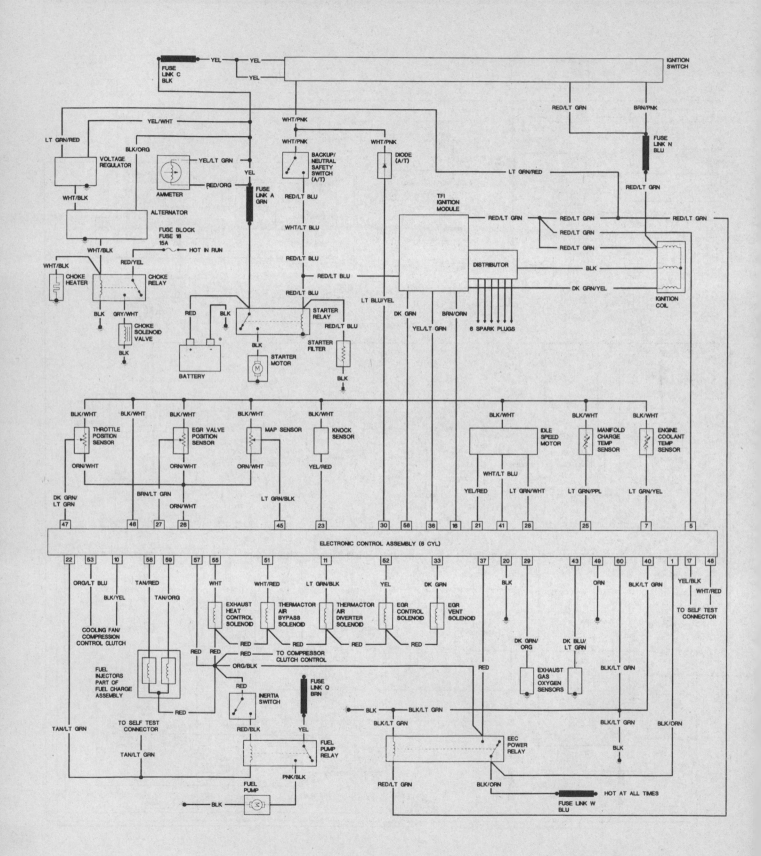

Wiring diagram for 1985 V6 models (3 of 6)

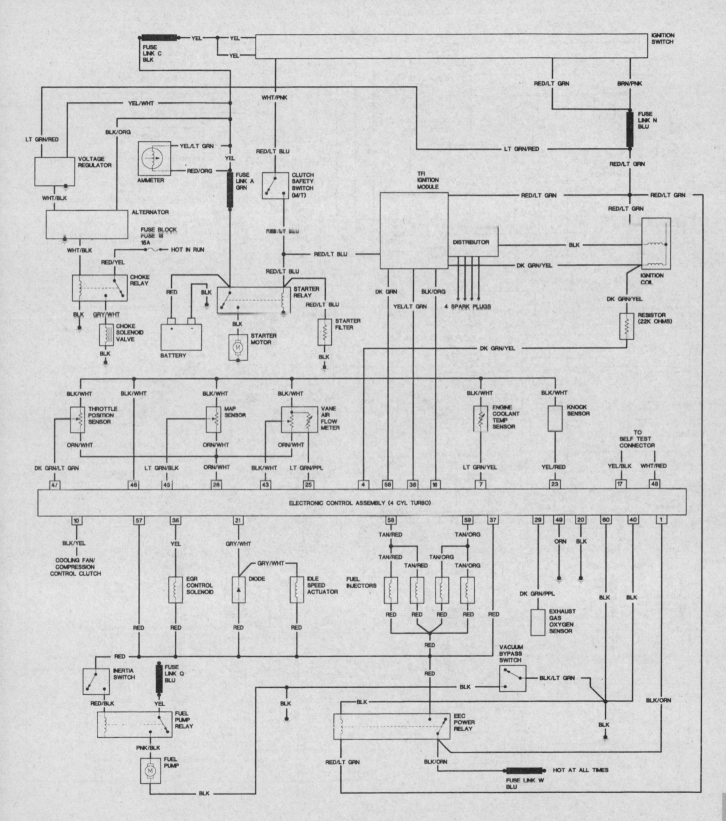

Wiring diagram for 1985 models, four-cylinder turbo (4 of 6)

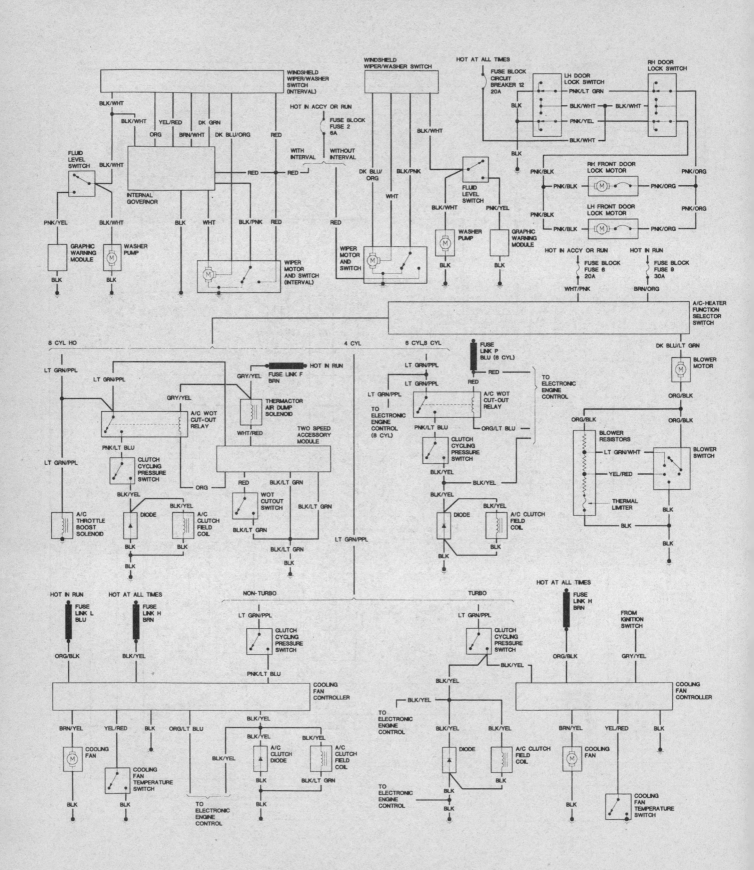

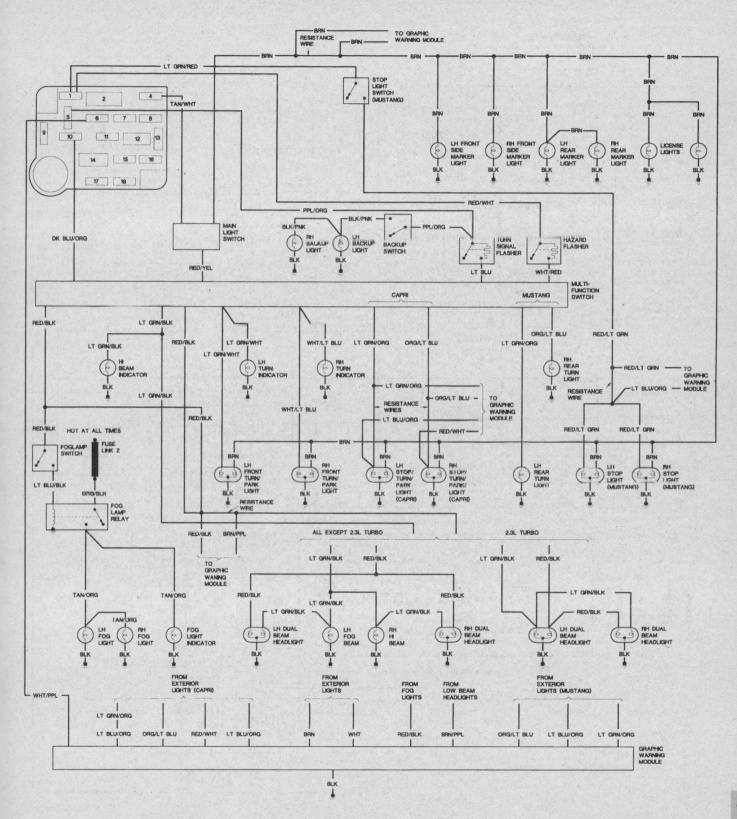

Wiring diagram for all 1985 models (6 of 6)

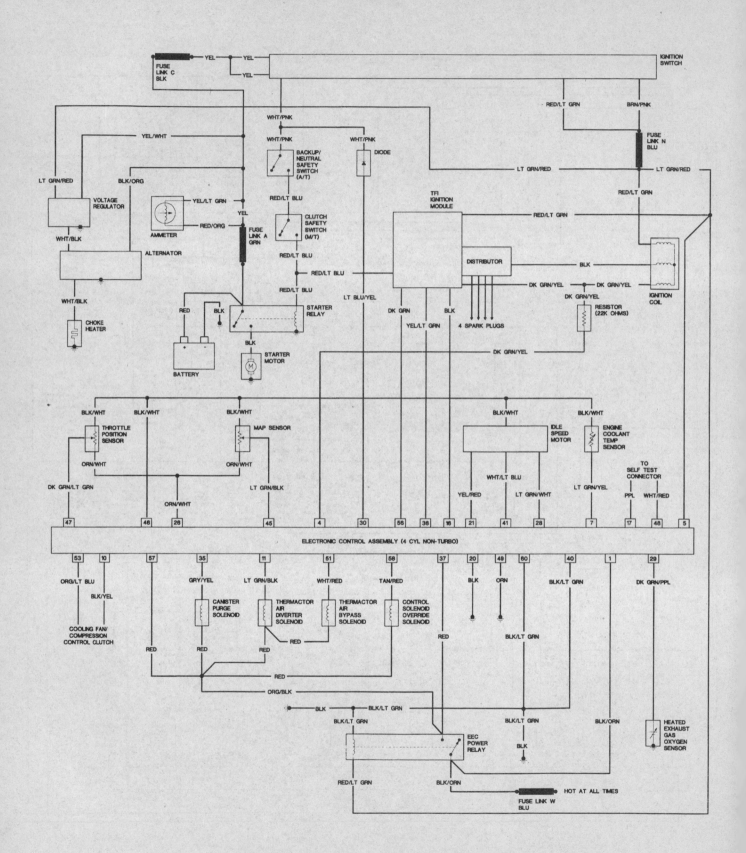

Wiring diagram for 1986 models, four-cylinder non-turbo (1 of 6)

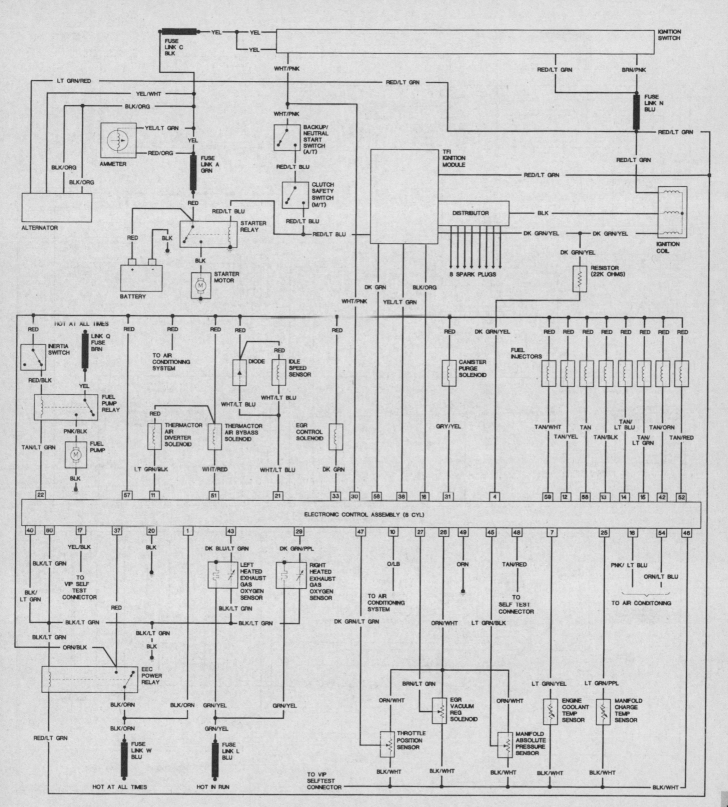

Wiring diagram for 1986 V8 models (2 of 6)

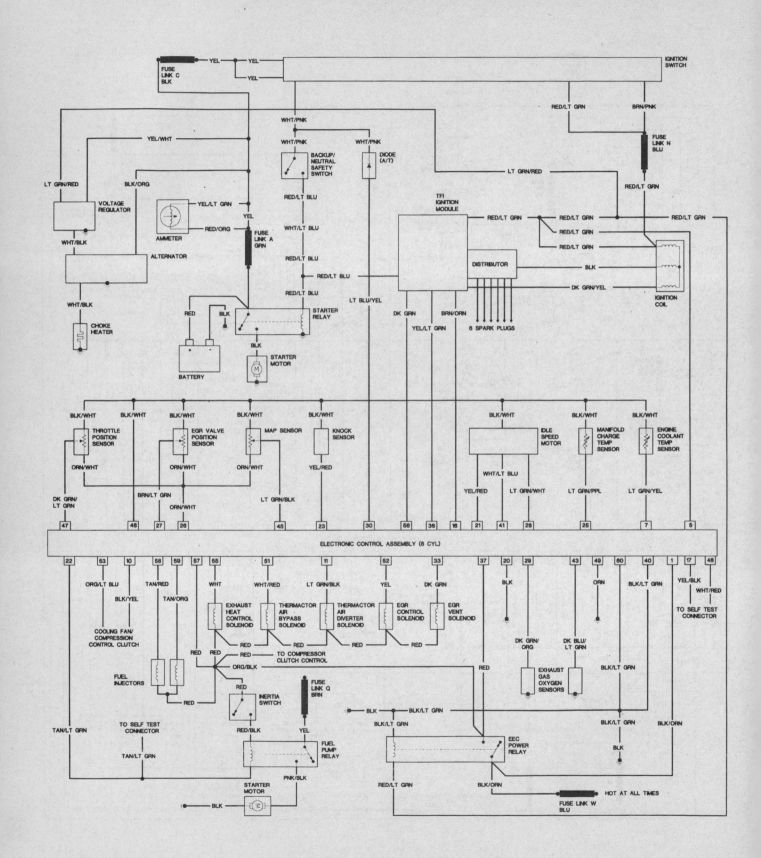

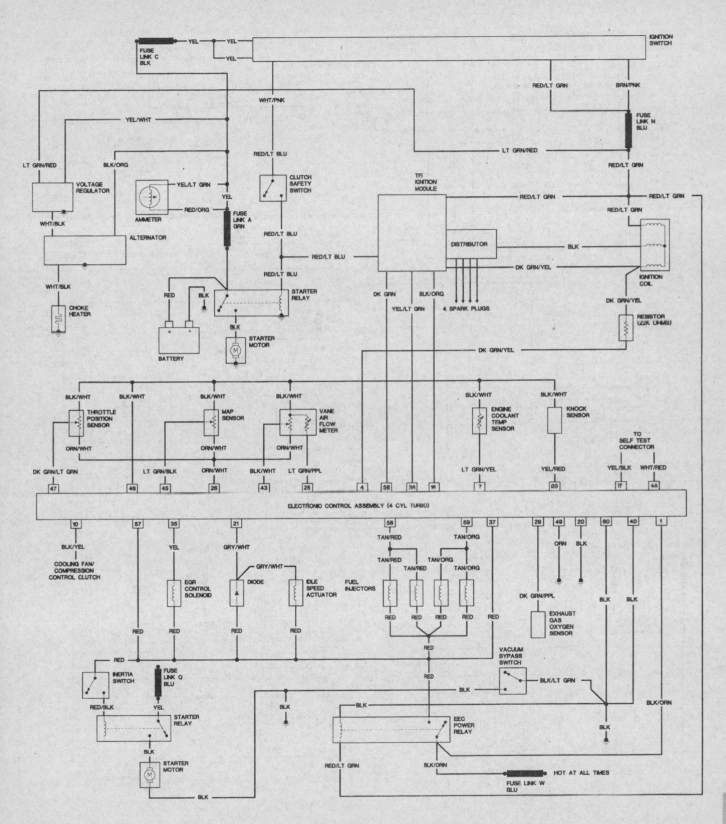

Wiring diagram for 1986 models, four-cylinder turbo (4 of 6)

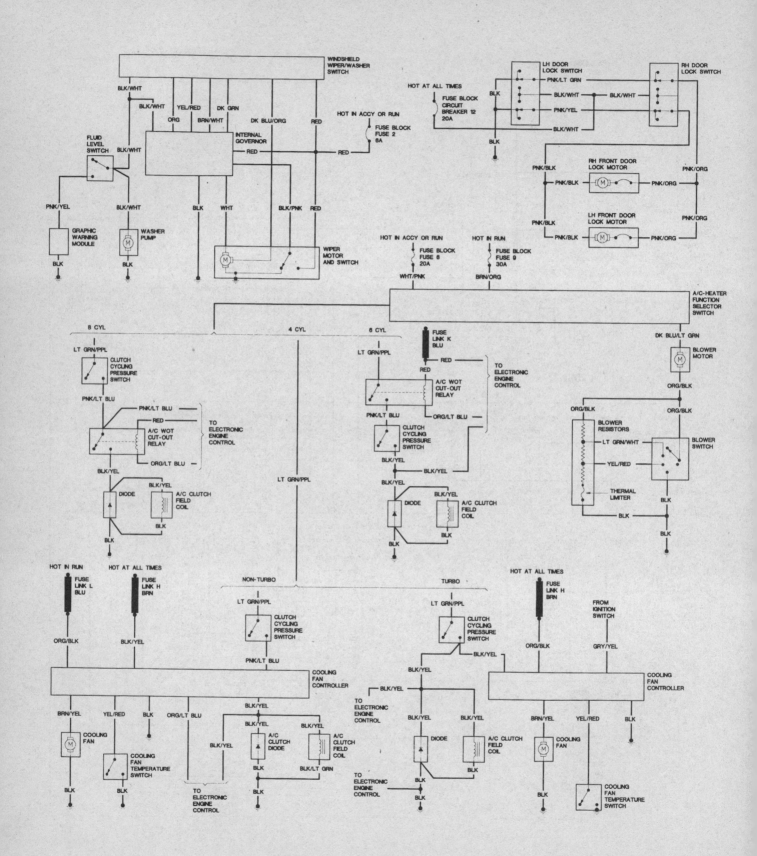

Wiring diagram for all 1986 models (5 of 6)

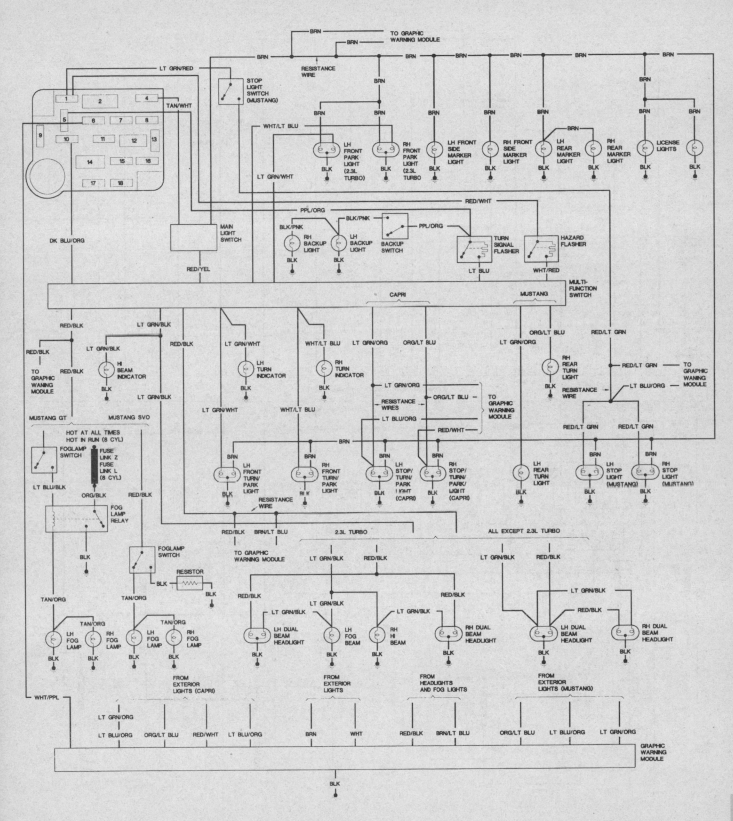

Wiring diagram for all 1986 models (6 of 6)

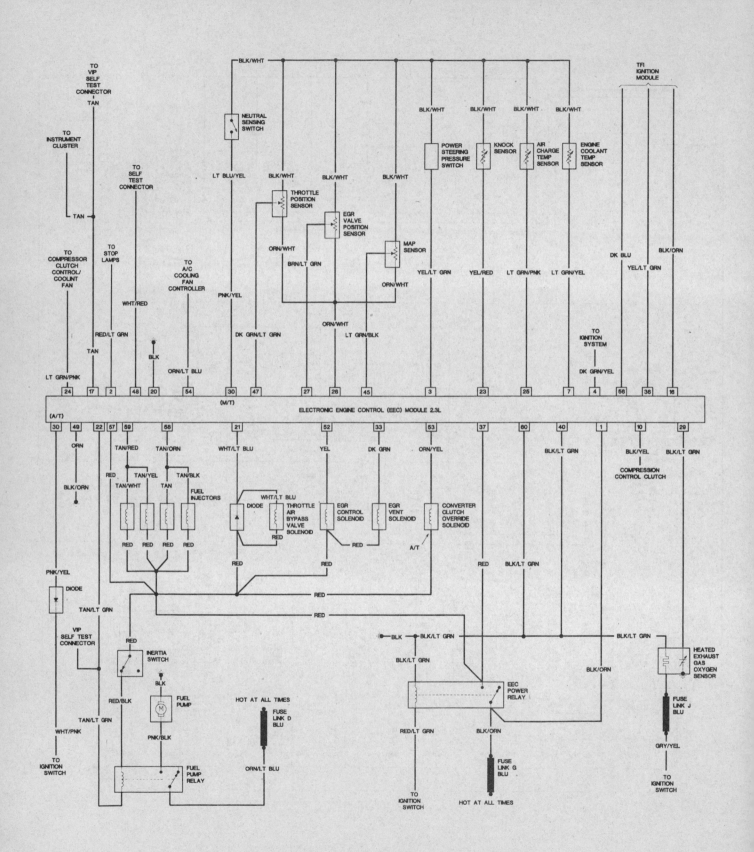

Wiring diagram for 1987 four-cylinder models (1 of 4)

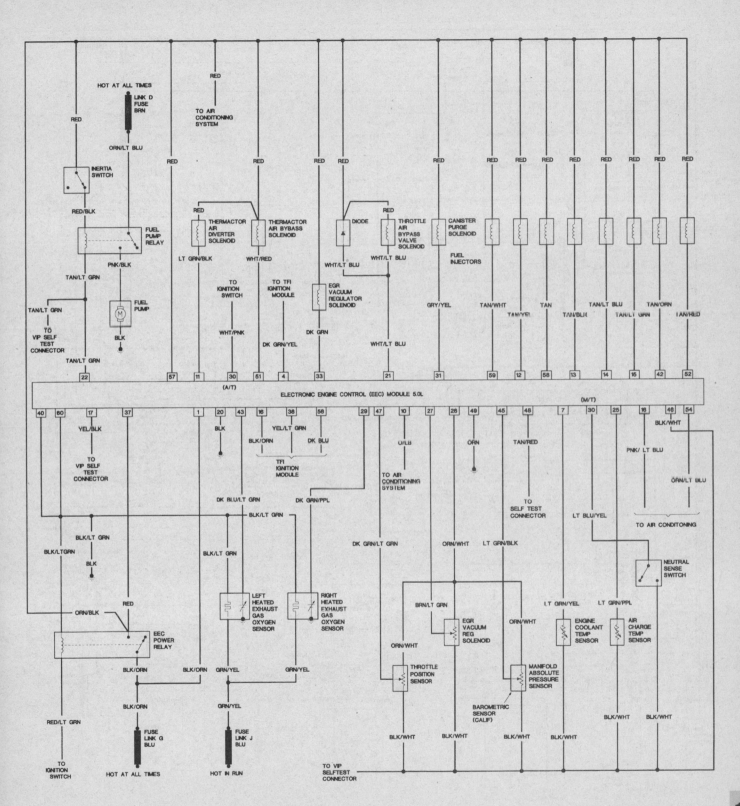

Wiring diagram for 1987 V8 models (2 of 4)

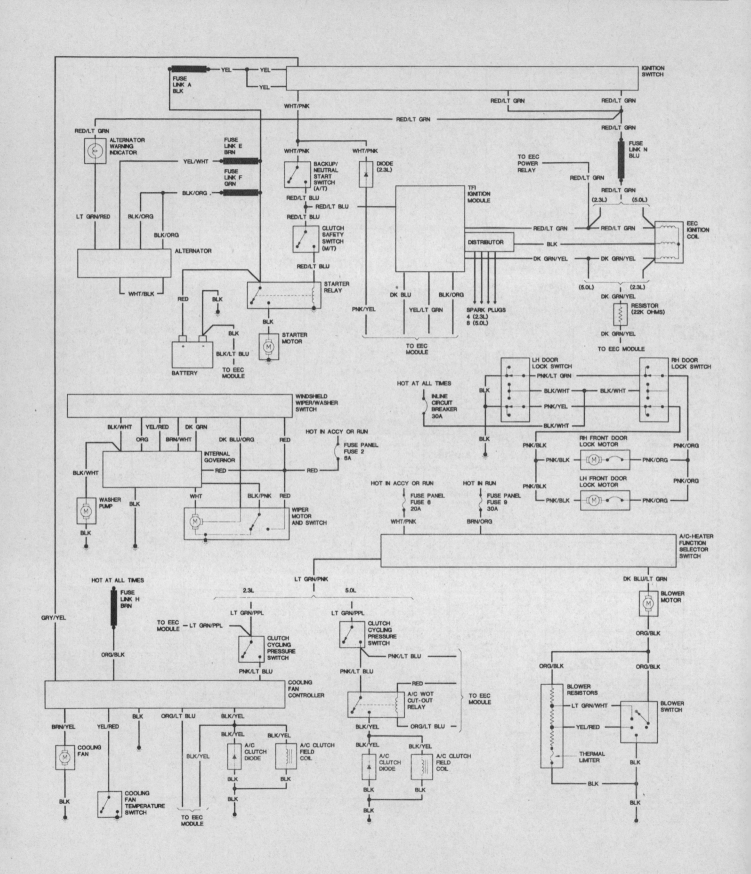

Wiring diagram for all 1987 models (3 of 4)

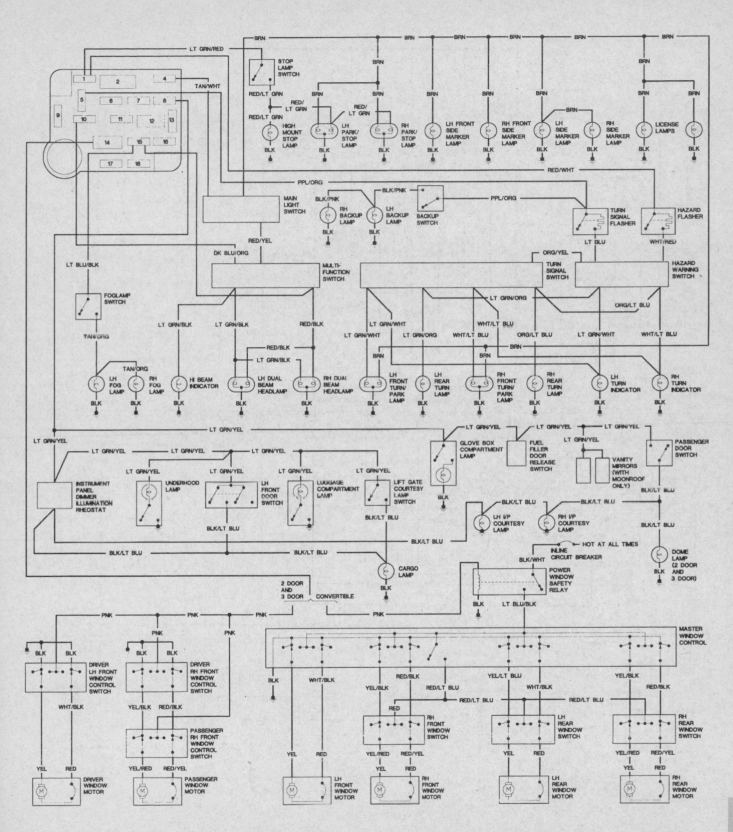

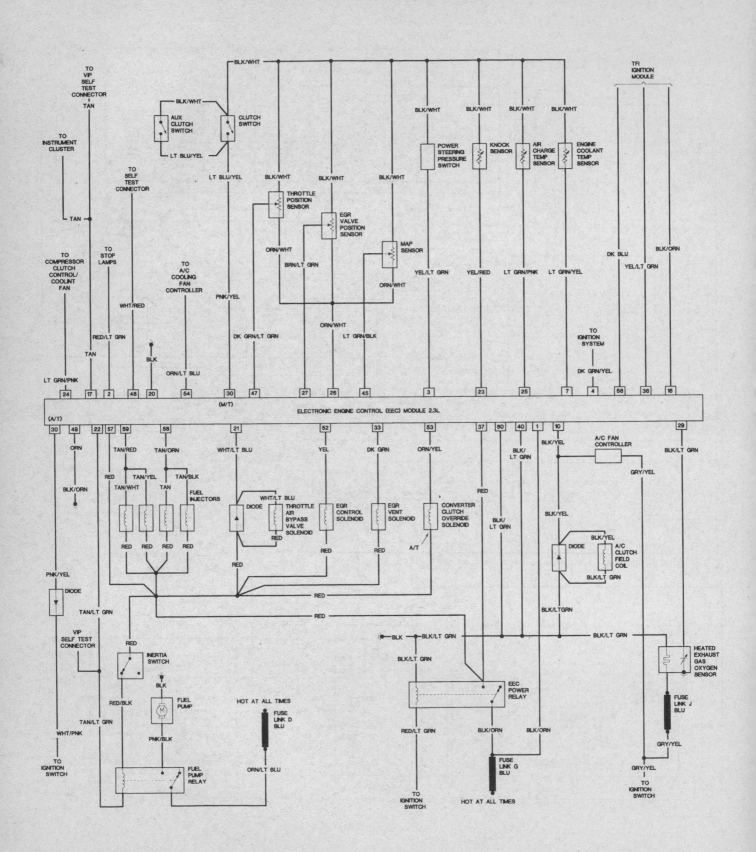

Wiring diagram for 1988 four-cylinder models (V8 similar) (1 of 3)

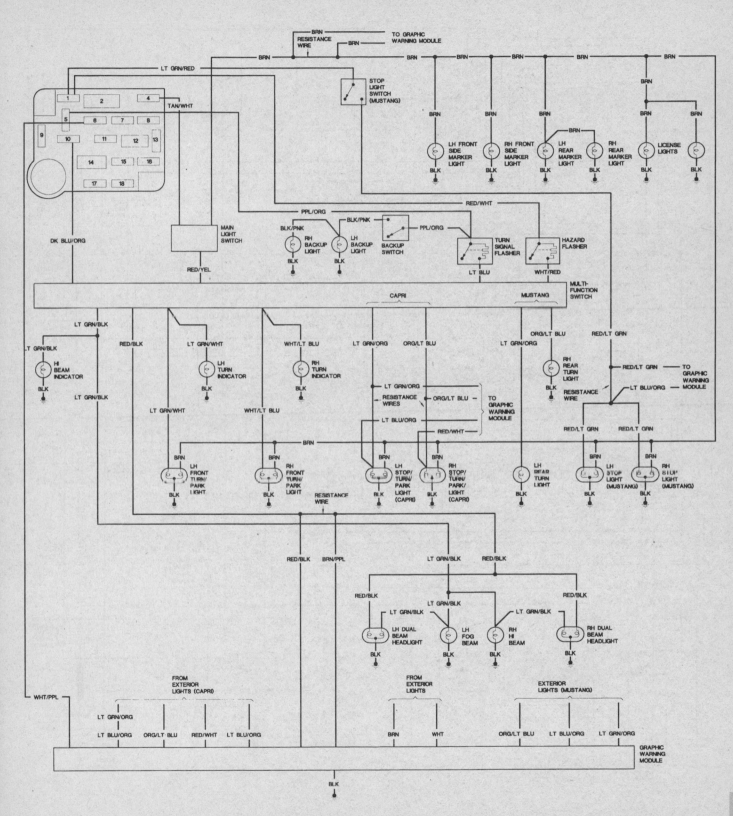

Wiring diagram for all 1988 models (2 of 3)

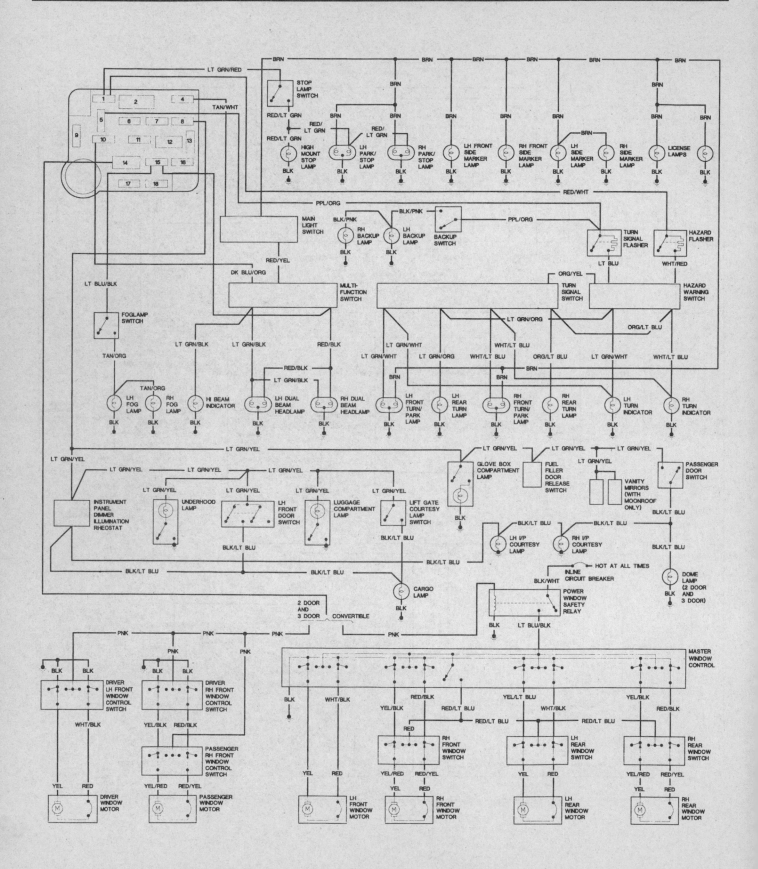

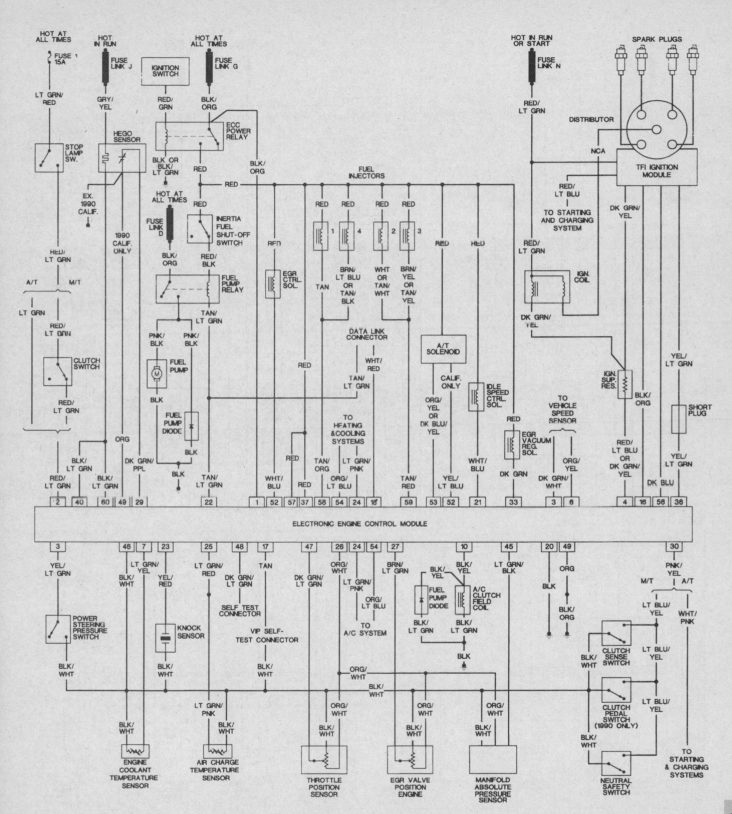

Wiring diagram for 1989 and 1990 four-cylinder models

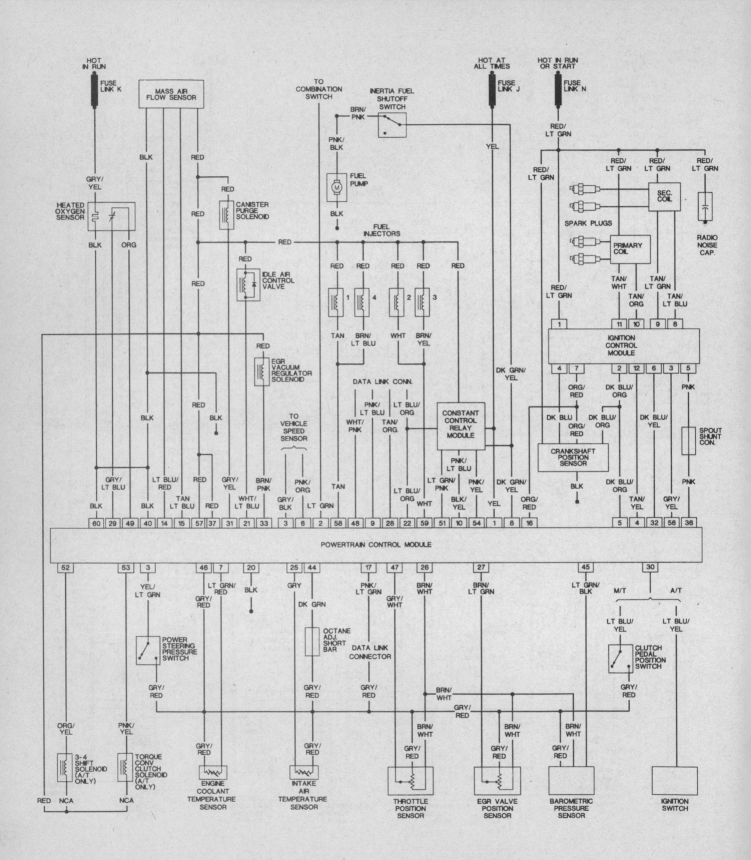

Wiring diagram for 1991 and later four-cylinder models

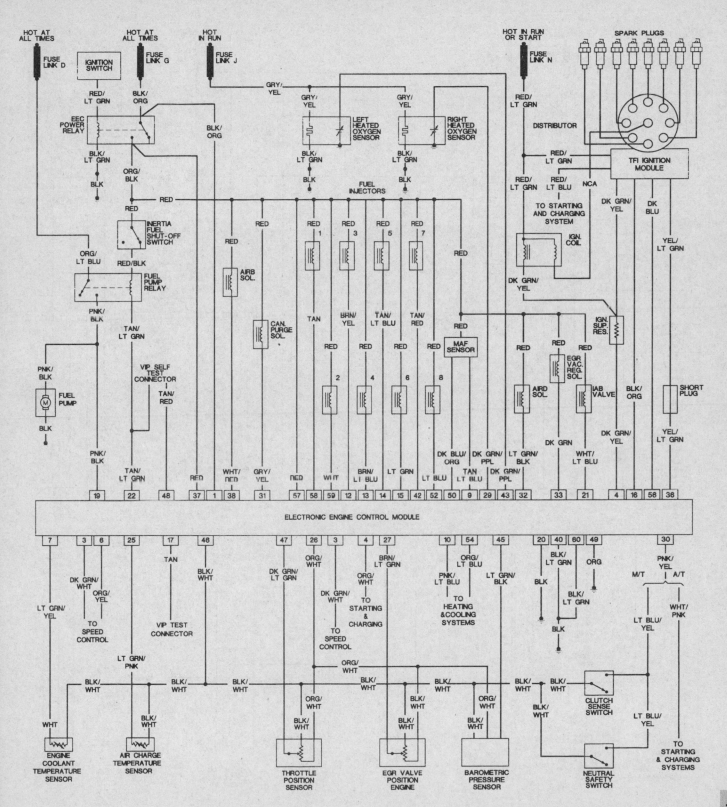

Engine controls wiring diagram for 1989 and 1990 V8 models

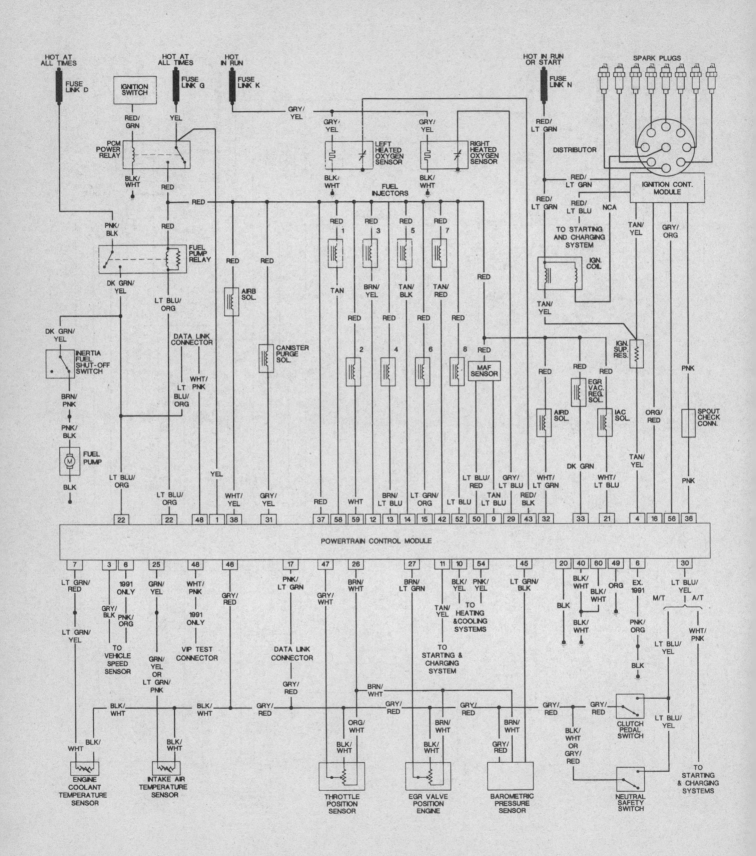

Engine controls wiring diagram for 1991 and later V8 models

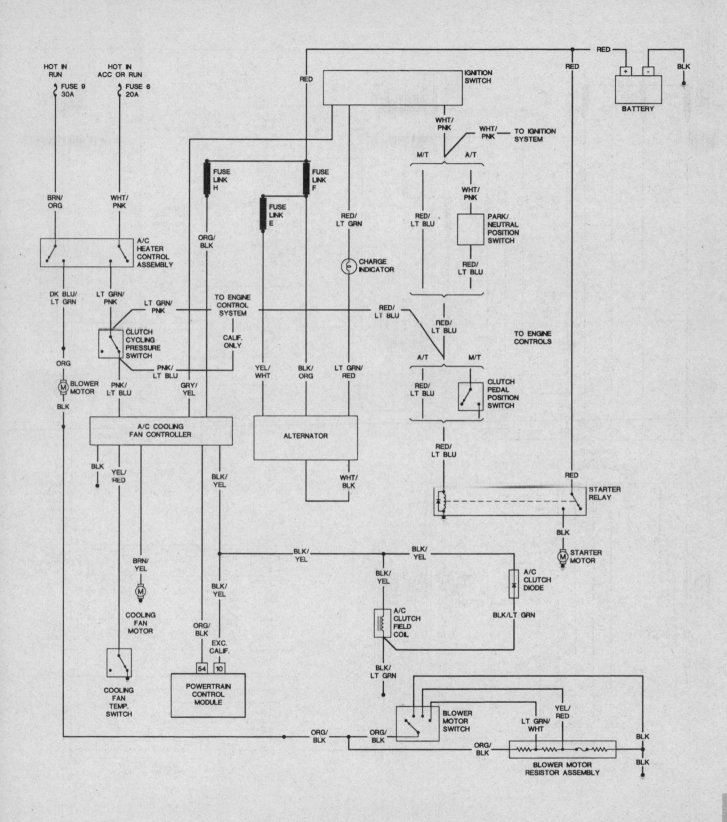

Body wiring diagram for 1989 and 1990 four-cylinder models

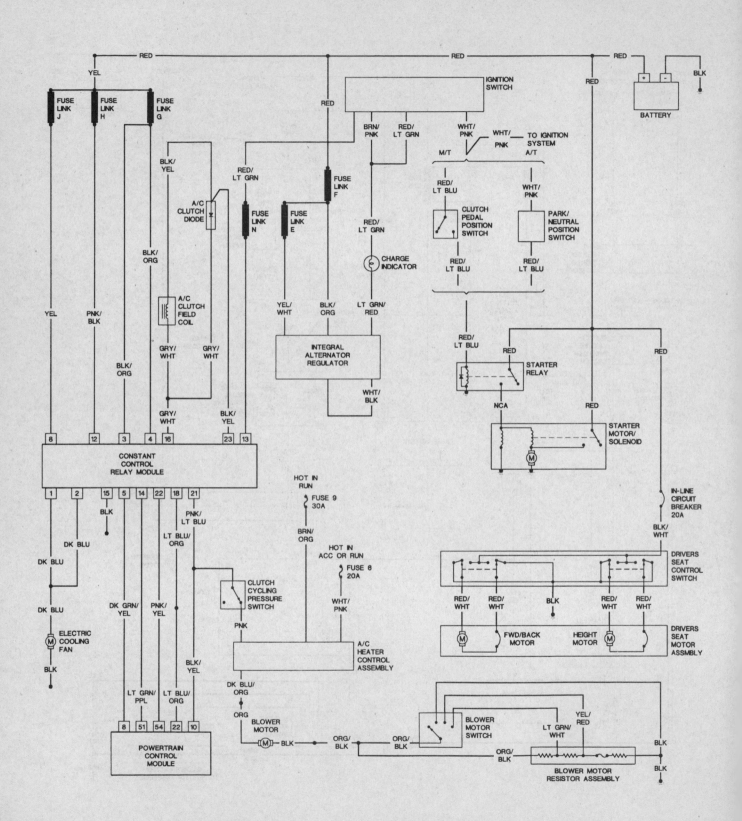

Body wiring diagram for 1991 and later four-cylinder models

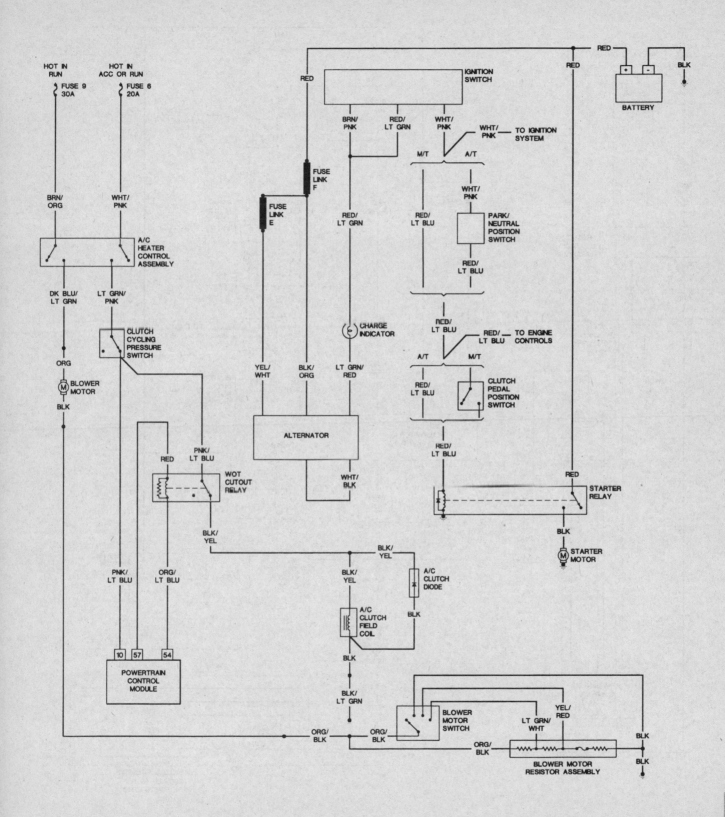

Body wiring diagram for 1989 and 1990 V8 models

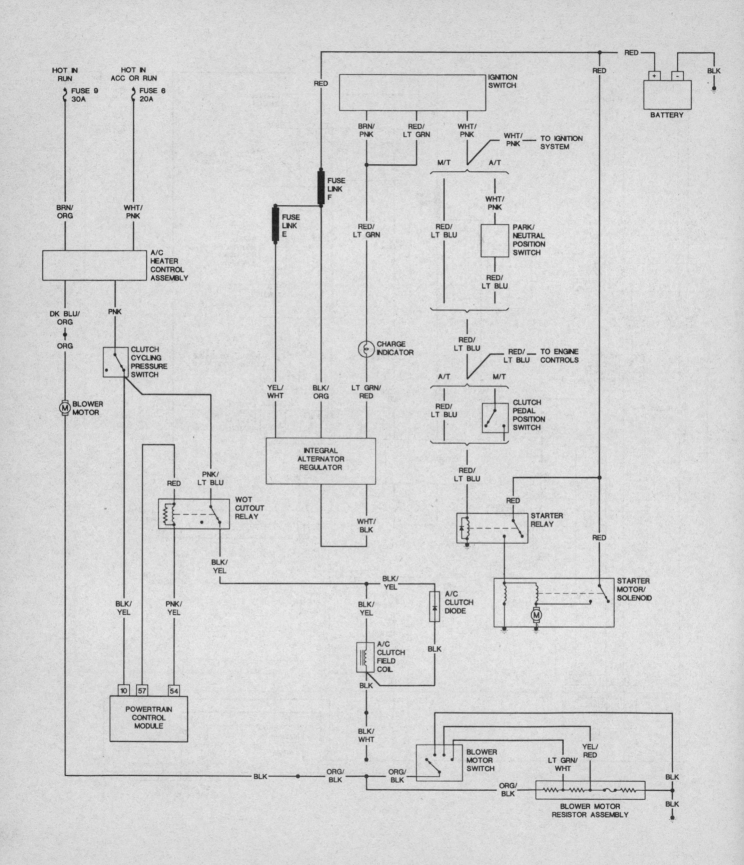

Body wiring diagram for 1991 and later V8 models

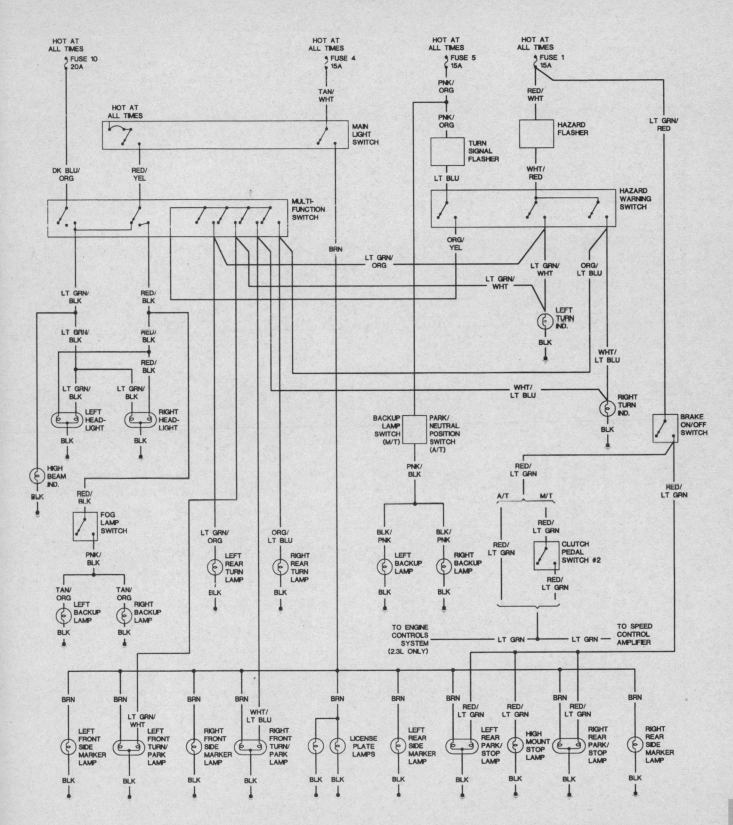

Body wiring diagram for all models

Notes

Index

Notes

Haynes Automotive Manuals

NOTE: New manuals are added to this list on a periodic basis. If you do not see a listing for your vehicle, consult your local Haynes dealer for the latest product information.

ACURA
12020 **Integra** '86 thru '89 & **Legend** '86 thru '90
12021 **Integra** '90 thru '93 & **Legend** '91 thru '95

AMC
Jeep CJ - see JEEP (50020)
14020 **Mid-size models** '70 thru '83
14025 **(Renault) Alliance & Encore** '83 thru '87

AUDI
15020 **4000** all models '80 thru '87
15025 **5000** all models '77 thru '83
15026 **5000** all models '84 thru '88

AUSTIN-HEALEY
Sprite - see MG Midget (66015)

BMW
*18020 **3/5 Series** not including diesel or all-wheel drive models '82 thru '92
18021 **3-Series** incl. Z3 models '92 thru '98
18025 **320i** all 4 cyl models '75 thru '83
18050 **1500 thru 2002** except Turbo '59 thru '77

BUICK
*19010 **Buick Century** '97 thru '02
Century (front-wheel drive) - see GM (38005)
*19020 **Buick, Oldsmobile & Pontiac Full-size** (Front-wheel drive) '85 thru '02
Buick Electra, LeSabre and Park Avenue; Oldsmobile Delta 88 Royale, Ninety Eight and Regency; Pontiac Bonneville
19025 **Buick Oldsmobile & Pontiac Full-size** (Rear wheel drive)
Buick Estate '70 thru '90, Electra '70 thru '84, LeSabre '70 thru '85, Limited '74 thru '79
Oldsmobile Custom Cruiser '70 thru '90, Delta 88 '70 thru '85, Ninety-eight '70 thru '84
Pontiac Bonneville '70 thru '81, Catalina '70 thru '81, Grandville '70 thru '75, Parisienne '83 thru '86
19030 **Mid-size Regal & Century** all rear-drive models with V6, V8 and Turbo '74 thru '87
Regal - see GENERAL MOTORS (38010)
Riviera - see GENERAL MOTORS (38030)
Roadmaster - see CHEVROLET (24046)
Skyhawk - see GENERAL MOTORS (38015)
Skylark - see GM (38020, 38025)
Somerset - see GENERAL MOTORS (38025)

CADILLAC
21030 **Cadillac Rear Wheel Drive** all gasoline models '70 thru '93
Cimarron - see GENERAL MOTORS (38015)
DeVille - see GM (38031 & 38032)
Eldorado - see GM (38030 & 38031)
Fleetwood - see GM (38031)
Seville - see GM (38030, 38031 & 38032)

CHEVROLET
*24010 **Astro & GMC Safari Mini-vans** '85 thru '02
24015 **Camaro V8** all models '70 thru '81
24016 **Camaro** all models '82 thru '92
24017 **Camaro & Firebird** '93 thru '00
Cavalier - see GENERAL MOTORS (38016)
Celebrity - see GENERAL MOTORS (38005)
24020 **Chevelle, Malibu & El Camino** '69 thru '87
24024 **Chevette & Pontiac T1000** '76 thru '87
Citation - see GENERAL MOTORS (38020)
24032 **Corsica/Beretta** all models '87 thru '96
24040 **Corvette** all V8 models '68 thru '82
24041 **Corvette** all models '84 thru '96
10305 **Chevrolet Engine Overhaul Manual**
24045 **Full-size Sedans** Caprice, Impala, Biscayne, Bel Air & Wagons '69 thru '90
24046 **Impala SS & Caprice and Buick Roadmaster** '91 thru '96
Impala - see LUMINA (24048)
Lumina '90 thru '94 - see GM (38010)
*24048 **Lumina & Monte Carlo** '95 thru '01
Lumina APV - see GM (38035)
24050 **Luv Pick-up** all 2WD & 4WD '72 thru '82
Malibu '97 thru '00 - see GM (38026)

24055 **Monte Carlo** all models '70 thru '88
Monte Carlo '95 thru '01 - see LUMINA (24048)
24059 **Nova** all V8 models '69 thru '79
24060 **Nova and Geo Prizm** '85 thru '92
24064 **Pick-ups '67 thru '87** - Chevrolet & GMC, all V8 & in-line 6 cyl, 2WD & 4WD '67 thru '87; Suburbans, Blazers & Jimmys '67 thru '91
24065 **Pick-ups '88 thru '98** - Chevrolet & GMC, full-size pick-ups '88 thru '98, C/K Classic '99 & '00, Blazer & Jimmy '92 thru '94; Suburban '92 thru '99; Tahoe & Yukon '95 thru '99
*24066 **Pick-ups '99 thru '01** - Chevrolet Silverado & GMC Sierra full-size pick-ups '99 thru '01, Suburban/Tahoe/Yukon/Yukon XL '00 thru '01
24070 **S-10 & S-15 Pick-ups** '82 thru '93, **Blazer & Jimmy** '83 thru '94,
*24071 **S-10 & S-15 Pick-ups** '94 thru '01, **Blazer & Jimmy** '95 thru '01, **Hombre** '96 thru '01
24075 **Sprint** '85 thru '88 & **Geo Metro** '89 thru '01
24080 **Vans - Chevrolet & GMC** '68 thru '96

CHRYSLER
25015 **Chrysler Cirrus, Dodge Stratus, Plymouth Breeze** '95 thru '00
10310 **Chrysler Engine Overhaul Manual**
25020 **Full-size Front-Wheel Drive** '88 thru '93
K-Cars - see DODGE Aries (30008)
Laser - see DODGE Daytona (30030)
25025 **Chrysler LHS, Concorde, New Yorker, Dodge** Intrepid, **Eagle Vision**, '93 thru '97
*25026 **Chrysler LHS, Concorde, 300M, Dodge** Intrepid, '98 thru '03
25030 **Chrysler & Plymouth Mid-size** front wheel drive '82 thru '95
Rear-wheel Drive - see Dodge (30050)
*25035 **PT Cruiser** all models '01 thru '03
*25040 **Chrysler Sebring, Dodge** Avenger '95 thru '02

DATSUN
28005 **200SX** all models '80 thru '83
28007 **B-210** all models '73 thru '78
28009 **210** all models '79 thru '82
28012 **240Z, 260Z & 280Z** Coupe '70 thru '78
28014 **280ZX** Coupe & 2+2 '79 thru '83
300ZX - see NISSAN (72010)
28016 **310** all models '78 thru '82
28018 **510 & PL521 Pick-up** '68 thru '73
28020 **510** all models '78 thru '81
28022 **620 Series Pick-up** all models '73 thru '79
720 Series Pick-up - see NISSAN (72030)
28025 **810/Maxima** all gasoline models, '77 thru '84

DODGE
400 & 600 - see CHRYSLER (25030)
30008 **Aries & Plymouth Reliant** '81 thru '89
30010 **Caravan & Plymouth Voyager** '84 thru '95
*30011 **Caravan & Plymouth Voyager** '96 thru '02
30012 **Challenger/Plymouth Saporro** '78 thru '83
30016 **Colt & Plymouth Champ** '78 thru '87
30020 **Dakota Pick-ups** all models '87 thru '96
*30021 **Durango** '98 & '99, **Dakota** '97 thru '99
30025 **Dart, Demon, Plymouth Barracuda, Duster & Valiant** 6 cyl models '67 thru '76
30030 **Daytona & Chrysler Laser** '84 thru '89
Intrepid - see CHRYSLER (25025, 25026)
*30034 **Neon** all models '95 thru '99
30035 **Omni & Plymouth Horizon** '78 thru '90
30040 **Pick-ups** all full-size models '74 thru '93
*30041 **Pick-ups** all full-size models '94 thru '01
30045 **Ram 50/D50 Pick-ups & Raider and Plymouth Arrow Pick-ups** '79 thru '93
30050 **Dodge/Plymouth/Chrysler** RWD '71 thru '89
30055 **Shadow & Plymouth Sundance** '87 thru '94
30060 **Spirit & Plymouth Acclaim** '89 thru '95
*30065 **Vans - Dodge & Plymouth** '71 thru '03

EAGLE
Talon - see MITSUBISHI (68030, 68031)
Vision - see CHRYSLER (25025)

FIAT
34010 **124 Sport Coupe & Spider** '68 thru '78
34025 **X1/9** all models '74 thru '80

FORD
10355 **Ford Automatic Transmission Overhaul**
36004 **Aerostar Mini-vans** all models '86 thru '97
36006 **Contour & Mercury Mystique** '95 thru '00
36008 **Courier Pick-up** all models '72 thru '82
*36012 **Crown Victoria & Mercury Grand Marquis** '88 thru '00
10320 **Ford Engine Overhaul Manual**
36016 **Escort/Mercury Lynx** all models '81 thru '90
36020 **Escort/Mercury Tracer** '91 thru '00
36024 **Explorer & Mazda Navajo** '91 thru '01
36028 **Fairmont & Mercury Zephyr** '78 thru '83
36030 **Festiva & Aspire** '88 thru '97
36032 **Fiesta** all models '77 thru '80
*36034 **Focus** all models '00 and '01
36036 **Ford & Mercury Full-size** '75 thru '87
36040 **Granada & Mercury Monarch** '75 thru '80
36044 **Ford & Mercury Mid-size** '75 thru '86
36048 **Mustang V8** all models '64-1/2 thru '73
36049 **Mustang II** 4 cyl, V6 & V8 models '74 thru '78
36050 **Mustang & Mercury Capri** all models Mustang, '79 thru '93; Capri, '79 thru '86
*36051 **Mustang** all models '94 thru '03
36054 **Pick-ups & Bronco** '73 thru '79
36058 **Pick-ups & Bronco** '80 thru '96
*36059 **F-150 & Expedition** '97 thru '02, F-250 thru '99 & **Lincoln Navigator** '98 thru '02
*36060 **Super Duty Pick-ups, Excursion** '97 thru '02
36062 **Pinto & Mercury Bobcat** '75 thru '80
36066 **Probe** all models '89 thru '92
36070 **Ranger/Bronco II** gasoline models '83 thru '92
*36071 **Ranger** '93 thru '00 & **Mazda Pick-ups** '94 thru '00
36074 **Taurus & Mercury Sable** '86 thru '95
*36075 **Taurus & Mercury Sable** '96 thru '01
36078 **Tempo & Mercury Topaz** '84 thru '94
36082 **Thunderbird/Mercury Cougar** '83 thru '88
36086 **Thunderbird/Mercury Cougar** '89 and '97
36090 **Vans** all V8 Econoline models '69 thru '91
*36094 **Vans** full size '92 thru '01
*36097 **Windstar Mini-van** '95 thru '03

GENERAL MOTORS
10360 **GM Automatic Transmission Overhaul**
38005 **Buick Century, Chevrolet Celebrity, Oldsmobile Cutlass Ciera & Pontiac 6000** all models '82 thru '96
*38010 **Buick Regal, Chevrolet Lumina, Oldsmobile Cutlass Supreme & Pontiac Grand Prix** (FWD) '88 thru '02
38015 **Buick Skyhawk, Cadillac Cimarron, Chevrolet Cavalier, Oldsmobile Firenza & Pontiac J-2000 & Sunbird** '82 thru '94
*38016 **Chevrolet Cavalier & Pontiac Sunfire** '95 thru '01
38020 **Buick Skylark, Chevrolet Citation, Olds Omega, Pontiac Phoenix** '80 thru '85
38025 **Buick Skylark & Somerset, Oldsmobile Achieva & Calais and Pontiac Grand Am** all models '85 thru '98
*38026 **Chevrolet Malibu, Olds Alero & Cutlass, Pontiac Grand Am** '97 thru '00
38030 **Cadillac Eldorado** '71 thru '85, **Seville** '80 thru '85, **Oldsmobile Toronado** '71 thru '85, **Buick Riviera** '79 thru '85
*38031 **Cadillac Eldorado & Seville** '86 thru '91, **DeVille** '86 thru '93, **Fleetwood & Olds Toronado** '86 thru '92, **Buick Riviera** '86 thru '93
38032 **Cadillac DeVille** '94 thru '02 & **Seville** - '92 thru '02
38035 **Chevrolet Lumina APV, Olds Silhouette & Pontiac Trans Sport** all models '90 thru '96
*38036 **Chevrolet Venture, Olds Silhouette, Pontiac Trans Sport & Montana** '97 thru '01
General Motors Full-size Rear-wheel Drive - see BUICK (19025)

GEO
Metro - see CHEVROLET Sprint (24075)
Prizm - '85 thru '92 see CHEVY (24060), '93 thru '02 see TOYOTA Corolla (92036)

(Continued on other side)

---

* Listings shown with an asterisk (*) indicate model coverage as of this printing. These titles will be periodically updated to include later model years - consult your Haynes dealer for more information.

Haynes North America, Inc., 861 Lawrence Drive, Newbury Park, CA 91320-1514 • (805) 498-6703

Haynes Automotive Manuals (continued)

NOTE: New manuals are added to this list on a periodic basis. If you do not see a listing for your vehicle, consult your local Haynes dealer for the latest product information.

40030 **Storm** all models '90 thru '93
Tracker - *see SUZUKI Samurai (90010)*

GMC
Vans & Pick-ups - *see CHEVROLET*

HONDA
42010 **Accord CVCC** all models '76 thru '83
42011 **Accord** all models '84 thru '89
42012 **Accord** all models '90 thru '93
42013 **Accord** all models '94 thru '97
*42014 **Accord** all models '98 and '99
42020 **Civic 1200** all models '73 thru '79
42021 **Civic 1300 & 1500 CVCC** '80 thru '83
42022 **Civic 1500 CVCC** all models '75 thru '79
42023 **Civic** all models '84 thru '91
42024 **Civic & del Sol** '92 thru '95
*42025 **Civic** '96 thru '00, **CR-V** '97 thru '00, **Acura Integra** '94 thru '00
42040 **Prelude CVCC** all models '79 thru '89

HYUNDAI
*43010 **Elantra** all models '96 thru '01
43015 **Excel & Accent** all models '86 thru '98

ISUZU
Hombre - *see CHEVROLET S-10 (24071)*
*47017 **Rodeo** '91 thru '02; **Amigo** '89 thru '94 and '98 thru '02; **Honda Passport** '95 thru '02
47020 **Trooper & Pick-up** '81 thru '93

JAGUAR
49010 **XJ6** all 6 cyl models '68 thru '86
49011 **XJ6** all models '88 thru '94
49015 **XJ12 & XJS** all 12 cyl models '72 thru '85

JEEP
50010 **Cherokee, Comanche & Wagoneer Limited** all models '84 thru '00
50020 **CJ** all models '49 thru '86
*50025 **Grand Cherokee** all models '93 thru '00
50029 **Grand Wagoneer & Pick-up** '72 thru '91
Grand Wagoneer '84 thru '91, Cherokee & Wagoneer '72 thru '83, Pick-up '72 thru '88
*50030 **Wrangler** all models '87 thru '00

LEXUS
ES 300 - *see TOYOTA Camry (92007)*

LINCOLN
Navigator - *see FORD Pick-up (36059)*
*59010 **Rear-Wheel Drive** all models '70 thru '01

MAZDA
61010 **GLC Hatchback (rear-wheel drive)** '77 thru '83
61011 **GLC (front-wheel drive)** '81 thru '85
61015 **323 & Protogé** '90 thru '00
*61016 **MX-5 Miata** '90 thru '97
61020 **MPV** all models '89 thru '94
Navajo - *see Ford Explorer (36024)*
61030 **Pick-ups** '72 thru '93
Pick-ups '94 thru '00 - *see Ford Ranger (36071)*
61035 **RX-7** all models '79 thru '85
61036 **RX-7** all models '86 thru '91
61040 **626 (rear-wheel drive)** all models '79 thru '82
61041 **626/MX-6 (front-wheel drive)** '83 thru '91
61042 **626** '93 thru '01, **MX-6/Ford Probe** '93 thru '97

MERCEDES-BENZ
63012 **123 Series Diesel** '76 thru '85
63015 **190 Series** four-cyl gas models, '84 thru '88
63020 **230/250/280** 6 cyl sohc models '68 thru '72
63025 **280 123 Series** gasoline models '77 thru '81
63030 **350 & 450** all models '71 thru '80

MERCURY
64200 **Villager & Nissan Quest** '93 thru '01
All other titles, see FORD Listing.

MG
66010 **MGB** Roadster & GT Coupe '62 thru '80
66015 **MG Midget, Austin Healey Sprite** '58 thru '80

MITSUBISHI
68020 **Cordia, Tredia, Galant, Precis & Mirage** '83 thru '93
68030 **Eclipse, Eagle Talon & Ply. Laser** '90 thru '94
*68031 **Eclipse** '95 thru '01, **Eagle Talon** '95 thru '98
68040 **Pick-up** '83 thru '96 & **Montero** '83 thru '93

NISSAN
72010 **300ZX** all models including Turbo '84 thru '89
72015 **Altima** all models '93 thru '01
72020 **Maxima** all models '85 thru '92
*72021 **Maxima** all models '93 thru '01
72030 **Pick-ups** '80 thru '97 **Pathfinder** '87 thru '95
*72031 **Frontier Pick-up** '98 thru '01, **Xterra** '00 & '01, **Pathfinder** '96 thru '01
72040 **Pulsar** all models '83 thru '86
Quest - *see MERCURY Villager (64200)*
72050 **Sentra** all models '82 thru '94
72051 **Sentra & 200SX** all models '95 thru '99
72060 **Stanza** all models '82 thru '90

OLDSMOBILE
73015 **Cutlass** V6 & V8 gas models '74 thru '88
For other OLDSMOBILE titles, see BUICK, CHEVROLET or GENERAL MOTORS listing.

PLYMOUTH
For PLYMOUTH titles, see DODGE listing.

PONTIAC
79008 **Fiero** all models '84 thru '88
79018 **Firebird** V8 models except Turbo '70 thru '81
79019 **Firebird** all models '82 thru '92
79040 **Mid-size Rear-wheel Drive** '70 thru '87
For other PONTIAC titles, see BUICK, CHEVROLET or GENERAL MOTORS listing.

PORSCHE
80020 **911** except Turbo & Carrera 4 '65 thru '89
80025 **914** all 4 cyl models '69 thru '76
80030 **924** all models including Turbo '76 thru '82
80035 **944** all models including Turbo '83 thru '89

RENAULT
Alliance & Encore - *see AMC (14020)*

SAAB
*84010 **900** all models including Turbo '79 thru '88

SATURN
*87010 **Saturn** all models '91 thru '02

SUBARU
89002 **1100, 1300, 1400 & 1600** '71 thru '79
89003 **1600 & 1800** 2WD & 4WD '80 thru '94

SUZUKI
90010 **Samurai/Sidekick & Geo Tracker** '86 thru '01

TOYOTA
92005 **Camry** all models '83 thru '91
92006 **Camry** all models '92 thru '96
*92007 **Camry, Avalon, Solara, Lexus ES 300** '97 thru '01
92015 **Celica Rear Wheel Drive** '71 thru '85
92020 **Celica Front Wheel Drive** '86 thru '99
92025 **Celica Supra** all models '79 thru '92
92030 **Corolla** all models '75 thru '79
92032 **Corolla** all rear wheel drive models '80 thru '87
92035 **Corolla** all front wheel drive models '84 thru '92
92036 **Corolla & Geo Prizm** '93 thru '02
92040 **Corolla Tercel** all models '80 thru '82
92045 **Corona** all models '74 thru '82
92050 **Cressida** all models '78 thru '82
92055 **Land Cruiser FJ40, 43, 45, 55** '68 thru '82
92056 **Land Cruiser FJ60, 62, 80, FZJ80** '80 thru '96
92065 **MR2** all models '85 thru '87
92070 **Pick-up** all models '69 thru '78
92075 **Pick-up** all models '79 thru '95
*92076 **Tacoma** '95 thru '00, **4Runner** '96 thru '00, **& T100** '93 thru '98
*92078 **Tundra** '00 thru '02 & **Sequoia** '01 thru '02

92080 **Previa** all models '91 thru '95
*92082 **RAV4** all models '96 thru '02
92085 **Tercel** all models '87 thru '94

TRIUMPH
94007 **Spitfire** all models '62 thru '81
94010 **TR7** all models '75 thru '81

VW
96008 **Beetle & Karmann Ghia** '54 thru '79
*96009 **New Beetle** '98 thru '00
96016 **Rabbit, Jetta, Scirocco & Pick-up** gas models '74 thru '91 & Convertible '80 thru '92
96017 **Golf, GTI & Jetta** '93 thru '98 & **Cabrio** '95 thru '98
*96018 **Golf, GTI, Jetta & Cabrio** '99 thru '02
96020 **Rabbit, Jetta & Pick-up** diesel '77 thru '84
96023 **Passat** '98 thru '01, **Audi A4** '96 thru '01
96030 **Transporter 1600** all models '68 thru '79
96035 **Transporter 1700, 1800 & 2000** '72 thru '79
96040 **Type 3 1500 & 1600** all models '63 thru '73
96045 **Vanagon** all air-cooled models '80 thru '83

VOLVO
97010 **120, 130 Series & 1800 Sports** '61 thru '73
97015 **140 Series** all models '66 thru '74
97020 **240 Series** all models '76 thru '93
97040 **740 & 760 Series** all models '82 thru '88
97050 **850 Series** all models '93 thru '97

TECHBOOK MANUALS
10205 **Automotive Computer Codes**
10210 **Automotive Emissions Control Manual**
10215 **Fuel Injection Manual, 1978 thru 1985**
10220 **Fuel Injection Manual, 1986 thru 1999**
10225 **Holley Carburetor Manual**
10230 **Rochester Carburetor Manual**
10240 **Weber/Zenith/Stromberg/SU Carburetors**
10305 **Chevrolet Engine Overhaul Manual**
10310 **Chrysler Engine Overhaul Manual**
10320 **Ford Engine Overhaul Manual**
10330 **GM and Ford Diesel Engine Repair Manual**
10340 **Small Engine Repair Manual, 5 HP & Less**
10341 **Small Engine Repair Manual, 5.5 - 20 HP**
10345 **Suspension, Steering & Driveline Manual**
10355 **Ford Automatic Transmission Overhaul**
10360 **GM Automatic Transmission Overhaul**
10405 **Automotive Body Repair & Painting**
10410 **Automotive Brake Manual**
10411 **Automotive Anti-lock Brake (ABS) Systems**
10415 **Automotive Detailing Manual**
10420 **Automotive Eelectrical Manual**
10425 **Automotive Heating & Air Conditioning**
10430 **Automotive Reference Manual & Dictionary**
10435 **Automotive Tools Manual**
10440 **Used Car Buying Guide**
10445 **Welding Manual**
10450 **ATV Basics**

SPANISH MANUALS
98903 **Reparación de Carrocería & Pintura**
98905 **Códigos Automotrices de la Computadora**
98910 **Frenos Automotriz**
98915 **Inyección de Combustible 1986 al 1999**
99040 **Chevrolet & GMC Camionetas** '67 al '87
Incluye Suburban, Blazer & Jimmy '67 al '91
99041 **Chevrolet & GMC Camionetas** '88 al '98
Incluye Suburban '92 al '98, Blazer & Jimmy '92 al '94, Tahoe y Yukon '95 al '98
99042 **Chevrolet & GMC Camionetas Cerradas** '68 al '95
99055 **Dodge Caravan & Plymouth Voyager** '84 al '95
99075 **Ford Camionetas y Bronco** '80 al '94
99077 **Ford Camionetas Cerradas** '69 al '91
99083 **Ford Modelos de Tamaño Grande** '75 al '87
99088 **Ford Modelos de Tamaño Mediano** '75 al '86
99091 **Ford Taurus & Mercury Sable** '86 al '95
99095 **GM Modelos de Tamaño Grande** '70 al '90
99100 **GM Modelos de Tamaño Mediano** '70 al '88
99110 **Nissan Camioneta** '80 al '96, **Pathfinder** '87 al '95
99118 **Nissan Sentra** '82 al '94
99125 **Toyota Camionetas y 4Runner** '79 al '95

Over 100 Haynes motorcycle manuals also available

8-03

* Listings shown with an asterisk (*) indicate model coverage as of this printing. These titles will be periodically updated to include later model years - consult your Haynes dealer for more information.

Haynes North America, Inc., 861 Lawrence Drive, Newbury Park, CA 91320-1514 • (805) 498-6703

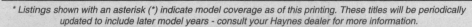